1959 C. Wright Mills's *The Sociological Imagination* published

1960 John F. Kennedy and Richard Nixon meet in the Great Debates

Television in 90 percent of all U.S. homes

Joseph Klapper's *Effects of Mass Communication* published

1961 Key's *Public Opinion and American Democracy* published

Kennedy makes nation's first live TV presidential press conference

Schramm team's *Television in the Lives of Our Children* published

1962 Festinger's cognitive dissonance article appears

Sidney Kraus's *Great Debates* published

Air Force commissions Paul Baran to develop a national computer network

1963 JFK assassinated

Albert Bandura's aggressive modeling experiments first appear

Networks begin one-half-hour newscasts

1964 McLuhan's *Understanding Media* published

1965 Color comes to all three commercial TV networks

Comsat satellite launched

1966 Mendelsohn's *Mass Entertainment* published

Berger and Luckmann's *The Social Construction of Reality* published

1967 Merton's *On Theoretical Sociology* published

1969 Blumer coins "symbolic interaction"

ARPANET, forerunner to Internet, goes online

1971 Bandura's *Psychological Modeling* published

1972 *Surgeon General's Report on Television and Social Behavior* released

McCombs and Shaw introduce "agenda-setting"

Gerbner's Violence Profile initiated

FCC requires cable companies to provide "local access"

Ray Tomlinson develops e-mail

1973 Watergate Hearings broadcast live

1974 Blumler and Katz's *The Uses of Mass Communication* published

Noelle-Neumann introduces "spiral of silence"

Goffman pioneers frame analysis

Home use of VCR introduced

Term "Internet" coined

1975 ASNE's *Statement of Principles* replaces *Canons*

Bill Gates and Paul Allen develop operating system for personal computers

1977 Steve Jobs and Stephen Wozniak perfect Apple II

Janus's Critical Feminist Theory article published

1978 Digital audio and video recording adopted as media industry standard

Faules and Alexander's *Communication and Social Behavior: A Symbolic Interaction Perspective published*

1981 IBM introduces the PC

Petty and Cacioppo's Elaboration Likelihood Model introduced

1983 *Journal of Communication* devotes entire issue to "Ferment in the Field"

CD introduced

1984 Radway's *Reading the Romance* published

Graber's *Processing the News published*

1985 Meyrowitz's *No Sense of Place* published

Ang's *Watching Dallas* published

Vallone et al.'s Hostile Media Effect introduced

1990 Signorielli and Morgan's *Cultivation Analysis* published

1991 Gulf War explodes, CNN emerges as important news source

1992 ACT disbands, says work is complete

1992 World Wide Web released

1993 Ten years after "Ferment," *Journal of Communication* tries again with special issue, "The Future of the Field"

Patterson's *Out of Order published*

1995 Anderson's General Aggression Model introduced

Launch of *Journal of Computer Mediated Communication*

1996 Telecommunications Act passes, relaxes broadcast ownership rules, deregulates cable television, mandates television content ratings

1998 *Journal of Communication* devotes entire issue to media literacy

MP3 introduced

1999 Mulvey's "Visual Pleasure and Narrative Cinema" published

2000 Name change of *Critical Studies in Mass Communication* to *Critical Studies in Media Communication*

Green and Brock's narrative persuasion and transportation theories

2001	Terrorist attacks on New York City and Washington, D.C.	2009	Internet overtakes newspapers as a source of news for Americans
2002	Slater and Rouner's Extended Elaboration Likelihood Model introduced		American Society of Newspaper Editors becomes American Society of News Editors
2003	FCC institutes new, relaxed media ownership rules		Radio and Television News Directors Association becomes Radio Television Digital News Association
	U.S. invasion of Iraq		Social networking use exceeds e-mail
	Social networking websites appear	2011	Sales of e-books exceed sales of print books on Amazon
	Bloggers' Code of Ethics formalized		Digital music sales surpass sales of physical discs
2004	*Journalism & Mass Communication Quarterly* focuses edition on media framing		Arab Spring and Occupy Wall Street
	American Behavioral Scientist devotes two entire issues to media literacy	2012	U.S. sales of tablets exceed those of laptop computers
	Facebook launched		Online movie transactions exceed number of physical disc transactions
	Sherry's call for a Neuroscience Perspective		U.S. Internet ad spending exceeds all U.S. print advertising
2005	YouTube launched		Audit Bureau of Circulations becomes Alliance for Audited Media
	News Corp (Rupert Murdoch) buys MySpace		Association of Alternative Newsweeklies becomes the Association of Alternative Newsmedia
2006	Google buys YouTube Twitter launched	2013	American Psychiatric Association adds "Internet Addiction Disorder" to *American Diagnostic and Statistical Manual of Mental Disorders*
2007	*Journal of Communication* publishes special issue on framing, agenda-setting, and priming		
2008	*Journal of Communication* publishes special issue on the "intersection" of different mass communication research methods and theoretical approaches		
	Moyer-Gusé's entertainment overcoming resistance model introduced		

From the Cengage Series in Mass Communication and Journalism

General Mass Communication

Belmas/Overbeck, *Major Principles of Media Law*, 2014 Edition

Biagi, *Media/Impact: An Introduction to Mass Media*, Eleventh Edition

Fellow, *American Media History*, Third Edition

Hilmes, *Connections: A Broadcast History Reader*

Hilmes, *Only Connect: A Cultural History of Broadcasting in the United States*, Fourth Edition

Lester, *Visual Communication: Images with Messages*, Sixth Edition

Straubhaar/LaRose/Davenport, *Media Now: Understanding Media, Culture, and Technology*, Eighth Edition

Zelezny, *Cases in Communications Law*, Sixth Edition

Zelezny, *Communications Law: Liberties, Restraints, and the Modern Media*, Sixth Edition

Journalism

Bowles/Borden, *Creative Editing*, Sixth Edition

Davis/Davis, *Think Like an Editor: 50 Strategies for the Print and Digital World*, Second Edition

Hilliard, *Writing for Television, Radio, and New Media*, Eleventh Edition

Kessler/McDonald, *When Words Collide: A Media Writer's Guide to Grammar and Style*, Eighth Edition

Kessler/McDonald, *Cengage Advantage Books: When Words Collide: A Media Writer's Guide to Grammar and Style + Exercise Book*, Eighth Edition

Rich, *Writing and Reporting News: A Coaching Method*, Seventh Edition

Public Relations and Advertising

Diggs-Brown, *Strategic Public Relations: Audience Focused Approach*

Diggs-Brown, *The PR Styleguide: Formats for Public Relations Practice*, Third Edition

Drewniany/Jewler, *Creative Strategy in Advertising*, Eleventh Edition

Hendrix, *Public Relations Cases*, Ninth Edition

Newsom/Haynes, *Public Relations Writing: Form and Style*, Tenth Edition

Newsom/Turk/Kruckeberg, *Cengage Advantage Books: This is PR: The Realities of Public Relations*, Eleventh Edition

Sivulka, *Soap, Sex, and Cigarettes: A Cultural History of American Advertising*, Second Edition

Research and Theory

Baran/Davis, *Mass Communication Theory: Foundations, Ferment, and Future*, Seventh Edition

Sparks, *Media Effects Research: A Basic Overview*, Fourth Edition

Wimmer/Dominick, *Mass Media Research: An Introduction*, Tenth Edition

MASS COMMUNICATION THEORY

Foundations, Ferment, and Future

SEVENTH EDITION

Stanley J. Baran, Ph.D.
Bryant University

Dennis K. Davis, Ph.D.
Pennsylvania State University

CENGAGE
Learning·

Australia • Brazil • Mexico • Singapore • United Kingdom • United States

CENGAGE Learning·

Mass Communication Theory: Foundations, Ferment, and Future, Seventh Edition
Stanley J. Baran and Dennis K. Davis

Product Director: Monica Eckman

Product Manager: Kelli Strieby

Associate Content Developer: Erin Bosco

Product Assistant: Katie Walsh

Media Developer: Jessica Badiner

Marketing Manager: Jillian Borden

Art and Cover Direction, Production Management, and Composition: PreMediaGlobal

Manufacturing Planner: Doug Bertke

Rights Acquisitions Specialist: Amber Hosea

Cover Image: © mareandmare/iStockphoto

For product information and technology assistance, contact us at **Cengage Learning Customer & Sales Support, 1-800-354-9706.**

For permission to use material from this text or product, submit all requests online at **www.cengage.com/permissions.**
Further permissions questions can be e-mailed to **permissionrequest@cengage.com.**

Library of Congress Control Number: 2013949097

Student Edition:

ISBN-13: 978-1-285-05207-6

ISBN-10: 1-285-05207-2

Cengage Learning
200 First Stamford Place, 4th Floor
Stamford, CT 06902
USA

Cengage Learning is a leading provider of customized learning solutions with office locations around the globe, including Singapore, the United Kingdom, Australia, Mexico, Brazil and Japan. Locate your local office at **www.cengage.com/global**.

Cengage Learning products are represented in Canada by Nelson Education, Ltd.

To learn more about Cengage Learning Solutions, visit **www.cengage.com**.

Purchase any of our products at your local college store or at our preferred online store **www.cengagebrain.com**.

Printed in the United States of America
2 3 4 5 6 7 17 16 15 14

To Sidney Kraus

His words and actions—indeed, how he has chosen to live his life and career—in the years since the first edition of this book have convinced us of the wisdom of our original decision to honor him—our friend, mentor, and colleague.

CONTENTS

PREFACE

We have been collaborating on media theory textbooks for over 30 years beginning with a book published in 1981 and continuing with seven editions of this textbook. During that time we have witnessed many changes in society, politics, the media, media theory, and the media research community. There have been times of prosperity and there have been economic crises. Euphoria greeted the end of the Cold War followed by the terror of 9/11. Dot-com companies boomed and crashed. The Internet was first a novelty and then a significant but hard-to-classify medium. Social media and smartphones appeared and added new complexity to an already chaotic media landscape.

We have witnessed many changes to media theory and research—from the ferment of debate over theory in the 1980s to the emergence of more nuanced perspectives on theory in recent years. We watched as researchers increasingly struggled with questions flowing from accelerating changes in media. They debated how best to understand the role of new media and to chart their place among the well-established mass media. Considerable research focused on mass media entertainment and its effects. Researchers asked whether new media-based entertainment would displace established mass media. Would the Internet replace television or would the tube absorb the Net? Did the protection of children from online smut require new laws? The rise of social media raised a new set of questions. Would interaction with mediated friends displace real-world interactions? Would content recommended by friends prove more persuasive?

The events of September 11, 2001, and the wars that followed had a sobering influence on the development of media theory. Suddenly, research on mass entertainment seemed less important and interest in political communication research surged. Many if not all of the reasons that sent us to combat, unexamined and unchallenged by much of the media we count on to help us govern ourselves, proved to be false. Where were the media when it counted, or in the words of Michael Massing in the *New York Review of Books*, "Now they tell us." But consider that five years after the start of what was supposed to be a "cake walk" and three years after President Bush himself told the public that there was no link between Iraq and September 11, "as many as four in 10 Americans [41 percent] continued to believe that Saddam Hussein's regime was directly involved in financing, planning, or carrying out the terrorist attacks on that horrible day" (Braiker, 2007). Growing awareness of the media industries' powers and responsibilities led to significant criticism of their performance in the run-up to war and its coverage, and more surprising, an unprecedented public outcry against media concentration. The American people, writes media critic Todd Gitlin, "rub their eyes and marvel that a nation possessed of such an enormous industry ostensibly specializing in the gathering and distribution of facts could yet remain so befogged" (2004, p. 58).

In our preface to the sixth edition we confessed to being challenged by the way that media theory was evolving in response to technological change and to globalization. When it comes to media theories, what is still relevant and what is unimportant? How can and should we understand the role media now play in the world that has been so radically altered? Those challenges have continued and have become even more serious. Trust in media continues to erode. Questions about the way media affect our system of self-governance and our ability to know ourselves, our neighbors, and our world have become even more difficult to address. Does social media bring us closer to politicians or is it simply another tool that elites can use to manipulate us?

Although this textbook features much less historical background than previous editions, it continues to place the discipline's advances (and missteps) in historical context. The value of this strategy resides in its ability to reveal how social theory generally—and media theory specifically—develops as an ongoing effort to address pressing technological, social, and political problems. Often the most important eras for media theory development have been those of crisis and social turmoil. These are the times when the most important questions about media are asked and the search for their answers is most desperate. For half a century after the 1940s, we relied on media theories forged in the cauldron of economic depression and worldwide warfare. But by the 1990s and the end of the Cold War, the concerns of earlier eras had faded. In earlier editions, we asked whether an era of dramatic technological change might give rise to new media theories for a world whose problems were different from those of the 1940s. Did we need new media theories to fit a stable and orderly world with rising economic prosperity and startling but beneficent technological change? This question took on new significance with the dot-com crash in 2000, the economic crisis of 2008, and the recent rise of social media. Thus far, there are no new theories but the evolution of several existing theories has accelerated.

After 9/11 we were confronted by the challenges of a world in which many old questions about the role of media suddenly had new urgency. Attention turned again to the persuasive power of media and the degree to which elites control our knowledge and understanding of the social world. As you read this edition, you will find that we devote considerable attention to theories of media cognition and framing. These theories provide tools for gaining insight into the subtle ways that media can be used to control and direct political and social change. Many of the most important media research questions raised by 9/11 have only begun to be addressed. But it is clear that media theory can provide crucial insights as we work to come to grips with a new kind of public discourse, a new kind of America, a new kind of world.

A UNIQUE APPROACH

One unique feature of this book is the balanced, comprehensive introduction to the two major bodies of theory currently dominating the field: the social/behavioral theories and the cultural/critical theories. We need to know the strengths and the limitations of these two bodies of theory. We need to know how they developed in the past, how they are developing in the present, and what new conceptions they might produce, because not only do these schools of thought represent the mass communication theory of today, but they also promise to dominate our understanding of mass communication for some time to come. This balanced approach is becoming even more useful as more and more prominent scholars are calling for the integration of these bodies of theory (Delli Carpini, 2013; Jensen and Neuman, 2013; Potter, 2009).

Many American texts emphasize social/behavioral theories and either ignore or denigrate cultural/critical theories; European texts do the opposite. Conversely, as critical/cultural theories have begun to gain popularity in the United States, there have been a few textbooks that explain these theories, yet they tend to ignore or disdain social/behavioral theories. Instructors and students who want to cover *all* types of media theories are forced to use two or more textbooks and then need to sort out the various criticisms of competing ideas these books offer. To solve this problem (and we hope advance understanding of all mass communication theory), we systematically explain the legitimate differences between these theories and the research based on them. We also consider possibilities for accommodation or collaboration. This edition considers these possibilities in greater depth and detail. It is becoming increasingly clear how these bodies of theory can complement each other and provide a much broader and more useful basis for thinking about and conducting research on media.

THE USE OF HISTORY

In this book, we assume that it is important for those who study mass communication theory to have a strong grounding in its historical development. Therefore, in the pages that follow, we trace the history of theory in a clear, straightforward manner. We include discussions of historical events and people we hope students will find inherently interesting, especially if instructors use widely available DVDs, video downloads, and other materials to illustrate them (such as political propaganda, the *War of the Worlds* broadcast, newsreels from the World War II era, and the early days of television, and so on).

Readers familiar with previous editions of this textbook will find that we've made some significant changes in the way that we present the unfolding of media theory. For example, one theme of this book ever since its first edition is that theory is inevitably a product of its time. You will see that this edition is replete with examples of media's performance during our ongoing "war on terror" and their own ongoing institutional upheaval, but you will also see that many individual conceptions of mass communication theory themselves have been reinvigorated, challenged, reconsidered, or otherwise altered.

We have made an important change in how we discuss the emergence of the two important bodies of media theory. We no longer refer to specific eras in theory development and we don't use the term "paradigm" to refer to them. Instead we talk about the development of trends in media theory. We think that the notion of "trends in theory" better represents the way that the field has evolved. We have identified three trends in theory development. The first trend—the mass society and propaganda theory trend—was dominant from the 1920s until the 1940s. It gradually gave way to the media-effects-theory trend—a trend that dominated media research from the 1950s until the 1980s when it began to be challenged by the critical cultural theory trend.

NEW TO THIS EDITION

Although we have substantially reduced our discussion of older theories, our condensed consideration of the history of the discipline is still much more extensive and detailed than other theory textbooks. This made room for a wide variety of new thinking in mass communication theory. Some of the ideas you'll encounter that are new to this edition are:

- the Dual Model of Social Responsibility Theory
- an expansion of Daniel Hallin's Sphere of Consensus, Legitimate Debate, and Deviance in the digital age
- Anderson and Dill's General Aggressive Model of media violence
- Super-Peer Theory of learning from media
- a discussion of the impact of sexual hip-hop
- the Downward Spiral Model of Media Effects and the desensitization to violence
- an expanded discussion of critical feminist scholarship and feminist reception studies
- Objectification Theory (drawn from feminist critical theory)
- the Empowered Child Model of Media Research/Development
- wishful and similarity identification in media effects
- an expanded discussion of Entertainment Theory and Mood Management Theory
- a detailed discussion of Schema Theory and information processing
- the Heuristic-Systematic Model of information processing

- Transportation Theory
- Narrative Persuasion Theory
- the Extended Elaboration Likelihood Model
- the Entertainment Overcoming Resistance Model
- the Delay Hypothesis of media effects
- Hostile Media Theory
- an examination of the literature on the neuroscience perspective of information processing
- Affective Intelligence
- Motivated Reasoning and the Backfire Effect
- the Top-Down/Bottom-Up Theory of Political Attitude Formation
- Entman's cascading activation model of framing
- a discussion of transactive memory and neural plasticity and Internet use
- the Dual-Factor Model of Facebook Use
- the Idealized Virtual Identity Hypothesis of social network use
- the Extended Real-life Hypothesis of social network use
- Parental Mediation Theory of children's digital media use, and
- new sections on health communication and computer-mediated communication.

THE USE OF TOPICS FOR CRITICAL THINKING

It is important, too, that students realize that researchers develop theories to address important questions about the role of media—enduring questions that will again become important as new media continue to be introduced and as we deal with a world reordered by September 11, the ongoing war on terrorism, systemic economic distress, and seemingly intractable political and cultural divides. We must be aware of how the radical changes in media that took place in the past are related to the changes taking place now.

We attempt this engagement with mass communication theory in several ways. Every chapter begins with a list of Learning Objectives designed to guide student thinking. Each chapter also includes a section entitled *Critical Thinking Questions*. Its aim, as the title suggests, is to encourage students to think critically, even skeptically, about how that chapter's theories have been applied in the past or how they are being applied today. Each chapter also includes at least two *Thinking about Theory* boxes. These pedagogical devices are also designed to encourage critical thinking. Some discuss how a theorist addressed an issue and tried to resolve it. Still others highlight and criticize important, issue-related examples of the application of media theory. Students are asked to relate material in these boxes to contemporary controversies, events, and theories. A few examples are Chapter 4's essay on drug arrests and race, Chapter 8's box on media coverage of workers and the working poor, and Chapter 9's essay on American climate change denialism. We hope that readers will find these useful in developing their own thinking about these issues. We believe that mass communication theory, if it is to have any meaning for students, must be used by them.

We have also sprinkled the chapters with *Instant Access* boxes, presenting the advantages and disadvantages of the major theories we discuss. The advantages are those offered by the theories' proponents; the disadvantages represent the views of their critics. These presentations are at best sketchy or partial, and although they should give a pretty good idea of the theories, the picture needs to be completed with a full reading of the chapters and a great deal of reflection on the theories they present. All chapters also provide marginal definitions of important terms, and chapter summaries. Finally, at the end of the text there is an extensive bibliography and a thorough index.

THE BIG PICTURE

This textbook provides a comprehensive, authoritative introduction to mass communication theory. We have provided clearly written examples, graphics, and other materials to illustrate key theories. We trace the emergence of three trends in media theory—mass society/propaganda, social/behavioral, and critical/cultural. Then we discuss how each of these bodies of theory contributes to our understanding of media and human development, the use of media by audiences, the influence of media on cognition, the role of media in society, and finally the links between media and culture. The book ends with a consideration of how media theory is developing to meet current challenges, especially those posed by the new interactive digital technologies. We offer many examples of social/behavioral and critical/cultural theory and an in-depth discussion of their strengths and limitations. We emphasize that media theories are human creations typically intended to address specific problems or issues. We believe that it is easier to learn theories when they are examined with contextual information about the motives of theorists and the problems and issues they addressed.

In the next few years, as mass media industries continue to experience rapid change and our use of media evolves, understanding of media theory will become even more necessary and universal. We've continued to argue in this edition that many of the old questions about the role of media in culture, in society, and in people's lives have resurfaced with renewed relevance. This book traces how researchers and theorists have traditionally addressed these questions and we provide insights into how they might do so in the future.

THE SUPPORTING PHILOSOPHY OF THIS BOOK

The philosophy of this book is relatively straightforward: Though today's media technologies might be new, their impact on daily life might not be so different from that of past influences. Changes in media have always posed challenges but have also created opportunities. We can use media to improve the quality of our lives, or we can permit our lives to be seriously disrupted. As a society, we can use media wisely or foolishly. To make these choices, we need theories—those explaining the role of media for us as individuals and guiding the development of media industries for our society at large. This book should help us develop our understanding of theory so we can make better use of media and play a bigger role in the development of new media industries.

ADDITIONAL RESOURCES

For Instructors: An **Online Instructor's Manual** is available to assist faculty teaching a mass communication theory or media and society course. The Instructor's Manual offers assignment ideas, suggestions for audiovisual materials and for using many of the text's special features, syllabus preparation tools, and a sample syllabus. A Test Bank features chapter-by-chapter test questions in both multiple-choice and discussion/essay formats. You can download the Instructor's Manual by accessing the text's password-protected Instructor Companion Site.

For Students: A **Student Companion Site** provides access to a rich array of study tools, including chapter-level tutorial quizzes, Critical Thinking exercises, a glossary, flashcards, and relevant Web links.

ACKNOWLEDGMENTS

In preparing this seventh edition, we have had the assistance of many people. Most important, we have drawn on the scholarly work of several generations of social and cultural theorists. Their ideas have inspired and guided contemporary work. It's an exciting time to be a communication scholar!

We work within a research community that, although in ferment, is also both vibrant and supportive. In these pages, we acknowledge and explain the contributions that our many colleagues across the United States and around the world have made to mass communication theory. We regret the inevitable errors and omissions, and we take responsibility for them. We are also grateful to our reviewers.

These reviewers helped us avoid some errors and omissions, but they bear no responsibility for those that remain. We also wish to thank our Cengage friends, whose encouragement and advice sustained us. Their task was made less difficult than it might otherwise have been by our first Wadsworth editor, Becky Hayden, and Chris Clerkin, the editor for the first edition of this text. These accomplished professionals taught us how to avoid many of the sins usually committed by novice authors. The editor who worked with us the longest, Holly Allen, is as sharp as her predecessors, and she became quite adept at using her gentle hand with what had become two veteran textbook authors. Our new editorial team, ably headed by Erin Bosco, continued the competence and professionalism to which we have become accustomed.

We must also thank our families. The Davis children—Jennifer, Kerry, Andy, Mike—are now scattered across the Midwest in Norman, Lincoln, Nashville, and Chicago, so they have been less involved with (or impacted by) the day-to-day development of this edition. Nonetheless, they often assisted with insights drawn from the academic fields in which they themselves have become expert: history, philosophy, Asian studies, marketing, and computer science. The Baran kids— Jordan and Matt Dowd—are scattered as well, but Internet and phone access when the authors had questions about those "new-fangled" technologies proved invaluable. They suffered our questions with charm and love.

It would be impossible to overstate the value of our wives' support. Nancy Davis continues to provide a sympathetic audience for efforts to think through media theory and brainstorm ways to apply it. Susan Baran, an expert in media literacy in her own right, has a remarkable ability to find the practical in the most theoretical. This is why more than a few of the ideas and examples in these pages found their refinement in her sharp mind. She keeps her husband grounded as a thinker and author while she lifts him as a man and father.

Finally, this book is the product of a collaboration that has gone on for over 40 years. We started our professional careers at Cleveland State University in 1973 in a communication department headed by Sidney Kraus. Sid inspired us, along with most other junior faculty, to become active, productive researchers. Today, a disproportionate number of active communication scholars have direct or indirect links to the Cleveland State program. Sid demonstrates the many ways that a single person can have a powerful impact on a discipline. Through his scholarship, his mentorship, and his friendship he has left a truly indelible mark.

S.J.B. & D.K.D.

Foundations: Introduction to Mass Communication Theory and Its Roots

UNDERSTANDING AND EVALUATING MASS COMMUNICATION THEORY

Social networking site Facebook debuted on the Internet in 2003. Within five years it grew to 100 million users, and in October 2012, the company proudly announced it had 1 billion members visiting monthly, networking in over 70 languages (Delo, 2012). Upon reaching that milestone, Facebook released a video likening its brand to bridges, airplanes, and the universe. Critics easily saw the connection to bridges and planes. Like social networking, they bring people together. But the universe? A billion folks is a lot, but it's hardly the universe. Maybe the point was that Facebook's "citizens" represent a universe unto themselves. But it must be a strange universe indeed, with all those kids posting what they had for lunch, gossiping, and posting party pictures ... if in fact that was who populated the world of Facebook. It's not. Forty-six percent of Facebookers are over 45 years old, and this, its fastest-growing age segment, is larger than the 0- to 34-year-olds (42 percent) everyone assumes are its heaviest users (Skelton, 2012).

So maybe the typical Facebooker isn't what we usually think of when we consider who uses the site. So, what else do we want to know about these 1 billion users? How many friends does a typical Facebooker have? About 130 (Skelton, 2012). But now this raises another question. What exactly is a *friend*? If you can have 130 of them, are they really friends? Of course they are, argue psychologists Ashwini Nadkarni and Stefan Hofmann, who argue that Facebook fosters a sense of belonging and lets people express themselves as they'd like, two obvious functions served by real friends (2012). But in a billion-person universe there have to be a lot of different kinds of people looking for different things from their online friendships. Of course there are. Psychologists Laura Buffardi and Keith Campbell (2008) claim that narcissists and people with low self-esteem spend more time on Facebook than do others. But according to another psychologist, Samuel D. Gosling and his research team, maybe personality differences have little to do with *why* people use Facebook, as they discovered that rather than using the site to compensate for aspects of their offline personalities, users simply carry those everyday characteristics over to their online selves (Gosling et al., 2011).

Clearly Facebook is a useful medium to lots of people. Many log onto the site several times every day and constantly post updates. Most users don't give much thought to what they are doing and why. If asked, most say they are simply passing time, being entertained or engaging in casual communication with friends and family. But could Facebook be more important than they realize? What about your own use of Facebook? Is it making an important difference in your life or is it just another way to pass time? How do you view the company that provides you with Facebook? Do you know how it earns a profit from the services it provides? If you regularly upload lots of personal information, you are trusting that the company will not misuse this information and will provide you with the level of privacy that you want. But should you be so trusting? Facebook is a private company and it aggressively seeks to earn profits by selling information and giving advertisers access to its users. Should you care more about what Facebook does with the information you provide?

Your answers to these questions are naturally based on *your* ideas or assumptions about Facebook, its users, and your own experiences. You can take into account what your friends say about Facebook and what you happen to read in the media. You might wonder if what you think is happening for you and your friends is the same for all those "old people" Facebook says are there. Psychologists Nadkarni, Hofmann, Buffardi, Campbell, and Gosling had their ideas and assumptions, too but they moved beyond their immediate personal experience to conduct research. They collected data and systematically assessed the usefulness of their ideas. They engaged in social science. Working together with others in a research community they are seeking to develop a formal, systematic set of ideas about Facebook and its role in the social world. They are helping to develop a mass communication theory.

LEARNING OBJECTIVES

After studying this chapter you should be able to

- Explain differences in the operation of the physical and social sciences.
- Describe the relationship between the scientific method and causality.
- Define theory.
- Differentiate the four broad categories of mass communication theory—postpositive, cultural, critical, and normative theory—by their ontology, epistemology, and axiology.
- Establish criteria for judging theory.
- Differentiate the four trends in media theory—the mass society and mass culture, limited-effects, critical cultural, and meaning-making trends.

OVERVIEW

In this chapter, we will discuss just what separates an idea, a belief, or an assumption from a theory. We will examine mass communication theories and media theories created by social scientists and humanists. We'll look at some of the difficulties faced by those who attempt to systematically study and understand human behavior. We'll consider the particular problems encountered when the concern involves human behavior *and* the media. We'll see, too, that the definition of *social science* can be quite elusive. We'll define *theory* and offer several classifications of communication theory, media theory, and mass communication theory. We'll trace the way that theories of mass communication have been created and we will examine the purposes served by these theories. Most important, we will try to convince you that the difficulties that seem to surround the development and study of mass communication theory aren't really difficulties at all; rather, they are challenges that make the study of mass communication theory interesting and exciting. As physicist John D. Barrow wrote, "A world that [is] simple enough to be fully known would be too simple to contain conscious observers who might know it" (1998, p. 3).

DEFINING AND REDEFINING MASS COMMUNICATION

In recent decades, the number and variety of mass communication and media theories have steadily increased. Media theory has emerged as a more or less independent body of thought in both the social sciences and the humanities. This book is intended as a guide to this diverse and sometimes contradictory thinking. You will find ideas developed by scholars in every area of the social sciences, from history and anthropology to sociology and psychology. Ideas have also been drawn from the humanities, especially from philosophy and literary analysis. The resulting ferment of ideas is both challenging and heuristic. These theories provide the raw materials for constructing even more useful and powerful theoretical perspectives.

If you are looking for a concise, definitive definition of theory, you won't find it in this book. We have avoided narrow definitions of theory in favor of an inclusive approach that finds value in most systematic, scholarly efforts to make sense of media and their role in society. We have included recent theories that some contemporary researchers consider unscientific. Some of the theories we review are **grand**; they try to explain entire media systems and their role in society. Others are narrowly focused and provide insight into specific uses or effects of media. Our selection of theories for inclusion in this book is based partly on their enduring historical importance and partly on their potential to contribute to future scholarship. This process is necessarily subjective and is based on our own understanding of media and mass communication. Our consideration of contemporary perspectives is focused on those that illustrate enduring or innovative conceptualizations. But before we embark on that consideration, we need to offer definitions of some important concepts.

When an organization employs a technology as a medium to communicate with a large audience, **mass communication** is said to have occurred. The professionals at the *New York Times* (an organization) use printing presses and the newspaper (technology and medium) to reach their readers (a large audience). The

grand theory
Theory designed to describe and explain all aspects of a given phenomenon

mass communication
When a source, typically an organization, employs a technology as a medium to communicate with a large audience

writers, producers, filmmakers, and other professionals at the Cartoon Network use various audio and video technologies, satellites, cable television, and home receivers to communicate with their audience. Warner Brothers places ads in magazines to tell readers what movies it is releasing and it distributes those movies to local theaters where they are viewed by audiences.

But as you no doubt know—and as you'll be reminded constantly throughout this text—the mass communication environment is changing quite radically. When you receive a piece of direct-mail advertising addressed to you by name, and in which your name is used throughout, you are an audience of one—not the large audience envisioned in traditional notions of mass communication. When you sit at your computer and post a comment to a news story that is read by thousands of other readers, you are obviously communicating with a large audience, but you are not an organization in the sense of a newspaper, cable television network, or movie studio. The availability of lightweight, portable, inexpensive video equipment—quite possibly your smartphone—combined with the development of easy-to-use Internet video sites like YouTube, makes it possible for an "everyday" person like you to be a television writer and producer, reaching audiences numbering in the tens of millions.

Although most theories we will study in this text were developed before our modern communications revolution, many are still quite useful. But we must remember that much has changed and is changing in how people use technologies to communicate. One useful way to do this is to think of **mediated communication** as existing on a continuum that stretches from **interpersonal communication** at one end to traditional forms of mass communication at the other. Where different media fall along this continuum depends on the amount of control and involvement people have in the communication process. The telephone, for example (the phone as traditionally understood—not the one you might own that has Internet access, GPS, and some 500 other "killer apps"), sits at one end. It is obviously a communication technology, but one that is most typical of interpersonal communication: At most, a very few people can be involved in communicating at any given time, and they have a great deal of involvement with and control over that communication. The conversation is theirs, and they determine its content. A big-budget Hollywood movie or a network telecast of the Super Bowl sits at the opposite pole. Viewers have limited control over the communication that occurs. Certainly, people can apply idiosyncratic interpretations to the content before them, and they can choose to direct however much attention they wish to the screen. They can choose to actively seek meaning from media content, or they can choose to passively decode it. But their control and involvement cannot directly alter the content of the messages being transmitted. Message content is centrally controlled by media organizations.

As you'll see when we examine the more contemporary mass communication theories, new communication technologies are rapidly filling in the middle of the continuum between the telephone and television. Suddenly, media consumers have the power to alter message content if they are willing to invest the time and have the necessary skill and resources. Audiences are choosing to be *active* in ways that are hard to anticipate, and the consequences of their activity may not be understood for decades to come. The rise of social networking and YouTube

mediated communication
Communication between a few or many people that employ a technology as a medium

interpersonal communication
Communication between two or a few people, typically face-to-face

demonstrates an ever-growing willingness to use media to share content and perspectives on content. The ongoing popularity of downloading music and the Apple iPod show a willingness to invest the time, acquire the skills, and purchase the technology necessary to take greater control over music. These forms of audience activity have enabled media companies like Apple, Google, and Facebook to become dominant forces in a media world previously dominated by the likes of Disney, News Corporation, and Time Warner. New media companies are competing to provide innovative and useful technologies that deliver more attractive services. These technologies and services will give us new ways to create and control media content that is important to us. As this happens, there will be profound consequences for our personal lives, the media industries, and the larger social world. As journalist and new media theorist Jeff Jarvis explains, "Back in the day, a decade … ago, we discovered media—news, information, or service—through brands: We went and bought the newspaper or magazine or turned on a channel on its schedule. That behavior and expectation was brought to the Internet: Brands built sites and expected us to come to them. Now there are other spheres of discovery—new spheres that are shifting in importance, effectiveness, and share. I believe they will overlap more and more to provide better—that is, more relevant, timely, and authoritative—means of discovery. These evolving spheres also change the relationships of creators and customers and the fundamental economics of media" (2010).

SCIENCE AND HUMAN BEHAVIOR

Ours is a society that generally respects and believes its scientists. Science is one of the fundamental reasons why we enjoy our admirable standard of living and have a growing understanding of the world around us. But not all scientists or the science that they practice are understood or revered equally. British astronomer and philosopher John D. Barrow opened his 1998 book, *Impossibility: The Limits of Science and the Science of Limits*, with this observation on the value of science and its practitioners:

> Bookshelves are stuffed with volumes that expound the successes of the mind and the silicon chip. We expect science to tell us what can be done and what is to be done. Governments look to scientists to improve the quality of life and safeguard us from earlier "improvements." Futurologists see no limit to human inquiry, while social scientists see no end to the raft of problems it spawns. (p. 1)

The physical *scientists* and engineers are the dreamers, the fixers, the guardians. They are the future—they have sent us photos of stars aborning, detailed the inner workings of the atom, and invented the microwave oven, the World Wide Web, and cell phones that take and send video. *Social scientists* are the naysayers, the Grinches of the world. They tell us that television corrupts our morals, political campaigns render us too cynical to participate meaningfully in our democracy, and parents rely too heavily on television to babysit their kids. Or, as columnist David Brooks reminds us, "A survey of the social science of the past century shows it to be, by and large, an insanely pessimistic field" (2002, p. 22). We tend to readily accept most of the good findings of Barrow's *scientists*. The universe is continually expanding? Of course. The existence of quarks? Naturally. At the same time, we tend to be more suspicious of the findings of the *social scientists*.

Playing with Barbies destroys little girls' self-esteem? I don't think so! Videogames teach violence? That's so Twentieth Century! Texting kills spelling and grammar? OMG! U r wrng. LOL!

There is another important difference that we often see between physical and social science. Physical science has allowed us to gain increasing control over the physical world. This control has had direct and very useful consequences for our daily lives. Powerful technologies have been invented that very effectively shelter us from our environment and enable us to do things that would have been seen as magical just a few decades ago. But what has social science done for us lately? Is the social world a better place as a result of social science? Do we understand ourselves and others better? Are there stunning achievements that compare to splitting the atom or landing on the moon? Compared to the physical science, the social sciences seem much less useful and their theories less practical and more controversial.

social scientists
Scientists who examine relationships among phenomena in the human or social world

Why does our society seem to have greater difficulty accepting the theories and findings of **social scientists**, those who apply logic and observation—that is, science—to the understanding of the social world, rather than the physical world? Why do we have trust in the people who wield telescopes and microscopes to probe the breadth of the universe and the depth of human cells but skepticism about the tools used by social observers to probe the breadth of the social world or the depth of human experience? You can read more about the levels of respect afforded to scientists of different stripes in the box entitled "All Scientific Inquiry Is Value-Laden."

causality
When a given factor influences another, even by way of an intervening variable

causal relationship
When the alterations in a particular variable under specific conditions always produce the same effect in another variable

One important basis for our society's reluctance to accept the theories of the social scientists is the *logic of* **causality**. We readily understand this logic. You've no doubt had it explained to you during a high school physics or chemistry class, so we'll use a simple example from those classes: boiling water. If we (or our representatives, the scientists) can manipulate an independent variable (heat) and produce the same effect (boiling at 100 degrees centigrade) under the same conditions (sea level) every time, then a **causal relationship** has been established. Heating water at sea level to 100 degrees will cause water to boil. No matter how many times you heat beakers of water at sea level, they will all boil at 100 degrees. Lower the heat; the water does not boil. Heat it at the top of Mount Everest; it boils at lower temperatures. Go back to sea level (or alter the atmospheric pressure in a laboratory test); it boils at 100 degrees. This is repeated observation under controlled conditions. We even have a name for this, the **scientific method**, and there are many definitions for it. Here is a small sample:

scientific method
A search for truth through accurate observation and interpretation of fact

hypothesis
A testable prediction about some event

1. "A means whereby insight into an undiscovered truth is sought by (1) identifying the problem that defines the goal of the quest, (2) gathering data with the hope of resolving the problem, (3) positing a **hypothesis** both as a logical means of locating the data and as an aid to resolving the problem, and (4) empirically testing the hypothesis by processing and interpreting the data to see whether the interpretation of them will resolve the question that initiated the research" (Leedy, 1997, pp. 94-95).

2. "A set of interrelated constructs (concepts), definitions, and propositions that present a systematic view of phenomena by specifying relations among variables, with the purpose of explaining and predicting phenomena" (Kerlinger, 1986, p. 9).

THINKING ABOUT THEORY | All Scientific Inquiry Is Value-Laden

Science writer Shawn Lawrence Otto would argue that the elevated respect afforded to the physical and social sciences, to the positivists and postpositivists, is not as high as this text's discussion might lead you to believe. "At its core, science is a reliable method for creating knowledge, and thus power," he wrote, "Because science pushes the boundaries of knowledge, it pushes us to constantly refine our ethics and morality, and that is always political. But beyond that, science constantly disrupts hierarchical power structures and vested interests in a long drive to give knowledge, and thus power, to the individual, and that process is also political … Every time a scientist makes a factual assertion—Earth goes around the sun, there is such a thing as evolution, humans are causing climate change—it either supports or challenges somebody's vested interests" (2011). Yes, as you read, physical *scientists* may be the dreamers, the fixers, the guardians, but their work is increasingly likely to be just as unsatisfying to some as that of the social scientists.

Public reaction to the theory of evolution and the science behind climate change offer two obvious examples. Vincent Cassone, chair of the University of Kentucky's biology department, defends evolution as the central organizing principle of all the natural sciences, "The theory of evolution is the fundamental backbone of all biological research. There is more evidence for evolution than there is for the theory of gravity, than the idea that things are made up of atoms, or Einstein's theory of relativity. It is the finest scientific theory ever devised." Yet the legislature of his state challenged the teaching of evolution in Kentucky public schools (Blackford, 2012). Across America, 46 percent of college graduates do not accept the theory of evolution; even 25 percent with graduate degrees deny its validity. Climate scientists do not fare much better. Despite overwhelming evidence that the earth is warming, that human activity contributes to that change, and that the oceans are rising, the Virginia legislature banned the term "sea-level rise" from a state-commissioned study of the problem because it was a "left-wing term." It replaced it with "recurrent flooding" (both in Pollitt, 2012).

Why the resistance to even traditional physical sciences? Mr. Otto answers, "The very essence of the scientific process is to question long-held assumptions about the nature of the universe, to dream up experiments that test those questions, and, based on the observations, to incrementally build knowledge that is independent of our beliefs and assumptions" (2011). Still, this doesn't explain why social scientists seem to suffer greater criticism than their physical science colleagues? Why do you think this is the case?

3. "A method … by which our beliefs may be determined by nothing human, but by some external permanency—by something upon which our thinking has no effect….The method must be such that the ultimate conclusion of every man [*sic*] shall be the same. Such is the method of science. Its fundamental hypothesis … is this: There are real things whose characters are entirely independent of our opinions about them" (Peirce, 1955, p. 18).

Throughout the last century and into this one, some social researchers have tried to apply the scientific method to the study of human behavior and society. As you'll soon see, an Austrian immigrant to the United States, Paul Lazarsfeld, was an important advocate of applying social research methods to the study of mass media. But although the essential logic of the scientific method is quite simple, its application in the social (rather than physical) world is necessarily more complicated. Philosopher Karl Popper, whose 1934 *The Logic of Scientific Discovery* is regarded as the foundation of the scientific method, explained, "Long-term prophecies can be derived from scientific conditional predictions only if they apply to systems which can be described as well-isolated, stationary, and recurrent. These systems are very rare in nature; and modern society is not one of them" (in Stevens, 2012).

Take, for example, the much-discussed issue of press coverage of political campaigns and its impact on voter turnout. We know that more media attention is paid to elections than ever before. Today, television permits continual eyewitness coverage of candidate activity. Mobile vans trail candidates and beam stories off satellites so that local television stations can air their own coverage. The Internet and Web offer instant access to candidates, their ideas, and those of their opponents. Twitter and YouTube let us continually track their every move. Yet, despite advances in media technology and innovations in campaign coverage, voter participation in the United States remains low. Not since 1968 has turnout in a presidential election exceeded 60 percent. Even in the 2008 race between Barack Obama and John McCain, considered "the most technologically innovative, entrepreneurially driven campaign in American political history," only 56.8 percent of registered voters cast ballots (Dickinson, 2009; U.S. Election Project, 2009). Should we assume that media campaign coverage suppresses potential voter turnout? This is an assertion that some mass communication observers might be quick to make. But would they be right? How could or should we verify whether this assertion is valid?

As we shall see, the pioneers of mass communication research faced this situation during the 1930s. There were precious few scientific studies of, but many bold assertions about, the bad effects of mass media. A small number of social scientists began to argue that these claims should not be accepted before making **empirical** observations that could either support them or permit them to be rejected. While these early researchers often shared the widely held view that media were powerful, they believed that the scientific method might be used to harness this power to avoid negative effects like juvenile delinquency. They hoped to produce positive effects such as promoting Americans' trust in their own democratic political system while subverting the appeal of totalitarian propaganda. In this way, scientific research would allow media to be a force for good in shaping the social world. If their dreams had been fulfilled we would be living in a very different sort of social world. Social scientists would be engineering the construction of social institutions in much the same way that physical scientists engineer the construction of skyscrapers or Mars Rovers. But that didn't happen. Why?

Social researchers faced many problems in applying the scientific method to the study of social world. When seeking to observe the effects of political news, how can there be repeated observations? No two audiences, never mind any two individuals, who see news stories are the same. No two elections are the same. News stories vary greatly in terms of content and structure. Even if a scientist conducted the same experiment on the same people repeatedly (showing them, for example, the same excerpts of coverage and then asking them if and how they might vote), these people would now be different each additional time because they would have learned from previous exposure and had a new set of experiences. Most would complain about having to watch the same story over and over. They might

empirical
Capable of being verified or disproved by observation

say whatever they think the researcher wants to hear in order to get out of the experiment.

How can there be control over conditions that might influence observed effects? Who can control what people watch, read, or listen to, or to whom they talk, not to mention what they have learned about voting and civic responsibility in their school, family, and church? One solution is to put them in a laboratory and limit what they watch and learn. But people don't grow up in laboratories or watch television with the types of strangers they meet in a laboratory experiment. They don't consume media messages hooked to galvanic skin response devices or scanned by machines that track their eye movements. And unlike atoms under study, people can and sometimes do change their behaviors as a result of the social scientists' findings, which further confounds claims of causality. And there is another problem. Powerful media effects rarely happen as a result of exposure to a few messages in a short amount of time. Effects take place slowly, over long periods of time. At any moment, nothing may seem to be happening.

This implementation of the scientific method is difficult for those studying the social world for four reasons:

1. **Most of the significant and interesting forms of human behavior are quite difficult to measure**. We can easily measure the temperature at which water boils. With ingenious and complex technology, we can even measure the weight of an atom or the speed at which the universe is expanding. But how do we measure something like civic duty? Should we count the incidence of voting? Maybe a person's decision not to vote is her personal expression of that duty. Try something a little easier, like measuring aggression in a television violence study. Can aggression be measured by counting how many times a child hits a rubber doll? Is gossiping about a neighbor an aggressive act? How do we measure an attitude (a predisposition to do something rather than an observable action)? What is three pounds of tendency to hold conservative political views or 16.7 millimeters of patriotism?

2. **Human behavior is exceedingly complex**. Human behavior does not easily lend itself to causal description. It is easy to identify a single factor that causes water to boil. But it has proved impossible to isolate single factors that serve as the exclusive cause of important actions of human behavior. Human behavior may simply be too complex to allow scientists to ever fully untangle the different factors that combine to cause observable actions. We can easily control the heat and atmospheric pressure in our boiling experiment. We can control the elements in a chemistry experiment with relative ease. But if we want to develop a theory of the influence of mediated communication on political campaigns, how do we control which forms of media people choose to use? How do we control the amount of attention they pay to specific types of news? How do we measure how well or poorly they comprehend what they consume? How do we take into account factors that influenced people long before we started our research? For example, how do we measure the type and amount of political socialization fostered by parents, schools, or peers? All these things (not to mention countless others) will influence the relationship between people's use of media and their behavior in an election. How can we be sure what

caused what? Voting might have declined even more precipitously without media coverage. Remember, the very same factors that lead one person to vote might lead another to stay home.

3. **Humans have goals and are self-reflexive.** We do not always behave in response to something that has happened; very often we act in response to something we hope or expect will happen. Moreover, we constantly revise our goals and make highly subjective determinations about their potential for success or failure. Water boils *after* the application of heat. It doesn't think about boiling. It doesn't begin to experience boiling and then decide that it doesn't like the experience. We think about our actions and inactions; we reflect on our values, beliefs, and attitudes. Water doesn't develop attitudes against boiling that lead it to misperceive the amount of heat it is experiencing. It stops boiling when the heat is removed. It doesn't think about stopping or have trouble making up its mind. It doesn't have friends who tell it that boiling is fun and should be continued even when there is insufficient heat. But people do think about their actions, and they frequently make these actions contingent on their expectations that something will happen. "Humans are not like billiard balls propelled solely by forces external to them," explained cognitive psychologist Albert Bandura. "Billiard balls cannot change the shape of the table, the size of the pockets, or intervene in the paths they take, or even decide whether to play the game at all. In contrast, humans not only think, but, individually and collectively, shape the form those external forces take and even determine whether or not they come into play. Murray Gell-Mann, the physicist Nobelist, underscored the influential role of the personal determinants when he remarked, 'Imagine how hard physics would be if particles could think'" (2008, pp. 95–96).

4. **The simple notion of causality is sometimes troubling when it is applied to ourselves.** We have no trouble accepting that heat causes water to boil at 100 degrees centigrade at sea level; we relish such causal statements in the physical world. We want to know how things work, what makes things happen. As much as we might like to be thrilled by horror movies or science fiction films in which physical laws are continually violated, we trust the operation of these laws in our daily lives. But we often resent causal statements when they are applied to ourselves. We can't see the expanding universe or the breakup of the water molecule at the boiling point, so we are willing to accept the next best thing, the word of an objective expert, that is, a scientist. But we can see ourselves watching cable news and not voting and going to a movie and choosing a brand-name pair of slacks and learning about people from lands we've never visited. Why do we need experts telling us about ourselves or explaining to us why we do things? We're not so easily influenced by media, we say. But ironically, most of us are convinced that other people are much more likely to be influenced by media (the **third-person effect**). So although we don't need to be protected from media influence, *others* might; they're not as smart as we are (Grier and Brumbaugh, 2007). We are our own men and women—independent, freethinking individuals. We weren't affected by those McDonald's ads; we simply bought that Big Mac, fries, and a large Coke because, darn it, we deserved a break today. And after all, we did need to eat something and the McDonald's did happen to be right on the way back to the dorm.

third-person effect
The idea that "media affect others, but not me"

DEFINING THEORY

theory
Any organized set of concepts, explanations, and principles of some aspect of human experience

Scientists, physical or social (however narrowly or broadly defined), deal in **theory**. "Theories are stories about how and why events occur.... Scientific theories begin with the assumption that the universe, including the social universe created by acting human beings, reveals certain basic and fundamental properties and processes that explain the ebb and flow of events in specific processes" (Turner, 1998, p. 1). Theory has numerous other definitions. John Bowers and John Courtright offered a traditional scientific definition: "Theories ... are sets of statements asserting relationships among classes of variables" (1984, p. 13). So did Charles Berger: "A theory consists of a set of interrelated propositions that stipulate relationships among theoretical constructs and an account of the mechanism or mechanisms that explain the relationships stipulated in the propositions" (2005, p. 417). Kenneth Bailey's conception of theory accepts a wider array of ways to understand the social world: "Explanations and predictions of social phenomena ... relating the subject of interest ... to some other phenomena" (1982, p. 39).

Our definition, though, will be drawn from a synthesis of two even more generous views of theory. Assuming that there are a number of different ways to understand how communication functions in our complex world, Stephen Littlejohn and Karen Foss defined theory as "any organized set of concepts, explanations, and principles of some aspect of human experience" (2011, p. 19). Emory Griffin also takes this broader view, writing that a theory is an idea "that explains an event or behavior. It brings clarity to an otherwise jumbled situation; it draws order out of chaos.... [It] synthesizes the data, focuses our attention on what's crucial, and helps us ignore that which makes little difference" (1994, p. 34). These latter two writers are acknowledging an important reality of communication and mass communication theories: There are a lot of them, the questions they produce are testable to varying degrees, they tend to be situationally based, and they sometimes seem contradictory and chaotic. As communication theorist Katherine Miller explained, "Different schools of thought will define *theory* in different ways depending on the needs of the theorist and on beliefs about the social world and the nature of knowledge" (2005, pp. 22–23). Scholars have identified four major categories of communication theory—(1) postpositivism, (2) cultural theory, (3) critical theory, and (4) normative theory—and although they "share a commitment to an increased understanding of social and communicative life and a value for high-quality scholarship" (Miller, 2005, p. 32), they differ in

ontology
The nature of reality, what is knowable

epistemology
How knowledge is created and expanded

axiology
The proper role of values in research and theory building

- Their goals
- Their view of the nature of reality, what is knowable and worth knowing—their **ontology**
- Their view of the methods used to create and expand knowledge—their **epistemology**
- Their view of the proper role of human values in research and theory building—their **axiology**

These differences not only define the different types of theory, but they also help make it obvious why a broader and more flexible definition of *social science* in mass communication theory is useful.

POSTPOSITIVIST THEORY

postpositivist theory
Theory based on empirical observation guided by the scientific method

When researchers first wanted to systematically study the role of mass media in social world, they turned to the physical sciences for their model. Those in the physical sciences (physics, chemistry, astronomy, and so on) believed in *positivism*, the idea that knowledge could be gained only through empirical, observable, measurable phenomena examined through the scientific method. But as we saw earlier in this chapter, the social world is very different from the physical world. Causality needs to be understood and applied differently. After a century of trial and error, social scientists committed to the scientific method developed **postpositivist theory**. This type of theory is based on empirical observation guided by the scientific method, but it recognizes that humans and human behavior are not as constant as elements of the physical world.

The goals of postpositivist theory are the same as those set by physical scientists for their theories: explanation, prediction, and control. For example, researchers who want to explain the operation of political advertising, predict which commercials will be most effective, and control the voting behavior of targeted citizens would, of necessity, rely on postpositivist theory. Its ontology accepts that the world, even the social world, exists apart from our perceptions of it; human behavior is sufficiently predictable to be studied systematically. (Postpositivists do, however, recognize that the social world does have more variation than the physical world; for example, the names we give to things define them and our reaction to them—hence the *post* of postpositivism.) Its epistemology argues that knowledge is advanced through the systematic, logical search for regularities and causal relationships employing the scientific method. Advances come when there is **intersubjective agreement** among scientists studying a given phenomenon. That is, postpositivists find confidence "in the community of social researchers," not "in any individual social scientist" (Schutt, 2009, p. 89). It is this cautious reliance on the scientific method that defines postpositivism's axiology— the objectivity inherent in the application of the scientific method keeps researchers' and theorists' values out of the search for knowledge (as much as is possible). They fear that values could bias the choice and application of methods so that researchers would be more likely to get the results that they want (results that are consistent with their values). Postpositivist communication theory, then, is theory developed through a system of inquiry that resembles as much as possible the rules and practices of what we traditionally understand as science.

intersubjective agreement
When members of a research community independently arrive at similar conclusions about a given social phenomenon

CULTURAL THEORY

cultural theory
Theory seeking to understand contemporary cultures by analyzing the structure and content of their communication

But many communication theorists do not want to explain, predict, and control social behavior. Their goal is to *understand* how and why that behavior occurs in the social world. This **cultural theory** seeks to understand contemporary cultures by analyzing the structure and content of their communication. Cultural theory finds its origin in **hermeneutic theory**—the study of understanding, especially through the systematic interpretation of actions or texts. Hermeneutics originally began as the study or interpretation of the Bible and other sacred works. As it evolved over the last two centuries, it maintained its commitment to the

hermeneutic theory
The study of understanding, especially by interpreting action and text

social hermeneutics
Theory seeking to understand how those in an observed social situation interpret their own lot in that situation

examination of "objectifications of the mind" (Burrell and Morgan, 1979, p. 236), or what Miller calls "social creations" (2005, p. 52). Just as the Bible was the "objectification" of early Christian culture, and those who wanted to understand that culture would study that text, most modern applications of hermeneutics are likewise focused on understanding the culture of the users of a specific text.

There are different forms of cultural theory. For example, **social hermeneutics** has as its goal the understanding of how those in an observed social situation interpret their own place in that situation. Ethnographer Michael Moerman explained how social hermeneutic theory makes sense of alien or unknown cultures. Social hermeneutic theory tries to understand how events "in the alien world make sense to the aliens, how their way of life coheres and has meaning and value for the people who live it" (1992, p. 23). Another branch of cultural theory looks for hidden or deep meaning in people's interpretation of different symbol systems—for example, in media texts. As you might have guessed from these descriptions, cultural theory is sometimes referred to as *interpretive theory*. It seeks to interpret the meaning of texts for the agents that produce them and the audiences that consume them. Another important idea embedded in these descriptions is that any **text**, any product of social interaction—a movie, the president's State of the Union Address, a series of Twitter tweets, a conversation between a soap opera hero and heroine—can be a source of understanding. Understanding can in turn guide actions.

text
Any product of social interaction that serves as a source of understanding or meaning

The ontology of cultural theory says that there is no truly "real," measurable social reality. Instead, "people construct an image of reality based on their own preferences and prejudices and their interactions with others, and this is as true of scientists as it is of everyone else in the social world" (Schutt, 2009, p. 92). As such, cultural theory's epistemology, how knowledge is advanced, relies on the subjective interaction between the observer (the researcher or theorist) and his or her community. Put another way, knowledge is local; that is, it is specific to the interaction of the knower and the known. Naturally, then, the axiology of cultural theory embraces, rather than limits, the influence of researcher and theorist values. Personal and professional values, according to Katherine Miller, are a "lens through which social phenomena are observed" (2005, p. 58). A researcher interested in understanding teens' interpretations of social networking websites like Facebook, or one who is curious about meaning-making that occurs in the exchange of information among teen fans of an online simulation game, would rely on cultural theory.

CRITICAL THEORY

critical theory
Theory seeking transformation of a dominant social order in order to achieve desired values

There are still other scholars who do not want explanation, prediction, and control of the social world. Nor do they seek understanding of the social world as the ultimate goal for their work. They start from the assumption that some aspects of the social world are deeply flawed and in need of transformation. Their aim is to gain knowledge of that social world so they can change it. This goal is inherently—and intentionally—political because it challenges existing ways of organizing the social world and the people and institutions that exercise power in it. **Critical theory** is openly political (therefore its axiology is aggressively value-laden). It assumes that by reorganizing society, we can give priority to the most important human values.

Critical theorists study inequality and oppression. Their theories do more than observe, describe, or interpret; they criticize. Critical theories view "media as sites of (and weapons in) struggles over social, economic, symbolic, and political power (as well as struggles over control of, and access to, the media themselves)" (Meyrowitz, 2008, p. 642). Critical theory's epistemology argues that knowledge is advanced only when it serves to free people and communities from the influence of those more powerful than themselves. Critical theorists call this emancipatory knowledge. Its ontology, however, is a bit more complex.

According to critical theory, what is real, what is knowable, in the social world is the product of the interaction between **structure** (the social world's rules, norms, and beliefs) and **agency** (how humans behave and interact in that world). Reality, then, to critical theorists, is constantly being shaped and reshaped by the **dialectic** (the ongoing struggle or debate) between the two. When elites control the struggle, they define reality (in other words, their control of the structure defines people's realities). When people are emancipated, *they* define reality through their behaviors and interactions (agency). Researchers and theorists interested in the decline (and restoration) of the power of the labor movement in industrialized nations or those interested in limiting the contribution of children's advertising to the nation's growing consumerism would rely on critical theory. Some critical theorists are quite troubled by what they view as the uncontrolled exercise of capitalist corporate power around the world. They see media as an essential tool employed by corporate elites to constrain how people view their social world and to limit their agency in it. They worry about the spread of what they see as a global culture of celebrity and consumerism that is fostered by capitalist dominated media.

structure
In critical theory, the social world's rules, norms, and beliefs

agency
In critical theory, how humans behave and interact within the structure

dialectic
In critical theory, the ongoing struggle between agency and structure

NORMATIVE THEORY

Social theorists see postpositivist and cultural theory as *representational*. That is, they are articulations—word pictures—of some other realities (for postpositivists, those representations are generalizable across similar realities, and for interpretive theorists, these representations are local and specific). Critical theory is *nonrepresentational*. Its goal is to *change* existing realities.

There is another type of theory, however. It may be applied to any type of social institution but our focus will be on media institutions. Its aim is neither the representation nor the reformation of reality. Instead, its goal is to set an ideal standard against which the operation of a given media system can be judged. A **normative media theory** explains how a media system *should* operate in order to conform to or realize a set of ideal social values. As such, its ontology argues that what is known is situational (or, like interpretive theory, local). In other words, what is real or knowable about a media system is real or knowable only for the specific social system in which that media system exists. Its epistemology, how knowledge is developed and advanced, is based in *comparative analysis*—we can only judge (and therefore understand) the worth of a given media system in comparison to the ideal espoused by the particular social system in which it operates. Finally, normative theory's axiology is, by definition, value-laden. Study of a media system or parts of a media system is undertaken in the explicit belief that there is an ideal mode of operation based in the values of the larger social system.

normative media theory
Theory explaining how a media system should be structured and operate in order to conform to or realize a set of ideal social values

Theorists interested in the press's role in a democracy would most likely employ normative theory, as would those examining the operation of the media in an Islamic republic or an authoritarian state. Problems arise if media systems based on one normative theory are evaluated according to the norms or ideals of another normative theory. Chapter 3 is devoted in its entirety to normative theory. You can more deeply investigate the role of values in the four broad categories of theory we've discussed when reading the box entitled "True Values: A Deeper Look at Axiology."

THINKING ABOUT THEORY | **True Values: A Deeper Look at Axiology**

As we've seen, different communication theorists deal differently with the role of values in the construction of their ideas. Inasmuch as they model their research on that of those who study the physical world, postpositivists would ideally like to eliminate values from their inquiry. But they know they can't, so objectivity becomes their regulatory ideal; that is, they rely on the scientific method to reduce the impact of values on their work as much as possible. They also distinguish between two types of values in their work. Postpositivists cherish **epistemic values**—they value high standards in the conduct of research and development of theory. But they also confront **nonepistemic values**—the place of emotion, morals, and ethics in research and theory development. There is little debate about the former among postpositivists—who wouldn't want high standards of performance? But what about emotions, morals, and ethics? Why, for example, would researchers want to study media violence? Certainly they believe a relationship exists between media consumption and human behavior on some level. But what if an individual theorist strongly believes in the eradication of all violence on children's television because of her own son's problems with bullies at school? How hard should she work to ignore her personal feelings in her research and interpretation of her findings? Should she examine some other aspect of mass communication to ensure greater objectivity? But why should anybody have to study something that he or she has no feeling about?

Interpretive theorists, even though they more readily accept the role of values in their work than do postpositivists, also wrestle with the proper application of those values. Accepting the impossibility of separating values from research and theory development, interpretive theorists identify two ends of a continuum. Those who wish to minimize the impact of their personal values on their work **bracket** their values; that is, they recognize them, set them aside by figuratively putting them in brackets, and then do their work. At the other end of the continuum are those who openly celebrate their values and consciously inject them into their work. In truth, most interpretive researchers and theorists fall somewhere in the middle. If you were really thinking about theory, though, you would have asked, "But if an interpretive theorist openly celebrates his or her values and injects them into the research or theory development, hasn't she moved into critical theory?" And you would be correct, because it is hard to conceive of someone willing to inject personal values into social research and theory who did not want, at the very least, to advance those values. And in advancing those values, the status quo would be altered—hence, critical theory.

Critical and normative theorists, in their open embrace of values, face fewer questions about objectivity than do other theorists. But they, like all social researchers and theorists, must employ high epistemic values. Critical theorists advocate change; normative theorists advocate media striving to meet a social system's stated ideals of operation. These open articulations of nonepistemic values, however, do not excuse sloppy data gathering or improper data analysis.

What should be clear is that all involved in the serious study of human life must maintain the highest standards of inquiry *within the conventions* of their research and theory development communities. Given that, which axiology do you find most compatible with your way of thinking about human behavior? Should you someday become a mass communication researcher or theorist, which set of values do you think would prove most valuable in guiding your efforts?

epistemic values High standards in the conduct of research and theory development
nonepistemic values The place of emotion, morals, and ethics in research and theory development
bracket In interpretive theory, setting values aside

EVALUATING THEORY

French philosopher Andre Gide wrote, "No theory is good unless it permits, not rest, but the greatest work. No theory is good except on condition that one uses it to go on beyond" (quoted in Andrews, Biggs, and Seidel, 1996, p. 66). In other words, good theory pushes, advances, improves the social world. There are some specific ways, however, to judge the value of the many theories we will study in this book.

When evaluating postpositivist theory, we need to ask these questions:

1. How well does it explain the event, behavior, or relationship of interest?
2. How well does it predict future events, behaviors, or relationships?
3. How testable is it? In other words, is it specific enough in its assertions that it can be systematically supported or rejected based on empirical observation?
4. How parsimonious is it? In other words, is it the simplest explanation possible of the phenomenon in question? Some call this *elegance*. Keep in mind that communication theories generally tend to lack parsimony. In fact, one of the reasons many social scientists avoid the study of communication is that communication phenomena are hard to explain parsimoniously.
5. How practical or useful is it? If the goals of postpositivist theory are explanation, prediction, and control, how much assistance toward these ends is provided by the theory?

When evaluating cultural theory, we need to ask these questions:

1. How much new or fresh insight into the event, behavior, or relationship of interest does it offer? In other words, how much does it advance our understanding?
2. How well does it clarify the values inherent in the interpretation, not only those embedded in the phenomenon of interest, but those of the researcher or theorist?
3. How much support does it generate among members of the scholarly community also investigating the phenomenon of interest?
4. How much aesthetic appeal does it have? In other words, does it enthuse or inspire its adherents?

When evaluating critical theory, we need to ask the same questions we do of cultural theory, but we must add a fifth:

1. How useful is the critique of the status quo? In other words, does it provide enough understanding of elite power so that power can be effectively challenged? Does the theory enable individuals to oppose elite definitions of the social world?

When evaluating normative theory, we need to ask the following questions:

1. How stable and definitive are the ideal standards of operation against which the media system (or its parts) under study will be measured?
2. What, and how powerful, are the economic, social, cultural, and political realities surrounding the actual operation of a system (or its parts) that must be considered in evaluating that performance?
3. How much support does it generate among members of the scholarly community also investigating a specific media system (or its parts)?

FLEXIBLE SOCIAL SCIENCE

Now that you've been introduced to the four broad categories of social scientific theory, you might have guessed another reason that those who study the social world often don't get the respect accorded their physical science colleagues. Sociologist Kenneth Bailey wrote, "To this day you will find within social science both those who think of themselves as scientists in the strictest sense of the word and those with a more subjective approach to the study of society, who see themselves more as humanists than as scientists" (1982, p. 5). In other words, and as you've just seen, not all who call themselves social scientists adhere to the same standards for conducting research or accepting evidence. But complicating matters even more is the fact that social science researchers and theorists often blend (or mix and match) categories as they do their work (Bennett and Holbert, 2008). To some observers, especially committed postpositivists, this seems unsystematic. It also generates disagreement among social scientists, not about the issue under examination, say the influence of video violence on children's behavior, but about the appropriateness of the methods used, the value of the evidence obtained, or the influence of values on the work (i.e., debates over ontology, epistemology, and axiology).

MASS COMMUNICATION THEORY

One way to approach the study of media theory is to consider how theories have developed over the past two centuries. Not surprisingly, theories have evolved in part as a reaction to changes in mass media technology and the rise of new mass media organizations that exploited this technology. Proponents for the four types of theories developed different but sometimes related theories. Specific issues or concerns such as the effects of violent content or elite control of media have motivated the development and evolution of theories. Whenever new forms of media have been developed they have been praised by some and condemned by others. Debates over the usefulness of new forms of media have spawned numerous theories.

FOUR TRENDS IN MEDIA THEORY

For some time those who study the shifting history of mass communication theory have pointed to large-scale paradigm shifts, as once-popular notions in one era gave way to very different views in the next. Critics have challenged this way of looking at media theory, arguing that these overarching perspectives were not as well integrated or as dominant as they might appear to have been in retrospect (e.g., Neuman and Guggenheim, 2011). These shifts were rarely as clear-cut as often assumed, and the retelling of the interaction between proponents of different types of theory tended to dwell on conflict between their advocates rather than on the potential for collaboration or corroboration. Here, instead of distinct eras of mass communication theory, we identify *trends* in theory development. To some extent these trends are similar to eras in that they trace the development of relatively stable perspectives on mass communication, and over time there has been a shift from one trend to another. At given points in time, however, trends overlap and to some extent influence each other.

THE MASS SOCIETY AND MASS CULTURE TREND IN MEDIA THEORY

Our description of the eras of mass communication theory begins with a review of some of the earliest thinking about media. These ideas were initially developed in the latter half of the nineteenth century, at a time when rapid development of large factories in urban areas was drawing more and more people from rural areas to cities. At the same time, ever more powerful printing presses allowed the creation of newspapers that could be sold at declining prices to rapidly growing populations of readers. Although some theorists were optimistic about the future that would be created by industrialization, urban expansion, and the rise of print media, many were extremely pessimistic (Brantlinger, 1983). They blamed industrialization for disrupting peaceful, rural communities and forcing people to live in urban areas, merely to serve as a convenient workforce in large factories, mines, or bureaucracies. These theorists were fearful of cities because of their crime, cultural diversity, and unstable political systems. For these social thinkers, mass media symbolized everything that was wrong with nineteenth-century urban life. They singled out media for virulent criticism and accused them of pandering to lower-class tastes, fomenting political unrest, and subverting important cultural norms. Most theorists were educated **elites** who feared what they couldn't understand. The old social order was crumbling, and so were its culture and politics. Were media responsible for this, or did they simply accelerate or aggravate these changes?

elites
People occupying elevated or privileged positions in a social system

mass society theory
Perspective on Western, industrial society that attributes an influential but often negative role to media

The dominant perspective on media and society that emerged during this period has come to be referred to as **mass society theory**. It is an inherently contradictory theory that is often rooted in nostalgia for a "golden age" that never existed, and it anticipates a nightmare future in which social order is broken down, ruthless elites seize power, and individual freedom is lost. Some version of mass society theory seems to recur in every generation as we try to reassess where we are and where we are going as individuals and as a nation wedded to technology as the means of improving the quality of our lives. Each new version of mass society theory has its criticisms of contemporary media. It is useful to recognize that this trend in media theory is still found today even though many earlier forms of mass society theory have been discarded.

penny press
Newspapers that sold for one penny and earned profits through newsstand sales and advertising

Mass society theory can be regarded as a collection of conflicting notions developed to make sense of what is happening whenever there is large-scale and/or disruptive social change. Mass society notions can come from both ends of the political spectrum. Some are developed by people who want to maintain the existing political order, and others are created by revolutionaries who wanted to impose radical changes. But these ideological foes often share at least one assumption—mass media are troublesome if not downright dangerous. In general, mass society ideas hold strong appeal for any social elite whose power is threatened by change. Media industries, such as the **penny press** in the 1830s, **yellow journalism** in the 1890s, movies in the 1920s, radio in the 1930s, and TV in the 1950s were easy targets for elites' criticisms. They catered to readers in middle and lower social classes

yellow journalism
Newspaper reporting catering to working and other lower social class audiences using simple, often sensational content

using simple, often sensational content. Content mostly entertained rather than informed or educated people. These industries were easily attacked as symptomatic of a sick society—a society needing to either return to traditional, fundamental values or be forced to adopt a set of totally new values fostered by media. Many intense political conflicts strongly affected thinking about the mass media, and these conflicts shaped the development of various forms of mass society theory.

An essential argument of mass society theory is that media subvert and disrupt the existing social order. But media are also seen as a potential solution to the chaos they engender. They can serve as a powerful tool that can be used to either restore the old order or institute a new one. But who should be trusted to use this tool? Should established authorities be trusted to control media—to produce or censor media content? Should media be freely operated by private entrepreneurs whose primary goal is to make money? Should radical, revolutionary groups be given control over media so they can pursue their dreams of creating an ideal social order? At the end of the nineteenth century and the beginning of the twentieth century, fierce debate erupted over these questions. This conflict often pitted traditional elites, whose power was based on an agrarian society, against urban elites, whose power was increasingly based on industrialization and urbanization.

Today, the fallacies of both the critics and advocates of older forms of media technology are readily apparent. Early mass society notions greatly exaggerated the ability of media to quickly undermine social order, just as media advocates exaggerated their ability to create an ideal social order. These ideas failed to consider that media's power ultimately resides in the freely chosen uses that audiences make of it. Most mass society thinkers were unduly paternalistic and elitist in their views of average people and the ability of media to have powerful effects on them. Those who feared media exaggerated their power to manipulate the masses and the likelihood they would bring inevitable social and cultural ruin. Technology advocates were also misguided and failed to acknowledge the many unnecessary, damaging consequences that resulted from applying technology without adequately anticipating its impact.

THE LIMITED-EFFECTS TREND IN MEDIA THEORY

In the late 1930s and early 1940s, mass society notions began to be empirically investigated by Paul Lazarsfeld, who would eventually overturn some of its basic assumptions. Trained in psychological measurement, Lazarsfeld fled the Nazis in Austria and came to the United States on a Ford Foundation fellowship (Lazarsfeld, 1969). For the emerging field of mass communication research, he proved to be a seminal thinker and researcher. Like many of his academic colleagues, Lazarsfeld was interested in exploring the potential of newly developed social science methods, such as surveys and field experiments, to understand and solve social problems. He combined academic training with a high level of entrepreneurial skill. Within a few years after arriving in the United States, he had established a very active and successful social research center, the Bureau for Applied Social Research at Columbia University.

Lazarsfeld provides a classic example of a transitional figure in theory development—someone well grounded in past theory but also innovative enough to consider other concepts and methods for evaluating new ideas. Though quite familiar with and very sympathetic to mass society notions (Lazarsfeld, 1941), Lazarsfeld was committed to the use of empirical social research methods in order to establish the validity of theory. He was a strong advocate of postpositivism as a basis for developing theory. He argued that it wasn't enough to merely speculate about the influence of media on society. Instead, he advocated the conduct of carefully designed, elaborate surveys and even field experiments in which he would be able to observe media influence and measure its magnitude. It was not enough to assume that political propaganda is powerful—hard evidence was needed to prove the existence of its effects (Lazarsfeld, Berelson, and Gaudet, 1944). Lazarsfeld's most famous research efforts, the "American Voter Studies," actually began as an attempt to document the media's power during election campaigns, yet they eventually raised more questions about the influence of media than they answered.

By the mid-1950s, Lazarsfeld's work and that of other empirical media researchers had generated an enormous amount of data (by precomputer standards). Interpretation of these data led Lazarsfeld and his colleagues to conclude that media were not nearly as powerful as had been feared or hoped. Instead, these researchers found that people had numerous ways of resisting media influence, and their attitudes were shaped by many competing factors, such as family, friends, and religious community. Rather than serving as a disruptive social force, media more often seemed to reinforce existing social trends and strengthen rather than threaten the status quo. They found little evidence to support the worst fears of mass society theorists. Though Lazarsfeld and others never labeled this theory, it came to be referred to as **limited-effects theory**.

limited-effects theory
View of media as having little ability to directly influence people. The dominant effect of media is to reinforce existing social trends and strengthen the status quo

Throughout the 1950s, limited-effects notions about media continued to gain acceptance within academia. These ideas dominated the new field of mass communication research as it was developing in the 1950s and 1960s. Several important clashes occurred between their adherents and those who supported mass society ideas (Bauer and Bauer, 1960). This is hardly surprising, since the rise of Communism across Eastern Europe seemed to provide ample evidence that media could be used as powerful tools to meld increasingly large masses of individuals into an ever more powerful totalitarian state. How could the United States expect to win the Cold War unless it could somehow find a way to use mass media to confront and overcome the Soviets?

In 1960, several classic studies of media effects (Campbell et al., 1960; Deutschmann and Danielson, 1960; Klapper, 1960) provided apparently definitive support for the limited-effects view. Limited-effects notions about mass communication theory had been supported by a decade of postpositivist research. By contrast, advocates of mass society notions came under increasing attack as "unscientific" or "irrational" because they questioned "hard scientific findings." Mass society notions were further discredited within academia because they became associated with the anti-Communist **Red Scare** promoted by Senator Joseph McCarthy in the early 1950s. McCarthy and his allies focused considerable attention on purging alleged Communists from the media. They justified these purges using mass society arguments—average people needed to be protected from media manipulation. Limited-effects theorists produced research showing that average people were well protected from media influence by opinion leaders who filtered out Communist propaganda before it reached their followers.

Red Scare
Period in U.S. history, late 1950s to early 1960s, in which basic freedoms were threatened by searches for "Reds," or communists, in media and government

By the mid-1960s, the debate between mass society and limited-effects advocates appeared to be over—at least within the postpositivist research community. The body of empirical research findings continued to grow, and almost all were consistent with the latter view. Little or no empirical research supported mass society thinking. Most postpositivist researchers stopped looking for powerful media effects and concentrated instead on documenting minimal, limited effects. Some of the original media researchers had become convinced that media research would never produce any important new findings and returned to work in political science or sociology. In a controversial essay, Bernard Berelson (1959), who worked closely with Paul Lazarsfeld, declared the field of communication research to be dead. There simply was nothing left to study when it came to the mass media.

Ironically, Berelson's essay was published just before the field of media research underwent explosive growth. As postpositivist researchers in sociology and psychology abandoned media research, they were quickly replaced by the increasing numbers of faculty members working in rapidly growing programs dedicated to the study of media and communication. As these programs grew so did the volume of postpositivist research on media. Initially this research largely replicated work done by sociologists and psychologists, but by the 1970s media researchers began to make important new contributions to our understanding of media.

THE CRITICAL CULTURAL TREND IN MEDIA THEORY

While postpositivist media research flourished in the 1970s and 1980s it came under increasing criticism from European researchers. In Europe both left-wing and right-wing scholars had concerns about the power of media that were deeply rooted in World War II experiences with propaganda. Europeans were also skeptical about the power of postpositivist, quantitative social research methods to verify and develop social theory (they saw this approach to research as reductionist—reducing complex communication processes and social phenomena to little more than narrow propositions generated from small-scale investigations). This **reductionism** was widely viewed as a distinctly American fetish. Some European academics were resentful of the influence enjoyed by Americans after World War II. They argued that American empiricism was both simplistic and intellectually sterile. Although some European academics welcomed and championed American notions about media effects, others strongly resisted them and argued for maintaining approaches considered less constrained or more traditionally European.

One group of European social theorists who vehemently resisted postwar U.S. influence was the **neo-Marxists** (Hall, 1982). Consistent with Communist theory first formulated by Karl Marx, these left-wing social theorists argued that media enable dominant social elites to consolidate and maintain their economic power. Neo-Marxist theory is a form of critical theory. Media provide the elite with a convenient, subtle, yet highly effective means of promoting worldviews favorable to their interests. Mass media can be understood, they contended, as a public arena in which cultural battles are fought and a dominant, or hegemonic, culture is forged and promoted. Elites dominate these struggles because they start with important advantages. Opposition is marginalized, and the status quo is presented as the only logical, rational way of structuring society. Values favored by elites are

reductionism
Reducing complex communication processes and social phenomena to little more than narrow propositions generated from small-scale investigations

neo-Marxists
Advocates of the social theory asserting that media enable dominant social elites to maintain their power

subtlety woven into and promoted by the narratives of popular programs—even children's cartoons. Within neo-Marxist theory, efforts to examine media institutions and interpret media content came to have high priority. Such theories differ from older forms of Marxism because they assume that culture can be influenced by people who don't hold economic power.

During the 1960s, some neo-Marxists in Britain developed a school of social theory widely referred to as **British cultural studies**. It focused heavily on mass media and their role in promoting a hegemonic worldview and a dominant culture among various subgroups in the society. British cultural studies drew on both critical theory and cultural theory to create **critical cultural theory**. Researchers studied how members of those subgroups used media and assessed how this use might serve group interests (cultural theory) or might lead people to develop ideas that supported dominant elites (critical theory). This research eventually produced an important breakthrough. As they conducted audience research, social scientists at Birmingham University discovered that people often resisted the hegemonic ideas and propagated new, alternative interpretations of the social world (Mosco and Herman, 1981). Although British cultural studies began with **deterministic assumptions** about the influence of media (i.e., the media have powerful, direct effects), their work came to focus on audience reception studies that revived important questions about the potential power of media in certain types of situations and the ability of active audience members to resist media influence—questions that 1960s postpositivist media scholars ignored because they were skeptical about the power of media and assumed that audiences were passive.

During the 1970s, questions about the possibility of powerful media effects were again raised in U.S. universities. Initially, these questions were advanced by scholars in the humanities who were ignorant of the limited-effects perspective, skeptical about postpositivism, and well trained in cultural theory. Their arguments were routinely ignored and marginalized by social scientists because they were unsupported by "scientific evidence." Some of these scholars were attracted to European-style critical cultural theory (Newcomb, 1974). Others attempted to create an "authentic" American school of cultural studies—though they drew heavily on Canadian scholars like Harold Innis and Marshall McLuhan (Carey, 1977). This **cultural criticism**, although initially greeted with considerable skepticism by "mainstream" effects researchers, gradually established itself as a credible and valuable alternative to limited-effects notions.

British cultural studies
Perspective focusing on mass media and their role in cultural groups and in promoting a public forum in which definitions of the social world are negotiated

critical cultural theory
An integration of critical theory and cultural theory first attempted by British cultural studies scholars

deterministic assumptions
Assumptions that media have powerful, direct effects

cultural criticism
Collection of perspectives concerned with the cultural disputes and the ways communication perpetuates domination of one group over another

THE MEANING-MAKING TREND IN MEDIA THEORY

During the 1970s and 1980s, there was increasing competition between postpositivist and critical cultural scholars in both the United States and Europe. During much of this period, postpositivist researchers were at a disadvantage because limited effects theories failed to address how media might be playing a role in the social movements that were obviously transforming society—the civil rights, antiwar and feminist social movements. Additionally, they could not address the possible consequences of the cumulative effect of exposure to popular media content (such as televised violence) or to advertising. Gradually, limited-effects notions were altered, partially because of pressures from critical cultural studies, but also because of the emergence of new communication technologies that forced a rethinking of traditional assumptions about how people use (and are used by) media. We are again living in an era when we are challenged by the rise of powerful new media that clearly are altering how most of us live our lives and relate to others. Postpositivists have developed new research strategies and methods (as explained in later chapters) that provide them with better measures of media influence and that have already identified a number of contexts in which media can have powerful effects (e.g., Gurevitch, Coleman, and Blumler, 2010; Holbert, Garrett, and Gleason, 2010; Scheufele, 2000).

At the same time that postpositivist researchers moved toward a focus on use of media rather than media effects, critical cultural scholars advanced a similar but slightly different focus. Their research traced the way that cultural groups rather than individuals use media to serve group purposes. They studied how groups used various forms of media content from music to news. They found that group members often band together to criticize and resist ideas being promoted by media, for example in this "public sphere" union members might criticize hostile news coverage of strikes and feminists could criticize advertising that presented women in problematic ways (Castells, 2008).

At the heart of the meaning-making trend in theory is a focus on a more or less *active audience that uses media content to create meaningful experiences*. Theorists recognize that important media effects often occur over longer time periods and these effects can be intended by users. People as individuals or as groups can make media serve certain purposes, such as using media to learn information, manage moods, promote group identity, or seek excitement. When audiences use media in these ways, they are intentionally working to induce meaningful experiences. The various meaning-making perspectives assert that when people use media to make meaning—when they are able to intentionally induce desired experiences—there often are significant results, some intended and others unintended. So when young adults download billions of songs from the net in order to alter or sustain a mood, there will be consequences. Some of these consequences are intended, but sometimes the results are unanticipated and unwanted.

Have you ever sought thrills from a horror movie and then been troubled afterward by disturbing visual images? Factors that intrude into and disrupt meaning-making can have unpredictable consequences. The trend in meaning-making theory implies that future research will focus on people's successes or failures in their efforts to make meaning using media, and on intended and unintended consequences. These consequences should be considered both from the point of view of individuals and from the point of view of groups or society.

REVITALIZED EFFECTS RESEARCH

The popularity of critical cultural studies, new postpositivist research methods, and the rise of meaning-making theory have intensified and renewed research on many different types of media effects. Postpositivist and critical cultural scholars are addressing a variety of important research questions involving these effects. Here are just a few that we will consider in later chapters. What are the short-term and long-term consequences of routine exposure to violent images and sexual behavior in videogames? Are these effects similar to those found for televised violence or are there important differences? How much do television commercials for fast food and blockbuster movie tie-ins for junk food contribute to our country's epidemic of obesity? Does media coverage of important issues such as war, elections, or the economy contribute to or diminish public understanding and democratic discourse? Is there a relationship between some kids' new media use and poor school performance? Do sexy television shows contribute to rising rates of teen pregnancy? Does political corruption grow and political participation decline when local newspapers are forced to cut staff or close altogether? How much responsibility must teen and fashion magazines take for young girls' dissatisfaction with their body image? Did online music piracy kill the record industry, or did listeners tire of record companies' overreliance on formulaic music and overpriced CDs? How much freedom of the press is too much—and who gets to decide?

Even though these and a thousand similar questions serve to stimulate increased research and the development of better theories, they are also generating renewed controversy about the role of media. Critics use research findings to unfairly attack media while defenders find ways to explain away problematic findings. We must better understand why it has been so hard to come to a clear understanding of media influence and why it has been so easy to promote fallacious ideas about media.

SUMMARY

As we move ever more deeply into the ever-evolving communication revolution, we need an understanding of media theory to guide our actions and decisions. It should recognize that all social theory is a human construction and that it is dynamic, always changing as society, technology, and people change. This dynamism can be readily seen in the transformation of our understanding of the process of mass communication itself. New communication technologies have changed traditional notions of the mass audience, the mass communicator, and the relationships between the two. To understand this change, we rely on social science and its theories.

Social science is sometimes controversial because it suggests causal relationships between things in the social world and people's attitudes, values, and behaviors. In the physical sciences, causal relationships are often easily visible and measurable. In the study of human behavior, however, they rarely are. Human behavior is quite difficult to quantify, often very complex,

and often goal-oriented. Social science and human behavior make a problematic fit. The situation is even further complicated because social science itself is somewhat variable—it has many forms and can serve very different purposes.

Nonetheless, any systematic inquiry into media relies on theory—an organized set of concepts, explanations, and principles of some aspect of human experience. The explanatory power of media theory, however, is constantly challenged by the presence of many media, their many facets and characteristics, their constant change, an always-developing audience, and the ever-evolving nature of the groups and societies that use them. Still, social theorists have identified four general categories of communication theory. Two are representational, postpositivist theory (theory based on empirical observation guided by the scientific method) and cultural theory (the study of understanding, especially by interpreting actions and texts). A third, critical theory, seeks emancipation and change in a dominant social order. A fourth, normative theory, states how media systems can be ideally structured to achieve valued objectives.

While these types of theory have a commitment to an increased understanding of the social world, they differ in their goals, their ontology (the nature of reality, what is knowable), their epistemology (how knowledge is created and expanded), and their axiology (the proper role of values in research and theory building). Postpositivist theory is traditionally social scientific; cultural theory is based on interpretation of texts (the product of any social interaction can serve as a text); and critical theory, in seeking to overturn the status quo, studies the struggle—the dialectic—between a society's structure (its rules, norms, and beliefs) and its agency (how people interact in the face of that structure). Finally, the fourth type of mass communication theory, normative theory, is neither representational nor seeking change. It is designed to judge the operation of a given media system against a specific social system's norms or ideals so that these values can be achieved.

Our contemporary understanding of mass communication theory is the product of four trends in theory development. The mass society trend is characterized by fears of media's influence on "average" people and optimistic views of their ability to bring about social good. The second trend in mass communication theory started when early postpositivist media research produced findings that led to the formulation of limited-effects notions. Postpositivist research discredited naive mass society theories as "unscientific." They were replaced with limited-effects theories that argued that because people could resist media's power and were influenced by competing factors such as friends and family, mass communication most often served to reinforce existing social trends and strengthen rather than threaten the status quo.

The third trend was led by critical and cultural scholars. It was driven initially by critical theorists in Europe who held to neo-Marxist assumptions. British cultural studies, focusing on the use of media by social groups and on mass media's role as a public forum in which understanding of the social world is negotiated, made important contributions to this trend.

Today there is a new trend in mass communication theory, the emergence of meaning-making perspectives. These perspectives acknowledge that mass communication can indeed be powerful, or somewhat powerful, or not powerful at all, because active audience members can (and often do) use media content to create meaningful experiences for themselves. Framing theory, asserting that people use expectations of the social world to make sense of that world, and the media literacy movement, calling for improvement in people's ability to access, analyze, evaluate, and communicate media messages, are two examples of recent meaning-making theory.

As you learn about contemporary theories and research, we encourage you to use these theories to develop your own views on media theory and research and to defend your views against alternate arguments. The theories in this book will remain abstract ideas until you incorporate them into your own views about media and their importance in your life and the lives of others. Ultimately, you are responsible for making media work for you and for guarding against negative consequences.

In the first decades of the twenty-first century, we are entering a period in history not unlike that at the close of the nineteenth—an era in which an array of innovative media technologies is being shaped into powerful new media institutions. Have we learned enough from the past to face this challenging and uncertain future? Will we merely watch as media entrepreneurs shape new media institutions to fill gaps created by the collapse of existing institutions? Or will we be part of an effort to shape new institutions that better serve our own needs and the long-term needs of the communities in which we live? We invite you to address these questions as you read this book, and we will pose them again as a final challenge.

Critical Thinking Questions

1. Can you think of any social science "findings" on media that you reject? What are they? On what grounds do you base your skepticism? Can you separate your personal experience with the issue from your judgment of the social scientific evidence?

2. How do you interact with and use new and legacy media? Can you identify "effects" that have occurred because of that use? Do you typically media multitask, that is, consume two or more media at the same time? If so, how do you think this influences the presence or absence of possible effects? Can you offer any possible negative effects to balance any positive effects that might have occurred from any of your media use?

3. How skilled are you at making meaning from media content? How media literate do you think you are? Do you often make meaning from content that is markedly different from that of your friends or do you share their experience and interpretations of media? If so, why do you suppose this happens?

Key Terms

grand theory

mass communication

mediated communication

interpersonal communication

social scientists

causality

causal relationship

scientific method

hypothesis

empirical

third-person effect

theory

ontology

epistemology

axiology

postpositivist theory

intersubjective agreement

cultural theory

hermeneutic theory

social hermeneutics

text

critical theory

structure

agency

dialectic

normative media theory

epistemic values

nonepistemic values

bracket

elites

mass society theory

penny press

yellow journalism

limited-effects theory

Red Scare

reductionism

neo-Marxists

British cultural studies

critical cultural theory

deterministic assumptions

cultural criticism

CHAPTER 2

ESTABLISHING THE TERMS OF THE DEBATE OVER MEDIA: THE FIRST TREND IN MEDIA THEORY—MASS SOCIETY AND PROPAGANDA THEORIES

Riots engulfed the Middle East on 9/11 in 2012 in response to an anti-Muslim YouTube video depicting the Prophet Muhammad as a fraud and womanizer. Scores of people were killed and injured in several Muslim nations. When the U.S. government condemned the video, calling for respect for people of all faiths, Fox News personality Todd Starnes agreed, demanding a federal investigation of the cartoon television show *South Park* which, he argued, "has denigrated all faiths" (Glasstetter, 2012). Boycotts, too, were in vogue during the first two decades of the new century. Retailer J. C. Penney was targeted for partnering with gay celebrity Ellen DeGeneres, and the Campbell Soup Company was boycotted for placing ads in the gay-oriented magazine *The Advocate*. Louis Sheldon, founder of the Traditional Values Coalition, complained that television shows "such as *Will and Grace*, *Queer as Folk*, *Queer Eye for the Straight Guy*, *The L Word*, and *Glee* have been designed to desensitize Americans to the genuine risks of the homosexual agenda. Again, homosexuals are invariably portrayed as funny, sensitive, and caring individuals" (2012). At that same time, television writer Harry Jessell praised the medium for airing those programs, "In the past, the cultural change agent was the popular novel: *Oliver Twist* (poverty), *Uncle Tom's Cabin* (slavery), *The Jungle* (poverty and business corruption), *The Grapes of Wrath* (social justice) and *To Kill a Mockingbird* (racism). At some point in last century, film surpassed the novel in filling this role in society, then, in the 1980s or 1990s, TV took over. And when it started accepting gays, so did the nation" (2012). Critics accused cartoon character SpongeBob SquarePants and animated movie *Happy Feet Two* of pushing the liberal environmental agenda and *Sesame Street*'s puppets of having a "radical, left-leaning political agenda" (Bond, 2011). Arguing that their State Constitution required "government to protect the virtue and purity of the home," legislators on the Idaho House State Affairs Committee passed a 2013 resolution to ask the federal government to prohibit talk about and the portrayal, even implied, of premarital sex on television dramas, comedies, reality and talk shows, and commercials in order to "stand up for the morality of what is best for the citizens of Idaho," in the words of Representative Darrell Bolz (in KBOI, 2013).

Hate-filled movies, federal investigations of cartoon shows, gays in the media—pro and con—sex on television, and tree-hugging puppets were not the only media controversies of the time. Among other things, researchers at the National Institute of Health discovered that 50 minutes of cellphone use could alter normal brain function (Kang, 2011); the scientific journal *Pediatrics* published one report tying teens' consumption of online and other media violence to subsequent "seriously violent behavior" (Ybarra et al., 2008) and another linking exposure to sexual content on television to teen pregnancy (Chandra et al., 2008); the journal *Archives of Pediatrics & Adolescent Medicine* presented evidence of lagging language development in children as a result of infant television viewing (Bryner, 2009); *Circulation: Journal of the American Heart Association* published research demonstrating that every daily hour spent watching television was linked to an 18 percent greater risk of dying from heart disease, an 11 percent greater risk from all causes of death, and a 9 percent greater risk of death from cancer (Dunstan et al., 2010); social media were accused of fostering loneliness (Brandtzæg, 2012) and credited with fueling and spreading the Middle East democracy movement.

A YouTube video incites murderous rioting in the Middle East and Facebook fosters democracy in the same region? Social networking leads to loneliness? Media portrayals of pleasant homosexuals are really bad? Media portrayals of pleasant homosexuals are really good? An occasional on-air swear word produces a coarsened culture? Cell phones mess with our brains? Watching television and going online creates violent kids, gets teens pregnant, stunts language acquisition, and increases the risk of death? Some say yes; some say no.

For more than a century now, society has debated the role of media. Conservatives lament the decline of values sped by a liberal media elite. Liberals fear the power of a media system more in tune with the conservative values of its owners than of its audiences. School boards and city councils in hundreds of towns debate installing filtering software on school and library computers, pitting advocates of free expression against proponents of child protection. Controversial rappers are celebrated on television while their music is banned on scores of radio stations because it is considered racist and misogynistic. Online tracking of our activities robs us of our privacy and our cell phones become tracking devices for use by companies and government alike. Media industries promise their sponsors significant impact for their advertising dollars but claim their fare has little or no influence when challenged on issues of violence, gender stereotyping, and drugs. Every company, government agency, and nonprofit group of any size maintains or retains a public relations operation. Why would anyone bother if media have little or no impact? Why would the **First Amendment** to our Constitution, our "First Freedom," protect the expression of media industries if they have no influence? Why do we grant media outlets and their personnel special protection if their contributions to our society are so insignificant?

First Amendment
Guarantees freedom of speech, press, assembly, and religion

LEARNING OBJECTIVES

After studying this chapter you should be able to

- Explain the social, cultural, and political conditions that led to the development of mass society theory and propaganda theory.
- Place the role of the mass media in scholars' conceptions of those theories.
- Understand mass society and propaganda theorists' perceptions of the audience and its ability to interact with mass media.
- Explain why and in what form contemporary articulations of mass society theory and propaganda theory exist.
- List mass society theory's assumptions about media and audiences.
- Detail some early examples of mass society theory.
- Trace the origins of propaganda from its earliest days to its arrival in the United States.
- Explain the details of behaviorism, Freudianism, and the propaganda theories of Harold Lasswell and Walter Lippmann, as well as those of John Dewey's alternative perspective.

OVERVIEW

Clearly, a lot is at stake when we debate the role of media and develop and test theory to guide that conversation. Controversy over media influence can have far-reaching consequences for society and for media institutions. In this chapter, we will trace the rise of *mass society theory*, a perspective on society that emerged at the end of the nineteenth century and was especially influential through the first half of the twentieth century. It is an all-encompassing perspective on Western industrial society that attributes an influential but largely negative role to media. It views media as having the power to profoundly shape our perceptions of the social world and to manipulate our actions, often without our conscious awareness. This theory argues that media influence must be controlled. The strategies for control, however, are as varied as the theorists who offer them.

propaganda
No-holds-barred use of communication to propagate specific beliefs and expectations

This chapter's second major section will consider the **propaganda** theories that were developed after World War I and share many of mass society theory's concerns and assumptions. Both are examples of what we have labeled as the mass society trend in media theory. We will discuss how political propaganda was initially used to manipulate mass audiences and then consider some of the theories developed to understand and control it. With the normative theories discussed in Chapter 3, these were the first true mass communication theories. Mass society theory saw media as only one of many disruptive forces. In propaganda theories, however, media became the focus of attention. Propaganda theorists specifically analyzed media content and speculated about its ability to influence people's thoughts and actions. They wanted to understand and explain the ability of messages to persuade and convert thousands or even millions of individuals to extreme viewpoints and engage in seemingly irrational actions.

Propaganda commanded the attention of early media theorists because it threatened to undermine the very foundation of the U.S. political system and of democratic governments everywhere. By the late 1930s, many, if not most, American leaders were convinced that democracy wouldn't survive if extremist political propaganda was allowed to be freely distributed. But censorship of propaganda meant imposing significant limitations on that essential principle of Western democracy, communication freedom. This posed a terrible dilemma. Strict censorship might undermine democracy just as corrosively as propaganda.

white propaganda
Intentional suppression of potentially harmful information and ideas, combined with deliberate promotion of positive information or ideas to distract attention from problematic events

Even though the threat of propaganda was great, some propaganda theorists believed there could be a silver lining to this cloud. If we could find a way to harness the power of propaganda to promote good and just ideals, then we would not only survive its threat but have a tool to help build a better social order. This was the promise of what came to be called **white propaganda**—a top-down communication strategy that used propaganda techniques to fight "bad" propaganda and promote objectives elites considered good. After World War II, these white propaganda techniques provided a basis for the development of strategic (promotional) communication methods that are widely used today in advertising, political communication, and public relations. In fact, propaganda theory is experiencing a resurgence of interest precisely for this reason: many contemporary observers argue that the techniques used in modern promotional efforts appear to be even more effective in our contemporary world of corporate media ownership (Laitinen and Rakos, 1997).

The social world in which propaganda was widely practiced and in which propaganda theory evolved was especially turbulent. Industrialization and urbanization were reshaping both Europe and the United States. Important books of the time had titles like Ortega y Gasset's 1930 *The Revolt of the Masses*, Elton Mayo's 1933 *Human Problems of an Industrial Civilization*, and Erich Fromm's 1941 *Escape from Freedom*. During this era many new forms of technology were invented and quickly disseminated. Electricity became available in cities and later in rural areas, and that opened the way for the spread of thousands of electrical appliances. This technological change, however, occurred with little consideration for its environmental, social, or psychological impact. Social change could be rationalized as progress, but a high price was paid—workers were brutalized, vast urban slums were created, and huge tracts of wilderness were ravaged.

Media were among the many technologies that shaped and were shaped by this modern era. An industrial social order had great need for the fast and efficient distribution of information. There was need to command and control factories that spread across the continent. The advantages of new media like the telegraph and telephone were soon recognized, and each new communication technology was quickly adopted—first by businesses and then by the public.

In the mid- and late nineteenth century, large urban populations' growing demand for cheap media content drove the development of several new media: the penny press, the nickel magazine, and the dime novel. High-speed printing presses and Linotype machines made it practical to mass-produce the printed word at very low cost. Urban newspapers boomed all along the East Coast and in major trading centers across the United States. Newspaper circulation wars broke out in many large cities and led to the development of sensationalistic journalism that seriously challenged the norms and values of most readers.

MASS SOCIETY CRITICS AND THE DEBATE OVER MEDIA

Changes in media industries often increase the pressure on other social institutions to change. Instability in the way we routinely communicate can have unsettling consequences for all other institutions. Some leaders of these institutions resent external pressures and are reluctant to alter their way of doing things. Consider how the widespread use of the Internet and smartphones has forced alterations in the way we do many routine and important things. The changes associated with new media in the first half of the last century were far more disruptive because people were less experienced at dealing with communication changes. Not surprisingly, conservative critics interpreted the rise of the media industries as threatening to subvert every other social institution, including political, religious, business, military, and educational institutions. Social critics even accused media of profoundly altering families—the most basic social institution of all. Many of these worrisome views are consistent with mass society theory. This venerable theory has a long and checkered history. Mass society theory is actually many different theories sharing some common assumptions about the role of media and society. You can judge for yourself the worthiness of the criticism that accompanied the arrival of some of the media we now enjoy in the box entitled "Fearful Reactions to New Media."

THINKING ABOUT THEORY | **Fearful Reactions to New Media**

The introduction of each new mass medium of the twentieth century was greeted with derision, skepticism, fear, and sometimes silliness. Here is a collection of the thinking of the times that welcomed movies, talkies, radio, and television. Can you find examples of mass society theory's most obvious characteristics—the conceit that the elite way is the right way and condescension toward others?

Once you have read through these examples, go online or to the library and find similar dire predictions about the Internet and the Web. No doubt you've already read or heard concerns about Internet addiction, loss of parental authority, child pornography, online gambling, poor writing skills and "mall speak" from instant messaging, the loss of community, reduced attention spans, violent and offensive online gaming, privacy invasion, and identity theft. Can you identify other concerns associated with the coming of the new communication technologies?

Movies and Talkies

When you first reflect that in New York City alone, on a Sunday, 500,000 people go to moving picture shows, a majority of them perhaps

children, and that in the poorer quarters of town every teacher testifies that the children now save their pennies for picture shows instead of candy, you cannot dismiss canned drama with a shrug of contempt. It is a big factor in the lives of the masses, to be reckoned with, if possible to be made better, if used for good ends. Eighty percent of present day theatrical audiences in this country are canned drama audiences. Ten million people attended professional baseball games in America in 1908. Four million people attend moving pictures theaters, it is said, every day. $50,000,000 are invested in the industry. Chicago has over 300 theaters, New York 300, St. Louis 205, Philadelphia 186, even conservative Boston boasts more than 30. Almost 190 miles of film are unrolled on the screens of America's canned drama theaters every day in the year. Here is an industry to be controlled, an influence to be reckoned with.

Source: *American Magazine*, September 1909, p. 498.

And if the speech recorded in the dialogue (of talking pictures) is vulgar or ugly, its potentialities

(Continued)

THINKING ABOUT THEORY | Fearful Reactions to New Media   (Continued)

for lowering the speech standard of the country are almost incalculable. The fact that it is likely to be heard by the less discriminating portion of the public operates to increase its evil effects; for among the regular attendants at moving picture theaters there are to be found large groups from among our foreign-born population, to whom it is really vitally important that they hear only the best speech.

Source: *Commonweal*, April 10, 1929, p. 653.

Radio

In general one criterion must be kept in mind: the radio should do what the teacher cannot do; it ought not to do what the teacher can do better. However radio may develop, I cannot conceive of the time when a good teacher will not continue to be the most important object in any classroom.

Source: *Education*, December 1936, p. 217.

Is radio to become a chief arm of education? Will the classroom be abolished, and the child of the future stuffed with facts as he sits at home or even as he walks about the streets with his portable receiving set in his pocket?

Source: *Century*, June 1924, p. 149.

Television

Seeing constant brutality, viciousness and unsocial acts results in hardness, intense selfishness, even in mercilessness, proportionate to the amount of exposure and its play on the native temperament of the child. Some cease to show resentment to insults, to indignities, and even cruelty toward helpless old people, to women and other children.

Source: *New Republic*, November 1, 1954, p. 12.

Here, in concept at least, was the most magnificent of all forms of communication. Here was the supreme triumph of invention, the dream of the ages—something that could bring directly into the home a moving image fused with sound-reproducing action, language, and thought without the loss of measurable time. Here was the magic eye that could bring the wonders of entertainment, information and education into the living room. Here was a tool for the making of a more enlightened democracy than the world had ever seen. Yet out of the wizardry of the television tube has come such an assault against the human mind, such a mobilized attack on the imagination, such an invasion against good taste as no other communications medium has known, not excepting the motion picture or radio itself.

Source: *Saturday Review*, December 24, 1949, p. 20.

ASSUMPTIONS OF MASS SOCIETY THEORY

Mass society theory first appeared late in the nineteenth century as traditional social elites struggled to make sense of the disruptive consequences of modernization. Some (i.e., the landed aristocracy, small-town shopkeepers, schoolteachers, the clergy, upper-class politicians) lost power or were overwhelmed in their efforts to deal with social problems. For them, the mass media were symbolic of all that was wrong with modern society. Mass newspapers of the yellow journalism era were viewed as gigantic, monopolistic enterprises employing unethical practices to pander to semiliterate mass audiences. Leaders in education and religion resented media's power to attract readers using content they considered highly objectionable, vulgar, even sinful (Brantlinger, 1983). "A new situation has arisen throughout the world," wrote the editors of *Public Opinion Quarterly* in 1937, "created by the spread of literacy among the people and the miraculous improvement of the means of communication. Always the opinion of relatively small publics have been a prime force in political life, but now, for the first time in history, we are confronted nearly everywhere by *mass* opinion as the final determinant of political, and economic, action" (in Beniger, 1987, pp. S46–S47).

Envy, discontent, and outright fear were often at the roots of mass society thinking. Note the use of the words "we are confronted." These emotions undergirded the development of a theory that is both radically conservative and potentially revolutionary. It fears the emergence of a new type of social order—a mass society—that would fundamentally and tragically transform the social world. To prevent this, technological change generally and changes in media specifically must be controlled or even reversed. A conservative effort must be made to restore an idealized, older social order, or revolutionary action must be taken so that technology and media are brought under elite control and used to forge a new and better social order.

The mass society theories that were developed in the last century make several basic assumptions about individuals, the role of media, and the nature of social change. As you read about these assumptions, think about whether you have recently heard any similar arguments. They may have been altered to fit contemporary society, but they exist. We no longer fear totalitarianism but that has not stopped us from fearing a future that seems beyond our control or the control of our leaders. Here we list the assumptions and then discuss each in some detail:

1. The media are a powerful force within society that can subvert essential norms and values and thus undermine the social order. To deal with this threat media must be brought under elite control.
2. Media are able to directly influence the minds of average people, transforming their views of the social world.
3. Once people's thinking is transformed by media, all sorts of bad long-term consequences are likely to result—not only bringing ruin to individual lives but also creating social problems on a vast scale.
4. Average people are vulnerable to media because in mass society they are cut off and isolated from traditional social institutions that previously protected them from manipulation.
5. The social chaos initiated by media will likely be resolved by establishment of a totalitarian social order.
6. Mass media inevitably debase higher forms of culture, bringing about a general decline in civilization.

The first assumption is that the media subvert essential norms and values and threaten the social order. Thus, elite control of media is necessary. Opponents of the new media have consistently proposed turning control of them over to elites who will preserve or transform the social order. In Europe, this argument won out during the 1920s, and broadcast media were placed under the control of government agencies. These efforts had disastrous consequences when Hitler narrowly won election in Germany. His Nazi party quickly turned radio into an effective propaganda tool that helped consolidate his power. In the United States, many schemes were proposed in the 1920s that would have turned control of broadcasting over to churches, schools, or government agencies. Ultimately, a compromise was reached and a free-enterprise broadcasting industry was created under the more-or-less watchful eye of a government agency—the Federal Radio Commission, which later evolved into the Federal Communications Commission.

But why are the media so dangerous to society? What makes them threatening? How are they able to subvert traditional norms and values? A second assumption is that media have the power to reach out and directly influence the minds of average people so that their thinking is transformed (Davis, 1976). Media can act independently of all the other things that influence people in their daily lives. This is also known as the **direct-effects assumption** and has been hotly debated since the 1940s. Sociologist James Carey offered this accurate articulation of mass society theory's view of the influence of mass communication: "The media collectively, but in particular the newer, illiterate media of radio and film, possessed extraordinary power to shape the beliefs and conduct of ordinary men and women" (1996, p. 22). Although each version of mass society theory has its own notion about the type of direct influence different media may have, all versions stress how dangerous this influence can be and the extreme vulnerability of average people to immediate media-induced changes.

direct-effects assumption
The media, in and of themselves, can produce direct effects

The third assumption is that once media transform people's thinking, all sorts of bad long-term consequences result—not only bringing ruin to individual lives but also creating social problems on a vast scale (Marcuse, 1941). Over the years, virtually every major social problem we have confronted has been linked in some way to media—from prostitution and delinquency to urban violence and drug usage to the "defeat" in Vietnam and our loss of national pride. Teenage delinquents have seen too many gangster movies. Disaffected housewives watch too many soap operas, teenage girls hate their bodies because of beauty magazines, and drug addicts have taken too seriously the underlying message in most advertising: the good life is achieved through consumption of a product, not by hard work.

Mass society theory's fourth assumption is that average people are vulnerable to media because they have been cut off and isolated from traditional social institutions that previously protected them from manipulation (Kreiling, 1984). Mass society theorists tend to idealize the past and hold romantic visions of what life must have been like in medieval villages in Europe or in small rural towns on the American frontier. They assume that these older social orders nurtured and protected people within communities whose culture gave meaning to their lives. Although these views have some validity (most social orders have some redeeming qualities), they neglect to consider the severe limitations of traditional social orders. Most premodern social orders limited individual development and creativity for most community members. People were routinely compelled to do the jobs their parents and grandparents had done. People learned specific social roles based on the accident of being born in a certain place at a certain time. The freedom to develop in ways that people find meaningful was unknown.

Yet the claims that mass society theorists make about the vulnerability to manipulation of isolated individuals are compelling. These arguments have been restated in endless variations with every revolution in media technology. They assert that when people are stripped of the protective cocoon provided by a traditional community, they necessarily turn to media for the guidance and reassurance previously provided by their communities. Thus when people leave sheltered rural communities and enter big cities, media can suddenly provide communication that replaces messages from social institutions that have been left behind. Media can become the trusted and valued sources of messages about politics, entertainment, religion, education, and on and on. Under these conditions, people tend to learn new information and develop different ideas.

The fifth assumption is that the social chaos initiated by media will be resolved by establishment of a totalitarian social order (Davis, 1976). This assumption was developed during the 1930s and flourished at the time of the war against Fascism, reaching its peak of popularity in the United States during the witch hunt for Communists in government and media of the 1950s. Mass society is envisioned as an inherently chaotic, highly unstable form of social order that will inevitably collapse and then be replaced by totalitarianism. Mass society, with its teeming hordes of isolated individuals, must give way to an even worse form of society—highly regimented, centrally controlled, totalitarian society. Thus, to the extent that media promote the rise of mass society, they pave the way for totalitarianism.

Throughout the twentieth century, fear of the spread of totalitarianism grew in most democracies. For many, it symbolized everything that was loathsome and evil, but others saw it as the "wave of the future." Fascist and Communist advocates of totalitarianism dismissed democracy as well-meaning but impractical because average people could never effectively govern themselves—they were too apathetic and ignorant to do that. Even people with a desire to be politically active simply don't have the time and energy to be involved on a day-to-day basis. The masses must be led by a totalitarian leader who can weld them into a powerful force to achieve great things. Cultivation of individuality leads to inefficiency, jealousy, and conflict. Democracies were perceived as inherently weak, unable to resist the inevitable rise of charismatic, strong, determined leaders. Across Europe, in Latin America, and in Asia, fledgling democracies faltered and collapsed as the economic Great Depression deepened. Fascism in Germany and Communism in Russia provided examples of what could be accomplished by totalitarian rule. The People could be led to rise from the pit of a lost war and economic depression to forge a seemingly prosperous and highly productive social order. The United States was not immune to totalitarian appeals. Radical political movements arose, and their influence spread rapidly. In several states, right-wing extremists were elected to political office. Pro-Fascist groups held gigantic public rallies to demonstrate their support for Hitler. The supremacist and anti-Semitic writings of automaker Henry Ford were translated and published in Nazi Germany. Radio propagandists like Father Coughlin achieved notoriety and acceptance. Radicals fought for control of labor unions. The thousand-year Reich envisioned by Hitler seemed a more realistic outcome than the survival of democracy in modern nation-states.

Why was totalitarianism so successful? Why was it sweeping the world just as the new mass media of radio and movies were becoming increasingly prominent? Was there a connection? Were radio and movies to blame? Many mass society theorists believed they were. Without these media, they thought, dictators wouldn't have gained popularity or consolidated their power. They argued that radio and later television were ideally suited for reaching out into homes and directly persuading average people so that vast numbers of them could be welded into a regimented, cohesive society. Movies were able to communicate powerful images that instilled the positive and negative associations those dictators desired.

What these critics failed to note is that when the Nazis or Communists were most successful, average people had strong reasons for *wanting* to believe the promises about jobs and personal security made by the extremists. Personal freedom has little value when people are starving and a wheelbarrow full of money won't buy a loaf of bread. The success of Nazi or Communist propaganda was also dependent on silencing critics and shutting down media that provided competing viewpoints. Hitler didn't gain popularity quickly. He methodically suppressed competing individuals and groups over a period of years, not days. He effectively used radio and movies, but he had at his disposal all the other weapons of suppression typically available to a ruthless demagogue. But viewing Hitler from across the Atlantic, American elites saw only what they most feared—a demagogue relying mostly on media to achieve and hold power.

Totalitarianism was the biggest fear aroused by mass society theorists, but they also focused attention on a more subtle form of societal corruption—mass culture. The sixth and final assumption of mass society theory, then, is that mass media inevitably debase higher forms of culture, bringing about a general decline in civilization (Davis, 1976). To understand this criticism, you must understand the perspective held by Western cultural and educational elites during the past two centuries. In the decades following the **Enlightenment** (an eighteenth-century European social and philosophical movement stressing rational thought and progress through science), these elites saw themselves as responsible for nurturing and promulgating a higher form of culture, high culture, not only within their own societies but also around the world. For example, British and other colonial elites believed they were carrying the light of civilization to the people they conquered in much the same way American elites viewed their conquest of the Indians.

Enlightenment
Eighteenth-century European social and philosophical movement stressing rational thought and progress through science

In retrospect, the high culture perspective suffers from some serious limitations. The literary canon, one of the tools used to promote high culture, consisted mostly of works written by white, male, Western, Anglo-Saxon, and Protestant authors. Symphony music, ballet and opera don't communicate effectively outside of the urban, higher class culture in which they developed. And as for those colonialized peoples, they had no say in the replacement of their local cultures by those of their conquerors.

For defenders of high culture, mass media represented an insidious, corrosive force in society—one that threatened their influence by popularizing ideas and activities they considered trivial or demeaning. Rather than glorify gangsters (as movies did in the 1930s), why not praise great educators or religious leaders? Why pander to popular taste—why not seek to raise it to higher levels? Give audiences Shakespeare, not Charlie Chaplin. Why give people what they want instead of giving them what they need? Why trivialize great art by turning it into cartoons (as Disney did in the 1930s)? Mass society theorists raised these questions—and had long and overly abstract answers for them.

EARLY EXAMPLES OF MASS SOCIETY THEORY

Now we'll summarize a few of the early examples of mass society theory. This set of theories is by no means complete. The ideas we describe and discuss were influential at the time they were written and provided important reference points for later theorists. It is important to remember, too, that even where not specifically mentioned, the emerging mass media were clearly implicated in most examples.

In the latter chapters of this book, we will consider important new theories that articulate innovative thinking about popular culture—including ideas about the influence of U.S.-style mass entertainment in other nations. These inevitably draw on older notions about mass society and mass culture, but most reject the simplistic assumptions and criticisms of earlier eras. These newer theories no longer accept elite high culture as the standard against which all others must be measured. Current criticism tends to focus on the inherent biases of media when it comes to developing new forms of culture. Media are no longer seen as corrupting and degrading high culture. Rather, they are viewed as limiting or disrupting cultural development. Media don't subvert culture, but they do play a major and sometimes counterproductive role in cultural change. Fear of totalitarianism has been replaced worldwide by growing disillusionment with consumerism and its power to undermine local cultures and national identities.

GEMEINSCHAFT AND GESELLSCHAFT

gemeinschaft
In Tönnies's conception, traditional folk cultures

gesellschaft
In Tönnies's conception, modern industrial society

Among the originators of mass society notions was a German sociologist, Ferdinand Tönnies. Tönnies sought to explain the critical difference between earlier forms of social organization and European society as it existed in the late nineteenth century. In an 1887 book, *Gemeinschaft und Gesellschaft*, he proposed a simple dichotomy—**gemeinschaft**, or folk community, and **gesellschaft**, or modern industrial society. In folk communities, people were bound together by strong ties of family, by tradition, and by rigid social roles— basic social institutions were very powerful. Gemeinschaft "consisted of a dense network of personal relationships based heavily on kinship and the direct, face-to-face contact that occurs in a small, closed village. Norms were largely unwritten, and individuals were bound to one another in a web of mutual interdependence that touched all aspects of life" (Fukuyama, 1999, p. 57). In addition, "a collective has the character of a gemeinschaft insofar as its members think of the group as a gift of nature created by a supernatural will" (Martindale, 1960, p. 83). Although folk communities had important strengths as well as serious limitations, Tönnies emphasized the former. He argued that most people yearn for the order and meaning provided by folk communities. They often find life in modern societies troublesome and meaningless. As far as mass society theorists were concerned, not only did the emerging mass media disrupt kinship and direct face-to-face contact, but they certainly were not gifts of nature.

In gesellschaft, people are bound together by relatively weak social institutions based on rational choices rather than tradition. Gesellschaft represents "the framework of laws and other formal regulations that characterized large, urban industrial societies. Social relationships were more formalized and impersonal; individuals did not depend on one another for support... and were therefore much less morally obligated to one another" (Fukuyama, 1999, pp. 57–58). Naturally, it was the established elites (the traditional wielders of power and the most vocal champions of mass society theory) who stood to lose the most influence in the move from gemeinschaft to gesellschaft, as "average" people came to depend less on their influence and more on formalized and more objectively applied rules and laws. For example, when you take a job, you sign a formal contract based on your personal decision. You don't sign it because you are bound by family tradition to work for a certain employer. You make a more or less rational choice.

Over the years, media have been continually accused of breaking down folk communities (gemeinschaft) and encouraging the development of amoral, weak social institutions (gesellschaft). The late Reverend Jerry Falwell, founder of the Moral Majority, and fellow televangelist Pat Robertson reflected this view in 2001 when they charged that the September 11 terrorist attacks on the World Trade Center and the Pentagon were the products, not of Islamic radicalism, but of the "American cultural elite's" systematic subversion of traditional family and social values (Adbusters, 2002). Popular television shows prominently feature unwed couples living together, homosexual unions, and unwed mothers bearing children. Do these programs merely reflect social changes, or are they somehow responsible for them? As we'll see throughout this text, there is no simple answer to this question.

MECHANICAL AND ORGANIC SOLIDARITY

In his 1893 *Division of Labor in Society*, which was translated into English in 1933, French sociologist Émile Durkheim offered a theory with the same dichotomy as that of Tönnies but with a fundamentally different interpretation of modern social orders. Durkheim compared folk communities to machines in which people were little more than cogs. These machines were very ordered and durable, but people were forced by a collective consensus to perform traditional social roles. Think for a moment about all the family names used today that are derived from professions: Farmer, Taylor, Hunter, Goldsmith, Forester, Toepfer, and Shumacher (German for Potter and Shoemaker). Your name was, literally, what you were: John the Smith. Or consider the many family names that end in "son" or "sen." People were identified by their father's name: Peterson is Peter's son. People were bound by this consensus to one another like the parts of a great engine—**mechanical solidarity**.

mechanical solidarity
In Durkheim's conception, folk cultures bound by consensus and traditional social roles

Durkheim compared modern social orders to animals rather than to machines. As they grow, animals undergo profound changes in their physical form. They begin life as babies and progress through several developmental stages on their way to adulthood and old age. The bodies of animals are made up of many different kinds of cells—skin, bone, blood—and these cells serve very different purposes. Similarly, modern social orders can undergo profound changes, and therefore the people in them can grow and change along with the society at large. In Durkheim's theory, people are like the specialized cells of a body rather than like the cogs of a machine. People perform specialized tasks and depend on the overall health of the body for their personal survival. Unlike machines, animals are subject to diseases and physical threats. But they are capable of using mental processes to anticipate threats and cope with them. Durkheim used the term **organic solidarity** to refer to the social ties that bind modern social orders together.

organic solidarity
In Durkheim's conception, modern social orders bound by culturally negotiated social ties

Social orders with organic solidarity are characterized by specialization, division of labor, and interdependence (Martindale, 1960, p. 87). Be warned, though, it is easy to confuse Durkheim's labeling of mechanical and organic solidarity, because we naturally associate machines with modernity. Remember that he uses the metaphor of the machine to refer to folk cultures—not modern society.

You can see worries about and hopes for traditional and modern society in the writings of two important mass society thinkers, Dwight Macdonald and Edward Shils, men holding markedly different perspectives on modernity. We can see hints of Tönnies disdain for modern, mass society (gesellschaft) in this quote from Macdonald's (1953) essay, *A Theory of Mass Culture*:

> Being in so far as people are organised [*sic*] (more strictly disorganised) as masses, they lose their human identity and quality. For the masses are in historical time what a crowd is in space: a large quantity of people unable to express themselves as human beings because they are related to one another neither as individuals nor as members of communities—indeed they are not related to each other at all but only to something distant, abstract, non-human. (p. 14)

And we see hints of Durkheim's optimism for the benefits of organic solidarity (modern, mass society) in this quote from Shils' (1962) essay, *The Theory of Mass Society*:

> Despite all internal conflicts ... there are, within the mass society, more of a sense of attachment to the society as a whole, more sense of affinity with one's fellows, more openness to understanding, and more reaching out of understanding among men [*sic*] than in any earlier society.... The mass society is not the most peaceful or "orderly" society that ever existed; but it is the most consensual (p. 53).... Mass society has witnessed a reinterpretation of the value of a human being. Simply by virtue of his quality or membership in the society he acquires minimal dignity. (p. 62)

MASS SOCIETY THEORY IN CONTEMPORARY TIMES

Although mass society theory has little support among contemporary mass communication researchers and theorists, its basic assumptions of a corrupting media and helpless audiences have never completely disappeared. Attacks on the pervasive dysfunctional power of media have persisted and will persist as long as dominant elites find their power challenged by media and as long as privately owned media find it profitable to produce and distribute content that challenges widely practiced social norms and values. Vestiges of mass society resonate today on three fronts,

---

INSTANT ACCESS

Mass Society Theory

Strengths	Weaknesses
1. Speculates about important effects	1. Is unscientific
2. Highlights important structural changes and conflicts in modern cultures	2. Is unsystematic
3. Draws attention to issues of media ownership and ethics	3. Is promulgated by elites interested in preserving power
	4. Underestimates intelligence and competence of "average people"
	5. Underestimates personal, societal, and cultural barriers to direct media influence

high culture proponents, opponents of media concentration, and in social science circle where researchers see the operation of a powerful mass media in conjunction with an increasingly uninterested and uninvolved citizenry.

The high culture canon's most influential contemporary champion is British social critic, philosopher, and intellectual Roger Scruton. In *An Intelligent Person's Guide to Modern Culture* (2000), he wrote, "Something new seems to be at work in the contemporary world—a process that is eating away the very heart of social life, not merely by putting salesmanship in place of moral virtue, but by putting everything—virtue included—on sale" (p. 55). This work also makes clear mass society's elitism and support of elite culture:

This book presents a theory of modern culture, and a defense of culture in its higher and more critical form. It is impossible to give a convincing defense of high culture to a person who has none. I shall therefore assume that you, the reader, are both intelligent and cultivated. You don't have to be familiar with the entire canon of Western literature, the full range of musical and artistic masterpieces or the critical reflections that all these things have prompted. Who is? But it would be useful to have read *Les fleurs du mal* by Baudelaire and T. S. Eliot's *Waste Land*. I shall also presume some familiarity with Mozart, Wagner, Manet, Poussin, Tennyson, Schoenberg, George Herbert, Goethe, Marx, and Nietzsche. (p. x)

concentration
Ownership of different and numerous media companies concentrated in fewer and fewer hands

The second factor in contemporary rearticulations of mass society theory involves **concentration** of ownership of different media companies in fewer and fewer hands. According to journalist and media critic Ben Bagdikian (2004), the number of corporations controlling most of the country's newspapers, magazines, radio and television stations, book publishers, and movie studios has shrunk from 50, when he wrote the first edition of his classic *The Media Monopoly*, to 5 today. He has this to say about the concentration of ownership of media industries:

Left to their own devices, a small number of the most powerful firms have taken control of most of their countries' printed and broadcast news and entertainment. They have their own style of control, not by official edict or state terror, but by uniform economic and political goals. They have their own way of narrowing political and cultural diversity, not by promulgating official dogma, but by quietly emphasizing ideas and information congenial to their profits and political preferences. Although they are not their countries' official political authorities, they have a disproportionate private influence over the political authorities and over public policy. (Bagdikian, 1992, pp. 239–240)

Bagdikian, a strong proponent of media freedom, is no mass society theorist. But his concern is shared by many who hold to traditional notions of an involved public able to avail itself of a wide array of entertainment, news, and opinion. Concentration, they argue, gives people merely the illusion of choice.

It is the media's limited presentation of the larger world that has some contemporary postpositivist researchers suggesting a reconsideration of some of mass society theory's themes. James Beniger, for example, points to a number of well-respected modern theories of media influence that, while not envisioning an atomized, adrift population, do indeed envision large-scale or mass control wielded by various elites (1987). We'll look at these theories in detail later, but for now ideas such as *agenda setting theory* (media may not tell us what to think, but they do tell us what to think about), *spiral of silence* (alternative points of view are spiraled into silence in the face of overwhelming expression of a dominant view in the media), *cultivation analysis* (a false "reality" is cultivated among heavy television viewers by the repetitive, industrially created stories that dominate the medium), and *framing* (news conventions present a dominant interpretive background for understanding events and policy) argue for a powerful, public discourse-shaping media. Media concentration and effects theories such as these have also given new life to another early conception of all-powerful media, propaganda theory.

THE ORIGIN OF PROPAGANDA

Throughout the first half of the twentieth century, social elites debated the meaning of propaganda. Was propaganda necessarily bad or was it a good form of communication that could be corrupted? Many forms of communication seek to persuade people—were all of them propaganda? Gradually, the term *propaganda* came to refer to a certain type of communication strategy. It involves the no-holds-barred use of communication to propagate specific beliefs and expectations. The ultimate goal of propagandists is to change the way people act and to leave them believing that those actions are voluntary, that the newly adopted behaviors—and the opinions underlying them—are their own (Pratkanis and Aronson, 1992, p. 9). To accomplish this, though, propagandists must first change the way people conceive of themselves and their social world. They use a variety of communication techniques to guide and transform those beliefs. During the 1930s, the new media of radio and movies provided propagandists with powerful new tools.

Fritz Hippler, head of Nazi Germany's film propaganda division, said that the secret to effective propaganda is to (a) simplify a complex issue and (b) repeat that simplification over and over again (*World War II*, 1982). J. Michael Sproule (1994) argues that effective propaganda is covert: it "persuades people without seeming to do so" (p. 3); features "the massive orchestration of communication" (p. 4); and emphasizes "tricky language designed to discourage reflective thought" (p. 5). The propagandist believes that the end justifies the means. Therefore, it is not only right but necessary that half-truths and even outright lies be used to convince people to abandon ideas that are "wrong" and to adopt those favored by the propagandist. Propagandists also rely on **disinformation** to discredit their opposition. They spread false information about opposition groups and their objectives. Often the source of this false information is concealed so that it can't be traced to the propagandist.

disinformation
False information spread about the opposition to discredit it

As U.S. theorists studied propaganda, they came to differentiate black, white, and gray propaganda, but definitions of these types of propaganda varied (Becker, 1949; Snowball, 1999;). **Black propaganda** was usually defined as involving deliberate and strategic transmission of lies—its use was well illustrated by the Nazis. White propaganda was, as we have seen, usually defined as involving intentional suppression of contradictory information and ideas, combined with deliberate promotion of highly consistent information or ideas that support the objectives of the propagandist. Sometimes white propaganda was used to draw attention away from problematic events or to provide interpretations of events that were useful for the propagandist. Becker asserts that to be white propaganda, it must be openly identified as coming from an "outside" source—one that doesn't have a close relationship to the target of the propaganda.

black propaganda
Deliberate and strategic transmission of lies

gray propaganda
Transmission of information or ideas that might or might not be false. No effort is made to determine their validity

Gray propaganda involved transmission of information or ideas that might or might not be false. The propagandist simply made no effort to determine their validity and actually avoided doing so—especially if dissemination of the content would serve his or her interest. Becker argues that the truth or falsity of propaganda is often hard to establish, so it isn't practical to use veracity as a criterion for differentiating types of propaganda. Today we find the attribution of labels like "black" and "white" to the concepts of bad and good propaganda offensive. But remember one of this book's constant themes: These ideas are products of their times.

Propagandists then and now live in an either/or, good/evil world. American propagandists in the 1930s had two clear alternatives. On one side were truth, justice, and freedom—in short, the American way—and on the other side were falsehood, evil, and slavery—totalitarianism. Of course, Communist and Nazi propagandists had their own versions of truth, justice, and freedom. For them the American vision of Utopia was at best naive and at worst likely to lead to racial pollution and cultural degradation. The Nazis used propaganda to cultivate extreme fear and hatred of minority groups.

Thus, for the totalitarian propagandist, mass media were a very practical means of mass manipulation—an effective mechanism for controlling large populations. If people came to share the views of the propagandist, they were said to be converted: they abandoned old views and took on those promoted by propaganda. Once consensus was created, elites could then take the actions that it permitted or dictated. They could carry out the "will of the people," who have become, in the words of journalism and social critic Todd Gitlin, "cognoscenti of their own bamboozlement" (1991).

Propagandists typically held elitist and paternalistic views about their audiences. They believed that people needed to be converted for their "own good"—not just to serve the interest of the propagandist. Propagandists often blamed the people for the necessity of engaging in lies and manipulation. They thought people so irrational, so illiterate, or so inattentive that it was necessary to coerce, seduce, or trick them into learning bits of misinformation. The propagandists' argument was simple: If only people were more rational or intelligent, we could just sit down and explain things to them, person to person. But most aren't—especially the ones who need the most help. Most people are children when it comes to important affairs like politics. How can we expect them to listen to reason? It's just not possible.

engineering of consent
Official use of communication campaigns to reach "good" ends

In the post-World War I United States, when propaganda theory was originally developed, the beneficial use of propaganda became known as the **engineering of consent**, a term coined by "the father of modern public relations," Edward L. Bernays. Social historian Andrew Marshall (2013) quotes Bernays' kind words about propaganda, "The conscious and intelligent manipulation of the organized habits and opinions of the masses is an important element in democratic society. Those who manipulate this unseen mechanism of society constitute an invisible government which is the true ruling power of our country." As a result, Bernays believed that traditional democratic notions of freedom of press and speech should be expanded to include the government's "freedom to persuade…. Only by mastering the techniques of communication can leadership be exercised fruitfully in the vast complex that is modern democracy." Why did Bernays see propaganda and democracy as a good fit? Because in a democracy, results "do not just happen" (Sproule, 1997, p. 213).

The propagandist also uses similar reasoning for suppressing opposition messages: Average people are just too gullible. They will be taken in by the lies and tricks of others. If opponents are allowed to freely communicate their messages, a standoff will result in which no one wins. Propagandists are convinced of the validity of their cause, so they must stop opponents from blocking their actions.

PROPAGANDA COMES TO THE UNITED STATES

Americans first began to give serious consideration to the power of propaganda in the years following World War I. The war had demonstrated that modern propaganda techniques could be used with startling effectiveness to assemble massive armies and to maintain civilian morale through long years of warfare. Never before had so many people been mobilized to fight a war. Never before had so many died with so little to show for it over such a long period of time and under such harsh conditions. Earlier wars had been quickly settled by decisive battles. But in this war, massive armies confronted each other along a front that extended for hundreds of miles. From their trenches they bombarded each other and launched occasional attacks that ended in futility.

Harold Lasswell, a political scientist who developed several early theories of media, expressed considerable respect for the propaganda efforts marshaled in the cause of World War I. He wrote:

> When all allowances have been made and all extravagant estimates pared to the bone, the fact remains that propaganda is one of the most powerful instrumentalities in the modern world.... In the Great Society [modern industrial society] it is no longer possible to fuse the waywardness of individuals in the furnace of the war dance; a newer and subtler instrument must weld thousands and even millions of human beings into one amalgamated mass of hate and will and hope. A new flame must burn out the canker of dissent and temper the steel of bellicose enthusiasm. The name of this new hammer and anvil of social solidarity is propaganda. (1927a, pp. 220–221)

Many social researchers in the 1920s and 1930s shared these views. Propaganda was an essential tool that had to be used to effectively manage modern social orders, especially when they are in deadly competition with other nations that rely on propaganda to mobilize their masses.

After World War I, the propaganda battle continued, and inevitably it spread beyond Europe, as nations sought to spread their influence and new political movements attracted members. During the 1920s, radio and movies provided powerful new media for propaganda messages. Hitler's rise to power in Germany was accompanied by consolidation of his control over all forms of media—beginning with radio and the film industry and ending with newspapers. In the United States, the battle lines in the propaganda war were quickly drawn. On one side were the elites dominating major social institutions and organizations, including the major political parties, businesses, schools, and universities. On the other side was a broad range of social movements and small extremist political groups. Many were local variants of Fascist, Socialist, or Communist groups that in Europe were much larger and more significant. From the point of view of the old-line elites, these groups were highly suspect. Foreign subversion was a growing fear. The elites believed the influence of these movements and groups had to be curbed before they ruined *our* way of life.

Extremist propagandists, whether foreign-based or domestically grown, found it increasingly easy to reach and persuade audiences during the 1930s. Only a part of this success, however, can be directly attributed to the rise of the powerful new media. In the United States, large newspapers, movies, and radio were controlled mainly by the existing elites. Extremists were often forced to rely on older media like pamphlets, handbills, and political rallies. When the social conditions were right and people were receptive to propaganda messages, however, even older, smaller media could be quite effective. And conditions were right (remember our discussion of gemeinschaft and gesellschaft from earlier in this chapter). Mass society theorists and the elites they supported believed that "average people" were particularly open to demagogic propaganda because those "unfortunates" lived in a rapidly industrializing world characterized by psychological and cultural isolation and the loss of the security once sustained by traditional, binding, and informal social rules and obligations. As the economic depression deepened in the 1930s, many people no longer had jobs to provide an income to support their families and their relationships with others.

American elites therefore watched with increasing horror as extremist political groups consolidated their power in Europe and proceeded to establish totalitarian governments wielding enormous control over vast populations. How could they remain complacent when madmen like Hitler's propaganda chief, Joseph Goebbels, could openly espouse such antidemocratic ideas as "It would not be impossible to prove with sufficient repetition and psychological understanding of the people concerned that a square is in fact a circle. What after all are a square and a circle? They are mere words and words can be molded until they clothe ideas in disguise" (quoted in Thomson, 1977, p. 111).

We will review the propaganda theories of three of the most prolific, imaginative, and complex thinkers of their time: Harold Lasswell, Walter Lippmann, and John Dewey. Given the number of books these men wrote, it is impossible to provide a complete presentation of their work. Instead, we will highlight some of their most influential and widely publicized ideas. In nearly every case, these men later refined or even rejected some of these ideas.

Most of the propaganda theories that developed during the 1930s were strongly influenced by two theories: behaviorism and Freudianism. Some combined both. Before presenting the ideas of the major propaganda theorists, we will first look at the two theories that often guided their thinking.

BEHAVIORISM

behaviorism
The notion that all human action is a conditioned response to external environmental stimuli

John B. Watson, an animal experimentalist who argued that all human action is merely a conditioned response to external environmental stimuli, first popularized stimulus-response psychology. Watson's theory became known as **behaviorism** in recognition of its narrow focus on isolated human behaviors. Behaviorists rejected psychology's widely held assumption that higher mental processes (i.e., conscious thought or reflection) ordinarily control human action. In contrast to such "mentalist" views, behaviorists argued that the only purpose served by consciousness was to rationalize behaviors *after* they are triggered by external stimuli. Behaviorists attempted to purge all mentalist terms from their theories and to deal strictly with observable variables—environmental stimuli on the one hand and behaviors on the other. By studying the associations that existed between specific stimuli and specific behaviors, behaviorists hoped to discover previously unknown causes for action. One of the central notions in behaviorism was the idea of conditioning. Behaviorists argued that most human behavior is the result of conditioning by the external environment. We are conditioned to act in certain ways by positive and negative stimuli—we act to gain rewards or avoid punishments.

Early mass communication theorists, who saw the media as providing external stimuli that triggered immediate responses, frequently used behaviorist notions. For example, these ideas could be applied to the analysis of Fritz Hippler's notorious Nazi propaganda film, *The Eternal Jew*. Its powerful, grotesque presentations of Jews, equating them to disease-bearing rats, were expected to trigger negative responses in their German audiences. Repeated exposure to these images would condition them to have a negative response whenever they see or think about people of the Jewish faith.

FREUDIANISM

Freudianism
Freud's notion that human behavior is the product of the conflict between an individual's Id, Ego, and Superego

Freudianism, on the other hand, was very different from behaviorism, though Sigmund Freud shared Watson's skepticism concerning people's ability to exercise effective conscious or rational control over their actions. Freud spent considerable time counseling middle-class women who suffered from hysteria. During hysterical fits, seemingly ordinary individuals would suddenly "break down" and display uncontrolled and highly emotional behavior. It was not uncommon for quiet and passive women to "break down" in public places. They would scream, have fits of crying, or become violent. Often these outbursts occurred at times when the likelihood of embarrassment and trouble for themselves and others was at its highest. What could be causing this irrational behavior?

Ego
In Freudianism, the rational mind

Id
In Freudianism, the egocentric pleasure-seeking part of the mind

Superego
In Freudianism, the internalized set of cultural rules

To explain hysteria, Freud reasoned that the self that guides action must be fragmented into conflicting parts. Normally one part, the rational mind, or **Ego**, is in control, but sometimes other parts become dominant. Freud speculated that human action is often the product of another, darker side of the self—the **Id**. This is the egocentric pleasure-seeking part of ourselves that the Ego must struggle to keep under control. The Ego relies on an internalized set of cultural rules (the **Superego**) for guidance. Caught between the primitive Id and the overly restrictive Superego, the Ego fights a losing battle. When the Ego loses control to the Id, hysteria or worse results. When the Superego becomes dominant and the Id is completely suppressed, people turn into unemotional, depressed social automatons who simply do what others demand.

Propaganda theorists used Freudian notions to develop very pessimistic interpretations of media influence. For example, propaganda would be most effective if it could appeal directly to the Id and short-circuit or bypass the Ego. Alternatively, if through effective propaganda efforts the cultural rules (the Superego) moved the self in the direction of the Id, people's darker impulses would become normal—a strategy that some propaganda theorists believed was skillfully used by the Nazis.

Behaviorism and Freudianism were combined to create propaganda theories that viewed the average individual as incapable of rational self-control. These theories saw people as highly vulnerable to media manipulation using propaganda; media stimuli and the Id could trigger actions that the Ego and the Superego were powerless to stop. Afterward, the Ego merely rationalizes actions that it couldn't control and experiences guilt about them. According to these notions, media could have instantaneous society-wide influence on even the most educated, thoughtful people.

HAROLD LASSWELL'S PROPAGANDA THEORY

Lasswell's theory of propaganda blended ideas borrowed from behaviorism and Freudianism into a particularly pessimistic vision of media and their role in forging modern social orders. Lasswell was one of the first political scientists to recognize the usefulness of various psychological theories and to demonstrate how they could be applied to understanding and controlling politics. The power of propaganda was not so much the result of the substance or appeal of specific messages but, rather, the result of the vulnerable state of mind of average people. Lasswell argued that economic depression and escalating political conflict had induced widespread psychosis, and this made most people susceptible to even crude forms of propaganda. When average people are confronted daily by powerful threats to their personal lives, they turn to propaganda for reassurance and a way to overcome the threat. When people are jobless and their homes are in foreclosure, propaganda appeals find a ready audience.

In Lasswell's view, democracy has a fatal flaw. It seeks to locate truth and make decisions through openly conducted debates about issues. But if these debates escalate into verbal or even physical conflict between advocates for different ideas, then widespread psychosis will result. Spectators to these conflicts will be traumatized by them. Lasswell concluded that even relatively benign forms of political conflict were inherently pathological. When conflict escalates to the level it did in Germany during the Depression, an entire nation could become psychologically unbalanced and vulnerable to manipulation. Lasswell argued that the solution was for social researchers to find ways to "obviate conflict." This necessitates controlling those forms of political communication that lead to conflict. In Lasswell's view, even routine forms of political debate could escalate into conflicts threatening the social order. Lasswell critic Floyd Matson wrote, "In short, according to Lasswell's psychopathology of politics, the presumption in any individual case must be that political action is maladjustive, political participation is irrational, and political expression is irrelevant" (1964, p. 91). But how do you maintain a democratic social order if any form of political debate or demonstration is problematic? Lasswell had an answer to this question: replace public discourse with democratic propaganda.

Lasswell rejected simplistic behaviorist notions about propaganda effects. Here is how he described the task of the propagandist in a 1927 article:

> The strategy of propaganda, which has been phrased in cultural terms, can readily be described in the language of stimulus-response. Translated into this vocabulary, which is especially intelligible to some, the propagandist may be said to be concerned with the multiplication of those stimuli which are best calculated to evoke the desired responses, and with the nullification of those stimuli which are likely to instigate the undesired

responses. Putting the same thing into terms of social suggestion, the problem of the propagandist is to multiply all the suggestions favorable to the attitudes which he wishes to produce and strengthen, and to restrict all suggestions which are unfavorable to them. (1927b, p. 620)

In other words, a few well-targeted messages wouldn't bring down a democratic social order. He argued that propaganda was more than merely using media to lie to people in order to gain temporary control over them. People need to be slowly prepared to accept radically different ideas and actions. Communicators need a well-developed, long-term campaign strategy ("multiplication of those stimuli") in which new ideas and images are carefully introduced and then cultivated. Symbols must be created, and people must be gradually taught to associate specific emotions such as love or hate with these symbols. If these cultivation strategies are successful, they create what Lasswell referred to as **master (or collective) symbols** (Lasswell, 1934). Master symbols are associated with strong emotions and possess the power to stimulate beneficial large-scale mass action if they are used wisely. In contrast to behaviorist notions, Lasswell's theory envisioned a long and quite sophisticated conditioning process. Exposure to one or two extremist messages would not likely have significant effects. And propaganda messages can be delivered through many different media, not just radio or newspapers. Lasswell wrote, "The form in which the significant symbols are embodied to reach the public may be spoken, written, pictorial, or musical, and the number of stimulus carriers is infinite.... Consider, for a moment, the people who ride the street cars. They may be reached by placards posted inside the car, by posters on the billboards along the track, by newspapers which they read, by conversations which they overhear, by leaflets which are openly or surreptitiously slipped into their hands, by street demonstrations at halting places, and no doubt by other means. Of these possible occasions there are no end" (1927b, p. 631).

Lasswell argued that successful social movements gain power by propagating master symbols over a period of months and years using a variety of media. For example, the emotions we experience when we see the American flag or hear the national anthem are not the result of a single previous exposure. Rather, we have observed the flag and heard the anthem in countless past situations in which a limited range of emotions were induced and experienced. The flag and the anthem have acquired emotional meaning because of all these previous experiences. When we see the flag on television with the anthem in the background, some of these emotions may be aroused and reinforced. Once established, such master symbols can be used in many different types of propaganda. The flag is used continually during political campaigns as a means of suggesting that political candidates are patriotic and can be trusted to defend the nation.

Lasswell believed that past propagation of most master symbols had been more or less haphazard. For every successful propagandist, there were hundreds who failed. Although he respected the cunning way that the Nazis used propaganda, he was not convinced that they really understood what they were doing. Hitler was an evil artist but not a scientist. Lasswell proposed combating Hitler with a new science of propaganda. Power to control delivery of propaganda through the mass media would be placed in the hands of a new elite, a **scientific technocracy** who would pledge to use its knowledge for good rather than evil—to save democracy

master (or collective) symbols
Symbols that are associated with strong emotions and possess the power to stimulate large-scale mass action

scientific technocracy
An educated social science–based elite charged with protecting vulnerable average people from harmful propaganda

rather than destroy it. Lasswell and his colleagues developed a term to refer to this strategy for using propaganda. They called it the "science of democracy" (Smith, 1941). But could a democratic social order be forged by propaganda? Wouldn't essential principles of democracy be sacrificed? Is democracy possible without free and open public discourse?

In a world where rational political debate is impossible because average people are prisoners of their own conditioning and psychoses (remember behaviorism and Freudianism) and therefore subject to manipulation by propagandists, Lasswell argued, the only hope for us as a nation rested with social scientists who could harness the power of propaganda for Good rather than Evil. It is not surprising, then, that many of the early media researchers took their task very seriously. They believed that nothing less than the fate of the world lay in their hands.

WALTER LIPPMANN'S THEORY OF PUBLIC OPINION FORMATION

Throughout the 1930s, many other members of the social elite, especially those at major universities, shared Lasswell's vision of a benevolent social science-led technocracy. They believed that physical science and social science held the keys to fighting totalitarianism and preserving democracy. As such, Lasswell's work commanded the attention of leading academics and opinion leaders, including one of the most powerful opinion makers of the time—Walter Lippmann, a nationally syndicated columnist for the *New York Times*.

Lippmann shared Lasswell's skepticism about the ability of average people to make sense of their social world and to make rational decisions about their actions. In *Public Opinion* (1922), he pointed out the discrepancies that necessarily exist between "the world outside and the pictures in our heads." Because these discrepancies were inevitable, Lippmann doubted that average people could govern themselves as classic democratic theory assumed they could. The world of the 1930s was an especially complex place, and the political forces were very dangerous. People simply couldn't learn enough from media to help them understand it all. He described citizens in his 1925 book, *The Phantom Public*, as a "bewildered herd" of "ignorant and meddlesome outsiders" who should be sidelined as "interested spectators of action" and no more (in Marshall, 2013). Even if journalists took their responsibility seriously, they couldn't overcome the psychological and social barriers that prevented average people from developing useful pictures in their heads. Political essayist Eric Alterman quoted and summarized Lippmann's position:

> Writing in the early twenties, Lippmann famously compared the average citizen to a deaf spectator sitting in the back row. He does not know what is happening, why it is happening, what ought to happen. "He lives in a world he cannot see, does not understand and is unable to direct." Journalism, with its weakness for sensationalism, made things worse. Governance was better left to a "specialized class of men" with inside information. No one expects a steel-worker to understand physics, so why should he be expected to understand politics? (2008, p. 10)

These ideas raised serious questions about the viability of democracy and the role of a free press in it. What do you do in a democracy if you can't trust the people to cast informed votes? What good is a free press if it is impossible to effectively transmit enough of the most vital forms of information to the public?

What can you do if people are so traumatized by dealing with everyday problems that they have no time to think about and develop a deeper understanding of global issues? The fact that Lippmann made his living working as a newspaper columnist lent credibility to his pessimism. In advancing these arguments, he directly contradicted the Libertarian assumptions (free speech and free press; see Chapter 3) that were the intellectual foundation of the American media system.

Like Lasswell, Lippmann believed that propaganda posed such a severe challenge that drastic changes in our political system were required. The public was vulnerable to propaganda, so some mechanism or agency was needed to protect them from it. A benign but enormously potent form of media control was necessary. Self-censorship by media probably wouldn't be sufficient. Lippmann shared Lasswell's conclusion that the best solution to these problems was to place control of information gathering and distribution in the hands of a benevolent technocracy—a scientific elite—who could be trusted to use scientific methods to sort fact from fiction and make good decisions about who should receive various messages. To accomplish this, Lippmann proposed the establishment of a quasi-governmental intelligence bureau that would carefully evaluate information and supply it to other elites for decision making. This bureau could also determine which information should be transmitted through the mass media and which information people were better off not knowing. He believed that these social engineers and social scientists, by enforcing "intelligence and information control," would be able to "provide the modern state with a foundation upon which a new stability might be realized" (in Marshall, 2013). Though this agency was never created, the notion that government should act as a gatekeeper for problematic information did gain broad acceptance among American elites during World War II and the Cold War. A good example was the way that information about atomic weapons and atomic energy was carefully controlled so that throughout the Cold War adverse public reactions were minimized.

REACTION AGAINST EARLY PROPAGANDA THEORY

Lasswell and Lippmann's propaganda theories seemed to carry the weight of real-world proof—the globe had been engulfed by a devastating world war. The War to End All Wars in fact, yet global turmoil continued to rage. These conflicts were infused with sophisticated and apparently successful propaganda. Yet there was opposition. One prominent critic of propaganda theory was philosopher John Dewey. In a series of lectures (Dewey, 1927), he outlined his objections to Lippmann's views. Throughout his long career, Dewey was a tireless and prolific defender of public education as the most effective means of defending democracy against totalitarianism. He refused to accept the need for a technocracy that would use scientific methods to protect people from themselves. Rather, he argued that people could learn to defend themselves if they were only taught the correct defenses. He asserted that even rudimentary public education could enable people to resist propaganda methods. Dewey "took violent issue" with Lippmann's "trust in the beneficence of elites," wrote Alterman, " 'A class of experts,' Dewey argued, 'is inevitably too removed from common interests as to become a class of private interests and private knowledge.'… He saw democracy as less about information than conversation. The media's job, in Dewey's conception, was 'to interest the public in the public interest' " (2008, p. 10).

Dewey's critics saw him as an idealist who talked a lot about reforming education without actually doing much himself to implement concrete reforms (Altschull, 1990, p. 230). Dewey did no better when it came to reforming the media. He argued that newspapers needed to do more than simply serve as bulletin boards for information about current happenings. He issued a challenge to journalists to do more to stimulate public interest in politics and world affairs—to motivate people to actively seek out information and then talk about it with others. Newspapers should serve as vehicles for public education and debate. They should focus more on ideas and philosophy and less on descriptions of isolated actions. They should teach critical thinking skills and structure public discussion of important issues. His efforts to found such a publication never got very far, however.

Pragmatism
School of philosophical theory emphasizing the practical function of knowledge as an instrument for adapting to reality and controlling it

Dewey based his arguments on **Pragmatism,** a school of philosophical theory emphasizing the practical function of knowledge as an instrument for adapting to reality and controlling it. We'll take a closer look at this theory in Chapter 10. James Carey (1989, pp. 83–84) contends that Dewey's ideas have continuing value. He argues that Dewey anticipated many of the concerns now being raised by cultural studies theories. And as you'll also read in Chapter 9, Dewey's belief that educating people to think critically about media content and how they use it is at the heart of the media literacy movement and current concerns about public education and public discourse.

Dewey believed that communities, not isolated individuals, use communication (and the media of communication) to create and maintain the culture that bonds and sustains them. When media assume the role of external agents and work to manipulate the "pictures in people's heads," they lose their power to serve as credible facilitators and guardians of public debate; they become just another competitor for our attention. The potentially productive interdependence between the community and media is disrupted, and the public forum itself is likely to be destroyed.

INSTANT ACCESS

Propaganda Theory

Strengths

1. Is first systematic theory of mass communication
2. Focuses attention on why media might have powerful effects
3. Identifies personal, social, and cultural factors that can enhance media's power to have effects
4. Focuses attention on the use of campaigns to cultivate symbols

Weaknesses

1. Underestimates abilities of average people to evaluate messages
2. Ignores personal, social, and cultural factors that limit media effects
3. Overestimates the speed and range of media effects

MODERN PROPAGANDA THEORY

Consider the Hippler and Sproule characterizations of propaganda from earlier in this chapter: simplify a complex issue and repeat that simplification; use covert, massively orchestrated communication; and use tricky language to discourage reflective thought. Some contemporary critical theorists argue that propaganda conforming to these rules is alive and well today and that it is practiced with a stealth, sophistication, and effectiveness unparalleled in history. They point to a number of "natural beliefs" that have been so well propagandized that meaningful public discourse about them has become difficult if not impossible. Political discourse and advertising are frequent areas of modern propaganda study, and the central argument of this modern propaganda theory is that powerful elites so thoroughly control the mass media and their content that they have little trouble imposing their Truth on the culture.

Close your eyes and think *welfare*. Did you envision large corporations accepting government handouts, special tax breaks for oil companies, bailouts for giant banks? Or did you picture a single mother, a woman of color, cheating the taxpayers so she can stay home and watch *Maury*? This narrowing of public discourse and debate is examined in works such as historian Herb Schiller's *Culture, Inc.: The Corporate Takeover of Public Expression* (1989); communication theorist Robert McChesney's *Corporate Media and the Threat to Democracy* (1997) and *The Problem of the Media* (2004); mass communication researchers Kathleen Hall Jamieson and Paul Waldman's *The Press Effect* (2003); and linguist Noam Chomsky's *American Power and the New Mandarins* (1969), *Deterring Democracy* (1991), and with Edward S. Herman, *Manufacturing Consent* (Herman and Chomsky, 1988). All offer a common perspective. In Jamieson and Waldman's words, it is, " 'Facts' can be difficult to discern and relate to the public, particularly in a context in which the news is driven by politicians and other interested parties who selectively offer some pieces of information while suppressing others" (p. xiii).

Take one such "interested party," advertisers and their advertising, as an example. Different ads may tout one product over another, but all presume the logic and rightness of consumption and capitalism. Our need for "more stuff" is rarely questioned: the connection between wealth/consumption and success/acceptance is never challenged; and concern about damage to the environment caused by, first, the manufacture of products and second, their disposal, is excluded from the debate. The point is not that consumption and capitalism are innately bad, but that as in all successful propaganda efforts, the alternatives are rarely considered. When alternatives *are* considered, those who raise them are viewed as out of the mainstream or peculiar. By extension, this failure to consider alternatives benefits those same economic elites most responsible for limiting that consideration and reflection. Sproule has written thoughtfully and persuasively on advertising as propaganda in *Channels of Propaganda* (1994) and *Propaganda and Democracy: The American Experience of Media and Mass Persuasion* (1997).

This current reconsideration of propaganda theory comes primarily from critical theorists and, as a result, its orientation tends to be from the political Left (Chapter 1). For example, economist and media analyst Edward S. Herman identified five *filters* that ensure the "multi-leveled capability of powerful business and government entities and collectives (e.g., the Business Roundtable; U.S. Chamber of Commerce;

industry lobbies and front groups) to exert power over the flow of information" (1996, p. 117). These filters enable powerful business and government elites "to mobilize an elite consensus, to give the appearance of democratic consent, and to create enough confusion, misunderstanding, and apathy in the general population to allow elite programs to go forward" (p. 118). The first two of Herman's elite-supporting filters are *ownership* and *advertising*, which "have made bottom line considerations more controlling.... The professional autonomy of journalists has been reduced" (p. 124). The next two are *sourcing* and *flack*, increasingly effective because "a reduction in the resources devoted to journalism means that those who subsidize the media by providing sources for copy gain greater leverage" (p. 125). Here he is specifically speaking of the power of corporate and government public relations. Finally, the fifth filter motivating media toward propagandists' support of the status quo is the media's "belief in the 'miracle of the market.' There is now an almost religious faith in the market, at least among the elite, so that regardless of the evidence, markets are assumed benevolent and non-market mechanisms are suspect" (p. 125). These themes, as you will see in Chapter 5 accurately mirror many of the core assumptions of critical cultural theory.

Behaviorists Richard Laitinen and Richard Rakos (1997) offer another critical view of contemporary propaganda. They argue that modern propaganda—in their definition, "the control of behavior by media manipulation" (p. 237)—is facilitated by three factors: an audience "that is enmeshed and engulfed in a harried lifestyle, less well-informed, and less politically involved, ... the use of sophisticated polling and survey procedures, whose results are used by the propagandists to increase their influence, ... [and] the incorporation of media companies into megaconglomerates" (pp. 238–239). These factors combine to put untold influence in the hands of powerful business and governmental elites without the public's awareness. Laitinen and Rakos wrote:

> In contemporary democracies, the absence of oppressive government control of information is typically considered a fundamental characteristic of a "free society." However, the lack of aversive control does not mean that information is "free" of controlling functions. On the contrary, current mechanisms of influence, through direct economic and indirect political contingencies, pose an even greater threat to behavioral diversity than do historically tyrannical forms. Information today is more systematic, continuous, consistent, unobtrusive, and ultimately powerful. (1997, p. 237)

There is also renewed interest in propaganda theory from the political Right. This conservative interest in propaganda takes the form of a critique of liberal media bias (see, for example, Coulter, 2006; Goldberg, 2003, 2009; Morris and McGann, 2008; Shapiro, 2011). Other than surveys indicating that a majority of journalists vote Democratic, there is little serious scholarship behind this assertion. In fact, what research there is tends to negate the liberal media bias thesis, as the large majority of media outlet managers and owners tend to vote Republican, the majority of the country's syndicated newspaper columnists write with a conservative bent, and the majority of "newsmakers" on network and cable public affairs talk shows are politically right-of-center. Media writer David Carr explains, "What is the No. 1 newspaper in America by circulation? That would be *The Wall Street Journal*, a bastion of conservative values on its editorial pages.

Three of the top five radio broadcasters—Rush Limbaugh, Sean Hannity and ... Michael Savage—have outdrawn NPR's morning and evening programs by a wide margin. In cable television, Fox News continues to pummel the competition" (2012a, p. B1). Robert McChesney raises the added dimension of media ownership, "The fundamental error in the conservative notion of the 'liberal' media [is] it posits that editors and journalists have almost complete control over what goes into news.... In conservative 'analysis,' the institutional factors of corporate ownership, profit-motivation, and advertising support have no effect on media content.... The notion that journalism can regularly produce a product that violates the fundamental interests of media owners and advertisers and do so with impunity simply has no evidence behind it" (1997, p. 60).

Finally, as we saw in the case of contemporary interest in mass society theory, some postpositivists are rethinking propaganda theory in light of effects theories such as agenda setting, framing, and spiral of silence. Writes Rebecca Curnalia,

> Propaganda involves using (a) rhetorical devices to frame an attitude object, (b) disseminating the message widely enough to influence the public agenda, making the issue (c) more accessible and, therefore, more salient to individuals, thereby (d) influencing perceptions of the issue as broadly supported. This process affects people as they (e) perceive the majority opinion to be more in favor of the attitude object and experience normative pressure to conform or be silent. This explanation of the process and effects of propaganda conforms to the definitions offered by propaganda analysts and empirical studies of media effects. (2005, p. 253)

These researchers point to the engineering of consent that sent the United States into an invasion of Iraq on what is now acknowledged as false premises (Suskind, 2004) and the media's complicity in hiding the economic conditions and practices that would eventually disable the world economy in 2008 (Mitchell, 2009) to support their contention that elites continue to utilize propaganda for their own ends.

LIBERTARIANISM REBORN

By the end of the 1930s, pessimism about the future of democracy was widespread. Most members of the old-line elites were convinced that totalitarianism couldn't be stopped. They pointed to theories like those of Lasswell and Lippmann as proof that average people could not be trusted. The only hope for the future lay with technocracy and science.

In Chapter 3, we will trace the development of theories that arose in opposition to these technocratic views. Advocates of these emerging ideas didn't base their views of media on social science; rather, they wanted to revive older notions of democracy and media. If modern democracy was being threatened, then maybe the threat was the result of having strayed too far from old values and ideals. Perhaps these could be restored and modern social institutions could somehow be purified and renewed. Theorists sought to make the **Libertarianism** of the Founding Fathers once again relevant to democracy. In doing so, they created views of media that are still widely held.

Libertarianism
A normative theory that sees people as good and rational and able to judge good ideas from bad

Mass society theory, propaganda theory, and the ideas discussed in Chapter 3, taken together, shaped the early research and initial development of mass communication theory, rightly or wrongly, for the first decades of the discipline's history (Jowett and O'Donnell, 1999; Sproule, 1987). The mass society trend in media theory is still important. As you've read, some contemporary scholars argue that its influence persists. Moreover, these early conceptions of media influence established the terms of the debate: media do or do not have significant influence; people are or are not capable of resisting media influence; and, as you'll soon read, the media do or do not have an obligation to operate in a way that limits their negative influence while serving the interests of the larger society.

SUMMARY

Criticism of media and new media technology is not a new phenomenon. For more than a century now, new media industries have inspired harsh criticism from a variety of sources. Media entrepreneurs have countered criticisms from traditional elites and from media scholars. Although some concerns about media have faded, many remain. Critics still argue that the quality of much mass entertainment content has been lowered to satisfy audiences' basest tastes and passions. Early news media attracted—and today's supermarket tabloids and reality TV still attract—huge audiences by printing speculative, overdramatized, and gossipy stories. Through much of the last two centuries, criticism of media took the form of mass society theory. Tönnies and Durkheim helped frame a debate over the fundamental nature of modernity that has not ended. For mass society theorists and media apologists, media were symbolic of modernity—representing either the worst or the best of modern life.

Early mass society theorists argued that media are highly problematic forces that have the power to directly reach and transform the thinking of individuals so that the quality of their lives is impaired and serious social problems are created. Through media influence, people are atomized, cut off from the civilizing influences of other people or high culture. In these early theories, totalitarianism inevitably results as ruthless, power-hungry dictators seize control of media to promote their ideology.

And in the early part of the twentieth century, totalitarian propagandists did in fact use media to convert millions to their ideas, lending support to these assumptions of an all-powerful mass media. Though Nazi and Communist propagandists wielded media with apparent effectiveness, the basis for their power over mass audiences was not well understood. Theorists like Harold Lasswell held that propaganda typically influenced people in slow and subtle ways. It created new master symbols that could be used to induce new forms of thought and action. Lasswell's theories assumed that media could operate as external agents and be used as tools to manipulate essentially passive mass audiences. Also believing in the propaganda power of mass media was columnist Walter Lippmann, whose skepticism at the self-governance abilities of average people and distrust of lazy media professionals brought him to the conclusion that the inevitably incomplete and inaccurate "pictures in people's heads" posed a threat to democracy.

John Dewey's solution to propaganda's threat relied on traditional notions of democracy. Because people were in fact good and rational, the counter to propaganda was not control of media by a technocratic elite, but more education of the public.

Contemporary propaganda theory, centered in critical theory, argues that public discourse is shaped and limited by powerful elites to serve their own ends. Advertising's underlying theme that consumption and capitalism are beneficial is another area of interest to propaganda theorists. And postpositivist-effects researchers, too, are reconsidering newer conceptions of propaganda. The mass society trend in media theory continues to flourish.

Critical Thinking Questions

1. Roger Scruton wants to tell us what it means to be an intelligent person. He assumes that he can do this only if we already have a basic understanding of the great works. "It would be useful to have read *Les fleurs du mal* by Baudelaire and T. S. Eliot's *Waste Land* ," he wrote; "I shall also presume some familiarity with Mozart, Wagner, Manet, Poussin, Tennyson, Schoenberg, George Herbert, Goethe, Marx, and Nietzsche." How many of these masters and masterworks are you familiar with? If you don't know many of them, does that make you an unintelligent person? Can you make an argument for different definitions of intelligence? What would you say to Scruton about his definition of an intelligent person should you run in to him on campus?

2. Founding Father Benjamin Franklin said that Americans who would exchange a bit of freedom in order to secure a bit of security deserve neither freedom nor security. What does he mean by this? Can you relate this sentiment to the debate over the role of propaganda in a democracy? Where would Franklin have stood on the issue?

3. Can the traditional news media ever be truly "liberal," given their corporate ownership? Doesn't the now widely accepted view that the media failed the country in the run-up to the invasion of Iraq prove that they are anything but liberal? Why or why not? What about the media's failure to detect the looming financial crisis that was about to nearly destroy the global economy? Wouldn't a media with an anticorporate bias—that is, a liberal media—have been more vigilant?

Key Terms

First Amendment	gesellschaft	gray propaganda	Superego
propaganda	mechanical solidarity	engineering of consent	master (or collective) symbols
white propaganda	organic solidarity	behaviorism	scientific technocracy
direct-effects assumption	concentration	Freudianism	Pragmatism
Enlightenment	disinformation	Ego	Libertarianism
gemeinschaft	black propaganda	Id	

3 | NORMATIVE THEORIES OF MASS COMMUNICATION

Among other things going on in the world in the fall of 2012, the presidential election was headed into its final weeks and thousands more state and local contests were underway. In all, candidates and their supporting organizations spent $9.8 billion on that year's campaigns (Abse, 2012). There was widespread economic hardship across the country; income inequality and child hunger were at historical levels. Although American soldiers were still in harm's way in Afghanistan, some U.S. politicians were calling for war with Iran and greater military involvement in the Syrian civil war. A breakout of meningitis across several states sickened more than 400 people, killing 80. And at a time when an informed citizenry capable of understanding and responding to these events could not have been more essential, a national survey of American adults showed that only 40 percent had a great deal or fair amount of trust in the mass media, compared to 72 percent in 1970 (Morales, 2012).

This is bad news for democracy, wrote the study's author, Lymari Morales, "Americans' high level of distrust in the media poses a challenge to democracy and to creating a fully engaged citizenry. Media sources must clearly do more to earn the trust of Americans, the majority of whom see the media as biased one way or the other" (2012). Making matters even worse, young Americans were the most disillusioned. That generation, wrote researcher Paula Poindexter, described news using terms like *garbage*, *lies*, *one-sided*, *propaganda*, *repetitive*, and *boring*. Moreover, not only did they refuse to use news to help them live their daily lives, they did not even consider being informed important (2012).

digital natives
People who have lived their entire lives in an Internet-connected world

But how could this be, especially for young, media-savvy **digital natives**, people who have lived their entire lives in an Internet-connected world? Maybe the Internet *is* the problem, suggested political scientist Jonathan Ladd, who wrote that people who distrust the media are more resistant to new information, instead relying on their prior beliefs to make judgments about the world. As a result, they tend to expose themselves "to different messages than those who trust the media.

They disproportionately choose media outlets that provide information reinforcing their partisan predispositions and are less likely to choose outlets they see as politically hostile." The Internet, of course, offers access to scores of "new outlets entering the news marketplace" (2012).

But maybe the reason that people do not trust the media is even simpler than that—the media do not deserve it. Perhaps the media, in an era of fragmenting audiences and contracting resources, simply are not worthy of our trust as they turn increasingly to entertainment, tabloid topics, and opinions to keep what audiences they may still have. For example, when Arthur Brisbane, public editor of the *New York Times*, wondered aloud on his blog if reporters should be "truth vigilantes," calling out the lies of politicians and other powerful people (2012), critics pounced. "How can telling the truth ever take a back seat in the serious business of reporting the news?" asks media critic Jay Rosen, "That's like saying medical doctors no longer put 'saving lives' or 'the health of the patient' ahead of securing payment from insurance companies. It puts the lie to the entire contraption. It *devastates* journalism as a public service and honorable profession" (emphasis in the original; 2012). "Facts has finally died," lamented *Chicago Tribune* reporter Rex Huppke, "survived by two brothers, Rumor and Innuendo, and a sister, Emphatic Assertion" (2012).

The operation of our modern media system is rife with troubles such as this. National Public Radio was attacked after it was revealed that its *Planet Money* host Adam Davidson regularly gave for-pay speeches to the financial institutions he covered on his show (Soundbites, 2012). *The Wall Street Journal* failed to disclose that 10 of its editorial page op-ed writers, who at the time had authored 23 pieces critical of President Barack Obama or in praise of his electoral opponent Mitt Romney, were in fact official advisers to the Romney campaign (Strupp, 2012). During the 2012 campaign Barack Obama and Mitt Romney debated for a total of six nationally televised hours, during which they did not have to face a single question about poverty, growing American income inequality, housing, race or racism, criminal justice, drug legalization, labor unions, or climate change (Jackson, 2013). For most of that same campaign many of the country's major news organizations were in the habit of granting politicians and their campaigns **quote approval**, that is, the right to check over a reporter's story before publication or airing to see if they were satisfied with what they had said during the interview and how it was being reported. What the practice produces, wrote *New York Times* media critic David Carr, "isn't exactly news and it isn't exactly a news release, but it contains elements of both" (2012b, p. B1). Critics found quote approval particularly troubling a time in the history of our media that public relations professionals outnumbered journalists 4 to 1—as opposed to 1.2 to 1 in 1980 (Greenslade, 2012). Even Superman's alter ego Clark Kent quit the newspaper business, leaving the *Daily Plant* after more than 70 years to start writing online, "Facts have been replaced by opinions, information has been replaced by entertainment, and reporters have become stenographers," Kent told his editor, "The fact is we need to stand up for truth … for justice … and yeah, I'm not ashamed to say it … the American way" (in Wright, 2012). Mr. Kent was correct about stenography. The Pew Research Center's Project for Excellence in Journalism reported that

quote approval
Granting news sources the right to approve their words and how they are reported in advance of a story's release

in the 2012 presidential election "campaign reporters were acting primarily as megaphones, rather than as investigators, of the assertions put forward by the candidates and other political partisans. That meant more direct relaying of assertions made by the campaigns and less reporting by journalists to interpret and contextualize them.... Only about a quarter of the statements in the media about the character and records of the presidential candidates originated with journalists in the 2012 race, while twice that many came from political partisans. That is a reversal from a dozen years earlier when half the statements originated with journalists and a third came from partisans" (Enda and Mitchell, 2013).

These media and journalistic controversies are not easily resolved. The American media system is in a state of massive upheaval and overhaul. Optimistic observers argue that the media are undergoing *disruptive transition*, that is, change is inevitable, especially in light of the explosive growth of the Internet, and it will produce a new, better media and a new, more powerful journalism. After all, there is evidence that despite widespread and growing distrust of "the media" and "the press," Americans, especially young Americans, are relying on their computers, smartphones, and tablets to access more news than ever before (Mitchell, Rosenstiel, and Santhanam, 2012; "YouTube & News," 2012).

What will the American media system look like in the immediate future and in a future that we might have difficulty envisioning, given the remarkable speed with which our communication technology are being transformed and new relationships between "the people formerly known as the audience" (Gilmor, 2004) and the mass media are developed? What will guide that development and how will we know if what it produces is good or bad, serves us or harms us, fosters or weakens our democracy? Normative theory will.

LEARNING OBJECTIVES

After studying this chapter you should be able to

- Explain the origins of normative media theories.
- Evaluate Libertarianism as a guiding principle for the operation of mass media.
- Recognize the strengths and limitations of the marketplace of ideas approach to media freedom.
- Judge the worthiness and continued utility of Social Responsibility Theory.

OVERVIEW

During the era of yellow journalism, most media professionals cared very little for the niceties of accuracy, objectivity, and public sensitivities. But in the first decades of the twentieth century, some media industry people and various social elites began a crusade to clean up the media and make them more respectable and credible. The watchword of this crusade was *professionalism*, and its goal was elimination of shoddy and irresponsible content.

Some sort of theory was needed to guide this task of media reform. The goal of this theory would be to answer questions such as these:

- Should media do something more than merely distribute whatever content will earn them the greatest profits in the shortest time?
- Are there some essential public services that media should provide even if no immediate profits can be earned?
- Should media become involved in identifying and solving social problems?
- Is it necessary or advisable that media serve as watchdogs and protect consumers against business fraud and corrupt bureaucrats?
- What should we expect media to do for us in times of crisis?

These broad questions about the role of media are linked to issues concerning the day-to-day operation of media. How should media management and production jobs be structured? What moral and ethical standards should guide media professionals? Do they have any obligation beyond personal and professional self-interest? Exactly what constitutes being a journalist? Are there any circumstances when it is appropriate or even necessary to invade people's privacy or risk ruining their reputations? If someone threatens to commit suicide in front of a television camera, what should a reporter do—get it on tape or try to stop it? Should a newspaper print a story about unethical business practices even if the company involved is one of its biggest advertisers? Should television networks broadcast a highly rated program even if it routinely contains high levels of violence?

Answers to questions like these are found in normative theory—a type of theory that describes an ideal way for a media system to be structured and operated. Normative theories are different from most of the theories we study in this book. They don't describe things as they are, nor do they provide scientific explanations or predictions. Instead, they describe the way things *should be* if some ideal values or principles are to be realized. Normative theories come from many sources. Sometimes media practitioners themselves develop them. Sometimes social critics or academics do. Most normative theories develop over time and contain elements drawn from previous theories. This is especially true of the normative theory that currently guides mass media in the United States; it is a synthesis of ideas developed over the past three centuries.

This chapter examines a variety of normative media theories, including some that are questionable or even objectionable. We proceed from earlier forms of normative theory to more recent examples. Our attention is on the normative theory that is predominantly used to guide and legitimize most media operation in the United States: **social responsibility theory**. For a long time the debate about normative theory was muted in the United States. Social responsibility theory seemingly provided such an ideal standard for media that further debate was simply unnecessary. But the past 40 years have seen unprecedented growth and consolidation of control in the media industries, and as a result, gigantic conglomerates—conceivably more committed to the bottom line than to social responsibility—dominate the production and distribution of media content. In addition, the Internet has greatly expanded the number and variety of "media outlets," all with varying commitments to traditional standards of social responsibility.

social responsibility theory
A normative theory that substitutes media industry and public responsibility for total media freedom on the one hand and for external control on the other

In this chapter, we will assess why social responsibility theory has had enduring appeal for American media practitioners. We contrast it with theories popular in other parts of the world. We will speculate about its future, as its assumptions are regularly challenged by an ever-evolving media landscape and new relationships between content creators and providers and their audiences. As new industries based on new media technologies emerge, will social responsibility theory continue to guide them or will alternatives develop? Social responsibility theory is suited to a particular era of national development and to specific types of media. As the media industries change, this guiding theory might very well have to be substantially revised or replaced.

THE ORIGIN OF NORMATIVE THEORIES OF MEDIA

radical Libertarianism
The absolute belief in Libertarianism's faith in a good and rational public and totally unregulated media

First Amendment absolutists
Those who believe in the strictest sense that media should be completely unregulated

technocratic control
Direct regulation of media, most often by government agency or commission

Since the beginning of the last century, the role of mass media in American society, as we've already seen, has been hotly argued. At one extreme of the debate are people who argue for **radical Libertarian** ideals. They believe that there should be no laws governing media operations. They are **First Amendment absolutists** who take the notion of "free press" quite literally to mean that all forms of media must be totally unregulated. These people accept as gospel that the First Amendment dictate—"Congress shall make no law … abridging the freedom of speech or of the press"—means exactly what it says. As Supreme Court Justice Hugo Black succinctly stated, "No law means no law."

At the other extreme are people who believe in direct regulation of media, most often by a government agency or commission. These include advocates of **technocratic control**, people like Harold Lasswell and Walter Lippmann. They argue that media practitioners can't be trusted to communicate responsibly or to effectively use media to serve vital public needs—especially during times of crisis or social upheaval. Some sort of oversight or control is necessary to ensure that media satisfy important public needs.

As we saw in Chapter 2, advocates of control based their arguments on propaganda theories. The threat posed by propaganda was so great that they believed information gathering and transmission had to be placed under the control of wise people—technocrats who could be trusted to act in the public interest. These technocrats would be highly trained and have professional values and skills that guaranteed that media content would serve socially valuable purposes—for example, stopping the spread of terrorism or informing people about natural disasters or warning the public of a coming pandemic.

Other proponents of regulation based their views on mass society theory. They were troubled by the power of media content to undermine high culture with trivial forms of entertainment. Their complaints often centered on media's presentation of sex and violence. These regulation proponents also objected to the trivialization of what they considered important moral values.

Thus, both propaganda and mass society theories can be used to lobby for media regulation. Both perspectives view media as powerful, subversive forces that must be brought under the control of wise people, those who can be trusted to act in the public interest. But who should be trusted to censor media? Social scientists? Religious leaders? The military? The police? Congress? The Federal Communications

Commission? Although many powerful people believed in the necessity of controlling media, they couldn't reach consensus about who should do it. Media practitioners were able to negotiate compromises by pointing out the dangers of regulation and by offering to engage in self-regulation—to become more socially responsible.

Eventually, social responsibility theory emerged from this debate. It represents a compromise between views favoring government control of media and those favoring total press freedom. This didn't satisfy everyone, but it did have broad appeal, especially within the media industries. Even today, most mainstream media practitioners use some variant of social responsibility theory to justify their actions. To fully understand social responsibility theory, we must review the ideas and events that led to its development.

THE ORIGIN OF LIBERTARIAN THOUGHT ON COMMUNICATION

Modern Libertarian thinking about communication can be traced back to sixteenth-century Europe—a time when feudal aristocracies exercised arbitrary power over the lives of most people. This era was also rocked by major social upheaval. International trade and urbanization undermined the power of these rural aristocracies and several social and political movements sprang up, most notably the Protestant Reformation that demanded greater freedom for individuals over their own lives and thoughts (Altschull, 1990).

authoritarian theory
A normative theory that places all forms of communication under the control of a governing elite or authorities

Libertarian communication theory arose in opposition to **authoritarian theory**—an idea that placed all forms of communication under the control of a governing elite or authorities (Siebert, Peterson, and Schramm, 1956). Authorities justified their power as a means of protecting and preserving a divinely ordained social order. In most countries, this control rested in the hands of a king, who in turn granted royal charters or licenses to media practitioners. These publishers could be jailed for violating their charters, and charters or licenses could be revoked. Censorship of all types, therefore, was easily possible. Authoritarian control tended to be exercised in arbitrary, erratic ways. Sometimes considerable freedom might exist to publicize minority viewpoints and culture, as long as authorities didn't perceive a direct threat to their power. Unlike totalitarianism, authoritarian theory doesn't prioritize cultivation of a homogeneous national culture. It only requires acquiescence to the governing elite.

In rebelling against authoritarian theory, early Libertarians argued that if individuals could be freed from the arbitrary limits on communication imposed by church and state, they would "naturally" follow the dictates of their conscience, seek truth, engage in public debate, and ultimately create a better life for themselves and others (McQuail, 1987; Siebert, Peterson, and Schramm, 1956). Libertarians blamed authorities for preserving unnatural, arbitrary social orders. They believed strongly in the power of unrestricted public debate and discussion to create more natural ways of structuring society. Many early Libertarians were Protestants rebelling against church restrictions on their freedom to communicate. They believed that without these restrictions, individuals could follow their conscience, communicate accordingly, and ultimately come to a knowledge of the Truth.

In *Areopagitica*, a powerful Libertarian tract on communication freedom published in 1644, John Milton asserted that in a fair debate, good and truthful arguments will always win out over lies and deceit. It followed that if this were

self-righting principle

Milton's idea that in a fair debate, good and truthful arguments will win out over lies and deceit

true, a new and better social order could be forged using public debate. This idea came to be referred to as Milton's **self-righting principle,** and it continues to be widely cited by contemporary media professionals as a rationale for preserving media freedom (Altschull, 1990). It is a fundamental principle within social responsibility theory. Unfortunately, most early Libertarians had a rather unrealistic view of how long it would take to find the "truth" and establish an ideal social order. This ideal order was not necessarily a democracy, and it might not always permit communication freedom. Milton, for example, came to argue that Oliver Cromwell had found "truth." After all, the Puritan leader's battlefield victories had been guided by God. Because he was convinced that the resulting social order was ideal, Milton was willing to serve as the chief censor in Cromwell's regime. He expressed few regrets about limiting what Catholic leaders could communicate (Altschull, 1990). As far as Milton was concerned, Catholic ideas had been demonstrated to be false and therefore should be censored so right-thinking people wouldn't be confused by them.

When it became clear during the eighteenth century that definitive forms of "truth" couldn't be quickly or easily established, some Libertarians became discouraged. Occasionally they drifted back and forth between Libertarian and authoritarian views. Even Thomas Jefferson, author of the Declaration of Independence, wavered in his commitment to press freedom and his faith in the self-righting principle. Jefferson, who famously affirmed Milton's self-righting principle in a letter to a friend—"Were it left to me to decide whether we should have a government without newspapers or newspapers without government, I should not hesitate to prefer the latter" (quoted in Altschull, 1990, p. 117)—voiced deep frustration with scurrilous newspaper criticism during the second term of his presidency. Nevertheless, he placed Libertarian ideals at the heart of the United States' long-term experiment with democratic self-government. The revolution of the American Colonies against Britain was legitimized by those ideals. As Jefferson himself wrote in 1779, "That truth is great and will prevail if left to herself, that she is the proper and sufficient antagonist to error, and has nothing to fear from the conflict, unless by human interposition disarmed of her natural weapons, free argument and debate" (in Packer, 2006b, p. 59).

John Keane (1991) identified three fundamental concepts underpinning the Founders' belief in press freedom:

1. Theology: media should serve as a forum allowing people to deduce between good and evil.
2. Individual rights: press freedom is the strongest, if not the only, guarantee of liberty from political elites.
3. Attainment of truth: falsehoods must be countered; ideas must be challenged and tested or they will become dogma.

Bill of Rights

The first 10 amendments to the U.S. Constitution

As such, the newly formed United States was one of the first nations to explicitly adopt Libertarian principles, as it did in the Declaration of Independence and the **Bill of Rights.** The latter asserts that all individuals have natural rights that no government, community, or group can unduly infringe upon or take away. Various forms of communication freedom—speech, press, and assembly—are among the most important of these rights. The ability to express dissent, to band together with others to resist laws that people consider wrong, to print or broadcast ideas, opinions, and beliefs—these rights are proclaimed as central to democratic self-government. You can test your own commitment to freedom of expression in the box entitled "A Stirring Defense of Free Expression."

Despite the priority given to communication freedom, however, it is important to recognize that many restrictions on communication—accepted by media practitioners and media consumers alike—do indeed exist. Libel laws protect against the publication of information that will damage reputations. Judges can issue gag orders to stop the publication of information they think will interfere with a defendant's right to a fair trial. Other laws and regulations protect against false advertising, child pornography, and offensive language. The limits to communication freedom are constantly renegotiated.

THINKING ABOUT THEORY | **A Stirring Defense of Free Expression**

Concurring with the majority in the 1927 Supreme Court decision in *Whitney v. California*, Justice Louis Brandeis penned this stunning defense for freedom of expression:

Those who won our independence believed that the final end of the State was to make men free to develop their faculties; and that in its government the deliberative forces should prevail over the arbitrary. They valued liberty both as an end and as a means. They believed liberty to be the secret of happiness and courage to be the secret of liberty. They believed that freedom to think as you will and speak as you think are means indispensable to the discovery and spread of political truth; that without free speech and assembly discussion would be futile; that with them, discussion affords ordinarily adequate protection against the dissemination of noxious doctrine; that the greatest menace to freedom is an inert people; that public discussion is a political duty; and that this should be a fundamental principle of the American government. They recognized the risks to which all human institutions are subject. But they knew that order cannot be secured merely through fear of punishment for its infraction; that it is hazardous to discourage thought, hope, and imagination; that fear breeds repression; that repression breeds hate; that hate menaces stable government; that the path of safety lies in the opportunity to discuss freely supposed grievances and proposed remedies; and that the fitting remedy for evil counsels is good ones. Believing in the power

of reason as applied through public discussion, they eschewed silence coerced by law—the argument of force in its worst form. Recognizing the occasional tyrannies of governing majorities, they amended the Constitution so that free speech and assembly should be guaranteed. (Gillmor and Barron, 1974, pp. 21–22)

Of course you see and support the wisdom of Justice Brandeis's powerful enunciation of our First Freedom. But the world was a much different place in 1927. In the wake of the terrorist attacks on the United States on September 11, 2001, many people questioned if freedom of speech, press, assembly, in fact, "freedom to think as you will and speak as you think" were luxuries we could still afford. Attorney General John Ashcroft told reporters that media professionals who question his decisions and tactics in defending the country against further attack "aid terrorists" and "give ammunition to America's enemies" (quoted in Naureckas, 2002, p. 2). When the late-night talk show *Politically Incorrect* was dropped by several ABC stations and eventually canceled by the network because of host Bill Maher's comments critical of U.S. military action, White House press secretary Ari Fleischer told journalists that those events "are reminders to all Americans that they need to watch what they say, watch what they do" (quoted in Hart and Ackerman, 2002, p. 6). Dissent equals aid to terrorists? Americans watching what they say, what they do? Can you reconcile these comments with the impassioned arguments of Justice Brandeis?

In some eras, the balance shifts toward expanding communication freedom, but at other times, most notably in times of war, freedom is curtailed. In the wake of the September 11, 2001, terrorist attacks, for example, Congress passed legislation known as the Patriot Act that imposed a variety of restrictions on Americans' communication freedom. And whenever new media technologies are invented, it becomes necessary to decide how they should be regulated. The debate over communication freedom never ends, as we see today in the ongoing and heated debates over Internet music and video file-sharing, offensive media content, press access to military activities in times of armed conflict, and the right of domestic Islamic groups to engage in activities that others worry may threaten national security.

Why is it necessary to place limits on communication freedom? The most common reason for limiting communication freedom is a conflict over basic rights. The Bill of Rights guarantees citizens many different rights in addition to communication freedom. But where do the rights guaranteed to you end and those of another person begin? Do you have the right to shout "Fire!" in a crowded movie theater if there is no fire? The U.S. Supreme Court has ruled you don't. If you did, many people would be hurt—don't they have a right to be protected against your irresponsible behavior? Similar questions arise when groups attempt to stir up hatred and resentment against racial or ethnic minorities. In 2012, Twitter for the first time censored an account denying a German neo-Nazi group access to its service, angering Internet freedom and free speech groups alike. Who has the moral high ground here? Should YouTube take down videos blamed for causing violence? Does a fundamentalist religious group have the right to raise giant billboards accusing the president of the United States of being the anti-Christ and exhorting citizens to pray for his descent into hellfire? Shouldn't such irresponsible forms of communication be controlled? Over the years, the U.S. Congress, state legislatures, and even many municipalities have addressed questions like this. They have written laws to restrict communication freedom so that other, seemingly equally important rights might be guaranteed. Courts have upheld many of these laws, and others have been struck down because they deemed communication freedom more important.

THE MARKETPLACE OF IDEAS: A NEW FORM OF RADICAL LIBERTARIANISM

Though Libertarian thought in the United States dates from the country's founding, it has undergone many transformations. An important variant emerged in the 1800s during the penny press and yellow journalism eras. Throughout this period, public confidence in both business and government was shaken by recurring economic depressions, widespread corruption, and injustice. As we noted in Chapter 2, large companies led by robber barons—most notably in the oil, railroad, and steel industries—created nationwide monopolies to charge unfair prices and reap enormous profits. Workers were paid low salaries and forced to labor under difficult or hazardous conditions. Public respect for newspapers also ebbed as publishers pursued profits and created news to sell papers. They ignored or suppressed news about the abuses of the robber barons. Several social movements, especially the Progressive (liberal) and Populist (champion of average folks) movements sprang up to call for new laws and greater government regulation (Altschull, 1990; Brownell, 1983). They were effective, as Congress eventually enacted antitrust legislation to break up the big monopolies.

But Libertarians feared that these laws and regulations would go too far. Wanting to rekindle public support for Libertarian ideals, media practitioners developed a cogent response to Progressive and Populist criticisms. They argued that media should be regarded as a *self-regulating* **marketplace of ideas**. This theory is a variation of a fundamental principle of capitalism—the notion of a self-regulating market. In classical capitalist theory as formulated by Adam Smith, there is little need for the government to regulate markets. An open and competitive marketplace should regulate itself. If a product is in high demand, prices will "naturally" rise as consumers compete to buy it. This encourages other manufacturers to produce the product. Once demand is met by increased manufacturing, the price falls. If one manufacturer charges too much for a product, competitors will cut their prices to attract buyers. No government interference is necessary to protect consumers or to force manufacturers to meet consumer needs. Another term used to refer to these ideas is the **laissez-faire doctrine**.

According to the marketplace-of-ideas theory, the laissez-faire doctrine should be applied to mass media; that is, if ideas are "traded" freely among people, the correct or best ideas should prevail. The *ideas* compete, and the best will be "bought." They will earn profits that will encourage others to compete and market similar good ideas. Bad ideas will have no buyers and thus there will be no incentive to produce and market them. But there are some difficulties in applying this logic to our large contemporary media. Media content is far less tangible than other consumer products. The meaning of individual messages can vary tremendously from one person to the next. Just what is being traded when news stories or television dramas are "bought" and "sold"? When we buy a newspaper, we don't buy individual stories; we buy packages of them bundled with features like comics and horoscopes. We can choose to ignore anything in the package that we find offensive. And there is no direct connection between our purchase of the paper and the fact that we may or may not find some useful ideas in it. When we watch commercial television, we don't pay a fee to the networks. Yet buying and selling are clearly involved with network programs. Advertisers buy time on these shows and then use the programs as vehicles for their messages. When they buy time, they buy access to the audience for the show; they do not necessarily buy the rightness or correctness of the program's ideas. Sponsors pay more to advertise on programs with large or demographically attractive audiences, not for programs with better ideas in them. Clearly, the media marketplace is a bit more complicated than the marketplace for refrigerators or toothpaste, as you can investigate in the box entitled "Which Model of the Marketplace?"

In the American media system, the marketplace of ideas was supposed to work like this: Someone comes up with a good idea and then transmits it through some form of mass medium. If other people like it, they buy the message. When people buy the message, they pay for its production and distribution costs. Once these costs are covered, the message producer earns a profit. If people don't like the message, they don't buy it, and the producer goes broke trying to produce and distribute it. If people are wise message consumers, the producers of the best and most

marketplace of ideas

In Libertarianism, the notion that all ideas should be put before the public, and the public will choose the best from that "marketplace"

laissez-faire doctrine

The idea that government shall allow business to operate freely and without official intrusion

THINKING ABOUT THEORY | **Which Model of the Marketplace?**

The marketplace-of-ideas theory sees the operation of the mass media system as analogous to that of the self-regulating product market. Take this example and judge for yourself the goodness-of-fit.

What do these models imply about the quality of candy in the United States? What do they say about the quality of television?

Product Producer	Product	Consumer
Model 1 A product producer	produces a product as efficiently and inexpensively as possible	for its consumers, who wield the ultimate power: to buy or not to buy.
Model 2 Hershey's	produces candy efficiently and inexpensively on a production line	for people like us. If we buy the candy, Hershey's continues to make similar candy in a similar way.
Model 3 NBC	produces people using programs (their production line)	for advertisers. If they buy NBC's product, NBC continues to produce similar audiences in similar ways.

useful messages will become rich and develop large media enterprises, and the producers of bad messages will fail. Useless media will go out of business. If the purveyors of good ideas succeed, these ideas should become more easily available at lower cost. Producers will compete to supply them. Similarly, the cost of bad ideas should rise and access to them should diminish. Eventually, truth should win out in the marketplace of ideas, just as it should triumph in the public forum envisioned by the early Libertarians. According to marketplace-of-ideas theory, the self-righting principle should apply to mass media content as well as to public debate. But what if advertiser support permits bad messages to be distributed for free? Will people be less discriminating if they don't have to pay directly to receive these messages? What if the bad messages are distributed as part of a large bundle of messages (e.g., a newspaper or television news program; a package of cable television channels)? If you want the good messages, you also pay to subsidize the bad messages. What is bad for you might be good for someone else. You might not like horoscopes or soap operas, but you have friends who do.

Just how useful is the marketplace-of-ideas theory? After all, government regulation of the consumer marketplace is now generally accepted as necessary. Few people question the need for consumer protection laws or rules regulating unfair business practices. The consumer marketplace benefited from regulation, so why not regulate the marketplace of ideas? Since 1930, media critics have asked this question more and more frequently, and the recent rampant concentration of media companies and rapid diffusion of digital technologies have added new urgency to the call for government intervention.

Even so, marketplace-of-ideas theory enjoys significant support within the media industries. That support resides in the "duality" inherent in the marketplace-of-ideas philosophy, one that "has allowed widely divergent interpretations of the metaphor

INSTANT ACCESS

Marketplace-of-Ideas Theory

Strengths

1. Limits government control
2. Allows "natural" fluctuations in tastes, ideals, and discourse
3. Puts trust in the audience
4. Assumes "good" content will ultimately prevail

Weaknesses

1. Mistakenly equates media content with more tangible consumer products
2. Puts too much trust in profit-motivated media operators
3. Ignores the fact that content that is intentionally "bought" is often accompanied by other, sometimes unwanted content
4. Has an overly optimistic view of audiences' media consumption skills
5. Mistakenly assumes audience-not advertiser-is consumer
6. Definition of "good" is not universal (e.g., what is "good" for the majority might be bad for a minority)

to develop" (Napoli, 1999, p. 151). Media policy researcher Philip Napoli identified two interpretations of the marketplace of ideas. He wrote:

> Economic theory-based interpretations of the marketplace of ideas emphasize efficiency, consumer satisfaction, and competition. Whereas democratic theory-based interpretations emphasize citizen knowledge, informed decision making, and effective self-government. Within discussions of the marketplace-of-ideas metaphor, economic theory-based interpretations typically have been associated with arguments against government regulation of the communications industry, whereas democratic theory-based interpretations typically have been associated with calls for such regulation. (1999, pp. 151–152)

Media practitioners are satisfied with this distinction because, as numerous researchers have demonstrated (e.g., Lavey, 1993; Simon, Atwater, and Alexander, 1988), government—especially agencies such as the Federal Communications Commission and the Federal Trade Commission, which regulates advertising—"historically has devoted much greater empirical attention to the economic effects of its policies than to the social and political effects" (Napoli, 1999, p. 165).

GOVERNMENT REGULATION OF MEDIA

During the 1920s and 1930s, a new normative theory of mass communication began to emerge that rejected both radical Libertarianism and technocratic control. One source of this theory was congressional hearings over government regulation of radio. In 1927, these debates led to the establishment of the Federal Radio Commission (FRC), which was the forerunner of the Federal Communications Commission. As the debates raged, some people—especially Progressive and Populist politicians—argued that the excesses of yellow journalism proved that self-regulation wasn't enough. Overdramatized and fictitious news was so profitable that publishers and broadcasters couldn't resist producing it. Without some sort of regulation, radio was not likely to serve the public interest as well as it should. Even so, Progressives were cautious about turning control of radio over to government technocrats. A compromise solution was needed.

By the 1920s, the American public had come to accept government regulation of public utilities as a means of ending wasteful competition while preserving private enterprise. Before government regulation of power and telephone companies, cities were blanketed with competing networks of wires. Anyone who wanted to talk to people on other networks had to buy phones from all the competing companies. The cost of building entirely independent networks increased the cost of phone service and electricity. The solution to these problems was to allow one company to have a monopoly on supplying these needed services. In return for the grant of that monopoly, the company accepted government regulation of prices and services. In this way, public utilities were created with government commissions to oversee their operation. Could a government commission be used to regulate radio as a public utility? The answer was yes. In fact, Secretary of Commerce (later President) Herbert Hoover himself was moved to remark that this was one of the few instances in history where the country—industry and public alike—was unanimous in its desire for more regulation (Barnouw, 1966).

In the debate over the establishment of the FRC, Secretary Hoover championed one especially important philosophy—the airwaves belong to the people. If airwaves are public property like other national resources (national forests, for example), then privately operated stations can never own them. Instead, they must be licensed from the people and used in the public interest. If license holders violate the public trust, their licenses can be revoked. The FRC was created to act on behalf of the public. But some historians claim that the "compromise solution" between Populist demands for freedom and technocrats' calls for control produced a somewhat limited definition of the "public interest." In fact, they argue, the intent of the legislation creating the FRC, the Radio Act of 1927, was *not* to encourage an open forum for public debate because such a freewheeling discussion was considered a threat to the very "public interest, convenience, and necessity" that Congress wanted broadcasters to serve. Congress specifically designed the 1927 act to "deny the public access to the ideas of their enemies, such as unions, socialists, communists, evolutionists, improper thinkers, non-Christians, and immigrants.... Broadcasters could have free speech as long as they served the public interest by denying access to speakers who did not serve the public interest as they [Congress] defined it" (Goodman, 2001).

Nonetheless, the relative success of the FRC encouraged efforts to regulate other media industries. Government censorship of movies was widely advocated, especially by religious groups. Over time, the movie industry adopted various forms of self-censorship in an effort to avoid government regulation. As the threat of propaganda grew, even regulation of newspapers was seriously considered. In 1942, for example, the Hutchins Commission on Freedom of the Press was established to weigh the merits of and necessity for newspaper regulation (we'll say more about this later).

PROFESSIONALIZATION OF JOURNALISM

As pressure for government regulation of media mounted in the 1920s, industry leaders responded with efforts to professionalize. Leaders in the newspaper industry lobbied for and occasionally subsidized the establishment of professional schools to train media practitioners. Rather than cede control of media to a government agency, media managers went on record with pledges to serve public needs. In 1923, the American Society of Newspaper Editors (ASNE) adopted a set of professional standards entitled *The Canons of Journalism* (which were replaced in 1975 by the *ASNE Statement of Principles*). Since then, virtually every association of media practitioners has adopted similar standards. In doing so, these associations are emulating professionals in fields like law and medicine. These standards typically commit media practitioners to serving the public as effectively as possible.

Industry codes of ethics began to formalize another important conception about the role of media—that of a watchdog guarding the welfare of the public. Media should continually scan the social world and alert the public to problems. This gave rise around the turn of the twentieth century to **muckrakers**, crusading journalists who typically challenged the powerful on behalf of those less so. Their investigations of corruption proved so popular that newspapers specializing in them came to dominate the markets in some large cities. The Scripps Howard newspaper chain adopted the lighthouse as its symbol and chose the phrase "Give light and the people will find their own way" as its motto. Gradually, the watchdog role was widely accepted as a necessary and appropriate one for news media.

In some ambitious formulations of this role, the media are envisioned as independent watchdogs, a social institution, the **Fourth Estate** of government, charged with making certain that all other institutions—the three branches of government, business, religion, education, and family—serve the public. In the words of social critic and veteran journalist Bill Moyers (2001, p. 13), properly functioning media are needed "to keep our leaders honest and to arm the powerless with the information they need to protect themselves against the tyranny of the powerful, whether that tyranny is political or commercial." This perspective assumes that once people are informed about wrongdoing, incompetence, or inefficiency, they will take action against it. But there has always been concern that the watchdog might be subverted by the powerful, becoming a lapdog. Or the watchdog could become irresponsible, exaggerating its criticism of government or business to sell newspapers. What type of watchdog coverage should we expect from media when most are owned by the very corporations they are expected to police? And how likely is it that these media will criticize governments having the power to make decisions that affect their profits? Is it still reasonable to expect our profit-oriented press to comfort the afflicted and afflict the comfortable? As timely as these questions may be today, eight decades ago they were at the heart of the search for a theory to guide the operation of a growing American mass media system and its interactions with its growing audiences. Social Responsibility Theory was the result.

muckrakers
Crusading journalists who typically challenged the powerful on behalf of those less so

Fourth Estate
Media as an independent social institution that ensures that other institutions serve the public

SOCIAL RESPONSIBILITY THEORY OF THE PRESS: A POSTWAR COMPROMISE

Despite moves toward professionalization and self-regulation, pressure for greater government regulation of media mounted throughout World War II and continued during the anti-Communist agitation that followed. In response, Henry Luce, CEO of Time Inc., provided funding for an independent commission to make recommendations concerning the role of the press. The Hutchins Commission on Freedom of the Press was established in 1942 and released a major report of its findings in 1947 (Davis, 1990; McIntyre, 1987). Its members consisted of leaders from many areas of society, including academics, politicians, and leaders of social groups.

Commission members were divided between those who held strongly Libertarian views and those who thought some form of press regulation was necessary. Those who favored regulation were fearful that the marketplace of ideas was much too vulnerable to subversion by antidemocratic forces. Several of these regulation proponents were guided by a philosophy of public communication developed by social researchers at the University of Chicago. The **Chicago School** envisioned modern cities to be "Great Communities" composed of hundreds of small social groups—everything from neighborhood social organizations to citywide associations. For these Great Communities to develop, all constituent groups had to work together and contribute. These were referred to as **pluralistic groups** in recognition of their cultural and racial diversity (Davis, 1990).

Chicago School
Social researchers at the University of Chicago in the 1940s who envisioned modern cities as "Great Communities" made up of hundreds of interrelated small groups

pluralistic groups
In a Great Community, the various segments defined by specific unifying characteristics

The Chicago School opposed marketplace-of-ideas notions and argued that unregulated mass media inevitably served the interests and tastes of large or socially dominant groups. In their view, *protecting* the right of expression was not equivalent to *providing* for it. They wanted a *positive* role for government regulation, "an interventionary role—to provide enabling structures for a healthy public sphere" (Pickard, 2010, p. 394). Their concern, reinforced by what they regularly saw in the media of their day, was that small, weak, pluralistic groups would be either neglected or denigrated. They also worried that ruthless elites could use media as a means of gaining personal political power. These demagogues could manipulate media to transmit propaganda to fuel hatred and fear among a majority and unite them against minorities. Hitler's use of media to arouse hatred of the Jews served as a prime example.

To prevent this tyranny-by-the-majority and to mandate support for pluralistic groups, some commission members favored creation of a public agency—a press council—made up of people much like themselves and having the power to prevent publication of hate propaganda. In the view of these Hutchins Commission members, this "new and independent agency [would] appraise and report annually upon the performance of the press." It would base that appraisal on its comparison of "the accomplishments of the press with the aspirations which the people have for it" (in Bates, 2001). A press council might, for example, have required that newspapers and radio stations devote a certain portion of their coverage to minority groups. Or it might have required that these groups be given regular columns or programs in which they could express whatever they wanted.

Commission members recognized that such regulations might impose additional costs on media outlets. If this happened, government subsidies might cover these expenses. By serving pluralistic groups, media would strengthen them and enable them to contribute to the Great Community. This fostering of pluralism and restraint on propaganda were seen as essential to preventing the spread of totalitarianism in the United States.

Although the majority of the Hutchins Commission members had some sympathy for Chicago School ideas, they opposed any direct form of press regulation (Davis, 1990; McIntyre, 1987). This meant they faced a serious dilemma. On the one hand, they recognized that the marketplace of ideas was not self-regulating and that the media were doing less than they could to provide services to minority groups. However, they feared that any form of press regulation would open the door to official control of media—the very thing they were trying to prevent. Ultimately, the Hutchins Commission members decided to place their faith in media practitioners, calling on them to redouble their efforts to serve the public:

> [They] endorsed professional responsibility ... [as] a way of reconciling market flaws with the traditional conception of the democratic role of the media. [The Hutchins Commission's report] asserted journalists' commitment to higher goals—neutrality, detachment, a commitment to truth. It involved the adoption of certain procedures for verifying facts, drawing on different sources, presenting rival interpretations. In this way, the pluralism of opinion and information, once secured through the clash of adversaries in the free market, could be recreated through the "internal pluralism" of monopolistic media. Market pressures to sensationalize and trivialize the presentation of news could be offset by a commitment to inform. (Curran, 1991, p. 98)

The synthesis of ideas put forward in the Hutchins Commission report has become known as the *Social Responsibility Theory of the Press* (Siebert, Peterson, and Schramm, 1956). It emphasized the need for an independent press that scrutinizes other social institutions and provides objective, accurate news reports. The most innovative feature of social responsibility theory was its call for media to be responsible for fostering productive and creative "Great Communities." It said that media should do this by prioritizing cultural pluralism—by becoming the voice of all the people—not just elite groups or groups that had dominated national, regional, or local culture in the past.

In some respects, social responsibility theory is a radical statement. Instead of demanding that media be free to print or transmit whatever their owners want, social responsibility theory imposes a burden on media practitioners. As the commission argued, "The press is not free if those who operate it behave as though their position conferred on them the privilege of being deaf to ideas which the processes of free speech have brought to public attention" (quoted in Bates, 2001).

Social responsibility theory appealed to the idealism and professionalism of many media practitioners and tried to unite them in the service of cultural pluralism—even when this might reduce their profits or antagonize existing social elites. Social responsibility theory challenged media professionals' ingenuity to develop new ways of serving their communities. It encouraged them to see themselves as frontline participants in the battle to preserve democracy in a world drifting inexorably toward totalitarianism. By helping pluralistic groups, media were building a wall to protect democracy from external and internal foes. Denis McQuail (1987) summarized the basic principles of social responsibility theory as follows:

- Media should accept and fulfill certain obligations to society.
- These obligations are mainly to be met by setting high or professional standards of informativeness, truth, accuracy, objectivity, and balance.
- In accepting and applying these obligations, media should be self-regulating within the framework of law and established institutions.
- The media should avoid whatever might lead to crime, violence, or civil disorder or give offense to minority groups.
- The media as a whole should be pluralist and reflect the diversity of their society, giving access to various points of view and to rights of reply.
- Society and the public have a right to expect high standards of performance, and intervention can be justified to secure the, or a, public good.
- Journalists and media professionals should be accountable to society as well as to employers and the market.

USING SOCIAL RESPONSIBILITY THEORY TO GUIDE PROFESSIONAL PRACTICE

The ideals of social responsibility theory have proved quite durable, even if their full implications are rarely understood by working journalists. In fact, many scholars argue, "social responsibility doctrine has always been relegated to the fringes of journalism education and the newsroom. More than 60 years after the Hutchins Commission report, news personnel generally remain hostile to its focus on the public good and on broad-based reporting about significant events of the day" (Christians, Ferre, and Fackler, 1993, p. 38). Furthermore, in the competing "ethos of news as business [and] that of news as socially responsible institution," social responsibility often comes in second (Lind and Rockier, 2001, p. 119). In our current era of large media corporations, "Friends of the 'liberty of the press' must recognize that *communication markets restrict freedom of communication* by generating barriers to entry, monopoly and restrictions upon choice, and by shifting the prevailing definition of information from that of a public good to that of a privately appropriated commodity" (Keane, 1991, pp. 88–89, emphasis in original).

So, if social responsibility theory is to remain a viable normative theory, greater effort might be needed to implement it. Compared with the vast amount of research conducted on media effects, relatively little work has examined whether existing news production practices, as intended, actually serve societal goals. For example, one primary goal is communicating accurate information about important events to the public. Research findings on this goal are mixed. Evidence indicates that people don't learn much from news reports and what they do learn is quickly forgotten (Graber, 1987). People become easily confused by stories that are poorly structured or use dramatic but irrelevant pictures. This research has had little or no impact on the practice of journalism. Its findings have been largely ignored or misinterpreted by media practitioners (Davis and Robinson, 1989).

In the 1970s and 1980s, sociologists published a series of studies that raised important questions about the value of routine news production practices (Bennett,

1988; Epstein, 1973; Fishman, 1980; Gans, 1979; Glasgow University Media Group, 1976, 1980; Tuchman, 1978). Journalists have consistently ignored most of this work as biased, irrelevant, and misguided. It deserves a more careful reading. Gaye Tuchman, for example, presents a well-developed argument concerning the role played by media in the discovery and cultivation of social movements. She sees news production as bound by "strategic rituals" and believes that these practices appear to satisfy the requirements imposed by social responsibility norms but fall far short of achieving their purpose. For example, journalists ritualistically construct "balanced" stories in which they contrast opposing views. However, these rites might actually undermine rather than advance pluralism. She maintains that "balanced stories" about minority groups frequently contain statements from social or political leaders that subtly or blatantly denigrate groups and their ideas. The emotionally charged opinions of little-known group leaders are contrasted with reasoned pronouncements from well-known credible officials. Reporters make little effort to create a context for new groups' broader goals or culture. Instead, their reports tend to focus on dramatic events staged by isolated group members. There's much more to be said about the impact of routine news production practices in Chapter 9.

LIMITATIONS OF PROFESSIONALIZATION

Practicing contemporary journalism in a manner consistent with social responsibility theory's norms of professionalism faces additional difficulties. In their move toward professionalization, media practitioners, like doctors and lawyers before them, pledge to uphold standards of professional practice. They promise to weed out irresponsible people and give recognition to those who excel. Those who violate standards should be censured. In extreme cases, they could be barred from professional practice. And as an alternative to direct government regulation, media professionalization has worked relatively well. Certain limitations, however, especially in our time of dramatic technological and economic change in the media industries, lead to recurring problems:

1. **Professionals in every field, including journalism, are been reluctant to identify and censure colleagues who violate professional standards.** To do so is often seen as admitting that problems exist. Public trust in all media professionals might be shaken if too many people are barred from practice. Professional societies tend to operate as closed groups in which members are protected against outside threats and criticism. Attacks from outsiders are routinely dismissed as unwarranted, even when evidence against a practitioner mounts. Often action is taken only in extreme cases, when it cannot be avoided. Even then, news media either avoid covering the case or provide brief and superficial coverage.

This problem is amply demonstrated by *New York Times* reporter Judith Miller and her reporting on weapons of mass destruction (WMD) in the run-up to the 2003 invasion of Iraq (Okrent, 2004). Once it became apparent that the WMD her sources had assured her were in Iraq were in fact imaginary, and well after her own newspaper's disavowal of her "flawed journalism," several of Miller's colleagues admitted that they were suspicious of much of her work on the issue, but they remained quiet because of her close ties with the paper's senior editors. But some colleagues did take their misgivings to *Times*' editors. But because Miller was a Pulitzer Prize–winning journalist with contacts high in the administration, they ignored those warnings, continuing to run her "well-sourced" stories on the paper's front page. Miller was "allowed to resign" only after she and her paper could no longer withstand the scrutiny and criticism that followed her role, however insignificant, in the illegal outing of undercover CIA agent Valerie Plame in 2005. Executive editor at the time, Bill Keller, eventually admitted, "People, I thought, did not need another scandal and so I let it fester for a year.... What I should have done when I came in was ... write that mea culpa and explain to readers, 'You know, look, we wrote some bad stories in the run-up to the war. I don't think it was out of any malice, I think it was we kind of fell for the conventional wisdom.... I think I could have saved the paper a lot of trouble and some damage by dealing with that much sooner" (Strupp, 2011).

2. **Professional standards can be overly abstract and ambiguous.** They can be difficult to implement and enforce. Mission statements and broad codes of ethics are notoriously vague. The Radio-Television News Directors Association's Code of Ethics and Professional Conduct (2000), for example, instructs its members to "pursue truth aggressively and present the news accurately, in context, and completely as possible." But news directors must make choices concerning allocation of resources. Increasingly, the news we see consists of corporate and government public relations **video news releases (VNRs)**. In fact, almost every American local television news operation makes use of these outsider-provided public relations pieces, and one recent study of 77 stations discovered that not a single one disclosed the source of the VNR (Farsetta, 2006). How do editors decide when to stop airing VNRs and start engaging in independent digging and reporting? There might be no reason to doubt the truth of a VNR unless a reporter takes the time to conduct an independent investigation.

But what if an independent journalistic investigation leads a large advertiser to cancel its account with the station? Why risk producing stories that might prove embarrassing to someone or some organization? In the news business, telling the truth can sometimes be difficult and expensive. Professional standards are vague, so nothing forces journalists to endanger relationships with friendly sources or the company's profit margins. In fact, it is a poorly kept broadcast industry secret that many stations maintain printed lists of people and issues that are untouchable—they may not be covered—"for fear of alienating an advertiser" (Potter, 2001, p. 68).

3. **In contrast with medicine and law, media professionalization doesn't include standards for professional training and licensing.** Other professions mandate that practitioners receive long and closely monitored professional training. For example, doctors and lawyers undergo from 4 to 10 years of specialized training in addition to completing 4 years of college. But media practitioners are unwilling to set requirements for professional training and have strongly resisted efforts to license journalists. They argue that these requirements would inevitably be used by government to control the press. If the press is to remain free from control, it must be free to hire anyone—no matter how untrained or unqualified. Anyone should be able to claim the title of journalist, start a newspaper, and exercise his or her rights to free press. No government agency should be able to step in and shut down a paper just because some of its reporters or editors are unlicensed.

But, as veteran journalist David Marsh asks, "What makes someone a journalist? As recently as 10 years ago, the answer would have been straightforward: journalists

video news release (VNR)

Report produced by an outside organization, typically a public relations firm, that is distributed free of charge to television stations made their living by producing editorial material (written or otherwise) that was then published or broadcast to an audience of readers, listeners, or viewers. In the new digital age of the web and social media, things are more complicated. If I tweet from a major news event—the Arab spring, say—is that journalism? If I start my own political blog, does that make me a journalist? If I'm a teacher, say, but contribute stories to a newspaper, does that make me a 'citizen journalist'? Does it make any difference whether people are paid, or not, for such work? Should **bloggers**, tweeters and 'citizen journalists' be held to, and judged by, the same standards as people working in more traditional journalistic roles" (2012)?

bloggers
Writers who maintain blogs, regularly updated online journals of news and opinion

4. **In contrast with other professions, media practitioners tend to have less independent control over their work.** Media practitioners don't work as autonomous practitioners and therefore have difficulty assuming personal responsibility for their work. They tend to work in big, hierarchically structured bureaucracies. Individual reporters, editors, producers, and directors have only a limited ability to control what they do. Reporters are given assignments by editors, advertising designers work for account executives, and television anchors and camera operators follow the instructions of news directors. Editors, account managers, and directors are all responsible to higher management. In these large bureaucracies, it is difficult to assign responsibility. Those at lower levels can claim that they are only "following orders," whereas people at higher levels can simply disavow any knowledge of what was going on below them. Earlier we discussed the example provided by Judith Miller and her misleading reporting about Iraq prior to the start of the war. Miller's editors claimed ignorance of her actions. Her colleagues suspected what she was doing but chose to ignore it. So is Miller fully responsible for misleading coverage, or do her colleagues and supervisors share blame?

5. **In the media industries, violation of professional standards rarely has immediate, directly observable consequences.** Thus it is hard for critics to cite violations or to identify the harm that has been done. When doctors fail, people die. When lawyers fail, people go to jail unnecessarily. The results of unethical or incompetent media practice are harder to see. "The media blew both of the major catastrophes of our time," wrote Greg Mitchell, editor-in-chief of *Editor & Publisher*, "I speak, of course, of the Iraq war and the financial meltdown." The outcome of "missing stories of this enormity" naturally had "consequences that will echo … for decades," but at the time of the initial failed reporting there was little way to know that would be the case (2009, p. 16).

Sometimes, unprofessional conduct might even do some good. The classic case of Janet Cooke is instructive. In 1980, Cooke, a reporter for the *Washington Post*, wrote a Pulitzer Prize-winning series about ghetto children (Altschull, 1990, pp. 361–364). Later these stories were found to be based on fabricated interviews. Cooke took personal details and comments from several people and then wove them together to create a fictitious interviewee. The resulting stories had great dramatic impact, educating readers about the reality of drugs in the inner city and spurring official action to clean up particularly troublesome areas. Nevertheless, her reports violated professional standards of truth and accuracy. Cooke was fired and the paper returned the Pulitzer. The *Post* expressed profound embarrassment and its legendary editor, Ben Bradlee, called it the worst failure of his long career.

THE DUAL RESPONSIBILITY MODEL

dual responsibility theory
Revision of social responsibility theory delineating a role for fiscal, as well as social, responsibility in news decision making

Communication researchers Terry Adams-Bloom and Johanna Cleary, acknowledging these pressures on journalists' professionalism, proposed an update of social responsibility theory that "upholds the high ideals and First Amendment considerations of social responsibility theory while recognizing the economic realities of today's mega-corporate environment" (2009, p. 2). Their revision, the **dual responsibility theory**, "acknowledges the reality of bottom-line considerations ... [and] delineates a place for fiscal, as well as social, responsibility in news decision making in a 24-hour news cycle world.... This orientation does not, in and of itself, necessarily produce poor quality content. However, it does represent a shift in prioritizing content that may be the more relevant question when looking at today's news media" (p. 6). You can visually examine the shift they propose in Figure 3.1.

stakeholder theory
Idea that companies should operate in the best interests of all those who depend on them—their stakeholders

They base their revision on **stakeholder theory**, the idea that companies should operate in the best interests of *all* those who depend on them—their stakeholders—not simply those who benefit financially. Maximizing profit, in and of itself, should not be companies' primary goal. They suggest that this orientation "allows a wide berth for ethical business practices and good corporate citizenship and lessens the importance of pure capitalism" (p. 3).

FIGURE 3.1A Traditional Model of Social Responsibility

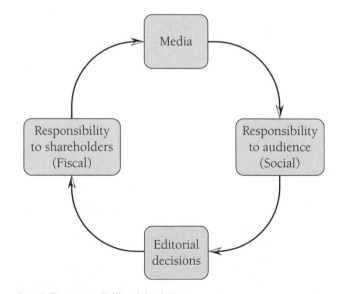

FIGURE 3.1B Dual Responsibility Model

Terry Bloom, International Journal on Media Management, 2009

Critics of social responsibility theory (Altschull, 1995; McQuail, 2005; Pickard, 2010) would argue that most media organizations, even without license from the dual responsibility model to grant even more consideration to profit, have long favored profit over responsibility. Maybe contemporary media companies are simply more obvious about it in what Adams-Bloom and Cleary call today's "mega-corporate environment," emboldened by "an atmosphere of deregulation and sweeping policy change" (p. 2). Nonetheless, these researchers have undertaken one of the few serious reexaminations of the normative theory that has ostensibly guided American media practices for more than half a century.

IS THERE STILL A ROLE FOR SOCIAL RESPONSIBILITY THEORY?

Although U.S. media have developed many professional practices in an effort to conform to the ideals of social responsibility theory, the long-term objective—the creation of "Great Communities"—has never seemed more elusive. Our cities have undergone decades of urban renewal, yet slums remain, and in some cities they continue to spread. There have been national "wars" to combat poverty, crime, pollution, disease, and drugs, but the quality of life for many Americans has not improved. Nondominant ethnic and racial cultures are still widely misunderstood. Minority group members continue to be discriminated against and harassed. There are millions of illegal immigrants in the United States whose work is critical to the economy but whom most Americans distrust and would deport if possible. There is evidence that hate groups are increasing in size and that their propaganda is effectively reaching larger audiences (Severson, 2012). Politicians still find it possible to win elections by stirring up public fear of various minorities.

Does this mean that social responsibility theory is wrong? Has it been poorly implemented? What responsibility can or should media practitioners assume on behalf of the Great Communities they serve? More important, how should this responsibility be exercised? With news helicopters circling over riot scenes? With inflammatory coverage of hate groups? With boring coverage of the routine work of neighborhood associations? With sensational coverage of political candidates when they demean and stereotype minorities? Was there merit in the Chicago School arguments concerning coverage of pluralistic groups? If so, what forms might that coverage take? Should group members be allowed some direct control of what is printed about them in newspapers or broadcast on television?

local origination (or mandatory access) rule
Rule requiring local cable television companies to carry community-based access channels

Our society's experience with local access channels on cable television suggests that it is not easy to use media to support pluralistic groups. In 1972, the Federal Communications Commission for the first time required local cable companies to provide local access channels in an effort to serve pluralistic groups, and although these **local origination (or mandatory access) rules** have been altered, suspended, and otherwise tinkered with during the last 40 years, they have generally failed to serve their intended purpose. Very few people watch the access channels, and few groups use them.

low power FM (LPFM) radio
Community-based, noncommercial stations broadcasting over small areas, typically three to seven miles

Many observers believe that social responsibility theory will be given new strength by emerging technologies that allow communities greater power to disseminate information. The FCC licenses **low power FM (LPFM) radio** stations, community-based, noncommercial stations broadcasting over small areas, typically

INSTANT ACCESS

Libertarianism

Strengths

1. Values media freedom
2. Is consistent with U.S. media traditions
3. Values individuals
4. Precludes government control of media

Weaknesses

1. Is overly optimistic about media's willingness to meet responsibilities
2. Is overly optimistic about individuals' ethics and rationality
3. Ignores need for reasonable control of media
4. Ignores dilemmas posed by conflicting freedoms (e.g., free press versus personal privacy)

three to seven miles. The more than 825 stations currently on-air are operated by community groups, labor unions, churches, and other nonprofit groups usually absent from the airwaves (Yu and Renderos, 2013). Cable television, though never approaching the reempowering-the-public revolution predicted for it in the 1960s, has at least made literally hundreds of channels available, many of which are dedicated to ethnic and specific-interest communities. Now, with the near total diffusion of the Internet and World Wide Web, audience size and ability to make a profit have become unimportant concerns for literally millions of "voices." The website for a tribe of Native Americans, for example, sits electronically side-by-side with those of the most powerful media organizations. What many theorists fear, however, is that this wealth of voices— each speaking to its own community—will **Balkanize** the larger U.S. culture. That is, rather than all Americans reading and viewing conscientiously produced content about all the Great Communities that make the United States as wonderfully diverse and pluralistic as it is, communities will talk only to

Balkanize
Dividing a country, culture, or society into antagonistic subgroups

INSTANT ACCESS

Social Responsibility Theory

Strengths

1. Values media responsibility
2. Values audience responsibility
3. Limits government intrusion in media operation
4. Allows reasonable government control of media
5. Values diversity and pluralism
6. Aids the "powerless"
7. Appeals to the best instincts of media practitioners and audiences
8. Is consistent with U.S. legal tradition

Weaknesses

1. Is overly optimistic about media's willingness to meet responsibility
2. Is overly optimistic about individual responsibility
3. Underestimates power of profit motivation and competition
4. Legitimizes status quo

people residing within their borders. The values, wants, needs, and ideas of others will be ignored. Journalist Bree Nordenson, for example, argues that "shared public knowledge is receding, as is the likelihood that we come in contact with beliefs that contradict our own. Personalized home pages, newsfeeds, and e-mail alerts, as well as special-interest publications lead us to create what sociologist Todd Gitlin disparagingly referred to as 'my news, my world.' Serendipitous news—accidently encountered information—is far less frequent in a world of TiVo and online customization tools" (2008, p. 37). William Gibson, author of *Neuromancer* and guru to the cybergeneration, predicts that there will indeed be Great Communities, but they will be communities built around brands—Planet Nike and the World of Pepsi—rather than around common values and aspirations (Trench, 1990).

THE PUBLIC INTEREST IN THE INTERNET ERA

More than 245 million Americans use the Internet; computers sit in more than 80 percent of their homes and 92 percent of these have Internet access ("Internet Users," 2013). Adult Internet users spend more than half of their online time reading news, and over 111 million people a month click onto a newspaper site (Hendricks, 2012; Sass, 2011). Yahoo! News draws 110 million unique readers a month; CNN 74 million; MSNBC 73 million; and Google News 65 million ("Top 15," 2012). Half of all Americans own smartphones or tablets, and more than 62 percent use those devices to access online news sites every week, the same frequency with which they play online games. Only e-mail exceeds reading news as a regular activity for these mobile users (Mitchell, Rosenstiel, and Santhanam, 2012).

There are, as we've already discussed, many other news sites, blogs. There are more than 180 million blogs, up from 36 million five years ago ("Buzz," 2012). While the vast majority often quickly go dormant, and many are no doubt personal diaries, family gathering sites, and other idiosyncratic outlets, many others are "citizen publishers," "stand-alone journalists," and "networks of dedicated amateurs" who do meaningful journalism (Stepp, 2006, p. 62). "Freedom of the press now belongs not just to those who own printing presses," wrote journalism scholar Ann Cooper, "but also to those who use cell phones, video cameras, blogging software, and other technology to deliver news and views to the world" (2008, p. 45). In addition, blogging itself has become professionalized. Scores of trained, paid journalists ply their trade on highly sophisticated, advertising-supported blogs. *Politico*, *Huffington Post*, and *JimRomenesko.com* are only three examples. Moreover, virtually every mainstream news outlet, from local newspapers to national television networks, requires its journalists to regularly blog on the company's website as well as maintain a presence on Twitter and Facebook. The *New York Times*, for example, has more than 60 news and opinion blogs on its website. As such, Internet news sites have assumed a growing news-gathering and dissemination function in our society as well as a central role in our democracy's public discourse.

Bloggers, for example, are routinely granted official access to major news events such as presidential press conferences and Supreme Court hearings; they have a professional association, the Online News Association (at *www.cyberjournalist.net*), and a code of ethics; online journalists are eligible for Pulitzer Prizes; and in 2009, in order to include online journalists among their members, both the Radio and Television News Directors Association (RTNDA) and the American Society of Newspaper Editors (ASNE) changed names. The RTNDA became the RTDNA—the Radio Television Digital News Association—and the ASNE dropped "paper" from its name to become the American Society of News Editors. And a 2012 McArthur Foundation study found that there were over 400 websites providing news and information relevant to Chicago-area residents. More than 300 formed what the study called "the core of the Chicago news and information ecosystem," and 80 percent received few if any links from other sites in the network, meaning that much of the information was unduplicated (Gordon and Johnson, 2012).

Internet news sites, then, are forcing a major reconsideration not only of the practice of journalism, but of social responsibility and the public interest. For example, where long-time journalist and retired Dean of the Columbia School of Journalism Nicholas Lemann can survey the digital media environment and proclaim, "As a consumer of news, this is the best time there has ever been" (in Moynihan, 2012), sociologist and historian Paul Starr expresses concern over the future of media's social responsibility in the era of digital technology:

> The digital revolution has been good for freedom of expression because it has increased the diversity of voices in the public sphere. It has been good for freedom of information because it has made government documents and data directly accessible to more people and has fostered a culture that demands transparency from powerful institutions. But the digital revolution has had mixed effects on freedom of the press. Yes, it has allowed new entrants into the media and generated promising innovations in journalism. But by undermining the economic basis of professional reporting and by fragmenting the public, it has weakened the ability of the press to act as an effective agent of public accountability. (2012, p. 234)

New-journalism theorist Jay Rosen acknowledges that the traditional media's social responsibility role has indeed been weakened, but offers an alternative, more optimistic view of what that means. His position is that the Internet can give more voice to more people, creating "great communities" built around information and ideas. "In the age of mass media," he wrote, "the press was able to define the sphere of legitimate debate with relative ease because the people on the receiving end were atomized—meaning they were connected 'up' to Big Media but not across to each other. But today one of the biggest factors changing our world is the falling cost for like-minded people to locate each other, share information, trade impressions and realize their number" (2009). He argues that "big media" limit public discourse by "deciding what does and does not legitimately belong within the national debate." He slightly modified political scientist Daniel Hallin's sphere-of-influence model (1986) to explain how this self-serving selection diminishes public discussion of important issues (Figure 3.2).

According to Rosen and Hallin, democratic public discourse consists of three spheres which are strictly policed by traditional, mainstream media journalists:

1. *Sphere of legitimate debate*—journalists recognize this "as real, normal, everyday terrain. They think of their work as taking place almost exclusively within this space.... Hallin: 'This is the region of electoral contests and legislative

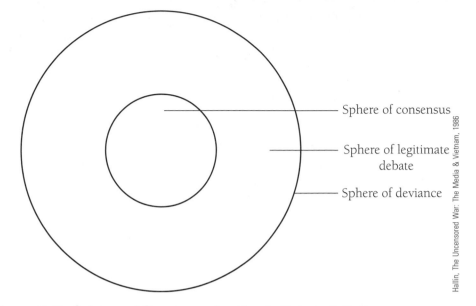

Sphere of consensus

Sphere of legitimate debate

Sphere of deviance

Hallin, The Uncensored War: The Media & Vietnam, 1986

FIGURE 3.2   Spheres of Consensus, Legitimate Debate & Deviance (adapted from Hallin, 1986)

debates, of issues recognized as such by the major established actors of the American political process.'"

2. *Sphere of consensus*—"the 'motherhood and apple pie' of politics, the things on which everyone is thought to agree. Propositions that are seen as uncontroversial to the point of boring, true to the point of self-evidence, or so widely held that they almost universally lie within this sphere. Here, Hallin writes, 'Journalists do not feel compelled either to present opposing views or to remain disinterested observers.'"

3. *Sphere of deviance*—here "we find 'political actors and views which journalists and the political mainstream of society reject as unworthy of being heard.' [J]ournalists maintain order by either keeping the deviant out of the news entirely or identifying it within the news frame as unacceptable, radical, or just plain impossible. The press 'plays the role of exposing, condemning, or excluding from the public agenda' the deviant view, says Hallin. It 'marks out and defends the limits of acceptable political conduct'" (Rosen, 2009).

Legitimate debate appears on the front pages of American newspapers, in their opinion sections, and on the Sunday morning television news roundtables. Objectivity and balance are the dominant norms. *Consensus* is "the American creed." Capitalism is good and the market serves all Americans well; America's global motives are always right and just. *Deviance* is disagreement with America's two major political parties, disbelief that what benefits Wall Street benefits Main Street, views that are never reflected in the news. "It's not that there's a one-sided debate," wrote Rosen, "there's no debate.... The established media ... are not passive agents here. They have an overt bias for consensus and against 'deviancy', which means they want the doughnut hole (what is off-limits to public debate) to be as big as possible and they want to exclude as much 'deviancy' as possible from admission to the sphere of 'legitimate' debate.... [A]lternative—or even worse, radical—points of view, which might enliven the sphere of 'legitimate' debate are consistently excluded" (2009).

Rosen's point about the new online journalism is not only that there are more voices, which is certainly the case, but that because of the Internet people are connected into issue or idea communities; they are no longer atomized. The net, he told Glenn Greenwald, "connects us to other people who feel the same way when they're watching the news, who have said to themselves: 'Wait, that's not the range of debate. Oh, wait a minute, that doesn't sound such a deviant idea to me, I know you're portraying it that way' " (2009). And once the mainstream media's authority to define the sphere of legitimate debate is weakened, a greater number and variety of issues will enter public discourse and they will be debated from a greater number of perspectives. This will enrich democracy, which, in the words of journalism scholars Stephan Coleman and Jay Blumler, suffers from a "deficit of deliberation." "The most exciting and innovative participatory exercises," they wrote, "have in common an aspiration to promote and utilise [sic] public discussion as a means of engendering the collective production of policy decisions worthy of public consent" (2009, p. 15). In other words, the Internet furthers social responsibility theory's goal of giving voice to all and fostering community. The question facing blogs and other Internet news outlets, then, is no longer whether they practice journalism; it is whether they can remain independent of the pressures that seem to limit more traditional outlets.

NONPROFIT JOURNALISM

One answer to that question, and another example of the Internet's ability to reinvigorate the ideals of social responsibility theory, rests in the development of nonprofit journalism. "There is considerable attention paid in the United States to the collapse of journalism—both in terms of the demise of the business model for corporate commercial news media, and the evermore superficial, shallow, and senseless content that is inadequate for citizens concerned with self-governance," wrote journalism scholar Robert Jensen, "This collapse is part of larger crises in the political and economic spheres, crises rooted in the incompatibility of democracy and capitalism. New journalistic vehicles for storytelling are desperately needed" (2010, p. 1). Those new vehicles are increasingly not-for-profit news organizations.

Hundreds of American foundations and individual contributors now give generously to primarily online news and information projects, much of that support directed specifically to investigative journalism. The Knight and the Sandler Foundations, for example, underwrite Spot.us, a website that invites journalists to pitch stories to people who then contribute small amounts of money to those they deem worthy, a practice known as **community-funded (or crowd-funded) journalism**. These foundations also fund ProPublica, a nonprofit investigative reporting group that partners with for-profit news outlets to do stories those media might not otherwise cover. ProPublica, winner of two Pulitzer Prizes in its first four years of operation, teamed with CBS to report on the spending of federal stimulus money and with the *New York Times* on coverage of the American reconstruction effort

community-funded (or crowd-funded) journalism
Journalists propose projects online to people who then contribute to those they deem worthy

in Iraq. The Knight Foundation, through its New Voices program administered by the Institute for Interactive Journalism at American University, also provides grants in support of the launch of local news organizations. Essex County Community Media in New Jersey and GrossePointToday.com in Michigan are two examples. The Center for Independent Media and its national portal, the *Washington Independent*, support a number of state-based political news websites, including the *Colorado Independent* and the *Minnesota Independent*. Scores of other local, non-profit journalism sites, using a variety of funding schemes and employing varying mixes of professional and citizen journalists, also operate. Among the more successful are MinnPost.com and NewJerseyNewsroom.com.

OTHER NORMATIVE THEORIES

Western concept
A normative theory combining aspects of Libertarianism and social responsibility theory

development concept
A normative theory describing systems in which government and media work in concert to ensure that the media aid the planned, beneficial development of a given nation

revolutionary concept
A normative theory describing a system in which media are used in the service of revolution

William Hachten (1992) provided the now-classic perspective on normative theories guiding the media systems of different countries and political systems. He identified five "concepts": (1) Western, (2) development, (3) revolutionary, (4) authoritarian, and (5) communism. The **Western concept**, exemplified by the United States, Great Britain, and most other well-developed industrial nations, combines aspects of Libertarianism and social responsibility theory. It recognizes that there are no completely free media systems and that even in the most profit-oriented systems, there exists not only a public expectation of service and responsibility, but an official expectation as well, one backed by "significant communication related activities of government"—in other words, regulation (Stevenson, 1994, p. 109).

The **development concept** describes systems in which government and media work in concert to ensure that media aid the planned, beneficial development of a given nation. This concept is exemplified by the media systems of most developing nations in Africa, Asia, the former Eastern bloc of Europe, and Latin America. Media and government officials work together to produce content that meets specific cultural and societal needs—for example, disease eradication and the dissemination of new farming techniques. There is more government involvement in the operation of the media than there is in the Western concept, but little overt official censorship and control.

The **revolutionary concept** describes a system in which media are used in the service of revolution. No country officially embraces this concept, but that doesn't mean that the people and media professionals cannot use a nation's communication technologies to upset the government. The goals of media in the revolutionary concept are to end government monopoly over information, building an opposition to the existing government, destroying the legitimacy of an existing government, and bringing down that government (Stevenson, 1994). The revolutionary concept was in clear evidence in the Polish democracy movement—Solidarity—and its adroit manipulation of that country's media system in its 1989 overthrow of its Communist regime.

More recently, the rise and success of democracy movements in several Middle Eastern and African countries—the Arab Spring—demonstrate how the Internet is forcing a reconsideration of the revolutionary concept just as it has led to new thinking on social responsibility theory. The tools of revolutionary media had long been pamphlets and newspapers, loud-speaker trucks, clandestine radio and television broadcasts from inside and outside a country's borders, and even guerilla takeover of government-controlled media. These methods are usually thwarted by arrests, military crackdowns, and electronic blocking of broadcast signals. The Internet, especially social media, has changed that. "The Arab Spring had many causes," wrote communication researcher Philip Howard and his colleagues, "One of these sources was social media and its power to put a human face on political oppression. [Tunisian vegetable merchant Mohammed] Bouazizi's self-immolation [in protest of government corruption] was one of several stories told and retold on Facebook, Twitter, and YouTube in ways that inspired dissidents to organize protests, criticize their governments, and spread ideas about democracy" to several countries in the region, including not only Tunisia, but Egypt, Libya, Algeria, Morocco, Syria, and Yemen" (2011).

Because there are now only three remaining communist countries (North Korea, China, and Cuba), the **authoritarian** and **communism concepts** are typically discussed as one. Both advocate the complete domination of media by the government for the purpose of forcing those media to serve, in the case of the authoritarian system, the government's desires, and in the case of the communism concept, the Communist Party's.

Recently, however, some scholars have been arguing for a less category-based, more flexible approach to normative theory. Chengju Huang, for example, argued for a **transitional media approach** to evaluating specific media systems, because "the post-Cold War era in the information age is witnessing an accelerated social and media transition across the world." As such, media researchers "confront more mixed social and media systems than the standard ones described by various normative models" (2003, p. 456). This approach would be *nonnormative*, making media system "change and adaptation its primary orientation." It would accept change and adaptation as "*a historical process occurring through both revolution and evolution.*" And it would be *culturally open-minded*, maintaining "that media transition in various societies may take different paths in different political, cultural, and socioeconomic contexts, and therefore may lead to different and often complex media systems" (pp. 455–456). Naturally, it is the changing global political environment, advances in communication technologies (especially "borderless" technologies such as satellite and the Internet), and rapid globalization encouraging this call for a more flexible approach to evaluating a given media system against that society's hypothetical ideal (the basis for normative theory).

authoritarian concept
A normative theory advocating the complete domination of media by a government for the purpose of forcing those media to serve the government

Communism concept
A normative theory advocating the complete domination of media by a Communist government for the purpose of forcing those media to serve the Communist Party

transitional media approach
A less category-based, more flexible approach to evaluating media systems than traditional normative theory

SUMMARY

During the 1940s, social responsibility theory emerged as the predominant normative theory of media practice in the United States. It represented a compromise between radical Libertarian views and calls for technocratic control. Social responsibility theory put control of media content in the hands of media practitioners, who were expected to act in the public interest. No

means existed, however, to compel them to serve the public. They were free to decide what services were needed and to monitor the effectiveness of those services. Since its articulation by the Hutchins Commission, most media practitioners have at least been introduced to the basic ideals of social responsibility theory. As such, when they are questioned about their work, most provide explanations based on social responsibility notions. In addition, many different news production practices have been developed in an effort to implement these ideas. Still, there seems to be little enthusiasm among many media professionals for social responsibility theory's focus on the public good and on broad-based reporting about significant events. In addition, as the conflict between social responsibility and profitability continues to grow in our increasingly concentrated and commercialized media, responsibility becomes less central to the mission of many media organizations. The dual responsibility version of social responsibility theory argues that rather than push back against this abdication of obligation, media organizations can find a better balance by serving all stakeholders, specifically citizens and owners.

Media critics such as Gaye Tuchman (1978) have charged that media coverage of minority groups and social movements actually impedes or subverts group activities. They argue that ritualistic balancing of news combined with overdramatized coverage has popularized false impressions of groups or reinforced negative stereotypes. Groups get little real assistance from media. Most media services are aimed at demographic segments favored by advertisers—not at those groups in greatest need of help. Media have chronicled the decay of cities but have done little to create "Great Communities." Their target audiences are generally in the affluent suburbs, not the inner-city ghettos. The harshest critics of social responsibility theory argue that this ideology simply legitimizes and rationalizes the status quo (Altschull, 1990).

Despite little revamping or reexamination, social responsibility theory remains the normative theory guiding most media operation in the United States today. But recent changes in media technology and world politics make it reasonable to reassess social responsibility theory's usefulness as currently applied. New media such as niche cable channels and LPFM are available at low cost to ethnic or other minority groups, and the Internet has made it possible for even the smallest groups to enter their voices into the marketplace of ideas and shift public discourse toward issues otherwise ignored by traditional media. But some critics see the rise of many such small groups as a Balkanization of the larger U.S. culture. Still others see the Internet expanding the range of public discourse across greater numbers of people, as it connects people otherwise connected "up" to traditional media rather than across to each other. Before we can judge the merits of these positions, however, the normative theory on which our media system is grounded must be reformulated, especially given technological and economic changes reshaping mass communication. This will require a critical reexamination of social responsibility theory and careful consideration of alternatives.

Alternative normative theories, however, already exist, although they may not be a good fit for our political and social system. Hachten offered five concepts: (1) Western, combining Libertarian and social responsibility ideals; (2) development, something akin to developmental media theory; (3) revolutionary, in which the people and media professionals use mass media to challenge an existing regime; and (4) authoritarian and (5) communism, in which media serve the dictates of those in power. Recently, however, there have been calls for a less category-based and more flexible approach to normative theories, a transitional media approach to evaluating a given society's media system.

Critical Thinking Questions

1. Do you read news blogs? If so, which ones? Which engage primarily in commentary and which do original reporting? Do you trust these online news sites more or less than you do more traditional media outlets? Why or why not? Do you think blogs have been successful in expanding the permissible range of issues that have entered public discourse and expanded the breadth of the conversation surrounding them? Defend your answer.

2. Libertarianism is based on the self-righting principle—if all the information is available, good ideas will survive and bad ideas will die. But this also assumes that the "debate" between the ideas is fair. Do you think fairness can be achieved in contemporary mass media? Libertarianism also assumes that people are good and rational, that they can tell good ideas from bad ideas. Do you think this highly of your fellow citizens? Why or why not?

3. Social responsibility theory assumes a press that balances profit and service under the watch of an interested public. Many critics, as you've read, believe the media have favored profit over service as the public has remained disinterested. But if journalism becomes the product of a primarily nonprofit or philanthropic system, how might social responsibility theory have to be reconfigured? What will it mean if profit is no longer essential? What additional demands, if any, will this place on the public?

Key Terms

digital natives

quote approval

social responsibility theory

radical Libertarian

First Amendment absolutists

technocratic control

authoritarian theory

self-righting principle

Bill of Rights

marketplace of ideas

laissez-faire doctrine

muckrakers

Fourth Estate

Chicago School

pluralistic groups

video news releases (VNRs)

bloggers

dual responsibility theory

stakeholder theory

local origination (or mandatory access) rule

low power FM radio (LPFM)

Balkanize

community-funded (or crowd-funded) journalism

Western concept

development concept

revolutionary concept

authoritarian concept

communism concept

transitional media approach

FERMENT: METHODOLOGICAL DISPUTES DIVIDE THE DISCIPLINE

THE MEDIA-EFFECTS TREND

In 1928 William Short and W.W. Charters assembled a group of prominent social scientists to conduct research that they hoped would provide definitive evidence concerning the effects of movies on children. Short was a Congregational minister and Charters held a degree in education research from the University of Chicago. Both men firmly believed that postpositivist research on the effects of movies could serve a very practical purpose. They saw movies as a dangerous influence on society and they strongly supported government regulation to limit this influence (Jowett, Jarvie, and Fuller, 1996). Unfortunately in their view, the film industry had developed a very effective strategy for blocking regulation, putting in place a self-regulation effort led by a former Postmaster General of the United States, Will Hays. How could they counter these strategies and convince policymakers that more rigorous regulation was necessary? They decided that empirical research findings would provide the best way to do this. The Payne Fund, an entity financed by Francis Bolton, supported their work. Bolton was the niece of a wealthy Cleveland industrialist and shared their concerns about the problematic influence of movies.

The Payne Fund research was the first well-funded effort to comprehensively study media effects using postpositivist methods (Jowett, Jarvie, and Fuller, 1996). Researchers used content analysis, surveys, and experiments to probe the way children were affected by movies. In 1933 they published 12 books reporting their findings. Though the researchers were reputable and their books provided the most in-depth look ever at the influence of a mass medium, their work was largely ignored and had no influence on efforts to regulate movies. Why? A number of reasons have been offered. For example, Charters wrote a summary of the research that focused on evidence of disturbing effects but ignored findings that showed benign or nonexistent influence. For example, he may have been postpositivist in method, but his mass society thinking is clear in this "Conclusion":

> A single exposure to a picture may produce a measurable change in attitude. Emotions are measurably stirred as the scenes of a drama unfold and this excitement may be recorded in deviations from the norm in sleep patterns, by visible gross evidences of bodily movement, and by refined internal responses. They constitute patterns of

conduct in daydreaming, phantasy, and action. The evidence of their influence is massive and irrefutable. (1933, p. 60)

In addition, many of those social scientists were young and they were using relatively new, crudely developed empirical methods. By the time the research was published, the flaws in their methods had become apparent. The usefulness of postpositivist research methods and the value of its findings were still to be established. That would take decades to achieve. Finally, the movie industry's plan for self-regulation, the 1930 Motion Picture Production Code, appeared not only reasonable, but successful. And this tempered even the most extreme criticism leveled at Hollywood's excesses (Jowett, Jarvie, and Fuller, 1996).

Thirty years after the Payne Fund research was published, the way many social scientists looked at mass media had been radically altered. Most scholars no longer feared media as potential instruments of political oppression and cultural subversion, but instead saw mass communication as a relatively unimportant force with limited potential for harm and some potential for social good. Research methods initially marshaled to reign in the power of media had instead revealed media to be a benign force. Researchers gradually came to see media's power over the public as limited—so limited that no government regulations were necessary to control bad effects. Social scientists viewed the public itself as resistant to such effects. The belief grew that most people were influenced by other people rather than by the media; opinion leaders in every community and at every level of society were responsible for guiding and stabilizing public views. Only a very small minority of people had psychological traits that made them vulnerable to direct manipulation by media. Media were conceptualized as relatively powerless in shaping public opinion in the face of more potent intervening variables like people's individual differences and their group memberships. This new view of media was grounded in an ever-increasing array of empirical research findings and persisted even after the new medium of television transformed and dominated American households. The postpositivist media-effects trend had become well established.

LEARNING OBJECTIVES

After studying this chapter you should be able to

- Chart the development of the postpositivist effects trend in mass communication theory.
- Appreciate the contributions of Paul Lazarsfeld and Carl Hovland to advances in social science in general, and mass communication theory in particular.
- Explain the relationship between the selective processes, cognitive consistency, and attitude change.
- Understand the strengths and weaknesses of several foundational but still important mass communication theories such as information-flow theory, two-step flow theory, phenomenistic theory, and mass entertainment theory.
- See the value and drawbacks of applying theories of the middle range, functionalism, and systems theory to explaining media influence.

OVERVIEW

media-effects trend

Media effects on individuals, because of their importance, should be the focus of research; postpositivist methods provide the best avenue of inquiry

In this chapter we trace the rise of a new way of conceptualizing and studying media—the **media-effects trend**. This trend is an approach to media theory and research that came to dominate the way many U.S. scholars studied and thought about media in the last half of the twentieth century. When research on media first began in the 1920s, scholars in many different fields used a broad array of research methods to study the media. Qualitative methods were widely used even in the social sciences. The disciplines of psychology, social psychology, and sociology were still relatively new, and the potential of empirical research methods was still unclear. Scholars in the more established humanities tended to dominate research on media. Media, especially newspapers, movies, and radio, were widely viewed as important forces in society but there was considerable disagreement over the best ways to study and understand them. Fifty years later, empirical research on media effects had become so well accepted that it was widely regarded (and criticized) as a "dominant paradigm"—the best if not the only way to study media (Tuchman and Farberman, 1980).

To understand how this *effects research* became so dominant, we consider the central roles played by two people in the development of postpositivist media research—Paul Lazarsfeld and Carl Hovland. Lazarsfeld was a pioneer in the use of survey research to measure media influence on how people thought and acted. In the 1940s, his surveys provided increasing evidence that media rarely had a powerful direct influence on individuals. The effects that did occur were quite limited in scope—affecting only a few people or influencing less important thoughts or actions. Other factors such as political party membership, religion, and social status were more important.

Hovland was also a methodological innovator. He demonstrated how experimental methods could be used to evaluate media influence. He too found that media lacked the power to instantly convert average people away from strongly held beliefs. Even in laboratory situations where the potential for media influence was exaggerated, he could only find modest effects. Effects varied depending on many factors including message structure and content, preexisting knowledge or attitudes, and the source of messages.

We will look at the initial theories that emerged out of the early postpositivist effects research. Proponents for these theories argued that they were far superior to speculative ideas about media power. In the late 1950s and early 1960s, data from an impressive array of empirical studies were assembled into reports that form a canon for postpositivst researchers (e.g., Bauer and Bauer, 1960; Campbell et al., 1960; DeFleur and Larsen, 1958; Katz and Lazarsfeld, 1955; Klapper, 1960). Most of these theories were functionalist theories of media—theories that saw media as one force among many that determine how society functions. In general, problematic functions of media were balanced or offset by positive functions. Media were conceptualized as having no power to threaten or undermine the social order.

We consider how functionalism became a dominant perspective among postpositivist social scientists. In their view, American technological know-how had helped win World War II, and in the 1950s it provided many citizens with a comfortable and independent lifestyle. At the heart of this success were increasingly complex large-scale social, economic, and technological systems. Surely factors such as new communication technologies, efficient superhighways, universally available home ownership and higher education, the population's migration to the suburbs, an exploding advertising industry, women entering the workforce in ever larger numbers, expanded leisure time, the rise of the youth culture with its new music and social styles, the geographic displacement of millions of General Issues (GIs) as they were ushered out of the military, the increased voice and visibility of racial minorities, and the Cold War with its threat of imminent global destruction (to name only a few) worked—or functioned—together to produce the America that offered so much that was good and so much that was troubling.

functionalism
Theoretical approach that conceives of social systems as living organisms whose various parts work, or function, together to maintain essential processes

As such, **functionalism** "became dominant in American [social] theory in the 1950s and 1960s. The cornerstone of functionalist theory is the metaphor of the living organism, whose parts and organs, grouped and organized into a system, function to keep its essential processes going. Similarly, members of a society can be thought of as cells and its institutions as organs whose functioning … preserves the cohesive whole and maintains the system's homeostasis" (Bryant and Miron, 2004, p. 677). Through functionalism, mass communication's obvious influence on the social world could be explained and understood, and at the same time that effect could be seen as "limited" by other parts of the system.

communication systems theory
Theory that examines the mass communication process as composed of interrelated parts that work together to meet some goal

But some researchers thought that functionalism could also be applied to the study of mass communication itself and not just to the social system it helped support. The resulting **communication systems theory** offered an alternative to those who were beginning to reject limited-effects notions. They argued that a communication systems theory could allow us to view the role of media in the society at large and assess the usefulness of the powerful new communications technologies. Perhaps media's power could be better assessed at the macroscopic level—that is, by understanding its *larger* role in the social system.

THE DEVELOPMENT OF THE POSTPOSITIVIST EFFECTS TREND

The people who developed media-effects theory and research during the 1940s and 1950s were primarily methodologists—not theorists. In this chapter we focus attention on two such men, Paul Lazarsfeld and Carl Hovland. Both social scientists were convinced that we could best assess the influence of media by employing objective empirical methods. They argued that new research methods such as experiments and surveys made it possible to make observations that would allow them to draw objective conclusions about the effects of media. These conclusions would guide the construction of more useful theory grounded in systematic observation, not wild speculation.

Both Lazarsfeld and Hovland were trained in the empirical research methods that had been developed in psychology. In addition, Lazarsfeld spent time as a social statistician in Austria and was trained in survey methods. Working independently, they demonstrated how their research techniques could be adapted to the study of media effects. Unlike the Payne Fund researchers, both were gradually successful in convincing others of the usefulness and validity of their approach. With ongoing backing from the Rockefeller Foundation, Lazarsfeld secured government and private funding that enabled him to conduct expensive large-scale studies of media influence at Columbia University. After conducting propaganda experiments for the Office of War Information during World War II Hovland established a research center at Yale, where hundreds of persuasion experiments were conducted for more than a decade. Both Columbia and Yale became very influential research centers, attracting and educating some of the most prominent social researchers of the time. These researchers spread across the United States and established similar research centers at major universities.

Neither Lazarsfeld nor Hovland set out to overturn the way mass communication was understood. They had broader objectives. During the war years, they, along with many other postpositivist scholars, were drawn into media studies as part of the larger effort to understand the power of propaganda—the threats it posed as well as the opportunities it offered. Government agencies looked to them for advice on how to control Nazi propaganda and to mobilize Americans to fight the Germans and the Japanese. Unlike many colleagues who automatically assumed that media were quite powerful, Lazarsfeld and Hovland were determined to conduct empirical research that might reveal how media influence worked. They hoped that if media's power could be better understood, it might be controlled and used toward good ends.

Lazarsfeld and Hovland were part of a new generation of empirical social researchers who argued that scientific methods provided the essential means to understand the social world and to control media's power over society. These researchers sought to remake their academic disciplines: to convert sociology, psychology, political science, and even history into what they regarded as true social sciences grounded in empirical research. They cited the tremendous accomplishments made in the physical sciences. Fields like physics and chemistry vividly demonstrated the ability of science to understand and control the physical world. Some of the most striking examples could be found in new military technology: amazing aircraft, highly destructive bombs, and unstoppable tanks. These weapons could be used for either good or evil, to defend democracy or bolster totalitarianism. Like Harold Lasswell (Chapter 2), these would-be social scientists believed that if democracy were to survive, it would have to produce the best scientists, and these people would have to do a better job of harnessing technology to advance that political ideology.

As the new social scientists conducted their research, they found that media were not as powerful as mass society or propaganda theory had suggested. Media influence over public opinion or attitudes often proved hard to locate. Typically it was less important than that of factors such as social status or education. Those media effects that were found seemed to be isolated and sometimes contradictory. Despite the weak findings—study after study provided growing insight into the limited power of media—funding for additional research was easy to secure. Much of this support was provided by a government anxious to maintain its control in a fearful nation under siege from Communist ideology and nuclear weapons that by comparison render pale today's threats from stateless Islamic radicals (Pooley, 2008).

During the 1950s, as the media-effects trend became increasingly dominant, new media research centers modeled after those at Yale and Columbia opened across the United States. One of the early leaders in the field, Wilbur Schramm, was personally responsible for establishing communication research centers at the

University of Illinois, Stanford University, and the University of Hawaii. By 1960, many of the "classic studies" of media effects had been published and become required reading for the first generation of doctoral students in the newly created field of mass communication research.

How did the creators of the media-effects perspective view the power of media? Most of their early research suggested that media influence was minimal except in rare situations. As we discuss the early research, we will illustrate the factors that combined to make development of the media-effects trend possible. We list these factors here, and we will refer to them in later sections.

1. **The refinement and broad acceptance of empirical social research methods was an essential factor in the emergence of the media-effects trend.** Throughout this period, empirical research methods were effectively promoted as an ideal means of measuring, describing, and ultimately explaining social phenomena. A generation of empirical social scientists working in several academic disciplines declared them to be the only "scientific" way of dealing with social phenomena. They dismissed other approaches as overly speculative, unsystematic, or too subjective.

2. **Empirical social researchers successfully branded people who advocated mass society and propaganda notions as "unscientific."** They accused mass society theory advocates of being fuzzy-minded humanists, religious fanatics, doomsayers, political ideologues, or biased against media. Also, mass society and propaganda notions lost some of their broad appeal as the threat of propaganda seemed to fade in the late 1950s and 1960s.

3. **Social researchers exploited the commercial potential of the new research methods and gained the support of private industry.** One of the first articles Lazarsfeld wrote after arriving in the United States was about the use of survey research methods as a tool for advertisers (Kornhauser and Lazarsfeld, 1935). Researchers promoted surveys and experiments as a means of probing media audiences and interpreting consumer attitudes and behaviors. Lazarsfeld coined the term **administrative research** to refer to these applications. He persuasively argued for the use of empirical research to guide administrative decision-making.

administrative research
Research that examines audiences to interpret consumer attitudes and behaviors; the use of empirical research to guide practical administrative decisions

4. **The development of empirical social research was strongly backed by various private and government foundations, most notably the Rockefeller Foundation and the National Science Foundation.** This support was crucial, particularly in the early stages, because large-scale empirical research required much more funding than previous forms of social research had required. Without support from the Rockefeller Foundation, Lazarsfeld might never have come to the United States or have been able to develop and demonstrate the validity of his approach. Government funding during World War II was critical to Hovland's research. Without the government funding provided during the Cold War, large mass communication research centers might never have been established at major universities.

5. **As empirical research demonstrated its usefulness, media companies began to sponsor and eventually conduct their own empirical research on media.** In time, both CBS and NBC formed their own social research departments and employed many outside researchers as consultants. Two of the most influential early media

researchers were Frank Stanton and Joseph Klapper—the former collaborated with Lazarsfeld on numerous research projects in the 1940s, and the latter was Lazarsfeld's student. Both Stanton and Klapper rose to become executives at CBS. As media corporations grew larger and earned sizable profits, they could afford to fund empirical research—especially when that research helped to justify the status quo and block moves to regulate their operations. Media funding and support were vital to the development of commercial audience ratings services such as Nielsen and Arbitron. These companies pioneered the use of survey research methods to measure the size of audiences and guide administrative decision-making in areas such as advertising and marketing. Media support was also crucial to the growth of various national polling services, such as Gallup, Harris, and Roper. Media coverage of polls and ratings data helped establish their credibility in the face of widespread commonsense criticism.

6. **Empirical social researchers successfully established their approach within the various social research disciplines—political science, history, social psychology, sociology, and economics.** These disciplines, in turn, shaped the development of communication research. During the 1960s and 1970s, several communication areas—for example, advertising and journalism—rapidly expanded to meet growing student interest in studying communication and preparing for careers in related industries. As these areas developed, empirical social researchers from the more established social sciences provided leadership. Social science theories and research methods borrowed from the more established disciplines assumed an important—often-dominant—role in structuring research conducted in university journalism, advertising, speech communication, and broadcasting departments. Empirical research became widely accepted as the most scientific way to study communication, even though this research rarely found conclusive evidence of media influence.

FROM PROPAGANDA RESEARCH TO ATTITUDE-CHANGE THEORIES

Although persuasion and attitude change have been speculated about almost since the beginning of recorded history, systematic study of these phenomena began only in the twentieth century, and World War II provided the "laboratory" for the development of a cohesive body of thought on attitude change and, by obvious extension, media and attitude change. As we saw in Chapter 2, the United States entered that conflict convinced it was as much a propaganda battle as it was a shooting war. The Nazis had demonstrated the power of the Big Lie. America needed to be able to mount an effective counteroffensive. Before the United States could confront the Japanese and the Germans on the battlefield, however, it had to change people's opinions on the home front. During the 1930s, there were powerful isolationist and pacifist sentiments in the country. These movements were so strong that in the election of 1940, Roosevelt promised to keep the United States out of the war, even though the Nazis were quickly conquering much of Western Europe. Aid to Britain was handled secretly. Until the bombing of Pearl Harbor, American and Japanese diplomats were engaged in peace negotiations.

Thus the war provided three important motivations for people interested in what would come to be known as attitude-change research. First, the success of the Nazi propaganda efforts in Europe challenged the democratic and very American notion of the people's wisdom. It seemed quite likely that powerful bad ideas could overwhelm inadequately defended good ideas. Strategies were needed to counter Nazi propaganda and defend American values. A second war-provided research motivation was actually more imperative. Large numbers of men and women from all parts of the country and from all sorts of backgrounds had been rapidly recruited, trained, and tossed together in the armed forces. The military needed to determine what these soldiers were thinking and to find a way to intellectually and emotionally bind them—Yankee and Southerner, Easterner and Westerner, city boy and country girl—to the cause.

The third motivation was simple convenience: Whereas the military saw soldiers in training, psychologists saw research subjects—well-tracked research subjects. The availability of many people about whom large amounts of background information had already been collected proved significant because it helped define the research direction of what we now call attitude-change theory.

CARL HOVLAND AND THE EXPERIMENTAL SECTION

The army's Information and Education Division had a research branch. Inside the research branch was the Experimental Section, headed by psychologist Hovland. Its primary mission "was to make experimental evaluations of the effectiveness of various programs of the Information and Education Division" (Hovland, Lumsdaine, and Sheffield, 1949, p. v). At first, the Experimental Section focused on documentary films and the war department's orientation movie series, *Why We Fight*, produced by Hollywood director Frank Capra. But because of the military's increasing use of media, the Experimental Section also studied "other media ... quite diverse in character" (p. vi). As the researchers themselves wrote, "The diversity of topics covered by the research of the Experimental Section made it unfeasible to publish a single cohesive account of all the studies. However, it did appear possible to integrate the group of studies on the effects of motion pictures, film strips, and radio programs into a systematic treatment concerning the effectiveness of mass communication media" (p. vii). The researchers called their account *Experiments in Mass Communication*, and it bore the mark of group leader Hovland.

controlled variation
Systematic isolation and manipulation of elements in an experiment

With his background in behaviorism and learning theory, Hovland's strength was in identifying elements in media content that might influence attitudes and devising straightforward experiments employing **controlled variation** to assess the strength of these elements. Hovland took some piece of stimulus material (a film, for example) and systematically isolated and varied its potentially important elements independently and in combination to assess their effects.

To meet the military's immediate needs, the Experimental Section began with evaluation research, simply testing whether the *Why We Fight* film series met its indoctrination goals. Prevailing notions about the power of propaganda implied that the researchers would find dramatic shifts in attitude as a result of viewing the films. According to mass society or propaganda theory, every soldier, no matter what his or her background or personality, should have been easily manipulated by the messages in the films. Military training should have induced an ideal form of mass society experience. Individual soldiers were torn from their families, jobs, and social groups. They were isolated individuals, supposedly highly vulnerable to propaganda.

Nevertheless, Hovland's group found that the military's propaganda wasn't as powerful as had been assumed. The researchers discovered that although the movies were successful in increasing knowledge about the subjects in the films, they were not highly effective in influencing attitudes and motivations (their primary function). Even the most effective films primarily strengthened (reinforced) existing attitudes. Conversions were rare. Typically, only the attitudes specifically targeted by the films showed any change. More global attitudes, such as optimism or pessimism about the war, were resistant to change.

The fact that the films produced little attitude change and that what change did occur was influenced by people's individual differences directly contradicted mass society theory and its assumption that media could radically change even strongly held beliefs and attitudes. If isolated soldiers being hurriedly prepared for battle were resistant to the most sophisticated propaganda available, were average people likely to be more susceptible? These empirical facts contradicted the prevailing theoretical notions and implied that it would be necessary to radically revise these conceptualizations.

A second outcome of the initial evaluation work was important in determining the direction of future attitude-change theory. In examining one of the three films in the series, the 50-minute *The Battle of Britain*, Hovland and his colleagues found that, although initially more effective in imparting factual information than in changing attitudes about the British, as time passed, factual knowledge decreased but attitudes toward the British actually became more positive. Time, the researchers discovered, was a key variable in attitude change. Possibly propaganda effects were not as instantaneous as mass society theory or behaviorist notions suggested. Hovland's group formulated various explanations for these slow shifts in attitude. But with no precise way to scientifically answer the question of why the passage of time produced increased attitude change in the direction of the original media stimulus, Hovland and his research team developed a new type of research design—controlled variation experiments—"to obtain findings having a greater degree of generalizability. The method used is that of systematically varying certain specified factors while other factors are controlled. This makes it possible to determine the effectiveness of the particular factors varied" (Hovland, Lumsdaine, and Sheffield, 1949, p. 179).

One of the most important variables the researchers examined was the presentation of one or two sides of a persuasive argument. Using two versions of a radio program, they presented a one-sided argument (that the war would be a long one) and a two-sided argument (the war would be long, but the alternative view that the war would be short was also addressed). Of course, those who heard either version showed more attitude change than those who had heard no broadcast, but there was no difference in attitude change between the groups who had listened to the two versions. Hovland had anticipated this. Accordingly, he had assessed the participants' initial points of view, and here he did find attitude change. What he demonstrated was that one-sided messages were more effective with people already in favor of the message; two-sided presentations were more effective with those holding divergent perspectives. In addition, Hovland looked at educational level and discovered that the two-sided presentation was more effective with those people who had more schooling.

Thus, this group of psychologists determined that attitude change was a very complex phenomenon and that attributes of the messages themselves can and often did interact with attributes of the people receiving them. An enormous number of significant research questions suddenly could be posed. What happens, for example, when two-sided presentations are directed toward people who are initially predisposed against a position but have low levels of education? Such questions fueled several decades of persuasion research and challenged two generations of researchers.

DO MASS MEDIA INFLUENCE THE WAY PEOPLE VOTE?

inductive

An approach to theory construction that sees research beginning with empirical observation rather than speculation

Lazarsfeld was not a theorist, yet by promoting empirical research, he did more than any of his peers to transform social theory generally and media theory specifically. Lazarsfeld believed theory must be strongly grounded in empirical facts. He was concerned that macroscopic social theories, including the various mass society and propaganda theories, were too speculative. He preferred a highly **inductive** approach to theory construction—that is, research should begin with empirical observation of important phenomena, not with armchair speculation. After the facts are gathered, they are sifted, and the most important pieces of information are selected. This information is used to construct empirical generalizations—assertions about the relationships between variables. Then researchers can gather more data to see whether these generalizations are valid.

This research approach is cautious and inherently conservative. It avoids sweeping generalizations that go beyond empirical observations and demands that theory construction be "disciplined" by data collection and analysis (observation leads to research ... and more research ... and more research leads to theory development). Theory, therefore, is never too far removed from the data on which it is based. The research process proceeds slowly—building step-by-step on one data-collection effort after another. You'll recognize this from Chapter 1 as the epistemology of postpositivism. Eventually, researchers will find and test a large number of empirical generalizations. These generalizations are "added up" and used to

middle-range theory

A theory composed of empirical generalizations based on empirical fact

build what Robert Merton (1967) referred to as **middle-range theory** (discussed in more detail later in this chapter). Unlike earlier forms of grand social theory—mass society theory or the propaganda theories, for example—middle-range theory comprises empirical generalizations that are solidly based on empirical facts. At the time, most social researchers thought that this was how theories were developed in the physical sciences. By emulating physical scientists, social scientists hoped they would be just as successful in controlling the phenomena that interested them. If so, the scientific methods that produced nuclear bombs might also eliminate poverty, war, and racism.

During the presidential election campaign of 1940, pitting incumbent Franklin Delano Roosevelt against Republican Wendell Willkie, Lazarsfeld had his first major opportunity to test the validity of his approach. He designed and carried out what was, at the time, the most elaborate mass communication field experiment ever conducted. Lazarsfeld assembled a large research team in May 1940 and sent it to Erie County, Ohio—a relatively remote region surrounding and including the town of Sandusky, west of Cleveland along the shores of Lake Erie. The total population of the county was 43,000, and it was chosen because it was considered to be an average American locality. Though Sandusky residents tended to vote Democratic, the surrounding rural area was strongly Republican. By the time the research team left in November, members had personally interviewed more than 3,000 people in their homes. Six hundred were selected to be in a panel that was interviewed seven times—once every month from May until November. The researchers estimated that an interviewer visited one out of every three of the county's households (Lazarsfeld, Berelson, and Gaudet, 1944).

In his data analysis, Lazarsfeld focused attention on changes in voting decisions. As people were interviewed each month, their choice of candidates was compared with the previous month's choice. During the six months, several types of changes were possible. Lazarsfeld created a label for each. *Early deciders* chose a candidate in May and never changed during the entire campaign. *Waverers* chose one candidate, then were undecided or switched to another candidate, but in the end they voted for their first choice. *Converts* chose one candidate but then voted for his opponent—they had been converted from one political ideology to another. *Crystallizers* had not chosen a candidate in May but made a choice by November. Their choice was predictable, based on their political party affiliation, their social status, and whether they lived on a farm or in the city. Lazarsfeld reasoned that for these people, mass media simply served as a means of helping them sort out a choice that was to some extent predetermined by their social situation.

Lazarsfeld used a very long and detailed questionnaire dealing extensively with exposure to specific mass media content, such as candidate speeches on radio. If propaganda was as powerful as propaganda theories predicted, his research should have allowed him to pinpoint media influence. If these notions were valid, he reasoned that he should have found that most voters were either converts or waverers. He should have observed people switching back and forth between candidates as they consumed the candidates' latest media messages. Those who showed the most change should have been the heaviest users of media.

But Lazarsfeld's results directly contradicted the outcome that propaganda theory might have predicted. Fifty-three percent of the voters were early deciders. They chose one candidate in May and never changed. Twenty-eight percent were crystallizers—they eventually made a choice consistent with their position in society and stayed with it. Fifteen percent were waverers, and only 8 percent were converts. Lazarsfeld could find little evidence that media played an important role in influencing the crystallizers, the waverers, or the converts. Media use by those in the latter two categories was lower than average, and very few of them reported being specifically influenced by media messages. Instead, these voters were much more likely to say that they had been influenced by other people. Many were politically apathetic. They failed to make clear-cut voting decisions because they had such low interest. Often they decided to vote as the people closest to them voted—not as radio speeches or newspaper editorials told them to vote.

Lazarsfeld concluded that the most important influence of mass media was to reinforce a vote choice that had already been made. Media simply gave people more reasons for choosing a candidate whom they (and the people around them) already favored. For some voters—the crystallizers, for example—media helped activate existing party loyalties and reminded them how people like themselves were going to vote. Republicans who had never heard of Willkie were able to at least learn his name and a few reasons why he would make a good president. On the other hand, Lazarsfeld found very little evidence that media converted people. Instead, the converts were often people with divided loyalties; as Lazarsfeld described this situation, they were "cross-pressured." They had group ties or social status that pulled them in opposing directions. Willkie was Catholic, so religion pulled some people toward him and pushed others away. Most Republican voters were rural Protestants; to vote for Willkie, they had to ignore his religion. The same was true of urban Catholic Democrats; they had to ignore religion to vote for Roosevelt who was Protestant.

By 1945, Lazarsfeld seemed quite convinced that media were unimportant during election campaigns. In a coauthored article summarizing his views on the prediction of political behavior in U.S. elections, he makes no reference to any form of mass communication (Lazarsfeld and Franzen, 1945). Changes in vote decisions are attributed to social and psychological variables, not exposure to media. But if media weren't directly influencing voting decisions, what was their role? As Lazarsfeld worked with his data, he began to formulate an empirical generalization that ultimately had enormous importance for media theory. He noticed that some of the hard-core early deciders were also the heaviest users of media. They even made a point of seeking out and listening to opposition speeches. On the other hand, the people who made the least use of media were most likely to report that they relied on others for help in making a voting decision. Lazarsfeld reasoned that the "heavy user/early deciders" might be the same people whose advice was being sought by more apathetic voters. These "heavy user/early deciders" might be sophisticated media users who held well-developed political views and used media wisely and critically. They might be capable of listening to and evaluating opposition speeches. Rather than be converted themselves, they might actually gain information that would help them advise others so that they would be more resistant to conversion. Thus, these heavy users might act as **gatekeepers**—screening information and only passing on items that would help others share their views. Lazarsfeld chose the term **opinion leaders** to refer to these individuals. He labeled those who turned to opinion leaders for advice as **opinion followers**. Later in this chapter we will look at the research he designed to follow-up on this insight and provide a clear confirmation of it.

gatekeepers
In two-step flow, people who screen media messages and pass on those messages and help others share their views

opinion leaders
In two-step flow, those who pass on information to opinion followers

opinion followers
In two-step flow, those who receive information from opinion leaders

THE COMMUNICATION RESEARCH PROGRAM

The concept of attitude change was so complex that Hovland proposed and conducted a systematic program of research that occupied him and his colleagues in the postwar years. He established the Communication Research Program at Yale University, which was funded by the Rockefeller Foundation. Its work centered on many of the variables Hovland considered central to attitude change. He and his colleagues systematically explored the power of both communicator and message attributes to cause changes in attitudes, and they examined how audience attributes mediated these effects (made effects more or less likely).

This work produced scores of scientific articles and a number of significant books on attitude and attitude change, but the most seminal was the 1953 *Communication and Persuasion*. Although a close reading of the original work is the best way to grasp the full extent of its findings, a general overview of this important research offers some indication of the complexity of persuasion and attitude change.

Examining the communicator, Hovland and his group studied the power of source credibility, which they divided into trustworthiness and expertness. As you might expect, they found that high-credibility communicators produced increased amounts of attitude change; low-credibility communicators produced less attitude change.

Looking at the content of the communication, Hovland and his group examined two general aspects of content: the nature of the appeal itself and its organization. Focusing specifically on fear-arousing appeals, the Yale group tested the logical assumption that stronger, fear-arousing presentations will lead to greater attitude change. This relationship was found to be true to some extent, but variables such as the vividness of the threat's description and the audience's state of alarm, evaluation of the communicator, and already-held knowledge about the subject either mitigated or heightened attitude change.

The Hovland group's look at the organization of the arguments was a bit more straightforward. Should a communicator explicitly state an argument's conclusions or leave them implicit? In general, the explicit statement of the argument's conclusion is more effective, but not invariably. The trustworthiness of the communicator, the intelligence level of the audience, the nature of the issue at hand and its importance to the audience, and the initial level of agreement between audience and communicator all altered the persuasive power of a message.

Regardless of how well a persuasive message is crafted, not all people are influenced by it to the same degree, so the Yale group assessed how audience attributes could mediate effects. Inquiry centered on the personal importance of the audience's group memberships and individual personality differences among people that might increase or reduce their susceptibility to persuasion.

Testing the power of what they called "counternorm communications," Hovland and his cohorts demonstrated that the more highly people value their membership in a group, the more closely their attitudes will conform to those of the group and, therefore, the more resistant they will be to changes in those attitudes. If you attend a Big Ten university and closely follow your school's sports teams, it isn't very likely that anyone will be able to persuade you that the Atlantic Coast Conference fields superior athletes. If you attend that same Big Ten university but care little about its sports programs, you might be a more likely target for opinion change, particularly if your team loses to an Atlantic Coast Conference team in a dramatic fashion.

The question of individual differences in susceptibility to persuasion is not about a person's willingness to be persuaded on a given issue. In persuasion research, *individual differences* refers to those personality attributes or factors that render someone generally susceptible to influence. Intelligence is a good example. It is easy to assume that those who are more intelligent would be less susceptible to persuasive arguments, but this isn't the case. These people are more likely to be persuaded if the message they receive is from a credible source and based on solid logical arguments. Self-esteem, aggressiveness, and social withdrawal were several of the other individual characteristics the Yale group tested. But, as with intelligence, each failed to produce the straightforward, unambiguous relationship that might have seemed warranted based on commonsense expectations. Why? None of a person's personality characteristics operates apart from his or her evaluation of the communicator, judgments of the message, or understanding of the social reward or punishment that might accompany acceptance or rejection of a given attitude. As we'll see, these research findings and the perspective on attitude change they fostered were to color our understanding of media theory and effects for decades.

THE MEDIA-EFFECTS TREND BECOMES DOMINANT

From the 1950s to the 1990s, persuasion research provided a predominant framework for conducting inquiry on media. Even after this dominance ended, researchers continued to use its model for effects experiments. Persuasion research represented an important shift away from concerns about the role of propaganda in society and toward a focus on what happens when people are exposed to a broad range of media content. Similarly, survey research on media focused on the consequences of exposure to various forms of media content from violent cartoons to political advertising. Following the models provided by the early persuasion studies as well as those of Lazarsfeld's group, empirical media research focused heavily on the study of media effects, and so the media-effects trend had become the dominant force in media research. Melvin DeFleur (1970, p. 118) wrote: "The all-consuming question that has dominated research and the development of contemporary theory in the study of the mass media can be summed up in simple terms—namely, 'what has been their effect?' That is, how have the media influenced us as individuals in terms of persuading us?"

The study of media effects was obviously a worthwhile focus for research, but should it have been the dominant focus? In their pursuit of insights into media-effects processes, researchers were turning their attention away from larger questions about the role of media in society. They were focused on administrative rather than critical issues. Some researchers defended this emphasis on effects by arguing that larger questions about the role of media can't be answered by empirical research. Others maintained that they could address these larger questions only after they had a thorough understanding of the basic processes underlying media effects. The pursuit of this understanding has occupied many mass communication researchers over the past 80 years. Effects research articles still fill the pages of most of the major academic journals devoted to mass communication research. The rise of new forms of media has sparked a new round of research to see if these media have effects that are different from legacy media. Improvements in experimental and survey methods along with powerful new data analysis methods have produced many new insights into media effects. These insights are detailed in Chapters 8, 9, and 10.

Although the individual findings of effects research were enormously varied and even contradictory, two interrelated sets of empirical generalizations emerged from the early research: (1) The influence of mass media is rarely direct, because it is almost always mediated by *individual differences*; and (2) the influence of mass media is rarely direct, because it is almost always mediated by *group membership or relationships*. These sets of generalizations emerged out of both survey and experimental research. They identify two factors that normally can serve as effective barriers to media influence, but they can also increase the likelihood of influence. Both sets of generalizations are consistent with the limited-effects perspective and thus serve to buttress it. Study after study confirmed their existence and expanded our understanding of how they operate. Over time, these sets of generalizations allowed construction of a body of middle-range theory that is widely referred to as the **limited- or minimal-effects theory** because of its assumption that the media have minimal or limited effects as those effects are mitigated by a variety of mediating or intervening variables. This body of theory includes the following specific theories as well as the other theories described in this chapter:

1. **Individual differences** theory argues that because people vary greatly in their psychological makeup and because they have different perceptions of things, media influence differs from person to person. More specifically, "media messages contain particular stimulus attributes that have differential interaction with personality characteristics of members of the audience" (DeFleur, 1970, p. 122).
2. **Social categories** theory "assumes that there are broad collectives, aggregates, or social categories in urban-industrial societies whose behavior in the face of a given set of stimuli is more or less uniform" (DeFleur, 1970, pp. 122–123). In addition, people with similar backgrounds (e.g., age, gender, income level, religious affiliation) will have similar patterns of media exposure and similar reactions to that exposure.

THE SELECTIVE PROCESSES

One central tenet of attitude-change theory that was adopted (in one way or another or under one name or another) by most mass communication theorists is the idea of **cognitive consistency**. We noted earlier that Lazarsfeld found that people seemed to seek out media messages consistent with the values and beliefs of those around them. This finding implied that people tried to preserve their existing views by avoiding messages that challenged them. As persuasion research proceeded, researchers sought more direct evidence. Cognitive consistency is "a tendency (on the part of individuals) to maintain, or to return to, a state of cognitive balance, and ... this tendency toward equilibrium determines ... the kind of persuasive communication to which the individual may be receptive" (Rosnow and Robinson, 1967, p. 299). These same authors wrote: "Although the consistency hypothesis is fundamental in numerous theoretical formulations, ... of all the consistency-type formulations, it is Leon Festinger's theory of **cognitive dissonance** which has been the object of greatest interest and controversy" (1967, pp. 299–300).

Festinger explained that the bedrock premise of dissonance theory is that information that is not consistent with a person's already-held values and beliefs will create a psychological discomfort (dissonance) that must be relieved; people generally work to keep their knowledge of themselves and their knowledge of the world

Margin glossary

limited- or minimal-effects theory
The theory that media have minimal or limited effects because those effects are mitigated by a variety of mediating or intervening variables

individual differences
Individuals' different psychological makeups that cause media influence to vary from person to person

social categories
The idea that members of given groups or aggregates will respond to media stimuli in more or less uniform ways

cognitive consistency
The idea that people consciously and unconsciously work to preserve their existing views

cognitive dissonance
Information that is inconsistent with a person's already-held attitudes creates psychological discomfort, or dissonance

somewhat consistent (Festinger, 1957). Later, and more specifically, Festinger wrote, "If a person knows various things that are not psychologically consistent with one another, he will, in a variety of ways, try to make them more consistent" (1962, p. 93). Collectively, these "ways" have become known as the **selective processes**. Some psychologists consider these to be defense mechanisms we routinely use to protect ourselves (and our egos) from information that would threaten us. Others argue that they are merely routinized procedures for coping with the enormous quantity of sensory information constantly bombarding us. Either way, the selective processes function as complex and highly sophisticated filtering mechanisms screening out useless sensory data while quickly identifying and highlighting the most useful patterns in this data.

selective processes
Exposure (attention), retention, and perception; psychological processes designed to reduce dissonance

Attitude-change researchers studied three forms of selectivity: (1) exposure, (2) retention, and (3) perception. Keep in mind that these notions have since been widely criticized and should be interpreted very carefully. We will point out some of the major limitations as we discuss each. It's important to note that many contemporary media researchers think that the emergence of new forms of polarized political content in traditional media and on the Internet have given renewed importance to the study of selectivity. There will be more to say about this in later chapters.

selective exposure
The idea that people tend to expose themselves to messages that are consistent with their preexisting attitudes and beliefs

Selective exposure is people's tendency to attend to (become exposed to) media messages they feel are in accord with their already-held attitudes and interests and the parallel tendency to avoid those that might create dissonance. Democrats will watch their party's national convention on television but go bowling when the GOP gala is aired. Paul Lazarsfeld, Bernard Berelson, and Hazel Gaudet, in their Erie County voter study, discovered that "about two-thirds of the constant partisans (Republicans and Democrats) managed to see and hear more of their own side's propaganda than the opposition's.... But—and this is important—the more strongly partisan the person, the more likely he is to insulate himself from contrary points of view" (1944, p. 89).

In retrospect, we now realize that during the 1940s people commonly had media-use patterns strongly linked to their social status and group affiliation. Newspapers had definite party connections. Most were Republican. Thus, Republicans read newspapers with a strongly Republican bias, and Democrats either read Democratic newspapers or learned how to systematically screen out pro-Republican content. Radio stations tried to avoid most forms of political content but occasionally carried major political speeches. These weren't hard to avoid if you knew you didn't like the politics of the speaker. Labor unions were very influential during this era and structured the way their members used media.

selective retention
The idea that people tend to remember best and longest those messages that are most meaningful to them

Selective retention is the process by which people tend to remember best and longest information consistent with their preexisting attitudes and interests. Name all the classes in which you've earned the grade of A. Name all the classes in which you've earned a C. The As have it, no doubt. But often you remember disturbing or threatening information. Name the last class you almost failed. Have you managed to forget it and the instructor, or are they etched among the things you wish you could forget? If selective retention always operated to protect us from what we don't want to remember, we would never have any difficulty forgetting our problems. Although some people seem able to do this with ease, others tend to dwell on disturbing information. Contemporary thinking on selective retention ties that retention to the level of importance the recalled phenomenon holds for individuals.

**selective
perception**

The idea that people
will alter the mean-
ing of messages so
they become con-
sistent with preex-
isting attitudes and
beliefs

Keeping in mind that these processes are not discrete (you cannot retain that to which you have not been exposed), **selective perception** is the mental or psychological recasting of a message so that its meaning is in line with a person's beliefs and attitudes. Gordon Allport and Leo Postman's now-classic 1945 study of rumor is among the first and best examples of selective perception research. The two psychologists showed a picture of a fight aboard a train to different groups of people (Figure 4.1). The combatants were a Caucasian male grasping a razor and an unarmed African American male. Those who saw the scene were then asked to describe it to another person, who in turn passed it on. In 1945 America, people of all races and ages who recounted the story of the picture inevitably became confused, saying the blade was in the hands of the black man, not the white man. Allport and Postman concluded, "What was outer becomes inner; what was objective becomes subjective" (1945, p. 81).

The attitude researchers who documented the operation of selective processes were good scientists. But their findings were based on people's use of a very different set of media and very different forms of media content than we know today. In the 1940s and 1950s, movies were primarily an entertainment medium; radio disseminated significant amounts of news, but typically as brief, highly descriptive reports that expressed no partisan opinion; newspapers were the dominant news medium; and television did not exist. Television moved all the media away from dissemination of information toward the presentation of images and symbols. Many contemporary movies sacrifice story line and character development for exciting and interesting visuals; your favorite radio station probably presents

Allport/Postman The Basic Psychology of Rumor, 1945

FIGURE 4.1 Allport and Postman's Stimulus Drawing

minimal news, if any; and newspaper stories are getting shorter and shorter, the graphics more colorful and interesting, and more than a few papers across the country regularly present pictures snapped from a television screen or the Internet in their pages. It's not surprising that we process information very differently today than our grandparents did in the 1940s. But are we being selective when we use media today? We'll look at this in detail in later chapters.

Let's transport the valuable Allport and Postman experiment to our times to explain why the selective processes categorized by the attitude researchers and quickly appropriated by mass communication theorists might be less useful now in understanding media influence than they were in Allport and Postman's time.

If a speaker were to appear on television and present the argument, complete with charts and "facts," that a particular ethnic group or race of people was inherently dangerous, prone to violent crime, and otherwise inferior to most other folks, the selective processes should theoretically kick in. Sure, some racists would tune in and love the show. But most people would not watch. Those who might happen to catch it would no doubt selectively perceive the speaker as stupid, sick, beneath contempt. Three weeks later, this individual would be a vague, if not nonexistent, memory.

But what if television news—because covering violent crime is easier, less expensive, and less threatening to the continued flow of advertising dollars than covering white-collar crime, and because violent crime, especially that committed downtown near the studio, provides better pictures than a scandal in the banking industry—were to present inner-city violence to the exclusion of most other crime? What if entertainment programmers, because of time, format, and other pressures (Gerbner, 1990), continually portrayed their villains as, say, dark, mysterious, different? Do the selective processes still kick in? When the ubiquitous mass media that we routinely rely on repeatedly provide homogeneous and biased messages, where will we get the dissonant information that activates our defenses and enables us to hold onto views that are inconsistent with what we are being told? Does this situation exist in the United States today? Do most mainstream media routinely provide inherently biased messages? We will return to these and similar questions in later chapters.

INSTANT ACCESS

Attitude-Change Theory

Strengths

1. Pays deep attention to process in which messages can and can't have effects
2. Provides insight into influence of individual differences and group affiliations in shaping media influence
3. Attention to selective processes helps clarify how individuals process information

Weaknesses

1. Experimental manipulation of variables overestimates their power and underestimates media's
2. Focuses on information in media messages, not on more contemporary symbolic media
3. Uses attitude change as only measure of effects, ignoring reinforcement and more subtle forms of media influence

Today, nearly 70 years after the Allport and Postman study, would the knife still find its way from the white man's hand into the black man's? Have the civil rights movement and the scores of television shows and movies offering realistic, rich, and varied representations of African Americans made a difference? Or does routine news coverage of violent crime continue to fuel our apprehensions and therefore our biases? Later chapters that deal with theories that view mass communication as more symbolically, rather than informationally, powerful will address these questions. But for now, you can explore the issue with the help from the box entitled "Drug Users: Allport and Postman Revisited."

THINKING ABOUT THEORY | **Drug Users: Allport and Postman Revisited**

What do Charles Stuart, Susan Smith, Bonnie Sweeten, Ashley Todd, and Robert Ralston have in common? All had committed crimes and then blamed them on young, black males. All were successful for a while in their deceit. Stuart shot his pregnant wife, supposedly during a carjacking. Smith drowned her two infant children; she told police they were in her stolen car. Sweeten embezzled money from her employer and claimed she had been abducted as her get-away. During the 2008 Presidential election, Todd, a John McCain supporter, scarred her own face, claiming she was assaulted and disfigured by a 6-foot 4-inch tall black Barak Obama supporter. Ralston, a Philadelphia policeman, shot himself on purpose, possibly to get a transfer, but said the shooter had dark, braided hair and a face tattoo.

Of course, what these five inept criminals were counting on was our culture's inclination to "put the razor" in the black man's hands—that is, to attribute violence and crime to African Americans, just as Allport and Postman had demonstrated more than half a century before. But there is other, real-world evidence that what the two psychologists discovered long ago has yet to disappear. Our country's uneven record of arresting and incarcerating users of illegal drugs exemplifies the operation of selective perception.

Test yourself by answering this question. Among white, black, and Hispanic youth, which group has the highest incidence of severe drug problems? The introduction to this essay may have clued you to choose a lower percentage, but are you surprised to know that 9 percent of white teens have serious drug problems, compared to 7.7 percent of Hispanic and 5 percent of African American teens (Szalavitz, 2011)? Are you surprised to learn that blacks are

much more likely than whites to be stopped by police, arrested, prosecuted, convicted, and incarcerated (Tonry, 2011), or that the cars of African Americans are twice as likely to be searched during routine traffic stops as are those of white drivers (Briggs, 2012)?

Despite the fact that marijuana is used at comparable rates by Caucasians and African Americans, African Americans are 3.5 times as likely to be arrested for possession as are Caucasians; in some U.S. counties the disparity is as high as 30 to 1 (American Civil Liberties Union, 2013). African Americans represent only 13 percent of the country's illegal drug users, but they represent 37 percent of all drug-related arrests and 53 percent of all convictions for illegal drug use (Human Rights Watch, 2009). If our justice system were truly color-blind—if the razor remained in the hand of its wielder—African Americans would represent 13 percent of all drug arrests and 13 percent of all drug-related convictions.

But how can this be? Do police, prosecutors, judges, and juries selectively perceive drugs (the razor) as a "black" problem? *Chicago Tribune* columnist Salim Muwakkil cited research from the Justice Policy Group that "found that media coverage of crime exaggerates its scope and unduly connects it to youth and race.... A disproportionate number of perpetrators on the news are people of color, especially African-Americans, [so much so] that the term 'young black males' was synonymous with the word 'criminal' " (2001).

Would Allport and Postman be surprised that the "reality" of illegal drug use that many Americans perceive is so out of tune with objective reality? Are you? Would they predict that drugs, like the razor, would pass from the white hands to the black? Would you?

INFORMATION-FLOW THEORY

During the 1950s, social scientists conducted many surveys and field experiments to assess the flow of information from media to mass audiences. Among them were studies of how quickly people found out about individual news stories (Funkhouser and McCombs, 1971). The overall objective of this work was to measure the effectiveness of media in transmitting information to mass audiences. The research was patterned after persuasion research, but instead of measuring shifts in attitudes, it investigated if information was learned. Survey research rather than controlled experiments was used to gather data. This work drew on methods pioneered by both Lazarsfeld and Hovland. It was based on the empirical generalizations growing out of their work, and it yielded similar empirical generalizations.

Information-flow research addressed questions researchers thought to be quite important. Many believed that if our democracy was to survive the challenges of the Cold War, it was critical that Americans be well informed about a variety of issues. For example, Americans needed to know what to do in the event of a nuclear attack. They also needed to know what their leaders were doing to deal with threats from abroad. Classic theories of democracy assume that people must be well informed so they can make good political decisions. As such, the effective flow of information from elites to the public was essential if the United States was to counter the Communist threat.

Persuasion research had identified numerous barriers to persuasion. News-flow research focused on determining whether similar barriers impeded the flow of information from media to typical audience members. It gathered generalizations derived from laboratory-based attitude-change research and assessed their usefulness in understanding real-world situations and problems. Some of the barriers investigated included level of education, amount of media use for news, interest in news, and talking about news with others. The researchers differentiated between "hard" and "soft" news. Hard news typically included news about politics, science, world events, and community organizations. Soft news included sports coverage, gossip about popular entertainers, and human-interest stories about average people.

News-flow research found that most U.S. citizens learned very little about hard news because they were poorly educated, made little use of media for hard news, had low interest in it, and didn't talk to other people about it (Davis, 1990). Except for major news events such as President Eisenhower's heart attack or the assassination of President John F. Kennedy, most people didn't know or care much about national news events. Soft news generally was more likely to be learned than hard news, but even the flow of soft news was not what might have been hoped. The most important factor accelerating or reinforcing the flow of news was the degree to which people talked about individual news items with others. News of the Kennedy assassination reached most people very rapidly because people interrupted their daily routine to tell others about it (Greenberg and Parker, 1965). Without talk, learning about most hard news events rarely reached more than 10 to 20 percent of the population and was forgotten by those people within a few days or weeks.

Studies of the flow of civil defense information identified similar barriers. In most cases, members of the public were even less interested in mundane civil defense information than they were in politics. In a series of field experiments

(DeFleur and Larsen, 1958), researchers dropped hundreds of thousands of leaflets on small, isolated towns in the state of Washington. They signaled their view of the importance of their research by titling it "Project Revere"—like Paul Revere, they were seeking ways to inform the nation about an impending attack. DeFleur and Larsen wanted to determine how effective leaflets would be in warning people about incoming Soviet bombers. For example, one set of leaflets announced that a civil defense test was being conducted. Every person who found a leaflet was instructed to tell someone else about it and then drop the leaflet in a mailbox.

The researchers were disappointed that relatively few folks read or returned the leaflets. Children were the most likely to take them seriously. To get the most useful effect, eight leaflets had to be dropped for every resident in town. Speculating that people were ignoring the leaflets because they only warned of a hypothetical attack, and threatening people with a real attack was considered unethical, the researchers designed another field experiment in which people were supposed to tell their neighbors about a slogan for a new brand of coffee. Survey teams visited homes in a small town and told people that they could earn a free pound of coffee by teaching their neighbors the coffee slogan. The survey team promised to return the following week, and if it found that neighbors knew the slogan, then both families would receive free coffee. The experiment produced mixed results. On the one hand, almost every neighboring family had heard about the coffee slogan and tried to reproduce it. Unfortunately, many gave the wrong slogan. The research confirmed the importance of motivating people to pass on information, but it suggested that even a free gift was insufficient to guarantee the accurate flow of information. If word of mouth was crucial to the flow of information, the possibility of distortion and misunderstanding was high. Even if media deliver accurate information, the news that reaches most people might be wrong.

The most important limitation of this **information-flow theory** is that it is a simplistic, linear, **source-dominated theory**. Information originates with authoritative or elite sources (the established media or the government, for example) and then flows outward to "ignorant" individuals. It assumes that barriers to the flow of information can be identified and overcome, but little effort is typically made to consider whether the information has any value or use for average audience

information-flow theory
Theory of how information moves from media to audiences to have specific intended effects (now known as information or innovation diffusion theory)

source-dominated theory
Theory that examines the communication process from the point of view of some elite message source

---

INSTANT ACCESS

Information-Flow Theory

Strengths

1. Examines process of mass communication in real world
2. Provides theoretical basis for successful public information campaigns
3. Identifies barriers to information flow
4. Helps the understanding of information flow during crises

Weaknesses

1. Is simplistic, linear, and source-dominated
2. Assumes ignorant, apathetic populace
3. Fails to consider utility or value of information for receivers
4. Is too accepting of status quo

members. Audience reactions to messages are ignored unless they form a barrier to that flow. Then those barriers must be studied only so they can be overcome. Like most limited-effects theories, information-flow theory assumes that the status quo is acceptable. Elites and authorities are justified in trying to disseminate certain forms of information, and average people will be better off if they receive and learn it. Barriers are assumed to be bad and, where possible, must be eliminated. Information-flow theory is also an example of a middle-range theory. It serves to summarize a large number of empirical generalizations into a more or less coherent explanation of when and why media information will be attended to and what sorts of learning will result.

PERSONAL INFLUENCE: THE TWO-STEP FLOW THEORY

Earlier in this chapter we noted that Lazarsfeld made some useful generalizations based on his 1940 Erie County research. In 1945, he conducted research to directly investigate these empirical generalizations concerning opinion leaders and followers. He refused to speculate about the attributes of opinion leaders or their role—he wanted empirical facts (Summers, 2006). To get these facts, he sent a research team to Decatur, Illinois, to interview more than 800 women about how they made decisions about fashion, product brands, movies, and politics. Decatur, a city in the heartland of America, was widely viewed as representative of most small- to medium-sized cities. His researchers used a "snowball" sampling technique, contacting an initial sample of women. During the interviews, they asked these women if they had influenced or been influenced by other people in their thinking about international, national, or community affairs or news events. The researchers then followed up, conducting interviews with those who had been identified as influential. In this way Lazarsfeld tried to empirically locate women who served as opinion leaders. Their nomination by themselves or others was taken as factual evidence of their opinion-leader status.

More than 10 years passed before the Decatur research was published. Lazarsfeld eventually turned to one of his graduate students, Elihu Katz, and together they used the Decatur data as the basis for their 1955 *Personal Influence*. It formally advanced the **two-step flow theory**—a middle-range theory that influenced communication research for more than two decades.

two-step flow theory

The idea that messages pass from the media, through opinion leaders, to opinion followers

Katz and Lazarsfeld provided a very positive depiction of American society and assigned a restricted and benign role to media. They reported that opinion leaders existed at all levels of society and that the flow of their influence tended to be horizontal rather than vertical. Opinion leaders influenced people like themselves rather than those above or below them in the social order. Opinion leaders differed from followers in many of their personal attributes—they were more gregarious, used media more, were more socially active—but they often shared the same social status.

Pooley (2006) argues that *Personal Influence* did more than introduce an innovative way of understanding why the power of media is limited. In its first 15 pages, *Personal Influence* offered a summary of the history of propaganda research that provided boilerplate language that would be used in media theory textbooks and literature reviews written over the next five decades. These few pages dismissed pre–World War II theory and research as naïve and overly speculative, erroneously

INSTANT ACCESS

Two-Step Flow Theory

Strengths

1. Focuses attention on the environment in which effects can and can't occur
2. Stresses importance of opinion leaders in formation of public opinion
3. Is based on inductive rather than deductive reasoning
4. Effectively challenges simplistic notions of direct effects

Weaknesses

a. Is limited to its time (1940s) and media environment (no television)
b. Uses reported behavior (voting) as only test of media effects
c. Downplays reinforcement as an important media effect
d. Uses survey methods that underestimate media impact
e. Later research demonstrates a multistep flow of influence

grounded in the myth of media power. They promoted empirical research as providing more accurate findings that encouraged useful skepticism of media's power.

JOSEPH KLAPPER'S PHENOMENISTIC THEORY

phenomenistic theory
Theory that media are rarely the sole cause of effects and are relatively powerless when compared with other social factors

reinforcement theory
More common name for phenomenistic theory, stressing the theory's view that media's most common effect is reinforcement

In 1960, Joseph Klapper finally published a manuscript originally developed in 1949 as he completed requirements for a Ph.D. at Columbia University and worked as a researcher for CBS. *The Effects of Mass Communication* was a compilation and integration of all significant media-effects findings produced through the mid-1950s and was intended for both scholars and informed members of the public. Klapper was concerned that average people exaggerated the power of media. Though informed academics (i.e., empirical researchers) had rejected mass society theory, too many people still believed that media had tremendous power. He wanted to calm their fears by showing how constrained media actually were in their ability to influence people.

Klapper introduced an excellent example of a middle-range theory of media that he called **phenomenistic theory** but has since been typically referred to as **reinforcement theory**. It states that media rarely have any direct effects and are relatively powerless when compared to other social and psychological factors such as social status, group membership, strongly held attitudes, and education. According to Klapper:

1. Mass communication ordinarily does not serve as a necessary and sufficient cause of audience effects but, rather, functions among and through a nexus of mediating factors and influences.
2. These mediating factors are such that they typically render mass communication as a contributory agent, but not the sole cause, in the process of reinforcing existing conditions (1960, p. 8).

These generalizations about media were not very original, but Klapper expressed them forcefully and cited hundreds of findings to support them. His book came to be viewed as a definitive statement on media effects—especially by postpositive researchers and those outside the media research community.

Klapper's theory is now referred to as reinforcement theory because its key assertion is that the primary influence of media is to reinforce (not change) existing attitudes and behaviors. Instead of disrupting society and creating unexpected social change, media generally serve as agents of the status quo, giving people more reasons to go on believing and acting as they already do. Klapper argued that there simply are too many barriers to media influence for dramatic change to occur except under very unusual circumstances.

Even today, some 55 years after its introduction, reinforcement theory is still raised by those unconvinced of media's power. Yet with benefit of hindsight, we can easily see its drawbacks. When published in 1960, Klapper's conclusions relied heavily on studies (from Lazarsfeld, Hovland, and their contemporaries) of a media environment that did not include the mass medium of television and the restructured newspaper, radio, and film industries that arose in response to television. Certainly Klapper's work did not envision a world of Internet, YouTube, Facebook, Twitter, and Google. Much of the research he cited examined the selective processes, but with the coming of television, media were becoming more symbolically than informationally oriented, producing potentially erroneous conclusions. In addition, the United States that existed after World War II looked little like the one that existed before. As we'll see in later chapters, Klapper's "nexus of mediating variables"—that is, church, family, and school—began to lose their powerful positions in people's socialization (and therefore in limiting media effects).

Finally, Klapper might have erred in equating reinforcement with no effects. Even if it were true that the most media can do is reinforce existing attitudes and beliefs, this is hardly the same as saying they have no effect. You'll see in Chapter 5, as you did in the Chapter 2's discussion of contemporary propaganda theory, many contemporary critical scholars see this as media's most negative influence. The box entitled "Joseph Klapper's Phenomenistic Theory" presents Klapper's own explanation of his theory and asks you to assess it in light of some recent momentous events.

INSTANT ACCESS

Phenomenistic Theory

Strengths

1. Combines impressive amount of research into a convincing theory
2. Highlights role of mediating variables in the mass communication process
3. Persuasively refutes lingering mass society and propaganda notions

Weaknesses

1. Overstates influence of mediating factors
2. Is too accepting of status quo
3. Downplays reinforcement as an important media effect
4. Is too specific to its time (pre-1960s) and media environment (no television)

THINKING ABOUT THEORY | Joseph Klapper's Phenomenistic Theory

Joseph Klapper's own summary of his reinforcement, or phenomenistic, theory makes it clear that his ideas are very much at home in the limited-effects perspective. The following is drawn directly from his landmark work, *The Effects of Mass Communication*, published in 1960 (p. 8).

Theoretical Statements

1. Mass communication ordinarily does not serve as a necessary and sufficient cause of audience effects but, rather, functions among and through a nexus of mediating factors and influences.
2. These mediating factors are such that they typically render mass communication a contributing agent, but not the sole cause, in a process of reinforcing the existing conditions.
3. On those occasions that mass communication does function to cause change, one of two conditions is likely to exist:

    a. The mediating factors will be found to be inoperative and the effect of the media will be found to be direct.
    b. The mediating factors, which normally favor reinforcement, will be found to be themselves impelling toward change.

4. There are certain residual situations in which mass communication seems to produce direct effects, or directly and of itself to serve certain psychophysical functions.
5. The efficacy of mass communication, either as a contributory agent or as an agent of direct effect, is affected by various aspects of the media and communications themselves or of the communication situation.

Your Turn

Can you find hints in Klapper's overview of his theory to the dominant thinking of its time on media effects? Can you identify his subtle explanation of why advertising seems to work, an important point to make for a fine scientist who was also chief researcher for broadcast network CBS? After reading his summary of phenomenistic theory, can you explain why it remains, even today, the clearest and most used articulation of media's limited effects? Based on point number 3 in Klapper's summary, can you develop an explanation for the power of media during times of war, for example in the Middle East? Are the factors that normally mediate the power of media "inoperative"? Or are these factors "themselves impelling toward change"? List some of the factors that normally mediate the power of media. These would include things like personal relationships with friends and family, relationships with opinion leaders, contacts with teachers and classmates, or contacts with church members or religious leaders. Klapper would likely label the power demonstrated by media during war as an anomaly—an exception to the rule that media power is constantly checked by "a nexus of mediating factors and influences." Do you agree? How would he (and you) explain the precipitous drop in support for the conflict in Iraq after broadcast and publication of the horrific images of detainee abuse at Abu Ghraib prison (Time/CNN, 2004), if not a media effect? Would you argue that media have somehow become more powerful since Klapper developed his theory in the 1940s? If so, how?

THEORIES OF THE MIDDLE RANGE AND THE FUNCTIONAL ANALYSIS APPROACH

One of the most influential social theorists of the 1940s and 1950s was Robert Merton, a sociologist who, when at Columbia University, collaborated with Paul Lazarsfeld. Merton was trained as a social theorist but was intrigued by Lazarsfeld's empirical research. Lazarsfeld rarely relied on social theory to plan his research. He used his surveys to investigate things that intrigued him, such as his fascination with opinion leaders. He looked for what he termed "natural field experiments"—situations where important decisions had to be made or social changes implemented. Elections were a logical focus for his research. His surveys generated hundreds of findings. But how should these findings be interpreted? Could they be used to construct theory? Was there a strategy that could be used to integrate findings so that the social structures underlying them might be revealed?

The questions posed by Lazarsfeld's findings were not unique. As funding and respect for empirical research grew, findings increased exponentially. In an era before computers revolutionized data analysis, results were generated in rooms filled with boxes of questionnaires and people punching numbers into tabulation machines. When results from several hundred questionnaires had to be compiled, it could take weeks to produce a set of cross-tabulation tables or to calculate a small set of correlation coefficients. And once the results were obtained, how could they be interpreted? Most empirical research wasn't based on theory. At best, researchers conceptualized attributes that could be measured using questionnaire items. Research could show that some attributes were related to other attributes, but it couldn't explain how or why these relationships existed. What was needed was a way to inductively develop theory based on these findings. Merton offered a solution.

In 1949 Merton wrote *Social Theory and Social Structure*, a book that established his reputation as a sociologist and earned him the gratitude of the first generation of empirical social scientists. He continued to develop his ideas, and eventually published *On Theoretical Sociology* (1967). For more than two decades, Merton tutored a host of thoughtful and reflective empirical researchers. He gave them a perspective from which to plan and then interpret their work. He taught them a practical way of combining induction with deduction.

Merton's solution to the dilemma posed by the rising tide of research findings was development of "theories of the middle range." Unlike grand social theories (e.g., mass society theory) that attempt to explain a broad range of social action, middle-range theories were designed to explain only limited domains or ranges of action that had been or could be explored using empirical research. These theories could be created by carefully interpreting empirical findings. According to Merton,

> Some sociologists still write as though they expect, here and now, formulation of the general sociological theory broad enough to encompass the vast ranges of precisely observed details of social behavior, organization, and change and fruitful enough to direct the attention of research workers to a flow of problems for empirical research. This I take to be a premature and apocalyptic belief. We are not ready. Not enough preparatory work has been done. (1967, p. 45)

Merton (1967, p. 68) described middle-range theory as follows:

1. Middle-range theories consist of limited sets of assumptions from which specific hypotheses are logically derived and confirmed by empirical investigation.
2. These theories do not remain separate but are consolidated into wider networks of theory.
3. These theories are sufficiently abstract to deal with differing spheres of social behavior and social structure, so that they transcend sheer description or empirical generalization.
4. This type of theory cuts across the distinction between microsociological problems.

5. The middle-range orientation involves the specification of ignorance. Rather than pretend to knowledge where it is in fact absent, this orientation expressly recognizes what must still be learned to lay the foundation for still more knowledge.

Middle-range theory provided a useful rationale for what most empirical researchers, including media scientists, were already doing. Many were determined to ignore what they considered unnecessary theoretical baggage and focus on developing and applying empirical research methods. They believed that the future of social science lay in producing and collating empirical generalizations. Following the examples set by Paul Lazarsfeld and Carl Hovland, researchers conducted endless surveys and experiments, gathering data to support or reject individual generalizations and constantly discovering new research questions requiring yet more empirical research. Merton argued that all this research work would eventually be brought together to first create an array of middle-range theories, and then to construct a comprehensive theory having the power and scope of theories in the physical sciences. Moreover, when it was finally constructed, this theory would be far superior to earlier forms of social theory that were not empirically grounded.

Thus middle-range theory provided an ideal rationale and justification for continuing small-scale, limited-effects studies. It implied that eventually all these individual-effects studies would add up, permitting the construction of a broad perspective on the role of media. Yet middle-range theory had important shortcomings that were not immediately apparent. Countless empirical generalizations were studied, but the effort to combine them into broader theories proved more difficult than had been expected. In this and later chapters we will consider numerous interesting and useful middle-range theories, but when broader theories were developed based on these middle-range notions, they had crucial limitations. The first few generations of empirical researchers had little success at integrating their empirical generalizations into broader theories. But that may be changing. During the last decade, media researchers have begun a serious effort to integrate findings into broader theories (Potter, 2009).

In *Social Theory and Social Structure* (1949), Merton proposed what he called a "paradigm for functional analysis" outlining how an inductive strategy centered on the study of social artifacts (such as the use of mass media) could eventually lead to the construction of theories that explained the "functions" of these items. Merton derived his perspective on functional analysis from carefully examining research in anthropology and sociology. Functionalism, as we've seen, assumes that a society can be usefully viewed as a "system in balance." That is, the society consists of complex sets of interrelated activities, each of which supports the others. Every form of social activity is assumed to play some part in maintaining the system as a whole. By studying the functions of various parts of such systems, a theory of the larger system might be developed. This would be a middle-range theory, because it would integrate research findings from the studies that examined the different parts of the system.

One feature of functional analysis that appealed to Merton and his followers was its apparent *value-neutrality*. Older forms of social theory had characterized various parts of society as either "good" or "evil" in some ultimate sense.

For example, mass society theory saw media as essentially disruptive and subversive, a negative force that somehow had to be brought under control. Functionalists rejected such thinking and instead argued that empirical research should investigate both the functions and dysfunctions of media. In that way a systematic appraisal could be made of media's overall impact by weighing useful outcomes of media use against negative outcomes. Functionalists argued that social science had no basis and no need for making value judgments about media. Rather, empirical investigation was necessary to determine whether specific media perform certain functions for the society. Merton also distinguished **manifest functions**—those consequences that are intended and readily observed—and **latent functions**—those unintended and less easily observed.

Functional analysis was widely adopted as a rationale for many mass communication studies during the late 1950s and 1960s. Researchers tried to determine whether specific media or forms of media content were functional or dysfunctional. They investigated manifest and latent functions of media. In his classic 1959 book, *Mass Communication: A Sociological Perspective*, Charles Wright identified what have become known as the **classic four functions of the media**. He wrote: "Harold Lasswell, a political scientist who has done pioneering research in mass communications, once noted three activities of communication specialists: (1) surveillance of the environment, (2) correlation of the parts of society in responding to the environment, and (3) transmission of the social heritage from one generation to the next" (Wright, 1959, p. 16). To these, he added a fourth: entertainment. In as much as any one of these functions could have positive or negative influence, and because each carried manifest as well as latent functions, it's clear that functional analysis could give rise to very complicated assessments of the role of media.

For example, various forms of media content can be functional or dysfunctional for society as a whole, for specific individuals, for various subgroups in the society, and for the culture. Media advertising for fast-food chains might be functional for their corporations and stockholders and for the economy as a whole, but dysfunctional for the growing number of obese children enticed by their music and images (Wilcox et al., 2004). As obesity-related health problems increase, insurance costs could spiral, a dysfunction for working parents, but functional for those selling weight-reduction programs and fitness camps to exasperated parents. Thus the functions for society can be offset by the dysfunctions for individuals or for specific groups of individuals.

Lance Holbert, Kelly Garrett, and Laurel Gleason offer a contemporary example. We can judge the self-selected, echo-chamber media consumption facilitated by cable television, talk radio, and the Internet as a dysfunction because it fosters antagonism toward the political system. This view assumes that "trust and confidence" in the political system are "unqualified goods." But, they argue, "Trust and confidence are *not* unqualified goods; they must be earned or warranted" (2010, p. 29). Loss of trust may be a dysfunction for individuals as they lose confidence in a system designed to support them (a micro-level assessment), but may ultimately be a beneficial function because it will force the system to improve (a macro-level assessment).

This thinking leads to one of functionalism's primary problems—it rarely permits definitive conclusions to be drawn about the overall functions or dysfunctions of media. For example, one of the first media effects to be studied in some depth

---

manifest functions
Intended and observed consequences of media use

latent functions
Unintended and less easily observed consequences of media use

classic four functions of the media
Surveillance, correlation, transmission of the social heritage, and entertainment

INSTANT ACCESS

Functionalism

Strengths

1. Positions media and their influence in larger social system
2. Offers balanced view of media's role in society
3. Is based on and guides empirical research

Weaknesses

1. Is overly accepting of status quo
2. Asserts that dysfunctions are "balanced" by functions
3. Asserts that negative latent functions are "balanced" by positive manifest functions
4. Rarely permits definitive conclusions about media's role in society

---

narcotizing dysfunction

Theory that as news about an issue inundates people, they become apathetic to it, substituting knowing about that issue for action on it

using functional analysis was the **narcotizing dysfunction**, the idea that as news about an issue inundates people, they become apathetic to it, substituting knowing about that issue for action on it (Lazarsfeld and Merton, 1948). The narcotizing dysfunction was used to explain why extensive, often dramatic coverage of 1950 congressional hearings concerning organized crime didn't lead to widespread public demands for government action. Although the heavily reported hearings went on for 15 months, were conducted in 14 cities, and featured more than 800 witnesses, researchers found that average Americans thought that nothing could be done to combat organized crime. These findings were disturbing because they suggested that even when media are effective at surveying the environment and calling attention to societal problems (a manifest function), the public may react by doing nothing. Instead of activating people to demand solutions to problems, media coverage might "narcotize" them so that they become apathetic and decide that they are powerless to do anything (a latent dysfunction). But what would account for this narcotizing effect? Researchers argued that members of the public will be narcotized when they are exposed day after day to dramatic negative news coverage dwelling on the threats posed by a problem and emphasizing the difficulty of dealing with it. This research was one of the first studies to suggest that media can fail to perform an important function even when practitioners do what their profession defines as the socially responsible thing to do.

THE ENTERTAINMENT FUNCTION OF MASS MEDIA

In general, functional analysis tends to produce conclusions that largely legitimize or rationalize the status quo. A classic example of how functional analysis leads to status quo conclusions is found in the work of Harold Mendelsohn (1966). He was concerned that people widely misunderstood the influence of television, the powerful new medium of his era. He blamed elite critics of media (mostly mass society theorists) for fostering misconceptions about television's entertainment function. He charged that these critics were protecting their own self-interests and ignoring empirical research findings, and he dismissed most criticisms as prejudiced speculation inconsistent with empirical data.

According to Mendelsohn, mass society critics were paternalistic and elitist. They were upset because television entertainment attracted people away from the boring forms of education, politics, or religion that they themselves wanted to promote. Mendelsohn argued that people needed the relaxation and harmless escapism that television offered. If this entertainment weren't available, people would find other releases from the tensions of daily life. Television simply served these needs more easily, powerfully, and efficiently than alternatives.

Instead of condemning television, Mendelsohn argued that critics should acknowledge that it performs its function very well and at extremely low cost. He was concerned that critics had greatly exaggerated the importance and long-term consequences of television entertainment, and he asserted that it had a limited and ultimately quite minor social role. Television entertainment did not disrupt or debase high culture; it merely gave average people a more attractive alternative to high-brow entertainment like operas and symphony concerts. It did not distract people from important activities like religion, politics, or family life; rather, it helped them relax so that they could later engage in these activities with renewed interest and energy.

mass entertainment theory

Theory asserting that television and other mass media, because they relax or otherwise entertain average people, perform a vital social function

Mendelsohn cited numerous psychological studies to support his **mass entertainment theory**. He admitted that a small number of people might suffer because they became addicted to television entertainment. These same people, however, would most likely have become addicted to something else if television weren't available. Chronic couch potatoes might otherwise become lounge lizards or fans of romance novels. Mendelsohn viewed addiction to television as rather benign compared to other alternatives: It didn't hurt other people and viewing might even be slightly educational.

Functionalist arguments continue to hold sway in many contemporary effects debates. Here, for example, is developmental economist Charles Kenny (2009) wondering about the impact of the world's more than one billion television households and the average of four hours a day consumed by each individual living in them. "So," he asks, "will the rapid, planetwide proliferation of television sets and digital and satellite channels, to corners of the world where the Internet is yet unheard of, be the cause of global decay [as] critics fear?" His near-perfect, "yes, but" functionalist answer: "A world of couch potatoes in front of digital sets will have its downsides—fewer bowling clubs, more Wii bowling. It may or may not be a world of greater obesity.... But it could also be a world more equal for women, healthier, better governed, more united in response to global tragedy, and more likely to vote for local versions of *American Idol* than shoot at people" (p. 68).

INSTANT ACCESS

Mass Entertainment Theory

Strengths

1. Stresses media's prosocial influence
2. Provides cogent explanation for why people seek entertainment from media

Weaknesses

1. Is too accepting of the status quo
2. Paints negative picture of average people and their use of media

Mass entertainment theory and the narcotizing dysfunction provide excellent examples of how functional analysis and its findings can legitimize the status quo. Harmful effects are balanced by a number of positive effects. Who can judge whether the harm being done is great enough to warrant making changes? Congress? The courts? The public? When the evidence is mixed, the best course of action would appear to be inaction, especially in a democratic system that seems to have functioned quite well in the two and a half centuries since the Founders penned the First Amendment.

Functionalism allows researchers and theorists to easily avoid drawing controversial conclusions by simply noting that dysfunctions are balanced by functions. After all, we wouldn't want media to avoid publishing news about organized crime just because some people will be narcotized. Sure, a few folks may abuse mass entertainment, but the benefits of such wonderful diversions surely outweigh this small problem. There is a conservative logic inherent in these arguments. It says that if the social world isn't literally falling apart with riots in the streets and people jumping off rooftops, things must be "in balance." Dysfunctions of media must certainly be balanced by other functions. If society is in balance, we can deduce that the overall influence of factors such as media must be either positive or only slightly negative. Obviously negative effects are offset by positive effects. If we eliminate the negative effects, we might also eliminate the positive effects balancing them. Are we willing to pay that price?

Functional analysis, middle-range theory, and limited-effects notions made a good fit. If media influence was modest, media couldn't be too dysfunctional. Findings from effects research could be combined to create a middle-range theory. For example, in their classic and influential 1961 book, *Television in the Lives of Our Children*, Wilbur Schramm, Jack Lyle, and Edwin Parker found that although viewing certain forms of violent television content encouraged *some* children to be aggressive, this was more than offset by *most* children, who showed little or no influence. And there were important positive functions. Children who watch TV read fewer violent comic books. Some might even learn how to anticipate and cope with aggressive peers. Thus, Schramm, Lyle, and Parker concluded that as far as the social system as a whole was concerned, violent television content makes little difference despite being dysfunctional for a few children (those "damned" by their "bad" parents to be manipulated by television violence).

Although it doesn't claim to do so, their book can be interpreted as presenting a reassuring, empirically grounded, middle-range theory that explains the role of television for children. By contrast, and as you'll see in the next chapter, at precisely the same time Schramm, Lyle, and Parker were explaining television's impact in such balanced terms, researchers from the field of psychology, bound by neither functionalism nor limited-effects findings, were making significant and persuasive arguments about the harmful effects of mediated violence.

SYSTEMS THEORIES OF COMMUNICATION PROCESSES

Other communication researchers were not so sanguine about media's "balancing" of effects. Systems engineers alerted them to the possibility of developing holistic explanations for societal, or macro-level, effects. Those engineers were concerned with designing and analyzing increasingly complex mechanical and electrical systems. They had achieved great successes during World War II and had laid the basis for many of the spectacular postwar technological breakthroughs in broad-casting and computers. It is no surprise, then, that their approach would be attractive to researchers interested in studying the most complex system of all: society.

system
Any set of interrelated parts that can influence and control one another through communication and feedback loops

A **system** *consists of a set of parts that are interlinked so that changes in one part induce changes in other parts.* System parts can be directly linked through mechanical connections, or they can be indirectly linked by communication technology. Because all parts are linked, the entire system can change as a result of alterations in only one element. Systems can be *goal-directed* if they are designed to accomplish a long-term objective. Some systems are capable of *monitoring the environment and altering their operations in response to environmental changes.*

During World War II, electronics engineers began to develop systems that were programmed to pursue goals, monitor the environment, and adjust actions to achieve those goals. One example occurs when a guided missile is able to make midcourse adjustments by monitoring internal and external changes. Engineers were concerned with designing systems in which communication links functioned efficiently and transmitted information accurately. Communication was a means to an end. If a communication link didn't work properly, then the solution was obvious: Communication technology had to be improved so the desired levels of effectiveness and accuracy were achieved. Thus, in designing and engineering systems of this type, communication problems could be solved by technological change.

Could communication problems in the society be solved in the same way? Could improving the accuracy, reliability, and range of communication solve societal problems? Would a nation bound together by networks of telephone cables be less troubled by regional disputes? Would a world bound together by satellite-based communication be less troubled by war? During the 1950s and 1960s, there was increasing optimism that important societal-level communication problems might also be solved by improving the accuracy of message transmissions.

THE RISE OF SYSTEMS THEORIES

Observing the successes achieved by systems engineers during World War II, social theorists became intrigued by systems notions as a way of conceptualizing both macroscopic and microscopic phenomena. Some decided that the idea of systems offered a means of constructing useful models of various social processes, including communication. Rather than merely adding more variables, these models altered how relationships between variables were understood. In developing these models, theorists drew on a variety of sources. But most 1960s social systems theorists acknowledged that the greatest and most recent impetus toward the development of systems theories came from an engineering subfield known as

cybernetics
The study of regulation and control in complex systems

cybernetics, the study of regulation and control in complex machines. Cybernetics investigates how communication links between the various parts of a machine enable it to perform very complex tasks and adjust to changes taking place in its external environment.

Cybernetics emerged as an important new field during World War II, partly because of its use for designing sophisticated weapons (Wiener, 1954, 1961). It proved especially useful for communications engineering—the design of powerful new communication systems for military applications, such as radar and guided missiles. Communications engineers had abandoned simple linear models of the communication process by the 1940s. They conceptualized a circular but evolving communication process in which messages come back from receivers to influence sources that in turn alter their messages. They referred to these circular processes as **feedback loops**. In these systems, ongoing mutual adjustment is possible, ultimately leading to the achievement of a long-term objective or function.

feedback loops
Ongoing mutual adjustments in systems

Feedback loops enable sources to monitor the influence of their messages on receivers. But just as important, receivers can in turn influence sources. If the effects are not what was expected or desired, a source can keep altering a message until the desired feedback is obtained. As World War II progressed, machines were built that used ever more powerful forms of communication technology, such as radar and television cameras, to monitor the environment. These provided sophisticated means of detecting subtle changes so that a weapons system could achieve its objective. We refer to these as **communication systems** if their function is primarily to facilitate communication. By this definition, a guided missile is not a communication system; it is a weapons system that contains a communication subsystem.

communication systems
Systems that function primarily to facilitate communication

MODELING SYSTEMS

The term *system* is used in communication engineering and cybernetics to refer to any set of interrelated parts that can influence and control one another through communication and feedback loops. Any representation of a system, whether in words or diagrams, is a **model**. In systems with many interrelated parts, a change in one part affects the others because all are interconnected through channels. Interdependence and self-regulation are key attributes of such systems. Each part can have a specialized role or function, but all must interrelate in an organized manner for the overall system to operate properly and regulate itself so that goals are achieved. Systems can be relatively simple or quite complex. They can display a high or low level of internal organization. They can operate in a static fashion, or they can evolve and undergo profound change over time. They can operate in isolation or be interconnected with a series of other machines to form an even larger system.

model
Any representation of a system, whether in words or diagrams

Another key attribute of systems is that they are **goal-oriented**. That is, they constantly seek to serve a specific overall or long-term purpose. We usually associate goals with thinking and planning. But, of course, machines can't think. Their goal-orientation is built in, hardwired, or otherwise programmed. Once a machine is started, it will seek its goal even if the goal is mistaken or can't be achieved. Like the robots in a science fiction movie, machines carry out their mission even if doing so makes no sense.

goal-oriented
Characteristic of a system that serves a specific overall or long-term purpose

Although complex systems can be hard to describe and understand, the basic principles of a self-regulating system can be illustrated by looking at the way the furnace in your home operates. That device is part of a self-regulating system that uses a simple feedback loop to adjust to the external environment. The furnace communicates with a thermostat monitoring the environment, signaling it when it needs to turn on or off. As long as the temperature in your home remains within a desired range, the furnace remains inactive. When the thermostat detects a temperature below the desired range, it sends an electronic message telling the furnace to turn on. The furnace communicates with the thermostat by heating the air in your home. The thermostat monitors the air temperature, and when that reaches the desired level, the thermostat sends another message telling the furnace to turn off. In this simple system, the furnace and the thermostat work together to keep the temperature in balance. Communication in the form of a simple feedback loop linking the furnace and the thermostat enables the system to operate effectively.

APPLYING SYSTEMS MODELS TO HUMAN COMMUNICATION

Even simple systems models can be used to represent some forms of human communication. You and a friend can be seen as forming a system in which your friend plays the role of "thermostat." By maintaining communication with your friend, you find out whether your actions are appropriate or inappropriate. Are these the right clothes to wear now? Should you go to a dance or join friends for a movie? During your conversation, you might not be trying to affect your friend but rather want your friend to guide you. You want your friend's feedback so you can adjust your actions.

This example also illustrates key limitations of systems models when they are used to represent human communication—the easiest models to create tend to be too simple and too static. Unless you and your friend have a very unusual relationship, you will play many other kinds of roles and communicate with each other across a very broad range of topics. If the only function your friend serves for you is that of a thermostat, you probably need to reexamine your relationship. Assuming that you do have a more complex relationship with your friend, you could probably spend weeks trying to map out a systems model to represent the intricacies of your interrelationship. By the time you finished, you would discover that significant changes have occurred and the model is no longer accurate. Unlike mechanical parts linked by simple forms of communication, both you and your friend can easily alter your roles, your communication links, and the content and purposes of your messages. In other words, you regularly and routinely transform the system that links you to others. New feedback loops spring up while old ones vanish. New purposes develop and old purposes are forgotten.

ADOPTION OF SYSTEMS MODELS BY MASS COMMUNICATION THEORISTS

Like other social scientists, mass communication researchers were drawn to systems models. They came to see moderately complex systems models as an ideal means of representing communication processes—a big advance over simplistic linear communication process models common before 1960. Gradually, systems models replaced the **transmissional model** implicit in most of the early effects research. Harold Lasswell (1949) provided a cogent, succinct version of this model when he described the communication process as *who says what to whom through what medium with what effect*. This transmissional model assumes that a message source dominates the communication process and that its primary outcome is some sort of effect on receivers—usually one intended by the source. Influence moves or flows in

transmissional model

The view of mass media as mere senders or transmitters of information a straight line from source to receivers. The possibility that the message receivers might also influence the source is ignored. Attention is focused on whether a source brings about intended effects and whether unintended negative effects occur. Mutual or reciprocal influence is not considered.

Communication theorists proposed new models of communication processes with feedback loops in which receivers could influence sources and mutual influence was possible. The potential for modeling mutual influence was especially attractive for theorists who wanted to understand interpersonal communication. Most conversations involve mutual influence. Participants send out messages, obtain feedback, and then adjust their actions. In everyday life, people are constantly adjusting to one another. The overall social environment can be understood as something created by ongoing negotiation between actors.

The usefulness of systems models for representing mass communication processes was less obvious. With most traditional forms of mass media, there are few if any *direct* communication links from receivers to sources. Message sources can be unaware of the impact of their messages or find out what that impact was only after days or weeks have elapsed. During the 1960s, however, refinement of media ratings systems and improved, more scientific public opinion polls allowed the establishment of indirect communication links between message sources and receivers. Ratings and opinion poll results provided message producers with feedback about audience reaction to their messages. For television ratings this feedback was quite crude—either people watch a show or they don't. If they don't, producers change the message without much understanding of what people want. If ratings are high, they provide more of the same—until people get so tired of the same programming that they finally tune to something else. With opinion polls, the feedback can provide a bit more information to message sources, but not much. Politicians, for example, are constantly experimenting with messages in an effort to alter voter opinions and produce favorable evaluations of themselves.

INSTANT ACCESS

Systems Theory

Strengths

1. Can be conceptualized as either micro- or macro-level theory
2. Represents communication as a process
3. Can be used to model a limitless variety of communication processes
4. Moves mass communication theory beyond simple linear-effects notions

Weaknesses

1. Has difficulty assessing causal relationships
2. Is often too simplistic to represent complex communication patterns
3. Is perceived by some as overly mechanistic and dehumanizing
4. Focuses attention on observable structures, ignoring the substance of communication
5. Is unparsimonious

FUNCTIONALISM'S UNFULFILLED PROMISE

Although they did indeed help advance mass communication theory beyond a focus on specific limited-effects findings and middle-range theory, functionalism and systems theory suffered much criticism and are not among the central schools of thought in contemporary thinking about media. However, as we will explain later in this book, they have influenced the development of some important theories. These approaches to theory have not been more influential because scholars who construct interpretive and postpositivist theories see them as having serious limitations.

Humanistic scholars who develop interpretive theories tend to reject the mechanistic or biological analogies inherent in functionalism and systems models. They are fundamentally opposed to the use of functional analysis and systems models because they perceive them to be dehumanizing and overly simplistic. They argue that systems models are often nothing more than elaborate metaphors—sets of descriptive analogies. They are dissatisfied with the ability of functional analysis and systems models to adequately represent complex human or societal interrelationships. After all, people aren't parts of machines. The relationships in a family aren't like the mechanism in an old-fashioned pocket watch. Even complex mechanical systems are simple when compared with the human relationships that are found within a family. Humanists are fearful that in applying functional or mechanistic analogies we demean or trivialize human existence and experience.

Social scientists who develop postpositivist theories argue that research must stay focused on development of *causal* explanations and predictions. They reject complicated systems models because they don't permit the assessment of causality. In our earlier heating system model, which is the causal agent and which agent is being affected? Does the furnace cause the thermostat to act? Yes. Does the thermostat cause the furnace to act? Yes. So which is dominant in this relationship? Which controls the other? In this model, neither agent is clearly *causal*. Each causes the other to change. Thus, in even this very simple process involving feedback, causality can be hard to assess. If we measure the furnace and the thermostat at only one point in time, we are likely to get a completely mistaken impression of their relationship. When these processes become more complicated with more agents and more feedback loops, we need a schematic diagram to sort out the flow of influence. The effort to assign causality soon becomes a meaningless exercise. For example, given the complexity of the systems we create when we interact with other people, it becomes literally impossible to sort out causality—except for the simplest and most narrowly defined systems or parts of systems.

Should we be concerned about the difficulty of assigning causality in systems models? Is assignment of causality necessary to have a truly scientific theory? Or should we be satisfied if our theories are useful for other purposes? If we could simulate a set of interrelationships that provides insight into people playing certain roles in a particular situation over a limited time span, is that enough? Do we need to be able to say that the person playing role X has 0.23 causal dominance over the person playing role Y, whereas the person in role Y has 0.35 dominance over person X? Just how precise must our understanding of these interrelationships be for the simulation to be of value? Just how precise can we afford to make our simulations, given the time and research effort necessary?

Researchers who assert the importance of assigning causality are concerned that if they lower their concern for causality, they will create and use systems models based on little more than informed speculation. Although sophisticated systems models might allow them to construct fascinating computer simulations, will they serve any practical purpose? How can the utility of these models be evaluated if causality is not used as an explanatory standard? It might appear that a model fits a particular set of relationships and gives insight into interconnections between particular parts, but how can they be sure? How can they choose between two competing models that seem to represent a particular set of relationships equally well? These critics are deeply skeptical of the value of constructing models that contain complex interconnections between agents. Critics view systems models as unparsimonious—containing too many unnecessary variables and overly complex interrelationships.

Finally, as we have already noted here, functionalism and systems theory have a third limitation that many find troublesome: they have a bias toward the status quo. Because they tend to concentrate attention on observable structures (e.g., the functioning parts of the organism or machine), functionalism and systems theory often lead to the assumption that the primary function or role of these structures is to maintain and serve the overall system.

SUMMARY

The 1933 Payne Fund research ushered in the postpositivist media-effects trend—a trend that concentrated media research attention on the search for specific effects on individuals caused by exposure to certain forms of media content. Development of this trend was led by Paul Lazarsfeld and Carl Hovland and benefited from the refinement of empirical research methods, the failure of the mass society and propaganda thinkers to offer empirical evidence for their views, the commercial nature of the new research methods and their support by both government and business, and the spread of these methods to a wide variety of academic disciplines.

Lazarsfeld championed the inductive approach to theory construction and employed it in his 1940 voter studies and other research to develop the idea of a two-step flow of media influence. With other research of the time, this helped produce important generalizations about media influence: Media rarely have direct effects; media influence travels from media, through opinion leaders, to opinion followers; group commitments protect people from media influence; and when effects do occur, they are modest

and isolated. Hovland and other psychologists also provided evidence of limited media influence. Using controlled variation, they demonstrated that numerous individual differences and group affiliations limited media's power to change attitudes. This led logically to the development of dissonance theory, the idea that people work consciously and unconsciously to limit the influence of messages running counter to their preexisting attitudes and beliefs. This dissonance reduction operated through selectivity in exposure (attention), retention, and perception.

The rise of functionalism, middle-range, and systems theories in the 1950s and 1960s encouraged theorists to move beyond simplistic, fragmented, linear models of mass communication. At a time when limited-effects research findings dominated, functionalism's value-neutrality was attractive to researchers and theorists studying media's influence, especially as functional analyses accepted the presence of latent as well as manifest functions. The strategy of developing middle-range theory offered hope of moving beyond the empirical generalizations produced by run-of-the-mill effects research. These generalizations could be "added up" to create broader theories of media. Ultimately, functionalism's promise to more meaningfully alter the direction of mass communication theory was weakened by its inability to draw definitive conclusions about effects and by what many saw as its status quo orientation, as exemplified by research on the narcotizing dysfunction and mass entertainment theory.

Some mass communication researchers looked to a concept related to functionalism developed by communications engineers, systems, which evolved from cybernetics, the study of the regulation and control of complex machines. Systems consist of sets of parts interlinked so changes in one part induce changes in other parts. Systems theory allows the creation of models demonstrating the interdependence, self-regulation, and goal-orientation of systems. The application of systems theories to mass communication raised many important questions that forced reconsideration of the media-effects trend.

Critical Thinking Questions

1. Are you typically an opinion leader or an opinion follower? Are there specific topics on which you are one or the other? Identify an issue (movies, music, sports, fashion, domestic politics) on which you can identify another whose opinion you usually seek. How well does that person fit the description of opinion leaders embodied in two-step flow? Has membership in a social networking site such as Facebook or Twitter altered your role as an opinion leader or follower or that of any of your friends? How?

2. Klapper's phenomenistic theory argues that media's greatest power rests in their ability to reinforce existing attitudes and values. At the time, this was evidence that media had limited effects—they were limited to reinforcement. But more contemporary thinking sees reinforcement as anything but a limited effect. Can you anticipate some of the arguments in support of this view?

3. Were you surprised by the drug and race data presented in the Allport and Postman "Thinking about Theory" box? Why or why not? If you were, that is, if you put the drugs in the African American's hand, why do you think that happened? If you were not, why not? Can and would you offer a third-person effect answer?

Key Terms

media-effects trend

functionalism

communication systems theory

administrative research

controlled variation

inductive

middle-range theory

gatekeepers

opinion leaders

opinion followers

limited- or minimal-effects theory

individual differences

social categories

cognitive consistency

cognitive dissonance

selective processes

selective exposure

selective retention

selective perception

information-flow theory

source-dominated theory

two-step flow theory

phenomenistic theory

reinforcement theory

manifest functions

latent functions

classic four functions of the media

narcotizing dysfunction

mass entertainment theory

system

cybernetics

feedback loops

communication systems

model

goal-oriented

transmissional model

THE EMERGENCE OF THE CRITICAL CULTURAL TREND IN NORTH AMERICA

CHAPTER 5

Close your eyes and imagine the 1960s anti-Vietnam war movement. What did the protesters look like? How old were they? How were they dressed? How did they protest? What about the folks on the other side of that debate? What did they look like? How old were they? How were they dressed? Keep your eyes closed and imagine the Women's Rights Movement of that same time. What did the feminist protesters look like? How old were they? How were they dressed? How did they protest? What about the folks on the other side of that debate? Today, some 45 or 50 years later and the answers are easy. The antiwar protesters were weirdly dressed hippies, mostly young, generally engaged in at best disruptive and at worse violent action. The other side? Good, upstanding Americans, the Silent Majority whose voices were drowned out by the raucous radicals. The feminist? Young hippies burning their bras. The other side? Good, upstanding Americans, the Silent Majority whose voices were drowned out by the raucous radicals. Both images are accurate ... and inaccurate. Yes, there were weirdly dressed antiwar radicals engaging in violent action, but there were many, many more people inveighing against the war who were nothing of the sort. And feminists may have thrown bras, along with girdles, curlers, popular women's magazines, and pageant brochures, into a Freedom Trash Can to protest the 1968 Atlantic City Miss America contest, but this produced what might be called "bra-smoldering," not "bra-burning" (Campbell, 2011). And there were many, many more people, male and female, fighting for equality for women who neither burned nor smoldered their bras.

So where did our myths of antiwar radicals and bra-burning feminists come from? Keeping in mind that myths usually combine elements of both truth and fantasy, these particular versions of our history were jointly created by the movements themselves and the mass media. "The media needed stories, preferring the dramatic; the movement[s] needed publicity for recruitment, for support, and for political effect. Each could be useful to the other; each had effects, intended and unintended, on the other" (Gitlin, 1980, p. 25). But there was more at work in the coverage of these important social movements than a symbiotic relationship gone awry. There was the operation of presumably objective reporting requirements in which every Viet Cong flag-waving hippie was balanced by "reasonable-sounding, fact-brandishing authorities" (Gitlin, 1980, p. 4). Audience demands—and media acquiescence to those demands—that stories be reported in terms of recognizable narratives were also at work, so feminist protestors "burned bras" just as antiwar protesters burned draft cards (Polo, 2012). And underlying both there is the natural and historic tendency of elites, in this case media, political, and social elites, to maintain power. As sociologist Herbert Gans wrote, "In any modern society in which a number of classes, ethnic and religious groups, age groups and political interests struggle among each other for control over society's resources, there is also a struggle for the power to determine or influence the society's values, myths, symbols, and information" (1972, p. 373). In agreement, sociologist Todd Gitlin wrote, "Calm and cautionary tones of voice affirm that all 'disturbance' is or should be under control by rational authority; code words like *disturbance* commend the established normality; camera angles and verbal shibboleths ('and that's the way it is') enforce the integrity and authority of the news anchorman and commend the inevitability of the established order. Hotheads carry on, the message connotes, while wiser heads, officials and reporters both, with superb self-control, watch the unenlightened ones make trouble" (1980, p. 4).

Now ask yourself why, in September 2011, did it take the *Washington Post* four days and New York–based ABC, NBC, and CBS more than a week to devote even minimal attention to the thousands of Occupy Wall Street protesters who were "shutting down the heart of the [New York] financial district to protest political and economic inequality and highlight the need for an American democracy movement?" (Naureckas, 2011, p. 7). And why was that coverage typically "dismissive … Look at the oddly dressed people acting out! So?" asked *New York Times* columnist Paul Krugman, "Is it better when exquisitely tailored bankers whose gambles brought the world economy to its knees—and who were bailed out by taxpayers—whine that President Obama is saying slightly mean things about them?" (2011). These questions about media myth-making can't be answered by the media effects theory trend but in this chapter we will consider how a different perspective—the critical cultural theory trend—can provide answers.

LEARNING OBJECTIVES

After studying this chapter you should be able to

- Describe the critical cultural media trend, contrast it with the media effects trend, and differentiate the types of research questions that can be answered by each.

- Draw distinctions between macroscopic and microscopic mass communication theory; between critical and cultural theories and those based on empirical research; and between the transmissional and ritual perspectives on mass communication.

- Identify the roots of critical and cultural theory in Marxism, neo-Marxism, the Frankfurt School, textual analysis and literary criticism, political economy theory, and critical feminist scholarship.
- Identify differences and similarities in political economy theory and cultural studies.
- Explain the central ideas of James, Carey, Harold Innis, and Marshall McLuhan and identify their contribution to mass communication theory.

OVERVIEW

During the 1950s and 1960s, interest in cultural theories of mass communication began to develop and take hold—first in Europe, then in Canada and other British Commonwealth nations, and finally in the United States. As we noted in previous chapters, the media effects theory trend made some questionable assumptions and had important limitations. It focused on whether specific types of media content could have an immediate and direct effect on individuals' specific thoughts and actions. Researchers typically looked for evidence of these effects using traditional postpositivist approaches, primarily highly structured quantitative experiments or surveys. But it eventually became apparent that it was possible to study mass communication in other ways, that is, through cultural studies and critical theory approaches. "The space for these newer models grew," explained researcher Joshua Meyrowitz, "as it became clearer that the stimulus-response concept (even when refined through studies of individual and group differences in response to messages and even when explored in terms of the modulating influence of the opinions of influential peers) did not sufficiently account for the complexity of interactions with media" (2008, p. 642). As a result, writes media scholar Jefferson Pooley, in the 1970s,

> With more or less force, every social science discipline registered a protest against the confident scientism of the postwar decades—a backlash against natural science envy and blind faith in quantitative methods. In each field, insurgents elevated history and particularity over explanation and the search for timeless laws. To their opponents they affixed pejoratives like "positivist" and "behaviorist." The new, more humanist and interpretive social science drew upon, and contributed to, a much broader recognition across many fields that knowledge and interest are entangled with one another. (2007, p. 469)

Now, instead of focusing on specific, measurable effects on individuals, theory could focus on changes in culture, on how shared understandings and social norms change. Instead of trying to locate hundreds of small effects and add them all up, researchers could ask whether the development of mass media has profound implications for the way people create, share, learn, and apply culture.

In this chapter, we will trace the emergence of the critical cultural theory trend that addresses questions about the way media might produce profound changes in social life through their subtle influence on the myriad of social practices that form the foundation of everyday life.

This theory trend argues that media might have the power to intrude into and alter how we make sense of ourselves and our social world. Media could alter how we view ourselves, our relationship to others, even the image that we have of our body. Social institutions, including political, economic, and educational institutions, might be disrupted and transformed as media institutions play an increasingly central role in contemporary societies. In 1941, when the media effects trend was at the height of its scientific certainty, the "Father of American Social Science" Paul Lazarsfeld challenged his colleagues to address these larger societal issues:

> Today we live in an environment where skyscrapers shoot up and elevateds (commuter trains) disappear overnight; where news comes like shock every few hours; where continually new news programs keep us from ever finding out details of previous news; and where nature is something we drive past in our cars, perceiving a few quickly changing flashes which turn the majesty of a mountain range into the impression of a motion picture. Might it not be that we do not build up experiences the way it was possible decades ago …? (p. 12)

But the media-effects trend couldn't conduct research or produce theories that could address these issues. A different approach to research and theory construction was needed. The theories developed to address issues like this are quite diverse and offer very different answers to questions about the role of media in social life. In all these theories, the concept of **culture** is central. As cultural theorist Jeff Lewis explains, "Media texts—music, TV, film, print, Internet—meet their audiences in a complex intersection of systems and personal imaginings. To this end, the transformation of the world into a *global media sphere* is the result of a dynamic interaction between macro processes (history, economy, technology, politics and modes of social organization) and the profoundly intimate and intricate microcosms of a person's life—the realm of the individual subject. Culture, in a very profound sense, is formed through these processes: an assemblage of dynamic engagements that reverberate through and within individual subjects and the systems of meaning-making of which they are an integral part" (2008, pp. 1–2).

Cultural theories, then, offer a broad range of interesting ideas about how media can affect culture and provide many different views concerning the long-term consequences of the cultural changes affected by media. The theories introduced in this chapter proved to be quite useful for raising questions about the role of media for individuals and for society and they provided intriguing, cogent answers.

culture
The learned behavior of members of a given social group

CHANGING TIMES

Modern mass media dominate everyday communication. From the time children learn to talk, they are mesmerized by the sounds and moving images of *Sesame Street*. By the age of three, nearly one-third of kids have a television in their bedrooms (Rettner, 2011). During the teen years, media supply vital information on peer group culture and—most important—the opposite sex. In middle age, as people rear families, they turn to video on an expanding number of technologies for convenient entertainment and to magazines and the Internet for tips on raising teenagers. In old age, as physical mobility declines, people turn to television for companionship and advice. As the screens delivering media content multiply and deliver an ever-changing array of content, our overall use of media continues to increase. As screen time rises, it displaces many important everyday activities and disrupts our lives in ways we rarely notice.

Media have become a primary means by which most of us experience or learn about many aspects of the world around us. The importance of media as a source of experience about the social world continues to increase. As we spend more time in front of screens, we have less and less time to experience things first hand. Even when we don't learn about these things directly from media, we learn about them from others who get their ideas of the world from media. With the advent of mass media, many forms of folk culture fell into sharp decline. Everyday communication was fundamentally altered. Storytelling, game playing, and music making ceased to be important for extended families. Instead, nuclear families gathered in front of an enthralling electronic storyteller, watching others play games and make music. Informal social groups dedicated to cultural enrichment disappeared, as did vaudeville and band concerts. It is no coincidence that our culture's respect for older people and the wisdom they hold has declined in the age of media. If respected theorists like Joshua Meyrowitz (1985) and Robert McChesney (2004) are correct, we're losing touch with locally based cultures and are moving into a media-based global cultural environment. If new media researchers like Gwenn Schurgin O'Keeffe and Kathleen Clarke-Pearson (2011) and Scott Caplan (2005) are correct, young adults who have inadequate social skills and difficulty with face-to-face communication will turn to e-mail, texting, and instant messaging as more comfortable ways of developing or maintaining social relations.

Mass society theory (see Chapter 2) greeted similar types of social change with alarm. It viewed mediated culture as inferior to elite culture. As mass culture spread, theorists feared it would undermine the social order and bring chaos. People's lives would be disrupted. The sudden rise of totalitarian social orders in the 1930s seemed to fulfill these prophecies. In Fascist and Communist nations alike, media were used to propagate new and highly questionable forms of totalitarian culture. But were media ultimately responsible for the creation and promotion of these forms of government? Was the linkage between the new forms of media and their messages so great that the drift into totalitarianism was inevitable? Or could media promote individualism and democracy as easily as they did collectivism and dictatorship? We have struggled with these questions throughout a century of mass communication theory.

During the 1960s and 1970s, as the overt threat of a totalitarian takeover of the United States and the world declined, mass society theory lost its relevancy. By 1960, research following the media effects trend had concluded that media rarely produce significant, widespread, long-term changes in people's thoughts and actions. Media effects trend researchers no longer assumed that mediated mass culture was inherently antidemocratic. American media had become highly effective promoters of capitalism, individualism, and free enterprise. Today some critics argue that newer media technologies, such as iPods, the Internet, and smartphones, are "personal media," inherently biased toward individualism and market economies rather than toward collectivism and state control. So the role of media in culture seems to be settled—doesn't it? After all, we've won the Cold War. Shouldn't we conclude that media are benign? Can't we safely ignore the warnings in books like *1984* and *Brave New World*? In *1984*, cameras mounted on television sets allowed Big Brother to constantly monitor people's viewing and spot those who reacted suspiciously to propaganda messages. Today's media monitor us in ways that are far more subtle. Should we trust Facebook and Google to use this data in ways that serve our interests as well as theirs?

THE CRITICAL CULTURAL THEORY TREND

cultural studies
Focus on use of media to create forms of culture that structure everyday life

hegemonic culture
Culture imposed from above or outside that serves the interests of those in dominant social positions

political economy theories
Focus on social elites' use of economic power to exploit media institutions

The various cultural theories of media can be identified in several ways. In this chapter, we use a dichotomy widely employed by cultural theorists to differentiate their scholarship (Garnham, 1995). *Microscopic interpretive theories* focus on how individuals and social groups use media to create and foster forms of culture that structure everyday life. As such they sit at "the borderland between textual and social research" (Jensen, 1991, p. 27). These theories are usually referred to as **cultural studies** theory. *Macroscopic structural theories* focus on how media institutions are structured within capitalist economies. These theories focus attention on the way social elites operate media to earn profits and exercise influence in society. They argue that elites sometimes use media to propagate **hegemonic culture** as a means of maintaining their dominant position in the social order, encouraging "subordinated groups [to] actively consent to and support belief systems and structures of power relations that do not necessarily serve—indeed may work against—those interests" (Mumbry, 1997, p. 344). But they also contend that elites use media to create and market seemingly apolitical cultural commodities that serve to earn profits for those elites. This set of theories is called **political economy theory** because these ideas place priority on understanding how economic power provides a basis for ideological and political power. Some researchers speculate about how alternate forms of culture and innovative media uses are systematically suppressed. These theories directly challenge the status quo by exposing elite manipulation of media and criticizing both hegemonic culture and cultural commodities.

MACROSCOPIC VERSUS MICROSCOPIC THEORIES

Cultural studies theories are less concerned with the long-term consequences of media for the social order and more concerned with looking at how media affect the lives of groups of people who share a culture. These theories are micro-level, or *microscopic*, because they deemphasize larger issues about the social order in favor of questions involving the everyday life of groups of average people. Political economy theories, by contrast, are *macroscopic* cultural theories. They are less concerned with developing detailed explanations of how individuals or groups are influenced by media and more interested with how the social order as a whole is affected. Ideally, these theories ought to be complementary. Individual- or group-level explanations of what media do to people (or what people do with media) should link to societal-level theories. Yet, until recently, macroscopic and microscopic cultural theories developed in relative isolation. Theorists were separated by differences in geography, politics, academic discipline, and research objectives.

Microscopic cultural studies researchers prefer to interpret what is going on in the world immediately around them. Many of them find the social world an endlessly fascinating place. They are intrigued by the mundane, the seemingly trivial, the routine. They view our experience of everyday life and of reality itself as an artificial social construction that we somehow maintain with only occasional minor breakdowns. They want to know what happens when mass media are incorporated into the routines of daily life and play an essential role in shaping our experience of the social world—are there serious disruptions or do media enhance daily experience? Could media be causing problems that are somehow being compensated for or concealed? If so, how does this happen? Will there eventually be a breakdown—are we being systematically desensitized and trained to be aggressive? Or is everyday life being transformed in useful ways—are we somehow becoming kinder and gentler?

Macroscopic researchers are troubled by the narrow focus of microscopic theory. So what if some people experience everyday life in certain ways? Why worry if everyday-life culture is enhanced by media? These researchers demand answers to larger questions. They view media as industries that turn culture into a commodity and sell it for a profit. They want to assess the overall consequences to the social order when these industries become a major part of national economies. In what ways do media affect how politics is conducted, how the national economy operates, how vital social services are delivered? Macroscopic researchers want to know if media are intruding into or disrupting important, large-scale social processes. For example, have media disrupted the conduct of national politics and therefore increased the likelihood that inferior politicians will be elected? Macroscopic researchers believe that such large-scale questions can't be answered if you focus on what individuals are doing with media.

CRITICAL THEORY

critical theories
Theories openly espousing certain values and using these values to evaluate and criticize the status quo, providing alternate ways of interpreting the social role of mass media

Some cultural studies and political economy theories are also referred to as **critical theories** because their axiology openly espouses specific values and uses them to evaluate and criticize the status quo. Those who develop critical theories seek social change that will implement their values (Chapter 1). Political economy theories are inherently critical, but many cultural studies theories are not. Critical theory raises questions about the way things are and provides alternate ways of interpreting the social role of mass media. For example, some critical theorists argue that media in general sustain the status quo—even, perhaps especially, when it is under stress or breaking down. Critical theory often provides complex explanations for media's tendency to consistently do so. For example, some critical theorists identify constraints on media practitioners that limit their ability to challenge established authority. They charge that few incentives exist to encourage media professionals to overcome those constraints and even more troubling, that media practitioners consistently fail to even acknowledge them.

Critical theory often analyzes specific social institutions, probing the extent to which valued objectives are sought and achieved. Naturally, then, mass media and the mass culture they promote have become an important focus for critical theory. Critical researchers link mass media and mass culture to a variety of social problems. Even when they do not see mass media as the source of specific problems, they criticize media for aggravating or preventing problems from being identified or addressed and solved. For example, a theorist might argue that content production practices of media practitioners either cause or perpetuate specific problems. A common theme in critical theories of media is that content production is so constrained that it inevitably reinforces the status quo and undermines useful efforts to effect constructive social change.

Consider, for example, the last time you read news reports about members of an American social movement strongly challenging the status quo. How were their actions described? How were movement members and their leaders portrayed? These are the questions raised in the chapter's opening paragraphs. Consider veteran journalist Daniel Schorr's (1992) personal recollection of media coverage of the civil rights movement:

> I found [in the mid-1960s] that I was more likely to get on the CBS *Evening News* with a black militant talking the language of "Burn, baby, burn!" … [Then], in early February 1968, the Rev. Martin Luther King, Jr. came to Washington…. I came to his news conference with a CBS camera crew prepared to do what TV reporters do—get the most threatening sound bite I could to ensure a place on the evening news lineup. I succeeded in eliciting from him phrases on the possibility of "disruptive protests" directed at the Johnson Administration and Congress.
>
> As I waited for my camera crew to pack up, I noticed that King remained seated behind a table in an almost empty room, looking depressed. Approaching him, I asked why he seemed so morose.
>
> "Because of you," he said, "and because of your colleagues in television. You try to provoke me to threaten violence and, if I don't, then you will put on television those who do. And by putting them on television, you will elect them our leaders. And if there is violence, will you think about your part in bringing it about?" (p. 5C)

Stories about social movements usually imply problems with the status quo. Movements typically arise because they identify social problems that go unaddressed, and they make demands for social change. Media professionals are caught in the middle of the confrontation. Movement leaders demand coverage of their complaints, and they stage demonstrations designed to draw public attention to their concerns. Elites want to minimize coverage or to exercise "spin control" so coverage favors their positions. How do journalists handle this? How should they handle it? Existing research indicates that this coverage almost always denigrates movements

INSTANT ACCESS

Critical Theory

Strengths

1. Is politically based, action-oriented
2. Uses theory and research to plan change in the real world
3. Asks big, important questions about media control and ownership

Weaknesses

1. Is too political; call to action is too subjective
2. Typically lacks scientific verification; based on subjective observation
3. When subjected to scientific verification, often employs innovative but controversial research methods

and supports elites (FAIR, 2005; Goodman, 2004; McChesney, 2004). Coverage focuses on the deviant actions or appearance of some movement members and ignores the way movements define problems and propose solutions for them.

COMPARING THE MEDIA THEORY TRENDS

It is useful to keep in mind both the strengths and the limitations of the theories introduced in this chapter. Many of the theorists whose ideas we discuss believe that media play a central role in modern social orders or our daily lives. Rather than presenting us with the types of empirical evidence favored by proponents of the media effects trend, they ask us to accept their view of media influence using logic, argument, and our own powers of observation. Some describe compelling examples to illustrate their arguments. Others offer empirical evidence for their belief in powerful media, but they use innovative research methods, and so their work is challenged and questioned by traditional postpositivist researchers. During the 1970s and 1980s, supporters of the media effects trend were especially troubled by the rise of the critical cultural trend. They were quick to question the evidence offered by critical cultural theorists. They saw cultural theories as new variations of mass society theory—a theory they felt they had quite effectively debunked in the 1950s and 1960s. Effects researchers believed that cultural theories were too speculative and the empirical research generated from these theories was too loosely structured and inherently biased.

Cultural studies and political economy theorists employ a broad range of research methods and theory-generation strategies, including some that are unsystematic and selective. As a result, critics believe that personal biases and interests inevitably motivate culture researchers and affect the outcome of their work. But, argue cultural theory's defenders, this is acceptable as long as researchers openly acknowledge those biases or interests.

qualitative methods

Research methods that highlight essential differences (distinctive qualities) in phenomena

In contrast with the quantitative empirical research methods described in previous chapters, the techniques used by many critical or cultural researchers are often **qualitative methods**; that is, they highlight essential differences (distinctive qualities) in phenomena. Epistemologically, knowledge is created or advanced through discourse (debate and discussion) involving proponents of contrasting or opposing theoretical positions. Theory is advanced through the formation of schools of thought in which there is consensus about the validity of a specific body of theory. Often rival schools of theory emerge to challenge existing theories while developing and defending their own. Proof of a theory's power often rests in its ability to attract adherents and be defended against attacks from opponents.

Not surprisingly, researchers who adopt a postpositivist approach find cultural theories hard to accept. They are skeptical of theories evaluated more through discourse than through empirical research. Postpositivist media researchers place far less stress on theory development or criticism. Their research methods are used to generate theory and to *test* theory rather than as a means of making qualitative differentiations. They argue that if empirical research is conducted according to prevailing standards, findings can be readily accepted throughout the research community. There is no need for competing schools of theory. If other researchers doubt the validity of specific findings, they can replicate (duplicate) the research and then report conflicting findings. But in truth, these conflicting reports are quite rare and provoke considerable controversy when they are published. Though there is verbal debate between those who espouse conflicting empirically based theories, these disagreements rarely appear in print. When they do, both sides present empirical findings to support their positions. Arguments often center on methodological disputes about the reliability and validity of research findings rather than the strength of the theoretical propositions—researchers disagree about whether appropriate methods were used, question the application of specific methods, or argue that the data were improperly analyzed. Much less attention is given to the structure and consistency of theoretical propositions. When theory is developed, it takes the form of middle-range theory—theory that summarizes sets of empirical generalizations and usually doesn't make strong assertions or assumptions about the role of media.

THE RISE OF CULTURAL THEORIES IN EUROPE

grand social theories
Highly ambitious, macroscopic, speculative theories that attempt to understand and predict important trends in culture and society

Despite its popularity in American social science, the media-effects trend was never widely accepted by social researchers in Europe. European social research has instead continued to be characterized by what U.S. observers regard as **grand social theories**—highly ambitious, macroscopic, speculative theories that attempt to understand and predict important trends in culture and society. Mass society theory was a nineteenth-century example of a European-style grand social theory. It illustrated both the strengths and the limitations of this type of theory. Dissatisfied with these limitations, American social researchers, especially those trained in the Columbia School of empirical social research, chose to construct more modest middle-range theories.

In Europe, the development of grand social theory remained a central concern in the social sciences and humanities after World War II. Mass society theory gave way to a succession of alternate schools of thought. Some were limited to specific nations or specific academic disciplines or even certain universities. Others achieved widespread interest and acceptance. Most were not theories of media—they were theories of society offering observations about media and their place in society or the lives of individuals. Some of the most widely accepted were based on the writings of Karl Marx. **Marxist theory** influenced even the theories created in reaction against it. Marx's ideas formed a foundation or touchstone for much post-World War II European social theory. Cold War politics made them quite controversial in the United States. Theories developed in France or Germany often remained untranslated into English until several years after they became popular in Europe. Even theories developed in Britain were treated with skepticism and suspicion in the United States.

Marxist theory
Theory arguing that the hierarchical class system is at the root of all social problems and must be ended by a revolution of the proletariat

In the 1970s and 1980s, at the very time that Marxism itself was being rejected as a practical guide for politics and economics all across Europe, grand social theories based in part on Marxist thought were gaining increasing acceptance (Grossberg and Nelson, 1988). We briefly summarize key arguments in the Marxist perspective and pay particular attention to ideas about media. Then we present some more recent theories based on these ideas.

MARXIST THEORY

Karl Marx developed his theory in the latter part of the nineteenth century, during one of Europe's most volatile periods of social change. In some respects, his is yet another version of mass society theory—but with several very important alterations and additions. Marx was familiar with the grand social theories of his era. He was a student of the most prominent German Idealist philosopher, Georg Wilhelm Friedrich Hegel. Early in his career, Marx drew on Hegel's ideas, but later he constructed his own in opposition to them. From Hegel he derived insights into the human construction of the social world and of human reason itself. But while Hegel attributed social change to a metaphysical force, a "World Spirit," Marx eventually adopted a materialist position—human beings shape the world using the technology and physical resources available to them. It is the availability of and control over technology and resources that limit and determine what people can achieve.

Like some mass society theorists, Marx identified the myriad problems associated with industrialization and urbanization as the consequence of actions taken by powerful elites. Industrialization and urbanization were not inherently bad. Problems resulted when unethical capitalists attempted to maximize personal profits by exploiting workers. On the basis of a similar analysis, conservative mass society theorists demanded restoration of traditional social orders, but Marx was a Utopian, calling for the creation of an entirely new social order in which all social class distinctions would be abolished. The workers should rise against capitalists and demand an end to exploitation. They should band together to seize the means of production (i.e., labor, factories, and land) so they might construct an egalitarian democratic social order—Communism. In Marx's theory, media are one of many modern technologies that must be controlled and used to advance Communism.

Marx argued that the hierarchical class system was at the root of all social problems and must be ended by a revolution of the workers, or proletariat. He believed that elites dominated society primarily through their direct control over the means of production, the **base (or substructure) of society**. But elites also maintained themselves in power through their control over culture (media, religion, education, and so on) or the **superstructure** of society. Marx saw culture as something elites freely manipulated to mislead average people and encourage them to act against their own interests. He used the term **ideology** to refer to these forms of culture. Ideology fostered a "false consciousness" in the minds of average people so they came to support elite interests rather than their own. Marx believed an ideology operated much like a drug. Those who are under its influence fail to see how they are being exploited—it blinds them or it distracts them. In the worst cases, they are so deceived that they actually undermine their own interests and do things that increase the power of elites while making their own lives even worse.

Marx concluded that the only realistic hope for social change was a revolution in which the masses seized control of the base—the means of production. Control over the superstructure—over ideology—would naturally follow. He saw little possibility that reforms in the superstructure could lead to social evolution, or if they could, the resulting transformation would be very slow in coming. These views stemmed in part from his rejection of German Idealist philosophy. Ideologies could be endlessly debated, and existing elites always had ways of making sure

base (or substructure) of society
In Marxist theory, the means of production

superstructure
In Marxist theory, a society's culture

ideology
In Marxist theory, ideas present in a culture that mislead average people and encourage them to act against their own interests

INSTANT ACCESS

Cultural Studies Theory

Strengths

1. Provides focus on how individuals develop their understanding of the social world
2. Asks big, important questions about the role of media for individuals
3. Respects content consumption and sharing by media users

Weaknesses

1. Has little explanatory power at the macroscopic level
2. Focuses too narrowly on individual compared with societal role of media
3. Typically relies on qualitative research; is based on unsystematic subjective observation

their ideas were dominant. Revolution was the quickest and most certain way to bring about necessary change. Elites would never willingly surrender power; it must be taken from them. Little purpose would be served by making minor changes in ideology without first dominating the means of production.

NEO-MARXISM

Most British cultural studies are called *neo-Marxist theories* because they deviate from classic Marxist theory in at least one important respect—they focus concern on the superstructure issues of ideology and culture rather than on the base. The importance that neo-Marxists attach to the superstructure has created a fundamental division within Marxist studies. Many neo-Marxists assume that useful change can be achieved through ideological battles—through discourse in the public arena—rather than by violent revolution. Some neo-Marxists have developed critiques of culture that demand radical transformations in the superstructure, whereas others argue that modest reforms can lead to useful changes. Tensions have arisen among Marxist scholars over the value of the work undertaken by the various schools of neo-Marxist theory. Nonetheless, since the end of the Cold War, neo-Marxist positions have achieved great popularity and broad acceptance in the social sciences.

TEXTUAL ANALYSIS AND LITERARY CRITICISM

Modern European cultural studies have a second, very different source—a tradition of humanist criticism of religious and literary texts based in hermeneutics (Chapter 1).

Humanists have specialized in analyzing written texts since the Renaissance. One common objective was to identify those texts having greatest cultural value and interpreting them so their worth would be appreciated and understood by others. These humanists saw texts as a civilizing force in society (Bloom, 1987), and hermeneutics was seen as a scholarly tool that could be used to enhance this force. Humanist scholars ranged from religious humanists, who focused on the

high culture
Set of cultural artifacts including music, art, literature, and poetry that humanists judge to have the highest value

Bible or the writings of great theologians, to secular humanists working to identify and preserve what came to be known as the "literary canon"—a body of the great literature. The literary canon was part of what theorists referred to as **high culture**, a set of cultural artifacts including music, art, literature, and poetry that humanists judged to have the highest value. By identifying and explaining these important texts, humanists attempted to make them more accessible to more people. Their long-term goal was to preserve and gradually raise the level of culture—to enable even more people to become humane and civilized. In this way it would be possible to advance civilization in Europe and its colonies.

Over the years, many different methods for analyzing written texts have emerged from hermeneutic theory. They are now being applied to many other forms of culture, including media content. They share a common purpose: to criticize old and new cultural practices so those most deserving of attention can be identified and explicated and the less deserving can be dismissed. This task can be compared with that of movie critics who tell us which films are good or bad and assist us in appreciating or avoiding them. But movie critics are typically not committed to promoting higher cultural values; most only want to explain which movies we are likely to find entertaining.

Contemporary critical theory includes both neo-Marxist and hermeneutic approaches. Hybrid theories combine both. Before examining these, we will look at some of the historically important schools of critical theory that have produced still-influential work.

THE FRANKFURT SCHOOL

Frankfurt School
Group of neo-Marxist scholars who worked together in the 1930s at the University of Frankfurt

One early prominent school of neo-Marxist theory developed during the 1920s and 1930s at the University of Frankfurt and became known as the **Frankfurt School**. Two of the most prominent individuals associated with the school were Max Horkheimer, its longtime head, and Theodor Adorno, a prolific and cogent theorist. In contrast with some later forms of neo-Marxism, the Frankfurt School combined Marxist critical theory with hermeneutic theory. Most Frankfurt School theorists were trained in humanistic disciplines but adopted Marxist theories as a basis for analyzing culture and society. Frankfurt School writings identified and promoted various forms of high culture such as symphony music, great literature, and art. Like most secular humanists, members of the Frankfurt School viewed high culture as having its own integrity and inherent value and thought that it should not be used by elites to enhance their personal power. Oskar Negt (1978, p. 62) has argued that Frankfurt School writing can best be understood from a political position that "takes a stand for people's needs, interests, and strivings toward autonomy and which also conscientiously undertakes practical steps toward making these things a reality today."

culture industries
Mass media that turn high culture and folk culture into commodities sold for profit

The Frankfurt School celebrated high culture while denigrating mass culture (Arato and Gebhardt, 1978). In one of their later and most influential books, Adorno and Horkheimer (1972) criticized mass media as **culture industries**—industries that turned high culture and folk culture into commodities sold for profit. The goal of that commodification was "to deceive and mislead ... [having]

only one real function: to reproduce incessantly the values of capitalist culture" (O'Brien and Szeman, 2004, p. 105). Here is how Adorno and Horkheimer themselves expressed this view:

> Under monopoly all mass culture is identical, and the lines of its artificial framework begin to show through. The people at the top are no longer so interested in concealing monopoly: as its violence becomes more open, so its power grows. Movies and radio need no longer pretend to be art. The truth that they are just business is made into an ideology in order to justify the rubbish they deliberately produce. They call themselves industries; and when their directors' incomes are published, any doubt about the social utility of the finished products is removed. (1972, p. 121)

Many of the specific criticisms of mass culture offered by Frankfurt School theorists were not that different from those of conservative humanistic scholars. But humanist critics tended to focus on specific media content, whereas Horkheimer and Adorno began to raise questions about the larger industries producing the content.

The Frankfurt School had a direct impact on American social research because the rise of the Nazis forced its Jewish members into exile. Horkheimer, for one, took up residency at the New School for Social Research in New York City. During this period of exile, Frankfurt School theorists remained productive. They devoted considerable effort, for example, to the critical analysis of Nazi culture and the way it undermined and perverted high culture. In their view, Nazism was grounded on a phony, artificially constructed folk culture cynically created and manipulated by Hitler and his propagandists. This hodgepodge of folk culture integrated many bits and pieces of culture borrowed from various Germanic peoples. But Nazism did appeal to a people humiliated by war and deeply troubled by a devastating economic depression. It helped them envision the Germany they longed to see—a unified, proud nation with a long history of achievement and a glorious future. As they rose to power, the Nazis replaced high culture with their pseudo-folk culture and discredited important forms of high culture, especially those created by Jews.

DEVELOPMENT OF NEO-MARXIST THEORY IN BRITAIN

During the 1960s and 1970s, two important schools of neo-Marxist theory emerged in Great Britain: British cultural studies and political economy theory. British cultural studies combines neo-Marxist theory with ideas and research methods derived from diverse sources, including literary criticism, linguistics, anthropology, and history (Hall, 1980a). It attempted to trace historic elite domination over culture, to criticize the social consequences of this domination, and to demonstrate how it continues to be exercised over specific minority groups and subcultures. British cultural studies criticizes and contrasts elite notions of culture, including high culture, with popular everyday forms practiced by minorities and other subcultures. It challenges the superiority of all forms of elite culture, including high culture, and compares it with useful, meaningful forms of popular culture. Hermeneutic attention is shifted from the study of elite cultural artifacts to the study of minority group "lived culture" and the way that media are used by groups to enhance their lives.

Graham Murdock (1989b) traced the rise of British cultural studies during the 1950s and 1960s. Most of its important theorists came from the lower social classes. The British cultural studies critique of high culture and ideology was an explicit rejection of what its proponents saw as alien forms of culture imposed on minorities. They defended indigenous forms of popular culture as legitimate expressions of minority groups. Raymond Williams was a dominant early theorist and a literary scholar who achieved notoriety with his reappraisals of cultural development in England. Williams pieced together a highly original perspective of how culture develops based on ideas taken from many sources, including literary theories, linguistics, and neo-Marxist writing. He questioned the importance of high culture and took seriously the role of folk culture. Not surprisingly, many of his colleagues at Cambridge University viewed his ideas with suspicion and skepticism. Throughout most of his career, he labored in relative obscurity at his own university while achieving a growing reputation among left-wing intellectuals at other academic institutions and in the British media.

Toward the end of the 1960s and into the 1970s, Williams (1967, 1974) turned his attention to mass media. Although media weren't the primary focus of his work, he developed an innovative, pessimistic perspective of mass media's role in modern society. His ideas inspired a generation of young British cultural studies scholars, first at the Centre for Contemporary Cultural Studies at the University of Birmingham and then at other universities across England and Europe. Williams was more broadly concerned with issues of cultural change and development, as well as elite domination of culture. Committed to certain basic humanistic values, including cultural pluralism and egalitarianism, he argued that mass media posed a threat to worthwhile cultural development. In contrast with most humanists of his time, Williams rejected the literary canon as a standard, and with it, traditional notions of high culture. But he was equally reluctant to embrace and celebrate folk culture—especially when it was repackaged as popular mass media content. If there were to be genuine progress, he felt, it would have to come through significant reform of social institutions.

The first important school of cultural studies theorists was formed at the University of Birmingham during the 1960s and was led first by Richard Hoggart and then by Stuart Hall. Hall (1982) was especially influential in directing several analyses of mass media that directly challenged limited-effects notions and introduced innovative alternatives. Building on ideas developed by Frankfurt School-trained Jurgen Habermas (1971, 1989) and Williams, Hall (1981b) understood ideology to be "those images, concepts, and premises which provide frameworks through which we represent, interpret, understand, and make sense of some aspect of social existence" (p. 31). As such, he argued that mass media in liberal democracies can best be understood as a **pluralistic public forum** in which various forces struggle to shape popular notions about social existence. In this forum, new concepts of social reality are negotiated and new boundary lines between various social worlds are drawn. Unlike traditional neo-Marxists, however, Hall did not argue that elites can maintain complete control over this forum. In his view, elites don't need total control to advance their interests. The culture expressed in this forum is not a mere superficial reflection of the superstructure but is instead a dynamic creation of opposing groups. To Hall (1981a, p. 228), popular culture "is the ground on

pluralistic public forum

In critical theory, the idea that media may provide a place where the power of dominant elites can be challenged which the transformations are worked." Elites, however, *do* retain many advantages in the struggle to define social reality. Counterelite groups must work hard to overcome them. Hall acknowledged that heavy-handed efforts by elites to promote their ideology can fail, and well-planned efforts to promote alternative perspectives can succeed even against great odds. Nevertheless, the advantages enjoyed by elites enable them to retain a long-term hold on power.

This disagreement over the immutability of ideology, "the relatively determined nature of social life and cultural forms under industrial capitalism" in the words of media theorist Klaus Bruhn Jensen, highlights the distinction between the more traditional Marxist **structuralist view** of culture and Hall's **culturalist view** (1991, p. 28). Where Hall saw culture as a site of social struggle and a place where change could occur, theorists such as Louis Althusser (1970) saw much less freedom, as elite control over the superstructure was near total. When culture becomes too free, elites enforce their ideology through that part of the superstructure he called *repressive state apparatuses*, for example the police and other law-making and enforcing institutions. But that is typically unnecessary because of their hegemonic control over *ideological state apparatuses*, the media and other social institutions like schools and religion.

structuralist view
Elite control over the superstructure through repressive and ideological state apparatuses

culturalist view
Culture is the site of social struggle and a place where change occurs

A key strength *and* limitation of some British cultural studies theorists is their direct involvement in various radical social movements. In keeping with their commitment to critical theory, they not only study movements but also enlist in and even lead them. Some cultural studies advocates argue that a person cannot be a good social theorist unless he or she is personally committed to bringing about change (O'Connor, 1989). Cultural studies theorists have been active in a broad range of British social movements, including feminism, youth movements, racial and ethnic minority movements, and British Labour Party factions. But active involvement can make objective analysis of movements and movement culture difficult. These cultural studies theorists usually don't worry about this because their axiology rejects the possibility of objectivity anyway and dismisses its utility for social research. Their intention is to do research that aids the goals of movements rather than conduct work that serves the traditional aims of scholarship or science.

INSTANT ACCESS

British Cultural Studies

Strengths

1. Asserts value of popular culture
2. Empowers "common" people
3. Empowers minorities and values their culture
4. Stresses cultural pluralism and egalitarianism
5. Developed audience reception research as a way of understanding media influence

Weaknesses

1. Is too political; call to action is too value-laden
2. Typically relies on qualitative research; is based on unsystematic subjective observation
3. Can overlook subtle, indirect ways that elites control media and audience reception

British cultural studies has addressed many questions and produced a variety of research on popular media content and the use that specific social groups make of it. Does this content exploit and mislead individuals or does it enable them to construct meaningful identities and experiences? Can people take ambiguous content and interpret it in new ways that fundamentally alter its purpose for them? Can useful social change be achieved through cultural reform rather than through social revolution?

In the United States, British cultural studies was an early influence on scholars in many fields, particularly the work of feminists (Long, 1989) and those who study popular culture (Grossberg, 1989). They saw it as offering an innovative way of studying media audiences that had many advantages over approaches grounded in limited-effects theory.

POLITICAL ECONOMY THEORY

Political economy theorists study elite control of economic institutions, such as banks and stock markets, and then show how this control affects many other social institutions, including the mass media (Murdock, 1989a). In certain respects, political economists accept the classic Marxist assumption that the base dominates the superstructure. They investigate the means of production by looking at economic institutions, expecting to find that these institutions shape media to suit their interests and purposes. For example, Herb Schiller, "one of the most widely recognized and influential political economists of communication" (Gerbner, 2001, p. 187), wrote for decades that "corporate influence pervades nearly every aspect of society. From simple things, like our daily diet and the clothes we wear, to matters of larger scale, like the way we communicate with each other" (Schiller, 2000, p. 101).

Political economists have examined how economic constraints limit or bias the forms of mass culture produced and distributed through the media. We've already seen Frankfurt School theorists express similar concerns. Political economists are not interested in investigating how mass culture influences specific groups or subcultures. They focus on how the processes of content production and distribution are economically and industrially constrained. Why do some forms of culture dominate prime-time television schedules whereas other forms are absent? Does audience taste alone explain those differences or can other, less obvious reasons be linked to the interests of economic institutions? Critical scholar Sut Jhally offers a near-perfect example of a political economy answer to these questions:

> All commodities have two fundamental features: they have *exchange-value* (that is, they are worth something and can be exchanged in the marketplace) and they have *use-value* (that is, they do something that makes them useful to human beings). What is the use-value of a cultural commodity? Its function, and its importance, stems from the *meaning* it generates. Records, films, newspapers, etc. provide meaning for their consumers. If a cultural commodity did not provide this then it would not be capable of being sold. People buy things for their use-value. Cultural commodities also have an exchange-value within the sphere of the marketplace—that is how profit is generated by the producers of the cultural commodities.... Are they of equal importance or is one more important than the other? ... Within the United States there has never been any questioning of the domination of use-value by exchange-value.... In the United States we

INSTANT ACCESS

Political Economy Theory

Strengths

1. Focuses on how media are structured and controlled
2. Offers empirical investigation of media finances and industry structure
3. Seeks link between media content production, media structure, and media finances

Weaknesses

1. Has little explanatory power at microscopic level
2. Is not concerned with causal explanation; is based on subjective analysis of industry structure and finances
3. Is not concerned with audience reception or media use

call government interference domination, and marketplace governance freedom. We should recognize that the marketplace does not automatically ensure diversity, but that ... the marketplace can also act as a serious constraint to freedom. (1989, pp. 80–81)

During the past four decades, compared to cultural studies theorists, political economy theorists have worked in relative obscurity. Although political economy theories gained respect in Europe and Canada, they were largely ignored in the United States. Later in this chapter we'll consider the work of Harold Innis, a Canadian economist who pioneered political economy research in Canada. Even though American communication theorists were intrigued by cultural studies theory, few found the views of political economists interesting or persuasive until quite recently, as we'll see in Chapter 9's discussion of news production research.

THE DEBATE BETWEEN CULTURAL STUDIES AND POLITICAL ECONOMY THEORISTS

Although the two schools of neo-Marxist theory—British cultural studies and political economy theory—appear to be complementary, there has been considerable rivalry between them (Murdock, 1989b). Some genuine theoretical differences separate the two, but they also differ in their research methods and the academic disciplines in which they are based. With their macroscopic focus on economic institutions and their assumption that economic dominance leads to or perpetuates cultural dominance, political economists were slow to acknowledge that cultural changes can affect economic institutions. Nor do political economists recognize the diversity of popular culture or the variety of ways in which people make sense of cultural content. Murdock suggested that the two schools should cooperate rather than compete. For this to happen, however, researchers on both sides would have to give up some of their assumptions and recognize that the superstructure and the base—culture and the media industries—can influence each other. Both types of research are necessary to produce a complete assessment of the role of media.

Other differences as well have led to serious debates between these two major schools of cultural theory. Cultural studies theorists tend to ignore the larger social and political context in which media operate. They focus instead on how individuals and groups consume popular culture content. Their research has led them to become increasingly skeptical about the power of elites to promote hegemonic forms of culture. Instead, they have found that average people often resist interpreting media content in ways that would serve elite interests (see the discussion of oppositional decoding in Chapter 7). Some cultural studies theorists have been less interested in making or influencing social policy, and their research often doesn't provide a clear basis for criticizing the status quo. Political economy theorists accuse some cultural studies researchers of abandoning the historical mission of critical theory in favor of an uncritical celebration of popular culture. They argue that it is important for theorists to actively work for social change. You can get some idea of why they think this is important by reading the box entitled "Media Coverage of Workers and the Working Poor."

Political economy theorists have remained centrally concerned with the larger social order and elites' ownership of media. They have criticized the growing privatization of European media, the decline of public service media institutions in Europe, and the increasing privatization and centralization of media ownership around the world. They take pride in remaining true to the mission of critical theory by remaining politically active and seeking to shape social policy. They have formed social movements and serve as leaders in others. Above all, political economy theorists are critical—they have an explicit set of values providing a basis for their evaluation of the status quo.

CULTURAL STUDIES: TRANSMISSIONAL VERSUS RITUAL PERSPECTIVES

transmissional perspective
View of mass communication as merely the process of transmitting messages from a distance for the purpose of control

ritual perspective
View of mass communication as the representation of shared belief where reality is produced, maintained, repaired, and transformed

James Carey was a leading American proponent of cultural studies, writing and speaking prolifically for the past three decades. At a time when U.S. media researchers viewed most cultural studies work with suspicion and skepticism, Carey, in a series of seminal essays (1989), drew on the work of British and Canadian scholars to defend cultural studies and contrast it with the media effects trend. One essential difference he found is that effects theories focus on the transmission of accurate information from a dominant source to passive receivers, whereas cultural studies is concerned with the everyday rituals people rely on to structure and interpret their experiences. Carey argued that the limited-effects view is tied to the **transmissional perspective**—the idea that mass communication is the "process of transmitting messages at a distance for the purpose of control. The archetypal case ... then is persuasion, attitude change, behavior modification, socialization through the transmission of information, influence, or conditioning" (Newcomb and Hirsch, 1983, p. 46). In the transmissional perspective, car commercials attempt to persuade us to buy a certain make of automobile, and political campaign messages are simply that: campaign messages designed to cause us to vote one way or another. They might or might not be effective in causing us to act as they intend.

The **ritual perspective**, on the other hand, links communication to "'sharing,' 'participation,' 'association,' 'fellowship,' and 'the possession of a common faith.'" It shares the same root with the words "'commonness,' 'communion,' 'community' ... A ritual view of communication is directed not toward the extension of messages in space but toward the maintenance of society in time; not the act of imparting

THINKING ABOUT THEORY | Media Coverage of Workers and the Working Poor

Think *labor unions*. What comes to mind? More than likely strikes (probably rowdy if not violent) and cigar-chomping, burly bosses. You're not alone. A recent poll found that attitudes toward unions are quite unfavorable: fewer than 45 percent of Americans expressed a favorable view toward unions; only 34 percent thought unions improved workplace productivity; and only 24 percent thought they improved the ability of U.S. companies to compete globally (Pew Research Center for the People and the Press, 2011). Critical theorists, especially political economy theorists, would tell you that these perceptions of labor are a product not only of the American media system, but of a national economy that devalues its poorest workers. "You could argue, without any shortage of compassion," wrote sociologist Barbara Ehrenreich, "that 'Low-Wage Worker Loses Job, Home' is nobody's idea of news." But at a time when the official national unemployment rate had reached double-digits and "blue-collar unemployment is increasing three times as fast as white-collar unemployment," stories such as the *Washington Post*'s "Squeaking by on $300,000" and "World's Wealthy Pay a Price in Crisis" seem coldly out of place (Ehrenreich, 2009, p. WK10; Hart, 2009, p. 5).

The working poor are invisible in the media, argue political economists, but all labor, especially organized labor, fares badly as well. When was the last time you read a news story about unions seeking ways to increase productivity or enhance global competitiveness, two ongoing efforts of the American labor movement? The media lauded the heroes of the 2009 "Miracle on the Hudson," the dramatic landing of a crippled US Airways jetliner on the Hudson River that saved 115 lives, yet not a single report mentioned that the plane's crew, captain Sully Sullenberger, and every one of the hundreds of rescue workers who came to their aid on that frigid morning were union members. The heroes of 9/11, the police and fire rescue personnel who rushed into the burning and crumbling Twin Towers? All union, every one (Wheeler, 2009).

What can we expect, argue political economists, from a system whose celebrity journalists consider $250,000 to be "middle-class" although only 2.0 percent of all U.S. households earn that much (Gross, 2010)? What can we expect, they argue, when the

characters in television's entertainment programming "compose a community far removed from our own: a town with a data-capture expert but no dishwasher, a rocket scientist but no sanitation worker, and a tech magnate but no truck driver. [Television] is full of people who run their own businesses, often inherited: an inn, a brew pub, a winery, a portrait gallery. Compared to the rest of us, they're much more likely to be wrangling with underlings or regulators rather than bosses" (Eidelson, 2011). "Who wants to become involved with characters fretting about losing their homes when there's fresh dirt on Britney?" asks *Variety*'s Cynthia Littleton (2008, p. 1).

Is this much ado about nothing? What does it matter if people with work-a-day jobs or a union card show up in the media? David Swanson (2005) of the International Labor Communications Association, answers, "News reports that pay any respect to the interests of working people or to organized labor are virtually non-existent on broadcast television, national cable television, and radio.… Labor news does not exist in the national media that provide most people with their understanding of public affairs. And it exists in the most marginalized, distorted, and silenced way in the corporate print medium?"

Mass communication researchers Christopher Martin (2004) and Federico Subervi (2013) collected empirical evidence for Swanson's observations, as did press critic Peter Hart (2005). Hart and his colleagues demonstrated that in one nineteen-month span of Sunday morning network television news shows featuring 364 different guests, only two were representatives of organized labor. Subervi's analysis showed that in the years 2008, 2009, and 2011, fewer than 0.3 percent of news stories aired on the four national news broadcasting networks involved labor unions or labor issues, and a majority of the stories that did run featured labor protests and pickets. "The narrative of labor is conflict," he wrote, "Even in stories about labor or unions, the main sources relied on are external to labor or unions.… Moreover, the discourse and framing continues to fault the workers and their representatives for any conflict or impasse, not the business, company or government."

Martin examined labor coverage in the three major television networks, *USA Today*, and the *New York*

(Continued)

THINKING ABOUT **THEORY** | **Media Coverage of Workers and the Working Poor**
(Continued)

Times, examining their reporting of several high-profile labor strikes in the 1990s, including work stoppages by flight attendants at American Airlines, delivery people at UPS, assembly line workers at a Michigan GM plant, and the 1994 baseball strike. He discovered that these outlets invariably based their presentations of labor disputes on five "key assumptions":

1. The consumer is always right; reports stress how strikes affect consumers while ignoring workplace issues and conditions leading to the action.
2. The public doesn't need to know about the "process of production," that is, how the workers do their jobs and how that fits into the overall functioning of their organizations.
3. Business leaders are the true heroes of the American economy (they keep costs down; they settle strikes).
4. The workplace is and should be a meritocracy (so why should all workers get a raise or better benefits?).
5. Collective action by workers distorts the market—we all pay more because workers want more.

These assumptions, according to Martin, produce coverage that is inevitably biased against workers because it sets them apart from and in opposition to those in the audience (who, of course, are themselves likely to be workers).

Similarly, Mark Harmon's (2001) examination of labor coverage demonstrated that in disputes between labor and management, network television news tells us that labor makes "demands" while management makes "offers"; it details workers' compensation while ignoring executive pay; and company, not union, logos typically appear onscreen over anchors' shoulders. David Madland (2008) studied coverage of four economic issues—employment,

minimum wage, trade, and credit card debt—in the five highest circulation American newspapers, the three major broadcast networks, and the three top cable news networks. He found that across all four issues, representatives of business were quoted or cited nearly two and a half times as frequently as workers or their union representatives. In coverage of the minimum wage and trade, the views of businesses were quoted more than one and a half times as frequently as those of workers. And in coverage of employment, businesses were quoted or cited more than six times as frequently as workers.

Outcomes such as these are inevitable, argue political economists, because American journalism "is founded on a couple of very bad ideas: It's a bad idea to have journalism mainly carried out by large corporations whose chief interest in news is how to make the maximum amount of money from it. And it's a bad idea to have as these corporations' main or sole source of revenue advertising from other large corporations" (Naureckas, 2009, p. 5). "You don't need to be a rocket scientist or a social scientist," explained syndicated columnist Norman Solomon, "to grasp that multibillion-dollar companies are not going to own, or advertise with, media firms that challenge the power of multibillion-dollar companies" (2009, p. 16). "It's not to the advantage to ABC or CBS or NBC to tell stories that make Walmart look bad, or make Calvin Klein look bad," explains Roberta Reardon, vice president of the AFL-CIO (in Ludwig, 2013).

Is the American media system capable of providing better journalism on workers and the working poor? Will it present workers and the working poor more frequently and realistically any time soon? Of course not, answer critical theorists; our media system is immersed in and enriched by a political economy that benefits from the devaluation of work and workers. Your turn. What do you think? Is this a realistic or pessimistic view of the American economic and media systems?

---

information but the representation of shared beliefs" (Carey, 1989, pp. 18–19). Carey believed, in other words, that "communication is a symbolic process whereby reality is produced, maintained, repaired, and transformed" (1975a, p. 177). According to Carey, a car commercial sells more than transportation. It is, depending on its actual content, possibly reaffirming the American sense of independence ("Chevy, the American Revolution!"), reinforcing cultural notions of male and female attractiveness (we don't see many homely actors in these ads), or extolling the personal value of consumption, regardless of the product itself ("Be the first on your block to have one"). Similarly, political campaign messages often say much more about our political system and us as a people than they say about the candidates featured in them.

Carey traced the origin of the ritual view to hermeneutic literary criticism. Scholars who study great literary works have long argued that these texts have far-reaching, long-lasting, and powerful effects on society. A classic example is the impact that Shakespeare has had on Western culture. By reshaping or transforming culture, these works indirectly influence even those who have never read or even heard of them. Literary scholars argue that contemporary cultures are analyzed and defined through their arts, including those arts that depend on media technology. These scholars have not been interested in finding evidence of direct media effects on individuals. They are more concerned with macroscopic questions of cultural evolution—the culture defining itself for itself. Thus ritual perspective theorists presume a grand-scale interaction between the culture, the media used to convey that culture, and the individual media content consumers of that culture.

During the 1970s and 1980s, a variety of communication theorists began to move away from more transmissionally oriented questions like "What effects do media have on society or on individuals?" and "How do people use the media?" toward broader examinations of how cultures become organized, how people negotiate common meaning and are bound by it, and how media systems interact with the culture to affect the way culture develops. This, as we'll see in Chapter 10 allowed cultural theories to become home for a variety of people who presumed the operation of powerful mass media—for example, advertising and market researchers, neo-Marxist media critics, and even sophisticated effects researchers. The primary focus was no longer on whether media have certain effects on individuals, but rather on the kind of people we are, we have become, or we are becoming in our mass-mediated world.

RESEARCH ON POPULAR CULTURE IN THE UNITED STATES

During the 1960s and 1970s, some American literary scholars began to focus their research on popular culture. By 1967, this group had grown large enough to have its own division (Popular Literature Section) within the Modern Language Association of America and to establish its own academic journal, *The Journal of Popular Culture*. These scholars were influenced by British cultural studies and by Canadian media scholar Marshall McLuhan. They adapted a variety of theories and research methods, including hermeneutics and historical methods, to study various forms of popular culture. Unlike British critical theorists, most have no links to social movements. They focus much of their attention on television and, now, the Internet as the premier media of the electronic era. Many express optimism about the future and the positive role of electronic media, rather than subscribing to the pessimistic vision of Williams.

Some of the best examples of popular culture research have been provided by Horace Newcomb in *TV: The Most Popular Art* (1974) and in his much-respected anthology, *Television: The Critical View*, which has had several updated editions (2007). These books summarize useful insights produced by researchers in popular culture, emphasizing that popular media content generally, and television programming specifically, are much more complex than they appear on the surface. Multiple levels of meaning are often present, and the content itself is frequently ambiguous.

Sophisticated content producers recognize that if they put many different or ambiguous meanings into their content, they will have a better chance of appealing to different audiences. If these audiences are large and loyal, the programs will have high ratings. Though Newcomb wrote long before the advent of *Modern Family*, *Big Bang Theory*, and *The Simpsons*, and cable television series such as *South Park*, *The Newsroom*, *Dexter*, and *Weeds*, these programs illustrate his argument. They make an art of layering one level of meaning on top of another so that fans can watch the same episode over and over to probe its meaning.

A second insight well articulated by Newcomb is that audience interpretations of content are likely to be quite diverse. The fact that some people make interpretations at one level of meaning, whereas others make their interpretations at other levels, is referred to as **multiple points of access**. Some interpretations will be highly idiosyncratic, and some will be very conventional. Sometimes groups of fans will develop a common interpretation, and sometimes individuals are content to find their own meaning without sharing it. We'll revisit this theme in Chapter 7's discussion of reception studies.

multiple points of access

Idea that some people make interpretations at one level of meaning, whereas others make their interpretations at others

One researcher whose work combines the popular culture approach with neo-Marxist theory is Larry Grossberg (1983, 1989). His take on popular culture "signals [the] belief in an emerging change in the discursive formations of contemporary intellectual life, a change that cuts across the humanities and the social sciences. It suggests that the proper horizon for interpretive activity, whatever its object and whatever its disciplinary base, is the entire field of cultural practices, all of which give meaning, texture, and structure to human life" (Grossberg and Nelson, 1988, p. 1). Although his synthesis proved controversial (O'Connor, 1989), it has gained wide attention. Part of its popularity stems from Grossberg's application of contemporary European theories to the study of popular culture. More recently, he has moved more toward neo-Marxist theory and has coedited two large anthologies of research, *Marxism and the Interpretation of Culture* (Nelson and Grossberg, 1988) and *Cultural Studies* (Grossberg, Nelson, and Treichler, 1992).

The serious study of popular culture poses a direct challenge to mass society theory, the limited-effects perspective, and notions of high culture for several reasons. In asserting the power of audiences to make meaning, popular culture researchers grant a respect to *average* people that is absent from mass society and limited-effects thinking. In treating popular culture as culturally important and worthy of study, they challenge high culture's bedrock assumption of the inherent quality of high-culture artifacts like symphonies and opera. In suggesting that individual audience members use media content to create personally relevant meaning, they open the possibility of media effects that are consumer-generated or -allowed. In short, in arguing the crucial cultural role played by the interaction of people and media texts, researchers studying popular culture lend support to all the cultural theories.

CRITICAL FEMINIST SCHOLARSHIP

Feminist popular culture researchers were instrumental in legitimizing and popularizing critical cultural theory in the United States. They adopted Carey's ritual perspective (communication is directed not toward the act of imparting information, but the representation of shared beliefs) rather than the effects trend's causal model of media influence. Some also worked in the neo-Marxist tradition of European cultural studies theory, making them open to a greater variety of research methods than those "approved" by traditional U.S. postpositivist effects researchers. Feminist critical scholars brought literary criticism, linguistics, anthropology, history, and even quantitative methods to their study of male domination of females and its consequences.

Naturally, however, it was the culture's ongoing and systematic sexism that motivated their research, as Noreene Janus explained in her classic 1977 "Research on Sex-Roles in Mass Media: Toward a Critical Approach":

> One of the most striking developments in American social life during the past decade is the growth of a feminist movement which has energetically and persistently challenged the sexist nature of our society. As part of a comprehensive attack on sexism, U.S. feminists have analyzed the major institutions—such as family, school, church, and mass media—to understand how sexism as an ideology is perpetuated. They have repeatedly charged that, of all these institutions, the mass media are especially potent mechanisms for the transmission of sexist ideas due to their ever-increasing role in our daily lives. (p. 19)

Although she readily acknowledged that there existed much good research on the portrayal of sex-roles in the media, Janus believed that not only was this not sufficient, it was detrimental to the cause of feminism. She argued for *critical* feminist research as a substitute for what she called the work of *liberal feminists*. For Janus, the way American liberal feminists posed their research problems, selected their methodologies, framed their questions, and drew their conclusions inevitably produced an "affirmation of the very framework" that produced the inequalities they were studying. "A liberal feminist, believing that the most important social division is between men and women," she wrote, "may set up research measuring the men against the women and then conclude that the research proves that the sexual division is the most fundamental" (1977, p. 22). But, she argued, "the most fundamental division within society is not that of men vs. women but rather than between the classes" (p. 24). Feminist cultural scholarship, therefore, would become feminist critical cultural scholarship when researchers focused their attention on larger social and economic structures. "The problem of sexism in the media must not be seen in terms of males oppressing females without at the same time demonstrating the historical development of sexism and its present relationship to capitalist relations of production.... A critical perspective will demonstrate not only that the women in the media are inferior to men, but also the limited and demeaning images of women are structurally related to the functioning of capitalism" (p. 29).

If Janus's neo-Marxism was a fruitful route of inquiry for critical feminist scholarship, so too was political economy theory. As Eileen Meehan and Ellen Riordan recently explained, "For the United States and the emerging global economy, sex plus money equals power. Addressing this equation in media studies requires the integration of feminism and political economy. This integrative approach is not simply a matter of adding one to the other. Rather, we argue that all media structures, agents, processes, and expressions find their raison d'être in the relationships shaped by sex and money" (2002, p. x).

Eventually, this feminist critical cultural scholarship would bring "new insights and a sense of crucial urgency to longstanding questions in communication research" (Wartella and Treichler, 1986, p. 4). Those insights tended to flow from four general approaches to feminist critical scholarship (Rakow, 1986). The *images and representations approach* attempted to answer the questions: what kinds of images of women are there in the media and what do they reveal about women's position in the culture; whose images are they and whom do they benefit; what are the consequences of those images; and, how do these images come to have meaning? The *recovery and reappraisal approach* asked: how have women managed to express themselves in a male-dominated culture; why is women's creativity overlooked, undervalued, or ignored; how do women and men's creativity differ; and, what are women's myths and stories? The *reception and experience approach* focused on female media consumers' experiences and perceptions, primarily of cultural products they found popular, as a means of granting women the means to speak for themselves about their own lives and experiences. Finally, *the cultural theory approach*, rather than examine content, as do the first three approaches, focuses on the organization and production of culture. It "stands back" from content to get a better view of the social and economic structures that produce culture in order to examine how they influence women's experiences and social positions.

Critical feminist media scholarship in the United States had another source, textual analysis of film and cinema based in **psychoanalytic theory**, which, drawn from Freudian psychology, argues that all human thought and action is driven by inner psychological and emotional factors, often outside of people's awareness. Its home in critical cultural theory is clear in Laura Mulvey's 1975 "Visual Pleasures and Narrative Cinema." Hollywood, she argued, "always restricted itself to a formal mise-en-scène reflecting the dominant ideological concept of the cinema" (Mulvey, 1975/1999, p. 834). And although, she admitted, Hollywood's monolithic grip on the film industry was at the time weakening, its ideology remained, typically presenting men and women differently, with men the active drivers of the movie's action and narrative and women existing primarily as passive objects for men's desire and fetishistic gazing. Deeply rooted in the pleasure humans find in looking at other people as objects, movies, as a capitalistic culture product, "portray a hermetically sealed world which unwinds magically, indifferent to the presence of the audience, producing for them a sense of separation and playing on their voyeuristic phantasy" (pp. 835–836). Because the world is "ordered by sexual imbalance," she writes, "the determining male gaze projects its phantasy on to the female figure which is styled accordingly" (p. 837). Why is the female figure "styled" to encourage the male gaze? Cinema, "artisanal as well as capitalist," seeks an audience. But why not also "style" male characters to attract female gaze? "According to the principles of the ruling ideology and the psychical structures that back it up, the male figure cannot bear the burden of sexual objectification" (p. 838). As a result, women are left with two options, identify with the onscreen males or identify with

psychoanalytic theory
All human thought and action is driven by inner psychological and emotional factors, often outside of people's awareness

the objectified females. Either way, their film viewing reinforces the very ideology that denigrates them. For Mulvey, women's image has "continually been stolen and used" to further traditional narrative film's "voyeuristic active/passive mechanisms" (p. 844). Her solutions? One is to make film less interesting, "It is said that analyzing pleasure, or beauty, destroys it. That is the intention of this article." The second, more reasonable and in line with the goals of critical theory, is emancipatory knowledge, "The alternative is the thrill that comes from leaving the past behind without rejecting it, transcending outworn or oppressive forms, or daring to break with normal pleasurable expectations in order to conceive a new language of desire" (p. 835).

MARSHALL MCLUHAN: THE MEDIUM IS THE MESSAGE AND THE MASSAGE

During the 1960s, a Canadian literary scholar, Marshall McLuhan, gained worldwide prominence as someone who had a profound understanding of electronic media and their impact on both culture and society. McLuhan was highly trained in literary criticism but also read widely in communication theory and history. Although his writings contain few citations to Marx (McLuhan actually castigated Marx for ignoring communication), he based much of his understanding of media's historical role on the work of Harold Innis, a Canadian political economist. Still, in his theory, McLuhan synthesized many other diverse ideas. We place him at the end of this chapter because his most influential writing was done in the 1960s, when cultural studies emerged as a serious challenge to limited-effects perspectives on media. But his work anticipates the development of the culture-centered theories that are the focus of Chapter 10 and so can be read as a preface to much of what is covered in that chapter.

With James Carey, whom many consider the founder of American cultural studies and who shared McLuhan's respect for Innis, McLuhan did much to inspire and legitimize macroscopic theories of media, culture, and society in North America. He wrote at a time when the limited-effects perspective had reached the peak of its popularity among academics in the United States, a time when most American communication researchers regarded macroscopic theory with suspicion, if not outright hostility. In the humanities, it was a time when the high-culture canon still consisted largely of "classic" work (European novels, symphonies, serious theater) produced by, white, Anglo-Saxon males, now dead. McLuhan's focus on the cultural role of popular media quickly posed a challenge both to limited-effects notions and to the canon.

McLuhan and his ideas are again in vogue. It is no small irony that McLuhan, hailed (or denigrated) in the 1960s as the "High Priest of Popcult," the "Metaphysician of Media," and the "Oracle of the Electronic Age," to this day is listed as "Patron Saint" on the masthead of *Wired* magazine, the "Bible of Cyberspace." "McLuhan came up with a theory of media generation and consumption so plastic and fungible that it describes the current age without breaking a sweat" writes technologist David Carr (2011, p. 10).

McLuhan's "theory" is actually a collection of lots of intriguing ideas bound together by some common assumptions. The most central of these, "All media, from the phonetic alphabet to the computer, are extensions of man [*sic*] that cause deep and lasting changes in him and transforms his environment" (1962, p. 13), argued that *changes in communication technology inevitably produce profound changes in both culture and social order.*

technological determinist

A person who believes that all social, political, economic, and cultural change is inevitably based on the development and diffusion of technology

Even though McLuhan drew on critical cultural theories such as political economy theory to develop his perspective, his work was rejected by political economists because it failed to provide a basis on which to produce positive social change. McLuhan had no links to any political or social movements. He seemed ready to accept whatever changes were dictated by and inherent in communication technology. Because he argued that technology inevitably causes specific changes in how people think, in how society is structured, and in the forms of culture that are created, McLuhan was a **technological determinist**.

HAROLD INNIS: THE BIAS OF COMMUNICATION

Harold Innis was one of the first scholars to systematically speculate at length about the possible linkages between communication media and the various forms of social structure found at certain points in history. In *Empire and Communication* (1950) and *The Bias of Communication* (1951), he argued that the early empires of Egypt, Greece, and Rome were based on elite control of the written word. He contrasted these empires with earlier social orders dependent on the spoken word. Innis maintained that before elite discovery of the written word, dialogue was the dominant mode of public discourse and political authority was much more diffuse. Gradually, the written word became the dominant mode of elite communication, and its power was magnified enormously by the invention of new writing materials (specifically paper) that made writing portable yet enduring. With paper and pen, small, centrally located elites were able to gain control over and govern vast regions. Thus new communication media made it possible to create empires.

Innis argued that written word-based empires expanded to the limits imposed by communication technology. Thus expansion did not depend as much on the skills of military generals as it did on the communication media used to disseminate orders from the capital city. Similarly, the structure of later social orders also depended on the media technology available at a certain point in time. For example, the telephone and telegraph permitted even more effective control over larger geographic areas. Everett Rogers paraphrased Innis: "The changing technology of communication acted to reduce the cost and increase the speed and distance of communication, and thus to extend the geographic size of empires" (2000, p. 126). As such, the introduction of new media technology gradually gave centralized elites increased power over space and time.

bias of communication

Innis's idea that communication technology makes centralization of power inevitable

Innis traced the way Canadian elites used various technologies, including the railroad and telegraph, to extend their control across the continent. As a political economist, he harbored a deep suspicion of centralized power and believed that newer forms of communication technology would make even greater centralization inevitable. He referred to this as the inherent **bias of communication**. Because of this bias, the people and the resources of outlying regions that he called *the periphery* are inevitably exploited to serve the interests of elites at *the center*.

MCLUHAN: UNDERSTANDING MEDIA

Although he borrowed freely from Innis, McLuhan didn't dwell on issues of exploitation or centralized control. His views on the cultural consequences of capitalist-dominated media were much more optimistic than those of the Frankfurt School. He was fascinated by the implications of Innis's arguments concerning the transformative power of media technology. He didn't fear the ways elites might exercise this power. If the technology itself determines its use, then there is nothing to fear from elites. If media could be used to create empires, what else could the elites do?

So McLuhan began asking different questions. Was it possible, for example, that media could transform our sensory experiences as well as our social order? After all, the acts of reading a book and viewing a movie or television program employ different sensory organs. During the 1960s, we were clearly moving from an era grounded in print technology to one based on electronic media. If communication technology plays such a critical role in the emergence of new social orders and new forms of culture, McLuhan wanted to know, what are the implications of abandoning print media in favor of electronic media?

McLuhan explained his vision of the implications of the spread of electronic media with catchy, and what proved to be lasting, phrases. He proclaimed that **the medium is the message** (*and the massage*). In other words, new forms of media transform (massage) our experience of ourselves and our society, and this influence is ultimately more important than the content that is transmitted in its specific messages—technology determines experience.

the medium is the message
McLuhan's idea that new forms of media transform our experience of ourselves and our society, and this influence is ultimately more important than the content of specific messages

He used the term **global village** to refer to the new form of social organization that would inevitably emerge as instantaneous electronic media tied the entire world into one great social, political, and cultural system. Unlike Innis, McLuhan didn't bother to concern himself with questions about control over this village or whether village members would be exploited. To McLuhan, these questions didn't matter. He was more concerned with microscopic issues, with the impact of media on our senses and where this influence might lead.

global village
McLuhan's conception of a new form of social organization emerging as instantaneous electronic media tie the entire world into one great social, political, and cultural system

McLuhan proclaimed, as we've seen, media to be **the extensions of man** [*sic*] and argued that media quite literally extend sight, hearing, and touch through time and space. Electronic media would open up new vistas for average people and enable us to be everywhere instantaneously. But was this an egalitarian and democratic vision? What would ordinary people do when their senses were extended in this way? Would they succumb to information overload? Would they be stimulated to greater participation in politics? Would they flee into the virtual worlds opened to them by their extended senses? In his writing and interviews, McLuhan tossed out cryptic and frequently contradictory ideas that addressed such questions. Occasionally, his ideas were profound and prophetic. More often, they were arcane, mundane, or just confusing.

the extensions of man
McLuhan's idea that media literally extend sight, hearing, and touch through time and space

Though he was often a cryptic prophet, McLuhan's observations concerning the global village and the role of electronic media in it are seen by many as anticipating the most recent developments in electronic media—this is precisely why the editors of *Wired* made McLuhan their patron saint. At a time when satellite communication was just being developed, he foretold the rise of 24-hour cable news networks and their ability to seemingly make us eyewitnesses to history as it's made on the battlefield or at the barricade. At a time when mainframe computers filled entire floors of office buildings, he envisioned a time when personal computers would be everywhere and the Internet would give everyone instant access to immense stores of information. But as one media critic (Meyrowitz, 1985) noted, to be everywhere is to be nowhere—to have no sense of place. To have access to information is not the same thing as being able to effectively select and use information. The global village isn't situated in space or time. Is it possible to adjust to living in such an amorphous, ambiguous social structure? Or will the global village merely be a facade used by cynical elites to exploit people? These questions go far beyond the paeans to electronic media that can be found throughout *Understanding Media.*

McLuhan's ideas achieved enormous public popularity. He became one of the first pop culture gurus of the 1960s. His pronouncements on the Nixon/Kennedy presidential race propelled him to national prominence. (Nixon was too "hot" for the "cool" medium of television; Kennedy was appropriately "cool.") McLuhan's ideas received serious attention but then fell into disfavor. Why the rise and sudden fall?

Initially, McLuhan's work fit the spirit of the early 1960s—"The Age of Camelot." In sharp contrast with political economists like Innis or neo-Marxist thinkers like those of the Frankfurt School, he was unabashedly optimistic about the profound but ultimately positive changes in our personal experience, social structure, and culture that new media technology would make possible. Unlike limited-effects theorists, he didn't dismiss media as unimportant. McLuhan was the darling of the media industries—their prophet with honor. For a brief period, he commanded huge fees as a consultant and seminar leader for large companies. His ideas were used to rationalize rapid expansion of electronic media with little concern for their negative consequences. They were corrupted to become broadcast industry gospel: So what if children spend most of their free time in front of television sets and become functionally illiterate? Reading is doomed anyway—why prolong its demise? Eventually, we will all live in a global village where literacy is as unnecessary as it was in preliterate tribal villages. Why worry about the negative consequences of television when it is obviously so much better than the old media it is replacing? Just think of the limitations that print media impose. Linear, logical thinking is far too restrictive. If the triumph of electronic media is inevitable, why not get on with it? No need for government regulation of media. The ideal form of media can be expected to evolve naturally, no matter what we try to do. No need to worry about media conglomerates. No need to complain about television violence. No need to resist racist or sexist media content. Adopt McLuhan's long-term global perspective. Think big. Think nonlinearly. Just wait for the future to happen. But was McLuhan *really* an optimist about the electronic future? You can judge for yourself by reading the box entitled "Was McLuhan Really an Optimist?"

But even as McLuhan's work became more accepted within the media industries, it aroused increasing criticism within academia. Perhaps the most devastating criticism was offered by other literary critics, who found his ideas too diverse and inconsistent. They were astounded by his notion that literacy was obsolete and found his praise of nonlinear thinking nonsensical or even dangerous. These critics thought nonlinear thinking was just an excuse for logically inconsistent, random thoughts. They called McLuhan's books brainstorms masquerading as scholarship.

THINKING ABOUT THEORY | Was McLuhan Really an Optimist?

McLuhan's writing could be pretty dense at times. But even his critics have had to admit that he was indeed way ahead of his time in anticipating much of the technology we now take for granted. Read what he had to say in *Understanding Media* (1964) about the relationship between the earth's growing population and how its inhabitants might coexist:

> The stepping-up of speed from the mechanical to the instant electric form reverses explosion into implosion. In our present electric age the imploding or contracting energies of our world now clash with the old expansionist and traditional patterns of organization. Until recently our institutions and arrangements, social, political, and economic, had shared a one-way pattern. We still think of it as "explosive," or expansive; and though it no longer obtains, we still talk about the population explosion and the explosion in learning. In fact, it is not the increase of numbers in the world that creates our concern with population. Rather, it is the fact that everybody in the world has to live in the utmost proximity created by our electric involvement in one another's lives. (p. 36)

It's safe to say that by "the utmost proximity created by our electric involvement in one another's lives," McLuhan is invoking the global village, where "proximity" would be enforced and maintained by instantaneous electronic media. But is he saying that this is necessarily a good thing? Remember, many of McLuhan's critics charged that he was overly optimistic about technology's influence. What do you make of "our concern" with population? To be "concerned" about something doesn't imply great optimism.

Technology optimist and McLuhan devotee Joseph C. R. Licklider relied on McLuhan's ideas when writing his seminal 1960 essay called *Man-Computer Symbiosis*. In it he predicted an America composed of citizens linked by "home computer consoles" and "informed about, and interested in, and involved in the process of government.... The political process would essentially be a giant teleconference, and a campaign would be a months-long series of communications among candidates, propagandists, commentators, political action groups, and voters. The key is the self-motivating exhilaration that accompanies truly effective interaction with information through a good console and a good network to a good computer" (quoted in Hafner and Lyon, 1996, p. 34). It was Licklider's, and therefore by extension McLuhan's, writing that encouraged scores of engineers and scientists to move toward the development of the Internet at a time when big, powerful mainframe computers were only just becoming available. McLuhan's and Licklider's optimism was rewarded.

Or was it? Are you an optimist or a pessimist about large numbers of people in close, electronic proximity? What has been your experience with the Internet, in general, and social networking websites like Facebook and Twitter in particular? Have these sites changed the social world of college students for better or worse? Has the Internet transformed the political process into a big, robust conversation, or has the screaming match only become more global and more unwieldy?

McLuhan himself might argue that he never was as optimistic about the "neighborliness" of the global village as his critics liked to assert. Speaking of our electronically imposed proximity, he said, "There is more diversity, less conformity under a single roof in any family than there is with the thousands of families in the same city. The more you create village conditions, the more discontinuity and division and diversity. The global village absolutely insures maximal disagreement on all points" (McLuhan and Steam, 1967, p. 279).

McLuhan answered by charging that these critics were too pedantic, too concerned with logic and linear thinking. They were too dependent on literacy and print media to be objective about them. They were the elitist defenders of the high-culture canon. Their jobs depended on the survival of literacy. He recommended that they work hard to free their minds from arbitrary limitations. Not surprisingly, few were willing to do so.

Effects trend media researchers were also uniformly critical of McLuhan, but for different reasons. Although a few tried to design research to study some of his notions, most found his assumptions about the power of media to be absurd. They were indoctrinated in effects theories and skeptical about the possibility that media could transform people's experience. Even if this was possible, how could research be designed to systematically study things as amorphous as "people's experience of the social world" or the "global village"? When early small-scale empirical studies failed to support McLuhan's assertions, their suspicions were confirmed. McLuhan was just another grand theorist whose ideas were overly speculative and empirically unverifiable.

McLuhan fared even less well with most critical cultural theorists. Although many of them respected Innis, they found McLuhan's thinking to be a perversion of Innis's basic ideas. Rather than attempt reform of the superstructure or lead a revolution to take control of the base, McLuhan seemed to be content to wait for technology to lead us forward into the global village. Our fate is in the hands of media technology, and we are constrained to go wherever it leads, he implied. Political economists saw this as a self-fulfilling prophecy, encouraging and sanctioning the development of potentially dangerous new forms of electronic media. These might well lead us to a painful future—a nightmare global village in which we are constantly watched and coerced by remote elites. As long as existing elites remained in power, political economists saw little hope for positive change. They condemned McLuhan for diverting attention from more important work and perverting the radical notions found in Innis's writing. Some political economists even saw McLuhan's ideas as a form of disinformation, deliberately designed to confuse the public so neo-Marxist work would be ignored or misinterpreted.

Despite these criticisms of McLuhan's work, much in it merits attention. Everett Rogers (2000) has argued that McLuhan's perspective deserves more attention by mass communication scholars, especially those interested in studying new media. Some young scholars find it an exciting starting point for their own thinking (Wolf, 1996). This is possible because McLuhan's work is so eclectic and open-ended.

INSTANT ACCESS

McLuhanism

Strengths

1. Is comprehensive
2. Is macroscopic
3. Resonated with the general public in the 1960s and 1970s
4. Elevates cultural value of popular media content
5. Anticipates a future in which media play a central role in fostering community
6. Enjoys longevity as a result of introduction of new electronic media

Weaknesses

1. Can't be verified by effects research
2. Is overly optimistic about technology's influence
3. Ignores important effects issues
4. Calls for nonlinear thinking, the value of which is questioned
5. Is overly apologetic of electronic media
6. Questions the value of literacy and argues for its inevitable decline

SUMMARY

Over the past four decades, the critical cultural theory trend has provided important alternative perspectives on the role of media in society. This trend includes theories that have their intellectual roots in Marxist theory, but they have incorporated and been influenced by other perspectives, including literary criticism. Theorists argue that mass media often support the status quo and interfere with the efforts of social movements to bring about useful social change. But they also argue that ordinary people can resist media influence and that media might provide a pluralistic public forum in which the power of dominant elites can be effectively challenged.

Many forms of theory and research examined in this book are produced by effect trend researchers who exclude values as irrelevant to the work at hand. Some cultural theory, however, is critical theory. It is more or less explicitly based on a set of specific social values. Critical theorists use these values to critique existing social institutions and social practices. They also criticize institutions and practices that undermine or marginalize important values. They offer alternatives to these institutions and practices and develop theory to guide useful social change.

Unlike earlier schools of Marxist theory, or even early neo-Marxist Frankfurt School theory, recent neo-Marxist cultural theorists reject the view that mass media are totally under the control of well-organized dominant elites who cynically manipulate media content in their own interest. Instead, they view media as a pluralistic public forum in which many people and groups can participate. However, they do recognize that elites enjoy many advantages in the forum because most media content, they believe, implicitly or explicitly supports the status quo. Also,

critical theorists reject simplistic notions of powerful and negative audience effects like those found in mass society theory. Even when media content explicitly supports the status quo, audiences can reinterpret or reject this content.

The ritual perspective of mass communication as articulated by James Carey sees the media as central to the representation of shared beliefs. This contrasts with the transmissional perspective that views media as mere senders of information, usually for the purpose of control. As dissatisfaction with media effects trend theories grew in the 1970s and 1980s, more and more communication theorists, even those with a postpositivist orientation, began to move toward this ritual perspective.

The rise of the critical cultural theory trend has produced research that is converging on a common set of themes and issues. Cultural studies and political economy theory have played an important role in identifying these themes and prioritizing these issues. Despite questions about the value of these approaches, they have proved heuristic. Cultural theorists make bold assertions and explicitly incorporate values into their work. They provide a useful challenge to mainstream media theory, as do popular culture researchers who grant much power to audiences and cultural value to such popular texts as television series and popular music. Critical feminist scholars, too, have raised important questions not only about media and women, but about the way the discipline has traditionally examined that relationship. Although controversial at the time, the ideas of Marshall McLuhan—many of which were based on the much-respected work of Harold Innis—underlie, at least implicitly, much contemporary critical and cultural theory.

Critical Thinking Questions

1. Critical theory, by definition, questions and challenges the status quo in hopes of changing it. But is this a proper role for any social scientific theory? After all, the status quo seems to be working for most of us; it certainly is for those who engage in critical theory. They probably have nice jobs at comfortable universities or think tanks.

Can you reconcile fundamental assumptions about the value of your social system with efforts to change it?

2. Does your hometown or state capital have a sponsored symphony, theater, or dance troupe, for example, the Boston Opera House, the New York Philharmonic, or the Houston Ballet? Why do municipal or state governments offer financial support to elite arts organizations such as these? Shouldn't the market decide? If these operations cannot survive on their own, why should taxpayers underwrite them? After all, does your city or state underwrite hip-hop or jazz clubs, rock 'n' roll, or R & B venues? What would someone from the Frankfort School say about this state of affairs? Someone from political economy theory?

3. What kind of car do you want, ideally, once you leave school? Why? What realities do you attribute to what is, in effect, little more than a sophisticated piece of steel, plastic, and glass? Where did these realities originate? How free are you to develop your own personally meaningful reality of the car you drive? And does it matter that you might not be as independent or idiosyncratic as you think? If you think cars are important primarily to men, why would this be the case? Does it suggest that the "reality" of cars is indeed constructed? If not, wouldn't men and women share the same reality? If the question asked you to consider style and fashion instead of cars, would your answers be the same?

Key Terms

culture

cultural studies

hegemonic culture

political economy theory

critical theories

qualitative methods

grand social theories

Marxist theory

base (or substructure) of society

superstructure

ideology

high culture

Frankfurt School

culture industries

pluralistic public forum

structuralist view (of culture)

culturalist view (of culture)

transmissional perspective

ritual perspective

multiple points of access

psychoanalytic theory

technological determinist

bias of communication

the medium is the message

global village

the extensions of man

6 | THEORIES OF MEDIA AND HUMAN DEVELOPMENT: CHILDREN AND ADOLESCENTS

In 1960, for every minute someone in an American household consumed media of any sort, there were a total of 82 minutes of content from which to choose. That may sound like information overload, but by 2005, the number had grown to 884 incoming minutes for every one minute consumed, an 1,000 percent increase in those 45 years (Neuman, Park, and Panek, 2012). In 1980, totaling all at-home media use, Americans received about seven hours of information a day. In 2009 they received 11.8 hours, or "3.6 zettabytes [a zettabyte is a billion trillion bytes]. Imagine a stack of paperback novels stacked seven feet high over the entire United States, including Alaska" (Young, 2009). Today, the gigabyte equivalent of all the movies ever made crosses global Internet networks every three minutes. It would take more than 6 million years to watch all the video that will travel the Internet in a single month. In 2016, 1.2 million minutes of video content will traverse the Internet every second (Cisco, 2012). Americans alone stream 3.8 billion minutes of video *advertising*—9.9 billion individual ads—a month (O'Malley, 2013).

As remarkable as these data may seem, they represent only a brief snapshot of the mass communication world into which contemporary kids are born and grow up. Today's children begin watching television attentively by the age of three. Nine-month-olds spend an hour a day in front of a television screen; kids under two spend twice as much time watching television than being read to. Forty-two percent of children under eight have a TV in their bedrooms, 29 percent a DVD player, 11 percent a video game console, and 4 percent a computer; 24 percent own their own handheld gaming device (Common Sense, 2011). Kids 2 to 11 watch a monthly total of 150 hours and 48 minutes of video, more than five hours a day. One-third of that time is on traditional TV and the rest on other video devices, including nearly four hours of Internet video ("On-Demand," 2013).

Before most children start school or form close relationships with peers, they have learned the names of countless television characters and are fans of particular programs. By the first day of elementary school, they are already watching nearly three hours a day. By eight years, they are watching four full hours. By the time they finish high school, average teenagers will have spent more time in front of their televisions than in school. Most children also spend more time with their television sets than they do communicating with their friends or family. If other forms of media like radio, MP3 players, movies, video games, magazines, the Internet, and smartphones are considered, the contrast between time spent with media and time with the "actual" world and "real" people becomes even more striking. As the authors of the Kaiser Family Foundation's study of "Generation M^2" (for "media") argued, "As anyone who knows a teen or a tween can attest, media are among the most powerful forces in young people's lives today. Eight- to eighteen-year-olds spend more time with media than in any other activity besides (maybe) sleeping—an average of more than seven-and-a-half hours a day, seven days a week. The TV shows they watch, video games they play, songs they listen to, books they read, and websites they visit are an enormous part of their lives, offering a constant stream of messages about families, peers, relationships, gender roles, sex, violence, food, values, clothes, and an abundance of other topics too long to list" (Rideout, Foehr, and Roberts, 2010, p. 2). Increasingly, children and young adults live in a mediated world where face-to-face communication with others is supplemented by and interwoven with a broad range of mediated communication. "The media environment that children grow up in has changed dramatically, and the amount of time they spend consuming media has exploded," writes media researcher Victoria Rideout, "Childhood and adolescence have been inundated with—and possibly transformed by—reality TV, smartphones, iPads, Facebook, Twitter, YouTube, *World of Warcraft*, *Angry Birds*, and texting, to name just a few" (2012a, p. 5). As a result, explains George Gerbner, "For the first time in human history most of the stories most of the time to most of the children are told no longer by the parents, no longer by the school, no longer by the church, no longer by the community, no longer hand-crafted, no longer community-based, no longer historically inspired, inherited, going from generation to generation, but essentially by a small group of global conglomerates that really have nothing to tell but have a lot to sell" (2010).

LEARNING OBJECTIVES

After studying this chapter you should be able to

- Explain how the social and technological changes that followed World War II paved the way for television and a theoretical reconsideration of media influence.

- Distinguish between various "violence theories" such as catharsis and social cognitive theory, as well as explain the operation of their many components such as aggressive cues, imitation and identification, observational learning, inhibitory and disinhibitory effects, priming effects, and the cognitive-neoassociationistic perspective.

- Identify the many important contextual variables that can influence the demonstration of media-influenced aggression.

- Recognize how the active theory of television viewing and the developmental approach have enriched the understanding of media effects.

- Explain how research on violent video games not only supports the television violence theories, but has produced deeper understandings of media effects on aggression.

- Follow the progression from this primarily children-oriented research to additional questions, asked by both effects and critical researchers, on the relationship between media consumption and young people's cognitive and emotional development.

- Appreciate cultural criticism of kinderculture and its redefining of childhood.

OVERVIEW

On August 6, 1945, the United States dropped an atom bomb on Hiroshima, effectively ending World War II. That four-year global conflict forced cataclysmic changes in the nation's economic, industrial, demographic, familial, and technological character, the impact of which would be felt most powerfully in the 1960s.

The mass medium that was to transform that decade—television—had an inauspicious introduction as a novelty at the 1939 World's Fair in New York. Its tiny picture, poor sound quality, and high cost led some to doubt its future as a popular medium. How could it compete with movies? Would people really want to sit at home and watch ghostly black-and-white images on a small screen when they could walk a few blocks to see powerful Technicolor images on a gigantic screen? During the next three years, a small number of experimental television stations began broadcasting a limited number and variety of programs to a minuscule audience. When the United States entered the war, television's already limited diffusion to the public halted, as the technologies and materials needed to improve and produce the medium went to the war effort. Technological research, however, did not stop. Therefore, when the war ended and materials were once again available for the manufacture of consumer goods, a technologically mature new medium was immediately available. Anticipating not only this, but also dramatic changes in American society that would benefit the new medium, the national commercial radio networks were already planning to move their hit shows and big stars to television.

This technological advance occurred simultaneously with profound alterations in U.S. society. The war changed the country from a primarily rural society boasting an agriculturally based economy into a largely urban nation dependent on an industrially based economy. After the war, more people worked regularly scheduled jobs (rather than the sunrise-to-sunset workday of farmers), and they had more leisure. More people had regular incomes (rather than the seasonal, put-the-money-back-into-the-land farmer's existence), and they had more money to spend on that leisure. Because the manufacturing capabilities developed for the war were still in existence, the economy had the ability to mass-produce items on which that money could be spent. Because more consumer goods were competing in the marketplace, there was a greater need to advertise, which provided the economic base for the new television medium. Because non-Caucasian Americans had fought in the war and worked in the country's factories, they began to demand their rightful share of the American dream. Because women entered the workforce while the men were off to battle, it was more common and acceptable to have both parents working outside the home. Because people had moved away from their small towns and family roots, the traditional community anchors—church and school—began to lose their dominance in the social and moral development of children who were present in the 1960s—in their teenage years—in inordinately large numbers because of the baby boom that occurred soon after war's end.

As in all periods of significant societal change, there were serious social problems. The rapid rise in the number of teenagers brought sharp increases in delinquency and crime. Critics blamed the schools for failing to educate children into responsible citizenship. Crime waves swept one city after another. Race riots broke out in several urban areas. Successive social movements captured the attention of the nation, especially the civil rights and the anti–Vietnam War movements. Some activists like the Black Panthers and the Weathermen became notorious for their willingness to use violence to pursue their objectives. Political instability reached new heights with the assassinations of President John F. Kennedy, Martin Luther King, Jr., and Robert Kennedy. Young people were behaving strangely. Many were listening more to new, unfamiliar music and less to their increasingly "old-fashioned, irrelevant" parents. Social scientists discovered the existence of a "generation gap" between conservative middle-class parents and their increasingly liberal, even radical children.

Media's role in all these changes was hotly debated. Although social researchers and media practitioners continued to put forward arguments based on limited-effects research findings, a new generation of observers charged that media were harming children and disrupting their lives. Evidence mounted that families, schools, and churches had become less important to children. As Urie Bronfenbrenner (1970) said, the backyards were growing smaller and the school yards growing bigger. In other words, young people were increasingly being socialized away from parents' influence. Bronfenbrenner's research demonstrated that, whereas parents and church had been the primary socializing agents for prewar American adolescents, by the mid-1960s, media and peers shared top billing in the performance of that crucial function.

It is no surprise, then, that the media, particularly television, became the target of increasing criticism and the object of intense scientific inquiry, especially where harmful effects were presumed. But these renewed efforts to probe the negative influence of mass media occurred when the effects trend was at the height of its influence among academics and virtually all research findings pointed to limited effects. An intense and continuing debate erupted between social researchers who had confidence in that approach to research and those skeptical of its conclusions despite the consistency of its empirical findings. Strong advocates of limited-effects notions were accused of being paid lackeys of the media industries, and overzealous critics of television were accused of being unscientific, oversimplifying complex problems, and ignoring alternative causes.

social cognitive theory
Theory of learning through interaction with the environment that involves reciprocal causation of behavior, personal factors, and environmental events

General Aggression Model (GAM)
Model of human aggression that argues that cognition, affect, and arousal mediate the effects of situational and individual personal variables on aggression

adultification of childhood
When children's value as consumers trumps their value as people, threatening their physical, psychological, social, emotional, and spiritual development

But psychologists working outside the prevailing media effects trend thought they could explain some of the contemporary social turmoil in microscopic—that is, individual—terms. Psychologists turned their attention to how people, especially children, learned from the mass media, especially television. What would eventually become known as **social cognitive theory** and its early attention to children moved communication theorists from their focus on the effects trend's findings of limited media influence. They directed much of their attention toward increases in the amount of real-world violence and the possible contribution of the new medium of television to that rise.

Social scientists developed several different perspectives on the effects of television violence, including catharsis, social learning, social cognitive theory, aggressive cues, and priming effects. Whereas the latter four perspectives see media as a possible factor in increasing the likelihood of actual violence, catharsis argues just the opposite. We will study these approaches as well as the context of mediated violence—that is, how violence and aggression are presented in the media. We will also examine differing understandings of how children interact with the media, specifically the active theory of television viewing and the developmental perspective. Additionally, we will look at recent interest in the media–violence link fueled by the explosion of realistic, participatory video games. This repurposing of the original television violence theories has produced a new model of media effects, the **General Aggression Model (GAM)**, which argues that "the enactment of aggression is largely based on knowledge structures (e.g., scripts, schemas) created by social learning processes" (Anderson and Dill, 2010, p. 773).

Violent video game play is also a factor in the discipline's contemporary focus on adolescents, or in other words, the relationship between media and development. Critical cultural scholars have also taken an interest in issues of young people's development, specifically in the relationship between their increased media consumption and the commercialization and **adultification of childhood**. Finally, as advances in mass communication theory and research are often driven by the development of new technologies and efforts to control their impact, we will also begin a discussion, to be continued in later chapters, of research and theory surrounding the use of new personal technologies.

FOCUS ON CHILDREN AND VIOLENCE

The argument about the media's role in fomenting social instability and instigating violence reached a peak in the late 1960s. After disruptive race riots in the Los Angeles suburb of Watts and in the cities of Cleveland, Newark, and Detroit, President Lyndon Johnson established two national commissions, the Kerner Commission in 1967 and the National Commission on the Causes and Prevention of Violence in 1968. They offered serious criticism of media and recommended a variety of changes in both news reporting and entertainment content. Writing in the preface to the 1968 commission's staff report, *Violence and the Media*, editor Paul Briand asked, "If, as the media claim, no objective correlation exists between media portrayals of violence and violent behavior—if, in other words, the one has no impact upon the other—then how can the media claim an impact in product selection and consumption, as they obviously affect the viewers' commercial attitudes and behavior? Can they do one and not the other?" (Baker and Ball, 1969, p. vii). This question reflected growing public and elite skepticism concerning effects trend–supported assumptions of a benign mass media.

The federal government itself tried to locate new answers to this problem by establishing the Surgeon General's Scientific Advisory Committee on Television and Social Behavior in 1969. Its purpose was to commission a broad range of research on television effects that might determine whether television could be an important influence on children's behavior. What did this collection of scientists conclude after two years and a million dollars of study? The surgeon general, Jesse L. Steinfeld, reported to a U.S. Senate subcommittee:

> While the ... report is carefully phrased and qualified in language acceptable to social scientists, it is clear to me that the causal relationship between televised violence and antisocial behavior is sufficient to warrant appropriate and immediate remedial action. The data on social phenomena such as television and violence and/or aggressive behavior will never be clear enough for all social scientists to agree on the formulation of a succinct statement of causality. But there comes a time when the data are sufficient to justify action. That time has come. (U.S. Congress, 1972, p. 26)

Nevertheless, this report did little to end the controversy over television's effects. Industry officials and lobbyists worked hard to block development and implementation of new Federal Communications Commission regulations for children's programming. They cited inconclusive research and restated limited effects arguments. Eventually the industry agreed to a self-imposed family viewing hour in which violent content was ostensibly minimized, and at the time, all three broadcast television networks tightened their programming standards and worked closely with program producers to limit gratuitous violence.

TELEVISION VIOLENCE THEORIES

The most important outcome of this television violence research was the gradual development of a set of theories that summarized findings and offered increasingly useful insight into the media's role in the lives of young people. Taken together, they now provide strong support for the link between television viewing and aggression. For example, nearly three decades ago (and 20 years after the surgeon general's call for action), after reviewing years of relevant research on the question, Aletha Huston and her colleagues wrote:

> The accumulated research clearly demonstrates a correlation between viewing violence and aggressive behavior—that is, heavy viewers behave more aggressively than light viewers.... Both experimental and longitudinal studies support the hypothesis that viewing violence is causally associated with aggression.... Field [naturalistic] experiments with preschool children and adolescents found heightened aggression among viewers assigned to watch violent television or film under some conditions. (1992, pp. 54–55)

Ten years after that Brad Bushman and Craig Anderson (2002) again reviewed the literature and concluded that the link between media violence and subsequent aggression has more scientific support than that of the relationship between self-examination and early detection of breast cancer, the amount of calcium intake and bone mass, and the use of condoms to prevent sexually transmitted disease. According to Brandon Centerwall in the *Journal of the American Medical Association*, "Manifestly, every violent act is the result of an array of forces coming together—poverty, crime, alcohol and drug abuse, stress—of which childhood exposure to television is just one. Nevertheless, the epidemiological evidence indicates that if, hypothetically, television technology had never been developed, there would today be 10,000 fewer homicides each year in the United States, 70,000 fewer rapes, and 700,000 fewer injurious assaults" (quoted in Vander Neut, 1999, p. 40).

Still, debate persists, or to be more precise, it persists inasmuch as a small number of scholarly skeptics (see Bushman, Rothstein, and Anderson, 2010) and many media industry spokespeople (see Tsukayama, 2013) continue to claim that the science is inconclusive. Even an overwhelming majority, 77 percent, of American parents accept the media violence–aggression connection (Mandese, 2013). You can assess for yourself the current state of thinking on media violence by reading the box entitled "Setting the Record Straight on Media Violence."

CATHARSIS

catharsis
Also called *sublimation*, the idea that viewing mediated aggression sates, or reduces, people's natural aggressive drives

The findings from the surgeon general's report on one aspect of the television violence debate, **catharsis**, were quite clear and did generate significant agreement. Testified CBS's Joseph Klapper, "I myself am unaware of any, shall we say, hard evidence that seeing violence on television or any other medium acts in a cathartic or sublimated manner. There have been some studies to that effect; they are grossly, greatly outweighed by studies as to the opposite effect" (U.S. Congress, 1972, p. 60). Yet catharsis (sometimes called sublimation)—the idea that viewing violence is sufficient to purge or at least satisfy a person's aggressive drive and therefore reduce the likelihood of aggressive behavior—has lived a long if not thoroughly respectable life in mass communication theory.

INSTANT ACCESS

Social Cognitive Theory

Strengths

1. Demonstrates causal link between media and behavior
2. Applies across several viewer and viewing situations
3. Has strong explanatory power (e.g., rejects catharsis, stresses importance of environmental and content cues)

Weaknesses

1. Laboratory demonstration raises question of generalizability
2. Experimental demonstration might overestimate media power
3. Has difficulty explaining long-term effects of media consumption
4. Underestimates people's active use of media messages
5. Focuses too narrowly on individual rather than on cultural effects

Common sense and your own media consumption offer some evidence of the weakness of the catharsis hypothesis. When you watch couples engaged in physical affection on the screen, does it reduce your sexual drive? Do media presentations of families devouring devilish chocolate cakes purge you of your hunger drive? If viewing mediated sexual behavior does not reduce the sex drive and viewing media presentations of people dining does not reduce our hunger, why should we assume that seeing mediated violence can satisfy an aggressive drive? Moreover, think back to when you attended movies like the *Die Hard* or *Transporter* or *Grindhouse* films. Did you walk out of the theater a tranquil, placid person? Probably not.

Yet it isn't difficult to see why the proposition seemed so attractive. For one thing, the philosopher Aristotle originally discussed catharsis in his *Poetics* to explain audience reaction to Greek tragedy. Even though he never wrote of the "purging" of an innate aggressive drive, but rather about audiences "purging" their own emotions of pity and fear because in a tragic play they saw misfortune befalling others (Gadamer, 1995), catharsis developed a conventional wisdom-based validity. For another, catharsis suggested that television violence had social utility—that is, it was functional, providing young people with a harmless outlet for their pent-up aggression and hostility. In television's early days, many people were anxious to rationalize their use of this attractive new medium, and the effect trend's embrace of functionalism (Chapter 4) supported that rationale.

There was even early scientific evidence suggesting that catharsis was indeed at work. Seymour Feshbach (1961) demonstrated what he said was catharsis by insulting college-age men with "a number of unwarranted and extremely critical remarks" in an experimental setting and then having them watch either filmed aggression (a brutal prize fight) or a neutral film (on the spread of rumors). The men were then asked to evaluate the experiment and the insulting experimenter. Those who had seen the prize fight were less aggressive in their attitudes than those who had seen the other film.

But, as F. Scott Andison wrote in 1977 after reviewing 20 years' worth of scientific evidence, "We can conclude on the basis of the present data cumulation that television, as it is shown today, probably does stimulate a higher amount of aggression in individuals within society. Therefore, it seems reasonable to tentatively accept the 'TV violence as a stimulant to aggression' theory and to reject the … 'cathartic' theories" (p. 323). Or as James D. Halloran (1964/65), then director of Britain's Center for Mass Communication Research at the University of Leicester, more directly put it, catharsis is a "phony argument."

But Feshbach *did* demonstrate a reduction in aggression after viewing, and he obtained similar results in a 1971 study (Feshbach and Singer, 1971) conducted with funding from NBC. The research was undertaken in a group home for preadolescent boys. For six weeks, half of the boys were restricted to watching television programs with little or no violence while the other half was allowed to watch violent content. A variety of behavioral measures indicated that the boys viewing the violent programs were less aggressive. These results may not have been caused by catharsis, however. The boys who were placed in the nonviolent programming group may have been frustrated because they were not allowed to watch some of their favorite shows. Heightened frustration might account for their increased aggressiveness.

What social scientists would eventually learn, however, is that certain presentations of mediated violence and aggression *can reduce* the likelihood of subsequent viewer aggression. But catharsis is not the reason. Rather, viewers *learn* that violence might not be appropriate in a given situation. Reconsider the first Feshbach study (1961). Maybe those who had seen the brutal boxing match, who had seen unnecessary pain inflicted on another human, simply said to themselves, "Aggression is not a good thing." Their aggressive drive might not have been purged, but they simply might have *learned* that such treatment of another human is inappropriate. In other words, their inclination toward aggression (remember, they had been insulted) was inhibited by the information in the media presentation. This leads us to the theory that is generally accepted as most useful in understanding the influence of media violence on individuals—social cognitive theory.

SOCIAL LEARNING

Humans learn from observation. There has been some question, however, about how much and what kinds of behaviors people learn from the media. This debate has been fueled, in part, by a definitional problem. No one questions whether people can imitate what they see in the media. **Imitation** is the direct mechanical reproduction of behavior. After watching Spike TV's *Ultimate Fighting Championship*, 23 Connecticut teens engage in a backyard slugfest/tournament that results in their arrest. Or two teenagers set fire to a New York subway toll-booth, killing its attendant, after seeing the movie *Money Train*. Both are true stories; both demonstrate imitation. The problem for mass communication theorists, however, is that these obvious examples of media influence, dramatic as they may be, are relatively rare. Moreover, such gross examples of media influence lend substance to the argument that negative effects occur only for those "predisposed" to aggression—in other words, those who are already more likely to act aggressively.

imitation
The direct reproduction of observed behavior

identification
A special form of imitation that springs from wanting to be and trying to be like an observed model relative to some broader characteristics or qualities

Identification, on the other hand, is "a particular form of imitation in which copying a model, generalized beyond specific acts, springs from wanting to be and trying to be like the model with respect to some broader quality" (White, 1972, p. 252). Although only one or a very few people might have *imitated* the behaviors seen in our *Ultimate Fighting Championship* and *Money Train* examples, how many others *identified* with their characters? How many others might choose different forms of violence against someone they might encounter? How many others identified with the characters' mode of problem solving, although they might never express it exactly as did our mediated aggressors? Imitation from media is clearly more dramatic and observable than is identification. But identification with media models might be the more lasting and significant of the media's effects. (For a detailed discussion of this distinction and its importance to media theory, see Baran and Meyer, 1974.)

The first serious look at learning through observation was offered by psychologists Neal Miller and John Dollard (1941). They argued that imitative learning occurred when observers were motivated to learn, when the cues or elements of the behaviors to be learned were present, when observers performed the given behaviors, and when observers were positively reinforced for imitating those behaviors. In other words, people could imitate behaviors they saw; those behaviors would be reinforced and therefore learned.

Instead of presenting a means of understanding how people learn from models (including media models), however, Miller and Dollard were simply describing an efficient form of traditional stimulus-response learning. They assumed that individuals behaved in certain ways and then shaped their behavior according to the reinforcement they actually received. The researchers saw imitation as replacing random trial-and-error behaviors. Imitation simply made it easier for an individual to choose a behavior to be reinforced. That actual reinforcement, they argued, ensured learning. But this insistence on the operation of reinforcement limited their theory's application for understanding how people learn from the mass media. Its inability to account for people's apparent skill at learning new responses through observation rather than actually receiving reinforcement limited its applicability to media theory.

social learning
Encompasses both imitation and identi-fication to explain how people learn through observation of others in their environments

Two decades later, Miller and Dollard's ideas about what they called **social learning** and imitation were sufficiently developed, however, to become valuable tools in understanding media effects. Whereas Miller and Dollard saw social learning as an efficient form of stimulus-response learning (the model provided information that helped the observer make the correct response to be reinforced), contemporary social cognitive theory (as social learning theory is now known) argues that observers can acquire symbolic representations of the behavior, and these "pictures in their heads" provide them with information on which to base their own subsequent behavior. Media characters (models) can influence behavior simply by being depicted on the screen. The audience member need not be reinforced or rewarded for exhibiting the modeled behavior.

SOCIAL COGNITION FROM MASS MEDIA

operant (or tradi-tional) learning theory
Asserts that learning occurs only through the making and subsequent rein-forcement of behavior

Operant (or traditional) learning theory as developed by the early behaviorists (see Chapter 2) asserts that people learn new behaviors when they are presented with stimuli (something in their environment), make a response to those stimuli, and have those responses reinforced either positively (rewarded) or negatively (punished). In this way, new behaviors are learned, or added to people's **behavioral repertoire**—the behaviors available to an individual in a given circumstance.

behavioral repertoire
The learned responses available to an individual in a given situation

Two things are clear, however. First, this is an inefficient form of learning. We all know, for example, how to deal with fire. If each of us had to individually learn our fire-related behavior, we would have overcrowded hospitals. According to operant learning theory, each of us, when presented with that stimulus (fire), would render a chance response (put our hand in it), and be burned. To ensure that we would not be scorched in the future, we would add avoidance of fire to our behavioral repertoire. Because that initial burned hand "increases the probabil-ity of a given behavior over time" (in our case, avoiding flames), the stimulus (the burned hand) is a **negative reinforcer** (Zimbardo and Weber, 1997, p. 215). This process is very inefficient. Instead we observe the operation of that stimulus-response-reinforcement chain in a variety of settings (mass-mediated and other-wise), and we in turn add avoidance to the store of behaviors that we can use when confronted in everyday life by the stimulus. In essence, then, we have

negative reinforcer
A particular stimulus whose removal, reduction, or prevention increases the probability of a given behavior over time

modeling
The acquisition of behaviors through observation

substituted a representation—a picture in our head—of an experience for an actual (and, in this case, painful) experience.

A second obvious point is that we do not learn in only this operant manner. We have all experienced learning through observation, even when we have not seen the stimulus-response-reinforcement chain—that is, when there has been no reinforcement, either to us or to the person in the representation. Observation of a behavior is sufficient for people to learn that behavior. Even people who have never shot an arrow from a bow, for example, know how it's done. **Modeling** from the mass media, then, is an efficient way to learn a wide range of behaviors and solutions to problems that we would otherwise learn slowly or not at all, or pay too high a price to learn in the actual environment.

This learning from observation of the environment, or social cognition, is the basis of social cognitive theory. According to Albert Bandura, "Social cognitive theory explains psychosocial functioning in terms of triadic reciprocal causation. In this model of reciprocal determinism, behavior; cognitive, biological, and other personal factors; and environmental events all operate as interacting determinants that influence each other bidirectionally" (1994, p. 61). In other words, things they experience in their environments (e.g., mass media) can affect people's behaviors, and that effect is influenced by various personal factors specific to those people and their situations.

This social cognition through the use of media representations operates in one or more of three ways (see Bandura, 1971, 1994, for excellent extended discussions):

observational learning
When the observation of a behavior is sufficient to learn that behavior

inhibitory effects
The effects of seeing a model punished for a behavior, thus reducing the likelihood that the observer will engage in that behavior

disinhibitory effects
The effects of seeing a model rewarded for a prohibited or threatening behavior, thus increasing the likelihood that the observer will engage in that behavior

1. **Observational learning.** Consumers of representations can acquire new patterns of behavior by simply watching these representations. We all know how to shoot a gun, although many of us have never actually performed or been reinforced for that act. Many of us probably even think that we can rob a convenience store. We've seen it done.

2. **Inhibitory effects.** Seeing a model in a representation punished for exhibiting a certain behavior decreases the likelihood that the observers will make that response. It is as if viewers themselves are actually punished. We see the villain brought low for evil deeds, or in *A Christmas Story* we observe Flick, challenged by Schwartz's triple-dog-dare, with his tongue painfully stuck to the frozen flag pole as the bell rings and his friends scurry away. Our likelihood of responding to various real-world stimuli in similar ways is reduced. Experimental studies using film and video of people being punished for various behaviors have shown that these representations can inhibit in observers such things as aggression, exploratory behavior, and antisocial interaction with peers.

3. **Disinhibitory effects.** A media representation that depicts reward for a threatening or prohibited behavior is often sufficient to increase the likelihood that the consumer of the representation will make that response. A young man sees Johnny Knoxville and his *Jackass* crew set themselves afire, apparently suffering no ill effects. His likelihood of responding to various real-world stimuli in similar ways is increased. Experimental studies using film and television representations of various threatening and prohibited encounters have successfully reduced fear of dentists, dogs, and snakes and increased aggression by reducing viewers' inhibitions regarding such action.

vicarious reinforcement

Reinforcement that is observed rather than directly experienced

reinforcement contingencies

The value, positive or negative, associated with a given reinforcer

Vicarious reinforcement is central to social cognition through the mass media. Although observational learning can occur in the absence of any reinforcement, vicarious or real, whether observers *actually engage in* that learned behavior is a function of the **reinforcement contingencies** (positive or negative) they associate with it. For example, when we see a television character rewarded or punished for some action, it is as if we ourselves have actually been rewarded or punished. This vicarious reinforcement tells us where to place the observationally learned behavior in our *behavioral hierarchy*—the likelihood that we will choose a given behavior. When presented with certain stimuli in our environment, we will be likely to choose a highly placed behavior for demonstration. One that promises punishment will be given a lower place in that hierarchy. We do not actually have to experience those rewards and sanctions; we have experienced them vicariously through the use of media representations.

Clearly, there are times when we ignore possible negative consequences and perform a behavior that we associate with punishment or restraints, such as running into a burning house. In these cases, sufficient incentive is present in the actual environment (saving a child from the flames, for example) to move that behavior up the hierarchy to a point where we choose it from among a number of alternatives. Bandura calls this **social prompting** of previously learned behaviors. This effect is "distinguished from observational learning and disinhibition because no new behavior has been acquired, and disinhibitory processes are not involved because the elicited behavior is socially acceptable and not encumbered by restraints" (2009, p. 108).

social prompting

Demonstration of previously learned behavior when it is observed as socially acceptable or without restraints

Bandura (1965) conducted what is now considered a classic experiment in modeling aggressive behavior from television, one having direct bearing on several aspects of the media effects debate. He showed nursery school children a television program in which a character, Rocky, was either rewarded for aggression (given candy and a soft drink and called a "strong champion") or punished for those same behaviors (reprimanded, called a "bully," and spanked with a rolled-up magazine). Those who saw aggression rewarded showed more aggressive activity in a

INSTANT ACCESS

Developmental Perspective

Strengths

1. Provides an age-based perspective on media effects
2. Respects children as competent, self-aware media consumers able to moderate media influence
3. Offers evidence of the eventual reduction of harmful effects and increase in positive media influence

Weaknesses

1. Misused to justify argument that as kids get older, likelihood of negative effects declines
2. Overestimates children's competence and self-awareness as media consumers in moderating media influence
3. Does not sufficiently appreciate role of media use in disrupting or otherwise influencing development

"free play" period (disinhibition), and those who saw it punished displayed less (inhibition). You can almost hear those people who believe that media have no effects on viewer aggression crowing, "See, the bad guy is punished, so media portrayals of violence actually reduce subsequent aggression."

But Bandura went one step further. He offered those in the inhibited group "sticker-pictures" for each of Rocky's aggressive acts they could demonstrate. Boys and girls alike could produce the "forbidden" behaviors (they moved up the behavioral hierarchy). The environment offered them sufficient reward to demonstrate those observationally learned but previously inhibited behaviors (social prompting). The response to the "TV violence apologists," then, is simple: The bad guy is usually "out-aggressed" by the good guy, who is rewarded for his or her more proficient display of aggression, and besides, that might not matter because the behaviors are observationally learned and can appear later when the conditions in the viewer's world call them (or similar ones) forward.

AGGRESSIVE CUES

aggressive cues
Information contained in media portrayals of violence that suggests (or cues) the appropriateness of aggression against specific victims

One direct outgrowth of social cognitive theory focuses on the **aggressive cues** inherent in media portrayals of violence. People who see mediated violence are believed to show higher levels of subsequent aggression. The question involves when and against whom do they aggress. The answer is that media portrayals of violence are almost always in some dramatic context, and that context provides information, or *cues*, telling viewers when and against whom violence is acceptable.

Leonard Berkowitz (1965) produced a representative piece of research in which male college students were shown a film of a brutal boxing scene (the closing sequence of the movie *The Champion*). To some, it was presented in the context of a story that said the loser deserved his beating—that is, the violence against him was justified. In a second version of the narrative, the defeated boxer was victimized—that is, the violence against him was unjustified.

The students were then given an opportunity to "grade" another student's design of "an original and imaginative floor plan for a house." Unbeknownst to them, all the participants were given the same floor plan from that other student (who was actually Berkowitz's accomplice). In half the cases, that accomplice introduced himself as a "college boxer," and in the other half as a "speech major." A "new form of grading" was to be used, grading by electrical shock: one shock was very good; ten was very bad. Of course, the accomplice was not actually zapped; the shocks administered by the participants were read by a metering device as the accomplice feigned a response. Any differences in shocking the accomplice would be the result of differences in what participants had seen on the screen. To confuse matters even more, half the participants were insulted (angered) by the experimenter before they began.

What happened? The "college boxer" was shocked more than the "speech major"; the angered subjects gave more shocks regardless of whom they were shocking; and those who had seen the justified version of the film also gave more shocks. Berkowitz's conclusions? First, viewers' *psychological state* can lead them to respond to cues in programs that meet the needs of that state. Second, viewers who see justified violence not only learn the behavior but also learn that it can be a good or useful problem-solving device (disinhibition). Third, cues associated with an on-screen victim, in this case a boxer, can disinhibit viewers toward aggression against similar people in the real world. Berkowitz said, "The findings show that the film context can affect the observer's inhibitions against aggression and that the people encountered soon afterwards vary in the extent to which they can evoke aggressive responses from the observer" (p. 368). In a later study (Berkowitz and Geen, 1966), Berkowitz produced similar results simply by having the real-world target of the viewers' aggression share little more than the same first name (Kirk) as the character in the film.

priming effects
The idea that presentations in the media heighten the likelihood that people will develop similar thoughts about those things in the real world

This idea of aggressive cues is supported by contemporary thinking on **priming effects,** which "maintains that the presentation of a certain stimulus having a particular meaning 'primes' other semantically related concepts, thus heightening the likelihood that thoughts with much the same meaning as the presentation stimulus will come to mind" (Jo and Berkowitz, 1994, p. 46). Berkowitz labeled this the **cognitive-neoassociationistic perspective,** explaining "that frequent viewing of violent media portrayals primes particular constructs (e.g., aggression, hostility) and thus makes these constructs more likely to be used in behavioral decisions as well as judgments about others" (Shrum, 2009, p. 56).

cognitive-neoassociationistic perspective
Frequent viewing of violent media portrayals primes particular constructs, making them more likely to be used in behavioral decisions

Aggressive cues, priming effects, and the cognitive-neoassociationistic perspective form the basis of some of the most interesting and controversial media violence research now being conducted. As the link between media violence and viewer aggression came to be generally accepted, attention turned to the issue of violence against a specific target—women. As Richard Frost and John Stauffer wrote, "But even though members of an audience for a violent film or television program may not be moved to actual behavioral imitation, do they not experience different levels of emotional arousal? ... Could arousal also be influenced by the type of violence being portrayed, such as violence against women as opposed to men?" (1987, p. 29).

In terms of aggressive cues, media portrayals cue viewers to consider women likely or appropriate targets of violence. In terms of priming effects and the cognitive-neoassociationistic perspective, media presentations of women as victims of violence heighten the likelihood that viewers, when confronted by real-life women, will have similar thoughts (constructs) about them; heavy viewing of such content primes those constructs, increasing the likelihood they will be employed.

The operation of all three concepts is evident in Michelle Kistler and Moon Lee's research on highly sexual hip-hop music videos. They demonstrated that college men who were exposed to this content "expressed greater objectification of women, sexual permissiveness, stereotypical gender attitudes, and acceptance of rape" than those who were not (2010, p. 67). In suggesting that these videos primed particular constructs "more likely to be used in behavioral decisions," the authors wrote, "The most disturbing finding ... is the significant effect of exposure on male participants' acceptance of rape myths. Men in the highly sexual hip-hop videos were portrayed as powerful, sexually assertive, and as having a fair degree of sexual prowess, whereas the women were portrayed as sexually available, scantily clad, and often preening over the men. This might have served as a cue to male participants that sexual coercion is more acceptable and that women exist for the entertainment and sexual fulfillment of men" (p. 83). Melinda Burgess and Sandra Burpos undertook a similar investigation, focusing not on hip-hop but on a "high sexualization/objectification" Top 40 music video from female country music artist Jessica Simpson. Their results mirrored those of Kistler and Lee's research: "For college males, viewing mainstream, commercially available music videos, the highly sexualized portrayal of a female artist is associated with judging a date rapist as less guilty. For both males and females, this portrayal was associated with less empathy for the victim. For women, this portrayal was associated with greater judgment of responsibility for the victim" (2012, p. 757).

Loss of empathy is an attitudinal or emotional effect, but closely related is **desensitization**, the mitigation or reduction of anxious physiological arousal in response to depictions of violence, both mediated and real-world, as the result of habitual consumption of mediated violence. Desensitization has been well documented, as research has consistently shown that "the more time individuals spent watching violent media depictions, the less emotionally responsive they became to violent stimuli" (Krahé et al., 2011, p. 631). For example, Barbara Krahé and her colleagues were able to identify reduced physiological reactivity to violent films in college students who admitted to a heavy diet of violent fare (Krahé et al., 2011).

desensitization
The idea that habitual consumption of mediated violence will mitigate or reduce anxious arousal in response to depictions of violence

THE CONTEXT OF MEDIATED VIOLENCE

Writing in 1994, Bandura summed the accumulated knowledge of social cognitive theory to conclude that television viewers "acquire lasting attitudes, emotional reactions, and behavioral proclivities towards persons, places, or things that have been associated with modeled emotional experiences" (p. 75). What is it about specific presentations of media violence that encourages this acquisition through modeling? W. James Potter (1997) identified seven important **contextual variables:**

contextual variables
The information (or context) surrounding the presentation of mediated violence

1. **Reward/punishment.** Rewarded aggression is more frequently modeled; punished aggression is less frequently modeled. We know these to be disinhibitory and inhibitory effects, respectively.
2. **Consequences.** Mediated violence accompanied by portrayals of negative or harmful consequences produces less modeling. Again, this shows inhibitory effects at work.
3. **Motive.** Motivated media aggression produces greater levels of modeling, and unjustified media violence results in less viewer aggression. Viewers are cued to the appropriateness (or inappropriateness) of using aggression.
4. **Realism.** Especially with boys, realistic media violence tends to produce more real-world aggression. As Potter explained, "Realistic [media] perpetrators are more likely to reduce inhibitions because their behaviors are more applicable to real life situations than are unrealistic perpetrators such as cartoon or fantasy characters" (p. 234).
5. **Humor.** Because it reduces the seriousness of the behavior, humorously presented media violence leads to the greater probability that viewers will behave aggressively in real life.
6. **Identification with media characters.** The more viewers identify with media characters (e.g., with those they consider like themselves or attractive), the

more likely it is that they will model the behaviors demonstrated by those characters.

7. **Arousal.** Potter explained: "Emotional appeals can serve to increase the dramatic nature of the narrative, and this can increase attention, ... positive dispositions toward the characters using violence, ... and higher levels of arousal." This dramatically induced arousal and emotional attachment to violent characters, according to Potter, are "likely to result in aggressive behavior" (p. 235).

ACTIVE THEORY OF TELEVISION VIEWING

active theory
View of television consumption that assumes viewer comprehension causes attention and, therefore, effects (or no effects)

viewing schema
Interpretational skills that aid people in understanding media content conventions

The operation of these contextual variables underscores the idea that media consumers do indeed bring something to the viewing situation. That is, they make judgments about what it is they are seeing as they consume: for example, Is this violence justified? Or What are the consequences of engaging in that behavior? Presenting "a theory of visual attention to television which has as its central premise the cognitively active nature of television viewing," Daniel Anderson and Elizabeth Lorch (1983, pp. 27–28), as well as several other researchers (e.g., Bryant and Anderson, 1983; Singer and Singer, 1983) challenged the idea that "television viewing is fundamentally reactive and passive."

This **active theory** of television viewing sees viewers in general—and in the violence debate, particularly children—as actively and consciously working to understand television content. The researchers argue that by the age of two and a half, children have sufficiently developed **viewing schema** that allow them to comprehend specific television content conventions. "Beyond two and a half years," they wrote, "visual attention to television increases throughout the preschool years ... and may level off during the school-age years.... We suggest this increase reflects cognitive development, increased world knowledge, and an understanding of the cinematic codes and format structures of television" (Anderson and Lorch, 1983, p. 13).

Those who argue for this active theory of viewing claim that social cognitive theorists generally subscribe "to the proposition that the child is an active, cognitive, and social being [but] television is seen as providing such an exceptionally powerful influence that the child becomes reactive in its presence" (Anderson and Lorch, 1983, p. 5). This pessimistic view of children's viewing and cognitive abilities, they claim, inevitably leads social cognition advocates to overestimate the power of the medium and underestimate the influence that individual viewers have in determining effects. Put another way, "reactive theory" assumes that attention causes comprehension and, therefore, effects. The active theory of television viewing assumes that comprehension causes attention and, therefore, effects (or no effects).

active-audience theories
Theories that focus on assessing what people do with media; audience-centered theories

As we will see in later chapters, this debate over the ability of individual television viewers to resist the influence of powerful content has emerged as a central theme in contemporary mass communication theory. One of the most important sets of these media theories is referred to as **active-audience theories**. These theories, which argue that average audience members can routinely resist the influence of media content and make it serve their own purposes, are opposed by other perspectives questioning people's ability to resist the influence of messages systematically structured to convey certain meanings. Both types of theories are increasingly supported by growing bodies of empirical evidence. It's quite possible that both are valid, even if they seem to offer contradictory views of the relative power of media over audiences. There is a third active-audience perspective, however, relevant especially when considering the media–violence link. It is that viewers are indeed active, but they are active in using violent content in support of the *increase* in their subsequent levels of aggression. For example, in demonstrating that young male and female adults who were exposed to media portrayals of aggression in romantic relationships showed higher levels of aggression in their real-life romantic relationships, Coyne and her colleagues (2011) offered the possibility that "more aggressive individuals turn to viewing more media violence for social comparison reasons, i.e. it makes them feel less abnormal in their own aggression." They pointed to the **downward spiral model** of media influence. "This model," they wrote, "posits that individuals tend to seek out violent media that is consonant with their aggressive tendencies, and, by extension, reinforces and exacerbates such tendencies" (p. 57).

downward spiral model

Model of media influence suggesting that individuals tend to seek out violent media that is consonant with their aggressive tendencies

THE DEVELOPMENTAL PERSPECTIVE

developmental perspective

The view of learning from media that specifies different intellectual and communication stages in a child's life that influence the nature of media interaction and impact

But obviously not all viewers, especially children, are active viewers, and not all are equally active. This understanding has led to support for the **developmental perspective**, one that assumes that children undergo "extensive and varied cognitive growth between birth and adulthood … that is extremely rich, complex, and multifaceted" (Flavell, 1992, p. 998). As such, this perspective also assumes that an important aspect of people's power to deal with television is their ability to comprehend it at different stages in their intellectual development. Logically, older children will "read" television differently than will younger children. As Ellen Wartella wrote, this developmental perspective "seeks to describe and explain the nature of the communicative differences between four-year-olds, six-year-olds, ten-year-olds, etc., and adults" (1979, p. 7).

Those differences certainly exist. For example, there is significant research evidence that children under eight are unable to understand advertising's intent, accept its claims as true, and are unable to distinguish between commercials and regular television programming. But, as Rozendaal, Buijzen, and Valkenburg demonstrate, their ability to recognize a variety of advertiser goals and tactics eventually develops around age 10, with understanding progressing steadily from 8 to 12, as they develop the ability to take the perspective of others and reason at an abstract level (2011). Likewise, Shade, Porter, and Sanchez (2005) demonstrated developmental differences in children's ability to understand the Internet's true nature, with preteens unable to comprehend that Internet content does not reside "inside" the computer itself. Yan found "significant age differences … in technical [the physical reality of computer networks] and social [the personal consequences of Internet use] understandings of the Internet across age groups 9–17" (2009, p. 112).

This notion of developmental stages in children's communicative abilities is drawn from developmental psychology, especially the work of Jean Piaget, who argued that children, as they move from infancy through adolescence, undergo qualitative changes in the level of cognitive and intellectual abilities available to them. Logically, then, it is easy to assume that older children's processing of television's messages is more developed and therefore somehow better at insulating them from television effects. But this is neither the conclusion of developmental research, nor is it the goal. Yes, wrote Ellen Wartella, the developmental perspective asks "new questions and [deals with] different sorts of communication issues regarding children's learning from television and use of television" (1979, pp. 8–9). But the misleading Piagetian assumption of ever-increasing cognitive competency produced the **empowered child model** of television effects research, which assumes that children eventually become "competent, self-aware users of television ... [and] tends to emphasize the positive aspects of children's engagement with television. Less emphasis in such studies is placed on questions of the consequences of media use for children's health and welfare, in particular, their cognitive, emotional, and physical development" (Wartella, 1999, pp. 84–85). In other words, the developmental perspective, rather than demonstrating that children pass through ordered stages of cognitive growth and eventually develop into competent users of the media, might actually suggest that media use can interfere with that development. Recall some of the data on children's engagement with media that opened this chapter—attentively watching before three years old, nine-month-olds averaging an hour a day in front of television, the number of little kids with televisions and game consoles in their bedrooms. *How* do children develop in this new media environment, especially as "the years from birth to age three are seen as crucial for development to proceed?" How does this engagement with media alter children's development, given that "new work studying sociocultural influences on development suggests that the ways in which children participate in structured social activities with their families, other adults, and children influence the rate and sorts of domain specific developmental progressions that occur?" (Wartella, 1999, p. 86). We'll return to this issue later in this chapter in our discussion of adolescents.

empowered child model

Television effects research that assumes that children eventually become competent, self-aware users of television

VIDEO GAMES REIGNITE INTEREST IN MEDIA VIOLENCE

The link between television and viewer aggression is accepted by all but the most ardent media defenders. As a result, most recent media violence research has focused on video games. This work, based in social cognitive theory, demonstrates the causal link between violent video games and subsequent player aggression and, as such, has expanded the field's confidence in the television violence findings. This research is uniform in its assessment. "Violent videogame play was positively related to aggressive behavior and delinquency" (Anderson and Dill, 2000, p. 772); "Videogame violence [is] positively correlated with trait hostility" (Gentile et al., 2004, p. 18); videogame exposure is "related to increases in aggressive behavior ... aggressive affect ... aggressive cognitions (i.e., aggressive thoughts, beliefs, and attitudes) ... and physiological arousal" (Anderson et al., 2003, p. 92).

Mounting research evidence aside, four factors drive this scholarly attention as well as public concern. First is the amount of video game play that children engage in. A nationwide Kaiser Family Foundation study revealed that nearly 9 in 10 young people have a game console at home, and half have a game device in their bedroom (Rideout, Foehr, and Roberts, 2010). Second is the "presence" of video games in high-profile school shootings such as those that occurred in 1999 at Columbine High School in Colorado and in 2012 in Aurora, Colorado, and the subsequent revelation that websites for shooter-games like *Medal of Honor* provide

THINKING ABOUT THEORY | Setting the Record Straight on Media Violence

In December 2003, a collection of the country's most prominent media effects researchers presented a major overview of the current state of thought on the influence of media violence on youth (Anderson et al., 2003). Published in the journal *Psychological Science in the Public Interest*, it attempted to do three things: (1) assess current thinking on the media–violence link in the wake of new interactive media such as video games and the Internet; (2) counter the "intransigent assertions made by a number of vocal critics" and "various interest groups" that the media–violence link does not exist; and (3) respond to "recent news reports [that] imply the scientific evidence is weaker" than it really is (p. 82). In other words, the researchers wanted to set the record straight. In fact, their report was to have been part of a surgeon general's report on youth violence in 2000 but was omitted from that government study after "editors sought heavy revisions," presumably because of its critical stance on the issue (Patterson, 2004, p. A4).

The researchers focused on five specific questions, listed here and accompanied by their conclusions. Can you find hints of social cognitive theory? Aggressive cues? Priming effects? Do you accept these findings? Why or why not? Do you fall prey to the third-person effect (Chapter 1)? Try to remember your reactions to these issues when you read later chapters dealing with the most current understandings of media influence. Revisit your thinking to see if you develop a new or different view of the media–violence link.

1. **What does research say about the relation—both short-term and long-term—between media violence and violent behavior?** The researchers offered five general observations:
   a. Media violence has a modest direct effect on serious forms of violent behavior.
   b. There is documented research evidence of the impact of media violence on aggression (including violence).
   c. The research base (scientific methods, samples of people, media genres) for these first two assertions is large and diverse, and the results are consistent.

d. For many people, the negative effects of heavy childhood exposure to mediated violence extend well into adulthood, even in the absence of continued consumption of violent fare.
e. Even people who are not highly aggressive are negatively affected by exposure to violent media, both in the short-term and over longer periods of time (Anderson et al., 2003, p. 104).

2. **How does media violence produce its effects on violent behavior?** "Media violence produces short-term increases in aggression by activating (priming) aggressive thoughts, increasing physiological arousal, and triggering an automatic tendency to imitate observed behaviors (especially among children). Media violence produces long-term increases in aggression and violence by creating long-lasting (and automatically accessible) aggressive scripts and interpretational schemas, and aggression-supporting beliefs and attitudes about appropriate social behavior" (p. 104).

3. **What characteristics of media violence are most influential, and who is most susceptible to such influences?** The causal relationship between media violence and behavior is influenced by: (a) viewer characteristics such as age, aggressiveness, perceptions of the realism of the content, and identification with aggressive characters; (b) viewers' social environment, that is, parents and family; and (c) aspects of the content itself, for example, perpetrator characteristics, realism of portrayal, justification of the violence, and the depiction of its consequences.

4. **How widespread and accessible is violence in the media?** The researchers identify "the abundant presence of electronic media" in our homes and the "extensive presence of violence" across those media. They document the "expansion of opportunities for children's exposure to media violence at home through the proliferation of new media, including

(Continued)

THINKING ABOUT **THEORY** | **Setting the Record Straight on Media Violence**   (Continued)

videogames, music videos, and the Internet." They also suggest that the interactivity of much of the new media may lead to even more powerful effects than those produced by traditional television (p. 104).

5. **How can individuals and society counteract the influence of media violence?** The scientific literature identifies several means of intervention. The most effective, obviously, is reduced exposure to violent content. There is some, but less, evidence of the effectiveness of counter-attitudinal interventions (structured lessons negating themes presented in media portrayals), parental interventions (adults watching and talking with young viewers), and increased media literacy (p. 105).

players with links to the home pages of the brand-name guns featured in those games. There players can peruse arms makers' catalogues, creating "a virtual showroom for guns" (Meier and Martin, 2012, p. A1). As a result, even before there is evidence of game play, as in the 2012 Newtown, Connecticut, grammar school massacre, public speculation quickly implicates violent video games (Knight, 2012). The later revelation that the Newtown shooter maintained a game-like scoreboard of competing mass murders served to fuel even more criticism of violent video games (Stanglin, 2013). Third is the sheer brutality of best-selling games such as the *Grand Theft Auto* series in which players control violent, criminal characters and first-person shooter games such as the popular *Call of Duty* games (employed by the U.S. military to desensitize soldiers to killing) in which players, from their personal point-of-view, employ a variety of weapons in virtual warfare. Fourth is video games' interactivity; that is, *players* are much more involved in the on-screen activity than are television *viewers*. They are participants, not merely observers, in the violence. This active involvement in the on-screen violence is problematic because, as social cognitive theory argues, "rehearsal" of observed behaviors greatly increases the amount of modeling (Bandura, 1994), and as Potter (1997) argues, identification and realism increase modeling. What could be more real than aggression in which players themselves participate? With whom could they identify more closely than themselves as they play? "It is true," wrote Anderson and his colleagues, "that as a player you are 'not just moving your hand on a joystick' but are indeed interacting 'with the game psychologically and emotionally.' It is not surprising that when the game involves rehearsing aggressive and violent thoughts and actions, such deep game involvement results in antisocial effects on the player" (Anderson et al., 2010, p. 171). Although his was a study of players' enjoyment in gaming rather than an examination of their effects, Daniel Shafer added support to this argument, demonstrating that gamers in player-versus-player contests demonstrated more hostility when playing than those playing against the game itself. This effect held whether the game was a first-person shooter or a puzzle game. But when player-versus-player gaming was combined with first-person shooting, there were "significant increases in state hostility" (2012, p. 731). It is also interesting to note that those greater levels of hostility actually reduced players' levels of enjoyment with the game.

Konijn, Bijvank, and Bushman (2007) specifically examined the issue of games' psychological and emotional interactivity by differentiating between two types of

similarity identification

Observer identifies with a character because they share some salient characteristic

wishful identification

Observer desires to emulate the character, either in general or specific terms

identification. Identification, as typically understood in social cognitive theory, is **similarity identification**, in which the observer identifies with a character because they share some salient characteristic. For example, both are male or both are American. However, a more powerful form of identification also exists, one particularly pertinent to participatory video games, **wishful identification**. Here the observer "desires to emulate the character, either in general terms (as a role model for future action or identity development) or in specific terms (extending responses beyond the viewing situation or imitating a particular behavior)." Because wishful identification provides a glimpse of "what if," wrote the researchers, "it is a powerful predictor of future behavior, especially in adolescents," especially boys, and as a result, "is closer to [Bandura's] concept of vicarious learning" (p. 1039). Their research did indeed demonstrate that wishful identification with violent characters in realistic games produced greater levels of aggression in players.

In sum, "research on violent television and film, videogames, and music reveals unequivocal evidence that media violence increases the likelihood of aggressive and violent behavior in both immediate and long-term contexts" (Anderson et al., 2003, p. 81).

GENERAL AGGRESSION MODEL

Considering the issue to be settled science, Craig Anderson and his colleagues attempted to provide a general framework for the argument that mediated violence does indeed increase viewer aggression (Anderson, Deuser, and DeNeve, 1995). Their goal was "to integrate existing mini-theories of aggression into a unified whole" (Anderson and Bushman, 2002, p. 33). The outcome, based primarily in social cognitive theory, is the General Aggression Model (GAM)—a model of human aggression that argues that cognition, affect, and arousal mediate the effects of situational and individual personal variables on aggression. It "incorporates biological, personality development, social processes, basic cognitive processes (e.g., perception, priming), short-term and long-term processes, and decision processes into understanding aggression" (DeWall, Anderson, and Bushman, 2011, p. 246).

To explain how exposure to mediated violence could have short-term effects (e.g., in the laboratory) and long-term effects (e.g., in real life when away from violent content), GAM assumes that "social behavior depends upon the individual's construal of events in the present environment, including the person's interpretation of these events, beliefs about typical ways of responding to such events, perceived competencies for responding in different ways, and expectations regarding likely outcomes. These cognitions provide a basis for some stability of behavior across a variety of situations (because each individual tends to resolve situational ambiguities in characteristic ways), but also allow considerable situational specificity (because of reality constraints upon possible construals).... Knowledge structures develop from experience; influence all types of perception, from basic visual patterns to complex behavioral sequences; can become automatized with use; are linked to affective states, behavioral programs, and beliefs; and guide interpretations and behavioral responses to the social and physical environments.... That is, decisions that initially require considerable conscious thought can, in fact, become effortless and occur with little or no awareness" (Anderson and Carnagey, 2004, p. 173).

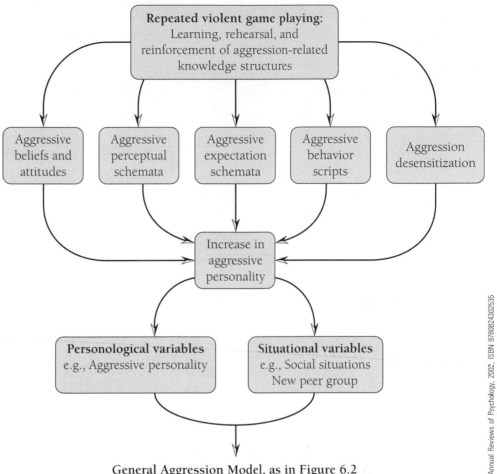

FIGURE 6.1 General Aggression Model: Developmental/Personality Processes (in the example of violent game play)

GAM has two parts, the *episode*—when a person is in a social situation and can behave either with or without aggression toward another—and *developmental/personality processes*—the aggression-related knowledge structures brought to that situation. In the episode (Figure 6.2), *Inputs* include *situation factors* that might increase or inhibit aggression. An insult, for example, might increase the likelihood of aggression; the presence of your parents might decrease it. *Person factors* "include all the characteristics a person brings to the situation, such as personality traits, attitudes, and genetic predispositions" (Anderson and Bushman, 2002, p. 35). *Routes* include the person's *present internal state*, its affect, cognition, or arousal (the dotted line between the three means they also influence one another). *Affect* refers to mood and emotion. *Cognition* refers to the accessibility of aggressive concepts or behavior scripts, that is, how easily (or not) aggressive thoughts are primed. *Arousal* refers to the level of physical and psychological excitement the person feels at the moment.

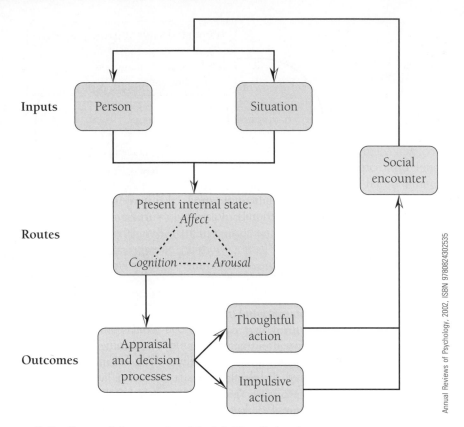

FIGURE 6.2   General Aggression Model: The Episode

Outcomes refer to what ultimately happens in the encounter. The person judges the situation, makes a decision, and responds either thoughtfully or impulsively. But remember, these *appraisal and decision processes* are the product of the inputs and the routes they traveled. The resulting social encounter now adds to the inputs brought to the next social encounter.

Media enter the model as part of a person's *developmental/personality processes* (Figure 6.1). The model asserts that *repeated violent game playing increases learning, rehearsal, and reinforcement of aggression-related cognitions.* These include *beliefs and attitudes* about aggression, the way aggression is *perceived*, *expectations* surrounding aggression, *scripts* or models for aggressive behavior, and *desensitization* to aggression. These five factors produce an *increase in aggressive personality* which influences *personal and situational variables*, which are, in fact, the person and situation inputs (at the top of The Episode, Figure 6.2) that produce either aggressive or nonaggressive behaviors in social encounters. Note, though, that Figure 6.1's topmost box could just as easily read "Repeated exposure to violent media content" or "Environmental modifiers" (Anderson and Bushman, 2002).

GAM is not without its critics. They contend that its reliance primarily on meta-analyses of laboratory experimental work reinforces that method's strong-effects bias; its scope makes empirical validation impossible; it cannot explain

INSTANT ACCESS

General Aggression Model (GAM)

Strengths

1. Provides a comprehensive overview of media–human aggression link
2. Incorporates a wide variety of personal and situational variables
3. Applies across several media user and media use situations
4. Explains both short-term and long-term effects

Weaknesses

1. Number and variety of elements and linkages make empirical investigation and validation impossible
2. Declines in real-world youth violence suggest model overstates media influence on aggression
3. Does not explain research showing no link between media violence and subsequent aggression
4. Reliance primarily on laboratory research reinforces experiments' built-in bias toward strong effects

research showing no media–aggression link; and, recent real-world declines in youth violence suggest GAM overstates media's influence on aggression.

MEDIA AND CHILDREN'S DEVELOPMENT

Mass communication researchers' focus on children extends beyond media use and aggression. The issue of media's contribution to children's development, that is, their evolution from children into functioning, competent adolescents and young adults has attracted significant theoretical attention. The American Academy of Pediatrics, for example, argues that media "present youth with common 'scripts' for how to behave in unfamiliar situations such as romantic relationships ... [and] **superpeer theory** states that the media are like powerful best friends in sometimes making risky behaviors seem like normative behavior" (Strasburger, Jordan, and Donnerstein, 2010, p. 758).

superpeer theory
Media serve as powerful best friends in sometimes making risky behaviors seem like normative behavior

Quite obviously, as we saw in the chapter's opening pages, young people grow up in a mass-mediated world, and that growing up—that development—has become a focus of interest from both effects and critical cultural researchers. Beyond the violence theories, there is quite a bit of postpositivist effects research demonstrating that media consumption, especially of television and video games, can impede young people's development. Typical of this work is that of Robert Weis and Brittany Cerankosky. They divided into two groups first-, second-, and third-grade boys who wanted, but did not yet have, video game consoles in their homes. They gave each family in the experimental group a game console and several Everyone-rated games to take home. The control group received nothing. Four months later they tested the boys on a number of school-related variables, and their results offered "support for the notion that videogame ownership among boys is associated with decreased academic achievement in the areas of reading and writing. Overall, boys who received the videogame system at the beginning of the study showed relatively stable and somewhat below average reading and writing achievement from baseline to follow-up. In contrast, boys in the control group showed increased reading and writing achievement across the duration of the study" (2010, p. 5). Among other negative developmental effects the postpositivists have investigated are attentional disorders (Christakis, et al., 2004); psychological distress (Page et al., 2010); limited vocabulary development (Christakis, et al., 2009); aggression in the classroom (Martins and Wilson, 2011); greater risk-taking while driving (Beullens, Roe, and Van den Bulck, 2011); lower social competence, greater impulsivity, depression, and social phobias (Gentile et al., 2011); loss of sleep and memory (Dworak et al., 2007); and carrying a weapon to school (Desai et al., 2010). Recall Ellen Wartella's contention from earlier in this chapter that any developmental perspective on young people's media use must consider the fact that it is impossible to separate that use from their development.

Despite their focus on causal effects models and limited concern for broader social and cultural issues, by the 1970s effects researchers were starting to show interest in the developmental aspects of adolescents' gender and sexual identities. Although that attention was modest compared to that of critical researchers, by the 1990s effects research was more fully invested in these issues. For example, in the 1970s, Baran demonstrated the relationship between adolescent and college student satisfaction with their sexual identities and consumption of film and television portrayals of physically romantic relationships (1976a, 1976b). In the 1980s, Courtright and Baran identified media portrayals of these relationships as a primary source of young people's acquisition of sexual information (1980). And in the 1990s, George Comstock (1991, p. 175) reviewed decades of research on young people's sex role socialization and concluded that a "modest but positive association" exists between television exposure and the holding of traditional notions of gender and sex roles. He also acknowledged that those who consume nontraditional portrayals of gender can and do develop similarly nontraditional perceptions of sex roles. Moreover, not only can media portrayals socialize children by encouraging certain expectations of themselves, these portrayals can encourage expectations of others. Comstock wrote: "Portrayals in television and other media of highly attractive persons may encourage dissatisfaction [with] or lowered evaluations of the attractiveness of those of the pertinent sex in real life" (1991, p. 176).

This line of inquiry is not only alive and well today, it is finding even stronger evidence of media influence than much of the early work. For example, Clark and Tiggemann (2007, p. 84) examined young girls' satisfaction with their own attractiveness. Searching for the sources of 9- to 12-year-old girls' "body dissatisfaction," they demonstrated that "increased exposure to appearance media (both television and magazines) and taking part in peer appearance conversations were related to body dissatisfaction and dieting behaviors." Bissell and Zhou, writing that there is "clear evidence that exposure to TDP (thinness depicting and promoting) media leads to distorted body-image perception in school-age females and college women," examined the effects specifically of entertainment and sports media exposure (2004, p. 5). They discovered that women who were frequently exposed to "thin ideal media" were more likely to be dissatisfied with the way they looked and to have taken "dangerous steps to modify their body shapes" (p. 17).

Vandenbosch and Eggermont demonstrated "direct relationships between sexually objectifying media and the internalization of beauty ideals [in adolescent girls], and indirect relationships between sexually objectifying media and self-objectification, and body surveillance through the internalization of beauty ideals" (2012, p. 869). Samson and Grabe studied the "sexual propensities of emerging adults," college students 17 to 25 years old, and their consumption of a wide variety of media (music videos, network and cable television, movies, and the Internet). Their results "point to media as a significant sexual socializing agent in shaping human psychosexual propensities. In fact, [their] study showed that media use has independent statistical associations with sexual excitation and inhibition mechanisms" (2012, p. 293). Stella Chia (2006) approached the issue from a somewhat different direction, demonstrating that young people use the media to make judgments about their friends' sexual behavior norms and then use those inferences when determining their own levels of sexual permissiveness.

Advertising's impact on children's development has been studied from a variety of perspectives. Research indicates that children younger than seven or eight cannot distinguish between program and advertising content. And although near seven or eight they can distinguish between commercials and other televised content, they do not necessarily understand the commercials' selling intent and that much advertising, especially premium advertising (ads that promise a gift or toy with purchase), can cause conflict between parents and children. In addition, the failure of many products to live up to the expectations created for them by children's advertising can lead to frustration and even cynicism (Wilcox et al., 2004). Much attention has centered on the advertising to kids of junk food and sugared snacks (Committee on Communications, 2006; Institute of Medicine, 2006), linking it to epidemic levels of obesity in American children (Hellmich, 2004). According to the Kaiser Family Foundation (2007, p. 3), American children aged 2 to 7 see more than 4,400 food ads a year on television alone; those aged 8 to 12 annually view more than 7,600; 13- to 17-year-olds watch more than 6,000. Half of all advertising time on children's television is devoted to food, and 34 percent of that is for candy and snacks, 28 percent are for cereal, and 10 percent are for fast food (Kaiser Family Foundation, 2007, p. 3). There is much research demonstrating a causal relationship between these commercials and children's preference of and request for "high-calorie and low-nutrient foods and beverages" (Gottesdiener, 2012). Not surprisingly, then, 30 percent of American children are overweight, and 15 percent meet the criteria for obesity. "When other variables are controlled," wrote Jennifer Derenne and Eugene Beresin, "TV exposure independently increases the odds of becoming overweight by 50%.... Furthermore ... excessive media consumption also may be correlated with the rate of childhood depression. This could be a function of negative body image, or may reflect the tendency of depressed kids to spend more time in front of the TV because of diminished energy" (2006, p. 259). Alcohol advertising to young children has also received research scrutiny. For example, Jerry Grenard and his colleagues demonstrated that younger adolescents are susceptible to the persuasive messages contained in televised alcohol commercials, and their positive response to those ads influences "some youth to drink more and experience drinking-related problems later in adolescence" (Grenard, Dent, and Stacy, 2013, p. e369).

early window
The idea that media allow children to see the world before they have the skill to successfully act in it

Critical cultural studies researchers have also been concerned about the influence of media on childhood and adolescence. They share effects-trend notions about media as young people's **early window**. That is, media allow children to see the world well before they are developmentally capable of competently interacting with it. As Joshua Meyrowitz, speaking specifically of television, explained, it "escorts children across the globe even before they have permission to cross the street" (1985, p. 238). What happens to young people's social development, he asks, when television treats them as "mini-adults"? Children's books, for example, are the only type of books that children are capable of reading, and their themes are geared to children's interests and experiences. Yet, as Meyrowitz argues, because all television is "educational television," there's no such thing as "children's television":

> [Television] allows the very young child to be "present" at adult interactions. Television removes barriers that once divided people of different ages and reading abilities into different social situations. The widespread use of television is equivalent to a broad social decision to allow young children to be present at wars and funerals, courtships and seductions, criminal plots and cocktail parties. Young children may not fully understand the issues of sex, death, crime, and money that are presented to them on television. Or, put differently, they may understand these issues only in childlike ways. Yet television nevertheless exposes them to many topics and behaviors that adults have spent several centuries trying to keep hidden from children. Television thrusts children into a complex adult world, and it provides the impetus for children to ask the meanings of actions and words they would not yet have heard or read about without television. (1985, p. 242)

Sociologist Neil Postman's argument for "the disappearance of childhood" rests in large part on this idea of the early window. He wrote, "Unlike infancy, childhood is a social artifact, not a biological category," one that is "difficult to sustain and, in fact, irrelevant," because ubiquitous connection to the media robs youngsters of "the charm, malleability, innocence, and curiosity" of childhood, leaving them "degraded and then transmogrified into the lesser features of pseudo-adulthood" (1994, pp. xi–xii). But critical theory attention to young people extends well beyond the early window. Its central theme is the corporate takeover of children's and adolescents' development.

kinderculture
The corporate construction of childhood

Developmental researcher Shirley Steinberg (2011) argues that effects research on young people's development is of limited value in the face of **kinderculture**, the corporate construction of childhood. The writers of children's and adolescents' "cultural curriculum," she argues, "are not educational agencies but rather commercial concerns that operate not for the social good but for individual gain. Cultural pedagogy is structured by commercial dynamics, forces that impose themselves into all aspects of our own and our children's private lives" (p. 18). She continues, "The study of power and kinderculture reveals insights into North American politics that may at first glance seem only incidental to parents and child professionals—especially those of the positivist paradigm. When one begins to explore child activist avenues, he or she is immediately confronted with the concentration of power into fewer and increasingly corporate hands … In light of the failure of oppositional institutions to challenge corporate hegemony, corporations to a large extent have free reign to produce almost any kinderculture that is profitable" (p. 31).

Journalist Susan Thomas investigated the children's marketing industry and identified its goal as "cradle-to-grave marketing" that produces "KGOY: Kids Getting Older Younger" (2007, p. 5). The product of this "hostile takeover of childhood," argues psychologist Susan Linn, is the "adultification of children," in which their "physical, psychological, social, emotional, and spiritual development are all threatened when their value as consumers trumps their value as people" (2004, p. 10). Young people, writes critical theorist Henry Giroux, arguably the most influential critic of the corporate takeover of youth, "now inhabit a cultural landscape in which, increasingly, they can only recognize themselves in terms preferred by the market … [Y]outh are educated to become consuming subjects rather than civic-minded and critical citizens … [and] the culture of the market displaces civic culture" (Giroux and Pollock, 2011). Elsewhere he continued, the "relentless expansion of a global market society" targets all children and youth, devaluing them by treating them as yet another "market" to be commodified and exploited and conscripting them into the system through creating a new generation of consuming subjects. "This low intensity war is waged by a variety of corporate institutions through the educational force of a culture that commercializes every aspect of kids' lives, using the Internet and various social networks along with the new media technologies such as cell phones to immerse young people in the world of mass consumption in ways more direct and expansive than anything we have seen in the past … this media is conscripting an entire generation into a world of consumerism in which commodities and brand loyalty become the most important markers of identity and primary frameworks for mediating one's relationship to the world … The stark reality here is that the corporate media are being used to reshape kids' identities into that of consumers rather than citizens … Kids may think they are immune to the incessant call to 'buy, buy, buy' and to think only about 'me, me, me,' but what is actually happening is a selective elimination and reordering of the possible modes of political, social and ethical vocabularies made available to youth" (2011).

Critical researchers, like their effects-trend colleagues, have also examined gender issues. **Objectification theory**, drawn from feminist critical theory, is central to this work. It "posits that girls and women are typically acculturated to internalize an observer's perspective as a primary view of their physical selves" (Fredrickson and Roberts, 1997, p. 173). Taking that perspective, Calogero and Tylka argue that people's "gendered experiences of the body constrain and impact body image." As a result, "human bodies are not allowed to naturally develop into a diverse range of shapes, sizes, and attributes. They are shaped by societal stressors and pressures that render the majority of people's natural bodies deficient in some capacity, and thus in need of chronic bodily evaluation and modification in order to produce bodies that meet prescriptive social roles, enhance social value, and secure social power. In other words, gender is critical not only for determining what people's bodies are capable of, but also for constructing how bodies should look and be looked at to meet societal expectations for what it means to be a heterosexual woman or man" (2010, p. 1). The product is low self-esteem, chronic body surveillance, and eating pathology. Boden argued that "contemporary consumer culture and its obsession with celebrity, the children's wear market and its transition from traditional children's clothing to more adult-like styling, and the

objectification theory
Theory arguing that females internalize others' perspective as a primary view of their physical selves

status of the 'tweenager' " combine to alter "children's self-styling and the presentation of their identity" (2006, p. 289).

Critical researchers have also taken on food advertising and other nutrition-related cultural factors and their implications for young people's physical development. "We are raising our children in a world that is vastly different than it was 40 or 50 years ago," explains obesity doctor Yoni Freedhoff, "Childhood obesity is a disease of the environment. It's a natural consequence of normal kids with normal genes being raised in unhealthy, abnormal environments." He identified as problematic school schedules that deny teens sufficient sleep, the ubiquity of fast food, developments in technology, the disappearance of home-cooked meals, the flood of food advertising aimed at kids, the ready availability of low-cost processed foods, the expansion of sugared-soda serving sizes, and ready access to unhealthy snacks in vending machines in every corner of a young person's life (in Haelle, 2013).

In fact, the United States has experienced a startling increase in childhood obesity in the last 30 years: "The prevalence of obesity among 12- to 19-year-olds has increased from 5 to 18 percent [in that time], overtaking smoking as the country's leading avoidable cause of morbidity and mortality" (Bickham et al., 2013, p. 2). Data such as these have, according to researcher Charlene Elliott, "prompted an increased scrutiny of the foodscape, along with the call for innovative strategies to make our social environments more supportive of healthy eating." Her approach to the issue was to examine the way supermarkets package child-targeted food to make them "fun" (2012, p. 303). Her semiotic analysis of 354 child-targeted products revealed that supermarkets employ bright colors, specialized fonts and graphics, labels on products identifying them as "fun foods," packaging for portability, and even though three out of four products she examined derived more than a fifth of their calories from sugar, nutrition claims to frame food as fun. Taking the food-is-fun critique in a somewhat different direction, Thomson examined online advergames (commercials disguised as video games). Analyzing the websites of two leading brands of sugared cereals, she argued that their "online cereal marketing disciplines the child (as) consumer/commodity through an immersive simulation of cereal marketing narratives. Both Frootloops.com and Luckycharms.com represent cereal as a valued (treasured, magical) item, and reward players not just for consuming/manipulating the desired food item, but also for mastering the marketing narratives/discourses guiding online play. Players are disciplined (through play) into a potentially unhealthy nutritional logic in which the most nutritionally bereft food items are most valuable and the consumptive possibilities are endless" (2010, p. 438). Her reading of these sites led her to argue, "It is thus imperative that cultural critics carefully unpack these emergent environments, along with their attendant discourses, narratives, and logics, not only in order to understand these new media forms, but also to expose their internal contradictions and raise important questions related to corporate ethics and public policy. This task is all the more pressing when it comes to the manipulation of childhood pleasures associated with digital game play as a persuasive agent to market food to children" (p. 441).

Finally, critical research and theory's ultimate goal is social change. As such, when considering media and young people's development, social critic Benjamin Barber calls for the creation of a truly civil society that acknowledges the real delights of childhood and helps children be children again by preserving them from the burdens of an exploitative and violent adult world. [That] refuses to "empower them" by taking away their dollies and blocks and toy wagons in which to haul them and replacing them with cell phones and video games and credit cards with which to pay for them. [That] refuses to "free" them from parents and other gatekeepers in order to turn them over to market-mad pied pipers who lead them over a commercial precipice down into the mall. Children should play not pay, act not watch, learn not shop. Where capitalism can, it should help protect the boundaries of childhood and preserve the guardianship of parents and citizens, otherwise it should get out of the way. Not everything needs to earn a profit, not everyone needs to be a shopper—not all the time. (2007, p 338)

You yourself can weigh in on an intriguing developmental argument against the commercialization of childhood in the box entitled, "Advertising to Kids: We Protect Adults, Why Not Children?"

THINKING ABOUT THEORY | **Advertising to Kids: We Protect Adults, Why Not Children?**

False or deceptive advertising is against the law. Section 5 of the Federal Trade Commission Act specifically states that unfair or deceptive advertising acts or practices are unlawful. And to make things clearer, Section 15 of that Act defines a false ad as one which is "misleading in a material respect." The Federal Communications Commission also has regulations covering deception in advertising. Section 317 of the Communications Act mandates that all broadcast advertising "be announced as paid for or furnished as the case may be." Most of the time the announcements are unnecessary. A commercial for a Chevy is a commercial, but less obvious commercials must be identified, for example teaser ads with no identifiable sponsor. Legal scholars Carter, Franklin, and Wright (2008) offer "On August 2, automotive history will be made" as an example of a violation because of its failure to convey to viewers or listeners the fact that it is a sponsored message. Of course, marketers are given wide latitude, as puffery, the little white lie, is permissible. No one really believes elves made those Keebler cookies.

So it's clear; our laws say people should be protected from clearly false or misleading advertising. "It is a long-standing principle in communication law that for advertising to be considered fair, it must be readily identifiable as such to its intended audience," argues the American Psychological Association Task Force on Advertising and Children, "The premise underlying this legal requirement is that it is unfair and deceptive for commercials to bypass the cognitive defenses against persuasion which adults are presumed to have when they understand that a given message consists of advertising content and can identify the source of the message. If it is unfair and deceptive to seek to bypass the defenses that adults are presumed to have when they are aware that advertising is addressed to them, then it must likewise be considered unfair and deceptive to advertise to children in whom these defenses do not yet exist" (Wilcox et al., 2004, p. 40). The argument is simple—all advertising to young children under eight is in fact illegal. The Task Force continues, "It is clear that the age-based constraints on children's comprehension of the nature and purpose of commercials are grounded in fundamental limitations in youngsters' cognitive abilities.... Thus, based upon the compelling evidence ... that documents young children's limited ability to recognize and defend against commercial persuasion, we believe the most obvious implication of this knowledge is that advertising specifically directed to audiences of children below the age of roughly 7–8 years should be considered unfair" (p. 40).

What do you think? We learned in Chapter 2 that the First Amendment is based in part on the philosophy that people are good and rational and can discern good messages from bad. But, by definition, young children cannot. So, should advertising to children who are developmentally incapable of judging

(Continued)

THINKING ABOUT THEORY | **Advertising to Kids: We Protect Adults, Why Not Children?**   (Continued)

the "goodness" of an ad's message—in fact, who are incapable of recognizing that an ad is an ad—be deserving of First Amendment protection as is other commercial speech?

Maybe looking at how other nations deal with the issue may help you formulate your answer. Would you be surprised to learn that of all the industrialized nations in the world, the United States is the only one that relies solely on industry self-regulation to protect young people from advertising? For example, Norway, Quebec, and Sweden ban all advertising during television programming aimed at kids; more than 30 countries, for example Australia, Malaysia, Korea, and Russia, have national laws that set various limits on television advertising to children; dozens of countries, among them the United Kingdom, Nigeria, Thailand, the Philippines, China, Denmark,

and Romania, regulate the advertising of junk and sugared foods to young people (Center for Science in the Public Interest, 2007). Quebec has a ban on fast-food advertising to kids. It has the lowest obesity rate of all the Canadian provinces and officials claim that the ban "decreases children's consumption by an estimated two to four billion calories" (Gottesdiener, 2012). Can you explain why the U.S. seems out of step with other countries in shielding young children from potentially harmful commercials? How would political economy theorists answer this question? What might critical scholars Henry Giroux and Shirley Steinberg say? So now back to you. Should American children have the same protections from commercial influence as do kids in most of the rest of the world?

GROWING UP CONNECTED: NEW PERSONAL TECHNOLOGIES AND DEVELOPMENT

Effects and critical cultural researchers and theorists alike have undertaken serious study of youthful use of personal technologies—smartphones, tablets, and social networking sites. We will devote part of Chapter 11 to the challenges new and emerging technologies pose for mass communication theory. Here, though, we briefly address some growing areas of interest. First, as we've seen earlier in this chapter, effects research has demonstrated a wide variety of harmful effects brought about by young people's interaction with screens rather than with other humans. The new personal communication technologies carry with them the same set of concerns, for example reduced human contact, especially with parents and peers, and lack of stimulation from their natural environments. Consumption data suggest these concerns are warranted. Kids 0 to 8 years old spend 27 percent of their daily screen time with these devices. Fifty-two percent of 5- to 8-year-olds have used at least one of the new digital technologies (Common Sense Media, 2011). One in five parents admits to using a smartphone or tablet to keep children distracted while running errands, and Apple and Google offer "tens of thousands of kid apps" with titles such as *BabyPlayFace* and *Elmo's Birthday* (Kang, 2011). Recognizing that 70 percent of tablet owners with children under 12 let their kids use their devices, Amazon offers Kindle Free Time Unlimited, a subscription service for children 3 to 8 that they can access on their parents' Kindles (Tsukayama, 2012). Ninety percent of American teens use social media; 75 percent belong to a social networking site, and one-third visit their social networking profile several times or more a day, and 51 percent do so every day (Rideout, 2012b).

While much research interest centers on time—every minute with a device is one minute less with a human (kids need laps, not apps)—alterations in the way young people interact and identify with these technologies also motivate much inquiry. "Younger generations," contends technologist Cathy Davidson, "don't just think about technology more casually, they're actually wired to respond to it in a different manner than we are" (in Rogers, 2011). The issues for young people's development that this raises are significant. This use of technology, writes Susan Maushart, "is not an activity—like exercise, or playing Monopoly, or bickering with your brother in the backseat. It's an environment: pervasive, invisible, shrink-wrapped around pretty much everything kids do and say and think.... Unfettered media use … is like breastfeeding on demand, resulting in an 'elongated toddlerhood' that creates a generation suffering from a 'global life-passivity that goes way beyond garden-variety teen cluelessness.'" Young people, she worries, may be doomed to live lives of "quiet digital desperation" (in Franklin, 2011). As it is, 43 percent of teens wish they could unplug sometimes and 36 percent sometimes wish they could go back to a time before social networking (Rideout, 2012b). According to the American Academy of Pediatrics, many young people express concern over cyberbullying and online harassment, sexting and other age-inappropriate messaging (O'Keeffe and Clarke-Pearson, 2011).

But not all research on these technologies is so pessimistic. For example, Grasmuck, Martin, and Zhao discovered that racial and ethnic minorities use Facebook to present "highly social, culturally explicit and elaborated narratives of self [to] reflect a certain resistance to the racial silencing of minorities by dominant color-blind ideologies of broader society" (2009, p. 158). Baker and Oswald demonstrated that "online social networking services may provide a comfortable environment within which shy individuals can interact with others" (2010, p. 873). Effects and critical researchers alike are also investigating developmentally important issues such as the online building and maintenance of identity, "branding" of digital self-presentations, the redefinition of friendship and community, and the interaction of technology and civic involvement. As these are not child and adolescent specific, we'll take them up in much more detail in Chapter 11.

SUMMARY

As the 1960s unfolded, bringing with them significant political, social, and cultural upheaval, television became the country's dominant mass medium, sitting in 90 percent of all American homes. Could there be a connection between the two? An obvious point of interest was the influence of mediated violence on subsequent viewer aggression. Psychologists, free of mass communication effects trend researchers' limited effects bias, attacked the issue, and children were the focus of their inquiry. Defense of the media came from proponents of catharsis, the idea that viewing violence substitutes for the actual

demonstration of aggression by the viewer. But this theory was ultimately discredited as social cognitive theory became widely accepted.

Social cognitive theory proved to be a useful way of understanding how people learn behaviors from television. By differentiating between imitation and identification and identifying several different modeling processes, such as observational learning, inhibitory and disinhibitory effects, and vicarious reinforcement, it helped explain how individuals learn from the media.

Research regarding aggressive cues and priming effects attempted to add some specificity to social cognitive theory, as did the developmental perspective. Another advance was the consideration of different contextual variables, aspects of the presentation of violence in the media content itself, in determining the amount of learning from viewing. Still another was a reconception of the young audience—the active theory of television viewing—that, although not dismissing media effects, did suggest that young viewers have more influence over their interaction with media than social cognitive theory seemed to imply. Yet some researchers made persuasive arguments that both the developmental perspective and active audience theories could in fact explain the presence, rather than the absence of effects.

Eventually these ideas were applied to "new" media such as video games, and the research linking consumption with subsequent aggression was equally convincing, especially as players of video game violence, unlike television viewers, participated in the mayhem and were rewarded for their aggression. Video game violence research was at the heart of the creation of the General Aggression Model, which, with its foundation in social cognitive theory, is a comprehensive representation of the connection between consumption of media violence and aggression in real-world social situations.

Acknowledging that media, especially television, were children's early window on a world they might not yet be equipped to engage, mass communication theorists began examining questions of how growing up in an increasingly mediated environment might affect their social and cognitive development. Effects-trend and critical cultural researchers alike took up questions of the development of young people's gender and sexual identity, the influence of advertising on their physical development (especially the link between advertising of junk food and sugared snacks and obesity), and how the corporate takeover of childhood has redefined the concept of childhood altogether.

Critical Thinking Questions

1. Are you convinced of the causal link between mediated violence and subsequent viewer aggression? Why or why not? Was your view altered by the information presented in this chapter? Why or why not? Where there are seemingly contradictory effects findings, might both be correct? Under what circumstances might those contradictory results both be valid?

2. Are you a video game player? If so, what is your reaction to the research presented in this chapter? If you think it does not apply to you, why is that? What about your friends?

   Is it possible you are engaging in the third-person effect we discussed in Chapter 1? Do you draw a distinction between different kinds of games or game play when you consider the issue of effects?

3. Do you think childhood has been redefined in contemporary times? Talk about this with your parents. Ask them if they think their childhoods were similar to the one you lived. If they see differences, ask them why they think those differences exist. How much attention do they pay to mass media issues? How much attention do you?

Key Terms

social cognitive theory

General Aggression Model (GAM)

adultification of childhood

catharsis

imitation

identification

social learning

operant (or traditional) learning theory

behavioral repertoire

negative reinforcer

modeling

observational learning

inhibitory effects

disinhibitory effects

vicarious reinforcement

reinforcement contingencies

social prompting

aggressive cues

priming effects

cognitive-neoassociationistic perspective

desensitization

contextual variables

active theory

viewing schema

active-audience theories

downward spiral model

developmental perspective

empowered child model

similarity identification

wishful identification

superpeer theory

early window

kinderculture

objectification theory

7 | AUDIENCE THEORIES: USES AND RECEPTION

Consider the ways we use media during a typical day. For most of us, that use is a routine activity that takes up a considerable amount of our free time and requires little planning. With the development of new media and new technology applied to old media, we can surround ourselves with powerful forms of entertainment and information wherever we go. In the past, we could carry print media with us, but now we can enjoy rich audiovisual media wherever and whenever we choose. If there are empty spaces in our daily routines, we can easily fill them with media content. We can check Facebook, send a text message, follow the latest meme on YouTube, or hurl an Angry Bird. But why do we use media the way we do? What are we seeking from media and are we getting what we want? Do media easily satisfy us, or do we constantly change our uses in search of something more? Has the increasing availability of new media enabled us to make changes so that media might better serve us? Or are we merely getting more of the same delivered to us in more convenient and attractive audiovisual packages?

During the past 15 years, the sharing of digital media content on the Internet has risen exponentially. This growth was initially driven by Internet music services (legal and otherwise) such as Napster, Mog, Rhapsody, iTunes, RealPlayer, Kazaa, and Morpheus. Today, more than 1.1 billion songs are downloaded monthly from Internet file-sharing sites (Morrissey, 2011). In addition, literally hundreds of millions of people use the Internet to share movies, television programs, photos, e-books; anything that can be digitized can be shared.

This sharing of digital content is revolutionizing how we use media. We can access media content any time we want using an ever-increasing array of devices. More than 170 million Americans have Internet-capable smartphones. One hundred and thirty million have tablet computers which, like desktop and laptop computers, can access not only the vast treasures of the Internet, but because of **cloud computing** (the storage of digital content, including personal information and system-operating software, on distant, third-party servers offering on-demand access) our own personally collected content ("Mobile Phone and Tablet Users," 2012). Sales of devices for

cloud computing
Storage of digital content on distant, third-party servers

196

storing, accessing, and playing digital files are rising exponentially. What is going on? Why are so many people becoming so active in their use of media that they are willing to buy expensive new forms of technology and learn somewhat complicated media-use skills? If we are collecting, organizing, and playing digital files, how satisfied are we with what we are doing? Do we enjoy experimenting with the technology? Do we compete with friends to download more files? Do we now have easy access to unusual, highly specialized music we can't get from the local music store (if there still is one)? Do we appreciate the ability to create highly personalized collections of movies or television shows? Do we rely solely on the pay-services, those that are completely legal, or do we wander to the legally questionable peer-to-peer options like BitTorrent, Gnutella, and MLDonkey (95 percent of those monthly 1.1 billion music downloads are illegal; Morrisey, 2011)?

The digital file-sharing phenomenon provides a dramatic example of how the availability of a new media technology can bring about widespread changes in what people do with media. In turn, these changes can have a powerful impact on the media industries, on technology manufacturers, and on ourselves and the people around us. Even if we don't change our uses of media, we can be affected if others change theirs.

It's important to remember that our personal uses of media are never unique to ourselves—millions of other people engage in the same activities—often at the same time. As we have seen in previous chapters, this widespread simultaneous use of media has long been of interest to media researchers. Media audience research dates from the beginning of the twentieth century. However, early researchers focused mostly on describing audiences and on determining whether media had direct effects on people. But by the 1960s, effects research was not producing many new insights. As a result, over the last 50 years, researchers have turned their attention to new questions and developed new theories of media that have produced a new understanding of why people use specific media and the meaning that use has for them.

active-audience theories

Theories that focus on assessing what people do with media; audience-centered theories

This simple idea—that people put specific media and specific media content to specific use in the hopes of having some specific need or set of needs gratified—forms the basis of the theories discussed in this chapter. Unlike many of the perspectives we've examined already, these **active-audience theories** do not attempt to understand what the *media do to people* but, rather, focus on assessing what *people do with media*. For this reason, they are referred to as audience-centered rather than source-dominated theories. Initially, most were micro-level theories rather than more macro-level perspectives. They were concerned with understanding how and why individuals use media and they have been developed by both empirical and critical or cultural studies researchers.

Much of the postpositivist research we reviewed in previous chapters was effects-trend research, which assumed that media do things to people, often without their consent or desire. This inquiry typically focused on negative effects—the bad things that happen to people because they are exposed to problematic media content. Effects were caused by a variety of content, from political propaganda to dramatized presentations of sex and violence. In this chapter we consider a very different type of media effect—effects we consciously or routinely seek every time we turn to media for some particular purpose.

Study of these effects was slow to develop. Mass society theory and fear of propaganda focused researchers' attention on the macroscopic, source-dominated, negative consequences of media. Audience members were assumed to be passively responding to whatever content media made available to them. There were some early critics of this viewpoint. For example, John Dewey (1927) argued that educated people could make good use of media. To him, propaganda was a problem that should be solved through public education rather than censorship; if people could be taught to make better use of media content, they wouldn't need to be sheltered from it (Chapter 2). Despite these arguments, empirical research remained focused on locating evidence of how average people were manipulated by media. Similarly, early political economy and cultural studies research assumed that mass audiences were easily manipulated by elites. Media content served to promote a false consciousness that led people to act against their interests. Elites used media to manipulate and control society (Chapter 5).

Eventually, the early effects research discovered that people weren't as vulnerable to propaganda as mass society theory had predicted. The evidence suggested that people were protected from manipulation by opinion leaders and their own well-formed, intensely held attitudes. They were selective in choosing, interpreting, and remembering media content. But even these seemingly optimistic conclusions were associated with a pessimistic view of the average person. Most people were irrational and incapable of critically evaluating and resisting propaganda messages. Researchers concluded that if the barriers protecting people were broken down, individuals could be easily manipulated. Scholars were slow to develop the perspective that average people can be responsible media consumers who use media for their own worthwhile purposes—an active audience.

The theories covered in this chapter tend to be microscopic and have limited concern for the larger social order in which media operate. They concentrate on understanding how audiences routinely use media and are affected by this use. They ask, "Why do people seek information from media or how do they cope with the flow of content from those media?" "Why do people seek entertainment and what purposes does it serve for them." They don't ask, "Should people be seeking information or entertainment from media or what are the consequences for society when people routinely choose to use media in certain ways each day?" This doesn't mean the findings generated by the theories covered in this chapter don't have larger implications or can't be used to answer questions about the consequences of media use for the social order. Active-audience theories can be quite compatible with macroscopic theories that can answer such questions, as you'll soon see.

LEARNING OBJECTIVES

After studying this chapter you should be able to

- Explain why postpositivist and cultural studies researchers became increasingly focused on media audiences rather than media effects and how the resulting active-audience theories differ from the effects theories dominant in earlier mass communication theory.

- Recognize the ways in which audiences can be active and how that activity can be measured.
- Identify and assess the propositions of Uses-and-Gratifications Theory.
- Differentiate media functions and media uses.
- Identify the types of media gratifications that have been found to be most common and/or important.
- Judge the contributions of Entertainment Theory to our understanding of people's use of entertainment content.
- Understand why Reception Studies posed a challenge to both effects-trend notions and older forms of neo-Marxist theory.
- Recognize feminist contributions to the development of Reception Studies.
- Recognize how the insights of active-audience theories can be used to assess your personal use of media.

OVERVIEW

During the 1970s and 1980s, postpositivist and cultural studies researchers became increasingly focused on media audiences. Their goal was to gain a more useful understanding of what people were doing with media in their daily lives. Television viewing was escalating during the 1960s and 1970s, but very little research was undertaken to examine what people were doing when they watched. Were viewers primarily passive consumers of entertainment, or was television viewing serving more important purposes? Were people couch potatoes or thoughtful, reflective viewers? As this research developed, new and less pessimistic conceptualizations of audiences were formed. Some postpositivist researchers reexamined limited-effects findings about audiences and concluded that people were not as passive as these effects theories implied. At the same time, some cultural studies researchers were conducting their own audience research and discovering that the power of elites to manipulate audiences was not as great as had been assumed by neo-Marxist theorists (Chapter 5).

Of course, the possibility of responsible audience activity was never totally ignored in early media research, but much of it gave audiences insufficient credit for selection, interpretation, and use of media content. We will see that early development of audience-centered theories was hampered by confusion about the concepts of "functions" and "functionalism" and by methodological and theoretical disputes. We will consider what it means to be an active-audience member and examine in detail several audience-centered approaches.

The theories introduced in the early part of this chapter are important because they were among the first to make a priority of studying audience activity, viewing it in a more or less positive way. As we shall see, this doesn't mean they ignored the possibility of long-term negative consequences. Active audiences can be misled by poorly constructed or inaccurate media presentations (e.g., Gerbner, 2010). Audience members need to be aware of what they are doing with media and take responsibility for their actions. We will explain how the development of audience-centered theories challenged limited-effects notions. In doing so, we revisit functional analysis and discuss how it formed the basis of much audience-centered theory. We describe the

uses-and-gratifications approach
Approach to media study focusing on the uses to which people put media and the gratifications they seek from those uses

entertainment theory
Examines key psychological mechanisms underlying audience use and enjoyment of entertainment-oriented media content

uses-and-gratifications approach, both as initially conceived and as it matured and developed. We explore some of its central notions—for example, the meaning of an active audience, how activity is measured, and the use of this approach to understand effects.

Then we look at **entertainment theory.** It seeks to understand what entertaining media content does to us. Sometimes, maybe even often, these effects occur without our awareness; however, other times we may have quite specific goals in mind and actively match our media use to a desired outcome. "Over time," explains James Potter, "people have developed strategies to use the media to manage their moods. They learn how to do this by trial and error, so that when they are in a mood they do not like they know what media and which messages to search out" (2012, pp. 208–209).

We will also consider another audience-centered perspective, reception studies, originally developed by cultural studies researchers in Britain. It also assumes that audiences are active, but it uses a different strategy for studying media consumers and reaches different but often complementary conclusions. Even though reception studies was consciously developed as a challenge to effects-trend notions, its conclusions aren't contradictory. In most cases, the findings provide an alternate set of insights that add to rather than refute postpositivist findings.

AUDIENCE THEORIES: FROM SOURCE-DOMINATED TO ACTIVE-AUDIENCE PERSPECTIVES

Propaganda theories are concerned with audiences. As we saw in Chapter 2, the power of propaganda resides in its ability to quickly reach vast audiences and expose them to the same simple but subversive messages. In these theories, the propagandist dominates the audience and controls the messages that reach it. Research focus is on how propagandists are able to manipulate audiences using messages that affect them as the propagandist intends. Most are source-dominated theories. They center their attention primarily on message sources and content, not on the interests or needs of the audiences those sources want to influence. Audience members' ability to resist messages is discounted or ignored. As media theories have developed, this focus has gradually shifted. As early as the 1940s, the work of people like Herta Herzog, Robert Merton, Paul Lazarsfeld, and Frank Stanton reflected at least the implicit concern for studying an active, gratifications-seeking audience. Lazarsfeld and Stanton (1942) produced a series of books and studies throughout the 1940s that paid significant attention to how audiences used media to organize their lives and experiences. For example, they studied the value of early-morning radio reports to farmers. They developed a device to measure audience reactions to radio program content as people were listening to it. As part of the Lazarsfeld and Stanton series, Bernard Berelson (1949) published a classic media-use study of the disruption experienced by readers during a newspaper strike. He reported convincing evidence that newspapers formed an important part of many people's daily routine.

Herta Herzog is often credited with being the originator of the uses-and-gratifications approach, although she most likely did not give it its label. Interested in how and why people listened to the radio, she studied fans of a popular quiz show (1940) and soap opera listeners (1944). This latter work, entitled "Motivations and Gratifications of Daily Serial Listeners," provides an in-depth examination of media gratifications. She interviewed 100 radio soap opera fans and identified "three major types of gratification." First, listening was "merely a means of emotional release"; "a second and commonly recognized form of enjoyment concerns the opportunities for wishful thinking"; and the "third and commonly unsuspected form of gratification concerns the advice obtained from listening to daytime serials" (pp. 51–55). Herzog wanted to understand why so many housewives were attracted to radio soap operas. In contrast with the typical effects research conducted in Lazarsfeld's shop, her work didn't try to measure the influence that soap operas had on women. She was satisfied with assessing their reasons and experiences—their uses and gratifications.

One of the first college mass communication textbooks, *The Process and Effects of Mass Communication*, also offered an early active-audience conceptualization. Author Wilbur Schramm (1954) asked this question, "What determines which offerings of mass communication will be selected by a given individual?" (p. 19). His answer was the **fraction of selection**:

fraction of selection
Graphic description of how individuals make media and content choices based on expectation of reward and effort required

$$\frac{\text{Expectation of Reward}}{\text{Effort Required}}$$

His point was that people weigh the level of reward (gratification) they expect from a given medium or message against how much effort they must make to secure that reward. Review your own news consumption, for example. If you are a regular television viewer, it's easier to watch the network news or flip on CNN than it is to get news online. Television news is presented attractively and dramatically. The images are usually arresting, and the narration and anchorperson's report are typically crisp and to the point. You never have to leave your chair to watch; once you settle on a specific news broadcast, you don't have to touch the remote again, and when the show you're watching ends, you're already in place for *American Idol*. This concerns only the denominator (effort required), and there is little effort required to consume a televised news program.

But if you routinely used the Internet, you might instead choose to get your news there because the reward you expect from your online news activity (news anytime you want it, ability to select just the stories you are interested in, more detail, greater depth, more variety of approach, more sophisticated reports, alternative perspectives, useful links, opportunity to comment) makes the additional effort (waiting for the server to connect you to your search engine, identifying the sites you're interested in, selecting specific reports, reading them, searching for alternative stories, accessing related links) worthwhile. You can develop your own fractions for your own media use of all kinds, but the essence of Schramm's argument remains: we all make decisions about which content we choose based on our expectations of having some need met, even if that decision is to not make a choice—say between two early evening situation comedies, for example, because we can't find the remote control and it's too much trouble to get up and change the channel—because all we really want is some background noise while we sit and daydream.

LIMITATIONS OF EARLY AUDIENCE-CENTERED RESEARCH

If this is all so seemingly logical and straightforward, why didn't early mass communication researchers create theories focused on active audiences? Why didn't such theories emerge as strong alternatives to limited-effects theories? Why were source-dominated theories so powerful and why did their influence persist so long? There are many possible answers. We have seen how mass society theory exaggerated the influence of media and centered widespread public concern on negative media effects. We looked at the Payne Fund studies of the effects of movies on children and teens. During World War II media research was used to meet the threat posed by totalitarianism. Since the 1930s, government agencies, private foundations, and the media industry all have been willing to provide funding to study a broad range of positive and negative effects, but they provided little money to study audience activity. Researchers also thought that it was possible to study effects more objectively and parsimoniously than was possible in the investigation of media gratifications. For example, behavioral or attitudinal effects might be observed in a laboratory following exposure to media content. Specific effects could be identified and measured. On the other hand, studying gratifications meant asking people to report on their subjective experiences of content. People might report hundreds of different gratifications which then needed to be sorted out and categorized. How could this be done objectively? Herzog (1940) recommended using qualitative research to study media gratifications. But during the 1940s and 1950s, postpositivist researchers were determined to avoid approaches that were unparsimonious and didn't meet what they regarded as scientific standards. They chose to focus their efforts on developing what they thought would be definitive, powerful explanations for the consequences of media use. Why bother to describe and catalog people's subjective reasons for using media?

Early postpositivist researchers thought studying people's subjective explanations would serve little purpose other than satisfying curiosity about why so many people wasted so much time using mass media. As far as they were concerned, the only things they needed to know about an audience was its size and **demographics** (the social attributes of audience members like age, gender, income, education). Early media researchers devoted considerable effort and expense to developing scientific methods for measuring audience size and composition. These were the things that advertisers wanted to know so they could better target ads and gauge their effectiveness. But most advertisers thought there was no practical reason to know why people sought out certain radio programs or read specific newspapers.

demographics
Social attributes of audience; that is, age, gender, income, education

Early media researchers were also concerned that the study of media gratifications would be difficult using available scientific methods. Most attitude researchers had strong behaviorist biases that led them to be suspicious of taking people's thoughts and experiences at face value. Did people really have any useful insight into why they use media? As we saw in Chapter 2, behaviorists believed that conscious thought only serves to provide rationalizations for actions people have been conditioned to make. To understand what really motivates people to act as they do, social scientists must observe how they have been conditioned through exposure to stimuli in past situations. But this would be very difficult and costly. Researchers worked hard to develop survey questionnaire items to measure specific attitudes using questions that only indirectly hinted at the underlying attitude being measured.

Postpositivist researchers criticized the early active-audience research as too descriptive—it did little more than take people's reasons for using media and group them into sets of arbitrarily chosen categories. Why one set of categories rather than another? Moreover, they dismissed the categorization process itself as arbitrary and subjective. For example, Herzog placed her listeners' reasons into three categories—why not five? Where did her categories come from, and how could we be certain she wasn't arbitrarily putting respondents' stated reasons into these categories? In contrast, experimental attitude-change research used what most researchers regarded as a scientifically sound set of procedures to develop attitude scales (Chapter 1). They believed that this type of research produced causal explanations rather than simple descriptions of subjective perceptions. As long as this empirical effects research offered the hope of producing significant new insight into the causal power of media, researchers had little motivation to test alternate approaches. They were anxious to prove the usefulness of their empirical methods and assert their standing as scientists rather than humanists.

CONFUSION OF MEDIA FUNCTIONS AND MEDIA USES

In Chapter 4, we described functional analysis and its use by early media researchers. By the 1960s, notions of an active and gratification-seeking audience had been absorbed into and confused with functional analysis. Failure to adequately differentiate media *uses* from media *functions* impeded the design and interpretation of audience-centered research. Charles Wright explicitly linked the active audience to functionalism in his 1959 book. This linkage to functions had a detrimental influence on the development of active-audience theories. Although Wright cautioned his readers to distinguish "between the consequences (functions) of a social activity and the aims or purposes behind the activity" (p. 16), functions were assumed by most communication theorists to be equivalent to (synonymous with) the aims or goals of the media industries themselves. To some extent this confusion over audience uses and societal functions also involves confusion about **levels of analysis** (the focus of research attention, ranging from individuals to social systems). As an individual audience member you may have certain personal purposes for reading a newspaper, and this activity should gratify some of these needs or you will stop reading. But you are only one of many people who will read that newspaper on a given day. Other people have other purposes that may be very different from your own. They will experience different gratifications. Functionalism is not concerned with individuals; it's concerned with overall functions for society that are served by mass media.

levels of analysis
The focus of research attention, ranging from individuals to social systems

As explained in Chapter 4, functionalism often serves to legitimize the status quo. It tends to assume that if the social order is stable, things are in balance—bad functions are offset by good functions—otherwise the social order will fall apart. To the extent that active-audience notions were conceptually confused with functionalism, critics judged them as merely another way to rationalize the way things are.

Let's use the classic four functions from Chapter 4's discussion of functionalism as an example. *Surveillance of the environment* refers to the media's collection and distribution of information. We know who was elected governor of Illinois because it was in the newspaper, and we know whether to wear a sweater to class because the radio weather forecaster said that it would be chilly today. *Correlation of parts of society* refers to the media's interpretive or analytical activities. We know that the failure of the highway bond proposition means that gasoline taxes will rise to cover necessary road repair because we read online reports and editorials explaining the connection. *Transmission of the social heritage* relates to the media's ability to communicate values, norms, and styles across time and between groups. How do you and your friends decide what clothes are fashionable or form expectations of what people normally do when they go out on dates? Media provide lots of information and advice about these topics. Finally, *entertainment* means media's ability to entertain or amuse.

These seem like perfectly reasonable aims of the media, but there is a problem. These might be goals of given media organizations, but (a) they might not necessarily be the purposes they serve for the people who consume those media, and (b) these functions can be different from the audience members' intended uses. For example, you might intentionally watch a horror movie to escape boredom, and you might even learn (unintentionally) a bit about how people deal with dangerous situations. In the course of watching you might also inadvertently learn how to use a knife as a weapon. The filmmaker's goal was to entertain, but the uses (the purpose) to which you ultimately put the content—escape boredom and unintentionally learn how to deal with danger and wield a knife—were much different. In other words, the source's aim is not always the ultimate function. If we confine our research to an investigation of functions intended by media practitioners (their goals), we are likely to ignore many negative effects. Because much early functional analysis was restricted to intended functions (again, goals), critics have charged that it is too apologetic to the media industries.

Wright, realizing how his conceptualization of media functions was misinterpreted, later wrote:

> Our working quartet of communications—surveillance, correlation, cultural transmission, and entertainment—was intended to refer to common kinds of activities that might or might not be carried out as mass communications or as private, personal communications. These activities were not synonymous for functions, which refer to the consequences of routinely carrying out such communication activities through the institutionalized processes of mass communications. (1974, p. 205)

The surveillance activity, its functions in our society, and the effects of those functions offer a good example of how Wright intended functionalism to be applied to media studies. Newspapers, magazines, television, and Internet news sites devote significant energy and effort to covering political campaigns and delivering the product of that effort to their audiences. If readers and viewers ignore (i.e., fail to use) the reports, no communication happens and the intended functions fail to occur. But if readers and viewers do consume the reports, the intended function we've been calling surveillance of the environment should take place. If so, there should be certain effects—readers and viewers should learn specific information from the news. They should use this information in ways that serve the larger society. Thus media cannot serve their intended function unless people make certain uses of their content. For surveillance to occur, routine transmission of news information about key events must be accompanied by active-audience use that results in widespread learning about those events and a willingness to act on this information. Thus news media can achieve this societal-level function only if enough individual audience members are willing and able to make certain uses of content and do so frequently and routinely.

dysfunction
A negative function

As was implied in Chapter 3's discussion of Libertarianism, one historically important and widely intended function of public communication is the creation and maintenance of an enlightened and knowledgeable electorate, one capable of governing itself wisely based on information gained from media and other people. But many of us might argue that most current-day news media transmit "infotainment" that actually serves a negative function (a **dysfunction**) in that it produces ill-educated citizens or citizens who actually become less involved in the political process because they substitute pseudo-involvement in overdramatized media depictions of campaign spectacles for actual involvement in real campaign activities (Edelman, 1988). The intended function of the reporting of those events and our intended use of the reports might be consistent with a normative theory (Libertarianism) underlying our political and media system. The overall consequences of that activity, however, might well be something completely different. As political campaigns cater more and more to the time, economic, and aesthetic demands of the electronic media (less complexity, more staging of campaign spectacles, less information about complex and controversial issues, more reliance on negative ads, and so on), voters might become cynical about politics, which might undermine support for government and inadvertently increase the influence of well-organized special interest groups (Gans, 1978). Voters' use of media might gradually change so instead of seeking information that isn't there, they turn to media for the mesmerizing spectacles that are available. In this example, the intended function of media hasn't changed, but its practical consequences have. These gaps between intended functions and observed societal consequences have impressed media critics, leading them to be suspicious of both functional analysis and theories that presume an active audience.

REVIVAL OF THE USES-AND-GRATIFICATIONS APPROACH

Interest in studying the audience's uses of the media and the gratifications the audience receives from the media had two revivals. The first occurred during the 1970s, partly as a response to the inconsequential and overqualified findings of run-of-the-mill effects research. As we discussed earlier, by the 1960s most of the important findings of effects research had been catalogued and demonstrated in study after study. In all this research, media's role was found to be marginal in comparison with other social factors. But how could this be true when media audiences were so vast and so many people spent so much time consuming media? Why were advertisers spending billions to purchase advertising time if their messages had no effect? Why were network television audiences continuing to grow? Didn't any of this media use have important consequences for the people who were engaging in it? If so, why didn't effects research document this influence? Was it overlooking something—and if so, what?

The media-effects trend had become so dominant in the United States that it was hard to ask questions about media that weren't stated in terms of measurable effects. There just didn't seem to be anything else worth studying, and no other approach to media research was considered useful. But if researchers restricted their inquiry to the study of effects, all they could obtain would be predictable, modest, highly qualified results. Though they were frustrated by this situation, few could see any practical alternative.

This first revival of interest in the uses-and-gratifications approach can be traced to three developments—one methodological and two theoretical:

1. **New survey research methods and data analysis techniques allowed the development of important new strategies for studying and interpreting audience uses and gratifications.** Researchers developed innovative questionnaires that allowed people's reasons for using media to be measured more systematically and objectively. At the same time, new data analysis techniques such as factor analysis provided more objective procedures for developing categories and for assigning reasons to them. Also, a large new generation of media researchers entered the academy in the 1970s. They were trained in the use of survey methods. As the decade advanced, the computer resources necessary to apply these methods were increasingly available—even to researchers working at smaller universities or colleges. These developments overcame some of the most serious methodological barriers to active-audience research.

2. **During the 1970s, some media researchers reached the conclusion that people's active use of media might be an important mediating factor making effects more or less likely.** They argued that a member of an active audience can decide whether certain media effects are desirable and set out to achieve those effects. For example, you might have decided to read this book to learn about media theories. You intend the book to have this effect on you, and you work to induce the effect. If you lack this intent and read the book for entertainment, use of the book is less likely to result in learning. Does the book cause you to learn? Or do you make it serve this purpose for you? If you hold the latter view, then you share the perspective of active-audience theorists. Your conscious decision to actively use the book is a necessary (mediating) factor that must occur so that the intended effect can take place.

3. **Some researchers began expressing growing concern that effects research was focusing too much on unintended negative effects of media while intended positive uses of media were being ignored.** By 1975, scholars knew a lot about the influence of television violence on small segments of the audience (most notably preadolescent boys), but much less about how most people were seeking to make media do things that they wanted.

The second and more recent revival of interest in uses and gratifications, as you might have guessed from this chapter's opening, is the product of the ongoing development and diffusion of new media technologies and Internet applications, most specifically because of the interactivity they encourage. Arguing that "uses-and-gratifications has always provided a cutting-edge theoretical approach in the initial stages of each new mass communications medium," Thomas Ruggiero (2000, p. 3) identified three characteristics of computer-mediated mass communication that "offer a vast continuum of communication behaviors" for uses-and-gratifications researchers to examine:

- *Interactivity* "significantly strengthens the core [uses-and-gratifications] notion of active user" (Ruggiero, 2000, p. 15) because interactivity in mass communication has long been considered "the degree to which participants in the communication process have control over, and can change roles in their mutual discourse" (Williams, Rice, and Rogers, 1988, p. 10).
- *Demassification* is "the ability of the media user to select from a wide menu.... Unlike traditional mass media, new media like the Internet provide selectivity characteristics that allow individuals to tailor messages to their needs" (Ruggiero, 2000, p. 16).
- *Asynchroneity* means that mediated messages "may be staggered in time. Senders and receivers of electronic messages can read mail at different times and still interact at their convenience. It also means the ability of an individual to send, receive, save, or retrieve messages at her or his convenience. In the case of television, asynchroneity meant the ability of VCR users to record a program for later viewing. With electronic mail [e-mail] and the Internet, an individual has the potential to store, duplicate, or print graphics and text, or transfer them to an online Web page or the e-mail of another individual. Once messages are digitized, manipulation of media becomes infinite, allowing the individual much more control than traditional means" (Ruggiero, 2000, p. 16).

In fact, people examining new technology have found uses-and-gratifications research to be quite helpful in studying a wide range of new media, especially e-mail and social networking sites. For example, Boneva, Kraut, and Frohlich (2001) report that women find e-mail more useful than do men in maintaining social relationships. They demonstrated increasing use of e-mail by women to keep in touch with family and friends. Quan-Haase and Young found that different goals drive people's choice to use either Facebook or instant messaging, "Facebook is about having fun and knowing about the social activities occurring in one's social network, whereas instant messaging is geared more toward relationship maintenance and development" (2010, p. 350). Another uses-and-gratifications analysis of Facebook demonstrated that females and males use the site differently, women for maintaining relationships, passing time, and being entertained and men for meeting new people and developing new relationships (Sheldon, 2008).

Uses-and-gratifications theory may also prove to be essential in assessing how and why various computer-based or wireless communication services are used to supplement and in some cases replace older media. For example, young adults, the demographic least likely to read a printed newspaper, actually consume more news and information content than do their parents, but they do so on their smartphones (Ellis, 2012), and telecommunications industry research indicates that smartphones have become "digital Swiss army knives," as their users continue to abandon traditional media to wirelessly play games, listen to music, watch television and movies, read books, and take photographs (O2, 2012). We will look at more of this social networking and use-of-Internet research in Chapter 11.

THE ACTIVE AUDIENCE REVISITED

Whether they are engaged in new or traditional media use, the question remains: How active are media audiences, and what forms does this activity take? Critics of uses-and-gratifications research have long charged that the theory exaggerates the amount of active use. They contend that most media use is so passive and habitual that it makes no sense to ask people about it. Mark Levy and Sven Windahl (1985) attempted to put the issue in perspective:

> As commonly understood by gratifications researchers, the term "audience activity" postulates a voluntaristic and selective orientation by audiences toward the communication process. In brief, it suggests that media use is motivated by needs and goals that are defined by audience members themselves, and that active participation in the communication process may facilitate, limit, or otherwise influence the gratifications and effects associated with exposure. Current thinking also suggests that audience activity is best conceptualized as a variable construct, with audiences exhibiting varying kinds and degrees of activity. (p. 110)

Jay G. Blumler (1979) claimed that one problem in the development of a strong uses-and-gratifications tradition is the "extraordinary range of meanings" given to the concept of *activity*. He identified several meanings for the term, including the following:

- **Utility:** Media have many uses for people, and people can put media to those uses.
- **Intentionality:** Consumption of media content can be directed by people's prior motivations.
- **Selectivity:** People's use of media might reflect their existing interests and preferences.
- **Imperviousness to influence:** Audience members are often obstinate; they might not want to be controlled by anyone or anything, even by mass media. Audience members actively avoid certain types of media influence.

Blumler's list summarized the forms of audience activity that the early uses-and-gratifications researchers studied. They related to overall choices of content and media-use patterns. These types of audience activity did not, however, consider what people actually did with media content once they had chosen it. Recent research has begun to focus on this type of audience activity—the manner in which people actively impose meaning on content and construct new meaning that serves their purposes better than any meaning that might have been intended by the message producer or distributor.

A good example is the many meanings fans and critics made from the all-time movie box office hit *Avatar*. Conservatives said the film encouraged viewers "to root for the defeat of American soldiers at the hands of an insurgency" and fed "hatred of the military and American institutions." The movie offered "an incredibly disturbing anti-human, anti-military, anti-Western world view." It "maligned capitalism, promoted animism over monotheism, and overdramatized the possibility of environmental catastrophe on earth" while "flirting with modern doctrines that promote the worship of nature as a substitute for religion" (all quotes from Leonard, 2010). Liberal critics condemned the film's imperialist/racist theme of the beautiful-but-flawed colored people saved by the white man. When conservative critics used *Avatar* to bolster their contention that Hollywood is liberal, liberals used it to argue that its proenvironment and antiwar themes resonated with the public—the fact that *Avatar* is history's most successful movie, earning nearly three billion dollars at the box office, means that people find gratification in those liberal themes; in other words, the market has decided. Or perhaps *Avatar* is something else, a special-effects laden, explosion-rich holiday blockbuster designed to amass billions of dollars for its creators and investors while providing a pleasurable few hours of diversion for those willing to pay the price of a ticket.

Two ways to clarify the issue are to distinguish between "activity" and "activeness" and to see the "active audience" as a relative concept. "Activity" and "activeness" are related, but the former refers more to what the audience does (e.g., chooses to read online news rather than watch television news), and the latter is more what the uses-and-gratifications people had in mind—that is, the audience's freedom and autonomy in the mass communication situation, as illustrated in the *Avatar* example. This activeness, no doubt, varies from one person to the next. Some audience members are more active, and some are more passive. This is obvious; we all know too many couch potatoes, people who live their lives through the movies, or people addicted to their iPhones, suffering from phantom-vibration syndrome, feeling their phones vibrate when in fact they are not (Dokoupil, 2012). But we also know many people who fit none of these descriptions. And an inactive user can become active. Our level of activity might vary by time of day and by type of content. We might be active users of the World Wide Web by day and passive consumers of late-night movies. What the uses-and-gratifications approach really does, then, is provide a framework for understanding when and how different media consumers become more or less active and what the consequences of that increased or decreased involvement might be.

The classic articulation of this framework is the one offered by Elihu Katz, Jay Blumler, and Michael Gurevitch (1974). They described five elements, or basic assumptions, of the uses-and-gratifications model:

1. **The audience is active and its media use is goal-oriented.** We've seen some confusion about exactly what is meant by *active*, but clearly various audience members bring various levels of activity to their consumption (if nothing else, at least in choice of preferred medium in given situations or preferred content within a given medium). You choose a printed magazine over its website because you like its portability and the feel of its glossy pages, and you know that when reading that magazine, you like biographies more than you do articles about finance.

2. **The initiative in linking need gratification to a specific media choice rests with the audience member.** Kristen Wiig and Melissa McCarthy, even teamed with Jon Hamm, cannot make you see *Bridesmaids*. Rachel Maddow and Anderson Cooper cannot compel you to be a news junkie.

3. **The media compete with other sources of need satisfaction.** This is what Joseph Klapper meant when he said that media function "through a nexus of mediating factors and influences" (Chapter 4). Simply put, the media and their audiences do not exist in a vacuum. They are part of the larger society, and the relationship between media and audiences is influenced by events in that

environment. If all your needs for information and entertainment are being satisfied by conversations with your friends, then you are much less likely to turn on a television set or go online for news. When students enter college, some forms of media use tend to sharply decline because these media don't compete as well for students' time and attention. In the current media environment, old media (television, radio, newspapers) increasingly compete for our attention with a growing range of new media that serve similar needs more cheaply, easily, or efficiently.

4. **People are aware enough of their own media use, interests, and motives to be able to provide researchers with an accurate picture of that use.** This, as we've seen earlier, is a much-debated methodological issue, explained succinctly here by James Potter, "Think about the experience of filling out a questionnaire that asks you how much time you spend on each type of [media] message, then asks you how much enjoyment you got from each type of message. Are you likely to say you spent a huge amount of time with a particular kind of media message yet received no enjoyment from it? Even if this were the case, you would not be likely to admit it to a researcher that you are such a loser" (2012, p. 134).

But as research methods are continually refined, social scientists are increasingly able to offer better evidence of people's awareness of media use. In fact, research suggests that as media choices grow with the continued diffusion of technologies like digital video recorders, cable and satellite, and the Internet, people are being forced to become more conscious of their media use (La Ferle, Edwards, and Lee, 2000). For example, you can blunder into watching television shows by flipping to a channel and leaving the set tuned there all night. You can fall into certain viewing habits if everyone around you is regularly watching certain shows. But if you pay to download a movie, you are more likely to make an active choice. You don't pick the first title in the video-on-demand menu. You scan the options, weigh their merits, read the provided descriptions, maybe watch the offered trailers, and then settle on a movie. Your choice is much more likely to reflect your interests than when you "zone out" viewing one channel or watched whatever was on the screen in the lounge in the student center.

5. **Value judgments regarding the audience's linking its needs to specific media or content should be suspended.** For example, the "harmful effects" of consumer product advertising on our culture's values might only be harmful in the researcher's eyes. If audience members want those ads to help them decide what's "cool," that's their decision. This is perhaps the most problematic of Katz, Blumler, and Gurevitch's assertions. Their point is that people can use the same content in very different ways, and therefore the same content could have very different consequences, not that researchers should not care about their findings. Viewing *Avatar* might reinforce antiwar attitudes for some people. Viewing movies that show violent treatment of minorities could reinforce some people's negative attitudes and yet lead others to be more supportive of minority rights. We each construct our own meaning of content, and that meaning ultimately influences what we think and do. Defenders of new media advocate the merits of using social networking websites, e-mail, and text messaging to maintain contact with a wide range of distant friends. But what if people never develop new friendships because they are satisfied with keeping superficial contact with old friends? When you started college, did you stay in touch with high school friends using e-mail or social media

websites? Did this affect your desire to make new friends? Or did you use new media to seek out and establish new relationships in college? Your decisions about how to use social media determined the purposes that these media served for you.

This synopsis of the uses-and-gratifications perspective's basic assumptions raises several questions. What factors affect audience members' level of activeness or their awareness of media use? What other things in the environment influence the creation or maintenance of the audience members' needs and their judgments of which media use will best meet those needs? Katz, Blumler, and Gurevitch (1974, p. 27) addressed these issues, arguing that the "social situations" that people find themselves in can be "involved in the generation of media-related needs" in any of the following ways:

1. **Social situations can produce tensions and conflicts, leading to pressure for their easement through media consumption.** You're worried about your body image and think you have a weight problem, so you read magazines that give advice about dieting or you watch movies or sitcoms in which characters struggle with similar problems. Or you decide to watch some of YouTube's anorexia-themed videos.

2. **Social situations can create an awareness of problems that demand attention, information about which might be sought in the media.** You're out with friends and you notice that the most popular people in that circle are those who are the most socially outgoing; you also see that they get invitations that you do not. You increase your consumption of style and fashion magazines to better understand the social scene, or you go online, knowing that Google can help you find in-depth information about most social problems.

3. **Social situations can impoverish real-life opportunities to satisfy certain needs, and the media can serve as substitutes or supplements.** Your student budget does not allow you to buy the "in" clothes or to pay the cover charge at the dance club, so the Style Network's *How Do I Look?* keeps you company. When you come to college, you might use social networking sites to stay in contact with old friends as a substitute until you make new ones. Talk shows on radio and television provide an endless stream of chatter to fill up spaces in our lives and create a sense of being involved with other people.

4. **Social situations often elicit specific values, and their affirmation and reinforcement can be facilitated by the consumption of related media materials.** The fact that you are a single young adult in college often means that you are part of a group that values going to parties. To check this out, do some research on Facebook and see the attention people your age give to their social lives. This media content not only promotes the party scene, it reinforces your attitudes toward it.

5. **Social situations can provide realms of expectations of familiarity with media, which must be met to sustain membership in specific social groups.** What? You don't watch *The Walking Dead*? You don't know how Justin Timberlake became famous? You didn't know that Aubrey Graham was Jimmy on *Degrassi: The Next Generation* before he became the rap artist known as Drake? You haven't seen the latest dating flick? Or what about sports? Who won the World Series? Can LeBron replace Michael? How about those Patriots, those Falcons, those 49ers?

Of course, if you see media as important sources of effects, you might ask whether the mass media themselves might have been instrumental in creating certain social situations (such as those in our examples); and for making the satisfaction of those situations' attendant needs so crucial; and for making themselves, the media, the most convenient and effective means of gratifying those needs. Would we worry so much about body image if the media didn't present us with an endless parade of slender, fit, attractive people? Would we care as much about sports if they weren't constantly being promoted by media? But that is typically not of concern in traditional uses-and-gratifications thinking because the members of the audience personally and actively determine what gratifications of what needs will and will not occur from their own exposure to media messages.

USES-AND-GRATIFICATIONS RESEARCH AND EFFECTS

This tendency to ignore the possibility of effects has led many researchers to dismiss uses-and-gratifications research as interesting but ultimately of little value. As a result, some contemporary proponents of the approach have taken on the challenge of linking gratifications and effects.

Windahl (1981) argued that a merger of uses-and-gratifications research and effects-trend research was overdue and proposed what he called a "uses and effects" model that viewed the product of the use of media content as "conseffects." In a similar vein, Palmgreen, Wenner, and Rosengren (1985) wrote, "Studies have shown that a variety of audience gratifications (again, both sought and obtained) are related to a wide spectrum of media effects, including knowledge, dependency, attitudes, perceptions of social reality, agenda-setting, discussion, and various political effects variables" (p. 31).

INSTANT ACCESS

Uses-and-Gratifications Theory

Strengths

1. Focuses attention on individuals in the mass communication process
2. Respects intellect and ability of media consumers
3. Provides insightful analyses of how people experience media content
4. Differentiates active uses of media from more passive uses
5. Studies the use of media as a part of everyday social interaction
6. Provides useful insight into adoption of new media

Weaknesses

1. Too often mistakenly associated with functionalism, which can create a bias toward the status quo
2. Cannot easily address the presence or absence of effects
3. Many of its key concepts are criticized as unmeasurable
4. Is too oriented toward the micro-level
5. Media gratifications are often not associated with effects

Blumler also presented his ideas on how the uses-and-gratifications and effects approaches could be harmonized. You'll notice that his perspective still centers responsibility for the control of effects with the consumer rather than the media. He wrote:

> How might propositions about media effects be generated from … gratifications? First, we may postulate that cognitive motivation will facilitate information gain…. Second, media consumption for purposes of diversion and escape will favour [sic] audience acceptance of perceptions of social situations in line with portrayals frequently found in entertainment materials…. Third, involvement in media materials for personal identity reasons is likely to promote reinforcement effects. (1979, pp. 18–19)

Renewed interest in uses-and-gratifications developed when the effects trend was dominant, so it is no surprise that theorists focused more on what unites rather than separates the two schools of thought. Alan Rubin writes that "the primary difference between the two traditions" is that effects researchers most often examine the mass communication process from the source's perspective, while uses-and-gratifications people begin with the audience member. But both "seek to explain the outcomes or consequences of communication such as attitude or perception formation (e.g., cultivation, third-person effects), behavioral changes (e.g., dependency), and societal effects (knowledge gaps). Uses and gratifications does so, however, recognizing the greater potential for audience initiative, choice, and activity" (2009, p. 172).

ENTERTAINMENT THEORY

As we saw in Chapter 4, Harold Mendelsohn pioneered an attempt to apply psychological theories to assess what entertainment media do for us and to us. The discipline now regards his functional analysis approach to entertainment as too heavily biased toward a status quo that was not literally in disarray. But his view of the need to understand how audiences actually do use entertainment resonates today in some important postpositivist research.

Dolf Zillmann is credited with leading the way in the development of contemporary entertainment theory (Bryant, Roskos-Ewoldsen, and Cantor, 2003). Its proponents place it within the larger context of a psychology of entertainment (Bryant and Vorderer, 2006). It seeks to conceptualize and explicate key psychological mechanisms underlying entertainment and to differentiate entertainment processes from those that underlie media's role in information, education, or persuasion (p. ix). What separates current entertainment theory from earlier notions is that it doesn't see entertainment as simply an affective consequence of exposure to certain forms of media content. According to Bryant and Vorderer (2006), it envisions an overall process in which entertainment activity is "influenced, triggered and maybe even shaped by the media product that is selected" (p. 4). Although audience members do voluntarily control their selection of entertainment content, there are often underlying psychological processes they don't consciously control. It is these conscious and unconscious processes that provide a comprehensive explanation of how and why we use entertainment media, and they help explain the consequences of this use.

Entertainment theory integrates findings from research examining the effects of many different types of entertainment content. Dolph Zillmann and Peter Vorderer (2000) summarize research on horror, comedy, conflict, suspense, sex, affect-talk, sports, music, and videogames. They assess gender and age differences and identify a range of effects resulting from exposure to these forms of content. Some effects are intended by users, but many are not. For example, research finds that there may be a health benefit when we laugh, so viewing situation comedies could make us healthier. Regular viewing of television programs featuring sexual content is linked to phenomena such as ambivalence toward marriage, perceived frequency of sexual activity by others, and attitudes toward homosexuality. It's not likely that most viewers would have intended these effects or been aware of them. On the other hand, as Oliver (2008) notes—and as your own experience no doubt confirms—it is clear that people often have **hedonistic motivations** for their media choices, intentionally selecting "content that serves to maintain and maximize pleasure and to diminish and minimize pain both in terms of intensity and duration" (p. 40). That must be the reason moviegoers flocked to *Bridesmaids* and *Ted*. But they also turned out for "difficult" movies like *In the Valley of Elah*, *Life is Beautiful*, *The Pianist*, and *The Hurt Locker*. This is because people also have **eudaimonic motivations**, choosing content that provides opportunities for personal insight, self-reflection, and contemplation of "the poignancies of human life" (p. 40).

A recent edited collection (Bryant and Vorderer, 2006) has chapters devoted to a large number of psychological processes thought to be involved in or associated with entertainment, including selective exposure, motivation, attention, comprehension, information processing, attribution, disposition, empathy, identification with characters, involvement, mood management, social identity, and **parasocial interaction** ("interaction" between audience members and characters in media content; for example, talking to the television set). Each can be studied individually or several can be combined and used to study one or more forms of entertainment content. Some processes are more likely to be involved with certain

hedonistic motivations
Choosing content to maintain and maximize pleasure and diminish and minimize pain

eudaimonic motivations
Choosing content that provides opportunities for personal insight, self-reflection, and contemplation

parasocial interaction
"Interaction" between audience members and characters in media content

INSTANT ACCESS

Entertainment Theory

Strengths

1. Stresses media's prosocial influence
2. Assesses cognitive, affective, and behavioral effects
3. Provides cogent multivariate explanations for why people seek entertainment from media
4. Is grounded in an expanding body of empirical media-effects research
5. Provides a useful basis for conducting experiments

Weaknesses

1. Tends to accept status quo uses of entertainment media as a starting point for research
2. Has so far found effects that are mostly limited and minimal
3. Tends to ignore and doesn't provide a good basis for assessing cumulative effects
4. Tends to consider entertainment effects in isolation from other types of effects

forms of content. One way that research can advance in the future is to assess which processes are most centrally involved with which forms of entertainment.

As entertainment theory evolved, "subtheories" were created that focused on the various psychological processes listed here. One of the most interesting of these is **mood management theory**. We'll take a closer look at this idea because you might find it useful in analyzing your own use of media. It argues that a predominant motivation for using entertainment media is to moderate or control our moods. It articulates some of our commonsense notions about what we are doing when we seek out entertainment. If we're in a "bad mood," we turn on our iPod and listen to music. When we're "stressing out" from studying, we can take a break and surf the net or turn on a televised comedy. Silvia Knobloch-Westerwick (2006) provides a description of this theory: "The core prediction of mood management theory claims that individuals seek out media content that they expect to improve their mood. Mood optimization in this sense relates to levels of arousal— plausibly, individuals are likely to avoid unpleasant degrees of arousal, namely boredom and stress. By selecting media content, media users can regulate their own mood with regard to arousal levels" (p. 240).

According to Knobloch-Westerwick, there are four types of media content attributes relevant to mood management: excitatory potential, absorption potential, semantic affinity, and hedonic valence. *Excitatory potential* involves the ability of content to arouse or calm emotion—to get us excited or to reduce stress. *Absorption potential* involves the ability of content to direct our thoughts away from things that induce a negative mood and toward other things that induce positive feelings. *Semantic affinity* concerns the degree to which entertaining content involves things that are similar to (mean the same as) the things that are inducing a bad mood. *Hedonic valence* refers specifically to the potential that content has to induce positive feelings.

It should be possible for you to think about your recent use of entertainment content and assess the extent to which mood management theory can explain what you did and what happened to you. First, did your use of the content change your mood in the way you desired? If your mood did change, why do you think this happened? Did the content get you excited? Did it divert your thoughts from things that were bothering you? Was the content unrelated to your personal problems and therefore able to direct your thoughts toward something that made you feel better? Was the content capable of inducing positive feelings—of making you feel good? Can you remember an instance when you went to a movie and expected to be entertained but the opposite happened? What went wrong? Was the movie boring? Did it fail to distract you from your problems, or worse, did it actually remind you of the problems? Did it fail to arouse positive feelings?

Mood management theory can help to explain why our efforts to manage our moods can fail or why media content can be entertaining even when it concerns seemingly unpleasant things—like chainsaw massacres or devastating earthquakes. We might assume that situation comedies should always make us feel better, but they could remind us of our problems or they might just be boring. Conversely, we might expect that a horror movie or a thriller will arouse bad feelings, but it could be quite diverting and exciting—it could have high excitation and absorption potential.

mood management theory
A predominant motivation for using entertainment media is to moderate or control moods

Mood management theorists argue that we don't have to be consciously aware of these content attributes. We don't need to use them to consciously select content. Instead, we can be guided by our feelings about content—our vague expectations about what will make us feel better as opposed to having a well-thought-out, rational strategy guiding our selection. We don't ponder the hedonic valance or the semantic affinity of the television shows we select. According to Knobloch-Westerwick, "Awareness of mood optimization needs does not have to be assumed [by the researcher] … mood management processes may go by-and-large unnoticed by those who act on them—at least very little cognitive elaboration usually takes place" (2006, p. 241).

This view of audience members can be contrasted with that of uses-and-gratifications theorists, who rely on audience members to report both uses and gratifications. Mood management theorists don't necessarily expect audience members to be able to report how they use content to manage moods. They don't ask people to fill out questionnaires rating the expected hedonic valence or the excitation potential of various types of entertainment content. They know people don't always consciously make these types of assessments about content.

Since they can't conduct surveys to study mood moderation, they base their conclusions primarily on findings produced by experiments. In these experiments, audience members are exposed to media content that mood management theory predicts should influence them in certain ways. Subjects are exposed to content with high or low excitation potential or semantic affinity. But these experiments can be difficult to design. Researchers need to develop stimulus materials containing the proper amount of the attributes they are manipulating. But how do you take people's moods into account? Research ethics would make it difficult to deliberately induce bad moods prior to exposure to content.

Some audience members (maybe you) would reject the mood management explanation of what audience members are doing when they seek out entertainment content. You might argue that you're choosing content that is aesthetically pleasing or just mindless entertainment. Altering your mood may be the furthest thing from your mind. But is it? Might you be more concerned about managing your mood than your conscious mind is willing to acknowledge? Could you have been "conditioned" by past experiences with media content to know which forms of content will induce feelings that you unconsciously want to experience? Maybe you should take another look at what you're doing when you choose to zone out in front of your television for an evening or surf the net until 4 in the morning.

Knobloch-Westerwick reminds us that it's also important to differentiate between moods that tend to endure over time and temporarily induced changes in feelings. Moods could often be due to long-term, enduring personal or situational factors. They may be altered only temporarily by media content. For example, if you recently broke up with a close friend, this could induce a long-term negative mood. Watching a situation comedy might make you feel better temporarily, but the negative mood will return. You'd be managing your mood, but it would be only a short-term fix. In seeking out media content, you would need to avoid material that shows good friends because it will have too much "semantic affinity." Maybe horror movies or thrillers would be preferable. They would be exciting and diverting but wouldn't dwell much on human relationships.

Like most ideas related to entertainment theory, mood management theory accepts media as a benign force in society. What could be wrong with providing people with solace for everyday troubles? These contemporary theories for the most part suggest that the status quo is acceptable—much as Mendelsohn did many years ago. Mood management theory implies that media can help us cope with problems in our lives—problems that regularly induce bad moods. We don't have to develop a complex strategy to make media be helpful to us; we can rely on what we've learned from past experience with media, from what media have taught us to expect, and from the way we've been conditioned by exposure to a lifetime of entertainment programming.

DEVELOPMENT OF RECEPTION STUDIES: DECODING AND SENSE-MAKING

At the same time that audience-centered theory was attracting the attention of American empirical social scientists, British cultural studies researchers were developing a different but compatible perspective on audience activity. As we've seen, uses-and-gratifications researchers challenged the effects trend, at the time the dominant approach in U.S. mass communication research. In Britain, innovative cultural studies researchers were challenging both Marxist film critics and British proponents of the postpositivist effects trend.

Chapter 5 introduced the Birmingham University Centre for Contemporary Cultural Studies and the work of Stuart Hall, its most prominent scholar. Initially, Hall (1973) produced a mimeographed report that proved important in developing and focusing the work of his center. It was later published as a book chapter (Hall, 1980a), arguing that researchers should direct their attention toward (1) analysis of the social and political context in which content is produced (encoding), and (2) the consumption of media content (decoding). Researchers shouldn't make unwarranted assumptions about either encoding or decoding, he argued, but instead should conduct research permitting them to carefully assess the social and political context in which media content is produced and the everyday-life context in which it is consumed.

Proctor (2004) and Rojek (2009) assert that Hall intended his model as a challenge to the American-style effects research being conducted at Britain's University of Leicester Centre for Mass Communication Research. In the early 1980s the Centre was headed by James Halloran who specialized in research on the effects of television violence. Hall rejected the linear model of effects and presented his view as a much more nuanced approach to understanding media audience activity.

According to Shaun Moores (1993), Hall also developed his approach in part as a reaction against the tradition of Marxist film criticism found in the film journal *Screen*, which viewed mainstream popular films as inherently deceptive and supportive of an elite-dominated status quo—a view pioneered by the Frankfurt School. *Screen's* writers favored avant-garde films in which there was no pretense about depicting a "real" social world. Hall objected to the cultural elitism inherent in this perspective. "The project of the left is directed at the future, at the socialism that has still to come," he wrote, "and that is at odds with the direct experience of pleasure here and now. That causes all sorts of mental blocks when theorizing about the problem" (in Ang and Simmons, 1982, p. 14). Hall also thought it wrong to assume that popular films necessarily served to deceive and subvert working-class audiences and that there might well be cases in which these films actually made moviegoers less supportive of the status quo. In fact, the popular and critically acclaimed American message movies and British New Wave films of the time offered explicit and strong challenges to a United States and Great Britain committed to business as usual in those post-war decades. For example, in the United States, *Blackboard Jungle* and *Rebel Without a Cause*, both released in 1955, provided stark, pessimistic views of the alienation of youth. *Twelve Angry Men* (1957), *Imitation of Life* (1959), and *To Kill a Mockingbird* (1962) challenged prejudice and racism in the "Land of the Free." *The Pawnbroker* (1964) examined the clash of class and culture in urban America. In Great Britain, *Room at the Top* (1959), *The Entertainer* (1960), *A Taste of Honey* (1961), *The L-Shaped Room* (1962), and *The Loneliness of the Long Distance Runner* (1962)—dark, brooding films—"emphasized the poverty of the worker, the squalor of working-class life, the difficulty of keeping a home and keeping one's self-respect at the same time, [and] the social assumptions that sentence a person with no education and a working-class dialect to a lifetime of bare survival.... In the midst of this gray world, the directors focus on a common man reacting to his surroundings—bitter, brutal, angry, tough" (Mast and Kawin, 1996, p. 412). In addition, Hall did not think that it was reasonable to expect that working-class audiences should embrace avant-garde films as providing a better way of understanding the social world.

reception studies
Audience-centered theory that focuses on how various types of audience members make sense of specific forms of content

polysemic
The characteristic of media texts as fundamentally ambiguous and legitimately interpretable in different ways

preferred, or dominant, reading
In reception studies the producer-intended meaning of a piece of content; assumed to reinforce the status quo (sometimes referred to as the dominant reading)

In laying out his views about decoding, Hall proposed an approach to audience research that became known as **reception studies**, or reception analysis. One of its central features is its focus on how various types of audience members make sense of specific forms of content. Hall drew on French semiotic theory to argue that any media content can be regarded as a *text* made up of *signs*. These signs are structured; that is, they are related to one another in specific ways. To make sense of a text—to *read* a text—you must be able to interpret the signs and their structure. For example, when you read a sentence you must not only decode the individual words but also interpret its overall structure to make sense of it as a whole. Some texts are fundamentally ambiguous and can be legitimately interpreted in several different ways; they are **polysemic**. To return to an earlier example, Rebecca Keegan, James Cameron's biographer, said of the director's *Avatar*, "Some of the ways people are reading it are significant of Cameron's intent, and some are just by-products of what people are thinking about. It's really become this Rorschach test for your personal interests and anxieties." The film's producer, Jon Landau, added, "Movies that work are movies that have themes that are bigger than their genre. The theme is what you leave with, and you leave the plot at the theater" (both in Itzkoff, 2010, p. A1).

Hall argued that although most texts are polysemic, the producers of a message generally intend a **preferred, or dominant, reading** when they create a message. As a critical theorist, Hall assumed that most popular media content had a preferred reading reinforcing the status quo. But in addition to this dominant reading, it is possible for audience members to make alternate interpretations. They

INSTANT ACCESS

Reception Studies

Strengths

1. Focuses attention on individuals in the mass communication process
2. Respects intellect and ability of media consumers
3. Acknowledges range of meaning in media texts and the likelihood of many different interpretations
4. Seeks an in-depth understanding of how people interpret media content
5. Can provide an insightful analysis of the way media content is interpreted in everyday social contexts

Weaknesses

1. Is usually based on subjective interpretation of audience reports
2. Doesn't address presence or absence of effects
3. Uses qualitative research methods, which preclude causal explanations
4. Has been too oriented toward the micro-level (but is attempting to become more macroscopic)

negotiated meaning

In reception studies when an audience member creates a personally meaningful interpretation of content that differs from the preferred reading in important ways

oppositional decoding

In reception studies when an audience member develops interpretations of content that are in direct opposition to a dominant reading

might disagree with or misinterpret some aspects of a message and come up with an alternative or **negotiated meaning** differing from the preferred reading in important ways. In some cases, audiences might develop interpretations in direct opposition to a dominant reading. In that case, they are said to engage in **oppositional decoding**. As explained by Jesus Martin-Barbero (1993), although people are susceptible to domination by communication technologies, "they are able to exploit contradictions that enable them to resist, recycle, and redesign those technologies, … and people are capable of decoding and appropriating received messages and are not necessarily duped by them" (p. 225).

A student and colleague of Hall, David Morley, published one of the first detailed studies applying Hall's insights (Morley, 1980). It served as a model for subsequent reception studies. Morley brought together 29 groups of people drawn from various levels of British society. They ranged from business managers to trade unionists and apprentices. These groups were asked to view an episode from *Nationwide*, a British television news magazine show, assessing the economic consequences of the government's annual budget on three families. Once the program ended, the groups discussed what they had watched and offered their interpretations. *Nationwide* was chosen because an earlier analysis had identified it as a program that routinely offered status quo explanations for social issues (Brunsdon and Morley, 1981). Moreover, it was produced in a way designed to appeal to lower- and middle-class audiences. Thus the researchers expected that the program would be able to communicate status quo perspectives to those audiences.

Morley tape-recorded the group discussions and analyzed them, placing them into one of three categories: (1) dominant, (2) negotiated, or (3) oppositional decoding. He found that although an upper-class group of business managers dismissed the program as mere entertainment, they had no complaints about the views it offered. Morley labeled their decoding as a dominant reading. At the other extreme, a group of union shop stewards liked the format of the program but objected to its message. They saw it as too sympathetic to middle management and failing to address fundamental economic issues. Morley labeled their decoding as oppositional. In the negotiated decoding category were groups of teacher trainees and liberal arts students. Very few groups articulated only a dominant reading of the program. Aside from managers, only a group of apprentices was found to merely repeat the views offered by the program. Most offered a negotiated reading, and several provided oppositional readings.

Because the reception studies approach has developed in cultural studies, researchers have been careful to differentiate their empirical audience research from that conducted by postpositive researchers. They stress their effort to combine macroscopic encoding research with microscopic decoding studies. They also point to their reliance on qualitative rather than quantitative research methods. Reception studies are often conducted with focus groups. For example, people who frequently use certain types of content (fans) are sometimes brought together to discuss how they make sense of the content. In other cases, groups of people who belong to certain racial or ethnic groups are chosen so that the researcher can assess how these groups are routinely interpreting media content. In some cases, researchers undertake in-depth interviews to probe how individuals engage in "meaning making." In others, the researcher tries to assess how a focus group reaches a consensus concerning the meaning of content.

Sociologist Pertti Alasuutari (1999) has argued that reception research has entered a third stage. The first stage was centered on Hall's encoding-and-decoding approach. The second stage was dominated by Morley's pioneering audience ethnography work. Alasuutari wrote:

> The third generation entails a broadened frame within which one conceives of the media and media use. One does not necessarily abandon ethnographic case studies of audiences or analyses of individual programmes [sic], but the main focus is not restricted to finding out about the reception or "reading" of a programme by a particular audience. Rather the objective is to get a grasp of our contemporary "media culture," particularly as it can be seen in the role of the media in everyday life, both as a topic and as an activity structured by and structuring the discourses within which it is discussed.... The big picture that one wants to shed light on, or the big question to pursue, is the cultural place of the media in the contemporary world. It may entail questions about the meaning and use of particular programmes to particular groups of people, but it also includes questions about the frames within which we conceive of the media and their contents as reality and as representations—or distortions—of reality.... The big research programme also includes questioning the role of media research itself. (pp. 6–7)

Thus, this third generation of reception studies attempts to return to some of the more macroscopic concerns that initially motivated critical theorists. It represents an effort to integrate these critical theory concerns with reception analysis to establish a challenging research agenda. You can read about what some critical theorists are calling reception studies' latest incarnation in the box entitled "Semiotic Disobedience."

THINKING ABOUT THEORY | Semiotic Disobedience

British cultural theorist John Fiske coined the phrase *semiotic democracy* to refer to audience members' ability to make their own meaning from television content. In his words, viewers possessed the skill— and the right—to produce personal "meanings and pleasures" when interacting with media texts (Fiske, 1987, p. 236). In "meanings" you can see evidence of reception studies, and in "pleasures" you can see hints of uses-and-gratifications theory. But a new generation of active-audience writers and thinkers takes a more critical theory approach to the concept of an active audience. They argue that semiotic democracy, quite naturally, is evolving into **semiotic disobedience**, individuals' ability to reinvent or subvert media content, not to impose a personally meaningful reading, but to oppositionally redefine that content for themselves and others.

Examples abound. In San Francisco, the Billboard Liberation Front "improves" billboard advertising so the new "preferred" reading is in direct opposition to the one intended by the original advertiser. The Media Foundation, best known for its Buy Nothing Day, Digital Detox Week, and its magazine *Adbusters*, produces a series of magazine and online ads featuring a smoking, cancerous Joe Chemo bearing a remarkable likeness to the cigarette icon Joe Camel. Its American flag, with 50 brand logos rather than 50 stars, has filled a full page of the *New York Times*. *Disaffected!* is an online videogame designed to "introduce" people to the copy company Kinko's. Developer Ian Bogost, who wants to show that "games can bite back" at "colonization" by advertisers, promotes the game on his company's website this way: "Feel the indifference of these purple-shirted malcontents first-hand and consider the possible reasons behind their malaise—is it mere incompetence? Managerial affliction? Unseen but serious labor issues?" (Walker, 2006, p. 18).

Hamburger giant McDonald's has also had its name and logo oppositionally subverted and redefined in online games. In *McDonald's Videogame* players decide how much rain forest to clear in order to raise more cows for slaughter. Thirty-thousand people submitted YouTube entries when automaker Chevrolet invited people to create commercials for its Tahoe sports utility vehicle in 2006. But it was those ads linking the big SUV to global warming and sexual inadequacy that received worldwide media attention (Manly, 2007).

These forms of protest have arisen, according to semiotic disobedience advocates such as technologist David Bollier, because in our contemporary hyper-commercialized, corporate-dominated media "we are being told that culture is a creature of the market, not a democratic birthright. It is privately owned and controlled, and our role is to be obedient consumers. Only prescribed forms of interactivity are permitted. Our role, essentially, is to be paying visitors at a cultural estate owned by major 'content providers'" (2005, p. 3). The new digital communication technologies, with their portability, ubiquity, and ease of use make possible this subversion of the preferred readings.

What do you think? Do you find value in the subversion of a content provider's intended reading? Do you think these activities serve any meaningful function? Do you see semiotic disobedience as the next logical cultural step for people in the Internet Age? After all, we are able to impose our own oppositional readings on various texts; now we have a ready technology permitting us to create our own preferred readings in opposition to some elite's idea of what is "preferred." But because we can, should we?

semiotic disobedience Individuals' ability to reinvent or subvert media content to oppositionally redefine that content for themselves and others

FEMINIST RECEPTION STUDIES

Janice Radway (1984/1991) was one of the first American cultural studies researchers to exemplify the shift away from an exclusive focus on textual analysis and toward an increased reliance on reception studies. Her work provided an influential model for American scholars and is frequently cited as one of the best examples of feminist cultural studies research. Radway initially analyzed the content of popular romance novels. She argued that romance characters and plots are derived from patriarchal myths in which a male-dominated social order is assumed to be both natural and just. These books routinely presented men as strong, aggressive, and heroic, whereas women are weak, passive, and dependent. Women in their pages must gain their identity through their association with a male character.

After completing her content analysis of romance novels, Radway (1986, 1984/1991) interviewed women who read them and met regularly in groups to discuss them. She was surprised to find that many readers used these books as part of a silent rebellion against male domination which they were able to express in an "eloquence about their own lives" (1984/1991, p. 6). They read them as an escape from housework or child rearing. Many romance readers rejected key assumptions of the patriarchal myths. They expressed strong preferences for male characters who combined traditionally masculine and feminine traits, for example, physical strength combined with gentleness. Similarly, readers preferred strong female characters who controlled their own lives but retained traditional feminine attributes. Thus romance reading could be interpreted as a form of passive resistance against male-dominated culture. Romance readers rejected the preferred reading and instead engaged in negotiated or oppositional decoding. Their personal meaning making, Radway wrote, was their "declaration of independence" (1984/1991, p. 11). Her work, she said, "was less an account of the way romances as texts were interpreted than of the way romance reading as a form of behavior operated as a complex intervention in the ongoing social life of actual social subjects, women who saw themselves first as wives and mothers" (1984/1991, p. 7). Research on female viewers of soap operas offered similar interpretations of their decoding of content. Dorothy Hobson discovered that, as with most media texts, "there is no overall intrinsic message or meaning in the work.... [I]t comes alive and communicates when the viewers add their own interpretation and understanding to the programme [sic]" (1982, p. 170).

Another feminist cultural studies researcher offers evidence that women routinely engage in oppositional decoding of popular media content. Linda Steiner (1988) examined 10 years of the "No Comment" feature of *Ms.* magazine in which readers submit examples of subtle and not-so-subtle male domination. She argued that *Ms.* readers routinely engage in oppositional decoding and form a community acting together to construct these readings. Magazine examples can teach women how to identify these texts and help them develop interpretations serving their own interests rather than those of a patriarchal elite. Angela McRobbie, committed to "research *on* or *with* living human subjects, namely women or girls" (italics in original; 1982, p. 46), came to a similar conclusion in her study of teenage girls' negotiated readings of the movies *Flashdance* and *Fame.* She concluded that young girls' "passion" for these films "had far more to do with their own desire for physical autonomy than with any simple notion of acculturation to a patriarchal definition of feminine desirability" (1984, p. 47). You can read more about one of mass communication theory's most influential pieces of feminist reception analysis and judge for yourself if it is worthy of the importance it's given in the box, "Ien Ang's *Watching Dallas.*"

THINKING ABOUT THEORY | Ien Ang's *Watching Dallas*

Ien Ang's *Watching Dallas* was first published in 1982 in Dutch and in 1985, just as Janice Radway was establishing the legitimacy of feminist reception studies in the United States, it was translated into English. At the time Ang's work was considered "revolutionary" because it established her "as one of the founders of the Empirical and 'critical' active audience research movement, a movement that has changed the way in which audiences are thought of in media studies" (Alexander, 2011). Because most feminist cultural studies research at the time was based on interpretivist readings of texts, *Watching Dallas*, like Radway's *Reading Romance*, helped move feminist interest in popular culture and the notion of **interpretive communities** (people sharing a similar life situation who develop specific interpretive strategies) into the mass communication theory mainstream. Recall that Radway had indeed conducted her own reading of romance novels popular with female readers, but she went further. She began meeting regularly with groups of female readers, asking them in person and through questionnaires, what they thought was happening in those bodice-rippers. She conducted quantitative analyses of their responses and combined them with her own reading of the books and her reading of the conversations she had with those female fans.

Ang approached her text, the wildly popular American prime-time soap opera, *Dallas*, somewhat differently. Admitting that she was a fan of the show, which at the time was reviled in Europe as a prime example of "American cultural imperialism" and "the perfect hate symbol" of the "cultural poverty against which [European critical theorists] struggle" (1985, p. 2), she wanted to know why it had achieved "almost inconceivable popularity" in the Netherlands (52 percent of the country regularly tuned in; pp. 1, 118). Her innovation was to solicit letters from other fans and combine her reading of the show with her reading of those letters. She placed an ad in a popular Dutch women's magazine, *Vita*, which read, "I like watching the TV serial *Dallas* but often get odd reactions to it. Would anyone like to write and tell me why you like watching it too, or dislike it? I should like to

assimilate these reactions in my university thesis. Please write to …" (1985, p. 10). She received 42 responses, all but 3 from women. Her conclusion, much like Radway's, was that women bring their own readings to the show, readings much different from those constructed by men. What one fan called her "flight from reality" was, to Ang "not so much a denial of a reality as playing with it. A game that enables one to place the limits of the fictional and the real under discussion, to make them fluid. And in that game an imaginary participation in the fictional world is experienced as pleasurable" (p. 49). For *Dallas'* female fans, the show provided a "tragic structure of feeling" that, like soap operas themselves, "life is characterized by an endless fluctuation between happiness and unhappiness. Life is a question of falling down and getting up again" (p. 46). That tragic structure of feeling "is not about the great suffering which plays such a prominent role in the history of human kind and which is generally known as human tragedy—the sufferings of war, concentration camps, famine, etc.—but is rather about what is usually not acknowledged as tragic at all and for that very reason is so difficult to communicate" (pp. 79–80).

Pretty good stuff, right? But are you troubled by the small number of replies to Ang's ad? Is 39 letters from female fans enough of a response on which to build her sophisticated arguments? After all, it's only 3 fewer than Radway's 42 romance novel readers. Can you argue that Radway's interaction with those women—questionnaires and face-to-face meetings—means that she was able to gather more insight than could be gleaned from a collection of letters? And did you question whether Ang's overwhelming proportion of female responders might have been a result of placing the ad in a woman's magazine rather than in a more general publication? Maybe that doesn't matter because Ang wanted to hear from women. But does it matter that she labeled herself a "fan" who wanted to incorporate some real-people letters in her thesis rather than as a scholar, or a critical scholar, or a critical feminist scholar? How might

(Continued)

THINKING ABOUT THEORY | Ien Ang's *Watching Dallas*   (Continued)

the responses have been different, if at all, or how many fewer (or more) might she have received had she characterized herself differently?

Watching Dallas was and still is influential for bringing a form of empiricism to cultural studies and for giving voice to women audience members. Is that enough to "forgive" its methodological shortcomings (if you consider them that), or is Ang's combination of

interpretive analysis and female fan commentary valuable in itself because it brings us closer to interpretive theory's goal of understanding, in this case, how female fans of this particular television program are active in making meaning?

interpretive communities People sharing a similar life situation who develop specific interpretive strategies

SUMMARY

The audience has never been completely absent from mass communication theory, but the uses-and-gratifications approach brought it to a more central position in thinking about media. The assertion that audiences are active proved valuable in refining our understanding of the mass communication process.

Audience activity can be defined in several ways—utility, intentionality, selectivity, imperviousness to influence, and meaning construction—but activity should be seen as a relative concept; that is, some people are more active media consumers than are others. For example, entertainment theory, while accepting that people match goals to the consumption of specific forms of entertainment content, does not assert that this matching is always conscious. But reception studies recognizes people's active ability to make meaning from specific forms of content, presumably for personally relevant ends. Readers of media texts often apply their own negotiated and oppositional meanings to the preferred readings intended by content producers.

The active-audience perspectives described in this chapter were developed as a counter to both mass society theory and limited-effects notions. Active-audience perspectives argue that the media do not do things to people; rather, people do things with media. The basic tenet is that audiences are active and make media do things to serve their purpose.

Still, of all the chapters in this book, this one may leave you the most unsatisfied. Social cognitive theory was easy: People learn from the mass media through a process called modeling. Attitude-change theory is simple: Cognitive dissonance helps people protect themselves from persuasive messages. But the active-audience theories introduced in this chapter often raise as many questions about the role of media in our lives as they answer. They suggest that our use of media is actually much more complicated than we might like to assume. When you relax by clicking the remote and watching *Modern Family* or *So You Think You Can Dance*, you might like to assume that you are only being amused by these shows. Theories arguing that this seemingly routine choice is the result of your seeking a particular set of gratifications from a quite specific use of media might seem to be making something out of nothing. Despite any reservations you might have about these theories, you should recognize that our everyday use of media is an infinitely complex process and an extremely important one.

In the next two chapters, we'll move beyond the focus of the theories covered in this chapter. First, we'll examine ideas that dig deeper into the microscopic processes that structure how we make sense of and remember media content. Then we'll look at theories that address larger questions concerning the role of media in the social order and in culture. Some of these theories move beyond simply seeking answers to questions about the role of media. They offer ways of addressing problems posed by media—of taking greater control over them. Proponents of media literacy, as we'll see in Chapter 11, offer ways to help us all become more skilled consumers and readers of media and their content. What media literacy proponents emphasize is that it's not enough for audiences simply to be active. Audience activity must be grounded on informed critical reflection. If we are going to rely on media to make sense of our social world, then we need to take more control over how we do this.

A second reason that audience theories leave many observers unsatisfied is the difficulty these theories have in explaining media effects. Several authors we've cited have argued that uses-and-gratifications theory developed as a "counter" to the effects research dominant at the time. Blumler, for example, wrote that it developed "at a time of widespread disappointment with the fruits of attempts to measure the short-term [media] effects on people" (1979, p. 10). Palmgreen, Wenner, and Rosengren (1985) wrote: "The dominance of the 'effects' focus in pre- and post-World War II communication research tended to overshadow … concern with individual differences" (p. 12). In a sense, proponents of active-audience theory could not allow themselves the luxury of demonstrating or even postulating effects because that would have been heresy to the then-dominant limited-effects perspective.

Critical cultural theorists like Stuart Hall had another reason for disregarding media effects. Hall was convinced that effects research was useless because it largely served the status quo. He regarded the American focus on postpositivist effects research with great suspicion, believing that it served primarily the interests of the media industries. If researchers found effects, as with advertising, their findings were exploited to manipulate audiences. If they demonstrated no effects or that the effects they did find were "limited," their work was used to fend off the regulation of media industries. Hall thought this was nonsense. He believed that the dominant readings

embedded in most media content were obviously propping up a status quo in which most people were exploited. But how could he demonstrate this in a way that would be convincing to someone other than a neo-Marxist? His answer was reception studies—a qualitative research strategy permitting in-depth exploration of how groups "read" popular media content from television sitcoms to punk rock videos. But political economists criticize reception analysis as providing a different kind of apology for the media industries because most reception analysis suggests that people cope quite nicely with problematic media content. Individuals negotiate meaning or they engage in oppositional decoding. Is this so different from the limited-effects findings produced by postpositivist effects researchers?

So where do we go from here? How can we move beyond the narrow focus of audience theories and address larger questions concerning the role of media in society or in culture? We will provide our answers to these questions in the next three chapters. But we will leave you now with hints provided by Blumler, Gurevitch, and Katz, the creators of the original 1974 volume *The Uses of Mass Communication*. When asked to write the concluding comments for a book to celebrate the tenth anniversary of that work, they had this advice, which can be applied to any of the audience theories we have reviewed in this chapter:

> Philosophically, lingering traces of "vulgar gratificationism" should be purged from our outlook. This implies the following:
>
> (1) Rejection of audience imperialism. Our stress on audience activity should not be equated with a serene faith in the full or easy realization of audience autonomy.
>
> (2) Social roles constrain audience needs, opportunities, and choices…. The individual is part of a social structure, and his or her choices are less free and less random than a vulgar gratificationism would presume.
>
> (3) Texts are also to some extent constraining. In our zeal to deny a one-to-one relationship between media content and audience motivation, we have sometimes appeared to slip into the less warranted claim that almost any type of content may serve any type of function. (1985, pp. 259–260)

Critical Thinking Questions

1. Where does the greater amount of power reside in the media/audience relationship? That is, do media do things to people, or do people do things with media? Are there circumstances when the "balance of power" might shift? That is, are there circumstances when audience members have greater control over their reading than others? Have the new digital media shifted the balance of power, giving individual audience members more power? How much control do you exercise over your meaning making when using digital media like video games and Facebook? Do you ever make meaning with your friends using these media's interactivity? Why or why not?

2. Choose a media consumption choice that you may often have to make, such as selecting a movie streamed to your laptop versus one at the multiplex, choosing an episode of your favorite situation comedy downloaded to your smartphone versus one on your big-screen television set, or scanning online headlines versus spending 30 minutes with the newspaper. Subject that decision to Schramm's fraction of selection. Which "wins"? Which elements in the numerator and denominator might you change to produce a different outcome? What does this tell you about your media uses and gratifications?

3. Why would you ever impose an oppositional reading of a piece of media content? After all, the producers went to great lengths to create a text that would bring you some satisfaction. Why not just enjoy it? There are always other texts that can provide you with the reading you prefer.

Key Terms

cloud computing

active-audience theories

uses-and-gratifications approach

entertainment theory

fraction of selection

demographics

levels of analysis

dysfunction

hedonistic motivations

eudaimonic motivations

parasocial interaction

mood management theory

reception studies

polysemic

preferred, or dominant, reading

negotiated meaning

oppositional decoding

semiotic disobedience

interpretive communities

Theories of Media Cognition and Information Processing

Immigration was among the more contentious issues facing the electorate during the 2012 presidential campaign. As a result, when that contest was in its primary stages *Newsweek* thought it would be interesting to conduct a national survey based on the very citizenship test that those hoping to become citizens are required to take. How did already-Americans fare? Twenty-nine percent could not name the sitting vice president; 73 percent could not explain why we fought the Cold War; and 44 percent did not know what the Bill of Rights was. Another poll near that time showed that 58 percent of the country could not identify the Taliban, although our war in Afghanistan against that group of religious terrorists was in its 10th year. "A 2010 World Public Opinion survey found that Americans want to tackle deficits by cutting foreign aid from what they believe is the current level (27 percent of the budget) to a more prudent 13 percent. The real number is under 1 percent," added political writer Andrew Romano, "A January 25 CNN poll, meanwhile, discovered that even though 71 percent of voters want smaller government, vast majorities oppose cuts to Medicare (81 percent), Social Security (78 percent), and Medicaid (70 percent). Instead, they prefer to slash waste—a category that, in their fantasy world, seems to include 50 percent of spending, according to a 2009 Gallup poll" (2011). Five months before election day, large numbers of Americans—63 percent of Republicans, 27 percent of independents, and 15 percent of Democrats—continued to believe that Iraq had weapons of mass destruction at the time of the 2003 invasion, despite President George Bush's public acknowledgment in 2006 that the weapons of mass destruction (WMD) did not exist, and fewer than half the country (47.2 percent) "always" believed President Obama was born in the United States despite the release of his birth certificate and contemporaneous Hawaiian newspaper announcements of his birth (Froomkin, 2012b).

These data were not anomalies, as "a substantial amount of scholarship ... has sought to determine whether citizens can participate meaningfully in politics. Recent work has shown that most citizens appear to lack factual knowledge about political matters … and that this deficit affects the issue opinions that they express" (Nyhan and Reifler, 2010, p. 303).

But how can this be? Are Americans simply not very bright? Given the country's impressive social, cultural, and technological achievements this seems unlikely. Is it that there is insufficient access to information and analysis? Improbable in the age of constant media connection and the Internet. Political writer Lee Harris suggested another possibility in his essay, "Are Americans Too Dumb for Democracy?" "The difficulty we human beings face in making the right decision is not owing to our lack of smarts" he wrote. "The challenge we face is one we all face together—it stems from the maddening complexity and relentless perversity of the world we live in. It is cognitive hubris to think that any degree of intelligence or expertise can do away with this most stubborn of all stubborn facts" (2012).

LEARNING OBJECTIVES

After studying this chapter you should be able to

- Explain the major ideas encompassed by information-processing theory, including the concept of limited cognitive resources.
- Apply information-processing theory to making sense of television news.
- Better appreciate how schema theory has enriched the study of mass communication, especially in the realm of processing political communication.
- Recognize the influence of the hostile media effect on processing information.
- Find value in the elaboration likelihood model's explanation of how people come to process information systematically and heuristically.
- Judge the value of newer theories of information processing, such as narrative persuasion theory and the extended elaboration likelihood model, especially to health-oriented media messages.
- Evaluate those information-processing theories that suggest people may not be completely rational when making meaning from media messages, ideas such as affective intelligence, motivated reasoning, and the backfire effect.
- Assess the value to mass communication theory of incorporating various neuroscience perspectives into our understanding of information processing.

OVERVIEW

These questions—What do Americans know and not know? How do they know it? Where do they get their information? How well do they remember information? How do they use that information? How well do they differentiate good ideas from bad?—have been at the heart of mass communication theory and research from the field's earliest days. You read in earlier chapters that the rise of propaganda and powerful new forms of mass media led many to argue that democracy was obsolete. Average people couldn't be trusted to govern themselves. Lippmann

(1922) claimed that the social world had become too complex for people to understand. These concerns motivated the first systematic investigation of the power of media messages to move people to action. Lazarsfeld's voting research and Hovland's research on attitude change just before and after World War II allayed some of the most serious concerns about the power of propaganda. They found that propaganda wasn't as powerful as many feared. Most people were protected from the influence of propaganda by their social relationships and preexisiting attitudes. But researchers didn't find that people had the ability to independently assess and reject problematic messages. Even better educated people were vulnerable to certain types of propaganda messages. The postpositivist tradition of media effects research begun by Lazarsfeld and Hovland continues to today, with important work on information processing and cognition that raises new questions as it attempts to answer decades-old questions. Fears of propaganda have faded but there is a host of new concerns. America seems to be dividing into two nations served by different sets of media outlets. Increasingly people seek out media that confirm and reinforce what they already believe and media outlets are evolving to serve this desire. Widespread ignorance persists in many important areas of science, health, safety and technology. Entertainment media continue to dominate our attention while information media are marginalized. Fanciful myths about the nature of the social world abound while scientifically based accounts are greeted with widespread skepticism. To what extent are media responsible for these problems? Is there something interfering with how people learn about and make sense of the social world? Could media do a better job of informing and educating the public concerning the social world?

In this chapter we'll look at a wide variety of microscopic-level theories of how individuals gather, process, and evaluate the flow of information, much of it from the media, that they continuously encounter. Most of the early research in this area came from cognitive psychologists, scientists interested in how an individual, employing mental structures and processes, "observes and makes sense out of a complex environment" (Axelrod 1973, p. 1249). These cognitive psychologists rejected behaviorist notions that people simply react to stimuli in their environments and later use their cognitions to justify those responses (Chapter 2). Clearly, much more was going on as people lived their lives. As Robert Axelrod explained, "The world is complex, and yet people are able to make some sense out of it. A national or international political arena, for example, is so huge and so complex that to make any sense out of it seems to be a superhuman task. And yet national leaders and even the man [sic] in the street do make more or less intelligent interpretations about political events and relationships. How do they do this?" (1973, p. 1248). Among the tools researchers have to answer that question is **information-processing theory**, a means of understanding how people deal with sensory information. But despite what we may like to believe, much of our information processing is out of our conscious control ... and that may indeed be a good thing ... sometimes.

information-processing theory
Theory for understanding how people deal with sensory information

Mass communication theory, as you've read, had its roots in the study of propaganda and persuasion, so it came to embrace the idea that people processed information—well or poorly, correctly or incorrectly—based on identifiable and measurable variables. But as the discipline matured, and as newer and newer media appeared, and as media content became increasingly visual and sophisticated, those early understandings had to be enriched. Mass communication scholars' appreciation of people's cognitive abilities and respect for their use of personal experience to make meaning began to grow. New theories came to the field from political science and psychology, themselves soon enriched and improved by the introduction of mass communication questions and variables. If people were indeed cognitive misers (naturally avoiding strenuous mental processing of information when they could), maybe theory could be used to guide the construction of media content that could take advantage of that seeming limitation to do some societal good. And at the same time, perhaps theory could help explain why some people, in the eyes of others, "just don't get it."

INFORMATION-PROCESSING THEORY

Cognitive psychologists have developed a perspective on the way individuals routinely cope with sensory information: information-processing theory. It is actually a large set of diverse and disparate ideas about cognitive processes and provides yet another avenue for studying media audience activity (Chapter 7). Researchers work to understand how people take in, process, store, and then use various forms of information provided by media.

Drawing on the same metaphors as systems theory (Chapter 4), information-processing theory often uses mechanistic analogies to describe and interpret how each of us takes in and makes sense of the flood of information our senses encounter every moment of each day. It assumes that individuals operate like complex bio-computers, with certain built-in information-handling capacities and strategies. Each day we are exposed to vast quantities of sensory information, but we filter this information so only a small portion of it ever reaches our conscious mind. We single out for attention and processing only a tiny fraction of this information, and we eventually store only a tiny amount of that in long-term memory. We are not so much information *handlers* as information *avoiders*—we have developed sophisticated mechanisms for screening out irrelevant or useless information. When our capacity to cope with sensory information is overwhelmed we make mistakes by failing to take in and process critical information.

Cognitive psychologists make an important distinction between cognitive processes and consciousness. Much of what takes place in our brain never reaches our consciousness. Although this activity often affects our conscious thoughts, it does so only very indirectly through its influence on other cognitive processes. Our consciousness acts as a supreme overseer of this cognitive activity but has very limited and typically quite indirect control over it. This perspective on cognition is contrary to what most of us would like to assume about our ability to control what goes on in our minds. It contradicts our personal experience, which is largely based on what conscious reflection is able to reveal to us. When we watch a televised news report, we have the sense that we are getting every bit of useful information from it that is there. But recent research finds that only a fraction of the original information reaches us, even when we pay close attention. We get distracted by compelling pictures and waste precious cognitive resources processing them while we miss important auditory information.

How can we have so little control over these important processes supplying us with such critical information? If we are making mistakes and missing important information, maybe all we need to do is concentrate harder; but are you always successful when you've tried to force yourself to remember something for an exam? Did it work? If cognitive theorists are right, we need to be much more distrustful of the experiences our consciousness weaves together for us based on the very limited and attenuated flow of information that eventually reaches it. Research is beginning to reveal just how easily and often consciousness fails to provide accurate or even useful representations of the social world.

Some cognitive psychologists argue that many of the processing mechanisms we use to screen in and screen out information must have developed when early human beings were struggling to adapt to and survive in a hostile physical environment (Wood and McBride, 1997). In that environment, it was critical that potential predators and prey be quickly identified so swift action could be taken. There was no time for conscious processing of such information and no need for conscious reflection before action. If you sensed a predator nearby, you ran away. If you sensed nearby prey, you attacked. Those who didn't either died at the hands of predators or died of starvation. Humans who developed the requisite cognitive skills survived.

These cognitive processing mechanisms became critical to adapting to and surviving in close social relationships with other human beings. For example, much of the cognitive processing capacity of the human brain is effectively devoted to taking in and unconsciously interpreting subtle body and facial movements enabling us to sense what others are feeling and anticipate how they are likely to act. We don't think about the information these cognitive processes produce. We experience this information as an intuition—we have a sense that others feel certain ways or will act certain ways. These processing mechanisms might have been more important to survival than processing information about prey and predators precisely because human beings are relatively weak and defenseless compared with many predators. Humans quickly die when food supplies fluctuate or temperatures vary. Human children require nurturing for much longer periods than do the young of other mammals. As a result, it is essential that humans form communities in which they can band together to survive. But living in communities requires cognitive skills far more sophisticated than those needed to sense predators and prey.

How relevant are these ideas for understanding how we deal with sensory information? Think about it for a moment. As you sit reading this book, consider your surroundings. Unless you are seated in a white, soundproof room with no other people present, there are many sensory stimuli around you. If you have been sitting for some time, your muscles might be getting stiff and your back might have a slight ache. Those around you might be laughing. A radio might be playing. All this sensory information is potentially available, but if you are good at focusing your attention on reading, you are routinely screening out most of these external and internal stimuli in favor of the printed words on this page.

Now consider what you do when you watch a television program. Unless you have a VCR or a DVR player and can review scenes in slow motion, you can't pay attention to all the images and sounds. If you do watch them in slow motion, the experience is totally different from viewing them at normal speed. Viewing television is actually a rather complex task using very different information-processing skills than reading a textbook. You are exposed to rapidly changing images and sounds. You must sort these out and pay attention to those that will be most useful to you in achieving whatever purpose you have for your viewing. But if this task is so complex, why does television seem to be such an easy medium to use? Because the task of routinely making sense of television appears to be so similar to the task of routinely making sense of everyday experience. And making sense of that experience is easy, isn't it?

Information-processing theory offers fresh insight into our routine handling of information. It challenges some basic assumptions about the way we take in and use sensory data. For example, we assume that we would be better off if we could take in more information and remember it better. But more isn't always better. Consider what happens when you fill the hard drive of your computer with more and more content. It becomes increasingly difficult to quickly find things. Some important documents may be lost among thousands of useless or trivial items.

It's not surprising, then, that some people experience severe problems because they have trouble routinely screening out irrelevant environmental stimuli. They are overly sensitive to meaningless cues such as background noise or light shifts. Others remember too much information. You might envy someone with a photographic memory—especially when it comes to taking an exam. But total recall of this type can pose problems as well. Recall of old information can intrude on the ability to experience and make sense of new information. A few cues from the present can trigger vivid recall of many different past experiences. If you've watched reruns of the same television show several times—*Family Guy* or *The Simpsons*, for example—you probably have found that as you watch one episode it triggers recall of bits and pieces of previous episodes. If you were asked to reconstruct a particular episode of either program, you would likely weave together pieces from several different shows. Everyday life is like that—if we remember too much, the past will constantly intrude into the present. Forgetting has advantages.

Another useful insight from information-processing theory is its recognition of the limitations of conscious awareness. Our culture places high value on conscious thought processes, and we tend to be skeptical or suspicious of the utility of mental processes only indirectly or not at all subject to conscious control. We associate consciousness with rationality—the ability to make wise decisions based on careful evaluation of all available relevant information. We associate unconscious mental processes with things like uncontrolled emotions, wild intuition, or even mental illness. We sometimes devalue the achievements of athletes because their greatest acts are typically performed without conscious thought—she's in the zone; he's a natural. No wonder we are reluctant to acknowledge our great dependency on unconscious mental processes.

The overall task of coping with information is much too complex for conscious control to be either efficient or effective. We have to depend on routinized processing of information and must normally limit conscious efforts to instances when intervention is crucial. For example, when there are signs of a breakdown of some kind, when routine processing fails to serve our needs properly, then conscious effort might be required.

One advantage of the information-processing perspective is that it provides an objective perspective on learning. Most of us view learning subjectively. We blame ourselves if we fail to learn something we think we should have learned or that appears to be easy to learn. We assume that with a little more conscious effort, we could have avoided failure. How often have you chided yourself by saying, "If only I'd paid closer attention"; "I should have given it more thought"; "I made simple mistakes that I could have avoided if only I'd been more careful"? But would a little more attention really have helped all that much? Information-processing theory recognizes that we have **limited cognitive resources**. If more resources are directed toward one task, another task will be performed badly. As a result, more attention to one aspect of information processing often leads to breakdown in some other aspect of processing. We typically deal with information in environments where it is coming at us from several different media at the same time. We're watching television, surfing the net, monitoring instant messaging, and talking on a cellphone—all at the same time. The current college generation is rightly labeled the "M" generation—both for its ubiquitous use of *media* and for its constant *multitasking*. No wonder our cognitive resources are pushed to the limit. No wonder we make mistakes and fail to learn what we intend.

limited cognitive resources
In information-processing theory, idea that as more resources are directed toward one task, another will suffer

For example, when we do something as simple as viewing television news, we are taking in visual and verbal information. We tend to place priority on processing visual information; as a result, complex, powerful visual images compel us to devote more cognitive resources to making sense of them. But if we do that, we miss the verbal information. Of course, sometimes additional conscious effort can do wonders. We can choose to ignore the compelling pictures and pay close attention to the verbal information. But what we might need is some overall revamping of our routine information-handling skills and strategies—a transformation of our information-processing system. This can take considerable time and effort—not just trying harder in one specific instance. Thus information-processing theory provides a means of developing a more objective assessment of the mistakes we make when processing information. These mistakes are routine outcomes from a particular cognitive process or set of processes—not personal errors caused by personal failings.

Information-processing theory doesn't blame audience members for making mistakes when they use media content. Instead it attempts to predict these mistakes based on challenges posed by the content and normal limitations in people's information-processing capacity. In some cases it links routine or common errors to breakdowns in information processing and suggests ways to avoid them. For example, research has repeatedly demonstrated that poorly structured news stories will routinely be misinterpreted even if journalists who write them are well intentioned and news consumers try hard to understand them (Gunter, 1987). Rather than retraining people to cope with badly structured stories, it may be more efficient to change the structure of the stories so more people can use them without making mistakes.

PROCESSING TELEVISION NEWS

Information-processing theory has been used extensively in mass communication research to guide and interpret research on how people decode and learn from television news broadcasts. Numerous studies have been conducted, and useful reviews

INSTANT ACCESS

Information-Processing Theory

Strengths

1. Provides specificity for what is generally considered routine, unimportant behavior
2. Provides objective perspective on learning; mistakes are routine and natural
3. Permits exploration of a wide variety of media content
4. Produces consistent results across a wide range of communication situations and settings

Weaknesses

1. Is too oriented toward the micro-level
2. Overemphasizes routine media consumption
3. Focuses too much on cognition, ignoring such factors as emotion

of this literature are now available (Davis, 1990; Davis and Robinson, 1989; Graber, 1988; Gunter, 1987; Robinson and Davis, 1990; Robinson, Levy, and Davis, 1986). Different types of research, including mass audience surveys and small-scale laboratory experiments, have produced remarkably similar findings. A rather clear picture of what people do with television news is emerging.

Though most of us view television as an easy medium to understand and one that can make us eyewitnesses to important events, it is actually a difficult medium to use. Information is frequently presented in ways that inhibit rather than facilitate learning. Part of the problem rests with audience members. Most of us view television primarily as an entertainment medium. We have developed many information-processing skills and strategies for watching television that serve us well in making sense of entertainment content but that interfere with effective interpretation and recall of news. We approach televised news passively and typically are engaging in several different activities while viewing. Our attention is only rarely focused on the screen. We depend on visual and auditory cues to draw our attention to particular stories. In fact, content producers are aware of the power of our **orienting response**, humans' instinctive reaction to sudden or novel stimulus. So they use the medium's technical conventions—edits, quick cuts, zooms, pans, sudden noises, and movements—to trigger involuntary responses, that is, to attract our attention (Reeves and Thorson, 1986).

orienting response
Humans' instinctive reaction to sudden or novel stimulus

We rarely engage in deep, reflective processing of news content that might allow us to assume more conscious control over this meaning making (Kubey and Csikszentmihalyi, 2002). So most news story content is never adequately processed and is quickly forgotten. Even when we do make a more conscious effort to learn from news, we often lack the information necessary to make in-depth interpretations of content or to store these interpretations in long-term memory.

But although we have many failings as an audience, news broadcasters also bear part of the blame. The average newscast is often so difficult to make sense of that it might fairly be called "biased against understanding." The typical broadcast contains too many stories, each of which tries to condense too much information into too little time. Stories are individually packaged segments typically composed of complex combinations of visual and verbal content (to better activate our orienting response). All too often, the visual information is so powerful that it overwhelms the verbal. Viewers are left with striking mental images but little contextual information. Often pictures are used that are irrelevant to stories—they distract and don't inform. Findings presented by Dennis Davis and John Robinson (1989) are typical of this body of research. They interviewed more than 400 viewers to assess what they learned or failed to learn from three major network news broadcasts. They identified numerous story attributes that enhanced or inhibited learning. Stories with complex structure and terminology or powerful but irrelevant visual images were poorly understood. Human-interest stories with simple but dramatic storylines were well understood. Viewers frequently confused elements of stories and wove together information drawn from similar reports. But how much blame is fairly aimed at news professionals? "The task that democratic theory prescribes for American general-purpose mass media is extremely difficult at best, and, in most instances, impossible," writes public opinion researcher Doris Graber, "To gain the attention of mass audiences, the media must tell political stories simply and interestingly. But most political stories are neither simple nor appealing to general audiences. Most cannot be condensed to fit the brief attention span of the public. The attempt to be both simple and interesting leads to oversimplification and an emphasis on sensational human interest features of events" (1984, pp. 214–215).

None of this, however, is to say that viewers cannot learn from television news. There is indeed evidence that the more conscious attention people give to the news the more accurate information they learn. As Steve Chaffee and Joan Schleuder demonstrated, "Attention to news media appears to be a consistent individual difference that accounts for substantial variation in learning beyond the effects of simple exposure. There is some evidence of fluctuation in attention from one medium to another, one kind of news to another, and one time to another, but these dimensions of variation are overshadowed by the general trait that we might call attentiveness to news media" (1986, p. 102). Researcher Mira Sotirovic explains, "The way people process information also has been found to have important implications for the effects of news media…. Information-processing strategies help individuals to cope with the vast amount of incoming news items and allow them to achieve meaning and understanding appropriate to their needs…. Basically, the strategies can be more effortful, elaborate, and analytic, or less demanding, simple, and heuristic. More elaborated active processing is related to greater recall of news and greater exclusion of irrelevant information" (2003, p. 125).

Information-processing theory has great potential to permit exploration of a wide variety of media content beyond news. Researchers apply it to such diverse topics as advertising (Lang, 1990), televised political content, and children's programming (Young, 1990). This research is rapidly revealing how we tailor our innate cognitive skills to make sense of and use media content. Our ability to do this is most strikingly demonstrated by children as they learn to watch television. Within a few years, children move from being dazzled by shifting colors and sound on the screen to making complex differentiations (good/bad, strong/weak, male/female) about program characters and making accurate predictions about the way story lines will unfold. For example, children come to recognize that Disney stories will have happy endings despite the efforts of evil characters. But underlying these seemingly simple and routine acts of meaning making are complex cognitive processes that have been adapted to the task of watching television.

SCHEMA THEORY

schema theory
Information-processing theory arguing that memories are new constructions constructed from bits and pieces of connected experiences and applied to meaning making as situations demand

schemas
Cognitive structures built up as people interact with the environment in order to organize their experience

Doris Graber, in *Processing the News*, her landmark effort to understand how people "tame the information tide," brought **schema theory** to the discipline (1984). Schema theory can be traced back to 1932 and cognitive psychologist Sir Frederic Bartlett's initially ill-received *Remembering*. His contemporaries rejected his assertion that remembering is not reproductive, but reconstructive; that is, people do not hold memories in their minds as details of things past, to be called forth when required. Instead, memories are new constructions cobbled together from bits and pieces of connected experiences and applied as situations demand. What make this construction possible are **schemas**, cognitive structures people build up that are abstracted from prior experience and used for processing new information and organizing experiences. Bartlett himself defined a schema as "an active organization of past reactions, or of past experiences" (p. 201). These complex, unconscious knowledge structures "are active, without any awareness at all" (p. 200). Moreover, schemas are "generic"; that is, after a person has encountered a phenomenon first once, then many times, he or she builds—and continues to build—an abstract, general cognitive representation (a schema) and all new incoming information related to that phenomenon is processed in terms of that schema. Schemas are also "generative"; that is, they can handle an indefinite number of new instances because individuals are constantly building and revising their schemas in response to new information (Brewer and Nakamura, 1984).

Consider your schema for something simple, for example, *boat*. Even if you have never been on a boat, your boat schema no doubt contains knowledge about boats in general (float, move, hulls, decks), and quite likely information about specific types of boats, such as motor boats (sleek, fast, powerful) and sailboats (sails, wind, ropes, masts, lean over). You might also think of boats in the larger context of water-bound transportation devices; for example, tankers, navy ships, container ships, and barges are large, functional boats propelled by motors; yachts are large pleasure boats; and submarines are a special class of boat that sometimes travels under water. You may have personal experience with boats, so those experiences are part of your boat schema—musty smell, sea sickness, vacationing at the ocean or lake, water skiing, swimming with friends, romance. Each new boat experience builds more information into your boat schema. So, when you hear a 45-second radio news report about a sailboat race through Capitol City's industrial harbor you can quite easily and efficiently make sense of the story and more than likely produce a fair account for a friend who later asks you about it.

But you also have schemas for much more complex phenomena. What is your Republican schema? Your Democrat schema? Your war-on-terror schema? Your democracy schema? How broad and deep are they? How were they built, that is, what experiences—real-world and mass mediated—contributed to their construction and the connections they call up when something in your experience activates them?

scripts

Form of schema, a standardized generalized episode

Some schemas are for events, rather than things or concepts. When these schemas are constructed episodically—if this ... then that ... then this ... then that—they are called **scripts**, "standardized generalized episode[s]" (Schank and Abelson, 1977, p. 19). People "understand what they see and hear" by matching those inputs to scripts, "pre-stored groupings of actions they have already experienced" (p. 67).

Now recall Graber's "defense" of American news media and their impossible task of trying to report on complex and unappealing events for an audience with a short attention span. In this situation, she argues, schemas serve four important functions for news consumers who, by nature, are cognitive misers:

1. They determine what information will be noticed, processed, and stored so that it becomes available for later retrieval from memory.
2. They help people organize and evaluate new information, fitting it into their already-established perceptions. People do not have to construct new concepts when familiar information is presented in the news.
3. They make it possible for people to go beyond the immediate information presented in a news report, helping them fill in missing information.
4. They help people solve problems because they contain information about likely scenarios and ways to cope with them; that is, they serve as scripts. This makes them important tools in helping people decide how to act (p. 24).

Her study of a panel of 21 registered voters/news consumers to see how people make sense of the news confirmed Professor Graber's assessment of the value of schema. "People tame the information tide quite well," she wrote, "They have workable, if intellectually vulnerable, ways of paring down the flood of news to manageable proportions" (1984, p. 201). "People from all walks of life, endowed with varying capabilities, can manage to extract substantial amounts of political knowledge from this flood of information," she continued, "All panelists had mastered the art of paying selective attention to news and engaging in the various forms of relatedness searches. All had acquired schemas into which they were able to fit incoming political information. All were able to work with an adequate array of schema dimensions, and all frequently used multiple themes in their various schemas" (p. 204).

In fact, Graber discovered, voters bring several well-formed schemas to their interpretation of political news (1988, p. 193):

- *Simple Situation Sequences*—people do not process news stories to remember precise details; instead, they condense the account to their bare essentials to understand what they mean in specific contexts.
- *Cause-and-Effect Sequences*—people link reported situations to their likely causes.
- *Person Judgments*—people easily process news about individuals in terms of their demographic groups because they have built schemas about human nature, goals, and behaviors.
- *Institution Judgments*—just as people have schemas for the behavior of individuals, they have schemas for the way institutions are supposed to operate.
- *Cultural Norms and American Interests*—people have a general "the American way" schema that includes the construction that democracy is the best form of government for the United States and for the world as a whole.

- *Human Interest and Empathy*—people interpret reports in terms of self-perception: "Is the situation depicted in the news story similar to what I have experienced directly or vicariously or similar to what I would do under the circumstances?" (p. 212).

You can read more about what happens when news frames bump up against people's schemas in the box, "Battle of the Competing Schemas."

THINKING ABOUT THEORY │ Battle of the Competing Schemas

One of the drawbacks of schema theory is that people from different disciplines, and sometimes from the same fields, often use the term a bit casually. For example, in his very fine work on news frames and consumers' schemas, Fuyuan Shen writes, "It is theorized here that, in response to news discourses, individuals will engage in active thinking and bring *their own mental frames or schemas* to the interpretative process (emphasis added; 2004, p. 401). Sometimes, as in this example, *frames* and *schemas* are used interchangeably; sometimes they represent different phenomena. Sometimes *scripts* and *schemas* are interchangeable; sometimes a script is a specific type of schema. Sometimes scholars try to refine the term *schema*, for example, employing constructs such as *propositions* or *frame keepers* (Brewer and Nakamura, 1984, p. 31). We'll revisit the many different definitions of frames and framing in Chapter 10.

In his classic work on media coverage of presidential elections, *Out of Order*, Thomas Patterson employs *schema* as this text does: "a cognitive structure that a person uses when processing new information and retrieving old information. It is a mental framework the individual constructs from past experiences that helps make sense of a new situation" (1993, p. 56). He also talks about *frames*, using that term just as Shen did, that is, to refer to how news reports are constructed around a specific theme.

Patterson argues that reporters and voters have differing schemas for elections, and this clash of mental frameworks produces such a disconnect between journalism and voters that "the United States cannot have a sensible campaign as long as it is built around the news media" (p. 25).

Regarding elections, voters have a "governing schema" that values "policy problems, leadership traits, policy debates, and the like." Patterson quotes another political scientist, Samuel Popkin, to say that this schema produces "voters [who] actually do reason about parties, candidates, and issues. They have premises, and they use those premises to make inferences from their observations of the world around them" (p. 59). But political reporters, according to Patterson, have a "game schema." "When journalists encounter new information during an election, they tend to interpret it within a schematic framework according to which candidates compete for advantage…. [C]andidates are strategic actors whose every move is significant…. [P]olitics is essentially a game played by individual politicians for personal advancement, gain, or power" (pp. 57–58).

What meanings of the electoral process do reporters construct using the game schema? When candidates speak about issues, the press hears ulterior motives. When candidates make promises, reporters hear pie-in-the-sky proposals that they can't possibly keep. For campaign reporters, elections are about the horse race: Who's ahead; how far; what do the polls say? "In the game schema, the focus is on a few individuals—the candidates—rather than on the larger interests they represent and the broader political forces that shape their campaign," writes Patterson, "To the press, strategy and maneuvers are not merely a component of the campaign; they are a decisive element" (p. 63).

What kind of reporting results from these constructions; in other words, how are news stories about elections framed? When Patterson wrote *Out of Order* in 1993, the horse-race frame (a news account's organizing structure) made up 35 percent of network television news coverage, and reporting on polls accounted for another 33 percent. Policy issues made up less than one-third of all reporting. Things did not improve much in the next 15 years.

(Continued)

THINKING ABOUT THEORY | **Battle of the Competing Schemas**   (Continued)

In the 2008 election, 71 percent of all political stories in all the major media were horse-race reports; only 13 percent dealt with policy. These data led William Hudson to write, "This journalistic 'schema' or 'frame' of an election as a strategic game between opposing campaign teams not only diminishes discussion of issues but also distorts such discussion at the rare times when issues are raised. Rather than portraying the candidates' issue statements as serious proposals for addressing the country's problems, the strategic game frame treats such statements merely as positions taken to attract the support of particular constituencies." The press's schema-driven framing of campaign news stories damages democracy because, just as Patterson argued, "[V]oters are intensely interested in learning about candidates' issue positions as a way of evaluating their capacity to address real problems, even though the journalists' strategic frame lets little of that information get through to them" (2013, p. 196).

Do you agree with researchers Patterson and Hudson? Do you think reporters and voters actually have these dramatically different schemas for elections? Is it possible that these scholars are overly generous in their view of American voters and maybe a little too negative about the press? Here are three pieces of data to help you with your answers. In the

2012 presidential election between Barack Obama and Mitt Romney, 60.6 percent of overall news coverage was dedicated to the candidates' personality and strategy and to the horse race. Coverage of policy accounted for 39.4 percent of reporting, and other than the economy (11.6 percent), no other issue made up more than 5 percent of the news. For example, education policy was the focus of only 0.5 percent and environmental policy only 0.2 percent of all reporting ("Election 2012 Coverage In One Word: Hollow," 2012). Also during that election, Americans' distrust of the press reached record highs, with 60 percent of adults saying they had little or no trust at all in the media to report the news fully, fairly, and accurately. The gap of 20 percentage points between negative and positive views of the press was the largest since the Gallup Organization first began asking the question in the 1990s (Morales, 2012). Finally, despite "a cliff-hanger presidential election, major issues at stake, an estimated $6 billion spent in the 2012 campaigns, and an eight million-person increase in the eligible voters," voter turnout fell from 62.3 percent of eligible citizens in 2008 to 57.5 percent. Ninety-three million eligible voters in the "Greatest Democracy on Earth" stayed home on Election Day, with every state in the country except Louisiana and Iowa showing a decline ("2012 Voter Turnout," 2012).

---

schema-inconsistent advertising

Advertising that intentionally violates people's expectations of that form of content

Schema theory has also been applied to advertising content, typically in assessing the impact of **schema-inconsistent advertising**, that is, advertising that intentionally violates people's expectations of that form of content. For example, arguing that advertisers' immediate goal is to attract consumers' attention and have them engage their commercial messages, Hazel Warlaumont reasoned that, "One aspect of schema theory is that if a text conforms to a person's expectations, or schema, then perception will be smooth and logical; if not, it will seem incongruous, or 'schema-inconsistent.' If the stimuli are not what was expected, it may arouse a mild 'perturbation' or a feeling of surprise that may motivate the viewer to attempt to make sense out of the discrepancy through involvement with the stimuli" (1997, p. 41). Her research demonstrated that this was indeed the case.

HOSTILE MEDIA EFFECT

What happens to information processing when individuals believe the media "favor or are hostile toward specific topics or groups? … [These] attitudes toward media have been shown to be important because they affect a host of social and political

INSTANT ACCESS

Schema Theory

Strengths

1. Focuses attention on individual cognitive processing in the mass communication process
2. Respects the information-processing ability of media consumers
3. Provides specificity in describing the role of experience in information processing
4. Provides exploration of a wide variety of media information
5. Provides consistent results across a wide range of communication situations and settings

Weaknesses

1. Too oriented toward micro-level
2. Suffers from label confusion (e.g., schema, frame, script)
3. Insufficiently accounts for neurological influences
4. More research is needed to understand the processes involved in schema formation and change

---

hostile media effect (HME)

Idea that partisans see media as less sympathetic to their side, more sympathetic to the opposing side, and generally hostile to their point of view

behaviors" (Tsfati and Cohen, 2013, p. 1). Research into the **hostile media effect (HME)** has consistently demonstrated that partisans—those who feel strongly about an issue—see media coverage of their topic of interest as less sympathetic to their side, more sympathetic to the opposing side, and generally hostile to their point of view. Specifically:

- Partisans, viewing the very same piece of media content, interpret it as biased against their position (Vallone, Ross, and Lepper, 1985).
- When asked to recall the contents of an account, partisans remember more negative references to their position than positive ones (Vallone et al., 1985).
- Partisans believe that neutral audiences will be persuaded against their point-of-view by hostile media coverage, although the evidence suggests that this is not necessarily the case (Perloff, 1989).

Albert Gunther and Cathleen Schmitt demonstrated that partisans' did indeed place their perceived hostility at the feet of the media. They presented people with the same neutral write-up on genetically modified foods drawn from actual newspaper stories. In one condition the account was presented as a newspaper article; in the other, as a student essay. They discovered that "partisans saw the information as disagreeably biased in a news story format. In student-essay format, however, the hostile media perception disappeared" (2004, p. 55). But why attribute hostility specifically to the media? Gunther and Liebhart demonstrated that it may be the media's *reach to a potentially larger audience* (a story on genetically modified food would or would not be published) that fueled partisans' perception of an account's hostility to their position. They wrote, "Partisans in both groups were virtually identical in their perceptions of content when the author was a student; the same uniform perception appeared when the context was a composition unlikely to reach any audience beyond the classroom. However, when either the author was a journalist or the context was a nationally circulated news article, partisan perceptions diverged conspicuously. Under those circumstances, participants on opposing sides saw identical information as significantly biased in opposite directions—a direction counter to their own point of view" (2006, p. 462).

But what happens when these partisans encounter media reports that are actually and clearly supportive of their positions? When it becomes impossible for these people to see the reporting as hostile, they tend to judge it as less supportive than do their opponents and even nonpartisans (Gunther and Chia, 2001). This is the *relative HME*, "to denote that while clearly favorable coverage is not seen as objectively hostile, the bias does not completely disappear but rather just becomes relative" (Tsfati and Cohen, 2013, p. 6).

Vallone, Ross, and Lepper explain that the HME is a product of people's routine cognitive processing—selective perception and systematic information processing:

> Partisans who have consistently processed facts and arguments in light of their preconceptions and prejudices (accepting information at face value, or subjecting it to harsh scrutiny, as a function of its congruence with these preconceptions and prejudices) are bound to believe that the preponderance of reliable, pertinent evidence favors their viewpoint. Accordingly, to the extent that the small sample of evidence and argument featured in a media presentation seems unrepresentative of this larger "population" of information, perceivers will charge bias in the presentation and will be likely to infer hostility and bias on the part of those responsible for it. (1985, p. 579)

This "investment" in their position leads to the *different standards mechanism* in which partisans' conviction that opposing arguments—by definition—are inferior renders their mere inclusion in a media account proof of biased or hostile reporting (Giner-Sorolla and Chaiken, 1994). You can read more about some people's response to what they consider hostile media in the box, "The Fox Effect."

ELABORATION LIKELIHOOD MODEL

elaboration likelihood model (ELM)

Model of information processing that seeks to explain the level of elaboration, or effort, brought to evaluating messages

Not all information-processing theory involves learning from news and advertising. Much of this work is devoted to how people interpret and react to persuasive messages. Psychologists Richard Petty and John Cacioppo (1986) developed a model of persuasion they called the **elaboration likelihood model** (ELM) which, while accepting the cognitive psychology view that people are "cognitive misers" (Taylor, 1981), acknowledges that when presented with a persuasive message, people will sometimes put a lot of effort into their cognition; sometimes, though, they rely on less demanding, simple analysis. As *social* psychologists, Petty and Cacioppo argued that there must be something more than the efficient use of cognitive capacity that motivates these different information-processing strategies. Their ELM (Figure 8.1), then, is based on the assumption that for social reasons, people are motivated to hold "correct" attitudes. Why? Because "incorrect attitudes are generally maladaptive and can have deleterious behavioral, affective, and cognitive consequences. If a person believes that certain objects, people, or issues are 'good' when they are in fact 'bad,' a number of incorrect behavioral decisions and subsequent disappointments may follow" (p. 127). But although "people want to hold

THINKING ABOUT THEORY | The Fox Effect

There is no doubt that the American public is politically polarized. For example, there is a "widening partisan chasm between Republicans and Democrats; the percentage of partisans who respond at the extremes ("strong approval" or "strong disapproval") has increased significantly over time. In fact, polarized assessments of presidential performance are higher today than at any other time in recent history, including the months preceding the resignation of President Nixon. In this sense at least, mass public opinion is polarized" (Iyengar and Hahn, 2009, p. 20). And it is equally true that political partisans, particularly conservatives, consider the traditional or mainstream media biased against their world view (Morris, 2007). In fact, Republicans are twice as likely as Democrats to classify the three broadcast network evening newscasts, the weekly news magazines, and both public radio and public television as liberally biased (Pew Research Center for the People and Press, 2004). In other words, conservatives tend to view the traditional national media as hostile.

Dissonance theory, specifically selective perception, and the HME would suggest that searching out attitude-friendly news sources is a logical response to this judgment, and that is precisely what has happened. Conservatives, for example, have flocked to cable television's Fox News, primarily because of its "distinctive reputation for delivering a proconservative perspective on issues and events" (Iyengar and Hahn, 2009, p. 22). Moreover, while there is only one news source that Americans in general trust more than they distrust—PBS—Democrats trust everything *except* Fox and Republicans trust *nothing but* Fox (Jensen, 2013).

What are the effects of this avoidance of potentially hostile media, if any? One outcome, demonstrated by Iyengar and Hahn, is *ideology-based polarization in news selection*. They presented political partisans with identical stories, all drawn from liberal-leaning MSNBC's daily newswire, and labeled them as originating from one of these four outlets: Fox News, NPR, CNN, and the BBC. Conservatives overwhelming chose to read the Fox News versions, while liberals showed no preference … other than to avoid Fox News (2009). A second outcome is that some media sources intentionally become more partisan in their reporting in order to attract these growing segments of the audience, as there is a financial incentive for news outlets to cater to them. As economists Sendhil Mullainathan and Andrei Schleifer explain, "[G]reater competition typically results in more aggressive catering to such prejudices as competitors strive to divide the market" (2005, p. 1042). And this contributes to a third outcome, the *echo chamber effect*. For example, Morris demonstrated that "Fox News watchers have perceptions of political reality that differ from the rest of the television news audience" (2007, p. 707). Fox viewers consistently report more erroneous knowledge than viewers of other news outlets on the Iraq War (e.g., the United States found weapons of mass destruction and Saddam Hussein collaborated with al Qaeda), climate change, and what is contained in the Affordable Care Act, otherwise known as Obamacare (e.g., free health care for illegal immigrants; Mooney, 2012). Annual surveys have consistently identified what has come to be known as "the Fox effect," the idea that watching Fox News renders people less knowledgeable about public affairs than if they had watched no news at all (Cassino, 2011, 2012).

But can these phenomena—ideology-based selection of what news to encounter (sometimes called **siloing**), increasingly, openly partisan news outlets, and an echo chamber that reinforces misperception of the facts—really be good for democracy? How can political leaders talk to the citizens they represent if those citizens have markedly different views of the facts, of reality? How can citizens talk to one another? Do you think that the growing partisan divide in America contributed to the rise of partisan media or do you think partisan media contributed to that divide? Do you think the Internet, with its wealth of possible sources, will move people to encounter a greater array of news sources, or will they move even more deeply into an increased number of supporting sources?

siloing Ideology-based selection of news sources

correct attitudes, the amount and nature of issue-relevant elaboration in which they are willing or able to engage to evaluate a message vary with individual and situational factors" (p. 128). In other words, not everyone is willing or able to process information in a way that will get them to that correct attitude, at least not all the time. Sometimes they take an easier, more automatic route to their opinion. You can hear echoes of dissonance theory and social categories from our earlier discussion of attitude change (Chapter 4). This is because this **peripheral route** of information processing (the right side of Figure 8.1) does not rely on elaboration (scrutiny) of the message as much as it does on cues unrelated to the information—for example, attractive sources, catchy jingles, or political party labels—exactly as dissonance theory and social categories suggest. These cues are often called **heuristics**, simple decision rules that substitute for more careful analysis of persuasive messages. This happens for a very good reason. As Richard Miller and his colleagues explained, it would be "irrational to scrutinize the plethora of counterattitudinal messages revived daily. To the extent that one possesses only a limited amount of information-processing time and capacity, such scrutiny would disengage the thought processes from the exigencies of daily life" (Miller, Brickman, and Bolen, 1975, p. 623).

But obviously there often are circumstances when people actively, willingly work through an argument or issue. When motivated by the relevance of the information, a need for cognition, or a sense of responsibility, people will use the **central route** of information processing (the left side of Figure 8.1) in which they bring as much scrutiny to the information as possible. They engage in "issue-relevant thinking" and the "elaboration likelihood" is high. ELM sees the likelihood of elaboration as running along a continuum from no thought about the information at hand to "complete elaboration of every argument, and complete integration of the elaborations into the person's attitude schemas" (Petty and Cacioppo, 1986, p. 8). Attitudes that are the product of this more stringent elaboration tend to be more deeply held, more enduring, and more predictive of subsequent behavior. Attitudes developed through the peripheral route tend to be less deeply held, less enduring, and less predictive of behavior.

The **heuristic-systematic model** of information processing, much like ELM, argues that people process information systematically and heuristically, but it sees these two processes as often working together. In other words, it is a dual-process model that recognizes concurrent modes of information processing that are qualitatively different (Chaiken and Trope, 1999). As a result, if the two processes produce a judgment that is congruent, that is, similar, the outcome is *additive*. It produces more stable attitude change that is a better predictor of later behavior. If they are incongruent or in opposition, systematic processing *attenuates*, or diminishes, the strength of the heuristics. When the information or arguments under consideration are ambiguous, heuristics tend to *bias* the information processing, even biasing people's systematic processing.

ELM has been tested in scores of research trials in scores of settings and has enjoyed widespread acceptance. So it is no surprise that mass communication researchers find it useful, especially because much media consumption, even of

peripheral route
In ELM, information processing that relies on cues unrelated to the issue at hand

heuristics
Simple decision rules that substitute for more careful analysis of persuasive messages

central route
In ELM, information processing characterized by heightened scrutiny of information related to the issue at hand

heuristic-systematic model
Dual-process model of information processing that argues for the parallel operation of systematic and heuristic processing

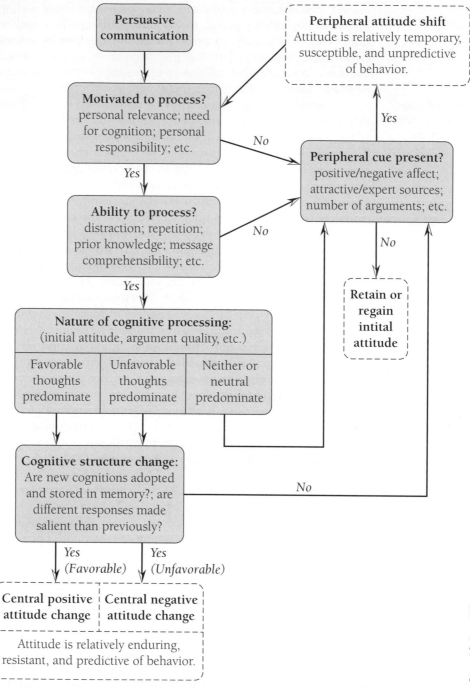

FIGURE 8.1   The Elaboration Likelihood Model

Petty and Cacioppo, 1986.

obvious persuasive messages such as commercials, occurs routinely (without much elaboration) and, as we've already seen, theorists have identified difficulties in information processing even when audience members do attempt to pay attention to (elaborate) messages. ELM's most frequent application to mass communication, then, is in the realm of information campaigns. Petty, Brinol, and Priester explain:

> If the goal of a mass media influence attempt is to produce long-lasting changes in attitudes with behavioral consequences, the central route to persuasion appears to be the preferred persuasion strategy. If the goal is immediate formation of a new attitude, even if it is relatively ephemeral (e.g., attitudes toward the charity sponsoring a telethon), the peripheral route could prove acceptable.... [Research] on mass media persuasion has come a long way from the early optimistic (and scary) notion that the mere presentation of information was sufficient to produce persuasion, and the subsequent pessimistic view that media influence attempts were typically ineffective. We now know that media influence, like other forms of influence, is a complex, though explicable process. (2009, pp. 153–154)

Lance Holbert, Kelly Garrett, and Laurel Gleason attempt to reduce that complexity by arguing that the new digital media make clear ELM's value to mass communication theory and research. Traditional media, they argue, are *push media*; they push information toward audience members, who either accept it or don't accept it. But new media are *pull media*; audience members pull from them the information they seek. "When you have the user in control, pulling down political media content, what do you have from the standpoint of ELM?" they write. "You have *motivation*—audience members who want to consume politically persuasive media messages. In addition, audience members in a pull media environment are more likely to consume their chosen political media messages at desirable times, in preferred places/contexts, and utilizing formats that best match their particular learning styles. Each of these characteristics of the media-use experience facilitates greater *ability* to process political information" (2010, p. 27).

INSTANT ACCESS

Elaboration Likelihood Model

Strengths

1. Focuses attention on individuals in the mass communication process
2. Respects intellect and ability of media consumers
3. Provides specificity in describing process of information processing
4. Provides exploration of a wide variety of media information
5. Provides consistent results across a wide range of communication situations and settings

Weaknesses

1. Too oriented toward micro-level
2. Dismisses possibility of simultaneous, parallel information processing
3. Sacrifices testable causal relationships in favor of multiple cues present in messages
4. Less useful in explaining persuasive effects of entertainment media

NARRATIVE PERSUASION THEORY AND THE EXTENDED ELABORATION LIKELIHOOD MODEL

narrative persuasion theory
Idea that absorption into a media narrative is a key mechanism in the story's power to influence real-world beliefs and behaviors

transportation
When a person's mental systems and capacities become focused on the events in a media narrative

Narrative persuasion theory argues that being "absorbed" into a media narrative "is a key mechanism whereby the story can influence one's real-world beliefs and behaviors…. Once individuals become immersed in the story, perceive it as realistic, and identify with story characters, there is a greater probability that narrative-based belief change will occur" (Kim et al., 2012, p. 473). Engagement with a media narrative consists of transportation, perceived similarity to characters in the story, and empathetic feeling toward those characters. **Transportation** is "a convergent process, where all the person's mental systems and capacities become focused on the events in the narrative" (Green and Brock, 2000, p. 701). Transportation theory's developers, Melanie Green and Timothy Brock, explain how transportation differs from ELM but can ultimately produce the same degree of attitude change:

> In conditions that promote high elaboration, central or systematic route processing ensues: A message recipient thoughtfully considers the central arguments of the message. The alternative route, under low elaboration conditions, is to use peripheral or heuristic processing, whereby attitude change results from either shallow processing of cues or reliance on simple rules. Rather than amount of thought per se, transportation theory posits processing that is qualitatively different from the traditional systematic or heuristic modes described in dual-process models of persuasion…. Elaboration implies critical attention to major points of an argument whereas transportation is an immersion into a text. Elaboration leads to attitude change via logical consideration and evaluation of arguments, whereas transportation may lead to persuasion through other mechanisms. First, transportation may reduce negative cognitive responding. Transported readers may be less likely to disbelieve or counterargue story claims, and thus their beliefs may be influenced. Next, transportation may make narrative experience seem more like real experience. Direct experience can be a powerful means of forming attitudes … and to the extent that narratives enable mimicry of experience, they may have greater impact than nonnarrative modes. Finally, transportation is likely to create strong feelings toward story characters; the experiences or beliefs of those characters may then have an enhanced influence on readers' beliefs. (2000, p. 702)

Perceived similarity and empathy, while clearly involved in transportation, are more closely connected to identification. You may remember identification from social cognitive theory (Chapter 6), and it carries much the same meaning in narrative persuasion theory: "An imaginative process through which an audience member assumes the identity, goals, and perspective of a character" (Cohen, 2001, p. 261). Identification, then, involves a cognitive response (perceived similarity) and an emotional response (empathy). Moreover, transportation and identification, because they rely on the individual content consumer's imagination, operate similarly for fiction and nonfiction narratives alike. Sheila Murphy and her colleagues delineated the cognitive processes thought to occur during transportation: "First, the audience member loses awareness of his or her surroundings and all cognitive facilities are focused entirely on the mediated world. Second, transported viewers feel heightened 'emotions and motivations.'… A transported viewer is so completely immersed in the media world that his or her responses to narrative events are strong, as though they were actually experiencing those events. Third, when viewers emerge from the transported state, they are often changed as a result of being so deeply engrossed in the narrative" (Murphy et al., 2011, pp. 410–411).

Hyun Suk Kim and his colleagues demonstrated the persuasive power of media narratives using *newspaper articles* (not highly dramatic, involving television shows!) about people successfully quitting smoking. The articles in the experimental conditions presented "exemplars," former smokers with whom the participants (all smokers) could identify. Their results "consistently indicated that smokers who read a news article in which an exemplar served as a delivery vehicle for health information about successful smoking cessation experienced a greater degree of engagement with the story and its characters, which in turn was associated with elevated quit intentions, compared to those exposed to an article with no exemplar" (Kim et al. 2012, pp. 484–485). Another group of researchers compared the effectiveness of a specifically prepared dramatic narrative video (*The Tamale Lesson*) and a nonfiction narrative featuring doctors, health experts, and charts (*It's Time*) in imparting information about cervical cancer and the need for Pap tests. Although both were successful in raising awareness of cervical cancer and creating positive attitudes toward testing, the fictional narrative was more effective, especially as viewers' level of transportation increased (Murphy et al., 2013). A different, much more dramatically constructed and presented media narrative, a six-episode-long storyline in the network television show *Desperate Housewives* that focused on non-Hodgkin's lymphoma (cancer), proved effective in linking involvement with a specific character and the narrative itself with increased knowledge and even behavioral intention in the form of further information seeking and talking to friends and family about cancer (Murphy et al., 2011).

The value of narrative persuasion theory can be seen in another piece of research on the persuasive power of media narratives about health, but one that makes no reference to narrative persuasion theory. Susan Morgan and her colleagues studied the effect of entertainment television narratives on intention to become an organ donor. Employing actual episodes of prime-time network programs *CSI: NY*, *Numb3rs*, *House*, and *Grey's Anatomy*, each of which had organ donation as a plot line, they argued that "the influence of the media on modeling behaviors is likely to be dependent on how emotionally involving and absorbing people find a particular episode" (Morgan, Movius, and Cody, 2009, p. 137). As you might recognize from these words, these researchers pinned the power of television narratives to social cognitive theory (modeling), but their logic suggests that they just as easily might have made a narrative entertainment theory argument, especially as they demonstrated that emotional involvement in these programs (transportation and identification) significantly affected intention to talk to someone about organ donation, urging others to become organ donors, and deciding to become an organ donor.

extended elaboration likelihood model (E-ELM)

Absorption in a narrative and response to its characters in a narrative enhance persuasive effects and suppress counterarguing if the story's implicit persuasive content is counterattitudinal

Michael Slater and Donna Rouner made that very argument in their development of the **extended elaboration likelihood model (E-ELM)**. They wrote, "The impact of entertainment-education messages on beliefs, attitudes, and behavior is typically explained in terms of social cognitive theory principles. However, important additional insights regarding reasons why entertainment-education messages have effects can be derived from the processing of persuasive content in narrative messages. Elaboration likelihood approaches suggest that absorption in a narrative, and response to characters in a narrative, should enhance persuasive effects and suppress counterarguing if the implicit persuasive content is counterattitudinal"

INSTANT ACCESS

Narrative Persuasion Theory

Strengths

1. Focuses attention on individuals in the mass communication process
2. Can enrich the elaboration likelihood model
3. Respects people's cognitive processing of entertainment content
4. Provides exploration of a wide variety of media information
5. Provides a model for the construction of prosocial content
6. Accounts for the operation of affect and cognition

Weaknesses

1. Too oriented toward micro-level
2. Has not demonstrated that effects of entertainment content are enduring and significant
3. More needs to be known about the factors that enhance or prevent narrative persuasion effects

entertainment-education (EE)
Occurs when prosocial messages are imbedded in popular media content

(2002, p. 173). Traditional ELM, they argue, is "robustly" suited to obvious persuasive efforts, but "of limited use in understanding entertainment-education" (p. 174). **Entertainment-education (EE)** occurs when prosocial messages are imbedded in popular media content, either with the specific intent of influencing attitudes or behavior or simply as a dramatic device, but one that serves incidentally to promote a prosocial end.

Emily Moyer-Gusé went one step further, joining the extended elaboration likelihood model and social cognitive theory to create the **entertainment overcoming resistance model**. Note on Figure 8.2 where she identifies the contribution of each to her model. The basic premise of the entertainment overcoming resistance model is that there are "features of entertainment media that facilitate involvement with characters and/or narrative involvement [that] should lead to story-consistent attitudes and behaviors by overcoming various forms of resistance" (2008, p. 420). Involvement with entertainment-education narratives refers to viewers' interest in following the story as it plays out. In this sense it is the same as transportation and represents individuals as "primarily engaged in the storyline, rather than in one's immediate environment, and experiencing vicarious cognitive and emotional responses to the narrative as it unfolds" (p. 409).

entertainment overcoming resistance model
Entertainment media features can facilitate involvement with characters and/or narrative involvement leading to story-consistent attitudes and behaviors by overcoming various forms of resistance

Involvement with characters is a bit more complicated, as it involves identification, wishful identification, similarity, parasocial interaction, and liking. In the entertainment overcoming resistance model,

- *Identification* is an emotional and cognitive process in which individuals take on the role of a narrative's character, forgetting their own reality and for the time becoming the character and adopting the character's perspective. Identification has four dimensions—empathic (sharing feelings with the character); cognitive (sharing the character's perspective); motivational (internalizing the character's goals); and absorption (losing self-awareness during consumption of the narrative).

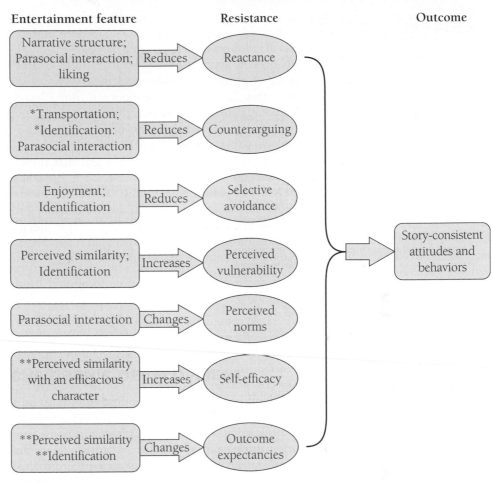

| Entertainment feature | Resistance | Outcome |

FIGURE 8.2 Entertainment Overcoming Resistance Model

Within the figure:

Entertainment feature → Resistance → Outcome

- Narrative structure; Parasocial interaction; liking — *Reduces* → Reactance
- *Transportation; *Identification: Parasocial interaction — *Reduces* → Counterarguing
- Enjoyment; Identification — *Reduces* → Selective avoidance
- Perceived similarity; Identification — *Increases* → Perceived vulnerability
- Parasocial interaction — *Changes* → Perceived norms
- **Perceived similarity with an efficacious character — *Increases* → Self-efficacy
- **Perceived similarity **Identification — *Changes* → Outcome expectancies

→ Story-consistent attitudes and behaviors

*Predicted by the extended elaboration likelihood model
**Predicted by social cognitive theory

- *Wishful identification* occurs when individuals want to be like, desire to emulate, and look up to the character (Chapter 6).
- *Similarity*, sometimes called homophily, is the degree to which individuals think that they are similar to a character. It can occur as similarity of physical attributes, demographic variables, beliefs, personality, or values.
- *Parasocial interaction* is individuals' interaction with a narrative's characters, forming a "pseudo relationship" (Chapter 7). Parasocial interactions seem like face-to-face relationships but, of course, they are not reciprocated by media characters.
- *Liking* is individuals' positive evaluations of a narrative's characters; it is sometimes called affinity or social attraction.

Not that all narrative persuasion research examines normative messages, or messages designed to generate positive health attitudes and behaviors. Juan-José Igartua and Isabel Barrios wanted to expand narrative persuasion theory and the E-ELM to explanations of attitude change when narratives deal with controversial or polemical topics or stories that otherwise deal with values that people hold important. No one, they argued, could be opposed to the health messages embedded in the narratives typically used in narrative persuasion and E-ELM research. They asked, what about "research into the impact of public narratives that sow controversy or agitate public opinion" (2012, p. 515). Using the film *Camino*, a Spanish movie about the death of a 14-year-old girl that presented the controversial Catholic religious group Opus Dei and religion in general in a negative light, they demonstrated that exposure to the film "induced a greater degree of agreement with the beliefs 'Opus Dei is an organization harmful for society' and 'religion is an obstacle to living a full life' " (p. 526). These judgments grew stronger with greater identification with the film's main character. The persuasive power of narratives, they argued, should be studied across a wider range of media, issues, and contexts than had been the case.

THE DELAY HYPOTHESIS

The persuasive power of narratives, as we've just seen, has been quite convincingly demonstrated, so much so that it has become the foundation of both the extended elaboration likelihood and the entertainment overcoming resistance models. But some scholars logically wonder if these narratives, so effective in influencing correct (i.e., prosocial and healthful) attitudes and behaviors may be just as effective in influencing incorrect ideas or judgments. In proposing the **delay hypothesis**, Jakob Jensen and his colleagues wrote, "People are bombarded by mass media every day all over the world, and a sizeable (and growing) body of mass communication research has demonstrated that much of this content is distorted in a multitude of ways. Media narratives provide misrepresentations or inaccurate information about gender, race, class, sexual orientation, and a variety of social behaviors.... Thus, the opportunity for delayed message effects in narrative situations—small or sizeable—is considerable" (Jensen et al., 2011, p. 523).

delay hypothesis
Idea that media effects can occur over time as people engage in information processing and recall, often leading to incorrect cognitions

The delay hypothesis contends that media effects can occur over time as people engage in information processing and recall. "Fictional media narratives," they wrote, "may produce small or no immediate effects on receiver beliefs that then increase or manifest over time as components of the message decay, become dissociated in memory, and/or are reappropriated in alternative ways by cognitive networks" (p. 509). The subsequent effect might be a *delayed drip*—a delayed cumulative effect—or a *delayed drench*—a delayed large effect. Nonetheless, "many effects will occur well after initial exposure to fictional narratives, especially those with vivid content and imagery" (p. 510).

sleeper effect
Idea that attitude change not immediately measurable after reception of a persuasive message might occur over time as recipients forget factors typically influencing persuasion

The logic of the delay hypothesis is similar to that of the **sleeper effect**, the idea that attitude change, while not immediately measurable after reception of a persuasive message, might occur over time as recipients forget factors that typically influence persuasion, such as source, evidence, and so on (Hovland, Lumsdaine, and Sheffield, 1949). The sleeper effect was originally a product of the World War II persuasion research accompanying the *Why We Fight* film series (Chapter 4) and has since had mixed research support. The delay hypothesis, however, in much the same way as narrative persuasion theory, contends that there is a fundamental difference between attitude change based on a persuasive message (where attention is on the argument being made) and that produced by narratives, where attention is on plot, characters, and action and where message consumers are transported into the narrative itself, especially as dramatized narrative fictions are typically more vivid and exciting than real life and therefore likely to distort people's memories (Shrum, 2009).

To test the delay hypothesis, Jensen and his colleagues showed college students an episode of the ABC television network program *Boston Legal*. And like the narrative persuasion research we've already discussed, it dealt with health and medicine; but unlike that work, it did so incorrectly (ABC eventually issued a public apology and explanation). The specific episode, entitled *Nuts*, incorrectly presented allergy autoinjectors (shots for the emergency treatment of life-threatening allergic reactions) as ineffective in treating severe peanut allergies. In this particular narrative a teacher who had administered the treatment a few seconds after a child was stricken was being sued because of the death of that child. The researchers demonstrated that when participants were queried two weeks after viewing they reported more false knowledge than they did immediately after seeing the program, confirming the delay hypothesis. The researchers also discovered that the perceived reality of the narrative influenced the delayed effect.

AFFECTIVE INTELLIGENCE, MOTIVATED REASONERS, AND THE BACKFIRE EFFECT

Over the last few decades a different perspective on information processing has begun to take hold. Political scientists James Kuklinski and Paul Quirk describe the trend this way, "The [cognitive] psychologist starts with the layperson's common-sense perception that people are generally rational.... Heuristic judgments disappoint such expectations, often profoundly. In describing their effects, therefore, psychologists highlight the error. Political scientists, on the other hand, start with the research showing that people are politically ignorant. They find evidence that political heuristics can save them from being strictly clueless. So unlike psychologists, they are inclined to stress the positive side" (2000, p. 166). In other words, many of the information-processing shortcuts to which humans are prone may be functional rather than dysfunctional. "Judging from anthropological research," they explain, "ancestral humans fought frequent wars and faced a high likelihood of death by homicide.... The hazardous conditions presumably rewarded stereotyping, ethnocentrism, and quick-trigger responses to fear and anger, major traits that frequently create conflict in modern politics.... [A]ncestral humans also lived in an information environment radically different from ours—with no writing or formal arithmetic, few concerns about remote consequences, and little or no specialized knowledge. This environment may account for the relative ineffectiveness of abstract and systematic information in persuasion.... [T]o the extent that we possess evolved processes for responding to persuasion, they are not adapted for this new-fangled information" (p. 165).

affective intelligence
Idea that affect (emotion) and reason beneficially work in concert in information processing

The theory of **affective intelligence** flows directly from this view of humans as "survivalist information processors." It sees affect (emotion) and reason, not in opposition when processing information, but as working in concert. The concept's originators, George Marcus, Russell Newman, and Michael MacKuen, explain:

> Affective intelligence is a theory about how emotion and reason interact to produce a thoughtful and attentive citizenry.... We focus particularly on the dynamics between feeling and thinking through which busy individuals come to pay some attention to the hubhub of the political world that swirls around them. Most of us are not policy wonks, political activists, or professional politicians. Most of the time, most of us literally do not think about our political options but instead rely on our political habits. Reliance on habit is deeply ingrained in our evolution to humanity. So when do we think about politics? When our emotions tell us to. We posit that individuals monitor political affairs by responding habitually, and for the most part unthinkingly, to familiar and expected political symbols; that is, by relying on past thought, calculation, and evaluation. But the central claim of our theory is that when citizens encounter a novel or threatening actor, event, or issue on the political horizon, a process of fresh evaluation and political judgment is activated. (2000, p. 1)

As a result, negative (or counterattitudinal) information encourages individuals to learn more by heightening their attention to the new information and increasing the effort they take to process it. Negative affect (emotion), then, motivates people to learn more about the stimulus and the environment, producing better decisions.

motivated reasoning
Idea that affect (emotion) and reason work in concert in information processing, but not necessarily beneficially as individuals are psychologically motivated to maintain and find support for existing evaluations

The theory of **motivated reasoning** assumes a relationship between emotion and reason similar to that described in affective intelligence, but argues that the outcome is not necessarily better decision making because individuals are psychologically motivated to maintain and find support for existing evaluations. David Redlawsk and his colleagues wrote:

> Motivated reasoners make an immediate evaluation of new information and use it to update an online tally that summarizes their evaluative affect. Newly encountered information carries with it an affective value. Given an existing evaluation (represented by the online tally), these affective components interact so that the online tally directly influences how the new information is evaluated *before* it is used to update the tally. This is the key insight missing from both the cognitive approaches and affective intelligence. Even anxious voters presumably motivated to learn more and make more accurate assessments may well be subject to the processing biases of motivated reasoning as they affectively evaluate *before* they begin to cognitively process new information. While a negative emotional response may be generated by incongruence between expectations (existing affect as summarized by the online tally) and new information, motivated reasoning suggests that this incongruence does not necessarily lead to greater accuracy in evaluation or greater information search. Instead voters committed to a candidate may be motivated to discount incongruent information; they may mentally argue against it, bolstering their existing evaluation by recalling all the good things about a liked candidate even in the face of something negative. Motivated reasoning describes an interaction between existing affective evaluations and new information, but unlike affective intelligence, the effect of affect may lead to *less* accurate updating, rather than more. (Redlawsk, Civettini, and Emmerson, 2010, p. 567)

You may hear echoes of dissonance theory in this explanation, and that is no surprise as the theory of motivated reasoning is based, in part, on that classic conception of information processing (Chapter 4).

backfire effect
People who receive unwelcome, correcting information not only resist that challenge to their views, they come to hold their original, erroneous position even more strongly

Brendan Nyhan and Jason Reifler produced evidence for motivated reasoning in their study of the **backfire effect**—when people who receive unwelcome, correcting information not only resist that challenge to their views, they actually come to hold their original, erroneous position even more strongly (2010). Individuals may simply selectively perceive the new information as consistent with their existing beliefs, but the backfire effect suggests something else is operating: as people cognitively counter-argue the challenging information, especially if they do so vigorously, they construct even more firmly held supporting opinions, leading them to positions that are more extreme than those originally held. In a series of experiments testing misconceptions about politically loaded topics such as the Iraq War and weapons of mass destruction, stem cell research, and tax cuts, Nyhan and Reifler demonstrated that corrections failed to reduce misconceptions for the most committed partisans and that "direct factual contradictions can actually *strengthen* ideologically grounded factual beliefs" (p. 323). The authors also noted that while it was conservatives who demonstrated the backfire effect in their experiments, "there is a great deal of evidence that liberals and Democrats [as demonstrated in other research] also interpret factual information in ways that are consistent with their political predispositions" (p. 323).

THE NEUROSCIENCE PERSPECTIVE

In 2004, mass communication researcher John Sherry wrote, "The field of mass communication and its most influential scholars emerged from [social scientific] traditions that were intellectually antagonistic to the idea that biology may play a role in determining behavior. As time went by, researchers moved toward even more environmentally based social interactional theories found in the human action perspective … sociocultural theories … or even theories that may share more with humanities than the sciences, such as semiotics and the critical/cultural studies schools (p. 91). But, he continued,

> there is no longer any question among most developmental psychologists, cognitive scientists, neuroscientists, and biologists that nature interacts with nurture to determine human behavior. Unlike other human sciences, communication has never seriously engaged the nature/nurture debate. As a result, communication researchers have developed a one-sided way of thinking about human communication that has major implications for the richness of our theory and for our ability to account for variance. If communication researchers continue to remain enamored of an early-20th-century ontology and ignore the building evidence of biological influence on behavior, our theories risk becoming outmoded. (p. 102)

neuroscience perspective
Views information processing as a complex system of interlinked and interdependent relationships of people's biological and social environment

He offered five areas long of interest to mass communication researchers that have suffered from the discipline's inattention to the **neuroscience perspective**—the view of human agency as a "complex system of interlinked and interdependent relationships of our biological and social environment" (Muuss, 1988, p. 300):

- *Attention*—Why is our attention drawn to media; how do we differently attend to different media and genres; why are there individual differences in attention?
- *Emotion*—How does emotion enhance media experiences; how do media and mood interact; where do medium and genre preferences originate; how and why do people become habituated or addicted to media and media content?

- *Learning and memory*—What is the connection between individual differences in learning ability and memory and media effects?
- *Motivation*—How does media use interact with basic human drives?
- *Perception*—How might differing perceptual abilities influence media experiences and preferences?

Here's an example. If the ELM's central-route processing is in part dependent on the individual's motivation and ability to process an argument, how can a researcher ignore the quite real possibility that different people are differently disposed, often by nature, to do so? But it isn't as if the field of mass communication has completely ignored the nature aspect of the **nature/nurture divide** (genetics and brain physiology vs. learning and culture). Sherry himself acknowledged several evolutionary and trait-based media effects studies from the 1990s, for example, Shoemaker's 1996 research on biological and cultural evolution and attraction to negative news, Malamuth's 1996 work on evolutionary differences in the appeal of erotic content to men and women, and Krcmar and Greene's 1999 investigation of young people's exposure to violent content and the trait of sensation seeking. You also saw in Chapter 6 that even earlier, in 1979, Ellen Wartella proposed a developmental perspective of children's television use that could be employed to describe and explain the communicative differences between children of different ages and differences between children and adults. Twenty years later, in 1999, she made the same argument, expressly linking this developmental perspective to the "neuropsychological effects of format characteristics and viewing styles of children" (p. 81). And for decades advertisers and marketers have been employing **neuromarketing research**—biometric measures like brainwaves, facial expressions, eye-tracking, sweating, and heart rate monitoring—to find the "magic keys" to bypassing consumers' reason and logic in order to directly reach their subconscious. For example, here is marketer Tim Riesterer offering advice to advertisers on the *Harvard Business Review* blog: "Breaking through the status quo is like breaking a habit. Your brain goes on autopilot when a habit is formed. To disrupt the status quo, you need to appeal to the part of the brain where decisions are actually made…. Your messaging needs to feed the old brain the thing it craves most to make a decision—contrast. This part of the brain relies exclusively on visual and emotional contrast to decide between what's unsafe and safe. For your prospects, this means they need to see a clear distinction between what they're already doing and what you're proposing" (2012).

The neuroscience perspective recognizes that the brain has several parts, each serving important functions. The part of the brain that governs survival is the *limbic system*. Sometimes people refer to it as the old brain, sometimes as the lizard or reptilian brain because it has been with all animal species since they first evolved onto land. The new brain (about 100 million years old), the conscious, reasoning part, is the *cerebral cortex*. It serves learning and memory. James Potter suggests we think of our brains as " 'hard wired' to perform certain functions, but they also include a lot of software that gives us the capability to think for ourselves" (2012 pp. 89–90). Nobel Prize–winning economist Daniel Kahneman adopts a similar metaphor in his book, *Thinking, Fast and Slow* (2011). He says the brain operates through two systems, System 1 and System 2. System 1 is the old brain, or

nature/nurture divide
Question of the source of human attitudes and behavior, genetics and brain physiology vs. learning and culture

neuromarketing research
Marketers' use of biometric measures to find the "magic keys" to consumer behavior

Potter's hard drive. It runs automatically, can never be turned off, and makes very quick, usually correct decisions based on very little information. System 1 loves heuristics, mental shortcuts. Why? Primitive people could not survive if they paused to ponder whether that rustle in the bushes was a lion or not, and if it was, might it be a nice lion, or maybe one in need. By the time they answered these questions they'd be lion food. System 1 works so naturally, so smoothly and quickly, that it usually overrules people's rational selves, System 2. System 2 is slow and inefficient. It requires attention, energy, and time. Kahneman doesn't say that people are cognitive misers, but his view of System 2 as deferring, even justifying System 1 (we would call it dissonance reduction) suggests he believes we are. This is why marketer Riesterer, mentioned just above, wants to target old, unreflective System 1. Why even bother with System 2? It's too much work and he might not get the results he wants. System 1, however, does have limitations. It has "biases," Kahneman explains, "systematic errors that it is prone to make in specified circumstances.... It sometimes answers easier questions than the one it was asked, and it has little understanding of logic and statistics" (p. 25). And while the fact that it can never be turned off might seem to be a good thing (for survival, at least), it may be a problem as well, as when the task at hand demands System 2's particular strengths.

But as Sherry explained, mass communication's disciplinary attention to learning and memory, those aspects of our rational selves, has caused the field to discount the questions raised by the influence of the old brain/System 1. To remedy this, he argues that mass communication theory and research must "account for the contribution of biology (e.g., sex, temperament, hormones, physical appearance, etc.) and of the social environment (e.g., parents, peers, culture, etc.). The neuroscience paradigm," he continues, "assumes that (a) all human behavior is rooted in neurophysiological processing, (b) one's neurophysiological makeup is genetically determined, but (c) is plastic across the life span (including in utero) and is therefore susceptible to environmental influence" (2004, pp. 92–93). Peter Hatemi, Enda Byrne, and Rose McDermott, a team of social scientists and geneticists, explain the interaction and plasticity of genetic makeup and environment:

> In a neurobiological view, the environment represents much more than simply the stimuli that the entire organism faces. Rather the environment refers to both internal cellular processes *and* the external forces operating on an individual. Specifically, the environment refers to many factors, including the cellular environment, in utero hormones and maternal stress during gestation, and all processes that manifest across the lifespan, including the environment one's parents were in when a person was conceived, the environment a person faces as both a child and an adult, diet, parenting, family environment, social and economic issues, emotional bonding, and random life events. In short, the environment can refer to everything both inside and outside the body before and after an individual was born. And, the same environmental stimulus, such as cold weather, or trauma, can have multiple effects on both the internal mechanisms and the overall person's behavior. Thus, different stimuli can exert similar effects under particular conditions as well, both within the same person and across individuals. At times, the same stimulus can trigger entirely different genetic mechanisms that may or may not work together or in opposition to one another. In this way, the actual objective nature of a given stimuli is less important than the subjective way in which it is interpreted and assimilated in light of a person's history and unique physiology. (2012, p. 309)

The relationship between genetics and attitudes has been amply demonstrated in studies of twins. Identical twins (monozygotic; siblings with the same genetic makeup, having been conceived from a single egg) are consistently more alike ideologically and attitudinally than fraternal twins (dizygotic; siblings conceived from two different eggs and thus genetically different) on issues such as the death penalty, ethnocentrism, morality, unions, unemployment, and abortion (Eaves and Eysenck, 1974). This distinction persists even when identical twins are raised apart from one another (Tesser, 1993). Twin studies have also demonstrated that fraternal twins tend to be ideologically and attitudinally similar while they are being raised in the same home (nurture is indeed powerful), but once they move away (and apart), they develop markedly different attitudes. This is as we would expect, as they are then free to choose their own friends, environments, and experiences, and their genetic dispositions can take them where they will in these interactions (nature is freer to express itself). But this does not happen for identical twins. Even when apart, even when free to choose their own friends, environments, and experiences, they remain attitudinally similar because they possess similar genetic dispositions (Hatemi et al., 2009).

We've seen how the evolution of the brain may influence how we react to the world, but as you have just read, the neuroscience perspective also includes consideration of genes and genetics. But keep in mind, genetics do not *determine* attitudes and behaviors. There no "gene for xxxxxx," for example, a "liberal gene," "conservative gene," or "media use gene." The effects of genetics in general on the propensity to demonstrate complex social traits and behaviors is indirect and the result of the interaction of literally thousands of genes in interaction with what is already going on in the body and in the surrounding environment (Hill, Goddard, and Visscher, 2008). Hatemi, Byrne, and McDermott explain:

> It can be overwhelming to consider how every single emotional or physical thought or action that we experience, even those we cannot see, such as the way our immune system reacts to the incursion of bacteria, the influence of a person's touch, a smile, or the feeling of warm sunlight on our face, is initiated by the combination of some stimulus and the concomitant expression of genes within our cells. This leads to the

INSTANT ACCESS

Neuroscience Perspective

Strengths

1. Focuses attention on individuals in the mass communication process
2. Brings clarity to the nature/nurture debate
3. Enriches traditional notions of communicative activity
4. Shows the value of automatic, unconscious information processing
5. Accounts for the operation of affect and cognition

Weaknesses

1. Too oriented toward micro-level
2. Can lack specificity, especially "if the environment can refer to everything"
3. Can appear overly deterministic
4. Usefulness for understanding important aspects of media influence needs to be demonstrated

reciprocal action of other cells which result in signals that govern the expression of other genetic and neurobiological systems, which eventually inspire feeling, thought, and behavior. Once we combine this fascinating interaction with the human ability to transcend our biology, to reason, to feel, to perceive, to question, to talk, to love, to empathize, and all other self-reflective dynamics that make us human, only then can we appreciate both the wonder and complexity of the human genome. (2012, p. 308)

Less poetically, genes regulate the environment of our bodies' cells; they provide the information that tells those cells which proteins to make, which then open or close other neurobiological pathways that encourage or discourage our states and traits. These states and traits "operate through a complex cognitive and emotive architecture." These processes "then become operationalized through a psychological architecture in a human organism that walks around, moves, and experiences the world, resulting in outcomes we observe at the macro level as behaviors, preferences, attitudes, and other recognizable measures" (Hatemi, Byrne, and McDermott, 2013, p. 309).

Mass communication researchers have begun to heed Professor Sherry's call. For example, Kirzinger, Weber, and Johnson employed a twin study to demonstrate that "a nontrivial portion of variation [in media consumption and communication behavior] is explained by genetic factors" (2012, p. 159). Theresa Correa, Amber Hinsley, and Homero de Zúñiga connected three elements of the "Big Five" model of personality traits—extraversion, neuroticism, and openness to experiences—to individual's use of social networking (2010). They discovered positive relationships between use of social networking and extraversion and openness to new experiences, and a negative relationship between social networking and neuroticism, or emotional stability. They also demonstrated gender and age differences.

Arguably, however, it is in the realm of political communication that scholars have been most active in linking genetics and internal dispositions to attitudes. Indicative is the work of Hatemi and his colleagues on political attitudes and fear, a "genetically informed, stable, but malleable trait-based disposition, as well as a transitory state-based response that can be elicited or manipulated by environmental conditions" (Hatemi et al., 2013, p. 280). They demonstrated a "latent genetic factor" that is part of a social phobic disposition that generates mistrust of unfamiliarity, the idea that social contexts can be dangerous, fear of social exposure and of being awkward, and feeling humiliated in social contexts, resulting in negative attitudes toward out-groups (people unlike themselves). They concluded that "political preferences represent a manifestation of a genetic disposition expressed within the context of modern circumstances" (p. 12). But although they found that "common genetic disposition mutually influences social fear and out-group attitudes," they cautioned that "the relationship between any specific gene, fear disposition, and a particular social or political attitude is not likely to be hard-wired. Indeed, people may have divergent dispositions to be fearful of unfamiliar others, but long-term exposure to the unfamiliar makes it unfamiliar no more" (p. 13). Brad Verhulst and his colleagues applied the **top-down/bottom-up theory of political attitude formation** to demonstrating that "ideological preferences within the American electorate are contingent on both the environmental conditions that provide the context of the contemporary political debate and the internal predispositions that motivate people to hold liberal or conservative policy preferences" (Verhulst, Hatemi, and Eaves, 2012, p. 375). Political attitudes, they argued, are a combination of social experiences (top-down) and genetic

top-down/bottom-up theory of political attitude formation

Ideological preferences are products of environmental conditions (top-down) and internal predispositions (bottom-up) that motivate people to hold liberal or conservative policy preferences pathways (bottom-up). The former are those things that we usually associate with political attitudes, such as life experience and exposure to news and political information. The latter exert stable influence on attitudes and behavior over time and across different situations.

Science writer David Roberts summarizes this work, explaining that there is general agreement that "conservatives and liberals do not merely disagree on matters of policy, but are *different kinds of people*, who process information differently. On average, conservatives prefer simplicity and clear distinctions, where liberals display 'integrative complexity' and are more comfortable with ambiguity and nuance. Conservatives are 'hierarchs' and highly sensitive to in-group/out-group distinctions, where liberals are egalitarians. Conservatives come to decisions quickly and stick to them; liberals deliberate, sometimes to the point of dithering. Conservatives are more sensitive to threats while liberals are more open to new experiences" (2012).

SUMMARY

This chapter examined several information-processing theories, all of which, because they deal with how *individuals* process and make sense of the overwhelming amounts of information present even in the simplest media message, are microscopic in scope. Much of that cognitive work is out of our conscious control, and as we've seen, because this automatic processing is evolutionary in its roots, this is not necessarily a bad thing. Schema theory, for example, suggests that our automatic filing and classifying of our experiences makes it possible for us to "tame the information tide," leading to the idea that we are more purposive in the creation and maintenance of our attitudes that we are sometimes given credit for. The ELM takes this argument a step further, demonstrating that we can and do process information systematically and thoughtfully when and if we want to, but that there are times when we make judgments more peripherally, relying on cues, often unrelated to the message. Imagine, though, if this was not the case and we had to seriously and deeply scrutinize every message that came our way. We would be immobilized.

While schema theory, ELM, and their related concepts have been used primarily to explain how we process and manage persuasive messages, their logic has been applied to a wide variety of cognitive tasks, foremost among them the processing of health-related messages embedded in entertainment programming. Sometimes those messages are intentionally included in dramatic narratives; sometimes they are an essential part of the storyline, but that makes them no less potentially persuasive. The E-ELM and the entertainment overcoming resistance model are two ways of understanding how our knowledge about how we process media messages can be applied in the service of good.

Political communication researchers and theorists have looked at this wealth of research on how we process information and have come to a split decision on whether the cognitive miser in us all speaks well or poorly for our ability to perform our duties as citizens. Proponents of affective intelligence contend that our decision making, although based on emotion as well as reason, is actually an effective way to deal with the complexity of our politics. Proponents of motivated reasoning, while accepting the interplay of affect and reason as thoroughly human, are a bit more skeptical of our ability to come to well-conceived conclusions.

Finally, there is no better indication that these individual-based theories are microscopic than the current movement to account for the influence of evolutionary brain structure and genetics on attitudes and behavior. This neuroscience perspective attempts to bring order to the nature/nurture debate by showing that our attitudes and behaviors are indeed products of our environments, but that our environments consist of our internal physiological processes and the external forces that operate on us. This approach has brought a great deal of insight to media choice and consumption questions as well as to questions of how we process—or fail to process—political messages. What links the information-processing theories in this chapter are three simple, related ideas. First, we are humans who must interact with and make sense of a complex world. Second, messages from the mass media constitute a very large part of that interaction and complexity. And third, we are actually pretty good at processing the content we consume. So, in the next chapter, we will look at media effects on society; that is, we will investigate theories that attempt to explain the collective outcome of our individual processing of mass communication.

Critical Thinking Questions

1. Earlier in the chapter you were asked, "What is your war-on-terror schema?" Information-processing theory predicts that you did not spend much cognitive energy on that question at the time because you applied the example-posed-as-a-question heuristic. But now take a moment to answer the question. Much of this country's internal politics have been driven by the war on terror, and much American foreign policy is based on those politics. In other words, the war on terror warrants your systematic cognitive effort. So again, what is your war-on-terror schema and from what experiences has it been constructed?

2. A large proportion of the American public has little or no trust at all in the media to report the news fully, fairly, and accurately. How much of this negative opinion do you think is a product of the hostile media effect? In other words, will people who hold strong political opinions inevitably and always find mainstream, more-or-less objective media as hostile? Do you?

3. How open are you to divergent media voices? Do you engage in siloing, limiting yourself to a few attitudinally comfortable media outlets? Why or why not? Do you think that our democracy would be better served if more people exposed themselves to differing points of view? Explain your response in terms of the information-processing theories you studied in this chapter.

Key Terms

information-processing theory

limited cognitive resources

orienting response

schema theory

schemas

scripts

schema-inconsistent advertising

hostile media effect (HME)

siloing

elaboration likelihood model (ELM)

peripheral route

heuristics

central route

heuristic-systematic model

narrative persuasion theory

transportation

extended elaboration likelihood model (E-ELM)

entertainment-education (EE)

entertainment overcoming resistance model

delay hypothesis

sleeper effect

affective intelligence

motivated reasoning

backfire effect

neuroscience perspective

nature/nurture divide

neuromarketing research

top-down/bottom-up theory of political attitude formation

9 | THEORIES OF THE EFFECT OF MEDIA ON SOCIETY

How do we keep up on news about what is going on in our neighborhood, our city, our state, our nation, or around the world? How do we find out about the latest fashions, movies, technology, and diets? We live at a time when a lot is happening everywhere and all at once. Information about products, peers, family, community, state, nation, and the world constantly comes at us from an ever-growing array of media. News is created and packaged by an impressive collection of sources ranging from journalists to bloggers to YouTube enthusiasts. In our news we face an ever-growing amount of promotional information produced by advertisers, public relations agents, and others engaging in strategic communication. This information is often integrated with actual news so it's hard to tell what's news and what's not.

The way we receive and use information is being radically transformed by new media technologies, creating a very difficult situation for traditional news providers. Print newspapers are rapidly losing readers, especially younger ones, and they are hemorrhaging advertisers. More than a few have shuttered their operations. Many have reduced the physical size of their pages to cut the cost of paper. Some are publishing fewer days per week. A few have decided to exist only on the Internet. Some are becoming nonprofit corporations to reduce taxes, enabling them to stay in business.

Yet news on the Internet has been quite successful, as traffic on many news-oriented sites rapidly and steadily increases. Combining all newspaper reading, print and Internet, the American newspaper audience is actually expanding (Starkman, 2012). And although newspapers often offer free Internet access to much of the content published in their print editions, income from advertising on those online editions doesn't remotely make up for revenue lost by their print versions. Industry research indicates that although the online newspaper audience is at a record high—110 million unique visitors a month—and income from online advertising is equally robust—$20 billion a year—income from online ad sales is growing at only one-fiftieth the pace of print papers' ad sales decline (Thompson, 2012). Making matters even worse, on the Internet those same newspapers are competing against each other for regional and national audiences (and advertising sales). They also compete against many other news sources, such as blogs and sites maintained by other media organizations and specialty information interest groups. The outcome of this competition is uncertain, but as you saw in Chapter 3, it already is having important consequences for us and for society.

If the news business is troubled, strategic communicators appear to be thriving. As we saw in Chapter 3, public relations professionals now outnumber journalists 4 to 1—as opposed to 1.2 to 1 in 1980 (Greenslade, 2012). Promotional communicators generally see new media as offering them great potential for delivering their messages more effectively to more narrowly targeted audiences at lower cost. Facebook advertising is a good example. The social networking site provides advertisers with detailed information about users, allowing them to target their messages directly to people who like certain things or regularly engage in certain activities. Frequent moviegoers get regular updates on showings in their area, while those who like certain types of music are sent ads for bands and new releases.

How do you deal with the flood of information that threatens to inundate you? If you are typical, this is a question you rarely ask yourself. As you read in the last chapter, you deal with information by filtering most of it out. Most of it never reaches you because you don't pay any attention to the media that could deliver it. When you do attend to information, some of it is hard to understand and you skip over it and forget it. This may be information that you know is important but it really doesn't seem relevant to your life. But there is some information that you do find relevant. This is information that you seek out, information that you share with others face-to-face or by text or social networking. This is information that you care enough about to want to be constantly updated, information that makes a difference in your life and the lives of those you care about. Our use of information—and entertainment as we saw in the last chapter—does much to determine who we are, and the way most of us use that media content does much to shape the society we live in.

The theories discussed in this chapter are theories about media content and the role it plays for us and others. They are primarily macroscopic-level theories; they deal with how *we* use mass communication to interact with and shape the institutions that shape our realities and thereby shape our everyday lives. As James Potter explains, macroscopic theory and effects are "concerned with aggregates rather than individuals. An aggregate is a combined whole that is formed by the gathering together of all the particular elements. The public is an aggregate because it is the collection of all individuals" (2012, p. 237). In other words, you may have a very specific, well-constructed, and stable terrorism schema (to borrow an example from the last chapter), but so do the millions of other people with whom you must share your world. What is the macroscopic—or aggregate—effect of all those people holding opinions and making judgments based on their own micro-level schemas?

These theories offer varying perspectives. Some are cautiously optimistic while others are pessimistic. They provide different ways of understanding how and why information affects us and how that translates into larger social understandings and action. They also explain how content such as news can shape the social world. We don't often think of news as something that can—or should—alter the social world. News is supposed to be a report about things that are happening; it's not supposed to influence what is happening. Journalists continue to tell us that they only provide objective news coverage. As Fox News insists, "We report, you decide." The theories in this chapter reject this simple assertion and challenge us to look differently at news—not as a mirror that simply reflects the social world, but as a force capable of shaping that world.

Even if we personally don't pay attention to politics, we will live in a world shaped by the way news reports politics. Even if we personally dislike celebrity culture and sports, for example, our lives are affected by them because so many people around us are influenced by them. Many of us may not know the name Umar Farouk Abdul Mutallab; we might not even have paid attention to the news of his Christmas Day, 2009, attempt to bring down an airliner by exploding a bomb in his underwear; but whether we did or didn't follow this story, we still have to deal with long lines, full body scans, heightened security at airports, and election campaigns that turn on which political party makes the best promises about keeping us safe from the terrorists.

LEARNING OBJECTIVES

After studying this chapter you should be able to

- Explain the social, cultural, and political role played by the mass media, given the interaction between the construction of their content and our consumption of that material.

- Appreciate how mass media's attention to specific events and issues influences the importance we assign to those events and issues, how we interpret them, how those interpretations come to shape the political agenda, and how some people are moved to speak less openly about them.

- Better understand how routine news production practices, including journalists' commitment to objectivity at all costs, shape the content of the news and subsequently people's perceptions of the world.

- Find value in a number of contemporary mass communication theories that offer evidence of media's ability to produce macro-level effects, such as innovation diffusion theory, social marketing theory, media system dependency theory, and the knowledge-gap hypothesis.

- Detail the nature of cultivation analysis and its contributions to our understanding of media influence.

- Assess the potential for media literacy and media literacy interventions to enhance positive media effects and limit those that may be harmful.

OVERVIEW

The media theorists we consider in this chapter argue that the failings of news and other media content raise important questions about the motives of media practitioners and their professional norms. Are they really doing everything they can and should to provide us with useful services, or are they part of the problem? To what extent do their professional norms and newsroom culture inadvertently lead them to be socially irresponsible? These questions about the social role of media are much like those raised in Chapter 3's discussion of normative theories. More-over, they imply that our media system's dominant normative theory, social responsibility theory, is no longer serving as a useful guide to media professionals as they go about their work. Does this theory need to be replaced, or at least seri-ously reconsidered? We'll look at alternatives in Chapter 10.

The earliest mass communication theories arose out of a concern for the pres-ervation of social order in the face of the threat posed by propaganda. Ever since the appearance of modern mass media in the middle of the nineteenth century, social theorists have speculated about the power of media to create community on the one hand and disrupt important social institutions on the other. They embraced technology as a panacea or they feared it as a corrupting force. In Chapter 2 we traced the rise of mass society theory and that of the mass media industries. At its height, mass society theory painted a dire picture of a totalitarian future in which a cynical elite, bent on creating and maintaining absolute power, manipulated media.

In this chapter, we consider theories addressing many of the same questions and issues that sparked the development of mass society theory. We live today in a world transformed by powerful new media—by communications satellites encir-cling the globe while computer-based media invade not only our homes, but every corner and every minute of our days. These technologies give rise to unrealistic hopes and inspire inordinate fears. Like our ancestors at the end of the nineteenth century, we harbor doubts about our political system. Though we aren't threatened by totalitarian propaganda, we are regularly deluged by negative news, political advertising, and even narrative entertainment that feed our cynicism about politics and "the way things are."

The contemporary media theories we consider might seem familiar to you based on your reading of previous chapters. Most draw on older theories to offer cogent and insightful analyses of the role of media in society. For the most part the theories discussed in this chapter are grounded in empirical social research. Although this work is quite diverse, the theories it supports have many similarities. As you will see, the assessment these theories provide of contemporary media and their social role is mostly negative. Several argue that media routinely disrupt important social institutions such as politics or education. Others argue that our dependency on media leads to important effects.

It is important to keep in mind that despite their negative tone, none of these contemporary media theories should be confused with mass society theory. None argues that media will inevitably destroy high culture, bring an end to democracy, and plunge us into a dark age of totalitarianism. Their view of the social order is far more sophisticated than the mass society thinking central to many earlier theo-ries. Their understanding of individuals is similar to the perspectives presented in Chapter 8. It's generally positive but mixed, based in part on active audience assumptions but tempered by the recognition that much human behavior is habit-ual and not consciously controlled. People don't always do what's reasonable or most useful when it comes to media. On the other hand, media don't easily manip-ulate passive individuals. Instead, media's power rests in their ability to provide communication services that we routinely use and that are central to the maintenance of our personal identities and our social order. And as you'll also see, that power can be enhanced or limited by individuals literate in the use of those communication services.

AGENDA-SETTING

What were the crucial issues in the 2012 presidential election? The United States was faced with an escalating federal budget deficit and a slowly recovering economy. Billions of dollars were being spent to pursue war and reconstruction in Afghanistan. The country, actually the Earth, was in the last quarter of what would become the warmest year in recorded history. Income inequality was at its highest since the Great Depression of the 1930s. College loan obligation was nearing unsustainable levels, threatening to sink into endless debt even those graduates who could find jobs worthy of their degrees. The nation led the world in childhood obesity, Type II diabetes, infant mortality, the proportion (and real number) of the population in prison, and military spending. What do you remember from the mass media as the important issues and images of that campaign? Mitt Romney's five houses, his wife's Olympic horse, Clint Eastwood yelling at an empty chair, "Corporations are people my friends," and the 47 percent? Barack Obama's plan to take away your guns, "You didn't build that," government money paying for birth control, Obamacare, and socialism? Of all the issues that should or could have been aired and examined, only a few became dominant. Only a few were viewed by many Americans as the most important issues facing the United States. This is **agenda-setting**.

agenda-setting
The idea that media don't tell people what to think, but what to think about

Although he did not specifically use the term, Bernard Cohen (1963) is generally credited with identifying the process, which would later be called agenda-setting. "The press is significantly more than a purveyor of information and opinion," he wrote. "It may not be successful much of the time in telling people what to think, but it is stunningly successful in telling its readers what to think about. And it follows from this that the world looks different to different people, depending not only on their personal interests, but also on the map that is drawn for them by the writers, editors, and publishers of the papers they read" (p. 13). Cohen's perspective might have lingered in obscurity had it not been empirically confirmed by the research of Maxwell E. McCombs and Donald Shaw (1972). They explained their interpretation of agenda-setting: "In choosing and displaying news, editors, newsroom staff, and broadcasters play an important part in shaping political reality. Readers learn not only about a given issue, but how much importance to attach to that issue from the amount of information in a news story and its position.... The mass media may well determine the important issues—that is, the media may set the 'agenda' of the campaign" (p. 176).

During September and October of the 1968 presidential election, these researchers interviewed 100 registered voters who had not yet committed to either candidate (presumably these people would be more open to media messages). By asking each respondent "to outline the key issues as he [sic] saw them, regardless of what the candidates might be saying at the moment," they were able to identify and rank by importance just what these people thought were the crucial issues facing them. They then compared these results with a ranking of the time and space accorded to various issues produced by a content analysis of the television news, newspapers, newsmagazines, and editorial pages available to voters in the area where the study was conducted. The results? "The media appear to have exerted a considerable impact on voters' judgments of what they considered the major issues of the campaign.... The correlation between the major item emphasis on the main campaign issues carried by the media and voters' independent judgments of what were the important issues was +.967," they wrote. "In short, the data suggest a very strong relationship between the emphasis placed on different campaign issues by the media ... and the judgments of voters as to the salience and importance of various campaign topics" (McCombs and Shaw, 1972, pp. 180–181).

This important and straightforward study highlights both the strengths and limitations of agenda-setting as a theory of media effects. It establishes that there is an important relationship between media reports and people's ranking of public issues. On the negative side, we can see that the logic of agenda-setting seems well suited for the question of news and campaigns, but what about other kinds of content and other kinds of effects? More important, though, is the question of the actual nature of the relationship between news and its audience. Maybe the public sets the media's agenda and then the media reinforce it. The McCombs and Shaw analysis, like most early agenda-setting research, implies a direction of influence from media to audience—that is, it implies causality. But the argument that the media are simply responding to their audiences can be easily made. Few journalists have not uttered at least once in their careers, "We only give the people what they want." McCombs (1981) himself acknowledged these limitations.

It is important not to judge the utility of the agenda-setting approach based on the earliest studies. For example, Shanto Iyengar and Donald Kinder attempted to overcome some of the problems of earlier work in a series of experiments designed to test the "agenda-setting hypothesis: Those problems that receive prominent attention on the national news become the problems the viewing public regards as the nation's most important" (1987, p. 16). Their series of experiments examined agenda-setting, the vividness of news reports, the positioning of stories, and what they called **priming**.

priming
In agenda-setting, the idea that media draw attention to some aspects of political life at the expense of others

- *Agenda-setting:* Iyengar and Kinder demonstrated causality. They wrote: "Americans' view of their society and nation are powerfully shaped by the stories that appear on the evening news. We found that people who were shown network broadcasts edited to draw attention to a particular problem assigned greater importance to that problem—greater importance than they themselves did before the experiment began, and greater importance than did people assigned to control conditions that emphasized different problems. Our subjects regarded the target problem as more important for the country, cared more about it, believed that government should do more about it, reported stronger feelings about it, and were much more likely to identify it as one of the country's most important problems" (Iyengar and Kinder, 1987, p. 112).
- *Vividness of presentation:* The researchers found that dramatic news accounts undermined rather than increased television's agenda-setting power. Powerfully presented personal accounts (a staple of contemporary television news) might

focus too much attention on the specific situation or individual rather than on the issue at hand.

- *Position of a story:* Lead stories had a greater agenda-setting effect. Iyengar and Kinder offered two possible reasons for this result. First, people paid more attention to the stories at the beginning of the news, and these were less likely to fall victim to the inevitable interruptions experienced when viewing at home. Second, people accepted the news program's implicit designation of a lead story as most newsworthy.

- *Priming:* This is the idea that even the most motivated citizens cannot consider all that they know when evaluating complex political issues. Instead, people consider the things that come easily to mind, or as the researchers said, "those bits and pieces of political memory that are accessible." You can hear echoes of schema theory here. Iyengar and Kinder's research (1987) strongly demonstrated that "through priming [drawing attention to some aspects of political life at the expense of others] television news [helps] to set the terms by which political judgments are reached and political choices made" (p. 114). Writing in a later study, Iyengar (1991) offered this distinction: "While agenda-setting reflects the impact of news coverage on the perceived importance of national issues, priming refers to the impact of news coverage on the weight assigned to specific issues in making political judgments" (p. 133). We'll return to a consideration of priming in the next chapter when we discuss it as part of framing theory.

agenda-building
A collective process in which media, government, and the citizenry reciprocally influence one another in areas of public policy

Agenda-setting has an important macro-level implication: **agenda-building**, "the often complicated process by which some issues become important in policy making arenas" (Protess et al., 1991, p. 6). Kurt Lang and Gladys Lang (1983) defined "agenda-building—a more apt term than agenda-setting—[as] a collective process in which media, government, and the citizenry reciprocally influence one another" (pp. 58–59). Agenda-building presumes cognitive effects, an active audience, and societal-level effects. Its basic premise—that media can profoundly affect how a society (or nation or culture) determines what are its important concerns and therefore can mobilize its various institutions toward meeting them—has allowed this line of inquiry, in the words of David Protess and his colleagues (1991), to "flourish."

framing theory
Idea that people use sets of expectations to make sense of their social world and media contribute to those expectations

second-order agenda-setting
The idea that media set the public's agenda at a second level or order—the attribute level ("how to think about it"), where the first order was the object level ("what to think about")

Agenda-setting pioneer McCombs has undertaken an effort to expand and develop the concept by linking it to a broad range of other media theories—for example, **framing theory** (McCombs and Ghanem, 2001). He called his new theory **second-order agenda-setting**. McCombs argued that agenda-setting operates at two levels, or orders: the *object level* and the *attribute level*. Conventional agenda-setting research has focused at the object level and has assessed how media coverage could influence the priority assigned to objects (e.g., issues, candidates, events, and problems). In doing this, media told us "*what* to think about." But media can also tell us "*how* to think about" some objects. Media do this by influencing second-order "attribute agendas." They tell us which object attributes are important and which ones are not, and for this reason second-order agenda-setting is sometimes called *attribute agenda-setting*. Balmas Meital and Tamir Sheafer tested attribute agenda-setting for candidates, rather than issues (2010), demonstrating that those candidate attributes most emphasized in the news, coupled with their evaluative tone (positive or negative), do indeed predict the public's general evaluation of the candidate's suitability for office. Moreover, the researchers were able to show causality: "When the saliency of a candidate's attributes changed in the news agenda, similar changes also appeared in the public's agenda; when there were no changes in the news agenda, there were no changes in the public agenda as well." This led them to identify the *affective priming of candidate attributes*—"the most salient candidate attributes in the public's mind will become the criterion for evaluating the candidate. And, the evaluative tone of that attribute in the memory of the voter will be a decisive factor that will generate the direction (positive vs. negative) of candidate evaluation" (pp. 222–223).

hierarchy-of-effects model

Practical theory calling for the differentiation of persuasive effects relative to the time and effort necessary for their accomplishment

Another advance on the original agenda-setting theory is its influence on behavior. Soo Jung Moon, for example, combined agenda-setting and the **hierarchy-of-effects model**. Although there is more to be said about the hierarchy-of-effects model later in this chapter, at its most basic level it argues that people move through a series of stages between their initial awareness or an issue and any subsequent, ultimate behavior toward it. It is typically modeled as the **C-A-B sequence**: cognitive effects (C) lead to affective effects (A), which lead to behavioral effects (B). Studying media coverage during the 2004 presidential campaign, Moon was able to link first- and second-order agenda-setting effects to political behaviors such as voting, engaging in political discussions, donating to candidates, and attending political meetings. He concluded, "In the learning hierarchy of CAB, people give more thought to those objects or attributes that they regard as important—and the greater the amount of thought, the stronger the attitudes. In turn, strong attitudes function as predictors of behaviors" (2011, p. 14).

C-A-B sequence

Persuasion model that assumes cognitive effects (C) lead to affective effects (A) which lead to behavioral effects (B)

Still, conceptual overlap between agenda-setting, priming, and framing continues to cloud a fuller understanding of agenda-setting, leading Dietram Scheufele to argue that agenda-setting and priming are compatible, but framing is quite different because it involves activation of entire interpretive schemas—not merely prioritization of individual objects or attributes. He wrote:

> Agenda-setting and priming rely on the notion of attitude accessibility. Mass media have the power to increase levels of importance assigned to issues by audience members. They increase the salience of issues or the ease with which these considerations can be retrieved from memory.... Framing, in contrast, is based on the concept of prospect theory; that is, on the assumption that subtle changes in the wording of the description of a situation might affect how audience members interpret this situation. In other words, framing influences how audiences think about issues, not by making aspects of the issue more salient, but by invoking interpretive schemas that influence the interpretation of incoming information. (2000, p. 309)

In Chapter 10, we will provide a much more detailed explanation of framing theory and return to this disagreement over the link between framing and agenda-setting. Still, both theories continue to be widely applied and often are used together as a way of developing a comprehensive strategy for examining the production, dissemination, and comprehension of news stories.

INSTANT ACCESS

Agenda-Setting

Strengths

1. Focuses attention on audience interaction with media
2. Empirically demonstrates links between media exposure, audience motivation to seek orientation, and audience perception of public issues
3. Integrates a number of similar ideas, including priming, story positioning, and story vividness

Weaknesses

1. Has roots in mass society theory
2. Is most applicable to (and often limited to) studies of news and political campaigns
3. Direction of agenda-setting effect is questioned by some

THE SPIRAL OF SILENCE

spiral of silence
Idea that people holding views contrary to those dominant in the media are moved to keep those views to themselves for fear of rejection

A somewhat more controversial theory of media and public opinion is the concept of the **spiral of silence**. This can be regarded as a form of agenda-setting but one clearly focused on societal-level consequences. In the words of its originator, Elisabeth Noelle-Neumann (1984), "Observations made in one context [the mass media] spread to another and encourage people either to proclaim their views or to swallow them and keep quiet until, in a spiraling process, the one view dominated the public scene and the other disappeared from public awareness as its adherents became mute. This is the process that can be called a 'spiral of silence'" (p. 5).

In other words, because of people's fear of isolation or separation from those around them, they tend to keep their attitudes to themselves when they think they are in the minority. The media, because of a variety of factors, tend to present one (or at most two) sides of an issue to the exclusion of others, which further encourages those people to keep quiet and makes it even tougher for the media to uncover and register that opposing viewpoint. Spiral of silence provides an excellent example of a theory that argues for cumulative effects of media. Once a spiral of silence is initiated, the magnitude of media influence will increase to higher and higher levels over time. If various viewpoints about agenda items are ignored, marginalized, or trivialized by media reports, people will be reluctant to talk about them. As time passes, those viewpoints will cease to be heard in public and therefore cannot affect political decision making.

The way news is collected and disseminated, Noelle-Neumann argued (1973), effectively restricts the breadth and depth of selection available to citizens. She identified three characteristics of the news media that produce this scarcity of perspective:

1. *Ubiquity:* The media are virtually everywhere as sources of information.
2. *Cumulation:* The various news media tend to repeat stories and perspectives across their different individual programs or editions, across the different media themselves, and across time.

3. *Consonance:* The congruence, or similarity, of values held by journalists influences the content they produce.

This view of media effects suggests that two different social processes, one macroscopic and one microscopic, simultaneously operate to produce effects. Audience members, because of their desire to be accepted, choose to remain silent when confronted with what they perceive to be prevailing counteropinion. Journalists, because of the dynamics of their news-gathering function, present a restricted selection of news, further forcing into silence those in the audience who wish to avoid isolation.

Spiral of silence theory has been the recipient of much criticism. For example, Katz (1983) saw it as little more than an updating of mass society theory, "Even in the democracies, media—like interpersonal communication—can impose acquiescence and silence in defiance of the free flow of information" (1983, p. 91). Charles Salmon and F. Gerald Kline (1985) wrote that the effects explained by the spiral of silence could just as easily be understood as the product of the bandwagon effect (everybody wants to join a winner) or projection (people's natural tendency to use their own opinions to form perceptions of the general climate of opinion around them). In addition, these critics argued that individual factors, such as a person's degree of ego-involvement in an issue, should be considered (regardless of the climate of opinion surrounding you, if you feel very strongly about the issue, you might not want to remain silent, even if isolation is a threat). Drawing on the notion that pluralistic groups can mediate media effects, Carroll Glynn and Jack McLeod (1985) faulted the spiral of silence for underestimating the power of people's communities, organizations, and reference groups in mitigating media influence on the larger society. Glynn and McLeod also questioned the generalizability of Noelle-Neumann's research (initially conducted almost exclusively in what was then West Germany) to the American situation, and they raised the possibility of situations in which media can actually move people to speak up rather than remain silent.

Noelle-Neumann (1985) responded simply that the media, especially television, adopt a prevailing attitude in any controversy as a matter of course, and as a result, they present a "dominant tendency." Holders of the minority viewpoint are willing to speak out if they feel that they are supported by the media dominant tendency (as during the civil rights movement).

Despite these disagreements, spiral of silence continues to hold research interest and enjoy empirical support. For example, Andrew Hayes and his colleagues tested Noelle-Neumann's idea of media activating the "quasi-statistical organ," something of a sixth sense allowing people, in her words, to assess the "distribution of opinions for and against his ideas, but above all by evaluating the strength (commitment), the urgency, and the chances of success of certain proposals and viewpoints" (1974, p. 44). In a cross-cultural study of eight nations, they demonstrated that "those who reported relatively greater FSI [fear of social isolation] reported relatively more attention to public opinion polls [suggesting] that such fear does serve to stimulate the quasi-statistical organ to tune into the signal of public opinion transmitted through the mass media in the form of public opinion poll results" (Hayes et al., 2011, p. 18).

INSTANT ACCESS

The Spiral of Silence

Strengths

1. Has macro-and micro-level explanatory power
2. Is dynamic
3. Accounts for shifts in public opinion, especially during campaigns
4. Raises important questions concerning the role and responsibility of news media

Weaknesses

1. Has overly pessimistic view of media influence and average people
2. Ignores other, simpler explanations of silencing
3. Ignores possible demographic and cultural differences in the silencing effect
4. Discounts power of community to counteract the silencing effect

NEWS PRODUCTION RESEARCH

During the past five decades, several important studies have been conducted on the production and consumption of news content (Crouse, 1973; Epstein, 1973; Fishman, 1980; Gans, 1979; Gitlin, 1980; Tuchman, 1978; Whiten, 2004). Most of this research was undertaken by British and American sociologists during the 1970s and 1980s. Their purpose was to critically analyze how journalists routinely cover news.

news production research
The study of how the institutional routines of news production inevitably produce distorted or biased content

W. Lance Bennett (1988, 2005a) surveyed this **news production research** literature and summarized four ways in which current news production practices distort or bias news content:

1. *Personalized news:* Most people relate better to individuals than to groups or institutions, so most news stories center around people. According to Bennett (1988), "The focus on individual actors[s] who are easy to identify with positively or negatively invites members of the news audience to project their own private feelings and fantasies directly onto public life" (p. 27). Thus personalization helps people relate to and find relevance in remote events. It does this, however, at a cost. "When television news reports about poverty focus on an individual's situation rather than on poverty more generally," wrote *New York Times Magazine* editor Alexander Star, "viewers look for someone (the poor person or someone else) who caused the hardship. But this … is to avoid the whole complicated process that brought someone grief. Stories call our attention away from chance, the influence of institutions or social structures, or the incremental contributions that different factors typically make to any outcome. And they follow conventions that verge on melodrama: events are caused by individuals who act deliberately, and what those individuals do reflects their underlying character. This, to put it mildly, is not how most things happen" (2008, p. 10). In short, reality becomes little more than a series of small, individual soap operas.

2. *Dramatized news:* Like all media commodities, news must be attractively packaged, and a primary means of doing this involves dramatization. Edward

Jay Epstein (1973) provided the following quotation from a policy memorandum written by a network television news producer: "Every news story should, without any sacrifice of probity or responsibility, display the attributes of fiction, of drama. It should have structure and conflict, problem and denouement, rising action and falling action, a beginning, a middle, and an end. These are not only the essentials of drama; they are the essentials of narrative" (pp. 4–5). So the all-too-frequent federal budget crises become dramatic contests between the president and the opposition party ... Who will blink first ... Who will prevail ... Who was most damaged? There is little reporting on what these conflicts mean for everyday people or for the future of representative democracy.

3. *Fragmented news:* The typical newspaper and news broadcast is made up of brief capsulized reports of events—snapshots of the social world. By constructing news in this way, journalists attempt to fulfill their norm of objectivity. Events are treated in isolation with little effort to interconnect them. Connection requires putting them into a broader context, and this would require making speculative, sometimes controversial linkages. Is there a link between three isolated plane crashes, or between three separate toxic waste spills? Should journalists remind readers of a candidate's three divorces when reporting on that politician's opposition to gay unions in the name of "preserving the sanctity of marriage"? By compartmentalizing events, news reports make it difficult for news consumers to make their own connections. Bennett argued that when journalists attempt to do analysis, they create a collage. They assemble evidence and viewpoints from conflicting sources and then juxtapose these pieces in a manner that defies interpretation, especially by news consumers who lack interest or background knowledge. These stories might meet the norm of being "balanced," but they don't assist people in making sense of things.

4. *Normalized news:* Stories about disasters or about social movements tend to "normalize" these potential threats to the status quo. Elite sources are allowed to explain disasters and to challenge movement members. Elites are presented as authoritative, rational, knowledgeable people who are effectively coping with threats. They can be trusted to bring things back to normal. If there is a problem with aircraft technology, it will be repaired—the Federal Aviation Administration (FAA) has the flight recorder and will pinpoint the cause of the crash as soon as possible. If social movements make legitimate demands, they will be satisfied—the governor has announced that she is forming a blue-ribbon commission to study the problem. Threat of terrorist attack? Don't worry, the government will protect you (just don't ask too many questions).

There are several reasons for this tendency. One is availability; reporters can always easily find officials. Another is the need to maintain access to valued news sources (more on this later). A third reason for normalization resides in the political economy of the news business (Chapter 5), and it is evident in this 2009 *Newsweek* cover story by reporter Evan Thomas on why liberals were upset with President Obama's handling of the economic recovery. He wrote, "If you are of the establishment persuasion (and I am), reading [these criticisms] makes you uneasy.... By definition, establishments believe in propping up the existing order. Members of the ruling class have a vested interest in keeping things pretty much the way they are. Safeguarding the status quo, protecting traditional institutions, can be healthy and useful, stabilizing and reassuring" (p. 22).

Gaye Tuchman (1978) conducted a now-classic example of news production research. She studied how the values held by journalists influence news, even when they make considerable effort to guard against that influence. She observed journalists as they covered social movements and concluded that production practices were implicitly biased toward support of the status quo. She found that reporters engage in **objectivity rituals**—they have set procedures for producing unbiased news stories that actually introduce bias.

For example, when leaders of a controversial movement were interviewed, their statements were never allowed to stand alone. Journalists routinely attempted to "balance" these statements by reporting the views of authorities who opposed the movements. Reporters frequently selected the most unusual or controversial statements made by movement leaders and contrasted these with the more conventional views of mainstream group leaders. Reporters made little effort to understand the overall philosophy of the movement. Lacking understanding, they inevitably took statements out of context and misrepresented movement ideals. Thus, though reporters never explicitly expressed negative views about these groups, their lack of understanding, their casual methods for selecting quotes, and their use of elite sources led to stories harmful to the movements they covered. Tuchman's arguments have been corroborated in research by Mark Fishman (1980) and Todd Gitlin (1980).

Environmental news, especially coverage of climate change, offers another example of how these objectivity rituals routinely support the status quo. Whereas the world scientific community overwhelmingly believes in global warming and the greenhouse effect, with some estimates as high as 95 percent of all scientists working in climatology, astronomy, and meteorology accepting these phenomena as scientific fact, when they are covered in the popular press, the issue is presented as in scientific dispute. Reporters, in their efforts to be "fair" and "objective," seek out spokespeople from "both sides," often turning to groups like the Global Climate Coalition, a public relations creation of the world's leading chemical companies. *Science* magazine's executive editor-in-chief, Donald Kennedy, explained the process to science writer Chris Mooney. "There's a very small set of people who question the consensus," he said. "And there are a great many thoughtful reporters in the media who believe that in order to produce a balanced story you've got to pick one commentator from side A and one commentator from side B. I call it the two-card Rolodex problem" (Mooney, 2004, p. 29). In fact, the United States press stands alone among the world's media industries in granting legitimacy to climate skeptics (Painter and Ashe, 2012).

In a 30-second television news spot that presents two experts, the logical audience reading is that this issue is in some scientific dispute. "The trouble with this conception of journalism," argues media critic Marty Kaplan, "is that it inherently tilts the playing field in favor of liars, who are expert at gaming this system. It muzzles reporters, forbidding them from crying foul, and requiring them to treat deception with the same respect they give to truth. It equates fairness with even-handedness, as though journalism were incompatible with judgment.

objectivity rituals
In news production research, the term for professional practices designed to ensure objectivity that are implicitly biased toward support of the status quo

INSTANT ACCESS

News Production Research

Strengths

1. Provides recommendations for potentially useful changes in news production practices
2. Raises important questions about routine news production practices
3. Can be used to study production of many different types of news
4. Can be combined with studies of news uses and effects to provide a comprehensive understanding of news

Weaknesses

1. Focuses on news production practices but has not empirically demonstrated their effect
2. Has pessimistic view of journalists and their social role
3. Has been ignored and rejected as impractical by practicing journalists
4. Needs to be updated since journalistic practices are being radically altered by the Internet and social media

'Straight news' isn't neutral. It's neutered—devoid of assessment, divorced from accountability, floating in a netherworld of pseudo-scientific objectivity that serves no one except the rascals it legitimizes" (2008). You can read more about news production research as it applies to coverage of climate change in the box, "We're Number 1! The American Press and Climate Change."

MEDIA INTRUSION THEORY

media intrusion theory
Idea that media have intruded into and taken over politics to the degree that politics have become subverted

Another body of research dealing with political communication is **media intrusion theory** (Davis, 1990). It is not a clearly articulated set of ideas but rather exists as a loosely connected set of assumptions underlying a broad range of empirical research in political science and communication. It assumes that the political system operates best when a responsible and informed political elite mediates between the public and its elected leaders. This elite, however, has a grassroots base. Leaders work their way into positions of power through their involvement in local, regional, and national social organizations—from local parent-teacher groups to the national Red Cross. Political parties serve as umbrella organizations in which leaders of various groups broker power. Most members of this elite don't hold political office but work behind the scenes serving the interests of their constituencies. Researchers are concerned because there is growing evidence that this political system is breaking down.

social capital
The influence potential leaders develop as a result of membership and participation in social groups

One worry is that many social groups that typically develop these leaders are losing membership and influence. Theorists refer to this as a decline in **social capital**, and a growing body of research has documented this decline in most Western nations. Media intrusion theorists blame media for this because many people stay home to consume media content rather than participate in local groups. The rise of television as a popular medium directly parallels this decline in social capital, so there is at least a plausible, if possibly spurious, link (Putnam, 2000).

The decline in social capital is seen as having many detrimental consequences. When politicians can no longer rely on local groups to which they had or have a

| THINKING ABOUT THEORY | We're Number 1! The American Press and Climate Change |

In 2004 the journal *Science* published a review of the existing scientific climate change research, 928 relevant studies, and discovered that not a single one denied that climate change was a reality. Additionally, most of the studies attributed that change to anthropogenic (human-made) influence. Author Naomi Oreskes, after listing scores of leading scientific organizations from around the world that had publically endorsed the existence of anthropogenic climate change, concluded, "Many details about climate interactions are not well understood, and there are ample grounds for continued research to provide a better basis for understanding climate dynamics. The question of what to do about climate change is also still open. But there is a scientific consensus on the reality of anthropogenic climate change. Climate scientists have repeatedly tried to make this clear" (p. 1686). Repeatedly? Why, with so much scientific certainty, must climate scientists have to work so hard? We all accept the science that cures our illnesses, keeps our planes aloft, and delivers the wonders of television and the Internet. What is different about the science surrounding climate change? Unless there is some grand conspiracy among the globe's tens of thousands of scientists that is visible only to a courageous band of nonscientists who know better, why is there still any dispute? News production researchers would argue that a, if not *the* culprit is the way we practice journalism in this country. Look at these examples of news coverage of climate change and decide for yourself.

February 17, 2013 saw the biggest environmental protest in history descend on Washington, D.C. Massive crowds gathered at the White House to protest the proposed Keystone pipeline that would carry oil from tar sand pits in northern Canada across America to the Gulf of Mexico. The headline for the *New York Times*' account of the action was "Obama Faces Risks in Pipeline Decision" (Broder, Krauss, and Austin, 2013, p. B1). This massive and controversial construction and technological undertaking, with its enormous and disputed environmental and economic implications, was reduced to a single question: the political risks it posed for President

Obama (*personalized news*). The first paragraph of the story read, "President Obama faces a knotty decision in whether to approve the much-delayed Keystone oil pipeline: a choice between alienating environmental advocates who overwhelmingly supported his candidacy or causing a deep and perhaps lasting rift with Canada." The framing of the story, from its first words, pitted American environmentalists against the nation of Canada (*dramatized news*). Although the story did quote portions of the activists' speeches, not a single environmentalist or protestor was interviewed. The only four people whom the reporters actually interviewed and quoted were a fellow from the Council on Foreign Relations, the vice-president of the Canadian Association of Petroleum Producers, the Canadian Ambassador to the United States, and the president of the Shell Canada oil company (*normalized news*). Nowhere in the story was there mention of earlier protests or actions against the pipeline. In addition, although the authors explained that pipeline proponents "say its approval would be an important step toward reducing reliance on the [Middle East] Organization of the Petroleum Exporting Countries for Energy," they failed to connect this claim (*fragmented news*) to the fact that U.S. oil consumption has declined every year since 2006 and that in 2011 fuel became America's top export for the first time in 21 years (Plumer, 2011).

Critics of media coverage of climate change also contend that journalists' insistence on maintaining "objectivity" actually introduces bias into their work. For example, here is an exchange from a May 2012 National Public Radio *NewsHour* report on climate change. Reporter Hari Sreenivasan offered that the National Academy of Sciences "says 97 percent to 98 percent of the most published climate researchers say humans are causing global warming. Still, persistent skeptics remain unconvinced.... A well-known conservative think tank, the Heartland Institute, doesn't trust the science behind the upcoming standards." He then introduced James Taylor—an attorney, not a scientist—who said, among other things, "Across the board, we have seen that warmer climate, warmer temperatures have always benefited

(Continued)

humans, and continue to do so." Mr. Taylor offered no evidence, scientific or otherwise, to which Mr. Sreenivasan added, "These are views challenged by scientific evidence." But he, too, offered no science (in Naureckas, 2012, pp. 6–7). "Objective" reporting that presents the positions of both sides as equally valid—National Academy of Sciences says "X," Heartland Institute says "Y." We report, you decide. But is it just the American press?

Researchers James Painter and Teresa Ashe asked that very question, conducting a comparison of newspaper coverage of climate change in six countries—Brazil, China, France, India, the United Kingdom, and the United States. They discovered that American papers are far more likely to publish uncontested claims from climate-change deniers than are those in other countries. Moreover, U.S. papers are "almost exclusively alone" in granting space to spokespeople who deny that the planet is warming at all. They called these deniers *trend skeptics*. U.S. papers are also Number 1 in granting coverage to *attribution skeptics*, people who agree the planet is warming but question if it is because of humans, and to *impact skeptics*, those who say that our warming planet is a good thing (2012).

But why should this be? Do you have an explanation beyond American media's self-imposed objectivity rituals, or their routine methods of collecting and reporting the news, as news production researchers argue? Could it be that there is insufficient audience interest in climate change news, so journalism outlets feel no real need to upset either side of the debate? For example, in January 2013 the *New York Times* closed its environment desk, saying that the issues it usually covered would now be taken up by other bureaus, for example, the business or Capitol Hill desks. Two months later, it shut down its environmentally based Green blog, leaving intact nine sports blogs, nine fashion and lifestyle blogs, an automobile blog, four technology blogs, and a host of others. These moves led journalism critic Kevin Drum (2013) to write, "Obviously the *Times* editors are going to come in for plenty of criticism over this, and that's fine. They deserve it. But let's face it: the reason they did this is almost certainly that the blog wasn't getting much traffic (and, therefore, not generating much advertising revenue). So a more constructive question is: Why do readers—even the well-educated, left-leaning readers of the *Times*—find environmental news so boring? Is it because we all write about it badly? Is it something inherent in the subject itself? Is it because most people think we don't really have any big environmental problems anymore aside from climate change? Or is it because it's just such a damn bummer to read endlessly about all the stuff we should stop doing because, somehow, it will end up destroying a rain forest somewhere?" Might Mr. Drum have ignored another likely possibility—that the routine National Academy of Sciences says "X," Heartland Institute says "Y" journalism serves no real value for people really interested in climate change?

connection to rally grassroots support for them, they are forced to turn to political consultants who advise them on how to use media to appeal to voters. But the televised political advertising and dramatic news coverage required to rally apathetic supporters come with a high price. Elites must devote precious time to raising money and then spend it on questionable forms of campaign communication.

The decline in social capital also has a direct impact on political parties. Ideally, parties function as "grand coalitions" of a broad range of social interest groups. They serve as a means by which these groups are able to achieve their goals. But as social capital has eroded, grassroots political party activity has also declined. This falloff has been well documented, as has been the drop in political affiliation and voting (Entman, 1989). Again, these changes in political parties occurred at the same time that television became a dominant medium.

Media intrusion theorists frequently cite the findings of the news production researchers to support their positions. They claim that political reports are too personalized, too dramatized, and too fragmented. Politics is often reported as a game between opposing teams, with the major politicians viewed as star players (Chapter 8). Stories focus on media-hyped spectacles—on big plays, on life-and-death struggles to score points. These reports don't help news consumers—in other words, citizens—develop useful understandings of politics. They don't systematically inform people about issues and how candidates would deal with issues. Rather, they encourage consumers to become political spectators, content to sit on the sidelines while the stars play the game.

Some journalists reject the media intrusion argument, asserting that they have little control over elections. They don't intrude into politics. Instead, their reporting efforts are being disrupted by political consultants. They point out that the political parties chose to give up control over presidential nominations when they decided to permit primary elections to be held across the nation. As the power of political parties has declined and the influence of political consultants has grown, manipulation of media by politicians has increased. Political consultants have developed very effective strategies for obtaining favorable news coverage for their candidates (Davis, 1990; Enda and Mitchell, 2013). During campaigns, journalists rely on particular production practices for gathering and generating news stories. Consultants are quite knowledgeable about these practices and skilled at supplying useful (to them) information and convenient events. These "anticipated" events make it very easy for journalists to cover the candidate as the consultant wants and hard for them to find material for alternate stories.

Robert Entman (1989) argues that a solution can be reached only if politicians, journalists, and the public change their behavior. Politicians must stop relying on manipulative and expensive strategies; journalists must cover issues rather than spectacles; the public must give serious attention to issues, not campaign spectacles and personalities. But how likely is it that these solutions can actually be implemented? Politicians and journalists are reluctant to change patterns of behavior that serve their immediate purposes—getting elected to office and attracting audiences to campaign coverage. And after every election campaign in recent years, private foundations have sponsored major conferences at which politicians and journalists have pledged to improve the quality of campaign communication. But the same mistakes are repeated in campaign after campaign. For example, campaign spending in the 2012 elections was a record $9.8 billion. Television stations were happy to reap windfall profits from campaign advertising and journalists expressed frustration about the way political consultants manipulate news coverage … and little changes. Soon after that election, political scientist Norman Ornstein had this advice to those who head news organizations, "I understand your concerns about advertisers. I understand your concerns about being labeled as biased. But what are you there for? What's the whole notion of a free press for if you're not going to report without fear or favor and you're not going to report what your reporters, after doing their due diligence, see as the truth? … And if you don't do that, then you can expect I think a growing drumbeat of criticism that you're failing in your fundamental responsibility. Your job is to report the truth" (in Froomkin, 2012a).

INSTANT ACCESS

Media Intrusion Theory

Strengths	Weaknesses
1. Explains how media may be disrupting important social institutions	1. Focuses on operation of news media but has not empirically demonstrated its effect
2. Provides a critical analysis of the operation of news media organizations during elections	2. Has overly pessimistic view of news media and their social role
3. Explains why political parties have been losing control over political primaries	3. Focuses too much on intrusion into politics
	4. Assumes that political parties should dominate politics

INFORMATION (INNOVATION) DIFFUSION THEORY

information diffusion theory
Theory that explains how innovations are introduced and adopted by various communities

meta-analysis
Identifies important consistencies in previous research findings on a specific issue and systematically integrates them into a fuller understanding

early adopters
In information/innovation diffusion theory, people who adopt an innovation early, even before receiving significant amounts of information

In 1962, Everett Rogers combined information-flow research findings with studies about the flow of information and personal influence in several fields, including anthropology, sociology, and rural agricultural extension work. He developed what he called diffusion theory. Rogers's effort at integrating information-flow research with diffusion theory was so successful that information-flow theory became known as **information diffusion theory** (and when it is applied to the diffusion of something other than information—that is, technologies—it is called *innovation diffusion theory*). Rogers used both labels to title subsequent editions of his book.

Rogers's work also illustrates the power of **meta-analysis** when it comes to developing a more useful middle-range theory. A meta-analysis identifies important consistencies in previous research findings on a specific issue and systematically integrates them into a fuller understanding. If previous research has been grounded in several different but related low-level theories, these can be combined to create new, more macroscopic theories. Rogers assembled data from numerous empirical studies to show that when new technological innovations are introduced, they pass through a series of stages before being widely adopted. First, most people become aware of them, often through information from mass media. Second, the innovations will be adopted by a very small group of innovators, or **early adopters**. Third, opinion leaders learn from the early adopters then try the innovation themselves. Fourth, if opinion leaders find the innovation useful, they encourage their friends—the opinion followers. Finally, after most people have adopted the innovation, a group of laggards, or late adopters, makes the change.

Information/innovation diffusion theory is an excellent example of the strength and the limitations of a middle-range theory (Chapter 4). It successfully integrates a vast amount of empirical research. Rogers reviewed thousands of studies. Information/innovation diffusion theory guided this research and facilitated its interpretation. Nevertheless, it has some serious limitations. Like information-flow theory and social marketing theory (discussed later in this chapter), information/innovation diffusion theory is a source-dominated theory that sees the communication process from the point of view of an elite who has decided to diffuse specific information or an innovation. Diffusion theory "improves" on information-flow theory by providing more and better strategies for overcoming barriers to diffusion.

Information/innovation diffusion theory assigns a limited role to mass media: they mainly create awareness of new innovations. But it does assign a very central role to different types of people critical to the diffusion process. Media *do* directly influence early adopters, but these people are generally well informed and careful media users. Early adopters try out innovations and then tell others about them. They directly influence opinion leaders, who in turn influence everyone else. **Change agents** are also key people involved with diffusion. Their job is to be highly informed about innovations and assist anyone who wants to make changes. Rogers recommended that change agents lead diffusion efforts; for example, they could go into rural communities and directly influence early adopters and opinion leaders about new agricultural practices. In addition to drawing attention to innovations, media can also be used to provide a basis for group discussions led by change agents.

Information/innovation diffusion theory represented an important advance over earlier effects-trend theories. Like other classic work of the early 1960s, it drew from existing empirical generalizations and synthesized them into a coherent, insightful perspective. Information/innovation diffusion theory was consistent with most findings from effects surveys and persuasion experiments; above all, it was very practical, as it laid the foundation for numerous promotional communication and marketing theories and the campaigns they support even today.

But the limitations of information/innovation diffusion theory were also serious. It had some unique drawbacks stemming from its application. For example, it facilitated the adoption of innovations that were sometimes not well understood or even desired by adopters. To illustrate, a campaign to get Georgia farm wives to can vegetables was initially judged a great success until researchers found that very few women were using the vegetables. They mounted the glass jars on the walls of their living rooms as status symbols. Most didn't know any recipes for cooking preserved vegetables, and those who tried using canned vegetables found that family members didn't like the taste. This sort of experience was duplicated around the

change agents
In information/innovation diffusion theory, those who directly influence early adopters and opinion leaders

---

INSTANT ACCESS

Information/Innovation Diffusion Theory

Strengths

1. Integrates large amount of empirical findings into useful theory
2. Provides practical guide for information campaigns in United States and abroad
3. Has guided the successful adoption of useful innovations in the United States and abroad

Weaknesses

1. Is linear and source-dominated
2. Underestimates power of media, especially contemporary media
3. Stimulates adoption by groups that don't understand or want the innovation

world: corn was grown in Mexico and rice was grown in Southeast Asia that no one wanted to eat; farmers in India destroyed their crops by using too much fertilizer; farmers adopted complex new machinery only to have it break down and stand idle after change agents left. Mere top-down diffusion of innovations didn't guarantee long-term success.

SOCIAL MARKETING THEORY

social marketing theory
Collection of middle-range theories concerning the promotion of socially valuable information

During the early 1970s, a new macroscopic theory of media and society began to take shape that shared important similarities with diffusion theory. It is known as **social marketing theory**. It is not a unified body of thought but rather a more or less integrated collection of middle-range theories dealing with the process of "creating, communicating, and delivering benefits that a target audience(s) wants in exchange for audience behavior that benefits society without financial profit to the marketer" (Kotler and Lee, 2008, p. 7). Public health practitioners have been especially drawn to this theory and use it to promote or discourage many different behaviors; and as you might imagine, elaboration likelihood and narrative persuasion theory figure quite prominently in contemporary social marketing theory. But rather than describing each of the theories that make up social marketing theory, we will look at the overarching theoretical framework and then discuss some of its important features. Readers interested in a more extended discussion of these theories and their application might consult other sources (Grier and Bryant, 2004; Kotler and Lee, 2008).

Like diffusion theory, social marketing theory is practically oriented and essentially source-dominated. It assumes the existence of a benign information provider seeking to bring about useful, beneficial social change. It gives these providers a framework for designing, carrying out, and evaluating information campaigns. In its most recent forms, it pays increased attention to audience activity and the need to reach active audiences with information they are seeking.

In addition to sharing many assumptions and concerns with diffusion theory, social marketing theory is also a logical extension of the persuasion theories outlined in Chapter 8. It represents an effort to increase the effectiveness of mass media–based information campaigns through greater understanding and manipulation of aspects of societal and psychological factors. Social marketing theory does this by identifying a variety of social system–level and psychological barriers to the flow of media information and influence. It anticipates these barriers and includes strategies for overcoming them. Some strategies are ingenious; others involve the brute force of saturation advertising. Social marketing theory has several key features:

1. **Methods for inducing audience awareness of campaign topics.** A key first step in promoting ideas is to make people aware of their existence. The easiest but most costly way to do this is with a saturation television advertising campaign. As social marketing theories have gained sophistication, other methods have been developed that are almost as effective but much less costly. These include using news coverage, embedding messages in entertainment narratives, and new media channels to induce awareness.

2. Methods for targeting messages at specific audience segments most receptive or susceptible to those messages. Limited-effects research demonstrated how to identify audience segments most vulnerable to specific types of messages (Chapter 4). Once identified, messages can be targeted at them. **Targeting** is one of several concepts borrowed from product marketing and converted to the marketing of beneficial ideas or behaviors. By identifying the most vulnerable segments and then reaching them with the most efficient channel available, targeting strategies reduce promotional costs while increasing efficiency.

targeting
Identifying specific audience segments and reaching them through the most efficient available channel

3. Methods for reinforcing messages within targeted segments and for encouraging these people to influence others through face-to-face communication. Even vulnerable audience members are likely to forget or fail to act on messages unless those messages are reinforced by similar information coming from several channels. Various strategies have been developed to make certain that multiple messages are received from several channels. These strategies include visits by change agents, group discussions, messages placed simultaneously in several media, and social network site reinforcement of messages delivered by traditional media.

4. Methods for cultivating images and impressions of people, products, or services. These methods are most often used when it is difficult to arouse audience interest. If people aren't interested in a topic, it is unlikely that they will seek and learn information about it. Lack of interest forms a barrier to the flow of information. One prominent method used to cultivate images is image advertising that presents easily recognizable, visually compelling images designed to imply a relationship between these attractive images and the attitude or behavior being promoted. Current social marketing thinking naturally accepts that these relationships can be easily, and more successfully, made through entertainment narratives.

5. Methods for stimulating interest and inducing information seeking by audience members. Information seeking occurs when a sufficient level of interest in ideas can be generated. Social marketers have developed numerous techniques to do just this. Using popular prime-time television programs is one example, but so too are devices such as 5K races, bus tours, colored-ribbon and wristband campaigns, and celebrity involvement.

6. Methods for inducing desired decision making or positioning. Once people are aware and informed, or at least have formed strong images or impressions, they can be moved toward either a conscious decision or an unconscious prioritization or positioning. Media messages can be transmitted through a variety of channels and used to highlight the value of choosing a specific option or prioritizing one service or behavior relative to others. Change agents and opinion leaders can also be used, though these are more expensive. This is a critical stage in any communication campaign because it prepares people to take an action desired by social marketers.

7. Methods for activating audience segments, especially those who have been targeted by the campaign. Ideally, these audiences will include people who are properly positioned but have not yet found an opportunity to act. In other cases, people will have prioritized an attitude, service, or behavior but must be confronted with a situation in which they are compelled to act. These are *contemplators*; they are *awake*, but not yet *in action* (Kotler and Lee, 2008, p. 273). Many communication campaigns fail because they lack a mechanism for stimulating action. People seem to be influenced by campaigns, but that influence isn't effectively translated into action. Social marketers employ a variety of techniques to activate people, for example, change agents, free merchandise, free and convenient transportation, free services, moderate fear appeals, and broadcast or telephone appeals from high-status sources.

One of the simplest yet most comprehensive social marketing theories is the hierarchy-of-effects model, because "it makes sense to posit that before people consume most goods and services, they have some information about these goods and services and form some attitude, no matter how weak that attitude or how quickly the attitude was formed" (Barry, 2002, p. 46). The hierarchy-of-effects model assumes that it is important to differentiate a large number of persuasion effects—some easily induced and others taking more time and effort. It permits development of a step-by-step persuasion strategy in which the effort begins with easily induced effects, such as awareness, and monitors them using survey research. Feedback from that research is used to decide when to transmit messages designed to produce more difficult effects, such as decision making or action. Thus the effort begins by creating audience awareness, then cultivates images or induces interest and information seeking, reinforces learning of information or images, aids people in making the "right" decisions, and then activates those people. At each step, the effectiveness of the campaign to that point is monitored, and the messages are changed when the proper results aren't obtained.

The hierarchy-of-effects model was first developed by product marketers (note "goods and services" from just above) but is now widely applied to social marketing. Critics argue that its assumption that certain effects necessarily precede others in time is unwarranted. Some people, for example, can be moved to act without ever being informed or even making a decision about an issue, especially one beneficial to her or his health. Social marketers respond that although they can't hope to induce all the desired effects in every targeted person, they have evidence that a well-structured, step-by-step campaign using survey data to provide feedback is much more successful than persuasion efforts based on simple linear effects models.

INSTANT ACCESS

Social Marketing Theory

Strengths

1. Provides practical guide for information campaigns in United States and abroad
2. Can be applied to serve socially desirable ends
3. Builds on attitude change and diffusion theories
4. Is accepted and used by media campaign planners

Weaknesses

1. Is source-dominated
2. Doesn't consider ends of campaigns
3. Underestimates intellect of average people
4. Ignores constraints to reciprocal flow of information
5. Can be costly to implement
6. Has difficulty assessing cultural barriers to influence

Critics of social marketing point to limitations very similar to those raised in our discussion of information-flow theory and of diffusion theory. Though social marketing theory squeezes some benefit out of the older source-dominated linear-effects models, it also suffers many of their limitations. In social marketing models, sources use feedback from target audiences to adjust their campaigns. This use is generally limited to changes in messages; however, long-term persuasion or information goals don't change. If audiences seem resistant, social marketers try new messages in an effort to break down resistance. They give little thought to whether the audience might be justified or correct in resisting information or influence. If the effort fails, they blame the audience for being apathetic or ignorant—people simply don't know what's good for them.

Thus the social marketing model is tailored to situations in which elite sources are able to dominate elements of the larger social system. These powerful sources can prevent counter-elites from distributing information or marshaling organized opposition. The theory doesn't allow for social conflict and thus can't be applied to situations in which conflict has escalated to even moderate levels. It applies best to routine forms of beneficial information.

MEDIA SYSTEM DEPENDENCY THEORY

media system dependency theory Idea that the more a person depends on having needs gratified by media use, the more important the media's role will be in the person's life and, therefore, the more influence those media will have

In its simplest terms, **media system dependency theory** asserts that the more a person depends on having his or her needs met by media use, the more important will be the role that media play in the person's life, and therefore the more influence those media will have on that person. From a macroscopic societal perspective, if more and more people become dependent on media, media institutions will be reshaped to serve these dependencies, then the overall influence of media will rise, and media's role in society will become more central. Thus there should be a direct relationship between the amount of overall dependency and the degree of media influence or centrality at any given point in time.

Melvin DeFleur and Sandra Ball-Rokeach (1975, pp. 261–263) have provided a fuller explanation using several assertions. First, the "basis of media influence lies in the relationship between the larger social system, the media's role in that system, and audience relationships to the media." Effects occur not because all-powerful media or omnipotent sources compel them, but because the media operate in a given way in a given social system to meet given audience wants and needs.

Second, "the degree of audience dependence on media information is the key variable in understanding when and why media messages alter audience beliefs, feelings, or behavior." The ultimate occurrence and shape of media effects rests with audience members and is related to how necessary a given medium or message is to them. The uses people make of media determine media's influence. If we rely on many sources other than media for our information about events, then the role of media is less than if we rely exclusively on a few media sources.

Third, "in our industrial society, we are becoming increasingly dependent on the media (a) to understand the social world, (b) to act meaningfully and effectively in society, and (c) for fantasy and escape." As our world becomes more complex and as it changes more rapidly, we not only need the media to a greater degree to help us make sense, to help us understand what our best responses might be, and to help us relax and cope, but we also ultimately come to know that world largely through those media. Note the emphasis on meaning-making (discussed more fully in Chapter 10) in this assertion. As we use media to make sense of the social world, we permit media to shape our expectations.

Finally, "the greater the need and consequently the stronger the dependency … the greater the likelihood" that the media and their messages will have an effect. Not everyone will be equally influenced by media. Those who have greater needs and thus greater dependency on media will be most influenced.

Recall our discussion of what constitutes an active audience (Chapter 7); we know that the best way to think of activity is to think of it as existing on a continuum, from completely inactive media consumers to very active ones. Because they tied audience activity to audience dependence, DeFleur and Ball-Rokeach described media dependency in just that way. Moreover, they explained that an individual's (or society's) level of dependency is a function of (1) "the number and centrality (importance) of the specific information-delivery functions served by a medium," and (2) the degree of change and conflict present in society.

These assertions can be illustrated with an example involving media use during a crisis. Think of your own media use the last time you found yourself in a natural crisis—in other words, in a time of change or conflict (earthquake, tornado, hurricane, or serious rainstorm or snowstorm). You probably spent more time watching television news than you did watching comedy shows. Now consider what happens when electricity fails during a crisis and cell phone networks are overwhelmed by callers trying to locate family and friends. Your portable radio would likely assume the greater "number and centrality of information delivery functions." Radio and radio news would become your medium and content of choice, respectively. And no doubt, if the crisis deepened, your dependence would increase. So might your attentiveness and willingness to respond as "directed" by that medium and its messages. The point of media system dependency theory is that we have developed a range of routine uses for various media, and we can easily adapt these uses to serve our needs. If one medium fails or is temporarily unavailable, we have no difficulty turning to others. What is important is how we come to depend upon the range of media available to us.

DeFleur and Ball-Rokeach refined and expanded their media system dependency theory a number of times (e.g., DeFleur and Ball-Rokeach, 1989) to account for such "system change," but their thesis never varied much beyond their initial assertion that media can and do have powerful effects. Media dependency has been measured by postpositivist researchers in a variety of ways, and each has its drawbacks. It has not yet been conclusively demonstrated that the experience of media dependency by average people is strongly related to a broad range of effects. Can we be dependent on media without *experiencing* dependency? Can we experience dependency when we are actually quite independent? If so, maybe we should gauge dependency with behavioral rather than attitudinal measures. Or maybe we need to conduct experiments rather than collect survey data. Is this theory better at explaining the consequences of short-term, situationally induced dependency (i.e., reaction to a crisis) than long-term chronic dependency?

Finally, the theory doesn't directly address the question of whether there is some ideal level of media dependency. Are Americans currently too dependent on media or too independent? Is the trend toward increased or decreased dependency? Will new media increase our dependency or make us more independent? How will new user-directed technologies like the Internet and smartphones reshape dependence and independence? "You see these tethered souls everywhere: The father joining in an intense Twitter debate at his daughter's dance recital. The woman cracking wise on Facebook while strolling through the mall. The guy on a date reviewing his fish tacos on Yelp. Not to mention drivers staring down instead of through their windshields," says technology writer Michael Rosenwald, "The stereotype of the computer-addicted recluse in the basement has been blown away; smartphones make it possible to turn off the physical world while walking through it. A recent Pew Research Center study found that 'a significant proportion of people who visit public and semipublic spaces are online while in those spaces.' Parks. Libraries. Restaurants. Houses of worship" (2010, p. A1). Because of these lingering questions, researchers interested in audience-use questions are increasingly turning toward uses and gratification and entertainment theory (Chapter 7) rather than media system dependency theory. Nonetheless, its importance to directing the discipline's attention to the presence of powerful media effects and to the relationship between micro-level and macro-level effects should not be dismissed. Ball-Rokeach explained the theory's genesis, "I became convinced that a media effects theory had to be able to explain both the occurrence and nonoccurrence of media effects ... and, second, the theory had to have cross-level applicability ... because media effects at macrolevels had consequences for microlevels and vice versa.... Finally, MSD theory is a theory of media power" (1998, pp. 12–13).

THE KNOWLEDGE GAP

A team of researchers at the University of Minnesota (Donohue, Tichenor, and Olien, 1986; Tichenor, Donohue, and Olien, 1970, 1980) developed a theory of society in which mass media and the use of media messages play a central role. Their original research focused on the role of news media in cities and towns of various sizes. It viewed these areas as subsystems within larger state and regional social systems. The team began by empirically establishing that news media systematically inform some segments of the population, specifically persons in higher

INSTANT ACCESS

Media Systems Dependency Theory

Strengths

1. Is elegant and descriptive
2. Allows for systems orientation
3. Integrates microscopic and macroscopic theory
4. Is especially useful in explaining the role of media during crisis and social change

Weaknesses

1. Is difficult to verify empirically
2. Meaning and power of dependency are unclear
3. Lacks power in explaining long-term effects

knowledge gap
Systematic differences in knowledge between better-informed and less-informed segments of a population

socioeconomic groups, better than others, producing a **knowledge gap**. "As the infusion of mass media information into a social system increases, segments of the population with higher socioeconomic status tend to acquire this information at a faster rate than the lower segments, so that the gap in knowledge between these segments tends to increase rather than decrease" (Tichenor, Donohue, and Olien, 1970, pp. 159–160). The knowledge-gap hypothesis assumes that there is a preexisting gap between these segments of the population, one that is exacerbated by audience and media factors. While there are differences in each group's ability to process and interpret information, and those of higher socioeconomic status tend to be more motivated to pay attention to political information in the media, most public affairs information is delivered by print media, which are intentionally demographically targeted at more affluent audiences.

Yoori Hwang and Se-Hoon Jeong (2009) conducted a meta-analysis of 46 "primary" investigations of the knowledge gap, demonstrating support for its central assertion, that there were indeed knowledge disparities between different social strata. They also discovered that the gap was greatest for "socio-political" and international topics, but less so for health-related and local information. Their analysis did challenge knowledge gap's original contention that the gap widens over time, instead finding support for the *constant gap*, that is, a preexisting gap that is not increased, but also is not reduced. The researchers acknowledged that the presence of a constant gap is "disappointing particularly when it exists despite planned media campaigns that attempt to provide useful health or political information. This constant gap among high and low SES individuals can be problematic as a health knowledge gap can lead to health disparities and a political knowledge gap can result in differences in participatory behaviors" (p. 533).

Thomas Holbrook (2002) examined knowledge gap on a national level, finding that the gaps actually narrowed during the course of presidential campaigns. He analyzed data from the National Election Studies from 1976 to 1996 and found that specific events such as political debates were linked to decreases in knowledge gaps. Holbrook's findings are consistent with earlier findings linking reduction of gaps to increases in social conflict that spark widespread public discussion and information seeking.

Naturally, the Internet, with its presumed "democracy" and all-information-all-the-time orientation, has reignited interest in knowledge-gap theory. Heinz Bonfadelli (2002) offered a pessimistic view of the Internet's potential role. In

digital divide
The lack of access to communication technology among people of color, the poor, the disabled, and those in rural communities

Switzerland, he found a **digital divide** between affluent, better-educated young adults who regularly use the Internet for information and their less-affluent, less-educated peers who either don't have access to the Internet or use it only for entertainment. Not surprisingly, this divide was linked to gaps in knowledge. In the United States, discussion of the knowledge gap is increasingly accompanied by talk of a persistent digital divide—the chronic lack of access to new communication technologies by specific groups of people. For example, although more than 80 percent of Americans have computers in their homes ("Internet Users in the World," 2013), that number lags for less-educated, lower-income, rural, Hispanic, and African American households and households in the East South Central region of the country. One-third of Americans, 100 million people, do not have broadband Internet access, many because of cost or location. Only 40 percent of adults with household incomes under $20,000 have broadband, and another 19 million people living in rural areas go without that service because cable and telecom companies do not find it sufficiently profitable to serve their locales (Smith, 2012). The Knight Commission on the Information Needs of Communities in a Democracy (2009) discovered that there are two Americas—one completely wired, one not very well—that produced not only a knowledge gap, but also literacy and social participation gaps as well. But even when people are wired, a social participation gap remains. A Pew Internet & American Life Project national study discovered that "contrary to the hopes of some advocates, the Internet is not changing the socio-economic character of civic engagement in America. Just as in offline civic life, the well-to-do and well-educated are more likely than those less well-off to participate in online political activities such as emailing a government official, signing an online petition, or making a political contribution" (Smith et al., 2009).

However, it is not only variable access to media technologies that produces knowledge gaps. Individual differences such as information-processing ability and level of cognitive complexity (McLeod and Perse, 1994) and perceived value of being informed (Ettema and Kline, 1977) also widen gaps, as does the quality of the information presented by news organizations. In a comparative study of knowledge gaps in four nations—the United States, Britain, Denmark, and Finland—James Curran, Shanto Iyengar, Brink Lund, and Inka Salovaara-Moring discovered a significant knowledge gap between American television news viewers and viewers of news in those other lands. They attributed the gap to the public service orientation of television news in those latter three countries, which "devotes more attention to public affairs and international news … gives greater prominence to news [broadcasting news several times an evening in what Americans would call prime time] … and encourages higher levels of news consumption" (2009, p. 5). These factors were strong enough to minimize the knowledge gap in those countries between the well-educated and less-educated and between those who were financially well-off and those who weren't.

INSTANT ACCESS

The Knowledge Gap

Strengths

1. Identifies potentially troublesome gaps between groups
2. Provides ideas for overcoming gaps
3. Presumes reciprocity and audience activity in communication
4. Is grounded in systems theory

Weaknesses

1. Assumes gaps are always dysfunctional; not all researchers agree
2. Limits focus to gaps involving news and social conflicts
3. Can't address fundamental reasons for gaps (e.g., poor schools, differences in cognitive skills, or limited access to information sources)

CULTIVATION ANALYSIS

cultivation analysis
Theory that television "cultivates" or creates a worldview that, although possibly inaccurate, becomes the reality because people believe it to be so

Cultivation analysis, a theory developed by George Gerbner during the 1970s and 1980s, addresses macro-level questions about the media's role in society, although it represents a hybrid combining aspects of both macroscopic and microscopic cultural theories. Some researchers regarded it as a likely prototype for future research, whereas others considered it a poor example of how to do research. This controversy was a pivotal one in the development of mass communication theory. It came when the limited-effects perspective was strong but beginning to show signs of waning and cultural theories were receiving more serious attention from media scholars. The controversy reveals a great deal about various opposing perspectives, some of which are still widely held. As you'll see from our review of this theory, it has undergone and continues to undergo important changes. The cultivation theory employed by most researchers today is very different from that originally formulated by Gerbner. As the theory has evolved it has attracted growing interest from postpositivist researchers. Somewhat ironically, a theory that was rejected by many postpositivists three decades ago is now widely accepted as a useful way to understand and explain media effects.

You can begin your own evaluation of cultivation analysis by answering three questions:

1. In any given week, what are the chances that you will be involved in some kind of violence: about 1 in 10 or about 1 in 100? In the actual world, about 0.41 violent crimes occur per 100 Americans, or less than 1 in 200. In the world of prime-time television, though, more than 64 percent of all characters are involved in violence. Was your answer closer to the actual or to the television world?

2. What percentage of all working males in the United States toil in law enforcement and crime detection: 1 or 5 percent? The U.S. Census says 1 percent; television says 12 percent. What did you say?

3. Of all the crimes that occur in the United States in any year, what proportion is violent crime, like murder, rape, robbery, and assault? Would you guess 15 or 25 percent? If you hold the television view, you chose the higher number. On television, 77 percent of all major characters who commit crimes commit the violent kind. The *Statistical Abstract of the United States* reports that in actuality only 10 percent of all crime in the country is violent crime.

These questions come from Gerbner and his colleagues, but their point was much more complex than simply stating that those who watch more television give answers more similar to the "TV answer" than to answers provided by official data. Their central argument is that television is a "message system" that "cultivates" or creates a worldview that, although possibly inaccurate, becomes the reality simply because we, as a people, believe it to be the reality and base our judgments about our own everyday worlds on that "reality."

You'll remember from Chapter 6 that during the 1960s and early 1970s interest in television as a social force, especially the medium's relationship to increasing individual and societal violence, reached its zenith. Two very important national examinations of the media, again especially television, were undertaken. The first was the National Commission on the Causes and Prevention of Violence, held in 1967 and 1968, and the second was the 1972 Surgeon General's Scientific Advisory Committee on Television and Social Behavior. One scientist involved in both efforts was Gerbner. His initial task was simple enough: produce an annual content analysis of a sample week of network television prime-time fare—the **Violence Index**—that would demonstrate, from season to season, how much violence was actually present in that programming. The index, however, was not without critics, and serious controversy developed around it. *TV Guide* magazine even called it the "million-dollar mistake."

Violence Index
Annual content analysis of a sample week of network television prime-time fare demonstrating how much violence is present

Debate raged about the definition of *violence*. How was "television violence" defined? Was verbal aggression really violence? Were two teenagers playfully scuffling violence? Was cartoon violence a problem? Critics raised other issues. Why examine only network prime-time? After school, early evening, and weekends are particularly heavy viewing times for most children. Why count only violence? Why not racism and sexism? Nonetheless, Gerbner and his associates attempted to meet the demands of their critics and each year refined their definitional and reporting schemes.

Regardless of the attacks on the researchers' work, one thing did not change: Year in, year out, violence still appeared on prime-time television to a degree unmatched in the "real world," and it was violence of a nature unlike that found in that "real world." If television was truly a mirror of society, or if that medium did simply reinforce the status quo, this video mirror, the Violence Index seemed to say, was more like one found in a fun house than in a home. In their 1982 analysis of television violence, for example, Gerbner and his colleagues discovered that "crime in prime time is at least ten times as rampant as in the real world [and] an average of five to six acts of overt physical violence per hour involves over half of all major characters" (Gerbner et al., 1982, p. 106).

Although the Violence Index identified similar disparities between real-world and televised violence from its very start, the single most important criticism of that annual measure—"So what?"—was finally addressed in 1973. To demonstrate a causal link between the fluctuating levels of annual televised mayhem and viewers' aggressive behavior, the Gerbner team moved beyond the Violence Index, redefining its work as the **Cultural Indicators Project**. In it the researchers conducted regular periodic examinations of television programming and the "conceptions of social reality that viewing cultivates in child and adult audiences" (Gerbner and Gross, 1976, p. 174). And now that they were addressing the "so what" question, they extended their research to issues well beyond violence.

Cultural Indicators Project
In cultivation analysis, periodic examinations of television programming and the conceptions of social reality cultivated by viewing

The cultural indicators research made five assumptions. First, *television is essentially and fundamentally different from other forms of mass media*. Television is in more than 98 percent of all American homes. It does not require literacy, as do newspapers, magazines, and books. Unlike the movies, it's free (if you don't count the cost of advertising added to the products we buy). Unlike radio, it combines pictures and sound. It requires no mobility, as do places of worship, movies, and theaters. Television is the only medium in history with which people can interact at the earliest and latest years of life, not to mention all those years in between.

Because of television's accessibility and availability to everyone, the second assumption of the Cultural Indicators Project is *the medium is the "central cultural* arm" of American society; it is, as Gerbner and his colleagues argued, "the chief creator of synthetic cultural patterns (entertainment and information) for the most heterogeneous mass publics in history, including large groups that have never shared in any common public message systems" (1978, p. 178).

The third assumption flows logically from this shared reality: "*The substance of the consciousness cultivated by TV is not so much specific attitudes and opinions as more basic assumptions about the 'facts' of life and standards of judgment on which conclusions are based*" (Gerbner and Gross, 1976, p. 175).

Because most television stations and networks are commercially supported (and therefore entrenched in the status quo) and target more or less the same audiences, and because they depend on relatively generic, formulaic, cyclical, repetitive forms of programs and stories, the fourth cultural indicators assumption is the idea that *television's major cultural function is to stabilize social patterns, to cultivate resistance to change*; it is a medium of socialization and enculturation. Again, Gerbner and his cohorts said it well:

> The repetitive pattern of television's mass-produced messages and images forms the mainstream of the common symbolic environment that cultivates the most widely shared conceptions of reality. We live in terms of the stories we tell—stories about what things exist, stories about how things work, and stories about what to do—and television tells them all through news, drama, and advertising to almost everybody most of the time. (Gerbner et al., 1978, p. 178)

If you're reading closely, you can hear echoes of Carey's call to understand television as a ritual rather than transmissional medium. In adopting this more ritualistic view, however, the cultural indicators researchers' fifth assumption—*the observable, measurable, independent contributions of television to the culture are relatively small*—caused additional controversy. In explaining this position, Gerbner used his **ice-age analogy**: "But just as an average temperature shift of a few degrees can lead to an ice age or the outcomes of elections can be determined by slight margins, so too can a relatively small but pervasive influence make a crucial difference. The 'size' of an 'effect' is far less critical than the direction of its steady contribution" (Gerbner et al., 1980, p. 14). The argument was not that television's impact was inconsequential, but rather that although television's measurable, observable, independent effect on the culture at any point in time might be small, that impact was, nonetheless, present and significant. Put somewhat differently, television's impact on our collective sense of reality is real and important, even though that effect might be beyond clear-cut scientific measurement, might defy easy observation, and might be inextricably bound to other factors in the culture.

ice-age analogy
In cultivation analysis, idea that the degree of television's influence is less critical than the direction of its steady contribution

THE PRODUCTS OF CULTIVATION ANALYSIS

To scientifically demonstrate their view of television as a culturally influential medium, cultivation researchers depended on a four-step process. The first they called **message system analysis**, detailed content analyses of television programming to assess its most recurring and consistent presentations of images, themes, values, and portrayals. The second step is the formulation of questions about viewers'

message system analysis
In cultivation analysis, detailed content analyses of television programming to assess recurring and consistent presentations of images, themes, values, and portrayals

cultivation
In cultivation analysis, television's contribution to the creation of a culture's frameworks or knowledge and underlying general concepts

mainstreaming
In cultivation analysis, the process, especially for heavier viewers, by which television's symbols monopolize and dominate other sources of information and ideas about the world

resonance
In cultivation analysis, when viewers see things on television that are congruent with their own everyday realities

first-order cultivation effects
Viewers' estimates of the occurrence of some phenomenon; probability judgments

social realities. Remember the earlier questions about crime? Those were drawn from a cultivation study. The third step is to survey the audience, posing the questions from step two to its members and asking them about their amount of television consumption. Finally, step four entails comparing the social realities of light and heavy viewers. The product, as described by Michael Morgan and Nancy Signorielli, should not be surprising: "The questions posed to respondents do not mention television, and the respondents' awareness of the source of their information is seen as irrelevant. The resulting relationships ... between amount of viewing and the tendency to respond to these questions in the terms of the dominant and repetitive facts, values, and ideologies of the world of television ... illuminate television's contribution to viewers' conceptions of social reality" (1990, p. 99).

What is television's contribution? Cultivation theorists argue that its major contribution is **cultivation**, a cultural process relating "to coherent frameworks or knowledge and to underlying general concepts ... cultivated by exposure to the total and organically related world of television rather than exposure to individual programs and selections" (Gerbner, 1990, p. 255). This cultivation occurs in two ways. The first is **mainstreaming**, where, especially for heavier viewers, television's symbols monopolize and dominate other sources of information and ideas about the world. People's internalized social realities eventually move toward the mainstream, not a mainstream in any political sense, but a culturally dominant reality more closely aligned with television's reality than with any objective reality. Is the criminal justice system failing us? It is if we think it is. The second way cultivation manifests itself is through **resonance**, when viewers see things on television that are most congruent with their own everyday realities. In essence, these people get a "double dose" of cultivation because what they see on the screen resonates with their actual lives. Some city dwellers, for example, might see the violent world of television resonated in their deteriorating neighborhoods. These effects manifest themselves in two ways. **First-order cultivation effects** are viewers' estimates of the occurrence of some phenomenon (e.g., violence or political corruption) typical of early cultivation research. These are probability judgments about the world. **Second-order cultivation effects** are the attitudes and beliefs that are formed as a result of those judgments (e.g., reluctance to go out at night or increased disdain for politicians; Shrum, 2004). You can test your own probability judgments about the world in the box, "How Do I See the World: My Reality vs. the Data."

Researchers have employed cultivation analysis to investigate the impact of television content on issues beyond violence and crime. It has been used in examinations of people's perceptions of affluence, divorce, and working women (Potter, 1991); acceptance of sexual stereotypes (Ward and Friedman, 2006); materialism (Reimer and Rosengren, 1990); values (Potter, 1990); mental health (Diefenbach and West, 2007); political participation (Besley, 2006); feelings of alienation (Signorielli, 1990); environmental concern (Shanahan, Morgan, and Stenbjerre, 1997); work (Signorielli and Kahlenberg, 2001); female body image (Van Vonderen and Kinnally, 2012); welfare (Sotirovic, 2001); and marital expectations (Segrin and Nabi, 2002). The assumptions of cultivation are supported throughout, though the strength of findings and the quality of the research

THINKING ABOUT THEORY | How Do I See the World: My Reality vs. the Data

Central to cultivation analysis is the idea that media cultivate, or grow, a generally held, mainstreamed picture of reality. One way it examines this effect is by comparing media consumers' judgments about the world against official data, demonstrating that heavier consumers typically offer probability judgments of real-world phenomena that are closer to the media's representations of those things than are actually the case. So, take this quiz and let's see how good your judgments about the world are. Then we can speculate about why you are so accurate … or not.

1. Poor people in America (the bottom 20 percent in household income) receive what percentage of all federal dollars from entitlements and other mandatory programs?
   a. 14%
   b. 32%
   c. 58%
   d. 90%
2. African Americans, who make up 22 percent of the poor, receive what proportion of these government benefits?
   a. 14%
   b. 32%
   c. 58%
   d. 90%
3. What percentage of the U.S. population is gay or lesbian?
   a. 3.5%
   b. 10.0%
   c. 25.5%
   d. 38.2%
4. Which of these states has the *lowest* divorce rate?
   a. Arkansas
   b. Oklahoma
   c. Massachusetts
   d. New York
5. Which category of Americans has the *highest* rate of substance abuse?
   a. Caucasian
   b. Hispanic
   c. African American
   d. Asian American
6. Of these four states, which has the *highest* rate of teenage pregnancy?

   a. New Hampshire
   b. Mississippi
   c. Texas
   d. Massachusetts
7. Which of these cities has the *lowest* crime rate?
   a. Detroit
   b. New York
   c. Baltimore
   d. Memphis

Answers:

1. b, 32% (The middle 60% receives 58%; Sherman, Greenstein, and Ruffing, 2012)
2. a, 14% (Poor non-Hispanic whites receive 69%; Sherman, Greenstein, and Ruffing, 2012)
3. a, 3.5% (On average, Americans estimate 25%; Morales, 2011)
4. c, Massachusetts (2.2 per 1,000 adults, compared to 2.7/1,000 for New York, 4.9/1,000 for Oklahoma, and 7/1,000 for Arkansas; U.S. Census Bureau, 2012)
5. a, Caucasians (9% of Caucasians, 7.7% of Hispanics, and 5% of African Americans are substance abusers; Szalavitz, 2011)
6. c, Texas (Its rate is 88 per 1,000 teenage girls; Mississippi's is 85/1,000; Vermont's is 40/1,000, and New Hampshire's is 33/1,000; Guttmacher Institute, 2010)
7. b, New York (New York is the 3rd safest big city in America; Columbus, Oklahoma City, and Memphis are among the 10 least safe; Mennem, 2013)

How did you do? While this, of course, is not a true cultivation study (we did not ascertain your levels of media consumption, nor did we compute the "media answer"), it is clear that you made your judgments based on some set of assumptions. Where did they come from? Finally, think about the way the media represent the phenomena covered by this little exercise. What is the media's typical representation of the working poor? Of gays and lesbians? Of drug abuse? Of "The Heartland" cities and states compared to those on the East and West Coasts? Do you think you might have offered different answers if you were a lighter consumer of the mass media? Why or why not?

second-order cultivation effects
Attitudes and beliefs that are formed as a result of viewers' probability judgments

vary greatly. These consistent results led Professor Gerbner to identify what he called the **3 Bs of television:**

1. Television *blurs* traditional distinctions of people's views of their world.
2. Television *blends* their realities into television's cultural mainstream.
3. Television *bends* that mainstream to the institutional interests of television and its sponsors.

3 Bs of television
In cultivation analysis, the idea that television blurs, blends, and bends reality

Gerbner's assessment of the way in which television dominates our social world is reminiscent of arguments about popular culture made by Max Horkheimer and Theodor Adorno more than half a century ago (Chapter 5):

> The historical circumstances in which we find ourselves have taken the magic of human life—living in a universe erected by culture—out of the hands of families and small communities. What has been a richly diverse hand-crafted process has become—for better or worse, or both—a complex manufacturing and mass-distribution enterprise. This has abolished much of the provincialism and parochialism, as well as some of the elitism, of the pretelevision era. It has enriched parochial cultural horizons. It also gave increasingly massive industrial conglomerates the right to conjure up much of what we think about, know, and do in common. (Gerbner, 1990, p. 261)

Clearly, Gerbner does not seem to think that this is a particularly fair trade-off, and as such, he places cultivation analysis in the realm of critical theory. Others do the same. James Shanahan and Vicki Jones, for example, state:

> Cultivation is sometimes taken as a return to a strong "powerful effects" view of mass media. This view isn't completely incorrect, but it misses the point that cultivation was originally conceived as a critical theory, which happens to address media issues precisely and only because the mass media (especially television) serve the function of storytelling…. Television is the dominant medium for distributing messages from cultural, social, and economic elites…. Cultivation is more than just an analysis of effects from a specific medium; it is an analysis of the institution of television and its social role. (1999, p. 32)

INSTANT ACCESS

Cultivation Analysis

Strengths

1. Combines macro- and micro-level theories
2. Provides detailed explanation of television's unique role
3. Enables empirical study of widely held humanistic assumptions
4. Redefines effect as more than observable behavior change
5. Applies to wide variety of effects issues
6. Provides basis for social change

Weaknesses

1. Early research had methodological limitations
2. Assumes homogeneity of television content
3. Focuses on heavy users of television
4. Is difficult to apply to media used less heavily than television

Since Gerbner's death in 2005, cultivation research has steadily moved away from attributing effects to amounts of television exposure to studying the influence of specific forms of media content. Segrin and Nabi (2002), for example, applied cultivation analysis to romance-oriented genres such as soap operas, romantic comedies, and relationship-based reality television, and Grabe and Drew (2007) studied exposure to different crime genres, specifically fictional narrative crime drama and nonfictional, "reality TV" violence. This specific content can be delivered by a variety of different media, including new media. One way of looking at new media is that to some extent they give each of us the power to shape the message system that cultivates our understanding of the social world. We're no longer at the mercy of three TV networks, but that doesn't mean that media have ceased to cultivate our understanding of ourselves and the people around us. "There is little evidence," write Michael Morgan, James Shanahan, and Nancy Signorielli, "that proliferation of channels has led to any substantially greater diversity of content. Indeed, the mere availability of more channels does not fundamentally change the socio-economic dynamics that drive the production and distribution of programs. On the contrary, that dynamic is intensified by increased concentration of ownership and control.... Even when new digital delivery systems threaten dominant interests, they are quickly swallowed up within the existing institutional structure. The much ballyhooed rise of user-generated video services such as YouTube have [*sic*]been absorbed by dominant players (Google) and are already being exploited for their benefits to advertisers" (2009, pp. 45–46). "As long as there are popular storytelling systems and purveyors of widely shared messages," write Michael Morgan and James Shanahan, "Gerbner's main ideas are likely to persist" (2010, p. 350).

MEDIA LITERACY

Implicitly or explicitly, communication scholars are responding to the many theories and research findings discussed in this and preceding chapters. There is a growing sense that the role of media for individuals and for society is problematic—but not beyond people's control. Many scholars feel that our current understanding of the role of media for individuals and society is sufficiently developed that action can and should be taken. This view is no longer restricted to critical theorists—it is generally expressed by leading postpositivist as well as critical cultural researchers. One way scholars are taking action is that they are leading the drive to improve media literacy.

media literacy
The ability to access, analyze, evaluate, and communicate messages

The media literacy movement is based on insights derived from many different sources. We list some of the most important here:

- Audience members are indeed active, but they are not necessarily very aware of what they do with media (uses and gratifications).
- The audience's needs, opportunities, and choices are constrained by access to media and media content (critical cultural studies).
- Media content can implicitly and explicitly provide a guide for action (social cognitive theory, schema theory, cultivation, and as you'll see in the next chapter, social construction of reality, symbolic interaction, and framing).

- People must realistically assess how their interaction with media texts can determine the purposes that interaction can serve for them in their environments (cultural theory).
- People have differing levels of cognitive processing ability, and this can radically affect how they use media and what they are able to get from media (information-processing theory and knowledge gap).

From a postpositivist perspective, the best way to ensure functional (rather than dysfunctional) use of media is to improve individuals' media-use skills. From a cultural studies perspective, we all need to develop our ability to critically reflect on the purposes media and media content serve for us. We need to be able to decide which media to avoid and which to use in ways that best serve our purposes. From the perspective of normative theory, we as citizens of a democracy must make good and effective use of our free press. This is media literacy.

Anthropologists, sociologists, linguists, historians, communication scientists—researchers from virtually all disciplines that study how people and groups communicate to survive and prosper—have long understood that as humans moved from preliterate, or oral, culture to literate culture, they assumed greater control over their environments and lives. With writing came the ability to communicate across time and space. People no longer had to be in the presence of those with whom they wished to communicate (Eisenstein, 1979; Inglis, 1990; Innis, 1951).

The invention of the movable-type printing press in the mid-1400s infinitely expanded the importance and reach of the written word, and power began to shift from those who were born into it to those who could make the best use of communication. If literacy—traditionally understood to mean the ability to read and write—increases people's control over their environments and lives, it logically follows that an expanded literacy—one necessitated by a world in which so much "reading" and "writing" occurs in the mass media—should do the same. Critical theorist Stuart Ewen writes:

> Historically, links between literacy and democracy are inseparable from the notion of an informed populace, conversant with the issues that touch upon their lives, enabled with tools that allow them to participate actively in public deliberation and social change. Nineteenth-century struggles for literacy and education were never limited to the ability to read. They were also about learning to write and thus about expanding the number and variety of voices heard in published interchanges and debates. Literacy was about crossing the lines that had historically separated men [sic] of ideas from ordinary people, about the social enfranchisement of those who had been excluded from the compensation of citizenship. (2000, p. 448)

As such, he argues elsewhere:

> In a society where instrumental images are employed to petition our affections at every turn—often without a word—educational curricula must … encourage the development of tools for critically analyzing images. For democracy to prevail, image making as a communicative activity must be undertaken by ordinary citizens as well. The aesthetic realm—and the enigmatic ties linking aesthetic, social, economic, political, and ethical values—must be brought down to earth as a subject of study. (1996, p. 413)

Alan Rubin (1998) offered three definitions of media literacy: (1) from the National Leadership Conference on Media Literacy—the ability to access, analyze, evaluate, and communicate messages; (2) from media scholar Paul Messaris—knowledge about how media function in society; and (3) from mass communication researchers Justin Lewis and Sut Jhally—understanding cultural, economic, political, and technological constraints on the creation, production, and transmission of messages. Rubin added: "All definitions emphasize specific knowledge, awareness, and rationality, that is, cognitive processing of information. Most focus on critical evaluations of messages, whereas some include the communication of messages. Media literacy, then, is about understanding the sources and technologies of communication, the codes that are used, the messages that are produced, and the selection, interpretation, and impact of those messages" (Rubin, 1998, p. 3).

Communication scholars William Christ and W. James Potter offer an additional overview of media literacy: "Most conceptualizations [of media literacy] include the following elements: Media are constructed and construct reality; media have commercial implications; media have ideological and political implications; form and content are related in each medium, each of which has a unique aesthetic, codes, and conventions; and receivers negotiate meaning in media" (1998, pp. 7–8). A careful reader can easily find evidence in these two summations of all the audience- and culture-centered theories we've discussed in this book.

TWO VIEWS OF MEDIA LITERACY

Mass communication scholar Art Silverblatt provided one of the first systematic efforts to place media literacy in audience- and culture-centered theory and frame it as a skill that must and can be improved. His core argument parallels a point made earlier: "The traditional definition of *literacy* applies only to print: 'having a knowledge of letters; instructed; learned.' However, the principal channels of media now include print, photography, film, radio, and television. In light of the emergence of these other channels of mass communications, this definition of literacy must be expanded" (1995, pp. 1–2). As such, he identified five elements of media literacy (1995, pp. 2–3):

1. An awareness of the impact of the media on the individual and society
2. An understanding of the process of mass communication
3. The development of strategies with which to analyze and discuss media messages
4. An awareness of media content as a "text" that provides insight into our contemporary culture and ourselves
5. The cultivation of an enhanced enjoyment, understanding, and appreciation of media content

Potter (1998) takes a slightly different approach, describing several foundational or bedrock ideas supporting media literacy:

1. **Media literacy is a continuum, not a category.** "Media literacy is not a categorical condition like being a high school graduate or being an American.... Media literacy is best regarded as a continuum in which there are degrees.... There is always room for improvement" (p. 6).
2. **Media literacy needs to be developed.** "As we reach higher levels of maturation intellectually, emotionally, and morally we are able to perceive more in media

messages.... Maturation raises our potential, but we must actively develop our skills and knowledge structures in order to deliver on that potential" (pp. 6–7).

3. **Media literacy is multidimensional.** Potter identifies four dimensions of media literacy. Each operates on a continuum. In other words, we interact with media messages in four ways, and we do so with varying levels of awareness and skill:

a. The cognitive domain refers to mental processes and thinking.
b. The emotional domain is the dimension of feeling.
c. The aesthetic domain refers to the ability to enjoy, understand, and appreciate media content from an artistic point of view.
d. The moral domain refers to the ability to infer the values underlying the messages (p. 8).

4. **The purpose of media literacy is to give us more control over interpretations.** "All media messages are interpretations.... A key to media literacy is not to engage in the impossible quest for truthful or objective messages. They don't exist" (p. 9).

The *Journal of Communication* devoted a special issue to media literacy (Media Literacy Symposium, 1998), and the *American Behavioral Scientist* devoted two entire issues to the topic, entitled " 'Disillusioning' Ourselves and Our Media: Media Literacy in the 21st Century" (Galician, 2004a, 2004b). These publications reflect wide scholarly interest in media literacy and the hundreds of empirical investigations of its tenets. This work typically takes the form of evaluating the effectiveness of **media literacy interventions**, efforts "to reduce harmful effects of the media by informing the audience about one or more aspects of the media, thereby influencing media-related beliefs and attitudes, and ultimately preventing risky behaviors" (Jeong, Cho, and Hwang, 2012, p. 454). The content subjected to these intervention efforts runs the entire range of that offered by the media, for example, food advertising (Livingstone and Helsper, 2006), alcohol advertising (Austin et al., 2002), racist portrayals (Ramasubramanian and Oliver, 2007), health narratives (Bergsma and Carney, 2008), portrayals of tobacco use (Gonzales et al., 2004), violence (Cantor and Wilson, 2003), and crime (Romer, Jamieson, and Aday, 2003). Se-Hoon Jeong, Hyunyi Cho, and Yoori Hwang applied meta-analysis to this body of work. Examining 51 empirically evaluated interventions, they demonstrated that "media literacy interventions may be an effective approach for reducing potentially harmful effects of media messages. Intervention effects were found across divergent topics for diverse audiences, for a broad range of media-related (e.g., knowledge) and behavior-related (e.g., attitudes and behaviors) outcomes. The results that intervention effects did not vary according to target age, the setting, audience involvement, and the topic suggest that interventions can be equally effective across a spectrum of settings (e.g., school, community, or lab), age groups, levels of audience involvement, and topics (e.g., alcohol, violence, and sex; 2012, p. 464). Smita Banerjee and Robert Kubey's review of the short-term and long-term effects of media literacy interventions came to a similar conclusion. Although not all interventions are successful, they wrote, "Some media literacy interventions do seem to help participants to become better 'critical thinkers' about media content, processes, and effects.... Media literacy instruction also appears to trigger some thought about media content and its comparison to 'the real world' " (2013, p. 14).

media literacy interventions
An effort to reduce harmful effects of the media by informing the audience about one or more aspects of those media

SUMMARY

The theories reviewed in this chapter are diverse but provide a surprisingly coherent and complementary vision of contemporary American society. Even though they are grounded in postpositivist research, they have produced research findings demonstrating that media do indeed have effects. Yet the picture of the role of media these theories provide is troubling. What we know about public issues, the terms we use to define them, and the importance we assign to them all might be strongly influenced by media.

But if media can't cause *immediate* conversion of vast audiences to new ideologies, just how powerful can they be? In Chapter 10, we will provide an answer to this question by expanding and extending the mantra of agenda-setting theory to encompass a set of meaning-making theories. Agenda-setting theory states that media don't tell people what to think (i.e., media don't directly influence attitudes), but media do tell people what to think about—they can and do affect the importance we assign to various public issues. If we take this a little further, we can argue (as McCombs does in his second-order agenda-setting theory) that media also tell people how to think about issues specifically and the social world generally. We'll revisit this theme in Chapter 10's look at how media frame issues for us so we are more likely to make sense of things in some ways rather than others.

Finally, media can have a profound influence on the accessibility and quality of information we use as we try to think, talk, and act in our social world. If the only information we can easily access is the information provided in "infotainment" or political spectacle, or if it is limited to a small range of agreed-upon legitimate (and legitimized) issues and perspectives, there will be many important things we never learn about from the media. Moreover, our impressions of the things that we do learn about might be strongly affected by the "packaging" of the information.

So how do you answer the questions raised about media by the theories in this chapter? Are you optimistic or pessimistic concerning the role of media? Will the rise of new communication technology like the Internet lead to important changes in how electronic media influence our views of the social world? Should media strive to serve the purposes that Libertarian thinkers (Chapter 3) assigned to them? Should we be demanding that media provide a range of public services, or should we be satisfied with the service that a competitive market provides? Or were these purposes too idealistic in the first place, given the necessity for media to earn profits in an increasingly competitive marketplace? Is it a problem if media act as a powerful agent for the status quo? To what extent do media shape your own view of your world?

Critical Thinking Questions

1. Have your opinions about a controversial issue in the news ever been spiraled into silence? If so, what was the situation? Might you have hesitated to defend your position on an issue or a favored political candidate? If not, have you ever had to resist the temptation to remain silent in the face of opposing opinion? If so, what were the circumstances? Do you pay attention to opinion polls so you can avoid talking about things that are becoming unpopular? Has the emergence of the Internet, with its distance and anonymity, altered your willingness to speak out or remain silent?

2. Do you vote? Why or why not? How important do you think your participation in the democratic process really is? That is, can one citizen make a difference? If you answer yes, do you find the theories presented in this chapter troubling? Why or why not? If you answer no, can you find an explanation for that response in the theories discussed here? Are there forms of political participation that do not involve traditional activities like

voting or political party activities that you do engage in? What are they? Why do you choose these over more traditional forms of activity?

3. When it comes to technology (e.g., a new Internet application, the latest recording equipment, or an innovative automotive device) are you a change agent, an early adopter, an opinion leader, or an opinion follower? What is it about you that determines where you stand in the process of the diffusion of innovation? Do you know any technological early adopters? What makes them similar to or different from you? Do you think there are gender differences—that is, are there some innovations in which one gender rather than the other might be more likely to take the lead? Why or why not?

Key Terms

agenda-setting

priming

agenda-building

framing theory

second-order agenda-setting

hierarchy-of-effects model

C-A-B sequence

spiral of silence

news production research

objectivity rituals

media intrusion theory

social capital

information diffusion theory

meta-analysis

early adopters

change agents

social marketing theory

targeting

media system dependency theory

knowledge gap

digital divide

cultivation analysis

Violence Index

Cultural Indicators Project

ice-age analogy

message system analysis

cultivation

mainstreaming

resonance

first-order cultivation effects

second-order cultivation effects

3 Bs of television

media literacy

media literacy interventions

Media and Culture Theories: Meaning-Making in the Social World

How would you describe your experience the last time you attended an athletic event or a party involving lots of strangers? Were you fearful because there were lots of strangers who were yelling or drinking heavily? What about your last visit to a big shopping mall? Were there unusual things going on that you didn't expect? When you're out in public do you often feel like events might spin out of control, or are you confident that nothing dangerous will happen to you? If you're a college student attending classes on a large campus, then you are constantly encountering people you don't know in places you haven't been before. Do you worry about that? Do you frequently find yourself in bizarre situations that are impossible to understand? These may seem like odd questions since most of us rarely have difficulty adjusting to everyday situations, even in new places where there are crowds of unfamiliar people. We routinely move through a wide range of everyday-life situations without any serious difficulties. But think about it. Why is it so easy for you to anticipate and plan for situations even when they involve strangers or new places, even when those strangers are screaming or drunk? It's easy because you share an everyday culture with others that enables you to anticipate and make sense of most situations and the people in them.

You're constantly learning about everyday culture, a culture that is constantly changing in subtle but important ways. For most of human history, everyday culture was learned through face-to-face communication with a handful of other people in a relatively small number of situations. Everyday culture was relatively static but varied so greatly from one place to another that even people living fairly close to one another found it hard to understand strangers. Even when people shared a common language, the dialects differed so dramatically from village to village that it limited communication and discouraged travel. Today we live in a world where people step off airliners in remote places around the globe and expect to encounter people and situations that they can understand. They expect to be understood and these expectations are usually met.

The world has become the global village that Marshall McLuhan enthused about in the 1960s (Chapter 5). There are a number of reasons why this has happened, but one of the most important is that media have become central to how we—and almost everyone else around the world—learn about everyday culture. It's likely that before you ever attended a football game or went to a bar, television and movies showed you how people acted in these places. Television constantly shows you many different types of people in a wide range of situations. Your consumption of media content has helped you form useful expectations (and reinforced problematic stereotypes). And now the Internet and social media have increased the ways you can learn about quite complex forms of everyday culture. It's not your great grandparents' social world anymore.

If you have grown up with the Internet and social media, these seem like very natural and normal ways to learn about and relate to other people. Facebook and Twitter provide a constant flow of information about friends, family, celebrities, and even politicians. But as we have pointed out frequently in previous chapters, not everyone is convinced that these new media are a benign force. How can we begin to understand what these new media are doing to transform our experience of the social world? Can theories developed to understand television be adapted for social media when the way new media are used and the content they deliver are so different? Remember from Chapter 3 that Dan Gilmor has labeled you "the people formerly known as the audience." Media writer Steve Smith adds to the recasting of today's media users, explaining that the people formerly known as the audience have also become programming executives, "I now think about where certain kinds of content fit into my routines and life, just as I push podcasts of different kinds and lengths to car, gym, walking, or other use cases where I want to experience them" (2013). In Chapter 11 we'll look at how media researchers are addressing these changes. Some of the theories we've looked at in earlier chapters are being adapted to new media while others are employed less and less. Media theory is changing. In this chapter we'll look at theories that are increasingly being used to understand new and old media how they affect everyday culture. If you want to understand how new media are changing the way people understand and experience the social world, these theories provide an excellent starting point.

LEARNING OBJECTIVES

After studying this chapter you should be able to

- Describe symbolic interactionism and pragmatism and explain how they differ from behaviorist or stimulus-response theory. Be able to explain how they differ from social constructionism.

- Be able to describe the notions of self-identity and social identity and how they are formed through communication.

- Describe framing theory and discuss its increasing popularity for studying news media and their effects.

- Be able to list key findings from framing research and discuss the insight they provide into the way news shapes our views of the social world.

- Explain commodification-of-culture notions and discuss the way commodification systematically alters how the social world is presented in media content.

- Be able to describe common ways that advertising commodifies culture and systematically misrepresents everyday life.

OVERVIEW

In Chapter 5, we traced the rise of cultural theories of media, giving particular attention to early schools of critical theory and cultural studies. This chapter looks at contemporary critical cultural studies theories as well as other theories focusing on culture. Cultural theory has a long and, as we've seen, controversial history in the field of mass communication. It predates the rise of postpositivist theories examining media effects on individuals. During the 1920s and 1930s, scholars at the University of Chicago advanced theories of community with a central focus on the role of communication in shaping everyday culture. From the 1950s to the 1980s, these cultural theories were marginalized by American mass communication scholars in favor of media-effects theories. The media-effects trend in theory development pushed aside competing approaches. Media theory textbooks written in the United States during this era often omitted any mention of cultural theories or gave them little attention. They tended to be categorized with mass society theory and their usefulness was questioned.

In the 1980s, when cultural theories began to be taken seriously in the discipline, a furious debate broke out between adherents and postpositivist opponents. The field was declared to be in ferment ("Ferment in the Field," 1983). Advocates of media-effects perspectives said their theories were more scientific because they were based on highly structured empirical observations and they were falsifiable—new findings could lead to their rejection. They attacked cultural theories as too speculative, too complex, and based on loosely structured qualitative research methods. There was no way to test their causal assertions. But since that time, cultural theories have gained acceptance, as have qualitative methods. There is growing respect between postpositivists and advocates for cultural theories. Textbooks, like this one, increasingly consider the strengths and limitations of both types of theories and the research methods on which they are based.

We will first consider micro-level cultural theories and then move to theories dealing with more macro-level concerns. The former examine the everyday use of media by individuals and local communities; the latter look at media's role in the larger social order. We use two terms to refer to the theories in this chapter. We refer to them as *culture-centered* because they study culture as a primary means of understanding the social world and the role media play in it. They provide different perspectives on how media influence culture and what the consequences of that influence are for individuals and society. We also refer to them as *meaning-making* theories because they are focused on understanding the way media influence how we make sense of the social world and our place in it—how we make meaning. Despite their common focus on culture and meaning-making, these theories are quite diverse. Some were developed by American scholars, whereas others originated in Europe. Some are critical—they assess how media frustrate our efforts to pursue valued objectives. Others are satisfied to provide in-depth descriptions of what we do with media and how our experiences of and actions in the social world are affected.

SYMBOLIC INTERACTIONISM

symbolic interactionism
Theory that people give meaning to symbols and that those meanings come to control those people

social behaviorism
View of learning that focuses on the mental processes and the social environment in which learning takes place

Symbolic interactionism was one of the first social science theories to address questions of how communication is involved with the way we learn culture and how culture structures our everyday experience. Symbolic interaction theory developed during the 1920s and 1930s as a reaction to and criticism of behaviorism (see Chapter 2), and it had a variety of labels until Herbert Blumer gave it its current name in 1969. One early name was **social behaviorism**. Unlike traditional behaviorists, social behaviorists rejected simplistic conceptualizations of stimulus-response conditioning. They were convinced that attention must be given to the cognitive processes mediating learning. They also believed that the social environment in which learning takes place must be considered. Traditional behaviorists tended to conduct laboratory experiments in which animals were exposed to certain stimuli and conditioned to behave in specific ways. Social behaviorists judged these experiments too simplistic. They argued that human existence was far too complex to be understood through conditioning of animal behavior.

George Herbert Mead (1934), a University of Chicago philosopher and social activist, provided a way of understanding social life that differed profoundly from behaviorist notions. Rather than observe rats running through mazes, he proposed a better way to understand how people learn to make sense of everyday life and structure their actions. He suggested we look at how people learn to play baseball (or any team sport). How do we learn to play these games? Surely not by reading textbooks titled *The Theory of Playing Second Base*. Not simply through stimulus-response conditioning as we get rewarded or punished for specific actions. Mead argued that what occurs on a playing field is a sophisticated form of mutual conditioning: the players teach each other how to play the game while they are playing it. Players must learn to structure their actions in very complex ways to cover their positions effectively. But each position must be played differently, so teammates can't rely on simple mimicry of one another. According to Mead, each player learns a social role—the pitcher role, the catcher role, or the left fielder role. Each role is learned by observing and modeling good players and by interacting with other team members. As they play, team members receive encouragement and friendly criticism from teammates and fans. If they play well, they have the satisfaction of being accepted by others as a productive member of a social unit—a community.

Mead saw a baseball team as a microcosm of society. Each of us learns many different social roles through interaction with others. We are members of many different communities. Our actions are constantly being subtly "conditioned" by others, while at the same time we are affecting their actions. The goal is not to manipulate or dominate each other but to create and sustain a productive social unit—a community providing its members with certain rewards in return for their willingness to take on specific roles. As we grow up we try out various roles, and then ideally we are able to select those that best fit our interests and personal abilities. Social roles and many other aspects of culture are learned through interaction—through experiences in daily life situations. Over time, we internalize the rules inherent in various situations and structure our actions accordingly.

Only in rare cases do we consciously reflect on and analyze our actions. If asked to explain what we are doing and why we are doing it, we are puzzled—the question seems strange, much like those that opened this chapter. Why don't you call your mother by her first name? Why do you ride an elevator facing forward and not backward? Why do you text rather than phone? Why post a status update on Facebook rather than send an e-mail? We are doing something because it is common sense; it's the way everybody does it; it's the normal, the logical, the right way to do things. Once internalized, these roles provide us with a powerful means of controlling our actions. In time, our identity becomes bound up with them: we understand ourselves, both emotionally and mentally, in terms of the roles we play and the personal identities that are associated with these roles. We value ourselves to the extent that these roles are respected by others. And sometimes, like athletes whose physical skills inevitably fail, we experience identity crises because we can't play a role as we or others expect us to or because we aspire to a role that proves to be beyond our ability or resources.

Mead's analogy is insightful and powerful, but it has some important limitations common to microscopic theories. Mead assumes that baseball teams operate as a sort of minidemocracy. But where do the teams come from? How do they get established? Who defines the rules of baseball games? Who sells the tickets, pays expenses, and profits from the game? Yes, team members mutually influence each other, but often coaches and a few older or more experienced players will dominate the team. And what about the team as a whole? It has a manager and owner who hire and fire team members.

The baseball team analogy also isn't very helpful for understanding how mass media might affect socialization. Ball players directly interact with one another. What happens when communication occurs through media—when people use Facebook or Twitter to relate to dozens or even hundreds of friends? Unlike baseball players who confront each other physically on the field, Facebook and Twitter users meet each other in cyberspace. They use tablets or tap away at their smartphones to exchange messages with friends. They post information about themselves (express their personal identity), but often this information provides a very fragmentary or even fictional description of who they are. They get constant updates of the activities of friends and they post descriptions of what they are doing. How is everyday culture being created and shared on Facebook or Twitter? Certainly not the way teammates do it.

Mead offered another important insight into the socialization process. Unlike animals conditioned to respond to stimuli in a predetermined manner, humans are socialized in ways that permit more or less conscious interpretation of stimuli and planned responses. What is the secret that enables us to do what animals cannot? Symbols.

Symbols, in general, are arbitrary, often quite abstract, representations of unseen phenomena. Think of the words you use—all are arbitrary vocalizations

symbols
In general, arbitrary, often abstract representations of unseen phenomena

that are essentially meaningless except to others who know how to decode them. When we write, we cover pages with complicated markings. To read them, someone must be literate in our language. According to Mead, the use of symbols transforms the socialization process—freeing it from the bonds of both space and time. Using symbols, we can create vivid representations of the past and we can anticipate the future. We can be transported anywhere on the globe or even into the far reaches of space.

In *Mind, Self, and Society*, Mead (1934) argues that we use symbols to create our experience of consciousness (mind), our understanding of ourselves (self), and our knowledge of the larger social order (society). In other words, symbols mediate and structure all our experience because they structure our ability to perceive and interpret what goes on around us. This argument is similar to the one made by information-processing theorists (see Chapter 8). In information-processing theory, *schemas* (sets of symbols) that we have learned in the past enable us to routinely make sense of the new sensory information we take in. Mead believed that mind, self, and society are internalized as complex sets of symbols. These sets of symbols serve as filtering mechanisms for our experiences.

This might seem to be an extreme argument. Most of us take for granted our ability to look at the world around us and see the things that are obviously there. We might assume that we were born with this ability. But think about it. Why do we notice certain things and not others? As we move through daily life we're constantly encountering ambiguous, complex situations. Unless we are unusually fastidious, for example, we will not notice small amounts of dust and dirt when we enter a room. We'll ignore most of the background sounds. According to Mead, human perceptual processes are extremely malleable and can be shaped by the sets of symbols we learn so that we will see only what our culture has determined is worth seeing. (Has your perception of Middle Eastern cultures changed since the United States' involvement in Iraq and Afghanistan? Are you more likely now to notice a woman wearing a head scarf? What mental images spring to mind when you hear the word *terrorist*? Twenty years ago the image might have been of an Irish Republican Army bomber or a Latin American drug criminal—now it's most likely a Middle Eastern male.) Mead's arguments anticipated cognitive psychology research, which, as you saw in Chapter 8, is beginning to empirically demonstrate much of what he hypothesized.

Thus symbolic interactionism posits that our actions in response to symbols are mediated (or controlled) largely by those same symbols. Therefore, our understanding of and relation to physical or objective reality is mediated by the symbolic environment—the mind, self, and society we have internalized. Put another way, the meanings we give to symbols define us and the realities we experience. As we are socialized, culturally agreed-upon meanings assume control over our interactions with our environments.

Consider the meaning that you attach to the stitched red, white, and blue cloth that constitutes an American flag. A flag is, in reality (objectively), little more than a piece of colored cloth. That is, it is little more than a piece of cloth until someone attaches symbolic meaning to it. We have decided that a particular array and formulation of colors and shapes should become our flag. Each of us experiences the flag differently, yet there is shared meaning as well. To many who support the conflict in the Middle East that began in Iraq in 2003, the flag flying over the 27-building, $800 million U.S. embassy that opened in 2010 symbolizes America's strength and its quest for democracy for all people. But for many who oppose that conflict, that same flag symbolizes America's occupation and quest for empire. Regardless of the meaning we individually attach to our flag, however, we are not free from its power. When a color guard passes before us at a sporting event, how free are we to remain sitting? At a school function, how free are we to continue chatting with our friends during the Pledge of Allegiance to that tricolored piece of fabric?

PRAGMATISM AND THE CHICAGO SCHOOL

pragmatism
Philosophical school of theory emphasizing the practical function of knowledge as an instrument for adapting to and controlling reality

Mead developed symbolic interactionism by drawing on ideas from **pragmatism**, a philosophical school of theory emphasizing the practical function of knowledge as an instrument for adapting to reality and controlling it. Pragmatism developed in America as a reaction against ideas gaining popularity at home and in Europe at the end of the nineteenth century—simplistic forms of materialism such as behaviorism and German idealism. Both behaviorism and idealism rejected the possibility of human *agency*, the idea that individuals could consciously control their thoughts and actions in some meaningful and useful way (Chapter 1). Idealism argued that people are dominated by culture, and behaviorism argued that all human action is a conditioned response to external stimuli. From the preceding description of Mead's ideas, you can see how he tried to find a middle ground between these two perspectives—a place that would allow for some degree of human agency. If we consider Mead's arguments carefully, they suggest that individuals do have some control over what they do, but he is really arguing that agency lies with the community (or in the baseball example, with the team). Communities rather than individuals create and propagate culture, those complex sets of symbols that guide and shape our experiences. When we act in communities, we are mutually conditioned so we learn culture and use it to structure experience. These pragmatist notions about culture and human agency are at the heart of many of the cultural theories developed in the United States. As a school of thought, pragmatism continues to attract interest in a number of disciplines. In philosophy, Richard Rorty (1991; Rorty, Schneewind, and Skinner, 1982) has popularized neo-pragmatism. In political science a number of scholars have advocated John Dewey's pragmatism as a way of moving that field in a useful direction (Farr, 1999). Chris Russill (2006, 2008, 2012) and Robert Craig (2007) discuss the ongoing relevance of pragmatism for contemporary communication theory.

For pragmatists, the basic test of the power of culture is the extent to which it effectively structures experience within a community. When some aspect of culture loses its effectiveness, it ceases to structure experience and becomes a set of words and symbols having essentially no meaning. For example, we can still find certain words in a dictionary and we could use them to decode old media content, but they would have no force in our lives—no connection to our experience. What does "twenty-three skidoo" mean? Do you have "the skinny"? You might understand these as "let's bounce" and "the 411," respectively. Or maybe not, depending on your experience. Culture is constantly changing—new elements are developed and old elements are abandoned. This change doesn't typically happen because it's planned by elites who manipulate culture to serve their interests. Rather, culture changes as situations in which communities act change. Culture can also change when people use media to relate to each other in new ways. Consider how quickly *hashtag*, *sexting*, *snapchat*, and *to poke someone* entered our consciousness.

Many of the most productive symbolic interactionists were, like Mead, located at the University of Chicago. They became known as the Chicago School. We discussed the Chicago School in Chapter 3 when we considered the argument they made concerning social responsibility of the press. These ideas, pragmatism and social interactionism, were at the heart of that normative theory.

Chicago School theorists in the 1920s saw the city that housed their campus as a gigantic social experiment—a place where many folk cultures were suddenly thrown together in situations where people were forced to understand and relate to others whose culture was very different from their own. As you may recall, they used the term *great community* to refer to Chicago. It's useful to contrast this term with another used quite a bit in this textbook: *mass society*. The difference highlights some key differences between pragmatism and mass society theory—between a theory that's optimistic about the future of large-scale social orders and one that's quite pessimistic. Mass society theorists worried that individuals would become "atomized" in large-scale social orders. The networks of social relationships holding people together would necessarily break down as people moved from rural communities to urban ghettos. High culture would give way to mass culture so people's existence would be degraded and dehumanized. Media would just make things worse by providing a more efficient mechanism for transmitting mass culture.

If mass societies are places where human existence is degraded, great communities are places where the potential for human existence is explored and new opportunities for developing culture are found. One of the most creative members of the Chicago School was Robert E. Park, a man who worked as a journalist, studied philosophy with John Dewey in Michigan, and sociology with Georg Simmel in Germany, exposed colonialism in the Belgian Congo, and served as an aide to educator, author, and early African American civil rights leader Booker T. Washington (Goist, 1971). With his colleagues, Park developed a perspective on urban life that was essentially optimistic while at the same time acknowledging that there were many problems. Cities were places where new forms of culture could be created—where many new and dynamic communities could be formed. Cities were made up of thousands of more or less interconnected local communities. It is this interconnection that allows for or compels the creation of more innovative forms of culture.

Not surprisingly, Park saw newspapers as playing an essential role in interconnecting the communities making up great communities. The most important thing about the newspaper, he thought, was that it served as a means of transmitting "news." This was an example of a

> non-spatially defined, yet community-oriented phenomenon which functioned to hold the larger society together. The news, as Park presented it, played the dual role—making communication within the local area possible, but also acting to integrate

individuals and groups into the wider society. He illustrated his point by indicating the function of the immigrant press. The effect of city life is to destroy the provincialism of the immigrant, and the foreign-language newspaper is the chief means of replacing older ties with a wider national loyalty. The press also makes it possible for the immigrant group to participate in American life, thus providing a first step in Americanization.

Park understood the metropolitan press to serve essentially the same function. Public opinion rests on news, on people talking about present events, and that is what newspapers make possible. While news is primarily local in character, the real power of the press, and other means of mass communication as well, is in providing the basis for public opinion and political action. Compatible with both permanence of location and with mobility, the metropolitan newspaper is an important means of holding together a city organism made up of various distinct parts. (Goist, 1971, p. 57)

Park's arguments concerning the function of the press in cities were abstract, and the Chicago School was not able to develop a theory clearly explaining how and why newspapers performed their role. Systematic research was never conducted to validate Park's ideas. As we saw in Chapter 3, members of the Hutchins Commission on Freedom of the Press argued for extensive local coverage that would permit people living in different communities to learn more about other communities. Unfortunately, Chicago newspapers didn't see much reader interest in this type of news. They ignored or rejected the Hutchins Commission's advice as impractical. In the 1950s and 1960s, big urban papers earned increasing amounts of money from sales in the growing and more affluent suburbs. Other than to report bad news about crime and social unrest, they ignored inner-city ethnic neighborhoods, often neglecting to deliver there as their residents depressed the papers' suburb-enriched, advertiser-attractive, up-scale demographics (Kirkhorn, 2000). It's doubtful that these newspapers played the role Park envisioned for them. But they undoubtedly contributed to (and disrupted) urban culture in other ways. We'll return to a consideration of Park's ideas in Chapter 11 when we look at how journalism is being reconceptualized to increase its usefulness to communities.

CURRENT APPLICATIONS OF SYMBOLIC INTERACTIONISM

Although Mead first articulated his ideas in the 1930s, it was not until the 1970s and 1980s that mass communication researchers began paying serious attention to symbolic interaction. Given the great emphasis that Mead placed on interpersonal interaction and his disregard for media, it is not surprising that media theorists were slow to see the relevancy of his ideas. Michael Solomon (1983), a consumer researcher, provided a summary of Mead's work that is especially relevant for media research:

1. Cultural symbols are learned through interaction and then mediate that interaction.
2. The "overlap of shared meaning" by people in a culture means that individuals who learn a culture should be able to predict the behaviors of others in that culture.
3. Self-definition is social in nature; the self is defined largely through interaction with the environment.

4. The extent to which a person is committed to a social identity will determine the power of that identity to influence his or her behavior.

Among the most notable efforts by communication scholars to apply this symbolic interactionist thinking to our use of mass media was the book *Communication and Social Behavior: A Symbolic Interaction Perspective*, written by Don F. Faules and Dennis C. Alexander in 1978. Basing their analysis on their definition of communication as "symbolic behavior that results in various degrees of shared meaning and values between participants," they offered three fundamental propositions on symbolic interaction and communication:

1. **People's interpretation and perception of the environment depend on communication.** In other words, what we know of our world is largely a function of our prior communication experiences in that world. This conforms to Solomon's idea of interaction with cultural symbols. As Faules and Alexander wrote, "Communication allows for the reduction of uncertainty without direct sensory experience. The media are a prime source of indirect experience, and for that reason have impact on the construction of social reality" (p. 23).

2. **Communication is guided by and guides the concepts of self, role, and situations, and these concepts generate expectations in and of the environment.** Put differently, our use of communication in different settings is related to our understanding of ourselves and others in those situations. This is analogous to Solomon's point about learning a culture and predicting the behavior of others.

3. **Communication consists of complex interactions "involving action, interdependence, mutual influence, meaning, relationship, and situational factors"** (p. 23). Here we can see not only a communication-oriented restatement of Solomon's precepts three and four but also a rearticulation of James Carey's ritual perspective (see Chapter 5). Faules and Alexander are clearly reminding us that our understanding of our world and our place in it are created by us in interaction and involvement with media symbols.

Before we get any further into symbolic interactionism, however, we must mention some definitional differences between this perspective and its close relative, social construction of reality, discussed in the next section of this chapter. In symbolic interaction theory, a **sign** is any element in the environment used to represent another element in the environment. Signs can be classified in two ways: **natural signs**, those things in nature (like the changing color of leaves) that represent something else in nature (like the coming of autumn); **artificial signs**, those that have been constructed (like a handshake) to represent something else in the social world (like a friendly greeting). These artificial signs work only if the people using them agree on their meaning—that is, if they are "interactive"; two or more people must agree on their meaning and must further agree to respond to that sign in a relatively consistent fashion. Social construction of reality uses the concept of signs somewhat differently, as you'll soon see.

Another difference between symbolic interactionism and social constructionism is the distinction between signals and symbols. In symbolic interactionism **signals** are artificial signs that produce highly predictable responses, like traffic signals. **Symbols,** on the other hand, are artificial signs for which there is less certainty and

sign
In symbolic interaction, any element in the environment used to represent another element in the environment

natural signs
In symbolic interaction, things occurring in nature that represent something else in nature

artificial signs
In symbolic interaction, elements that have been constructed to represent something else in the social world

signals
In symbolic interaction, artificial signs that produce highly predictable responses

symbols
In symbolic interaction, artificial signs for which there is less certainty of response

INSTANT ACCESS

Symbolic Interactionism

Strengths

1. Rejects simple stimulus-response conceptualizations of human behavior
2. Considers the social environment in which learning takes place
3. Recognizes the complexity of human existence
4. Foregrounds individuals' and the community's role in agency
5. Provides basis for many methodologies and approaches to inquiry

Weaknesses

1. Gives too little recognition to power of social institutions
2. In some contemporary articulations, grants too much power to media content

more ambiguity of response, like the flag. As Faules and Alexander (1978) explained, "Signals are used to regulate normative behavior in a society, and symbols are used to facilitate communicative behavior in a society" (p. 36).

SOCIAL CONSTRUCTIONISM

social constructionism

School of social theory that argues that individuals' power to oppose or reconstruct important social institutions is limited

social construction of reality

Theory that assumes an ongoing correspondence of meaning because people share a common sense about its reality

What almost all theories classified as culture-centered have in common is an underlying assumption that our experience of reality is an ongoing social construction in which we have some responsibility, not something that is only sent, delivered, or otherwise transmitted by some authority or elite. But although there is general agreement that human communities construct the social world, there is disagreement concerning the level of agency individual humans have in the processes by which this world is constructed and maintained. We've seen that symbolic interactionists are strong believers in the power of individuals to have a significant level of control over culture and their social world. If culture is forged on a daily basis in the millions of situations in which we all participate, there should be great potential for cultural innovation and change. If nothing else, people make mistakes, and that alone should lead to innovation.

Another school of social theory, **social constructionism**, questions the amount of control individuals have over culture. Social constructionism argues that once social institutions such as schools, churches, businesses, and military organizations are constructed, individuals' power to oppose or reconstruct these institutions is limited. Its proponents see these institutions dominating the practice of culture on a day-to-day basis.

This school of social theory is also known as the **social construction of reality**. According to social constructionists, social institutions wield enormous power over culture because they view the culture propagated by institutions as having a reality beyond our control. Here's an example. Students are often told that when they graduate they will get jobs in the *real* world. Implicit in this assertion is the assumption that college life is somehow *unreal*, whereas the world of work is *real*. But what does *reality* mean in this context? Your daily life at college is not a fantasy world. There are classes to attend and exams to take. But you do have quite a bit of control over how you play your role as a student. You have the autonomy to decide what you will do and when you will do it. You can skip classes without risk of being expelled. Your grades must be consistently very low over a number of semesters before you might be asked to leave. On the other hand, a primary reason why the world of work is *real* is that individuals have much less control over their actions and any consequences they might produce. Although the rules governing work are becoming more flexible, most jobs still require people to work certain hours of the day. Between those hours, employees are required to do whatever tasks are assigned. Many workplaces are still hierarchically structured, with a few people at the top dictating what everyone else does. Unlike the university, even occasional violations of the rules of the workplace can get you fired. *Real*, in this example, then, means that work is externally structured with little or no input from us and therefore beyond our personal control.

Social constructionism's view of the role of media contrasts sharply with both mass society theory and the limited-effects notions. Mass society theory envisioned vast populations living in nightmare realities dominated by demagogues. Limited-effects research focused on the more or less effective transmission of ideas, attitudes, and information from dominant sources to passive receivers. When social constructionism is applied to mass communication, it makes assumptions similar to those of symbolic interactionism; it assumes that audiences are active. Audience members don't simply passively take in and store bits of information in mental filing cabinets; they actively process this information, reshape it, and store only what serves culturally defined needs. They are active even when this activity largely serves to reinforce what they already know—to make them more willing to trust and act on views of the social world communicated to them by media. Thus, media can serve as an important way for social institutions to transmit culture to us; they let us know what social roles and personal identities are appropriate.

Active audience members use the media's symbols to make sense of their environments and the things in it, but those definitions have little value unless others share them—that is, unless the symbols also define things for other people in the same way. A Lexus, for example, can be as expensive an automobile as a Porsche, and both are functionally the same thing: automobiles that transport people from here to there. Yet the "realities" that surround both cars (and the people who drive them) are quite different. Moreover, how these different drivers are treated by other people may also vary, not because of any true difference in them as humans, but because the "reality" attached to each car is used to define their drivers (Baran and Blasko, 1984). We'll discuss this more later. For now, it's worth noting that your power as an individual to control the "realities" surrounding these cars is limited. But if you can afford to buy one then you can choose to participate in the "reality" that surrounds it.

Alfred Schutz (1967, 1970), a banker whose avocation was sociology, provided some early systematic discussions of ideas that have become central to social constructionism. Like many meaning-making theorists, he was fascinated by what he regarded as the mysteries of everyday existence. For example, as a banker, he was conscious of how dependent our economic system was on people's willingness to routinely accept that money—identically printed on standardized pieces of paper, differing only slightly, primarily on the numbers printed on their face and back—could have radically different value. But money is just one everyday mystery. Schutz sought a broader understanding of how we make sense of the world around us in order to structure and coordinate our daily actions. He asked, "How are we able to do this with such ease that we don't even realize we are doing it?"

phenomenology
Theory developed by European philosophers focusing on individual experience of the physical and social world

For answers to riddles about the origin and maintenance of social order, Schutz turned to a body of social theory developed in Europe, **phenomenology**. Relying on phenomenological notions, he asks that we bracket, or set aside, our common sense, taken-for-granted explanations for what we do and recognize that everyday life is actually much more complicated than we assume. Schutz argues that we conduct our lives with little effort or thought because we have developed stocks of social knowledge that we use to quickly make sense of what goes on around us and then structure our actions using this knowledge. Our knowledge of how to use money, with our attitudes toward and feelings about money, are just one example of a small part of these stocks of social knowledge.

It's important to note that we usually don't have much conscious awareness of this knowledge. When we are questioned about how or why we are engaging in a wide range of everyday actions, we find the questions puzzling or absurd. There are no obvious answers to these questions, but why would anyone even bother to ask them?

typifications
"Mental images" that enable people to quickly classify objects and actions and then structure their own actions in response

Schutz labeled one of the most important forms of knowledge we possess: **typifications**. Typifications enable us to quickly classify objects and actions we observe and then quickly and routinely structure our own actions in response. But typifications operate to some extent like stereotypes—though they make it easy to interpret even ambiguous situations, they also distort and bias our experience of these situations. Typifications we've learned before can be applied over and over again as long as we have the sense that they enable us to see things as they "really" are. We're likely to go on applying typifications even when problems arise and our interpretations cause trouble.

The concept of typifications is similar to Mead's idea of symbols and the notion of schemas in information-processing theory. It differs from these in emphasizing that these elements of culture can be beyond our conscious control even when they are quite crucial in making sense of things and guiding our actions. Mead thought of symbols as created in face-to-face interaction. But are the roles on his hypothetical baseball team really that flexible? Maybe they might better be conceived of as made up of Schutz's typifications. A little league team might tolerate a lot of innovation, but on a "real" team, when the game is being played "for real," players' actions are expected to closely adhere to certain norms, including such seemingly minor things as how to warm up or chatter from the bench. Batters who have an unusual stance at the plate or who swing the bat in unusual ways are closely scrutinized and told they should change their behavior.

Typifications may get communicated in face-to-face interactions, but they are propagated by social institutions and serve to preserve the power and authority of those institutions. What would happen to our banks if lots of people suddenly had doubts about the value of paper money? Consider what happens to people who joke about bombs or weapons while going through airport security checks because they find it hard to take the security procedures seriously. They are lucky if all that happens is that they miss their flights. If we don't apply typifications correctly, our actions may be punished. We could be kicked off the team or wind up being grilled as potential terrorists.

Social constructionism also calls attention to the problematic consequences of taking typifications too seriously. When we rely on typifications to routinely structure our experience, we can make serious mistakes. You can test the power of typifications for yourself when reading the box entitled "Typifications Shaping Reality? Not Mine!"

Schutz's ideas were elaborated in *The Social Construction of Reality* by sociologists Peter Berger and Thomas Luckmann. Published in 1966, the book made virtually no mention of mass communication, but with the explosion of interest in the media accompanying the dramatic social and cultural changes of that turbulent decade, mass communication theorists (not to mention scholars from numerous other disciplines) quickly found Berger and Luckmann's work and identified its value for developing media theory.

In explaining how reality is socially constructed, the two sociologists assumed first that "there is an ongoing correspondence between my meanings and their meanings in the world [and] that we share a common sense about [their] reality" (Berger and Luckmann, 1966, p. 23). Let's use a common household article as our example. Here are three symbols for that object:

1. Knife

2.

3.

symbol
In social construction of reality, an object that represents some other object

In social construction of reality, a **symbol** is an object (in these instances, a collection of letters or drawings on paper) representing some other object—what we commonly refer to as a knife. Here are three other symbols for that same object:

1. Messer
2. Cuchillo

3.

But unless you speak German or Spanish, respectively, or understand the third symbol to be a drawing of a butter knife, these symbols have no meaning for you; there is no correspondence between our meaning and yours. We share no common sense about the reality of the object being symbolized.

But who says that *knife* means what we all know it to mean? And what's wrong with those people in Germany and Mexico? Don't they know that it's *knife*, not *messer* or *cuchillo*? In English-speaking countries, the cultural consensus has been formed that *knife* means that sharp thing we use to cut our food, among other things, just as the folks in German- and Spanish-speaking lands have agreed

THINKING ABOUT THEORY | Typifications Shaping Reality? Not Mine!

Typifications, Alfred Schutz tells us, are the common-sense stocks of social knowledge that help us quickly make sense of the world around us and shape our actions accordingly. Because they help us interpret our experiences, it is important that we build accurate, useful typifications for the significant events, people, and things in our worlds. But consider recent talk of "Blue America" and "Red America," two "realities" of our country so different that there seems to be little civil discourse, never mind consensus between them. America seems torn by a "great cultural divide." For example, where do you stand on issues such as the right of homosexuals to marry? The war on drugs? Sex education in schools? These are only three of the many difficult issues dividing us from one another. Our realities of these matters are composed of our experiences with them, but how "accurate" are the typifications defining those experiences (and therefore, our realities), and where do they come from?

Let's test ourselves by answering these five quiz items:

1. Which of these three states has the highest divorce rate: Arkansas, Oklahoma, or Massachusetts?
2. Which religious category has the highest divorce rate: Baptists, nondenominational Christians, or atheists and agnostics?
3. Considering the country's white, black, and Hispanic teens, which group has the highest incidence of severe drug problems?
4. Among New Hampshire, Mississippi, and Texas, which two states have the higher rates of teenage pregnancy?
5. Put these three cities in order of their crime rates, highest to lowest: Atlanta, New York, Memphis.

Of course, you know that only liberals and atheists on the Atlantic and Pacific coasts favor gay marriage. They don't hold the institution as sacred as do those in the heartland. And of course, drugs are a problem of the inner city, so tougher criminal sentencing is necessary to make the point for those people. And speaking of the city, at least heartland people have better morals than those East Coast blue-staters,

especially someplace like that modern-day Gomorrah, New York City.

But the divorce rate is lowest in northeast, liberal Massachusetts (2.2 out of every 1,000 people), lower than the national average (3.4/1,000) and far lower than that of Arkansas (5.7/1,000) and Oklahoma (4.9/1,000; U.S. Census Bureau, 2012). Atheists and agnostics divorce at a rate of 21 percent, well below that of Baptists (27 percent) and nondenominational Christians (34 percent; "U.S. Divorce Rates," 2009). Drug problems? Nine percent of white teenagers have serious drug problems; that's compared to 7.7 percent of Hispanic and 5 percent of African American teens (Szalavitz, 2011). Teenage pregnancy rates are highest in Mississippi (90 pregnancies for every 1,000 girls 15 to 19 years old) and Texas (85/1,000). New Hampshire (33/1,000) has the lowest, joined by all the other New England states with teen pregnancy rates well below the national average of 68 births per 1,000 teen women (Kost and Henshaw, 2013). New York City is the safest big city in America, with a per capita crime rate of 4.2 percent, compared to Memphis (18 percent) and Atlanta (16 percent; Ott, 2009).

What was your reality of different locales' and believers' commitment to marriage, the demographics of problematic drug use, rates of teen pregnancy, and the prevalence of crime? Did it surprise you to learn that Massachusetts, the first state to legally permit homosexuals to marry, has the lowest divorce rate in America? How well did your typifications match the statistical actuality of the "real world"? How much do your individual realities contribute to your stance on gay marriage, the "drug war," teen pregnancy, and crime? Where and how were your, and the larger culture's, realities of these issues constructed (a social-construction-of-reality question)? What do marriage or atheists or people from the northeast and "the heartland" symbolize for you (a symbolic interaction question)? How have media covered these social issues and the advocates of their varying positions (a framing question)? Now that you have more accurate data on these controversial issues, will you reassess your opinions about them? Why or why not? Can you cite other theories from this or earlier chapters to support your answer?

on something else. There is no inherent truth, value, or meaning in the ordered collection of the letters k-n-i-f-e giving it the reality that we all know it has. *We* have given it meaning, and because we share that meaning, we can function as a people (at least when the issue is household implements).

But Berger and Luckmann (1966, p. 35) recognized that there is another kind of meaning we attach to the things in our environments, one that is subjective rather than objective. They call these **signs**, objects explicitly designed "to serve as an index of subjective meaning"; this is analogous to symbolic interaction's concept of symbols. If you were to wake up tomorrow morning, head on your pillow, to find a knife stuck into the headboard inches above your nose, you'd be fairly certain that this was some sort of sign. In other words, people can produce representations of objects that have very specific, very subjective agreed-upon meanings. What does the knife in the headboard signify? Says who? What does a Lexus signify? Says who? What do several pieces of cloth—some red, some white, some blue—sewn together in a rectangle in such a way to produce thirteen alternating red and white stripes and a number of stars against a blue field in the upper-left-hand corner signify? Freedom? Democracy? Empire? The largest car dealer on the strip? A place to buy breakfast? Says who?

Remember that symbolic interaction defines signs and symbols in precisely the opposite way as does social-construction-of-reality theory. This small problem aside, how do people use these signs and symbols to construct a reality that allows social order to be preserved? Berger and Luckmann (1966) developed Schutz's notion of typifications into what they refer to as **typification schemes**, collections of meanings we assign to some phenomenon that come from our stock of social knowledge to pattern our interaction with our environments and the things and people in it. A bit more simply, we as a people, through interaction with our environment, construct a "natural backdrop" for the development of "typification schemes required for the major routines of everyday life, not only the typification of others ... but typifications of all sorts of events and experiences, both social and natural" (p. 43).

Of course, media theorists and practitioners, especially advertisers and marketing professionals, understand that whoever has the greatest influence over a culture's definitions of its symbols and signs has the greatest influence over the construction of the typification schemes individuals use to pattern their interactions with their various social worlds. In other words, social institutions have the most influence in or control over the social world because they often are able to dominate how typification schemes get created and used. Why, for example, is one beer more "sophisticated" than another? Are we less likely to serve an inexpensive local beer to our houseguests than we are to serve Michelob or Heineken? Why? What makes brand-name products or clothes with designer labels better than generic alternatives?

Alternately, consider the example of airport security checks. We as individuals don't have much control over what we're able to do during these checks. If we travel frequently, we've probably worked out strategies to enable ourselves to move efficiently through the security checks. We go to the airport early, expecting that there could be a long wait. As we wait, we remove all metal objects from our pockets to our luggage. We wear shoes that slip off easily. We place our photo ID

signs
In social construction of reality, objects explicitly designed to serve as an index of subjective meaning

typification schemes
In social construction of reality, collections of meanings assigned to some phenomenon, which come from a social stock of knowledge to pattern interaction with the environment and things and people in it

and ticket where we can easily access them. We know not to joke about guns and bombs. But even after all this preparation, an alarm may go off as we pass through the metal detector. We know to stop immediately and allow ourselves to be scanned with an intrusive hand wand. If we happen to travel on a day when security is especially tight, our carry-on luggage may be opened and searched. We may be asked to turn on our electronic equipment to make certain it is operational. In many other situations we would consider this kind of treatment demeaning, frustrating, or humiliating. But now it's just a routine part of flying. We have learned and accepted a typification scheme enabling us to cope.

So who's right about the amount of agency exercised by individuals in the social world? Are symbolic interactionists correct when they argue that important ways of interpreting things (symbols) get created through everyday interaction? Or are social constructionists correct when they argue that typifications are handed down to us primarily by institutions that dominate the social world? Could both of these perspectives provide useful insights into different aspects of the social world? What about the role of media? Is advertising a powerful tool in the hands of social elites because it enables them to communicate and reinforce typifications so that they are widely accepted and applied? Could social media give us greater control over meaning-making by allowing us to easily and routinely share the meanings *we* attach to things with others? If social media did give us greater control, might that subvert elite control and undermine social stability in the larger society? Could it enable us to form new communities with others?

Because he based his ideas on concepts derived from both symbolic interactionism and social constructionism, we'll look next at framing theory as developed by Erving Goffman. His was the first theory of framing that became widely accepted and applied. We'll then look at several other framing theories that have in recent years gained popularity. While these theories share important features, they also have important differences. We'll assess those differences and weigh the strengths and limitations of the various framing theories.

INSTANT ACCESS

Social Constructionism

Strengths	Weaknesses
1. Rejects simple stimulus-response conceptualizations of human behavior	1. Gives too little recognition to power of individuals and communities
2. Considers the social environment in which learning takes place	2. In some contemporary articulations, grants too much power to elites who control media content
3. Recognizes the complexity of human existence	
4. Foregrounds social institutions' role in agency	
5. Provides basis for many methodologies and approaches to inquiry	

As we'll see, Goffman's theory is an interesting combination of symbolic inter-actionism and social constructionism. It allows for a certain amount of individual agency, but it also grants a fair amount of power to institutions. As we'll also see, Goffman asserted that social institutions can dictate the rules of the game, but we still have the power to decide how or even whether we will play the game. If we opt out of the game, we may wind up categorized as screwballs or mentally ill, but from Goffman's perspective that might mean that we have more sanity than the people who take the game too seriously.

FRAMING AND FRAME ANALYSIS

While critical cultural researchers were developing reception analysis during the 1980s, a new approach to audience research was taking shape in the United States. It had its roots in symbolic interaction and social constructionism. As we've seen, both argue that the expectations we form about ourselves, other people, and our social world are central to social life. You have probably encountered many terms in this and other textbooks that refer to such expectations—stereotypes, attitudes, typification schemes, and racial or ethnic bias. All these concepts assume that our expectations are socially constructed. They share the following assumptions concerning expectations:

1. Expectations are based on previous experience of some kind, whether derived from a media message or direct personal experience (in other words, we aren't born with them).
2. Expectations can be quite resistant to change, even when they are contradicted by readily available factual information.
3. Expectations are often associated with and can arouse strong emotions such as hate, fear, or love.
4. We typically are not consciously aware of our expectations and so can't make useful predictions about how we will feel or act in future situations based on these expectations.
5. Expectations guide our actions without our conscious awareness, especially when strong emotions are aroused or there are distractions that interfere with our ability to focus our attention and consciously interpret new information available in the situation.

Are you skeptical about these assumptions? Do you think you have more awareness and conscious control over your expectations? Try paying close attention to your actions over the next few hours. Try predicting what you will do and how others will act before you enter a new situation. How useful were your predictions? Did you act precisely as you thought you would? Did others act as you predicted? If your predictions weren't very good, did this mean you had difficulty making sense of the situation and taking action in it? Did the actions of others seem unusual or abnormal? Even when we can't consciously make useful predictions about situations, we usually have no difficulty making sense of them and acting in them in ways.

Developing and using expectations is a normal and routine part of everyday life. As human beings, we have cognitive skills allowing us to continually scan our environment, make sense of it, and then act on these interpretations. Our actions are routinized and habitual. Our inability to adequately understand these skills in no way prevents them from operating, but it does impede our ability to make sense of or even gain an awareness of our own meaning-making. We constantly make interpretations of the world around us. Sometimes we will understand what we are doing, but more often we won't—typically it doesn't matter whether we do or not. But if we would like to or want to assume more responsibility for our actions, then we should be concerned.

Based in part on Ludwig Wittgenstein's linguistic philosophy—particularly his notion of language games, sociologist Erving Goffman (1974) developed **frame analysis** to provide a systematic account of how we use expectations to make sense of everyday-life situations and the people in them (the theory is graphically represented in the box entitled "The Framing Process"). Goffman was a keen observer of everyday-life interactions. He wondered how we manage to cope so easily with the complicated situations that we constantly encounter. He decided that the best way to gain insight into everyday situations was to focus on the mistakes we make as we go through daily life—including the mistakes we never notice, such as when one person mistakes another's courtesy for flirting, or when someone's effort to move quickly through an airport is seen as suspicious. Goffman was especially intrigued by the way magicians and con artists are able to trick people. All a magician has to do is distract our attention so that he or she can perform a trick without detection. Why are people often so gullible? Why have Nigerians been able to scam Americans out of millions of dollars using what appear to most people to be outrageous e-mail scams? Like Alfred Schutz, Goffman was convinced that daily life is much more complicated than it appears and that we have ways of dealing with these complications (Ytreberg, 2002).

Although Goffman agreed with social constructionist arguments concerning typification schemes, he found them too simple. He argued that we constantly and often radically change the way we define or typify situations, actions, and other people as we move through time and space. We are able to adjust the schemes to fit specific circumstances and other individuals. We don't have only one typification scheme—we have whole sets of schemes ranging along various dimensions. But we usually won't have any conscious awareness of when we are making these changes. In other words, our experience of the world can be constantly shifting, sometimes in major ways, yet we may not notice these shifts. We can step from one realm of experience to another without recognizing that a boundary has been crossed. We don't operate with a limited or fixed set of expectations about social roles, objects, or situations. Thus, we don't have a simple stock of institutionally controlled knowledge as most social constructionists contend. Rather, we have enormous flexibility in creating and using expectations. Goffman argued that our experience of reality is bound up with our ability to move effortlessly through daily life making sense of situations and the people in them. If we do encounter problems, we have strategies for resolving them so routinely that we can proceed as though nothing unusual had happened.

Goffman used the term **frame** to refer to a specific set of expectations used to make sense of a social situation at a given point in time. Frames are like Berger and Luckmann's typification schemes, but they differ in certain important respects. According to Goffman, individual frames are like notes on a musical scale—they

frame analysis
Goffman's idea about how people use expectations to make sense of everyday life

frame
In frame analysis, a specific set of expectations used to make sense of a social situation at a given point in time

spread along a continuum from those structuring our most serious and socially significant actions to those structuring playful, trivial actions. Like the notes on a musical scale, each is different, even though there is underlying structural continuity. For social action, the continuity is such that we can learn how to frame serious actions by first learning frames for playful actions. Using the musical scale analogy, we first learn to play simple tunes using a narrow range of the scale in preparation for playing complex musical scores. Likewise, many of our games and sports provide useful preparation for more serious forms of action. We can learn from playing little league baseball and then apply it when we play a more serious game—a real game of life in which there's more at stake. If we can perform well under the pressures of a big game, we may handle the demands of other life situations better. Goffman argued that we are like animal cubs that first play at stalking frogs and butterflies and then are able to transfer these skills to related but more serious situations.

downshift or upshift

In frame analysis, to move back and forth between serious and less serious frames

When we move from one set of frames to another, we **downshift or upshift**. We reframe situations so we experience them as more or less serious. Remember when you pretended to fight with a friend as a child, but someone got hurt and the fight turned serious? Suddenly, you no longer pulled punches but tried to make them inflict as much pain as possible; you downshifted. You used many of the fighting skills learned during play but with a different frame—now you were trying to hurt your friend. Perhaps, as you both got tired, one of you told a joke and cued the other that you wanted to upshift and go back to a more playful frame. In the airport security example, an alarm going off is likely to bring about a quick downshift in our framing.

Let's consider that example of airport security checks again. We may be traveling with a group of friends. It's a nice day and we've been having fun. We find it hard to take the security check seriously or it slips our mind that we need to be careful. We forget some of the things we normally do when we're taking a security check seriously. But then the alarm goes off. Suddenly things get serious. We have to make fast readjustments but we do it fairly easily. Our smile vanishes. We stand up straight and pay close attention to the security agents. It's likely that we blame ourselves for making stupid mistakes; we forgot to take off our shoes or to remove our keys from our pockets. According to Goffman, we've gone from framing the situation playfully to imposing a serious frame.

If the symbolic interactionists are right and our meaning-making ability is so great, so innovative, and so flexible, why is there any pattern or order to daily existence? How are we able to coordinate our actions with others and experience daily existence as having order and meaning—how can we routinely adjust ourselves to life within the boundaries set by social institutions, as social constructionists believe we do? Life, Goffman argued, operates much like a staged dramatic performance. We step from one social realm or sphere to another in much the same way that actors move between scenes. Scenes shift, and as they shift we are able to radically alter how we make sense of them. As the scenes shift, we locate and apply new sets of expectations. Sometimes, as in the example of the problematic security check, we don't make the proper shift and then we're forced to do so by the people around us.

Framing involves shifting expectations. But just how do we and the people around us know when to make shifts? How do we know when one scene is ending and another beginning and act jointly so a shift can be made so seamlessly that we don't even notice that it has happened? According to Goffman, we are always monitoring the social environment for **social cues** that signal when we are to make a change, and we ourselves are often quite skilled at using these cues. For example, when we view a play in a theater, we rely on many conventional cues to determine when a shift in scenes takes place. One of the oldest and most obvious cues involves the curtain—it rises when a scene begins and falls when a scene ends. Other cues are more subtle—shifts in lighting and music tempo often signal changes. As lights dim and music becomes ominous, we know danger threatens. Movies employ many similar conventions. Goffman believed we use the same cognitive skills to make sense of daily life that we do to make sense of plays or movies. His theory implies that we can learn social cues through everyday interaction and from observing how these cues are used in media content. Again, you can see this represented graphically in the box, "The Framing Process."

Back to the airport. What if security agents dressed in street clothes or in beachwear? What if they casually stood around and ignored scanner alarms? What if they were joking with each other instead of carefully monitoring equipment? Would we take them seriously or would we frame the situation playfully? Social cues can make a big difference in how we structure our actions—especially when we aren't paying attention to what we are doing.

social cues
In frame analysis, information in the environment that signals a shift or change of action

---

THINKING ABOUT THEORY | The Framing Process

In a different book (Davis and Baran, 1981), we developed this version of Goffman's theory of framing. Can you explain how it allows for upshifting and downshifting? Can you speculate on how errors in framing can occur?

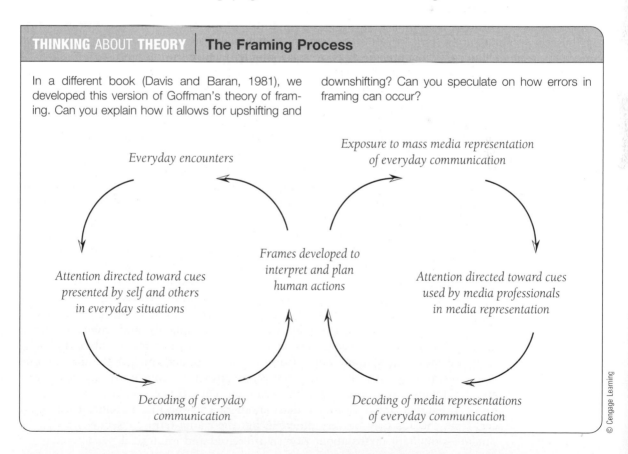

Everyday encounters

Exposure to mass media representation of everyday communication

Frames developed to interpret and plan human actions

Attention directed toward cues presented by self and others in everyday situations

Attention directed toward cues used by media professionals in media representation

Decoding of everyday communication

Decoding of media representations of everyday communication

So how do media come into this theory? Goffman made several heuristic explorations of the way media might influence our development and use of frames, including an essay entitled "Radio Talk" appearing in his book *Forms of Talk* (1981) and in another book, *Gender Advertisements* (1979). In the latter work he presented an insightful argument concerning the influence advertising could have on our perception of women. According to Goffman, ads are **hyperritualized representations** of social action (Ytreberg, 2002). They are edited to highlight only the most meaningful actions. Advertising using the sex appeal of women to attract the attention of men could inadvertently teach or reinforce social cues that might have inadvertent but serious consequences. Goffman showed how women in many ads are presented as less serious and more playful than men. They smile, place their bodies in nonserious positions, wear playful clothing, and in various ways signal deference and a willingness to take direction from men. Not only are they vulnerable to sexual advances, they signal their desire for them. No wonder these ads attract the attention of men. No wonder they are useful in positioning products. But could these representations of women be teaching or reinforcing social cues that have difficult consequences? Feminist theorists have made similar arguments (Walters, 1995).

We might be learning more than product definitions from these ads. We could be learning a vast array of social cues, some blatant but others quite subtle. Once learned, these cues could be used in daily life to make sense of members of the same or opposite sex and to impose frames on them, their actions, and the situations in which we encounter them. Or it's possible that these ads simply reinforce the cues we've already learned in daily life. But the constant repetition of the cues in the ads leads us to give them greater importance or priority. As we'll see later in this chapter, some researchers would argue that media cues can prime us to frame subsequent situations one way rather than another. For example, exposure to advertising could prime men to be overly sensitive to playful cues from women and increases the likelihood that they will upshift in ways that women don't expect or intend. Men learn such a vast repertoire of these cues that it might be hard for women to avoid displaying them. Men could routinely misinterpret inadvertent actions by women. Advertising might make it hard for women to maintain a serious frame for their actions. If they smile, bend their elbows in a particular way, or bow their heads even briefly, men might perceive a cue when none was intended. The more physically attractive the woman, the more likely this problem will arise, because most advertising features good-looking women.

Goffman's theory provides an intriguing way of assessing how media can elaborate and reinforce a dominant public culture. Advertisers didn't create sex-role stereotypes, but, Goffman argued, they have homogenized how women are publicly depicted. This is the danger of hyperritualization. Goffman contrasted the variety of ways that women are represented in private photos with their standardized (hyperritualized) depiction in advertising. Marketers routinely use powerful visual imagery to associate products with women who explicitly and implicitly signal their willingness to be playful sexual partners. There are many subtle and not-so-subtle messages in these ads. "Consume the product and get the girl" is one dominant message. Another is that physically attractive women are sexually active and fun-loving. Ads both teach and reinforce cues. They regularly prime us to frame situations one way rather than another. The specific messages each of us gets from the ads may be very different, but their long-term consequences may be similar—dominant myths about women are retold and reinforced.

hyperritualized representations
Media content constructed to highlight only the most meaningful actions

primary, or dominant, reality

In frame analysis, the real world in which people and events obey certain conventional and widely accepted rules (sometimes referred to as the dominant reality)

Compared with the other theories we have examined in this chapter, Goffman's is the most open-ended and flexible. He was convinced that social life is a constantly evolving and changing phenomenon, and yet we experience it as having great continuity. Though we have the capacity to constantly reframe our experience from moment to moment, most of us can maintain the impression that our experiences are quite consistent and routine. According to Goffman, we do this by firmly committing ourselves to live in what we experience as the **primary, or dominant, reality**—a real world in which people and events obey certain conventional and widely accepted rules. We find this world so compelling and desirable that we are constantly reworking our experience and patching up flaws in it, and we don't notice when rule violations occur.

Goffman argued that we work so hard maintaining our sense of continuity in our experience that we inevitably make many framing mistakes. We literally see and hear things that aren't—but should—be there according to the rules we have internalized. For example, most college campuses in America today face the problem of date rape. And ultimately, what is the basic issue in most of these occurrences? Goffman might answer that the issue involves upshifting and downshifting problems between men and women as they attempt to frame the situations (dating) they find themselves in. Alcohol consumption is often associated with date rape, increasing the likelihood that social cues will be misread or ignored. Or consider the even more common problem on campuses of binge drinking. Most students have a hard time taking drinking seriously. They've learned to frame drinking as an essentially playful activity. Advertising continually reinforces this frame along with its related social cues. The unwanted consequences of drinking too much don't appear in advertising. When these consequences are portrayed in the anti-binge-drinking advertising, students have a hard time taking these ads seriously.

From Goffman's viewpoint, primary reality is the touchstone of our existence—the real world in every sense of that term. We do permit ourselves constant and socially acceptable escapes into clearly demarcated alternative realities we experience as recreational or fantasy worlds. These are worlds where we can escape the pressures of being center stage in an unfolding drama we know can have long-term consequences. Not many students would expect to earn a high grade on an important

INSTANT ACCESS

Frame Analysis

Strengths

1. Focuses attention on individuals in the mass communication process
2. Micro-level theory but is easily applicable to macro-level issues
3. Is highly flexible and open-ended
4. Is consistent with recent findings in cognitive psychology

Weaknesses

1. Is overly flexible and open-ended (lacks specificity)
2. Postpositivists and critical cultural researchers have different versions of this theory
3. Causal explanations are only possible when there is a narrow focus on framing effects
4. Assumes individuals make frequent framing errors; questions individuals' abilities

essay exam by writing jokes about the instructor, but as the date rape example suggests, when we make framing mistakes in a playful reality, the results can be devastating to our real world.

THE DEVELOPMENT OF THEORIES OF FRAMES AND FRAMING

Frame analysis theory as developed by Goffman is a micro-level theory focusing on how individuals learn to routinely make sense of their social world. After Goffman's work in the 1960s and 1970s, framing theory continued to gain interest and acceptance. Today it has become one of the leading theories of mass communication. Other scholars took Goffman's ideas and extended them to create a conceptual framework that considers (1) the social and political context in which framing takes place, (2) how journalists develop and impose frames on ambiguous events to create news stories, (3) how news readers learn and apply frames to make sense of news, and (4) the long-term social and political consequences of news media frames.

The increasing popularity of framing theory has resulted in the development of differing versions of the theory. Critical cultural researchers have developed forms of framing theory that differ radically from those of postpositivist scholars. Postpositivist researchers have focused on identifying and measuring specific effects of certain types of frames on audiences or readers. They have identified "generic" frames that are frequently found in news stories and fundamentally alter how events are viewed by news audiences. These include conflict or contest frames, horse-race frames (Chapter 8), strategic frames, economic frames, moral frames, thematic frames, and episodic frames. Critical cultural researchers have focused on elite control over framing, how social movements use frames to advance their goals, and how people's understanding of the social world is shaped by frames learned from media. We will describe both types of framing theory, and we will consider the strengths and limitations of each. In general, postpositivists and critical cultural scholars have produced compatible findings even though their approaches are quite different. Research projects are being developed that use both approaches to produce more comprehensive findings (de Vreese, 2012).

Early examples of framing research applied to journalism can be found in the scholarship of two sociologists whom you met in the last chapter, Todd Gitlin (1980) and Gaye Tuchman (1978). Their work is frequently cited and has played an important early role in extending Goffman's ideas. Tuchman and Gitlin are critical cultural studies scholars with an interest in elite control over framing and how journalists frame events. Gitlin, as you saw in Chapter 5, focused on news coverage of politically radical social movements during the late 1960s. He argued that media framing of these movements demeaned their members, criticized their activities, and ignored their ideas. These representations made it impossible for movements to achieve their objectives. Tuchman focused on routine news production work and the serious limitations inherent in specific strategies for coverage of events (Chapter 8). Although the intent of these practices is to provide objective news coverage, the result is news stories in which events are routinely framed in ways that eliminate much of their ambiguity and instead reinforce socially accepted and expected ways of seeing the social world. Both Gitlin and Tuchman concluded that news mainly serves to perpetuate the status quo and to undermine social movements.

One of the most productive and creative contemporary framing researchers is William Gamson (1989; Gamson et al., 1992). He authored and coauthored a series of books, book chapters, and articles that have helped shape current perspectives on framing theory and its explanation of how news has influence in the social world. Gamson argues that framing of many societal issues and events is highly contested. Increasingly, frames used in public discourse are developed and promoted by individuals and groups having an interest in advancing certain ways of seeing the social world rather than others. He has traced the success and failure of social movements in promoting frames consistent with their ideological interests, specifically in the realm of nuclear power and global warming (Gamson and Modigliani, 1989).

Gamson's interest is in the ability of activist movements to bring about social change. He shares the social constructionist view that social institutions and the elites who lead them are able to dominate the social world by propagating frames serving their interests. But he believes that social movements have the ability to generate and promote alternate frames that can bring about important change in the social order. But for this to happen, movements need to develop cogent frames expressing their views, and they need to persuade journalists to produce news stories that present these frames effectively and sympathetically. Only then will such frames be disseminated to a larger audience so that more people begin to view the social world the way that movement members do. If enough people change their views, public pressure may build so that leaders of social institutions make changes. Still, Gamson concedes that cultural and political elites maintain the advantage, because "some frames have a natural advantage because their ideas and language resonate with a broader political culture. Resonances increase the appeal of a frame by making it appear natural and familiar. Those who respond to the larger cultural theme will find it easier to respond to a frame with the same sonoroties" (1992, p. 135). Charles Rowling and his colleagues elaborate, "As a result, culturally resonant messages possess high potential to cascade through the framing hierarchy.... [F]rames that tap into and resonate with cultural values—by celebrating or reinforcing them—will be more difficult to challenge; meanwhile, frames that do not engage with, or go so far as to overtly challenge, prevailing cultural values will be more likely to elicit contestation by other political actors, journalists, and the public" (Rowling, Jones, and Sheets, 2011, p. 1046). They base their argument on Robert Entman's (2004) **cascading activation model** of framing that posits that there is a "framing hierarchy in public discourse, with executive branch officials at the highest level, Congress followed by policy experts and ex-government officials at the middle level, and the press at the lowest level" (p. 1045). Using this model, these authors were able to demonstrate how elite frames dominated journalists' framing and therefore public perception of the debate surrounding torture by American military forces at Abu Ghraib prison in Iraq, rendering the complaints of antiwar and human rights activist groups ineffective.

Robert Benford and David Snow (2000) have provided a useful summary of social movement research grounded in framing theory, as have Johnston and Noakes (2005). You can read about how one contemporary social movement attempted to frame itself, how its opponents hoped to frame it, and how it was eventually framed by the traditional media in the box, "Framing Occupy Wall Street."

cascading activation model
Perspective on framing that posits a framing hierarchy in public discourse, with powerful public officials at the top and the press at the lowest level

THINKING ABOUT THEORY | Framing Occupy Wall Street

In mid-2011, as prodemocracy protests were erupting across the Middle East, ushering in what was to become known as "The Arab Spring," activists at the anticonsumerism organization Adbusters sent an e-mail to their subscribers suggesting similar action on New York's Wall Street, the real and symbolic heart of the American financial industry. Fueled by Twitter, Facebook, and Tumblr, the idea took off and soon there were Occupy Wall Street (OWS) protests in more than 900 cities around the world (Garofoli, 2012). The movement's physical and philosophical Wall Street home was in Zuccotti Park, where thousands of protesters set up a community, complete with a kitchen, library, and professionally staffed medical facility. Their goal was to raise public awareness of the country's growing level of income disparity—the gap between the richest Americans and those in the shrinking middle class and the swelling ranks of the poor. OWS's slogan, "We are the 99%," was designed to highlight the fact that the income and opportunity gap between the richest people in the country (the 1 percent) and everyone else was rapidly growing and becoming a permanent part of American life (Panousi et al., 2013). Making New York's financial district the site of its main activities was intended to signify that it was the activities of the nation's financial elites that were responsible for Americans' increasing economic insecurity. OWS had no leader; all decisions were made by consensus. It made no demands; its aim was to raise awareness, and through its actions make the moral argument for economic fairness. It espoused nonviolence.

Then the framing began. Conservative political consultant Frank Lutz advised anti-OWS politicians, when asked about the movement and its issues, to avoid expressions like *capitalism* (use *economic freedom* and *free market*), *tax the rich* (use *take from the rich*), *middle class* (use *hardworking taxpayers*), and *government spending* (use *government waste*). Never disagree with OWS's goals; instead say, " 'I get it.' … 'I *get* that you're angry. I *get* that you've seen inequality. I *get* that you want to fix the system.' " Opponents' goal was to frame OWS as well-intentioned but occupying the wrong place—occupy the White House, not Wall Street, because that's who's actually responsible for the country's financial woes (in Moody, 2011).

Liberal linguist George Lakoff, warning OWS to "frame yourself before others frame you," suggested the movement frame itself as "a moral and patriotic movement. It sees Democracy as flowing from citizens caring about one another as well as themselves, and acting with both personal and social responsibility. Democratic governance is about The Public, and the liberty that The Public provides for a thriving Private Sphere. From such a democracy flows fairness, which is incompatible with a hugely disproportionate distribution of wealth. And from the sense of care implicit in such a democracy flows a commitment to the preservation of nature" (2011). OWS's own framing would stress its love for America and desire to fix it.

How did the media frame OWS? "The media's initial portrayal of the Occupy protests was as airily dismissive," writes anthropologist and OWS activist David Graeber, "a collection of confused kids with no clear conception of what they were fighting for. The *New York Times*, the self-proclaimed paper of historical record, wrote absolutely nothing about the occupation [which was occurring only a few city blocks from its offices] for the first five days. On the sixth, they published an editorial disguised as a news story in the Metropolitan section, titled 'Gunning for Wall Street, with Faulty Aim,' by staff writer Ginia Bellafante, mocking the movement as a mere pantomime of progressivism with no discernible purpose" (2013). Margaret Cissel's content analysis comparing mainstream and alternative news coverage of the movement's first three weeks confirms Graeber's view. "While the mainstream media used confusion over the event as their dominant frames, alternative media focused on what the demonstrators were actually trying to accomplish," she discovered. And "while both news sources highlighted various conflicts surrounding the events of Occupy, they did so differently. The mainstream media placed the protesters at fault of the violence, and conversely, the alternative media sources focused on the brutality of the police and their violent acts on the peaceful protestors…. Occupy Wall Street highlights the differences between these two media sources. On the one hand, the mainstream media portrayed Occupy as a directionless and confused gathering of 'hippies'; on the other, alternative media focused on how the police, corporations, government,

(Continued)

and mass media are preventing them from having a voice by prohibiting their free speech through legalities and logistics" (2012, pp. 74–75).

But did OWS's "general refusal to identify clear leaders ... or even express focused demands" (Greenberg, 2011) doom its own framing efforts? Did the absence of identifiable spokespeople leave reporters with no one to interview but city and police officials, denying journalists the convenience of personalizing OWS and facilitating their tendency to seek out normalizing, elite voices, as news production (Chapter 9) as well as framing researchers might have predicted? Did the lack of movement demands mean that reporters had to find other ways to represent OWS, for example, with constant video of drum circles? Or, as Todd Gitlin—because of the media's natural elite bias—and Gaye Tuchman—because of journalism's routine, status quo–oriented news gathering practices—might have argued, could nothing have helped OWS control the way it was framed by the traditional media?

Despite the framing wars and media neglect, the movement quickly earned the support of a majority of the public. One month after it began, 54 percent of likely voters held a positive view of OWS, and 80 percent agreed with its declaration that the country's wealth disparity was too large (Greenberg, 2011). And what about those 900 other worldwide OWS protests? And what explains the fact that the movement endures today as a national and state-based movement, with issue-specific offshoots such as Occupy Our Homes (to help foreclosed and other home owners deal with their banks)? Is it possible that opposition and traditional media framing failed to shape the public's meaning-making of the movement? Is it possible that social media limited the traditional media's ability to impose a status-quo frame on OWS, or even forced them to reconsider that reflexive framing of movements? While acknowledging the power of the movement's message with a nation grown weary of an out-of-control and unaccountable financial industry, activist Graeber (2013), with two years of hindsight, argues that that elite framing of OWS failed because

by 2011 the omnipresence of phone cameras, Twitter accounts, Facebook, and YouTube

ensured such images [of movement activities] could spread instantly to millions. The image of [police officer] Tony Bologna casually blasting two young women behind a barricade with a chemical weapon appeared almost instantly on screens across the nation.... As a result, our numbers grew dramatically. What's more, union support materialized and rallies became larger and larger—instead of a couple thousand people coming to Zuccotti to rally or assemble for marches during the day, the crowds swelled to the tens of thousands. Thousands across America began trying to figure out how to send in contributions and started calling in an almost unimaginable wave of free pizzas. The social range of the occupiers also expanded: The crowd, which in the first few days was extremely white, soon diversified, so that within a matter of weeks we were seeing African-American retirees and Latino combat veterans marching and serving food alongside dreadlocked teenagers. There was a satellite General Assembly conducted entirely in Spanish. What's more, ordinary New Yorkers, thousands of whom eventually came to visit, if only out of curiosity, were astonishingly supportive: According to one poll, not only did majorities agree with the protests, 86 percent supported the protesters' right to maintain the encampment. Across the country, in just about every city in America, unlikely assortments of citizens began pitching tents, and middle-aged office workers listened attentively to punk rockers or pagan priestesses lecturing on the subtleties of consensus and facilitation or arguing about the technical differences between civil disobedience and direct action or the truly horizontal way to organize sanitation. In other words, for the first time in most of our living memories, a genuine grassroots movement for economic justice had emerged in America. What's more, the dream of contaminationism, of democratic contagion, was, shockingly, starting to work.

We'll return in the next chapter to the issue of the power of the new personal communication technologies to aid individual meaning-making and effect macro-level, cultural change.

EFFECTS OF FRAMES ON NEWS AUDIENCES

Over the past 20 years, postpositivist researchers have used effects research to document the influence frames can have on news audiences. The most common finding is that exposure to news coverage results in learning that is consistent with the frames that structure the coverage. If the coverage is dominated by a single frame, especially one originating from an elite source, learning will tend to be guided by this frame (Ryan, Carragee, and Meinhofer, 2001; Valkenburg and Semetko, 1999). What this research has also shown is that news coverage can strongly influence the way news readers or viewers make sense of news events and their major actors. This is especially true of news involving an ongoing series of highly publicized and relevant events, such as social movements (McLeod and Detenber, 1999; Nelson and Clawson, 1997; Terkildsen and Schnell, 1997). Research findings have confirmed many of the assertions made by Gitlin (1980). Typically, news coverage is framed to support the status quo, resulting in unfavorable views of movements. The credibility and motives of movement leaders are frequently undermined by frames that depict them as overly emotional, disorganized, or childish. Demonstrations organized by social movements are depicted as potentially violent so that police action is justifiable. Revisit Martin Luther King's lament over the coverage of his peaceful civil rights activities in Chapter 5, and in that same chapter, revisit Paul Krugman's "confusion" over the difference between protesters in Communist China's Tiananmen Square ("heroes of democracy") and those in America's anti-war demonstrations ("the usual protesters" and "serial protesters" whose "rallies delight Iraq").

Both postpositivist and critical cultural framing research provides a pessimistic assessment of news and the role that journalism plays in society. Frames used to structure news about major events are chosen based on journalistic traditions and newsroom norms with little consideration of how information structured by these frames will be interpreted and used by news audiences (Bennett, Lawrence, and Livingston, 2007; Patterson, 1993). Frames continue to be widely used even though research has shown that they are misleading or problematic. Journalists continue to frame election campaigns as horse races with a focus on who is winning or losing (Aalberg, Strömbäck, and de Vreese, 2012; Gulati, Just, and Crigler, 2004). Attention is focused on the strategies used by candidates to gain advantages over their opponents. Elections are framed primarily as contests in which conflict is central. Limited attention is given to framing public issues while considerable attention is given to framing the tactics, personalities, and personal lives of candidates (Van Aelst, Sheafer, and Stanyer, 2012). When issues are covered they are often portrayed merely as tools to be used to gain advantages in the contest. This type of coverage has been found to foster political apathy and cynicism, in part because it portrays politicians as egotists willing to do anything to garner votes, defeat opponents, and gain power (Cappella and Jamieson, 1997). Similarly, news reporting of health crises or threats to individual safety or national security tends to rely on frames that exaggerate threats but provide little practical advice on how to take actions that can minimize danger (Berger, 2001; Mazzarella, 2010). In fact, science news often leads to widespread public misunderstanding of science (Hargreaves and Ferguson, 2000). Overall, reporting of many issues tends to arouse undue public concerns while providing people with no way to alleviate these concerns aside from putting trust in public officials and official agencies. On the one hand, news fosters cynicism about politicians; on the other, it tells us there is no alternative but to trust these officials.

POSTPOSITIVIST VS CRITICAL CULTURAL APPROACHES TO FRAMING

The increasing popularity of framing research has been accompanied by arguments about ambiguity, limited scope, and inconsistency in framing theory. Some scholars argue that there are actually several different framing theories that should be carefully differentiated (Entman, 1993). Others want to integrate differing notions into a single theory (Scheufele, 1999, 2000). Critical cultural scholars complain that elite domination of framing is often neglected by postpositivist researchers (Carragee and Roefs, 2004). Postpositivists complain that the frames used in critical cultural research are too abstract and can't be studied systematically. In part, these differences in framing theory and the disagreements it generates stem from fundamentally different views of framing held by postpositivist and critical cultural researchers. Postpositivists are primarily interested in framing theory as a new and potentially more useful way to understand and predict media effects (Scheufele, 1999, 2000). They see framing research as closely related to the theories of media cognition and information processing (Scheufele and Tewksbury, 2007) that we considered in Chapter 8. They want to know if certain types of frames can affect how event information is processed and whether exposure to framed content will have specific effects. Postpositivists have not been interested in the origin of frames or why journalists choose certain frames to present events. They are not concerned about elite control over framing or the way frames get contested and negotiated. They focus on the effects of specific frames. They conduct quantitative research using experiments and surveys to demonstrate the existence of effects.

Critical cultural researchers reject the narrow focus of framing effects research. They have developed more macroscopic conceptualizations of framing that take into account elite efforts to control framing, framing done by journalists, and the way framing shapes public understanding of the social world. Critical cultural researchers have conducted qualitative research using field studies, content analysis, in-depth interviews or focus group research. They have found evidence of elite domination of framing and documented the problematic ways that news frames issues, politicians, and events. Some of their research focuses on framing contests in which elites are pitted against social movements in an effort to shape public understanding of certain aspects of the social world (Bennett, Lawrence, and Livingston, 2007; Entman, Livingston, and Kim, 2009). They have detailed the advantages that elites have over movements.

Framing theory appears likely to continue to develop and provide a basis for media research. In Chapter 11, we will discuss how framing research can be adapted to social media as well as to the ever increasing number and variety of Internet-based media. While news is the focus of most framing research today, framing theory could be readily applied to most other forms of media content. There is some framing research that deals with entertainment programming, but almost all current framing research examines news frames. Framing theory could be applied to content on Facebook or Twitter since these media have become central to the way that many people find out about and make sense of the world around them.

In Chapter 11, we also consider how framing theory can provide a basis for reforming journalism. Framing research findings have demonstrated serious limitations in many different journalism practices. Research consistently demonstrates that journalists routinely frame news events in ways that have problematic consequences. Framing research could be used to recommend and evaluate new strategies for news production. Currently there are two ongoing efforts to reform journalism—the civic journalism and the citizen journalism movements. We will discuss how framing research could be used to achieve the objectives of these movements.

MEDIA AS CULTURE INDUSTRIES: THE COMMODIFICATION OF CULTURE

commodification of culture

The study of what happens when culture is mass-produced and distributed in direct competition with locally based cultures

One of the most intriguing and challenging perspectives to emerge from critical cultural studies is the **commodification of culture**, the study of what happens when culture is mass-produced and distributed in direct competition with locally based cultures (Enzensberger, 1974; Gunster, 2004; Hay, 1989; Jhally, 1987). According to this viewpoint, media are industries specializing in the production and distribution of cultural commodities. As with other modern industries, they have grown at the expense of small local producers, and the consequences of this displacement have been and continue to be disruptive to people's lives.

In earlier social orders, such as medieval kingdoms, the culture of everyday life was created and controlled by geographically and socially isolated communities. Though kings and lords might dominate an overall social order and have their own culture, it was often totally separate from and had relatively little influence over the folk cultures structuring the everyday experience of average people. Only in modern social orders have elites begun to develop subversive forms of mass culture capable of intruding into and disrupting the culture of everyday life, argue commodification-of-culture theorists. These new forms function as very subtle but effective ways of thinking, leading people to misinterpret their experiences and act against their own self-interests.

Elites are able to disrupt everyday cultures by using a rather insidious and ingenious strategy. They take bits and pieces of folk culture, weave them together to create attractive mass culture content, and then market the result as a substitute for everyday forms of folk culture (Tunstall, 1977). Thus, elites not only subvert legitimate local cultures, but also earn profits doing so. People actually subsidize the subversion of their everyday culture. If you've ever debated hip-hop and rap artists "selling out," you've been part of a discussion of the commodification of culture. How did rap evolve from its roots in urban verbal warfare into a billion-dollar recording genre and vehicle for paid product placements (Kaufman, 2003)?

Commodification-of-culture theorists argue that this strategy has been especially successful in the United States, where media entrepreneurs have remained relatively independent from political institutions. Mass culture gained steadily in popularity, spawning huge industries that successfully competed for the attention and interest of most Americans. As a result, compared to what occurred in Europe, criticism of mass culture in the United States was muted. Most Americans accepted the cultural commodities emerging from New York and Hollywood as somehow their own. But these same commodities aroused considerable controversy when U.S. media entrepreneurs exported them to other nations (Gunster, 2004). The power of these commodities to reshape daily life was more obvious in most Third World nations, and even more disruptive.

In *The Media Are American* (1977), Jeremy Tunstall provided a cogent description of how American media entrepreneurs developed their strategy for creating universally attractive cultural commodities. He also traced how they succeeded internationally against strong competition from formerly dominant world powers France and Britain. In the late nineteenth and early twentieth centuries, American entrepreneurs had access to powerful new communications technology but no clear notion of how it could be used to make profits. Most big industrialists regarded media as no more than minor and highly speculative enterprises. Few were willing to invest the money necessary to create viable industries. How could messages broadcast through the air or crude black-and-white moving images on a movie screen be used to earn profits? Would people really pay to see or hear these things? How should industries be organized to manufacture and market cultural products? Most early attempts to answer these questions failed, but through trial and effort, wily entrepreneurs eventually developed a successful strategy.

According to Tunstall, the Tin Pan Alley "tune factory" in New York City provided a model later emulated by other U.S. media industries. The authors of popular music specialized in taking melodies from folk music and transforming them into short, attractive songs. These were easily marketed to mass audiences who didn't have the time or the aesthetic training to appreciate longer, more sophisticated forms of music. In its early days, Tin Pan Alley was a musical sweatshop in which songwriters were poorly paid and overworked, while sheet music and recording company entrepreneurs reaped huge profits. By keeping production and distribution costs low, rapid expansion was possible and profits grew accordingly. Inevitably, expansion carried the entrepreneurs beyond the United States. Because many were first-generation European immigrants, they knew how to return to and gain a foothold in Europe. World War II provided an ideal opportunity to further subvert European culture. The American military demanded and received permission to import massive quantities of U.S.-style popular culture into Europe, where it proved popular. American Armed Forces Radio was especially influential in its broadcasts of popular music and entertainment shows.

What are the consequences of lifting bits of the culture of everyday life out of their context, repackaging them, and then marketing them back to people?

Commodification-of-culture theorists provide many intriguing answers to this question:

1. **When elements of everyday culture are selected for repackaging, only a very limited range is chosen, and important elements are overlooked or consciously ignored.** For example, elements of culture important for structuring the experience of small minority groups are likely to be ignored, whereas culture practiced by large segments of the population will be emphasized. For a good illustration of

this, watch situation comedies from the 1960s like *Father Knows Best* and *Leave It to Beaver*. During this era, these programs provided a very homogeneous and idealized picture of American family life. They might make you wonder whether there were any poor people, working women, or ethnic groups living in the United States in the 1960s.

2. **The repackaging process involves dramatization of those elements of culture that have been selected.** Certain forms of action are highlighted, their importance is exaggerated, and others are ignored. Such dramatization makes the final commodity attractive to as large an audience as possible. Potentially boring, controversial, or offensive elements are removed. Features are added that are known to appeal to large audience segments. Thus, attention-getting and emotion-arousing actions— for example, sex and violence—are routinely featured. This is a major reason that car chases, gunfights, and verbal conflict dominate prime-time television and Hollywood movies, but casual conversations between friends are rare (unless they include a joke every 15 seconds—then we have comedy).

Rachel Dodes (2013) recently discussed the difficulties faced by movie producers as they seek to commodify various forms of social media. You can stage dramatic phone conversations by splitting the screen and showing two emotionally involved actors but what do you do with texting? Boxes of text on the movie screen are boring no matter how well written or presented. Movies featuring social media have failed at the box office. Critics blame the 2012 failure of *LOL* in part to its boring representation of social media. Dodes argued that an upcoming film, *Disconnect*, might provide more innovative and potentially interesting representations. By the time you read this, the box office will have delivered a verdict on this movie.

3. **The marketing of cultural commodities is undertaken in a way that maximizes the likelihood that they will intrude into and ultimately disrupt everyday life.** The success of the media industries depends on marketing as much content as possible to as many people as possible with no consideration for how this content will actually be used or what its long-term consequences will be. An analogy can be made to pollution of the physical environment caused by food packaging. The packaging adds nothing to the nutritional value of the food but is merely a marketing device—it moves the product off the shelf. Pollution results when we carelessly dispose of this packaging or when there is so much of it that there is no place to put it. Unlike trash, media commodities are less tangible and their packaging is completely integrated into the cultural content. There are no recycling bins for cultural packaging. When we consume the product, we consume the packaging. It intrudes and disrupts.

4. **The elites who operate the cultural industries generally are ignorant of the consequences of their work.** This ignorance is based partly on their alienation from the people who consume their products. They live in Hollywood or New York City, not in typical neighborhoods. They maintain ignorance partly through strategic avoidance or denial of evidence about consequences in much the same way the tobacco industry has concealed and lied about research documenting the negative effects of smoking. Media industries have developed formal mechanisms for rationalizing their impact and explaining away consequences. One involves supporting empirical social research and the limited-effects findings it produces. Another involves professionalization. Although this can have positive benefits (see Chapter 3), media practitioners can

---

INSTANT ACCESS

The Commodification of Culture

Strengths	Weaknesses
1. Provides a useful critique of commodification of culture by media	1. Argues for, but does not empirically demonstrate, effects
2. Identifies problems created by repackaging of cultural content	2. Has overly pessimistic view of media influence and the ability of average people to cope with cultural commodities
3. Identifies many subtle ways that advertising intrudes into everyday culture	3. Needs to be altered to take into account commodification of culture by new media

---

also use it to justify routine production practices while they reject potentially useful innovations.

5. **Disruption of everyday life takes many forms—some disruptions are obviously linked to consumption of especially deleterious content, but other forms are very subtle and occur over long periods.** Disruption ranges from propagation of misconceptions about the social world—like those cultivation analysis has examined (Chapter 9)—to disruption of social institutions. Consequences can be both microscopic and macroscopic and may take many different forms. For example, Joshua Meyrowitz (1985) argued that media deprive us of a sense of place. Neil Postman (1985) believes that media focus too much on entertainment, with serious long-term consequences. He has also examined media disruption in books entitled *The Disappearance of Childhood* (1994) and *The End of Education* (1996). Disruption of childhood, as you saw in Chapter 6, is also the focus of Susan Linn's *Consuming Kids* (2004), Benjamin Barber's *Consumed: How Markets Corrupt Children, Infantilize Adults, and Swallow Citizens Whole* (2007), and Shirley Steinberg's *Kinderculture: The Corporate Construction of Childhood* (2011). Kathleen Jamieson (1988) lamented the decline of political speech making brought about by electronic media and, with Karlyn Campbell (Jamieson and Campbell, 1997), media's corruption of the meaning of citizen action. Michael Parenti (1992), in *Make-Believe Media: The Politics of Entertainment*, also explores this theme.

ADVERTISING: THE ULTIMATE CULTURAL COMMODITY

Not surprisingly, critical cultural studies researchers direct some of their most devastating criticism toward advertising. They view it as the ultimate cultural commodity (Hay, 1989; Jhally, 1987). Advertising packages promote messages so they will be attended to and acted on by people who often have little interest in and often no real need for most of the advertised products or services. Marketers routinely portray consumption of specific products as the best way to construct a worthwhile personal identity, have fun, make friends and influence people, or solve problems (often ones we never knew we had). You deserve a break today. Just do it. Be the most interesting man in the world.

Compared to other forms of mass media content, advertising comes closest to fitting older Marxist notions of ideology. It is intended to encourage consumption that serves the interest of product manufacturers but may not be in the interest of individual consumers. Advertising is clearly designed to intrude into and disrupt routine buying habits and purchasing decisions. It attempts to stimulate and reinforce consumption, even if consumption might be detrimental to individuals' long-term health or their budget. For some products, such as cigarettes, alcohol, and even fast food, successful advertising campaigns move people to engage in self-destructive actions. In other cases, we are simply encouraged to consume things serving little real purpose for us or serving only the purposes that advertising itself creates. One obvious example is when we buy specific brands of clothing because their advertising has promoted them as status symbols. Clothing does indeed provide basic protection for our bodies, but used clothing from a thrift store provides the same protection as do the most well-known brands. Former ad agency executive turned anticommercialism activist Jelly Helm believes advertising's intrusion into American culture has created a country that is "sick.... We work too hard so that we can buy things we don't need, made by factory workers who are paid too little, and produced in ways that threaten the very survival of the earth." The United States "will be remembered as the greatest wealth-producer ever. It will be a culture remembered for its promise and might and its tremendous achievements in technology and health. It also will be remembered as a culture of hedonism to rival any culture that has ever existed, a culture of materialism and workaholism and individualism, a culture of superficiality and disposability, of poverty and pollution, and vanity and violence, a culture denuded of its spiritual wisdom" (Helm, 2002).

SUMMARY

This chapter has examined contemporary cultural and critical cultural theories. Some are primarily microscopic, examining individuals' and communities' everyday use of media, and others are more macroscopic, assessing media's role in the larger social order. But as you read, you saw that when dealing with cultural and critical cultural theory, the microscopic perspective has much to say about the macroscopic. The theories in this chapter are "culture-centered" because they focus on culture as a primary means of understanding the social world and media's role in it. They are also meaning-making theories because they examine the manner in which media influence how we make sense of the social world and our place in it.

One such theory is symbolic interaction, which assumes that our experience of reality is a social construction—as we learn to assign meaning to symbols, we give them power over

our experience. Early symbolic interactionism was an outgrowth of pragmatism, which emphasized individual agency as essential and influential in people's ability to adapt to and control reality. Another theory, social construction of reality, also assumes that people have a correspondence of meaning when they use symbols (an object that represents some other object) and signs (objects explicitly designed to serve as indexes of subjective meaning). These signs and symbols combine into collections of meanings, or typification schemes, that form the social stock of knowledge that patterns people's interactions with their environments.

Closely related to these is frame analysis, which assumes that people use their expectations of situations to make sense of them and to determine their actions in them. Individuals use the cues inherent in these situations to determine how to frame, or understand, situations and whether they should downshift or upshift: that is, the level of seriousness they should bring to their actions. Media's contribution to this framing is in influencing people's expectations, or readings, of those cues. Frame analysis has been applied with some success to journalists' production of news accounts, elites' power to shape the frames that journalists employ, and the meaning people make from those frames.

As such, media can have a profound influence on the *accessibility and quality of information* we use as we try to think, talk, and act in our social world. As our culture becomes increasingly commodified, the information we access is primarily that provided in infotainment or political spectacle. Because this content necessarily serves the interests of those who produce it, there may be many important things we never learn about from the media. Moreover, our impressions of the things that we *do* learn about might be strongly affected by the "packaging" of that information.

Critical Thinking Questions

1. Politicians were among the first professionals to understand the power of framing. What routinized or habitual meanings come to mind when you encounter terms like *pro-life, pro-choice, death tax, tax relief, tax and spend, socialized medicine, Obamacare, gun control, gun rights, politically correct, free markets*, or *bloated bureaucracy*. All are terms specifically designed to frame the meaning of the discussion that surrounds each. What meaning does each frame imply? What fuller or deeper meaning might be obscured? What is the intent of those who would employ these expressions? Is it consistent with honest democratic discourse? Why or why not?

2. Advertisers, through product positioning, make extensive use of symbolic interaction. Can you look around your life and find products (symbols) that you have intentionally acquired specifically to "position" yourself in others' meaning-making of you? For example, what car do you drive and why? Do you favor a specific scent or brand of clothes? What reality are you trying to create with your product choices?

3. Researchers have found that people become cynical about politics when the news they read frames politics in terms of conflict and strategy. How do you view politics and politicians? How do you react when you read about government gridlock or politicians voting in certain ways to gain reelection? Would you consider a career in politics? Could a politician who puts the public interest first ever be successful? Have you read or heard about this type of politician in the media recently?

Key Terms

symbolic interactionism

social behaviorism

symbols

pragmatism

sign

natural signs

artificial signs

signals

symbols

social constructionism

social construction of reality

phenomenology

typifications

symbol

signs

typification schemes

frame analysis

frame

downshift or upshift

social cues

hyperritualized representations

primary, or dominant, reality

cascading activation model

commodification of culture

FUTURE: RAPIDLY CHANGING MEDIA CHALLENGE A GLOBAL DISCIPLINE

THE FUTURE OF MEDIA THEORY AND RESEARCH

How would you describe yourself? What are your ideal personal attributes? Whom would you want to be like? How do you relate to other people? What expectations do others have of you, and what do you expect of them? How do you deal with difficult social situations? Where do you turn for information about your friends, and where do they find out about you? These are the sorts of questions we face every day as we work to find our place in the social world and develop relationships with other people. In Chapter 10 we looked at theories of everyday culture that provide insight into how we deal with questions like these. The theories we studied there explain that as we move through the many different situations that structure our everyday lives, our sense of ourselves undergoes continual change, as does our understanding of others. Still, most of us don't think much about these sometimes dramatic changes; rarely do we question who we are or our understanding of others. We have developed habits that help us ably cope with the social world.

One of the most important aspects of everyday culture consists of the personal identities we use to understand ourselves, to present ourselves to others, and to set the expectations we have that structure our communication and relationships with others. Everyday culture also involves the commonsense stock of knowledge about the social world that we have learned in order to cope with everyday problems and situations. Increasingly, media have become important to the way we develop this everyday culture. Media use has become central to developing and maintaining relationships with others. Texting and social networking sites (SNSs) like Facebook, SnapChat, and Twitter connect us with others in ways we find essential. For digital natives, people who have never lived in a world without the Internet, this is the way it is, the natural order of things. But what does it mean for our everyday interactions and realities? "Questions about the Internet's deleterious effects on the mind are at least as old as hyperlinks," wrote journalist Tony Dokoupil,

> but even among Web skeptics, the idea that a new technology might influence how we think and feel—let alone contribute to a great American crack-up—was considered silly

and naive, like waving a cane at electric light or blaming the television for kids these days. Instead, the Internet was seen as just another medium, a delivery system, not a diabolical machine. It made people happier and more productive. And where was the proof otherwise? Now, however, the proof is starting to pile up. (2012)

Researchers are indeed raising important questions about the changes that new media are producing on how we understand others and ourselves. They worry that there could be serious long-term consequences. Are they correct, or is this simply another panic induced by the introduction of new forms of media like those in Chapter 2's discussion of mass society theory? Or can we dismiss these concerns with a little bit of functionalism's "yes-but" strategy (Chapter 4)? For example, can we balance findings that "individuals who perceive themselves as lacking self-presentational skill would be especially likely to perceive online social interaction more favorable than [face-to-face] communication … [but this] preference for online social interaction leads to compulsive Internet use that results in negative outcomes" (Caplan, 2005, p. 730) with those suggesting that use of social networking sites is associated with "social capital" that can "strengthen social bonds as SNSs give free and easy communication with family, friends, and acquaintances regardless of time and place" (Brandtzæg, 2012, pp. 481–482)?

One thing that is certain in these debates is that people born after 1990 do use media much more often than those born earlier. Media have become an integral part of their daily lives. As we saw in Chapter 6, the typical 8- to 18-year-old uses media for seven-and-a-half hours each day. Since some of this use involves multi-tasking, their total media exposure amounts to 10¾ hours a day. Speaking only of cell phones, researchers Rideout, Foehr, and Roberts wrote, "Cell phones are the last thing they touch before falling asleep and the first thing they reach for upon waking. They spend the day accessing media using a variety of technologies that follow them everywhere they go" (2010, p. 2). "This generation doesn't make phone calls," writes journalist Clive Thompson, "because everyone is in constant, lightweight contact in so many other ways: texting, chatting, and social network messaging" (in Vanderbilt, 2012, p. 52). In fact, making calls ranks only fifth in Americans' time spent on their smartphones (O2, 2012). On their own, these are interesting data. But add the facts that 77 percent of 12- to 17-year-olds have a cell phone (Lenhart, 2012), cellphone ownership among 6- to 11-year-olds grew 68 percent between 2005 and 2010, that talking and texting over mobile devices account for the top two ways mothers communicate with their children, and that cellphone kids also are much more likely (84 percent) to say that their parents let them go anywhere they want online than do those without the devices (Kelly, 2010). Reading these data, keep in mind that if SNS Facebook, which first went online in 2004, was its own country, its more than a billion monthly active users would make it the third largest in the world, after only China and India (Delo, 2012). Two-thirds of American adults who are online are Facebook users, and since 2009 this site has been America's most-visited website, the destination of 9 percent of all visits to the Internet, accounting for one in every five page views on the Web (Duggan and Brenner, 2013; Tatham, 2012). Twitter, which debuted in 2006 and limits messages to 140 characters, has more than half-a-billion users, 142 million in the United States (Lunden, 2012). They send 175 million Tweets (messages) a day (Stadd, 2012).

The introduction of new media technologies has always been accompanied by unrealistic hopes and fears. Is this shift in media technology radically different from those that have happened before? Should concerns about high levels of media use by adolescents and young adults be taken seriously? The sheer amount of time spent with media bothers many critics. How can a "normal" life be lived if more than half of it involves the use of a technology? If much of our interaction with others, even our mothers, is mediated? Critics argue that media use can't help but be intrusive and disruptive. Technology proponents (and most young media users) respond that life hasn't really changed; it's been enhanced. Life now has a soundtrack courtesy of an iPod. Web surfing, Facebook, mobile video, texting, and portable video games keep boredom at bay. Google holds the answers to life's many questions and it can deliver them in a flash. You're never alone because friends are always a text message, a Facebook post, or an Instagram away. Media enable constant connection with others and provide useful frames for everyday situations. But could media be doing more for us and to us than we realize? There clearly are some very important questions about these media that need to be answered.

LEARNING OBJECTIVES

After studying this chapter you should be able to

- Recognize the profound alterations afoot in mass communication research and theory, largely brought about by the new digital communication technologies.

- Better understand Internet addiction, depression, and distraction.

- Assess the merits of the argument that the Internet, rather than expanding our interaction with the world, might actually be limiting it.

- Appreciate the intersection of mass and interpersonal communication, especially as demonstrated by advances in theories relating to computer-mediated communication and health communication.

- Appreciate the depth of journalism's disruptive transition into the digital era and assess possible new ways to practice journalism.

- Evaluate new thinking about media literacy in the digital age.

- Envision mass communication theory's global future.

OVERVIEW

In Chapter 10 we looked at cultural theories of media that provide insight into the many possible ways that media can alter personal identities, social roles, and understanding of the larger social world. In Chapter 9 we looked at media effects theories that provide a basis for assessing how media can affect cognition and action. In this chapter we summarize the insights that cultural and effects theories are providing about new media, and at the same time we'll consider the serious challenges that media researchers face as they study these new technologies. New media are constantly changing and as they change our use of them changes.

In Chapters 9 and 10 we reviewed both postpositivist and critical cultural research on news media and journalism. The overall conclusion from this research is that news fails to effectively inform people about events and that it frames important aspects of the social world in problematic ways. In this chapter we look at efforts to reconceptualize and reform journalism. These are troubled times for the news business. Newspapers are being forced to change because they have lost subscribers and advertising revenues have plunged. News media are widely distrusted. Media researchers have joined others to propose radical changes in how news media serve the public. Some reformers hope to restore interest and trust by involving newspapers more directly in local communities. Others seek to open up news media so that ordinary citizens become more directly involved in news production and distribution, an effort labeled **citizen journalism**.

citizen journalism
Direct involvement of ordinary citizens in news production and distribution

News researchers are directly involved in these journalism reform efforts. They are proposing changes, offering advice, setting up websites, organizing resources, and conducting relevant research. Not so long ago many researchers avoided efforts to bring about social changes based on theory or research. Postpositivist researchers believed that such efforts compromised their ability to be objective. But now, more and more scholars are applying their research to address problems associated with media. Journalism reform efforts are just one type of problem-solving research. Similar efforts are underway in a number of other areas including violent entertainment content (television and video games), educational content, science communication, and health communication.

Finally, the chapter concludes with a look at changes affecting the people and the organizations engaged in developing media theory and conducting media research. These changes are transforming the way that theory is developed and research is conducted. Not so long ago virtually all media researchers were Americans and most of them worked at large state universities in communication or journalism departments. There was a handful of journals devoted to publishing media research and almost all were located in the United States. Critics argued, not incorrectly, that media theory and research findings applied only to Americans and their peculiar system of privatized media. Increasingly, media research is a global enterprise with important work being conducted almost everywhere on the planet. The bulk of this work still tends to take place in the United States and Europe, but important centers for research are springing up in Asia, Australasia, Latin America, Africa, Russia, and the Middle East. The Internet facilitates collaboration between these researchers while providing a central focus for their research. Findings about the effects of Internet use in Korea can be quickly and easily compared to similar findings in Europe, New Zealand, and South Africa. An ever-growing array of journals scattered around the world focuses on media research. Interesting and useful findings are being replicated in many different nations and cultures. These findings provide a basis for developing and validating global theories of media.

NEW MEDIA THEORY AND RESEARCH: CHALLENGES AND FINDINGS

Over the last few years, the Radio and Television News Directors Association, founded in 1946, changed its name to the Radio Television Digital News Association; the American Society of Newspaper Editors, started in 1922, dropped "paper" from its name to become the American Society of News Editors; the Audit Bureau of Circulations, the print media's dominant circulation measurement operation since 1914, became the Alliance for Audited Media; and the Association of Alternative Newsweeklies, founded in 1978, transformed into the Association of Alternative Newsmedia. All these name changes and thousands more were the result of fundamental alterations in the nature of the mass media. Mass communication theory has likewise had to adapt. For example, the scholarly journal *Critical Studies in Mass Communication* changed its name to *Critical Studies in Media Communication*. After all, e-mail may well be mediated, but it's certainly not mass communication, and a lone blogger may not be a mass media outlet, but her posts accessed by more people than read a small-town daily newspaper may well be mass communication. But the challenges that the discipline faces as a result of the coming of the new communication technologies go well beyond name changes. For example, we've already seen in this chapter's opening that human relationships are being altered by new media. These changes—for good or bad—are certainly media effects. To what extent do young people share their personal and mediated experiences via social media and what are the consequences, and to what extent is face-to-face communication becoming an increasingly rare phenomenon that still somehow anchors the other forms of communication and the relationships that rely on them? And just as decades of mass communication theory and research had to be rethought with the advent and then dominance of television, they must adapt to a world where most television viewing no longer takes place on television sets (Fitzgerald, 2013). Do fundamental alterations in the use of television mean that the medium no longer has the same effects? What do changes in the number and diversity of channels, flexibility in screen size and portability, and competition from other media mean for "the effects of television"? Has television—maybe video is a better word—become mere wallpaper, simply more white noise in a babble of competing voices?

Throughout this book we have made occasional mention of how researchers and theorists with different interests have tried to address the new mediated communication environment. For example, Terry Adams-Bloom and Johanna Cleary suggested a rethinking of social responsibility theory in light of the economic havoc the Internet has wreaked on news organizations, and Jeffrey Rosen offered the idea that the Internet has so dramatically opened up public discourse to alternative views that social responsibility theory's vision of Great Communities may be close at hand (Chapter 3). Knowledge gap researchers are now investigating how Internet technology may help close the gap between rich and poor, and cultivation researchers have made efforts to dismiss the impact of the Internet's multitude of storytelling options on their theory's core assumptions (Chapter 9). And as we read in Chapter 7, Thomas Ruggiero believes that the Internet has opened up "a vast continuum of communication behaviors" for uses-and-gratifications researchers to study (2000, p. 3). It would have been impossible in previous chapters to discuss mass communication theory without taking stock of how the mass communication environment has been dramatically altered by new technology. But in this chapter we will look more deeply at several examples of contemporary media theory confronting the new communication technologies and outline the Internet-related findings they have produced.

INTERNET ADDICTION, DEPRESSION, DISTRACTION, AND ATOMIZATION

At several points in this text you've read that the introduction of new communication technologies is inevitably met with fears for the worst. This attitude, as you know, is the hallmark of mass society theory, and it has been on display ever since the Internet first appeared in the 1970s. Elite fear of the Net was certainly not misplaced, as executives of today's music, book, and newspaper industries can attest, as can the former leaders of those Middle Eastern regimes overthrown during the Arab Spring (Chapter 3). But there are more people making more music than ever before, just not on CDs bought at record stores (Pfanner, 2013); there are more people publishing books—often without the help of a publishing house—and more people reading them—often on an electronic device—than ever before (Piersanti, 2012); there are more people reading the daily newspaper than ever before, just not on the by-product of a dead tree (Starkman, 2012). And those Middle East regimes? They were overthrown by citizens weary of the oppression and corruption that kept them in power. It isn't that those expressing mass society fears were always wrong. In fact, they were correct in arguing that the coming of mass communication would mean profound alterations for the status quo. The deficiency in their thinking, though, was that their fear was based in new communication technologies' threat to *their interests*, not the well-being of those "regular" people whom they seemed so worried about. So while much of the early negative reaction to the Internet was quite self-interested, there are four early fears that do appear to have merit: Internet addiction, depression, distraction, and atomization.

Internet addiction
Spending 40 to 80 hours per week online, with individual sessions as long as 20 hours

Internet addiction is characterized by "spending 40 to 80 hours per week, with [individual] sessions that could last up to 20 hours. Sleep patterns are disrupted due to late night logins, and addicts generally stay up surfing until 2:00, 3:00, or 4:00 in the morning [despite] the reality of having to wake up early for work or school" (Young, 2004, p. 405). Several countries, China, Taiwan, and Korea for example, treat Internet addiction as a medically recognized psychiatric problem and operate government-funded treatment centers for addicts. In 2013, after years of debate, the American Psychiatric Association added "Internet Addiction Disorder" to its authoritative list of recognized mental illnesses, the *American Diagnostic and Statistical Manual of Mental Disorders*. And while teens may use the word "addiction" in a general rather than clinical sense, 60 percent of British teens say they are "highly addicted" to their cell phones (Sedghi, 2011) and American teens report similar levels; 41 percent say they are addicted to their phones and 20 percent to their social networking sites (Rideout, 2012b).

Addiction occurs because even in moderate Internet use, our brains rewire, that is, they alter physiologically. Americans average 30 hours a week on the Internet with 18- to 29-year-olds amassing more than 40 hours a week ("Demographics," 2012). Researcher Gary Small and his colleagues examined the brains of two groups of Internet users, veterans and novices. Looking at MRI images of participants' brains, they discovered that the Web users had "fundamentally altered prefrontal cortexes." They then instructed the novices to go home, spend five hours over the next week on the Internet, and then come back. When these participants did return, their brain scans showed changes similar to those of the veteran Internet users (Small et al., 2009). "The technology is rewiring our brains," said Nora Volkow, director of the National Institute of Drug Abuse. She compares the lure of digital stimulation not to that of drugs and alcohol; rather, the drive is more akin to that for food and sex, both essential but counterproductive in excess (in Richtel, 2010b, p. A1).

Studying the brains of diagnosed Internet addicts, Fuchun Lin and his colleagues discovered evidence of disruption to the connections in nerve fibers linking the brain areas involved in emotions, decision making, and self-control. "Overall," they wrote, "our findings indicate that IAD [Internet Addiction Disorder] has abnormal white matter integrity [extra nerve cells that speed up brain functioning] in brain regions involving emotional generation and processing, executive attention, decision making and cognitive control.... The results also suggest that IAD may share psychological and neural mechanisms with other types of substance addiction and impulse control disorders" (Lin et al., 2012).

Because depression is often tied to addiction, it too has drawn research attention. Raghavendra Katikalapudi and a team of researchers electronically monitored in real time the Internet usage of 216 college undergraduates, 30 percent of whom showed signs of depression. Their results showed that the depressed students were the most intense Web users. They exhibited more peer-to-peer file sharing, heavier e-mailing and online chatting, more video game play, and the tendency to quickly switch between many websites and other online resources than did the other students—all behaviors related to depression. Quickly switching between websites reflects anhedonia, an inability to experience emotions, as Web users desperately look for emotional stimulation. Heavy e-mailing and chatting signifies a relative lack of strong face-to-face relationships, as these students work to maintain contact either with distant friends or new people they met online (Katikalapudi et al., 2012). You can test yourself for Internet addiction in the box, "Internet Addiction Self-Analysis."

Facebook depression

Depression that develops when a great deal of time is spent on social media sites leading to exhibition of classic symptoms of depression

Depression and social networking has also received research attention. The American Academy of Pediatrics has identified **Facebook depression**, "depression that develops when preteens and teens spend a great deal of time on social media sites, such as Facebook, and then begin to exhibit classic symptoms of depression. Acceptance by and contact with peers is an important element of adolescent life. The intensity of the online world is thought to be a factor that may trigger depression in some adolescents" (O'Keeffe and Clarke-Pearson, 2011, p. 802). Psychologist Sherry Turkle reports that young people, those in their teens and early 20s, are exhausted by always having to be connected and are unable to look away for **fear of missing out, or FOMO**, a finding supported by research indicating that except for those over 50, most smartphone users check their text messages, e-mails, or social network sites "all the time" or "every 15 minutes" (in Dokoupil, 2012).

fear of missing out (FOMO)

Inability to disengage from social networking for fear of missing something

Addiction and depression are functions of abnormal or excessive use of the new communication technologies. Distraction, however, deals with more typical, everyday use, and it is a constantly raised issue, especially for young people. For example, American parents of kids 4 to 14 years old report that "time spent with digital devices" has reduced their children's ability to concentrate (23 percent), desire to use their imaginations (20 percent), time doing school work (20 percent), and development of critical thinking skills (17 percent; Boy Scouts of America,

---

THINKING ABOUT THEORY | **Internet Addiction Self-Analysis**

If you have ever worried that you spend too much time connected to the Internet, you may want to take this Internet addiction self-diagnostic, created by Kimberly S. Young of the *Center for Online Addiction* (2004, p. 404). Keep in mind that this is an analysis of *Internet addiction*, not *computer addiction*. So you must consider the entirety of your Internet use, not the time you spend with the individual devices—computers, smartphones, tablets, or game consoles—you use to connect to the Net. So think hard and honestly about your *Internet* use before you answer. Over the last six months ...

1. Did you feel preoccupied with the Internet (always thinking about previous online activity or anticipating the next online session)?
2. Did you feel the need to use the Internet with increasing amounts of time to achieve satisfaction?
3. Have you repeatedly made unsuccessful efforts to control, cut back, or stop Internet use?
4. Did you feel restless, moody, depressed, or irritable when attempting to cut down or stop Internet use?
5. Did you stay online longer than originally intended?
6. Have you jeopardized or risked the loss of a significant relationship, job, educational or career opportunity because of the Internet?
7. Have you lied to family members, therapists, or others to conceal the extent of involvement with the Internet?
8. Did you use the Internet as a way of escaping from problems or of relieving a dysphoric mood (e.g., feelings of helplessness, guilt, anxiety, depression)?

How should you interpret your answers? First, consider only nonessential computer and Internet usage. Business and school use should not be part of your computation. If you answer yes to five (or more) of the questions you are at risk of addiction. Dr. Young explains, "This list offers a workable definition of Internet addiction to help us differentiate normal from compulsive Internet use, but these warning signs can often be masked by the cultural norms that encourage and reinforce its use. That is, even if a person meets all eight criteria, signs of abuse can be rationalized away as 'I need this for my job' or 'It's just a machine' when in reality, the Internet is causing significant problems in a user's life" (2004, p. 404).

How did you do? Do you show signs of Internet addiction? If yes, what will you do about it? If no, how have you been able to avoid overreliance on this technology?

2012). Young people "tweet and blog and text without batting an eyelash. Whenever they need the answer to a question, they simply log onto their phone and look it up on Google. They live in a state of perpetual, endless distraction, and, for many parents and educators, it's a source of real concern. Will future generations be able to finish a whole book? Will they be able to sit through an entire movie without checking their phones? Are we raising a generation of impatient brats?" (Rogers, 2011). Certainly, digital screen time means less time spent interacting traditionally with the larger world and the people in it. But the issue of distraction deals with how our use of technology *influences* our interaction with the larger world and the people in it when we do leave the screen. As such, distraction has particular relevance to information processing theory. Research indicates that time spent with digital devices deprives our brains of needed downtime. "Downtime lets the brain go over experiences it's had, solidify them and turn them into permanent long-term memories," explains learning researcher Loren Frank. When the brain is constantly stimulated, "you prevent this learning process" (in Richtel, 2010a, p. B1). There is also research demonstrating that the speed of our digital communication technologies is conditioning us to be impatient and easily distracted in the offline world. Seventy-one percent of the nation's teachers say their students' attention spans are reduced "a lot" or "somewhat" because of their screen time (Rideout, 2012a).

There is little question that changes in how we interact with the actual world are occurring as a result of our use of the new digital technologies; otherwise, there would be no need to constantly reconsider the theories on which we rely to make sense of what is occurring. However, there are those who make a functionalist argument that while these changes may appear disruptive, they may also be beneficial. Some learning theorists argue that any individual loss of memory is more than compensated for by access to the Internet's vast repository of information and knowledge. Psychologist Daniel Wegner explains that rather than worry about distraction, we should "accept the role of the Web as a mind-expander and wonder not at the bad but at the good it can do us. There's nothing wrong, after all, with having our minds expanded. Each time we learn *who* knows something or *where* we can find information—without learning *what* the information itself might be—we are expanding our mental reach. This is the basic idea behind so-called **transactive memory**.... [N]obody remembers everything. Instead, each of us in a couple or group remembers some things personally—and then can remember much more by knowing who else might know what we don't. In this way, we become part of a transactive memory system. Groups of people commonly depend on one another for memory in this way—not by all knowing the same thing, but by specializing. And now we've added our computing devices to the network, depending for memory not just on people but also on a cloud of linked people and specialized information-filled devices. We have all become a great cybermind. As long as we are connected to our machines through talk and keystrokes, we can all be part of the biggest, smartest mind ever" (2012, p. SR6).

A second functionalist argument is that constant connection is indeed rewiring our brains, and this is as it should be. Our experience of the world is not *deficient*, but *different*. Digital learning researcher Kathy Davidson explains,

> The way we think about the brain has a lot to do with the technology of the era. Is the brain a machine, linear and orderly? Is the brain a mainframe computer, hardwired with fixed properties and abilities? Is the brain a network like the Internet, always changing and inherently interactive? Not surprisingly the metaphors for the brain have grown in complexity along with the evolution of ever more complicated technologies of interconnection.
>
> From contemporary neuroscience we know that the brain is a lot like an iPhone. It comes with certain basic communication functions bundled within it, and it has apps for just about everything. Those apps can be downloaded or deleted and are always in need of a software update. These iPhone apps represent the things we pay attention to, what counts for us, what we are interested in. Our interests shape what apps our personal iPhone has, but our interests aren't isolated. If my best friend says, "Find me on Gowalla," I then add the GPS-based Gowalla app so we can follow one another's comings and goings around L. A., and before I know it, I've added a dozen more apps to my phone from things I've learned through our game play and social networking as we travel the city, separate but connected. Our brain is similar. How we use our brain (what we pay attention to) changes our brain. Those things that most capture our attention—our learning and our work, our passions and our activities—change our

transactive memory

When the memory of the group benefits from each individual's contribution

neural plasticity
The brain's physical adaptation to the sensory stimuli it receives

actual brain biology. In this way the iPhone brain also corresponds nicely with recent advances in what we know about **neural plasticity**, the theory that the brain adapts physically to the sensory stimuli it receives. [The result] is the brain that changes itself. (2011, p. 22)

Dr. Davidson offered more detail elsewhere, "Younger generations don't just think about technology more casually, they're actually wired to respond to it in a different manner than we [non-digital natives] are, and it's up to us—and our education system—to catch up to them.... When my students go to the Web and they're searching and they're leaving comments and they're social networking and they're Facebooking and they're texting at the same time—those are their reflexes. They are learning to process that kind of information faster. That which we experience shapes our pathways, so they're going to be far less stressed by a certain kind of multitasking that you are or than I am, or people who may not have grown up with that" (in Rogers, 2011). In fact, Laura Mickes and her colleagues demonstrated that information on social networking sites, even strangers' Facebook status updates, are much more likely to be remembered than people's faces or sentences from books. Why? Because social networking's short posts are "largely spontaneous and natural emanations of the human mind;" they are "the sort of information that our memories are tuned to recognize....That which we readily generate," they said, "we also readily store" (Mickes et al., 2013).

atomization
Disconnecting individuals from one another and their communities

algorithms
Sets of data that, when combined, determine what content people see on the Internet

cookie
An identifying code added to a computer's hard drive by a visited website

Arguably the Internet effect that most closely echoes early mass society theory's fears is **atomization**, disconnecting individuals from one another and their communities. In essence, the argument is that the data the Web constantly and often surreptitiously collects on people is gathered into **algorithms**, sets of data that, when combined, determine what content people see on the Internet. Every time you visit a website, every time you strike a key, that information is collected and sent to someone by a **cookie**, an identifying code added to your computer's hard drive by a visited website. For example, if you search for the word depression on the site Dictionary.com, the site will install "223 tracking cookies on your computer so that other Web sites can target you with antidepressants" (Pariser, 2011, p. 6). Sometimes these cookies are for the site you are visiting; sometimes they are for third-party data gatherers; sometimes they disappear when you leave the site; sometimes they remain embedded on your hard drive. The European Union officially places strict control on the gathering, collecting, use, and sale of these data. There are no meaningful controls on this activity in the United States. But beyond the issues of what many consider to be the inappropriate invasion of our privacy and the unethical use of our private information (no small matters in their own right), how does this practice encourage individual atomization and what does it mean for mass communication theory? Internet freedom pioneer Eli Pariser explains, "The algorithms that orchestrate our ads are starting to orchestrate our lives. The basic code at the heart of the new Internet is pretty simple. The new generation of Internet filters looks at things you seem to like—the actual things you've done, or people like you like—and tries to extrapolate. They are prediction engines, constantly creating and refining a theory of who you are and what you'll do and want next. Together, these engines create a unique universe of information for each of us—what I've come to call a filter bubble—which fundamentally alters the way we encounter ideas and information" (2011, p. 9).

filter bubble
The ecosystem of information created by Web algorithms for each individual

That **filter bubble**—the ecosystem of information created by Web algorithms for each individual—determines not just what ads are sent your way when you search or visit a favorite site, it determines what news and information you see, based partly on what it has determined are your interests and partly on what information would be most hospitable to the ads, selected for you, that surround the information. What this does, explains mass communication scholar Joseph Turow, is call into question "a perspective with a lot of traction among contemporary academics: that the best way to think about audiences in the new age is to emphasize that individual audience members are exercising unprecedented control over the creation and distribution of media products" (2013, p. 1). In fact, just the opposite may be happening. "The surreptitiously constructed market-driven profiles are also central to media firms' increasing competitive need to personalize information, news, and entertainment. Built into the logic of these activities is social discrimination across a widening digital landscape. The trajectory raises a new version of the concerns about media's constructions of society for society that scholars first expressed in the late nineteenth and early twentieth centuries" (p. 2). Turow invokes not only early mass society theory (Chapter 2) notions in his critique, but critical theory (Chapter 5) as well, "The fundamental logic of the emerging media-buying system, though, privileges institutional power. It aims to constrain individuals' everyday media contexts, as well as to channel audience choices and initiatives toward the goals of marketers and of publishers—that is, the creators and distributors of content" (p. 6). Social responsibility theory (Chapter 3), too, enters his assessment, "Early twentieth-century sociologists from the Chicago School would undoubtedly see the market-driven social discriminations of the contemporary advertising industry as derailing their belief that media can encourage greater opportunities for democratic argumentation across broad populations" (p. 21). Technology writer Nicholas Carr, focusing specifically on Google, explains how we become atomized, isolated. He says that "Google's search engine doesn't push us outward; it turns us inward. It gives us information that fits the behavior and needs and biases we have displayed in the past, as meticulously interpreted by Google's algorithms. Because it reinforces the existing state of the self rather than challenging it, it subverts the act of searching. We find out little about anything, least of all ourselves, through self-absorption" (2013). As a result, explains Pariser, "while the Internet offers access to a dazzling array of sources and options, in the filter bubble we'll miss many of them. While the Internet can give us new opportunities to grow and experiment with our identities, the economics of personalization push toward a static conception or personhood. While the Internet has the potential to decentralize knowledge and control, in practice it's concentrating control over what we see and what opportunities we're offered in the hands of fewer people than ever before" (2011, p. 218).

This issue, people's access to the Internet's "dazzling array of sources and options," is at the heart of some researchers' prediction that the discipline would return to a belief in limited effects similar to that holding sway during the media-effects trend (Chapter 4). You can read about it in the box, "The Internet and the Return of Minimal Effects."

THINKING ABOUT THEORY | **The Internet and the Return of Minimal Effects**

The new mass communication environment, characterized by Internet-fueled declines in newspaper and news magazine readership, dwindling audiences for broadcast network television news, and growing audiences for partisan cable news channels and partisan websites and blogs, has forced a rethinking of many of the assumptions about media influence that the discipline has long held dear. Debate over the question of media's power to shape political attitudes and beliefs found its way into the pages of the *Journal of Communication*, pitting several of the discipline's most influential political communication scholars against one another.

W. Lance Bennett and Shanto Iyengar declared that mass communication theory is entering a new era of minimal media effects in which media are seen largely as reinforcing existing political views and inoculating partisan audiences against influence by opposing media. They were making the classic limited-effects argument. "Consider," they wrote

the famous earlier era of "minimal effects" that emerged from studies done in the 1940s and early 1950s.... The underlying context for this scholarship consisted of a premass communication media system and relatively dense membership in a group-based society networked through political parties, churches, unions, and service organizations.... At this time, scholars concluded that media messages were filtered through social preference processes.... Indeed, with the continued detachment of individuals from the group-based society, and increased capacity of consumers to choose from a multitude of media channels (many of which enable user-produced content), the effects picture may be changing again. As receivers exercise greater choice over both the content of messages and media sources, effects become increasingly difficult to produce or measure in the aggregate. (2008, pp. 707–708)

They based their view on five realities of modern mass communication:

1. *The impact of audience structure and communication technology.* "The principal impact of the revolution in technology has been to exponentially increase the supply of information. Today, citizens interested in the presidential election have access to thousands of online sources ranging from well-established news organizations to the candidates themselves and from the political parties to unknown individual bloggers" (p. 717).

2. *The fragmented audience in an era of selective exposure.* "There is a much wider range of media choices on offer, providing much greater variability in the content of available information. This means that something approaching information 'stratamentation' (stratification and fragmentation at the same time) is going on ... and more people are drifting away. People uninterested in politics can avoid news programming altogether by tuning into ESPN or the Food Network. And for political junkies, the sheer multiplicity of news sources demands they exercise discretionary or selective exposure to political information" (p. 717).

3. *The demise of the inadvertent audience.* In the pre-Internet era "television had a leveling effect on the distribution of information. The news reached not only those motivated to tune in but also people with generally low levels of political interest, thus allowing the latter group to 'catch up' with their more attentive counterparts. But once the networks' hold on the national audience was loosened ... exposure to news was no longer a given for the great majority of Americans" (p. 718).

4. *Partisan selective exposure among information seekers.* Although we have long known that "people will avoid information that they expect will be discrepant or disagreeable and seek out information that is expected to be congruent with their preexisting attitudes ... [i]n the days of old media, selecting conventional news sources on the basis of partisan preference was relatively difficult" (p. 719).

5. *Technology and the new partisan selectivity.* "It is not a coincidence that the increased availability of news sources has been accompanied by increasing political polarization.... The new, more diversified information environment makes it not only more feasible for consumers to seek out news they might find agreeable but also provides a strong economic incentive for news organizations to cater to their viewers' political preferences" (p. 720). The impact of this

(Continued)

phenomenon is exacerbated by the hostile media effect (Chapter 8).

R. Lance Holbert, R. Kelly Garrett, and Laurel Gleason (2010, p. 15) were not convinced, offering four rebuttals:

1. *Bennett and Iyengar are "too quick to dismiss the importance of attitude reinforcement."* This is the same argument that critics leveled at reinforcement theory (Chapter 4)—reinforcement is, in itself, a powerful effect. Contemporary mass communication theory "has identified persuasion as consisting of not only attitude *change*, but also attitude *formation* and attitude *reinforcement*" (italics in original; p. 17).

2. *They take "too narrow a view of the sources of political information, remaining fixated on news."* Political information permeates all forms of content, not just news. Baumgartner and Morris (2006), among many others, have demonstrated the influence on political attitudes of mock news shows like *The Daily Show* and *The Colbert Report*. Late night talk shows such as *The Late Show* and *The Tonight Show* make political humor and talk a nightly feature, and entertainment programming, cartoons like *South Park*, *Family Guy*, and *The Simpsons*, dramas like *Grey's Anatomy* and *The Good Wife*, and comedies like *The New Normal* and *Modern Family*, regularly present political topics. And there are hundreds of entertainment-oriented Web video channels such as *Funny or Die* that exist specifically to present current issue of importance wrapped in entertainment conventions.

3. *They "offer an incomplete portrayal of selective exposure, exaggerating the extent to which individuals avoid attitude discrepant information."* Yes, people do tend to gravitate toward material with which they agree, but there is little evidence of the opposite movement. That is, people "do not show much aversion to information with which they disagree" (p. 20). They offer research on online political news (Garrett, 2009), demonstrating that "the inclusion of attitude-consistent information promotes news item exposure … [but] attitude-discrepant information does not produce a significant decrease in the likelihood of examining a news item. Furthermore, it is

associated with substantially *longer* read times" (italics in original; p. 20).

4. *The demise of the inadvertent audience is meaningless in the age of pull media.* The inadvertent audience is an artifact of the push media era; when content was pushed onto audiences, some news and information content would inevitably be part of the flow. But we are now in the era of pull media, and it is in making this argument that Holbert, Garrett, and Gleason invoke the elaboration likelihood model (Chapter 8). They explain,

The pull media environment is where the user or receiver (not the sender) is in control.… When you have the user in control, pulling down political media content, what do you have from the standpoint of the ELM? You have *motivation*—audience members who want to consume potentially persuasive political media messages. In addition, audience members in a pull media environment are more likely to consume their chosen political media messages at desirable times, in preferred places/contexts, and utilizing formats that best match their particular learning styles. Each of these characteristics of the media-use experience facilitates greater *ability* to process political information. From the perspective of the ELM and political media effects, a solid case can be made that the pull media environment provides a stronger foundation for the emergence of the central route of persuasion than was possible in a push-media-dominated system. With a greater likelihood of central-route engagement comes increased opportunity for attitudinal and behavioral influences that are more robust and longer lasting and which are built to withstand subsequent counter persuasion. (italics in original; 2010, p. 27)

Where do you stand? Do you agree with the first set of authors, that people are increasingly self-selecting the political information to which they expose themselves, and as a result media impact on politics will become increasingly limited? Or do you favor the view of the second group of scholars, that if anything, the Internet will expand the media's influence? How might the issue of the filter bubble change this debate, if at all? Defend your answer, and don't be afraid to find support for your position in earlier chapters of this text.

COMPUTER-MEDIATED COMMUNICATION

The arrival of the new communication technologies accomplished a goal sought by many theorists since the late 1980s, the integration of scholarship on mass and interpersonal communication. Postpositivist media researchers of that time concluded that the discipline's constant ferment of competing ideas and research methods was impeding the development of a coherent approach to communication research. They proposed the creation of **communication science**, a perspective on research integrating all research approaches grounded in quantitative, empirical, behavioral research methods. They wanted to eliminate unfruitful fragmentation and provide a defining core philosophy for the scientific study of all forms of communication. Steve Chaffee and Charles Berger wanted this new approach "to embrace various communication contexts, including the production, processing, or effects of symbol or signal systems (including nonverbal) in interpersonal, organizational, mass, political, instructional, or other contexts" (1987, p. 17). They wanted media researchers to undertake the analysis of **intra-individual communication** (communication occurring within the person her- or himself) and **interpersonal communication** (communication between two or small groups of people) as part of their study of mass communication. Susan Pingree, John Weimann, and Robert Hawkins (1988) therefore saw communication science as rendering the mass versus interpersonal communication dichotomy obsolete (how, for example, can we understand the effects of violent video games without examining players' experiences and thought processes as well as the impact of those experiences and thought processes on the way two or more people might interact?). Unfortunately, communication science never really took hold, as methodological and scholarly territorial interests proved too strong. For example, communication science's roots in the postpositivist philosophy—grounded in quantitative, empirical, behavioral research methods—effectively shut out interpretive and critical mass communication researchers. More importantly, perhaps, is that there was just too big a conceptual divide between those interested in mass communication, the interaction of big media industries, their products, and large audiences of relatively autonomous individuals, and those interested in interpersonal communication, interaction between a mom and her child, two friends, a small group of strangers, or a boss and her subordinates. Now, though, much of this interpersonal communication is indeed technologically mediated. That's why *Critical Studies in Mass Communication* became *Critical Studies in Media Communication* and why the International Communication Association launched the *Journal of Computer Mediated Communication* in 1995. The Internet, then, has married interest in mass and interpersonal communication and has created at least two fruitful lines of inquiry, the technology's role in identity construction and maintenance and its influence on interpersonal communication itself.

One question at home in the uses-and-gratification tradition is why do people use social networking sites to interact with others, especially when distance isn't a factor? Given that there are more than a billion users on Facebook alone, there must be some gratification sought and met by online interaction with others. Psychologists Ashwini Nadkarni and Stefan Hofmann offer a **dual-factor model of Facebook (FB) use**, which can be applied to SNS use in general. They explain, "FB use is primarily motivated by two basic social needs: (1) *the need to belong*, and (2) the *need for self-presentation*. The *need to belong* refers to the intrinsic

---

communication science
Perspective on research integrating all research approaches grounded in quantitative, empirical, and behavioral research methods

intra-individual communication
Communication occurring within the person her- or himself

interpersonal communication
Communication between two or small groups of people

dual-factor model of Facebook (FB) use
Social networking site use is primarily motivated by the need to belong and the need for self-presentation

drive to affiliate with others and gain social acceptance, and the *need for self-presentation* to the continuous process of impression management. These two motivational factors can co-exist, but can also each be the single cause for FB use" (italics in the original; 2012, p. 245). This need to belong is important because people are highly dependent on social support from others, and exclusion can cause loss of self-esteem and emotional well-being. Self-esteem, according to Nadkarni and Hofmann, serves as a *sociometer*, a monitor of acceptability by others. Because social network sites foster a sense of belonging, their use can increase self-esteem and therefore feelings of acceptability. In fact, Gonzales and Hancock (2011) demonstrated that simply updating and reading one's own profile on a social networking site was sufficient to boost self-esteem. People's need for self-presentation online is the same as offline. We know ourselves through our interaction with others, and if others who are of importance to us are online, that's where we must be to present ourselves. But this raises a question of obvious interest to researchers working in the symbolic interactionism tradition (Chapter 10), *how* do we present ourselves on social networking sites? Does our understanding of ourselves and others operate on the Internet as it does in face-to-face encounters? Can and do we work to shape the sense of self we build from the responses of our online "teammates"?

Social network site users routinely employ "screen names, profiles, and messages" as a means to "foster others' impression formation about them" and these SNS "users may select what information they want to include in a profile to highlight their most positive qualities" (Zywica and Danowski, 2008, p. 6). But how and why do they do this? These researchers offered as their explanation the **idealized virtual identity hypothesis**, the tendency for creators of social network site profiles to display idealized characteristics that do not reflect their actual personalities. Mitja Back and his colleagues tested this hypothesis and discovered it happens far less likely than most people think. In fact, they demonstrated that for most users, online social networking (OSN) "may constitute an extended social context in which to express one's actual personality characteristics, thus fostering accurate interpersonal perceptions. OSNs integrate various sources of personal information that mirror those found in personal environments, private thoughts, facial images, and social behavior, all of which are known to contain valid information about personality." In opposition to the idealized virtual identity hypothesis, they proposed the "**extended real-life hypothesis** [which] predicts that people use OSNs to communicate their real personality" (Back et al., 2010, p. 372). But why don't SNS users routinely create idealized virtual identities? The researchers offered two answers, "Creating idealized identities should be hard to accomplish because (a) OSN profiles include information about one's reputation that is difficult to control (e.g., wall posts) and (b) friends provide accountability and subtle feedback on one's Profile" (p. 372). Communication scholar Katie Ellis offers an example, writing that users "selecting their profile pictures have knowledge of how others in the network will respond, even if this is only on an unconscious level. When users select a profile picture of themselves on their wedding day or with their partner, or with a group of people at a party or in a nightclub, they are communicating something significant. This act of choosing a profile picture demonstrates the way 'I' chooses a 'me'. The woman choosing a picture of herself on her wedding day takes the perspectives of other people, knowing they will interpret her as a wife

---

idealized virtual identity hypothesis
Tendency for creators of social network site profiles to display idealized characteristics that do not reflect their actual personalities

extended real-life hypothesis
People use social networking sites to communicate their real personality

or perhaps a 'beautiful bride,' which then invites all sorts of other social meanings. Finally, this picture means something to the individual who is negotiating their personal identity among the available social identities. Identity as it emerges in the mind of an individual cannot be separated from social processes and interactions" (2010, p. 39). This is exactly as symbolic interaction would have predicted: Identity is constructed and maintained through interaction with others; we peer into the responses of others for "accountability and subtle feedback" to know who we are. Online or off, we present ourselves based on who others think we are, which itself is based on the responses from others that we have already received.

How do SNS users direct others' attention to specific aspects of themselves? According to Zhao, Grasmuck, and Martin they use the power of selection to present not false, but *hoped-for* identities. They wrote, the "hoped-for possible selves users projected on Facebook were neither the 'true selves' commonly seen in [anonymous] MUDs or Chat Rooms, nor the 'real selves' people presented in localized face-to-face interactions. The Facebook selves appeared to be highly socially desirable identities individuals aspire to have offline but have not yet been able to embody for one reason or another" (2008, p. 1830).

Another uses-and-gratifications inspired question is what are the interpersonal communication advantages and disadvantages of using this particular medium for interacting with others? Petter Brandtzæg assessed the "social costs and benefits" of social networking and determined that SNS use builds "social capital and might strengthen social bonds as SNSs give free and easy communication with family, friends, and acquaintances regardless of time and place.... Examining the results [of his research] in light of the current media debate, they do not support the anxiety about 'antisocial networking' or low social involvement. SNSs communication does not seem to replace intimacy or face-to-face interaction. In fact, SNS users are actually more likely to socially interact face-to-face and report more social capital compared to nonusers" (2012, pp. 481–482). Social capital in this instance is the building of social connections and networks and the resulting norms and trust that are built enabling people to act together more effectively.

But are we acting together more efficiently? The "anxiety" Brandtzæg referred to is the oft-stated concern that the new communication technologies are connecting us to the world as they disconnect us from each other. The argument is that we are losing our sense of community. We are increasingly socially isolated, spending time out with smaller numbers of people, and those we do associate with are very much like ourselves. "The implications of such a trend are alarming" write Keith Hampton and his colleagues, "They indicate a decline in the availability of broad social support within social networks in the form of companionship and instrumental and emergency aid and an increased likelihood that important matters are discussed only within small, closed groups" (Hampton, Sessions, and Her, 2010, p. 131). Their analysis of more than 20 years' worth of data from the U.S. General Social Survey (a standard core of demographic, behavioral, and attitudinal questions asked annually and overseen by the National Science Foundation) suggests that these fears of isolated Americans, while not completely unreasonable, are exaggerated. They found that "neither Internet nor mobile phone use is associated with having fewer core discussion confidants or having less diverse ties with whom to discuss important matters" (2010, p. 148). In fact, their analysis demonstrated that smartphone ownership and some SNS activity actually increased the number of close confidants, and Internet users were far more likely to discuss important issues with people outside their immediate families and even with those of different politics.

There is indeed evidence, however, justifying critics' "anxiety" over growing social isolation. Robert Kraut and his colleagues undertook an early study of what they called "the Internet paradox," writing in 1998 that, "the Internet could change the lives of average citizens as much as did the telephone in the early part of the 20th century and television in the 1950s and 1960s. Researchers and social critics are debating whether the Internet is improving or harming participation in community life and social relationships." They studied 169 Internet users in 73 different households during their first one to two years online and discovered that "the Internet was used extensively for communication. Nonetheless, greater use of the Internet was associated with declines in participants' communication with family members in the household, declines in the size of their social circle, and increases in their depression and loneliness" (Kraut et al., 1998, p. 1017). More recently, John Cacioppo (of elaboration likelihood renown) has taken up this line of inquiry. He examined "the proportion of interactions [people had] with friends that were face-to-face, on social networking sites, in chat rooms, on gaming sites, or on dating sites. The greater the face-to-face percentage, the less lonely people were. Now, most people use Facebook to leverage face-to-face interactions, but some use it as a substitute. Metaphorically, that's like eating celery. If you're hungry, it's better than nothing, but it doesn't provide enough nutrition" (in Aamodt, 2012). So, asked journalist Stephen Marche (2012), doesn't this mean that Facebook and the new communication technologies actually do make people lonelier? Cacioppo replied with a different analogy, "If you use Facebook to increase face-to-face contact, it increases social capital," he said. "Facebook can be terrific, if we use it properly. It's like a car. You can drive it to pick up your friends. Or you can drive alone."

Psychologist Barbara Fredrickson and her colleagues approached the issue of the new communication technologies and waning human interaction from a health and well-being perspective, citing neural plasticity and **vagal tone**, the strength of the body's connection between the heart and brain by way of the vagus nerve (Kok et al., 2013). Researcher Fredrickson explained,

vagal tone
Strength of the body's connection between the heart and brain by way of the vagus nerve

> Most of us are well aware of the convenience that instant electronic access provides. Less has been said about the costs.... [O]ne measurable toll may be on our biological capacity to connect with other people. Our ingrained habits change us.... [E]xperiences leave imprints on our neural pathways, a phenomenon called neuro plasticity. Any habit molds the very structure of your brain in ways that strengthen your proclivity for that habit. Plasticity, the propensity to be shaped by experience, isn't limited to the brain. You already know that when you lead a sedentary life, your muscles atrophy to diminish your physical strength. What you may not know is that your habits of social connection also leave their own physical imprint on you.... Your brain is tied to your heart by your vagus nerve. Subtle variations in your heart rate reveal the strength of this brain-heart connection, and as such, heart-rate variability provides an index of your vagal tone. By and large, the higher your vagal tone the better. It means your body is better able to regulate the internal systems that keep you healthy, like your

cardiovascular, glucose and immune responses.... In short, the more attuned to others you become, the healthier you become, and vice versa. This mutual influence also explains how a lack of positive social contact diminishes people. Your heart's capacity for friendship also obeys the biological law of "use it or lose it." If you don't regularly exercise your ability to connect face-to-face, you'll eventually find yourself lacking some of the basic biological capacity to do so. (2013, p. SR14)

HEALTH COMMUNICATION

health communication
Employing various forms of communication to inform and influence people's decisions that enhance health

The new digital technologies have also united interpersonal and mass communication researchers in their study of **health communication**, employing various forms of communication to inform and influence people's decisions that enhance health. Among the most promising venues of inquiry are the use of the Internet as a substitute for a traditional visit to a health professional and the use of the new communication technologies in the service of public health campaigns.

Seventy-two percent of all Internet users search online for health information; a third of Americans go to the Web to diagnose medical conditions. Eight in ten of those efforts begin at a search engine rather than at a health-specific site (Heussner, 2013), and more than 40 percent of people's self e-diagnoses are eventually confirmed by a clinician (only 18 percent are disconfirmed), suggesting people are using the technology with some level of skill (Fox and Duggan, 2013). In fact, more people visit the digital doctor every day than visit actual health professionals. As a result, many health-care providers are taking advantage of the Internet deliver care. Many hospitals, clinics, and physicians maintain blogs to help people navigate, evaluate, and interpret online health information, often in advance of a visit. Many doctors offer—and most health plans pay for—e-visits, in which physicians and patients interact virtually instead of face-to-face. Used primarily to eliminate office visits for routine illnesses, patients simply enter their symptoms into an online system, and doctors, typically with the patients' health records electronically accessible, use that information to send a diagnosis and, when necessary, a prescription. Evaluation of e-visits undertaken by the American Medical Association suggests that the resulting diagnoses are accurate and far less costly to render (Mehrotra et al., 2013). E-visits are not only effective and cost-efficient, they facilitate health communication in other ways as well. Doctors can attach to their replies information such as patient-education materials, lab results, prescriptions, referrals, and links to well-vetted websites.

e-visits
Physicians and patients interacting virtually instead of face-to-face

Social networking is another site of health communication research interest, especially the use of information shared among social networking friends to improve health outcomes. For example, medical professionals have developed an app that searches for keywords in users' newsfeeds to alert them to their increased risk of catching the flu. If, for example, four of your SNS friends post that they missed class and three others post that they're kind of achy, you're likely to receive the message, "You have a chance of getting the flu *today*." Other researchers have applied a similar approach to sexually transmitted infections (STI). "Real-world social networks—in other words, a person's circle of friends and sexual partners—have already proved to be strong predictors of STI risk. It follows that sites like Facebook, which convene all of those real-world connections in one virtual setting, have huge potential in this arena." The logic is that if keywords in SNS posts suggest sexually risky behavior or social contact with an infected individual, users will get a message to exercise extra care. Alternatively, in states where sexual partner notification is the law, people diagnosed with an STI can be asked for a list of sexual partners and friends whom they think might benefit from testing. Those people can be contacted using Facebook with an alert that someone they know has been diagnosed with an STI, they might be at risk, and they should be tested (Clark-Flory, 2012).

As you read in Chapter 8 narrative persuasion theory, the extended elaboration likelihood model, and the entertainment overcoming resistance model were either developed for or enriched by use in health campaigns. Other examples of the marriage of interpersonal communication and mass communication in the service of these campaigns abound. For example, in 2012 Facebook, recognizing that its users have a need to belong and a need for meaningful self-presentation, began offering them a simple way to indicate their status as an organ donor on their Facebook page's Timeline, under Life Event. "We believe that by simply telling people that you're an organ donor, the power of sharing and connection can play an important role," Facebook founder Jeff Zuckerberg explained (in Jacobs, 2012). Facebook is also being used to promote safe sex among high school and college students. Sheana Bull and her colleagues conducted an experiment in which they sent different messages to different recipients. Those who received News Feed messages about sexual health—items about "condom negotiation," HIV testing, and healthy sexual relationships in a weekly feature called Just/Us—showed better rates of condom use. The researchers chose to use News Feed rather than information from more formal SNS safe-sex advocates because "there is little evidence to suggest a majority of youth actively seek out and engage with organizations on Facebook. Thus, approaches like that of Just/Us to 'push' messages out through RSS feed offer one way to get messages in front of a large number of youth" (Bull et al., 2012, pp. 472–473).

JOURNALISM'S DISRUPTIVE TRANSITION

Throughout history new communication technologies have consistently challenged the dominance of the existing media. For example, when television became the national medium of news and entertainment, radio had to change. Where radio had itself been the national medium of news and entertainment, it became a local medium of talk and disc-jockeys playing music. No medium was untouched by the new video medium: newspapers began to focus as much on analysis as reporting and became more local in their orientation; television could bring pictures and sound to the home and for free, so film had to find a new way to survive. Movies became bigger, louder, favoring spectacle over character and nuance. This is **functional displacement**, when the functions of an existing medium are replaced by a newer technology, the older medium finds new functions. But the Internet's impact on the existing mass media has not only been more dramatic than that of television on its predecessors, it has been far more disruptive because there are few new functions to be found that cannot be provided and often improved-on by the Internet. Whatever newspapers can do, they can do online as well as on paper.

functional displacement
When the functions of an existing medium are replaced by a newer technology, the older medium finds new functions

Whatever television and radio stations and networks can do, they can do online as well as over the air or via cable. But while these functions have moved online, the advertising dollars that support them have not. For example, even though newspaper readership is at an all-time high (combining paper and digital readership), American newspapers took in $207 million online ad dollars in 2011 but lost $2.1 billion in print advertising revenue in that same year (Rosenblum, 2013). This is a problem for journalism, as described by the Pew Research Center for the People and the Press's (2013) annual state of the news media report:

> A continued erosion of news reporting resources converged with growing opportunities for those in politics, government agencies, companies, and others to take their messages directly to the public,... Estimates for newspaper newsroom cutbacks in 2012 put the industry down 30% since 2000 and below 40,000 full-time professional employees for the first time since 1978. In local TV ... sports, weather, and traffic now account on average for 40% of the content produced on the newscasts studied while story lengths shrink. On CNN, the cable channel that has branded itself around deep reporting, produced story packages were cut nearly in half from 2007 to 2012. Across the three cable [news] channels, coverage of live events and live reports during the day, which often require a crew and correspondent, fell 30% from 2007 to 2012 while interview segments, which tend to take fewer resources and can be scheduled in advance, were up 31%. *Time* magazine, the only major print news weekly left standing, cut roughly 5% of its staff in early 2013 as a part of broader company layoffs,... A growing list of media outlets, such as *Forbes* magazine, use technology by a company called Narrative Science to produce content by way of algorithm, no human reporting necessary. And some of the newer nonprofit entrants into the industry, such as the Chicago News Cooperative, have, after launching with much fanfare, shut their doors. This adds up to a news industry that is more undermanned and unprepared to uncover stories, dig deep into emerging ones, or to question information put into its hands.... At the same time, newsmakers and others with information they want to put into the public arena have become more adept at using digital technology and social media to do so on their own, without any filter by the traditional media. They are also seeing more success in getting their message into the traditional media narrative. So far, this trend has emerged most clearly in the political sphere, particularly with the biggest story of 2012—the presidential election. [Our] analysis revealed that campaign reporters were acting primarily as megaphones, rather than as investigators, of the assertions put forward by the candidates and other political partisans. That meant more direct relaying of assertions made by the campaigns and less reporting by journalists to interpret and contextualize them... Only about a quarter of statements in the media about the character and records of the presidential candidates originated with journalists in the 2012 race, while twice that many came from political partisans. That is a reversal from a dozen years earlier when half the statements originated with journalists and a third came from partisans.

Recall the Adams-Bloom/Cleary dual-responsibility model of the press from Chapter 3. This new normative theory, while holding true the media's First Amendment obligation of public service, also openly recognizes media companies' need to maintain profitability. But "Where is that balance?" ask contemporary mass communication researchers, especially as "the Internet does not alleviate the tensions between commercialism and journalism; it magnifies them" (McChesney, 2013). Beyond the long list of issues identified by the Pew researchers, there are many other changes digging at the roots of American journalism. For example,

Pew and others have identified the flood of public relations material that makes up a large proportion of the content on cash-strapped news outlets. In fact, where the proportion of PR professionals to journalists was 1.2 to 1 in 1980, it rose to 3.6 to 1 in 2008 (Verel, 2010). And nearly all Americans, 98 percent, now say they have cause to distrust the information they find on the Internet (Bustamante, 2012). In response, the Sunlight Foundation developed and has made available for free software called *Churnalism*, "an open-source plagiarism detection engine. It will scan any text (a news article, e.g.) and compare it with a corpus of press releases and Wikipedia entries. If it finds similar language, you'll get a notification of a detected 'churn' and you'll be able to take a look at the two sources side by side" (R. Rosen, 2013).

To take advantage of the new communication technologies in this era of dwindling resources, many news outlets have begun to engage in what press scholar Jay Rosen calls the "**hamsterization of journalism.**" It is corrosive to journalism's mission, he says, because "expecting reporters to report, write, blog, tweet, shoot video, sift the web, raise their metabolism, and produce more without time and training is guaranteed to fail. Trading in print dollars for digital dimes has been an economic disaster for newsrooms that ran on those dollars. Online advertising will never replace what was lost. The editorial staff is the engine that makes the whole thing go. You cannot cut your way to the future" (2013). The problem, say Rosen and other critics of this trend, is that to increase online ad revenues outlets are attempting to attract as many "eyeballs" as they can to their various sites in order to up their click rates, the number of visitors to each one. But even if they are successful, those online visitors will never earn them the same levels of revenue their print or broadcast operations did. All they are accomplishing is cheapening their journalism. "The core problem with all these efforts to make journalism pay online," explains media industry scholar Robert McChesney, "is that they accelerate the commercialization of journalism, degrading its integrity and its function as a public service. The cure may be worse than the disease" (2013). Nowhere was this more evident than in the overwrought, often-incorrect real-time Twitter, Reddit, cable news, and Facebook reporting of the 2013 Boston Marathon bombing that produced false identifications of suspects, erroneous casualty reports, and announcements of the whereabouts of the police and their tactics, among other errors (Moynihan, 2013).

Another troublesome contemporary commercialization-of-online-news practice is **native advertising**, sometimes called branded or sponsored content. Because people tend to ignore banner and other typical online advertising, native advertising takes the form of a full-length story or article. Sometimes it's written by the outlet's journalists; sometimes it's provided by the sponsor or the sponsor's advertising agency. In either case, it takes the form—in tone and design—of the host site. "The reason sponsored content is so attractive to advertisers and marketers," explains media critic Andrew Leonard, "is that, done well, it's very difficult to tell what is actual news content and what is just a commercial." Many reputable and well-established media outlets engage in the practice, the *Washington Post*, *Forbes*, *The Atlantic*, and the *Huffington Post* are a few examples. Blogger Andrew Sullivan, who once wrote for the *Atlantic* and blogged for that magazine as well, offered his evaluation of the practice, "The very phrases—'sponsored content,'

hamsterization of journalism
Expecting reporters to report, write, blog, tweet, shoot video, sift the web, and produce more news without time and training

native advertising
Branded or sponsored online content that takes the form of a full-length story or article

'native advertising'—are as accurate as 'enhanced interrogation.' It's either an advertisement or your media company is producing content. Creating editorial content for advertisers for money, rather than for readers for its own sake, is a major shift in this industry. There is an obvious solution. It is to make the advertorials look more different from editorial than they now do and slap a clear word ADVERTISEMENT on top of it. If that ethical labeling ruins your business model, it's proof that your business model isn't ethical" (2013). Google, for one, is fighting this practice, demanding separation of news and advertising. The Internet colossus publically issued a "reminder about promotional and commerce journalism," warning news sites that "it's difficult to be trusted when one is being paid by the subject of an article, or selling or monetizing links within an article. Google News is not a marketing service, and we consider articles that employ these types of promotional tactics to be in violation of our quality guidelines. [Therefore], if a site mixes news content with affiliate, promotional, advertorial, or marketing materials (for your company or another party), we strongly recommend that you separate non-news content on a different host or directory, block it from being crawled with robots.txt, or create a Google News Sitemap for your news articles only. Otherwise, if we learn of promotional content mixed with news content, we may exclude your entire publication from Google News" (Gingras, 2013).

Although of obvious importance to normative theorists (Chapter 3), there is no aspect of mass communication theory that is not touched by such a dramatic disruption of the media system that sits at the root of its inquiry. Information processing theory, uses and gratifications, attitude change theory, political economy theory, to name only a few, will all have to be rethought in an era when the source, construction, reliability, and completeness of the media content people consume is dramatically different from what was typical at the time these classic theories were first developed and tested. Nonetheless, there are those who argue that this is indeed a "Golden Age" for consumers of journalism, a claim that is certainly contested. You can read more about this disagreement in the box, "Losing Money is Not a Business Model."

RECONCEPTUALIZING AND REFORMING JOURNALISM

The future of journalism is clearly threatened, and there is widespread consensus that journalism and the news media need to be drastically altered (Pickard, Sterns, and Aaron, 2009). As we've seen, the business model relied on over the past century by newspapers and other journalistic outlets has been undermined. Moreover, these economic problems come at a time when news media were already subject to widespread criticism. We saw in Chapter 3 that distrust of the media is at an all-time high (Morales, 2012). Taken together, these factors threaten the foundations of democratic self-governance (Jones, 2009, p. 55). "When a major news organization closes, civic engagement suffers ... without a vibrant press, democracy falters: A society without journalism is a society that invites corruption" (Pickard, Sterns, and Aaron, 2009, pp. 6–7). While the value of journalism is widely recognized, its usefulness as currently practiced is open to question. As you've seen throughout this text, researchers in traditions such as information processing, news framing, objectivity rituals, news production research, and political economy theory have

THINKING ABOUT THEORY | Losing Money Is Not a Business Model

The Pew Research Center for the People and the Press's 2013 annual state of the news media report discussed elsewhere in this chapter moved *Slate* technology writer Matthew Yglesias to call it "deeply pessimistic" and to counter, "American news media has never been in better shape. That's just common sense. Almost anything you'd want to know about any subject is available at your fingertips. You don't need to take my analysis of the Cyprus bank bailout crisis as the last word on the matter: You can quickly and easily find coverage from the *New York Times*, *Wall Street Journal*, *Financial Times*, and the *Economist*. Or if you don't want to see your Cyprus news filtered through an America/British lens, you can check out the take of distinguished Greek economist Yanis Varoufakis on his blog. Reuters created an interactive feature that lets you try out different formulae for making the Cypriot haircut work. A pseudonymous London-based fund manager using the name Pawel Morski has offered vital, deeply informed coverage on Twitter and his WordPress site. You can watch a Bloomberg TV interview on the situation with native Cypriot and former Federal Reserve adviser Athanasios Orphanides at your leisure." And like any good Web-savvy journalist, Yglesias provided links to every source he mentioned. He continued to herald journalism's new era: people can add depth and context to the news; there are more competing ideas than ever; distribution is "astonishingly" easy; it is "dramatically easier" to produce the news; the Internet never runs out of space or time. "In other words," he wrote, "any individual journalist working today can produce much more than our predecessors could in 1978. And the audience can essentially read *all* of our output. Not just today's output either. Yesterday's and last week's and last month's and last year's and so forth" (2013).

He did, however, admit that "for people trying to make a living in journalism, the problems are real enough," and that is what caught the eye of longtime media observer Bob Garfield who, as long ago as 2005, warned of the looming, digitally driven "chaos scenario" as media were entering the "post-advertising age" (2005, 2007). Garfield responded that today's news consumers are enjoying a fabulous new age of journalism "in exactly the way looters enjoy

an improved standard of living. Problem is, it only stays improved until the store is emptied out. The news industry has gone from being obscenely profitable to slightly profitable to—at least, in the case of newspapers—largely unprofitable. All of that fantastic content Yglesias was gushing about is paid for by venture capitalists making bad bets, established media companies digging into their savings accounts to pay the bills, displaced workers earning peanuts, amateurs, semi-pros, volunteers, and monks. I would say that the business model is unsustainable, but losing money is not a business model. It is a going-out-of-business model" (2013). He offered his readers "Journalism Economics 101." "Thanks to the pesky law of supply and demand," he explained, "there's an infinite amount of online content, and therefore an infinite amount of advertising inventory, and therefore prices are driven inexorably downward. The resulting revenue can't sustain robust news organizations. The revenue can't even sustain feeble news organizations." The result, just as the Pew researchers found, is that "a lot of smart, desperate people are smartly, desperately seeking cash elsewhere. To date, little good has come of this." He points to native advertising and "e-payola: pay-per-post, pay-per-tweet, pay-per-review—and their cousin, affiliate advertising, which gives bloggers and tweeters incentive to steer readers toward transaction. In broadcast TV, there's the serial incest between the news divisions and entertainment divisions, and on local TV, video news releases camouflaged as reportage" (2013).

His solution—paywalls and other subscription models. **Paywalls**, making online content available only through some form of payment, are now quite common for most American newspapers, but most online magazines and news sites have yet to take up the practice. His argument is that if you value journalism and its role in our democracy, *you* will have to pay for it. Are you willing? Under what, if any conditions? Maybe Mr. Garfield is wrong. What do you think? Are you enjoying this new "Golden Age" of journalism? How long do you think it can last if the economics of journalism stay as they are?

paywalls Making online content available only through some form of payment consistently demonstrated that journalists rarely attempt to systematically educate the public about important issues. They ignore persistent gaps in political knowledge and understanding. Simply assuming that what they do is useful, journalists don't worry about fostering civic engagement or supporting democratic self-governance. They focus instead on quick news reports about specific events that fall within their news net, a problem exacerbated by the new communication technologies. It's not surprising, then, that contemporary news researchers argue that journalism needs to be reconceptualized and its practices need to change.

One focus of journalism reform efforts involves examining the notions that journalists use to guide and justify their work. Researchers are questioning long-accepted and cherished tenets of journalism and reassessing their usefulness. In Chapter 10 we looked at news production research that examined how journalists routinely gather and report news. This work concluded that news production practices don't assure that news reports will be accurate, balanced, or objective. Recent critical cultural framing research has assessed the strategies used by political and social elites to control how journalists frame events. For example, a team of researchers led by Robert Entman (2009) analyzed news coverage of the Iraq war and concluded that official good-news frames tended to dominate coverage. Likewise, Bennett and his colleagues (2007) argued that press coverage of a long series of significant news events—from the war in Iraq to the human, economic, and environmental consequences of Hurricane Katrina—relied on official frames to such a heavy extent that that coverage failed to provide the public with crucial information.

Elite efforts to control news were startlingly evident in internal Marine memos that surfaced during the 2007 murder and dereliction-of-duty trials of the men involved in the 2005 killing of 24 Iraqi men, women, and children in Haditha. In response to a series of questions posed by *Time* reporter Tim McGirk as he worked to confirm the official account that the deaths "occurred during combat and were justified, if regrettable," the commanding officers of the unit involved met and developed "talking points" designed to shape McGirk's account. They wrote: "One common tactic used by reporters is to spin a story in such a way that it is easily recognized and remembered by the general population through its association with an event that the general population is familiar with or can relate to. For example, McGirk's story will sell if it can be spun as 'Iraq's My Lai massacre.' Since there was not an officer involved, this attempt will not go very far. We must be on guard, though, of the reporter's attempt to spin the story to sound like incidents from well-known war movies, like *Platoon*" (von Zielbauer, 2007, p. K5).

Obviously, like the authors of this Marine memo, other elites have extensive knowledge of how news is produced. They are also quite cognizant of how committed reporters are to their news production practices. This allows them to stage events likely to be framed as they choose and to effectively suggest to journalists how events should be framed. The conflict in Iraq—with its accounts of weapons of mass destruction, the mushroom cloud as smoking gun, the heroic private Jessica Lynch, the toppling of Saddam's statue, the Mission Accomplished aircraft carrier landing, President Bush's Thanksgiving visit, and the gallant death of football star-turned-army ranger Pat Tillman—provided numerous examples of journalists framing events exactly as elites wished them to (Baran, 2011, pp. 310–311). They

news reality frames

News accounts in which interested elites involve journalists in the construction of news drama that blurs underlying contextual realities

represent what W. Lance Bennett (2005b) calls **news reality frames**, because in each case, an interested elite "involves journalists in constructing news drama that blurs underlying contextual realities, ranging from passive reporting of routine pseudo-events (such as the campaign stop), to more active co-production on the part of the press (such as the carrier landing), to a growing stream of journalistically-driven rumor, spin, and speculation-based stories" (p. 174). The rise of public relations as an increasingly important profession has served to institutionalize this control over framing. All major social institutions, most notably corporations and government, employ public relations staff to promote frames that enable them to maintain or extend their control over the social world (Entman, 2004; Entman and Rojecki, 1993; Martin and Oshagen, 1997). The Pentagon alone, for example, employs more than 7,000 public relations specialists (Seitel, 2004).

Goffman (1979) observed that most news is about *frame violations*; that's what makes news newsworthy. Newscasts report deviations from normality: "Dog Bites Man" is not news; "Man Bites Dog" is. When journalists report frame violations, they are often implicitly serving as protectors of the status quo because many of the most important frame violations involve events that severely disrupt the status quo. These news stories provide detailed coverage of the disruption, but more important, they almost always document how elites go about restoring order (Gans, 1979). Bennett (1988, 2005a), as you saw in Chapter 9, refers to this coverage as "normalizing" news—news framing the social world so social issues and problems are smoothed over and made to appear as though they are routinely (and effectively) dealt with by those in power.

Disorder comes in many forms. It arises when storms cause widespread damage. It happens when technologies fail—when airliners crash or power supplies are cut off. It happens when disease epidemics strike or when the environment is polluted. And it happens when social movements stage protest events challenging those in power and advocating social change. Herbert Gans (1979) concluded that news coverage of social unrest was overwhelmingly dominated by official sources, which framed events from a status quo point of view. He argued that journalists tend to most effectively present the perspective of the upper-middle-class professional strata and defend this class against those above and below it. Recall *Newsweek*'s Evan Thomas from Chapter 9 explaining that in his work as a journalist, "Safeguarding the status quo, protecting traditional institutions, can be healthy and useful, stabilizing and reassuring" (2009, p. 22).

Gans has also examined how journalists covered social movements in their reporting of major American public policy issues: a steel industry shutdown, the Arab–Israeli conflict, affirmative action, abortion, and nuclear power. He demonstrated that in only one of these cases, abortion, was there consistent, ongoing coverage of social movements (2003). All the other issues involved some coverage of movements at certain stages, but in almost every case that coverage was curtailed when powerful elites made a decision and forced policy in a particular direction. Protests of such decisions were rarely covered. The major exception to this was nuclear power news, in which coverage of movement activities continued despite the existence of powerful elites favoring nuclear power. Elites were most effective in ending coverage of activist movements in affirmative action news stories. What do you think? Would you find more coverage of social movements useful or would it simply make news coverage more complicated and boring? Would you be more likely to become involved in social movements if they were featured in the news? Online news could easily provide links to movement websites but this is rarely done since readers might assume that journalists are endorsing or promoting these movements and journalists typically live in fear of appearing nonobjective. Recall, however, Chapter 10's Occupy Wall Street example of how that movement worked to limit elite framing and encourage those frames it thought most useful.

But do news audiences have a particular interest in and desire for normalizing news in which elites take action to restore order after social unrest or natural disasters? James Carey (1989) argued that one of the most important things news does for readers and viewers is to offer them ritualized messages providing reassurance that the world will go on as it always has. Framing research implies that there is a symbiotic relationship between journalists who use frames supporting the status quo and news consumers who typically want to be reassured that the status quo will endure and disruptions are only temporary. This relationship between journalists and consumers is likely to be especially strong during times when the status quo is severely challenged. At such times, it can be especially difficult for journalists to offer frames that contradict the status quo and raise questions about governing elites. Even if these frames are used to structure news, news consumers might well choose to ignore them or react against them.

participatory news
News that reports how citizens routinely engage in actions that have importance for their communities

Media scholars who have studied elite control over news production have advocated specific journalism reforms based on their research. Gans (2003) calls for more **participatory news** that reports how citizens routinely engage in actions that have importance for their communities. His research found that this type of coverage has vanished even from local newspapers, but it could be a vital part of encouraging more people to become politically engaged. Participatory news could range from covering conversations in coffee shops to reports on involvement in social groups. Reports on social movements could be "reframed" so they feature positive aspects rather than threats posed to the status quo. He argues that coverage of participation is the best way for journalists to effectively promote it.

explanatory journalism
News answering "why" questions

Gans also calls for **explanatory journalism**, which "seeks first and foremost to answer 'why' questions: to report why events and statements described by conventional journalism took place." Explanatory journalism involves offering frames for major events. It might mean presenting contrasting frames and providing news consumers a basis for choosing among them. Gans points out that "why stories" are vital "when visible, unusual changes take place in public life as well as private institutions, and people want to understand the effects of these changes on them" (2003, p. 99). If frames for these events aren't provided, people will make them up and circulate them as rumors.

collective action frames
News frames highlighting positive aspects of social movements and the need for and desirability of action

Gamson (2001) has also offered recommendations for news coverage to promote citizen engagement in politics. His advice centers on the use of what he calls **collective action frames**. These frames highlight positive aspects of social movements and would "offer ways of understanding that imply the need for and desirability of some form of action" (p. 58). To be effective, these frames should offer three components: injustice, identity, and agency. They need to reveal an existing harm or wrong (injustice), identify specifically who is doing the harm and who is being harmed (identity), and finally, explain the possibility of collective action to address the injustice (agency). News media typically focus on framing injustice but don't do as well with identity and agency. Gamson stresses the necessity of including agency in news frames. He argues that most Americans are discouraged about their ability to take collective action against injustice. Public policy is dominated by "centralized, hierarchical, national corporations and a national state" (p. 59). American political culture operates to produce quiescence and passivity. Injustice is often committed by government or corporations, institutions that most people find unassailable.

Some media scholars have gone beyond recommending changes in journalism practices and have become directly involved in reform efforts. Over the past 20 years, one of the leading efforts to reform journalism has been dubbed "public journalism or civic journalism" (Pew Center for Civic Journalism, 2002). It originated during the 1990s when the Internet's disruption of newspaper circulation first began to be taken seriously (Rosen, 1996). Civic journalism advocates reasoned that circulation was falling because people no longer found local news coverage useful or relevant. Newspapers had lost touch with their communities. To remedy this situation newspapers needed to put the public interest ahead of profits and become more directly involved in their communities. They should serve as forums for deliberation about important community issues. Funding from the Pew Foundation enabled a number of newspapers to experiment with various projects intended to achieve public journalism goals (Harwood, 2000). The success of these projects was mixed. In general there was little or no impact on readership, which continued its steady decline even in cities where newspapers made serious commitments to public journalism practices. Public journalism also met with considerable criticism from some journalists who argued it was either unnecessary or disruptive of their work. Involvement in communities jeopardized their objectivity, they complained, and risked turning them into advocates. How could newspapers be trusted as community watchdogs if they were themselves engaged in promoting changes in communities? As such, the movement lost momentum and its prime advocate and financial supporter, the Pew Center for Civic Journalism, closed its doors in 2003.

In its place journalism reform has taken the form of citizen journalism or participant journalism (Gilmor, 2004; Rosenberry and Burton, 2010). Citizen journalism is any journalism practice that is performed by non-journalists. It includes community-based online initiatives that aggregate news created by non-journalists. J-Lab, a news innovation center at American University has catalogued more than a thousand of these efforts (J-Lab, 2013). Bloggers who regularly aggregate, link to, or comment on news are considered citizen journalists. Anyone who regularly comments on news items online or recommends items to friends is a citizen journalist because he or she is engaging in editorial practices. Other citizen journalists work directly with professional journalists to cover local issues and events. Proponents of the various forms of citizen journalism argue that news will serve the public better if the public is more directly involved in determining what is newsworthy, helps to gather news, critically evaluates the way journalists cover news, and makes recommendations about news to others. Citizen journalism is possible largely because of new media that facilitate citizen involvement in news production, distribution, and evaluation.

Some journalists have embraced citizen journalism. They pay attention to comments posted to their news stories. They watch the frequency with which their stories are recommended to others. Using Internet-based applications and smartphone technology, they assemble and work with teams of volunteers as they cover and write news about topics in which team members are interested and knowledgeable. Teams provide feedback on early drafts of news stories and guide news editing. They check the accuracy of stories and assess their effectiveness in communicating information or ideas. But citizen journalism has encountered resistance from journalists who believe it threatens their independence and their status as professionals. They ask, "Would doctors or lawyers permit teams of amateurs to become directly involved in their work? If citizen journalists are such a good idea why not form teams of unlicensed health workers and call them citizen doctors?"

parental mediation theory
Theory of active parent involvement in the full array of children's media experiences

A NEW MEDIA LITERACY

The discipline has also begun to reframe media literacy to account for people's use of the new communication technologies. Lynn Clark details **parental mediation theory**, originally developed as a means of conceptualizing an active parental role in regulating and managing children's experiences with television. But as with so many other mass communication theories, it has had to evolve in the digital era to become "a hybrid communication theory that, although rooted primarily in social/psychological media effects and information processing theories, also implicitly foregrounds the importance of interpersonal communication between parents and their children" (2011, pp. 323–324). Clark argues that the parental mediation strategies that were effective with children's television viewing—**active mediation** (talking with children about television content), **restrictive mediation** (setting rules and limits on their viewing), and **co-viewing** (watching television with them)—need to be augmented in the digital age with a "fourth strategy of parental mediation as participatory learning [designed] to recognize that although children might encounter risks in the digital and mobile media environment, they might also engage with parents in activities that foster strengthened interpersonal relationships, individual and collaborative creativity, and even cognitive development" (2011, p. 335).

active mediation
Talking with children about television content as a media literacy strategy

restrictive mediation
Setting rules and limits on children's television consumption as a media literacy strategy

co-viewing
Watching television with children as a media literacy strategy

Sora Park approached the new media literacy from the perspective of social inclusion and exclusion, closely related to knowledge gap theory:

social inclusion
The ability to exercise control over the environment or resources that one might have in various dimensions of life

> Digital media literacy is related to potential social inclusion or exclusion. **Social inclusion** is the ability to exercise control over the environment or resources that a person might have in various dimensions of life. **Social exclusion** is not synonymous with poverty, but refers to a state where people cannot participate in key societal activities.... Information poverty increasingly is becoming an important indicator of social exclusion, especially in the digital era. The inability to use or access information and communications technology can lead to the widening of the gap between the socially included and excluded.... The enormous potential of the Internet to provide access to enormous amounts of data and information for those who are connected poses the traditional question of whether the media will enable people to access and use information that would have not been available if they were not connected. (2012, pp. 93–94)

social exclusion
A state where one cannot participate in key societal activities

Because interactivity is the central characteristic differentiating digital media from traditional mass media, Park insists that digital media literacy must include *device literacy* as well as *content literacy*. "A wider range of competencies is involved in using digital media compared with traditional mass media,"

TABLE 11.1 DIMENSIONS OF DIGITAL MEDIA LITERACY

	Device Literacy	Content Literacy
Access	Device ownership, access to service	Ability to search, find, and filter relevant content
Understand	Understand the basic nature of technology and know how to operate at a functional level	Ability to understand and critically analyze content
Create	Ability to produce, reproduce, and create content using digital technology	Ability to form opinions and ideas and convert them into digital content. Knowledge of content's social impact, cyber-etiquette, and ethics

Sora Park, Media International, Feb. 2012, p. 91

she explains, "While literacy skills of mass media focus on how people can critically understand mediated messages, digital media literacy skills expand beyond interpretation of content into the realm of controlling, altering, and appropriating content through various digital media channels. However, digital media literacy should not be regarded as replacing traditional media literacy; rather, it expands the literacy skills involved in reading, writing and understanding to encompass the new technologies" (p. 89). You can see her "dual-layered approach" to separating "the device with which the content is delivered and the content itself, since different skills are required to be able to use either" (p. 91) in Table 11.1.

FUTURE OF MEDIA THEORY AND RESEARCH: QUESTIONS AND DIRECTIONS

Charles Dickens began his novel about the French Revolution, *The Tale of Two Cities*, with the phrase, "It was the best of times, it was the worst of times...." Media theorists and researchers are living in that sort of time. On the one hand, their work has never been easier to accomplish. Online databases instantly bring journal articles and even books to their desktops. Powerful statistical analyses can be performed on the datasets obtained from large surveys or complex experiments. They can easily and instantly collaborate with colleagues across the nation or around the world. It's the best of times. On the other hand, media technology and applications are evolving rapidly and in unpredictable ways. Use of this technology is changing. Old uses persist while new uses spring up. Generation and gender gaps appear as older people struggle with new technology and women find different uses for media than men. Very young children spend hours a day interacting with screens. The flood of information from new media only seems to widen knowledge gaps and deepen misunderstanding of important issues. Polls show growing cynicism about politics and widespread distrust of mainstream journalism. Digital divides separate people with low and high incomes or with urban or rural residences. Older theories of mass communication originally developed to explain legacy media are no longer useful, and the usefulness of newer theories has not

been adequately demonstrated. New concepts and new research methods are introduced daily. It's the worst of times.

The future of media theory and research may be at a critical juncture point
similar to those we have considered in previous chapters. It's like the World War
II era when the media-effects trend emerged to dominate the field, and it's like the
early 1980s when the critical cultural trend challenged the effects trend. It's a time
when many media researchers are pondering the future and wondering how the
field will develop. They are investigating questions that are central to the discipline.
How will the effects trend and critical cultural trend develop? Are new theories or
methods needed to study the new communication media since they differ radically
from older forms of media? Which media theories will continue to be useful and
which should be discarded?

Here is a quick listing of some of the important changes that have occurred or
accelerated in the field of media theory and research over the past decade:

1. A community of researchers has emerged who are bound together in a global
   network that facilitates ongoing collaboration. International professional
   associations and journals provide support for this community.
2. Theory and research are shared in a growing number of academic journals and
   books, some of which are published only online. These journals tend to be
   increasingly specialized and focused on narrow lines of research in specific
   areas such as journalism practice, health communication, risk communication,
   and sports communication.
3. Media Ph.D. students are being educated to understand and use a common
   body of quantitative and qualitative theory and research methods at universities located around the world. This generation of academics will begin their
   careers in what they understand to be a global discipline and with the belief
   that their work can be useful beyond their own borders.
4. Conflicts between postpositivist and critical cultural researchers have
   dissipated—replaced by mutual respect and even collaboration. However,
   most academic journals and textbooks remain specialized along methodological lines.
5. American, European, and Asian researchers share leadership in key professional associations such as the International Communication Association and
   service on editorial boards of major academic journals such as the *Journal of
   Communication*.
6. Personal computers provide easy and low-cost access to powerful research
   tools for both qualitative and quantitative research.

Where will these changes lead? Is a global discipline being forged that might
have the ability to study what is becoming a globalized media system (Reese,
2010)? If so, what theories and research methods will be used by the scholars
working in this new discipline? Will qualitative and quantitative scholars continue
to work in relative isolation or will they begin to collaborate on large-scale projects
to address the many unanswered questions about the role of media for individuals
or for society?

In this book we have given considerable attention to two lines of theory
and research that are most promising—media cognition and framing. One is

firmly rooted in the effects trend and the other has roots in both the effects and critical culture trends. Each can be used to address important sets of research questions raised by new media. One leans toward microscopic analyses while the other is more macroscopic. Will these two lines of theory and research continue independently or could they merge? Merger would require cooperation between postpositivist and critical cultural researchers. Is that likely or even possible? Merger might require conducting large-scale research projects using both quantitative and qualitative methods. How would such projects be designed and who would pay for them? During World War II and the Cold War the effects trend was underwritten by large grants from the U.S. government and private foundations. Could funding for media research grow if it promised to answer the many important questions raised by new technology? Who would provide it and what sorts of findings would sponsors expect to get for their funding?

Recently, a number of prominent researchers have speculated about the future of the discipline and have addressed some of the questions we have posed concerning its future. Michael Delli Carpini (2013) has urged collaboration between quantitative and qualitative researchers in the area of entertainment and politics. He maintains that it isn't necessary to resolve methodological differences but to understand and even take advantage of them. In doing so, mass communication could become "a more integrated and influential discipline, and a more deliberative, vibrant intellectual community" (p. 536). He favors decoupling quantitative methods from positivism and combining them with qualitative methods to study the influence of entertainment media on the public's relationship to politics. He illustrates his argument by outlining how researchers using different methods could collaborate to study the critically acclaimed and hugely popular cable television series *The Wire*. He concludes, "Should this effort succeed, I believe it could remix ontological, epistemological, axiological, and praxeological underpinnings in exciting and groundbreaking ways, and in doing so, reap benefits for the collective understanding of the theory and practice of not only entertainment and politics, but also political communication more broadly" (p. 545).

Klaus Bruhn Jensen and W. Russell Neuman have argued that the "significant transformations in the media technologies of the digital age" are forcing researchers to reconsider and change the paradigms that underlie their work. Jensen is a European with background in qualitative research, while Neuman is an American trained as a quantitative researcher. After they offer the history of their field, they argue that the point of reference for both qualitative and quantitative researchers has "shifted from the image of the isolated and easily persuaded urban television viewer of the 1950s, to the always-connected—and perhaps always-distracted—Internet user of the new millennium" (2013, p. 232). They offer cautious optimism about the possibility that qualitative and quantitative researchers will join together to develop a common paradigm that can guide future research.

Denis McQuail (2013) discusses possibilities for a paradigm shift in the way communication is understood and studied. He cautions against the notion that such a shift would be driven by technological change. Older notions of media as powerful tools for social control are still widely prevalent and serve to guide considerable research—especially research conducted by media organizations and by elites who rely on media to influence audiences. There are many innovative notions about communication but they have not been integrated into a coherent alternative. He summarizes his view of this alternative, "Our new big idea is now much more complex and nuanced, even fragmentary and contested, but still has reference to ongoing changes in culture and society of a fundamental kind. As a result of new developments within the field of communication inquiry, we have a more adequate apparatus of concepts and ideas for relating the overarching ideas to the many new macroprocesses and microprocesses of communication that are now observable" (p. 227). If he is right, we may have the basis for developing a new perspective on media but we need to put all of the pieces together into a coherent vision if we are to forge a new paradigm for media research.

Frank Esser (2013) has called for increased cross-national research as a way of understanding how media are involved in the trend toward globalization. One example of this global research focuses on different models of journalism. He argues that comparison of different media systems can provide practical knowledge and problem solutions. This research can also lead to the development of theories that are broadly useful rather than relevant only for the nations in which they are developed. He argues for the development of better designs for comparative research. Though he personally favors postpositivist designs he acknowledges that "the field will benefit from increased triangulation, or the use of multiple methods and theories. With regard to methodological pluralism, I agree with Hallin and Mancini (2012, p. 217), who expect for the future 'many styles of comparative analysis' that coexist side by side—some large-scale and others small-scale, some quantitative and others qualitative, some descriptive and others hypothesis-based and explanatory. 'This is normal,' they state, and 'this is how a field should develop' " (p. 122).

These visions of the future of media theory and research all foresee a field that spans the globe as it works to describe and understand global media. It will use both qualitative and quantitative methods. It will rely on both postpositivist and critical cultural theories. These theories might be developed independently or they might be integrated into a powerful new paradigm for media theory and research. But there are many questions about this field that can't be answered. Could or should there be a new paradigm for theory and research? Existing media systems are deeply embedded in national politics and culture. Privately owned systems seek profits for shareholders while public systems serve publics in specific nations. Could or should these national media systems become increasingly integrated into a global system? Does the Internet already provide us with a global media system? Clearly there is much that can be learned about media systems by comparing them, but is comparison likely to lead to closer integration of these systems? On the one hand we now possess the technology that could permit us to forge a truly global media system. But on the other hand, our world remains deeply fragmented by political and cultural differences. Although the world increasingly shares the same media technology and similar forms of media content, it remains divided into competing and potentially hostile sets of nations.

SUMMARY

Mass communication theory, as is the case with any worthy scholarly pursuit, has been roiled by and benefitted from decades of ferment. The arrival of the new digital communication technologies has produced the discipline's latest round of self-examination and change. The debates surrounding the new media environment, however, are not mere intellectual battles of methodology or disciplinary turf. They will have profound influence on how we live as individuals and exist as communities. As you've read in this chapter, much of what we thought of as common sense, for example, that the Internet would expand our knowledge, better connect us, and make journalism faster, cheaper, and more democratic, now seems a bit optimistic. But many of the fears that accompanied the new technologies may also have been overstated. Theory is helping us sort out the real from the imagined and the wished-for from the can-do. But theory is useless unless we use it to guide our judgments and decisions.

Despite the breathtaking speed with which dramatic change has overtaken the mass media industries, communication technology, and our interaction with both, good mass communication theory can provide that guidance. We have seen over the short life (in scientific terms) of mass communication theory that media scholars have always found the resources necessary to address the challenges they faced in their times and circumstances. There is every reason to believe that contemporary thinkers and researchers are equally up to the task. Future theories—whether we call them mass communication or media theories—will need to address the full spectrum of mediated communication, from small-town newspapers to the Internet to social networking sites. These theories must assess how mediation takes place, the social context and social implications of using various media, the cognitive processes and skills necessary to encode and decode various types of messages from different types of media, and how individuals can take more control of the media they use to send and receive messages. These theories also need to critically assess the role media play in culture and society.

Despite the challenges facing media (or mass communication) theory, this is likely to be an exciting and productive era, one in which the conceptual and methodological tools developed over the past century and a quarter will be used to understand the rise of our entirely new media systems. We hope that this book has encouraged at least some of you to pursue careers as communication scholars, and we hope that all of you have gained an understanding of media that is useful to you.

Critical Thinking Questions

1. As a news consumer, do you think it is the best of times or the worst of times? Are you satisfied with the quality of the news you consume? How comfortable are you with its credibility? Do you access multiple sources of news, or do you impose your own bubble, visiting the same few websites, reading the same few publications, watching the same one or two television news channels? That is, how much do you take advantage of the wealth of options now available to you and others?

2. Are worries about Internet addiction, depression, and distraction overblown? How does your personal experience with the new digital technologies measure up against the research on these issues presented in this chapter? If you feel the findings presented here do not reflect your use of the Internet, why do you think that is the case? If your personal experience is reflected in these research findings, what changes in your interaction with the new media might you make?

3. What kind of social network site user are you? In your experience, does your use match that predicted by the idealized virtual identity hypothesis or the extended real-life hypothesis? Why is this the case? What about your friends? Which perspective best describes the way they present themselves?

Key Terms

citizen journalism

Internet addiction

Facebook depression

fear of missing out (FOMO)

transactive memory

neural plasticity

atomization

algorithms

cookie

filter bubble

communication science

intra-individual communication

interpersonal communication

dual-factor model of Facebook (FB) use

idealized virtual identity hypothesis

extended real-life hypothesis

vagal tone

health communication

e-visits

functional displacement

hamsterization of journalism

native advertising

paywalls

news reality frames

participatory news

explanatory journalism

collective action frames

parental mediation theory

active mediation

restrictive mediation

co-viewing

social inclusion

social exclusion

REFERENCES

"2012 Voter Turnout." (2012). *Bipartisan Policy Center*, November 8. (http://bipartisanpolicy.org/library/report/2012-voter-turnout).

Aalberg, T., J. Strömbäck, and C. H. de Vreese. (2012). "The Framing of Politics as Strategy and Game: A Review of Concepts, Operationalizations, and Key Findings." *Journalism*, 13: 162–178.

Aamodt, S. (2012). "An Interview with John Cacioppo: The Science of Loneliness." *Being Human.org*, September 26. (http://www.beinghuman.org/article/interview-john-cacioppo-science-loneliness).

Abse, N. (2012). "Big Data Delivers on Campaign Promise: Microtargeted Political Advertising in Election 2012." *IAB Presents*, October. (http://www.iab.net/media/file/Innovations_In_Web_Marketing_and_Advertising_delivery.pdf).

Adams-Bloom, T., and J. Cleary. (2009). "Staking a Claim for Social Responsibility: An Argument for the Dual Responsibility Model." *International Journal on Media Management*, 11: 1–8.

Adbusters. (2002). "The Rev. Jerry Falwell." *Adbusters*, January/February, no page number.

Adorno, T., and M. Horkheimer. (1972). *Dialectic of Enlightenment*. New York: Herder and Herder.

Alasuutari, P. (1999). "Introduction: Three Phases of Reception Studies." In P. Alasuutari, ed., *Rethinking the Media Audience*. Thousand Oaks, CA: Sage.

Alexander, G. (2011). "Ang in Retrospect." *Ien Ang: Theories in Media*, November 9. (http://angmediatheorist.blogspot.com/).

Allport, G. W. (1967). "Attitudes." In M. Fishbein, ed., *Readings in Attitude Theory and Measurement*. New York: Wiley.

Allport, G. W., and L. J. Postman. (1945). "The Basic Psychology of Rumor." *Transactions of the New York Academy of Sciences*, 8: 61–81.

Alterman, E. (2006). "Truth Is for 'Liberals.'" *The Nation*, June 26: 10.

Alterman, E. (2008). "The News from Quinn-Broderville." *The Nation*, February 24: 11–14.

Altschull, J. H. (1995). *Agents of Power: The Media and Public Policy*. White Plains, NY: Longman.

Altschull, J. H. (1990). *From Milton to McLuhan: The Ideas behind American Journalism*. New York: Longman.

Althusser, L. (1970). *For Marx*. Translated by Ben Brewster New York: Vintage.

American Civil Liberties Union. (2013). "The Journalists Guide to Criminal Justice Reform 2013." *Columbia Journalism Review*, March/April, Insert.

Anderson, C. A., L. Berkowitz, E. Donnerstein, L. R. Huesmann, J. D. Johnson, D. Linz, N. M. Malamuth, and E. Wartella. (2003). "The Influence of Media Violence on Youth." *Psychological Science in the Public Interest*, 4: 81–110.

Anderson, C. A., and B. J. Bushman. (2002). "Human Aggression." *Annual Review of Psychology*, 53: 27.51.

Anderson, C. A., and B. J. Bushman. (2001). "Effects of Violent Video Games on Aggressive Behavior, Aggressive Cognition, Aggressive Affect, Physiological Arousal, and Prosocial Behavior: A Meta-Analytical Review of the Scientific Literature." *Psychological Science*, 12: 353–359.

Anderson, C. A., and N. L. Carnagey. (2004). "Violent Evil and The General Aggression Model." In A. G. Miller, ed., *The Social Psychology of Good and Evil*. New York: The Guilford Press.

Anderson, C. A., W. E. Deuser, and K. DeNeve. (1995). "Hot Temperatures, Hostile Affect, Hostile Cognition, and Arousal: Tests of a General Model of Affective Aggression." *Personality and Social Psychology Bulletin*, 21: 434–448.

Anderson, C. A., and K. E. Dill. (2000). "Video Games and Aggressive Thoughts, Feelings, and Behavior in the Laboratory and in Life." *Journal of Personality and Social Psychology*, 78: 772–790.

Anderson, C. A., A. Shibuya, N. Ihori, E. L. Swing, B. J. Bushman, A. Sakamoto, H. R. Rothstein, and M. Saleem. (2010). "Violent Video Game Effects on Aggression, Empathy, and Prosocial Behavior in Eastern and Western Countries: A Meta-Analytic Review." *Psychological Review*, 136: 151–173.

Anderson, D. R., and E. P. Lorch. (1983). "Looking at Television: Action or Reaction?" In J. Bryant and D. R. Anderson, ed., *Children's Understanding of Television: Research on Attention and Comprehension*. New York: Academic.

Andison, F. S. (1977). "TV Violence and Viewer Aggression: A Culmination of Study Results, 1956–1976." *Public Opinion Quarterly*, 41: 314–331.

Andrews, R., M. Biggs, and M. Seidel. (1996). *The Columbia World of Quotations*. New York: Columbia University Press.

Ang, I. (1985). *Watching Dallas: Soap Opera and the Melodramatic Imagination*. London: Methuen.

Ang, I., and M. Simmons. (1982). "Interview with Stuart Hall." *Skrien*, 116: 14.

Arato, A., and E. Gebhardt. (1978). *The Essential Frankfurt School Reader*. New York: Urizen.

Auletta, K. (2010). "Non-Stop News." *New Yorker*, January 25: 38–47.

Austin, E. W., A. C. Miller, J. Silva, P. Guerra, N. Geisle, L. Gamboa, O. Phakakayai, and B. Kuechle. (2002). "The Effects of Increased Cognitive Involvement on College Students' Interpretations of Magazine Advertisements for Alcohol." *Communication Research*, 29: 155–179.

Axelrod, R. (1973). "Schema Theory: An Information Processing Model of Perception and Cognition." *American Political Science Review*, 67: 1248–1266.

Back, M. D., J. M. Stopfer, S. Vazire, S. Gaddis, S. C. Schmukle, B. Egloff, and S. D. Gosling. (2010). "Facebook Profiles Reflect Actual Personality, Not Self-Idealization." *Psychological Science*, 21: 372–374.

Bagdikian, B. H. (2004). "Print Will Survive." *Editor & Publisher*, March, 70.

Bagdikian, B. H. (2000). *The Media Monopoly*, 6th ed. Boston: Beacon.

Bagdikian, B. H. (1992). *The Media Monopoly*, 4th ed. Boston: Beacon.

Bailey, K. D. (1982). *Methods of Social Research*. New York: Free Press.

Baker, L. R., and D. L. Oswald. (2010). "Shyness and Online Social Networking Services." *Journal of Social and Personal Relationships*, 27: 883–889.

Baker, W. F. (2009). "How to Save the News." *The Nation*, October 12: 21–23.

Baker, R. K., and S. J. Ball. (1969). *Violence and the Media: A Staff Report to the National Commission on the Causes and Prevention of Violence*, vol. 9A. Washington, DC: U.S. Government.

Ball-Rokeach, S. J. (1998). "A Theory of Media Power and a Theory of Media Use: Different Stories, Questions, and Ways of Thinking." *Mass Communication & Society*, 1: 5–40.

Bandura, A. (2009). "Social Cognitive Theory of Mass Communication." In J. Bryant and M. B. Oliver, ed., *Media Effects: Advances in Theory and Research*. New York: Routledge.

Bandura, A. (2008). "The Reconstrual of 'Free Will' from the Agentic Perspective of Social Cognitive Theory." In J. Baer, J. C. Kaufman, and R. F. Baumeister, eds., *Are We Free? Psychology and Free Will*. Oxford: Oxford University Press.

Bandura, A. (1994). "Social Cognitive Theory of Mass Communication." In J. Bryant and D. Zillman, ed., *Media Effects: Advances in Theory and Research*. Hillsdale, NJ: Erlbaum.

Bandura, A. (1971). *Psychological Modeling: Conflicting Theories*. Chicago: Aldine Atherton.

Bandura, A. (1965). "Influence of Models' Reinforcement Contingencies on the Acquisition of Imitative Responses." *Journal of Personality and Social Psychology*, 1: 589–595.

Bandura, A., D. Ross, and S. A. Ross. (1963). "Imitation of Film-Mediated Aggressive Models." *Journal of Abnormal Social Psychology*, 66: 3–11.

Banerjee, S. C., and R. Kubey. (2013). "Boom or Boomerang: A Critical Review of Evidence Documenting Media Literacy Efficacy." In A. N. Valdivia and E. Scharrer, eds., *The International Encyclopedia of Media Studies: Media Effects/Media Psychology*. Hoboken, NJ: Blackwell.

Baran, S. J. (2011). *Introduction to Mass Communication: Media Literacy and Culture*. New York: McGraw-Hill.

Baran, S. J. (1976a). "How Television and Film Portrayals Affect Sexual Satisfaction in College Students." *Journalism Quarterly*, 53: 468–473.

Baran, S. J. (1976b). "Sex on Television and Adolescent Sexual Self Image." *Journal of Broadcasting*, 20: 1, 61-68.

Baran, S. J., and V. J. Blasko. (1984). "Social Perceptions and the Byproducts of Advertising." *Journal of Communication*, 34: 12–20.

Baran, S. J., and T. P. Meyer. (1974). "Imitation and Identification: Two Compatible Approaches to Social Learning from the Electronic Media." *AV Communication Review*, 22: 167–179.

Barber, B. R. (2007). *Consumed: How Markets Corrupt Children, Infantilize Adults, and Swallow Citizens Whole*. New York: W. W. Norton.

Barker, C. (2004). *Cultural Studies: Theory and Practice*. Thousand Oaks, CA: Sage.

Barnouw, E. (1966). *A History of Broadcasting in the United States: A Tower in Babel*, vol. 1. New York: Oxford University Press.

Barrow, J. D. (1998). *Impossibility: The Limits of Science and the Science of Limits*. New York: Oxford University Press.

Barry, T. E. (2002). "In Defense of the Hierarchy of Effects: A Rejoinder to Weilbacher." *Journal of Advertising Research*, 42: 44–47.

Bartlett, F. C. (1932). *Remembering: A Study in Experimental and Social Psychology*. Cambridge: Cambridge University Press.

Bates, S. (2001). "Realigning Journalism with Democracy: The Hutchins Commission, Its Times, and Ours." (http://www.annenberg.nwu.edu).

Baumgartner, J., and J. S. Morris. (2006). "The Daily Show Effect: Candidate Evaluations, Efficacy, and American Youth." *American Politics Research*, 34: 341–367.

Bauer, R. A., and A. H. Bauer. (1960). "America, Mass Society, and Mass Media." *Journal of Social Issues*, 10: 3–66.

Becker, H. (1949). "The Nature and Consequences of Black Propaganda." *American Sociological Review*, 14: 221–235.

Benford, R., and D. Snow. (2000). "Framing Processes and Social Movements: An Overview and Assessment." *Annual Review of Sociology*, 26: 611–639.

Beniger, J. R. (1987). "Toward and Old New Paradigm: The Half-Century Flirtation with Mass Society." *Public Opinion Quarterly*, 51: S46–S66.

Bennett, W. L. (2005a). *News: The Politics of Illusion*, 6th ed. New York: Longman.

Bennett, W. L. (2005b). "News as Reality TV: Election Coverage and the Democratization of Truth." *Critical Studies in Media Communication*, 22: 171–177.

Bennett, W. L. (1988). *News: The Politics of Illusion*, 2nd ed. New York: Longman.

Bennett, W. L., and M. Edelman. (1985). "Toward a New Political Narrative." *Journal of Communication*, 35: 128–138.

Bennett, W. L., and R. L. Holbert. (2008). "Empirical Intersections in Communication Research: Replication, Multiple Quantitative Methods, and Bridging the Quantitative-Qualitative Divide." *Journal of Communication*, 58: 615–628.

Bennett, W. L., and S. Iyengar. (2008). "A New Era of Minimal Effects? The Changing Foundations of Political Communication." *Journal of Communication*, 58: 707–731.

Bennett, W. L., R. G. Lawrence, and S. Livingston. (2007). *When the Press Fails: Political Power and the News Media from Iraq to Katrina*. Chicago, IL: University of Chicago Press.

Berelson, B. (1959). "The State of Communication Research." *Public Opinion Quarterly*, 23: 1–6.

Berelson, B. (1949). "What 'Missing the Newspaper' Means." In P. F. Lazarsfeld and F. N. Stanton, eds., *Communications Research, 1948–1949*. New York: Harper.

Berger, C. R. (2005). "Interpersonal Communication: Theoretical Perspectives, Future Prospects." *Journal of Communication*, 55: 415–447.

Berger, C. R. (2001). "Making It Worse Than It Is: Quantitative Depictions of Threatening Trends in The News." *Journal of Communication*, 46: 655–677.

Berger, P. L., and T. Luckmann. (1966). *The Social Construction of Reality: A Treatise in the Sociology of Knowledge*. Garden City, NY: Doubleday.

Bergsma, L. J., and M. E. Carney. (2008). "Effectiveness of Health-Promoting Media Literacy Literature Education: A Systematic Review." *Health Education Research*, 23: 522–542.

Berkowitz, L. (1965). "Some Aspects of Observed Aggression." *Journal of Personality and Social Psychology*, 2: 359–369.

Berkowitz, L., and R. G. Geen. (1966). "Film Violence and the Cue Properties of Available Targets." *Journal of Personality and Social Psychology*, 3: 525–530.

Bernays, E. L. (1928). *Propaganda*. New York: Liveright.

Besley, J. (2006). "The Role of Entertainment Television and Its Interactions with Individual Values in Explaining Political Participation." *Press/Politics*, 11: 41–63.

Beullens, K., K. Roe, and J. Van den Bulck. (2011). "Excellent Gamer, Excellent Driver? The Impact of Adolescents' Video Game playing on Driving Behavior: A Two-Wave Panel Study." *Accident Analysis and Prevention*, 43: 58–65.

Bickham, D. S., E. A. Blood, C. E. Walls, L. A. Shrier, and M. Rich. (2013). "Characteristics of Screen Media Use Associated with Higher BMI in Young Adolescents." *Pediatrics*, 131: 1–7.

Bissell, K. L., and P. Zhou. (2004). "Must-See TV or ESPN: Entertainment and Sports Media Exposure and Body-Image Distortion in College Women." *Journal of Communication*, 54: 5–21.

Blackford, L. B. (2012). "GOP Lawmakers Question Standards for Teaching Evolution in Kentucky." *Kentucky.com*, August 14. (http://www.kentucky.com/2012/08/14/2298914/gop-lawmakers-question-standards.html).

Bloom, A. D. (1987). *The Closing of the American Mind: How Higher Education Has Failed Democracy and Impoverished the Souls of Today's Students*. New York: Simon & Schuster.

Blumer, H. (1969). *Symbolic Interactionism*. Englewood Cliffs, NJ: Prentice Hall.

Blumer, H., and P. Hauser. (1933). *Movies, Delinquency, and Crime*. New York: Macmillan.

Blumler, J. G. (1979). "The Role of Theory in Uses and Gratifications Studies." *Communication Research*, 6: 9–36.

Blumler, J. G., M. Gurevitch, and E. Katz. (1985). "Reaching Out: A Future for Gratifications Research." In K. E. Rosengren, L. A. Wenner, and P. Palmgreen, eds., *Media Gratifications Research: Current Perspectives*. Beverly Hills, CA: Sage.

Blumler, J. G., and E. Katz, eds. (1974). *The Uses of Mass Communication: Current Perspectives on Gratifications Research*. Beverly Hills, CA: Sage.

Boden, S. (2006). "Dedicated Followers of Fashion? The Influence of Popular Culture on Children's Social Identities." *Media, Culture & Society*, 28: 289–298.

Bollier, D. (2005). *Brand Name Bullies*. New York: Wiley.

Boneva, B., R. Kraut, and D. Frohlich. (2001). "Using E-mail for Personal Relationships: The Difference Gender Makes." *American Behavioral Scientist*, 45: 530–550.

Bond, P. (2011). "Hollywood Studios Accused of Pushing Liberal Agenda through Children's Films." *Hollywood Reporter*, December 1. (http://www.hollywoodreporter.com/news/happy-feet-two-politics-childrens-movie-267827).

Bonfadelli, H. (2002). "The Internet and Knowledge Gaps: A Theoretical and Empirical Investigation." *European Journal of Communication*, 17: 65–85.

Bowers, J. W., and J. A. Courtright. (1984). *Communication Research Methods*. Glenview, IL: Scott Foresman.

Boy Scouts of America. (2012). "Environmental Scan 2012." (http://www.scouting.org/filestore/media/210-311.pdf).

Bradshaw, K. A. (2003). "Persuasive Communication/Collective

Behavior and Public Opinion: Rapid Shifts in Opinion and Communication/The Dynamics of Persuasion: Communication and Attitudes in the 21st Century." *Journalism and Mass Communication Quarterly*, 80: 754.

Braiker, B. (2007). "Poll: What Americans (Don't) Know." *Newsweek*, June 23. (http://www.msnbc.msn.com/id/19390791/site/newsweek).

Brandtzæ, P. B. (2012). "Social Networking Sites: Their Users and Social Implications—A Longitudinal Study." *Journal of Computer-Mediated Communication*, 17: 467–488.

Brantlinger, P. (1983). *Bread and Circuses: Theories of Mass Culture as Social Decay*. Ithaca, NY: Cornell University Press.

Brewer, W. F., and G. V. Nakamura. (1984). "The Nature and Functions of Schema." *Center for the Study of Reading, Technical report No. 325*. (https://www.ideals.illinois.edu/bitstream/handle/2142/17542/ctrstreadtechrepv01984i00325_opt.pdf?s).

Briggs, J. (2012). "Routine Justice: Research Shows How Racial and Gender Profiling Can Affect Outcome of Traffic Stops." *Kansas State University*, June 21. (http://www.k-state.edu/media/newsreleases/jun12/racialprofiling62112.html).

Brisbane, A. S. (2012). "Should *The Times* Be a Truth Vigilante?" *New York Times*, January 12. (http://publiceditor.blogs.nytimes.com/2012/01/12/should-the-times-be-a-truth-vigilante/).

Broder, J. M., C. Krauss, and I. Austen. (2013). "Obama Faces Risks in Pipeline Decision." *New York Times*, February 18: B1.

Bronfenbrenner, U. (1970). *Two Worlds of Childhood: U.S. and U.S.S.R.* New York: Sage.

Brooks, D. (2002). "Looking Back on Tomorrow." *Atlantic Monthly*, April: 20–22.

Brownell, B. A. (1983). "Interpretations of Twentieth-Century Urban Progressive Reform." In D. R. Colburn and G. E. Pozzetta, eds., *Reform and Reformers in the Progressive Era*. Westport, CT: Greenwood.

Brunsdon, C., and D. Morley. (1981). "'Crossroads' Notes on Soap Opera." *Screen*, 22: 327.

Bryant, J., and D. Miron. (2004). "Theory and Research in Mass Communication." *Journal of Communication*, 54: 662–704.

Buffardi, L. E., and W. K. Campbell. (2008). "Narcissism and Social Networking Web Sites." *Personality and Social Psychology Bulletin*, 34: 1303–1314.

"Buzz in the Blogosphere: Millions More Bloggers and Blog Readers." (2012). *NielsenWire*, March 8. (http://blog.nielsen.com/nielsenwire/online_mobile/buzz-in-the-blogosphere-millions-more-bloggers-and-blog-readers/).

Bryant, J., and D. R. Anderson. (1983). *Children's Understanding of Television: Research on Attention and Comprehension*. New York: Academic.

Bryant, J., D. R. Roskos-Ewoldsen., and J. Cantor. (2003). *Communication and Emotion: Essays in Honor of Dolf Zillmann*. Mahwah, NJ: Erlbaum.

Bryant, J., and R. L. Street. (1988). "From Reactivity to Activity and Action: An Evolving Concept and Weltanschauung in Mass and Interpersonal Communication." In R. P. Hawkins, J. M. Wiemann, and S. Pingree, eds., *Advancing Communication Science: Merging Mass and Interpersonal Processes*. Newbury Park, CA: Sage.

Bryant, J., and P. Vorderer. (2006). *Psychology of Entertainment*. Mahwah, NJ: Erlbaum.

Bryant, J., and D. Zillmann. (2002). *Media Effects: Advances in Theory and Research*. Mahwah, NJ: Erlbaum.

Bryner, J. (2009). "TV Causes Learning Lag in Infants." *Live Science*, June. (http://www.livescience.com/culture/090601–infants-television.html).

Bryson, L. (1954). *The Drive Toward Reason: In the Service of a Free People*. New York: Harper.

Bull, S. S., D. K. Levine, S. R. Black, S. J. Schmiege, and J. Santelli. (2012). "Social Media-Delivered Sexual Health Intervention." *American Journal of Preventative Medicine*, 43: 467–474.

Burgess, M. C. R., and S. Burpo. (2012). "The Effect of Music Videos on College Students' Perceptions of Rape." *College Student Journal*, 46: 748–763.

Burrell, G., and G. Morgan. (1979). *Sociological Paradigms and Organisation Analysis*. London: Heinemann.

Bushman, B. J., and C. A. Anderson. (2002). "Media Violence and the American Public: Scientific Facts versus Media Misinformation." *American Psychologist*, 56: 477–489.

Bushman, B. J., H. R. Rothstein, and C. A. Anderson. (2010). "Much Ado about Something: Violent Video Game Effects and a School of Red Herring: Reply to Ferguson and Kilburn." *Psychological Bulletin*, 136: 182–187.

Bustamante, H. (2012). "Mancx Survey: 98% of Americans Distrust Information on the Internet." *Business Wire*, July 17. (http://www.businesswire.com/news/home/20120717005277/en/Mancx-Survey-98-Americans1-Distrust-Information-Internet).

Calogero, R. M., and T. L. Tylka. (2010). "Fiction, Fashion, & Function: An Introduction to the Special Issue on Gendered Body Image, Part I." *Sex Roles*, 63: 1–5.

Campbell, A., P. W. Converse, W. E. Miller, and D. E. Stokes. (1960). *The American Voter*. New York: Wiley.

Campbell, W. J. (2011). "Bra-Burning, a Myth 'That Will Never Die.'." *Media Myth Alert*, June 8. (http://mediamythalert.wordpress.com/2011/06/08/bra-burning-a-media-myth-that-will-never-die/).

Cantor, J., and B. J. Wilson. (2003). "Media and Violence: Intervention Strategies for Reducing Aggression." *Media Psychology*, 5: 363–403.

Cantril, H., H. Gaudet, and H. Herzog. (1940). *Invasion from Mars*. Princeton, NJ: Princeton University Press.

Cappella, J. N., and K. H. Jamieson. (1997). *Spiral of Cynicism: The Press and the Public Good*. New York: Oxford University Press.

Caplan, S. E. (2005). "A Social Skill Account of Problematic Internet Use." *Journal of Communication*, 55: 721–736.

Carey, J. (1989). *Communication as Culture: Essays on Media and Society*. Winchester, MA: Unwin Hyman.

Carey, J. (1977). "Mass Communication Research and Cultural Studies: An American View." In J. Curran, M. Gurevitch, J. Woollacott, J. Marriott, and C. Roberts, eds., *Mass Communication and Society*. London: Open University Press.

Carey, J. (1975a). "Culture and Communications." *Communication Research*, 2: 173–191.

Carey, J. (1975b). *Sociology and Public Affairs: The Chicago School*. Beverly Hills, CA: Sage.

Carey, J. W. (1996). "The Chicago School and Mass Communication Research." In E. E. Dennis and E. Wartella, eds., *American Communication Research: The Remembered History*. New York: Routledge.

Carr, D. (2012a). "Tired Cries of Bias Don't Help Romney." *New York Times*, September 30: B1.

Carr, D. (2012b). "The Puppetry of Quotation Approval." *New York Times*, September 17: B1.

Carr, D. (2011). "Media Savant." *New York Times Book Review*, January 9: 1, 10–11.

Carr, N. (2013). "The Searchers." *Rough Type*, January 13. (http://www.roughtype.com/?p=2459).

Carragee, K. M., and W. Roefs. (2004). "The Neglect of Power in Recent Framing Research." *Journal of Communication*, 54: 214–233.

Carter, T. B., M. A. Franklin, and J. B. Wright. (2008). *The First Amendment and the Fifth Estate*. St. Paul, MN: West.

Cassino, D. (2012). "What You Know Depends on What You Watch: Current Events Knowledge across Popular News Sources." *Public Mind Poll*, May 3. (http://publicmind.fdu.edu/2012/confirmed/).

Cassino, D. (2011). "Some News Leaves People Knowing Less." *Public Mind Poll*, November 21. (http://publicmind.fdu.edu/2011/knowless/).

Castells, M. (2008). "The New Public Sphere: Global Civil Society, Communication Networks, and Global Governance." *Annals of the American Academy of Social Sciences*, 616: 78–93.

Center for Science in the Public Interest. (2007). "Food Marketing in Other Countries." *Cspinet.org*, February 16. (http://www.cspinet.org/nutritionpolicy/foodmarketing_abroad.pdf).

Chaiken, S., and Y. Trope. (1999). *Dual-Process Theories in Social Psychology*. New York: Guilford.

Chaffee, S. (2001). "Studying the New Communication of Politics." *Political Communication*, 18: 237–245.

Chaffee, S. H., and C. R. Berger. (1987). "What Communication Scientists Do." In C. R. Berger and S. H. Chaffee, eds., *Handbook of Communication Science*. Newbury Park, CA: Sage.

Chaffee, S. H., and J. Schleuder. (1986). "Measurement and Effects of Attention to Media News." *Human Communication Research*, 13: 76–107.

Chandra, A., S. C. Martino, R. L. Collins, M. N. Elliott, S. H. Berry, D. E. Kanouse, and A. Miu. (2008). "Does Watching Sex on Television Predict Teen Pregnancy? Findings from a National Longitudinal Survey of Youth." *Pediatrics*, 122: 1047–1054.

Charters, W. W. (1933). *Motion Pictures and Youth*. New York: Macmillan Company.

Chia, S. C. (2006). "How Peers Mediate Media Influence on Adolescents' Sexual Attitudes and Sexual Behavior." *Journal of Communication*, 56: 585–606.

Chomsky, N. (1991). *Deterring Democracy*. New York: Verso.

Chomsky, N. (1969). *American Power and the New Mandarins*. New York: Pantheon.

Christ, W. G., and W. J. Potter. (1998). "Media Literacy, Media Education, and the Academy." *Journal of Communication*, 48: 5–15.

Christakis, D. A., J. Gilkerson, J. A. Richards, F. J. Zimmerman, M. M. Garrison, D. Xu, S. Gray, and U. Yapanel. (2009). "Audible Television and Decreased Adult Words, Infant Vocalizations, and Conversational Turns: A Population-Based Study." *Archives of Pediatrics & Adolescent Medicine*, 163: 554–558.

Christakis, D. A., F. J. Zimmerman, D. L. DiGiuseppe, and C. A. McCarty. (2004). "Early Television Exposure and Subsequent Attentional Problems in Children." *Pediatrics*, 113: 708–713.

Christians, C. G., J. P. Ferre, and P. M. Fackler. (1993). *Good News: Social Ethics and the Press*. New York: Oxford University Press.

Cisco Systems. (2012). "Cisco Visual Networking Index: Forecast and Methodology, 2011–2016." *Cisco.com*, May 30. (http://www.cisco.com/en/US/solutions/collateral/ns341/ns525/ns537/ns705/ns827/white_paper_c11-481360.pdf).

Cissel, M. (2012). "Media Framing: A Comparative Content Analysis on Mainstream and Alternative News Coverage of Occupy Wall Street." *The Elon Journal of Undergraduate Research in Communications*, 3: 67–77.

Clark, L. S. (2011). "Parental Mediation Theory for the Digital Age." *Communication Theory*, 21: 323–343.

Clark, L., and M. Tiggemann. (2007). "Sociocultural Influences and Body Image in 9- to 12-Year-Old Girls: The Role of Appearance Schemas." *Journal of Clinical Child and Adolescent Psychology*, 36: 76–86.

Clark-Flory, T. (2012). "Facebook: The Next Tool in Fighting STDs." *Salon*, April 1. (http://www.salon.com/2012/04/01/facebook_the_next_tool_in_fighting_stds/).

Clawson, L. (2012). "Union Basics the Media Often Gets Wrong—And Ways Right-Wing Messaging Sneaks into Labor Coverage." *Daily Kos*, June 10. (http://www.dailykos.com/story/2012/06/10/1086581/-Union-basics-the-media-often-gets-wrong-and-ways-right-wing-messaging-sneaks-into-labor-coverage).

Cohen, B. C. (1963). *The Press and Foreign Policy*. Princeton, NJ: Princeton University Press.

Cohen, J. (2001). "Defining Identification: A Theoretical Look at the Identification of Audiences with Media Characters." *Mass Communication & Society*, 4: 245–264.

Cohen, J., and G. Weimann. (2000). "Cultivation Revisited: Some Genres Have Some Effects on Some Viewers." *Communication Reports*, 13: 99–115.

Coleman, S., and J. G. Blumler. (2009). *The Internet and Democratic Citizenship: Theory, Practice, and Policy*. New York: Cambridge University Press.

Committee on Communications. (2006). "Children, Adolescents, and Advertising." *Pediatrics*, 118: 2562–2569.

Common Sense Media. (2011). "Zero to Eight: Children's Media Use in America." *Common Sense Media*, Fall. (http://www.commonsense media.org/sites/default/files/research /zerotoeightfinal2011.pdf).

Comstock, G. (1991). *Television and the American Child*. San Diego: Academic.

Cooper, A. (2008). "The Bigger Tent." *Columbia Journalism Review*, September/October: 45–47.

Correa, T., A. W. Hinsley, and H. G. De Zúñiga. (2010). "Who Interacts on the Web? The Intersection of Users' Personality and Social Media Use." *Computers in Human Behavior*, 26: 247–253.

Coulter, A. (2006). *Godless: The Church of Liberalism*. New York: Crown.

Courtright, J. A., and S. J. Baran. (1980). "The Acquisition of Sexual Information by Young People." *Journalism Quarterly*, 57: 107–114.

Coyne, S. M., D. A. Nelson, N. Graham-Kevan, E. Tew, K. N. Meng, and J. A. Olsen. (2011). "Media Depictions of Physical and Relational Aggression: Connections with Aggression in Young Adults' Romantic Relationships." *Aggressive Behavior*, 37: 56–62.

Craig, R. T. (2007). "Pragmatism in the Field of Communication Theory." *Communication Theory*, 17: 125–145.

Crouse, T. (1973). *The Boys on the Bus*. New York: Random House.

Crowley, D. J., and P. Heyer. (1991). *Communication in History: Technology, Culture, Society*. New York: Longman.

Cunningham, B. (2003). "Re-thinking Objectivity." *Columbia Journalism Review*, July/August: 24–32.

Curnalia, R. M. L. (2005). "A Retrospective on Early Studies of Propaganda and Suggestions for Reviving the Paradigm." *Review of Communication*, 5: 237–257.

Curran, J. (1991). "Mass Media and Democracy: A Reappraisal." In J. Curran and M. Gurevitch, eds., *Mass Media and Society*. London: Edward Arnold.

Curran, J., S. Iyengar, B. Lund, and I. Salovaara-Moring. (2009). "Media System, Public Knowledge and Democracy: A Comparative Study." *European Journal of Communication*, 25: 5–26.

Daly, J. A. (2000). "Colloquy: Getting Older and Getting Better: Challenges for Communication Research." *Human Communication Research*, 26: 331–338.

Davidson, C. N. (2011). *Now You See It: How the Brain Science of Attention Will Transform the Way We Live, Work, and Learn*. New York: Viking.

Davis, D. K. (1990). "News and Politics." In D. L. Swanson and D. Nimmo, eds., *New Directions in Political Communication*. Newbury Park, CA: Sage.

Davis, D. K., and S. J. Baran. (1981). *Mass Communication and Everyday Life: A Perspective on Theory and Effects*. Belmont, CA: Wadsworth.

Davis, D. K., and J. P. Robinson. (1989). "Newsflow and Democratic Society in an Age of Electronic Media." In G. Comstock, ed., *Public Communication and Behavior*, vol. 3. New York: Academic.

Davis, R. E. (1976). *Response to Innovation: A Study of Popular Argument about New Mass Media*. New York: Arno.

DeFleur, M. L. (1970). *Theories of Mass Communication*. New York: David McKay.

DeFleur, M. L., and S. Ball-Rokeach. (1989). *Theories of Mass Communication*, 5th ed. New York: David McKay.

DeFleur, M. L., and S. Ball-Rokeach. (1975). *Theories of Mass Communication*, 3rd ed. New York: David McKay.

DeFleur, M. L., and O. N. Larsen. (1958). *The Flow of Information*. New York: Harper.

Delia, J. (1987). "Communication Research: A History." In C. Berger and S. Chaffee, eds., *Handbook of Communication Science*. Beverly Hills, CA: Sage.

Delli Carpini, M. X. (2013). "Breaking Boundaries: Can We Bridge the Quantitative Versus Qualitative Divide Through the Study of Entertainment and Politics?" *International Journal of Communication*, 7: 531–551.

Delo, C. (2012). "Facebook Hits Billionth User, Reveals First Major Ad from Global Agency of Record." *Advertising Age*, October 4. (http://adage.com/article/digital /facebook-serves-1-billion-makes-a -video-ad-celebrate/237571/).

"Demographics." (2012). *New Media Trend Watch*, December 19. (http:// www.newmediatrendwatch.com /markets-by-country/17-usa/123 -demographics).

Derenne, J., and E. Beresin. (2006). "Body Image, Media, and Eating Disorders." *Academic Psychiatry*, 30: 257–261.

Desai, R. A., S. Krishnan-Sarin, D. Cavallo, and M. Potenza. (2010). "Video-Gaming among High School Students: Health Correlates, Gender Differences, and Problematic Gaming." *Pediatrics*, 126: e1414–e1424.

Deutschmann, P. J., and W. A. Danielson. (1960). "Diffusion of Knowledge of the Major News Story." *Journalism Quarterly*, 37: 345–355.

de Vreese, C. H. (2012). "New Avenues for Framing Research." *American Behavioral Scientist*, 56: 365–375.

DeWall, C. N., C. A. Anderson, and B. J. Bushman. (2011). "The General Aggression Model: Theoretical Extensions to Violence." *Psychology of Violence*, 1: 245–258.

Dewey, J. (1927). *The Public and Its Problems*. New York: Holt.

Dickinson, T. (2009). "Shift+Control." *Mother Jones*, January/February: 15–19.

Diefenbach, D., and M. West. (2007). "Television and Attitudes toward Mental Health Issues: Cultivation Analysis and Third Person Effect." *Journal of Community Psychology*, 35: 181–195.

Dimmick, J., S. Patterson, and J. Sikand. (1996). "Personal Telephone Networks: A Typology and Two Empirical Studies." *Journal of Broadcasting and Electronic Media*, 40: 45–59.

Dodes, R. (2013). "From Talkies to Texties." *Wall Street Journal*, April 5, D1-2.

Dokoupil, T. (2012). "Is the Web Driving Us Mad?" *Daily Beast*, July 9. (http://www.thedailybeast.com /newsweek/2012/07/08/is-the -internet-making-us-crazy-what- the-new-research-says.html).

Donohue, G. A., P. J. Tichenor, and C. N. Olien. (1986). "Metro Daily Pullback and Knowledge Gaps, within and between Communities." *Communication Research*, 13: 453–471.

Drum, K. (2013). "Why Is the Environment So Boring?" *Mother Jones*, March. (http://www.motherjones.com/kevin-drum/2013/03/why-environment-so-boring).

Duggan, M., and J. Brenner. (2013). "The Demographics of Social Media Users—2012." *Pew Internet & American Life Project*, February 14. (http://www.pewinternet.org/Reports/2013/Social-media-users/The-State-of-Social-Media-Users.aspx).

Dunstan, D. W., E. L. M. Barr, G. N. Healy, J. Salmon, J. E. Shaw, B. Balkau, D. J. Magliano, A. J. Cameron, P. Z. Zimmet, and N. Owen. (2010). "Television Viewing Time and Mortality. The Australian Diabetes, Obesity and Lifestyle Study." *Circulation*, 121: 384–391.

Dworak, M., T. Schierl, T. Burns, and H. K. Struder. (2007). "Impact of Singular Excessive Computer Game and Television Exposure on Sleep Patterns and Memory Performance of School-Aged Children." *Pediatrics*, 120: 978–985.

Eaves, L. J., and H. J. Eysenck. (1974). "Genetics and the Development of Social Attitudes." *Nature*, 249: 288–289.

Edelman, M. (1988). *Constructing the Political Spectacle*, 3rd ed. Chicago: University of Chicago Press.

Editors. (2004). "*The Times* and Iraq." *New York Times*, May 26: A2.

Ehrenreich, B. (2009). "Too Poor to Make the News." *New York Times*, June 14: WK 10.

Eidelson, J. (2011). "Why Everyone on Television Is Richer than You." *Alternet*, July 14. (http://www.alternet.org/story/151647/why_everyone_on_television_is_richer_than_you).

Eisenstein, E. L. (1979). *The Printing Press as an Agent of Change: Communications and Cultural Transformations in Early-Modern Europe*. Cambridge, UK: Cambridge University Press.

"Election 2012 Coverage in One Word: Hollow." (2012). *4th Estate*, November 13. (http://election2012.4thestate.net/election-2012-coverage-in-one-word-hollow/).

Elliott, C. D. (2012). "Packaging Fun: Analyzing Supermarket Food Messages Targeted at Children." *Canadian Journal of Communication*, 37: 303–318.

Ellis, J. (2012). "Young-Adult Readers May Have Abandoned Print, but They'll Take News in Their Pockets." *Nieman Journalism Lab*, December. (http://www.niemanlab.org/2012/12/young-adult-readers-may-have-abandoned-print-but-theyll-take-news-in-their-pockets/).

Ellis, K. (2010). "Be Who You Want to Be: The Philosophy of Facebook and the Construction of Identity." *Screen Education*, 58: 36–41.

Enda, J., and A. Mitchell. (2013). "Many Americans Abandon News Outlets, Citing Less Information." *Pew Research Center's Project for Excellence in Journalism*, March 18. (http://stateofthemedia.org/2013/special-reports-landing-page/citing-reduced-quality-many-americans-abandon-news-outlets/).

Entman, R. M., S. Livingston, and J. Kim. (2009). "Doomed to Repeat: Iraq News, 2002-2007." *American Behavioral Scientist*, 52: 689–708.

Entman, R. M. (2004). *Projections of Power: Framing News, Public Opinion, and U.S. Foreign Policy*. Chicago: University of Chicago Press.

Entman, R. M. (1993). "Framing: Toward Clarification of a Fractured Paradigm." *Journal of Communication*, 43: 51–58.

Entman, R. M. (1989). *Democracy without Citizens: Media and the Decay of American Politics*. New York: Oxford University Press.

Entman, R. M., and A. Rojecki. (1993). "Freezing Out the Public: Elite and Media Framing of the U.S. Anti-Nuclear Movement." *Political Communication*, 10: 155–173.

Enzensberger, H. M. (1974). *The Consciousness Industry*. New York: Seabury.

Epstein, E. J. (1973). *News from Nowhere: Television and the News*. New York: Random House.

Esser, F. (2013). "The Emerging Paradigm of Comparative Communication Enquiry: Advancing Cross-National Research in Times of Globalization." *International Journal of Communication*, 7: 113–128.

Ettema, J. S., and F. G. Kline. (1977). "Deficits, Differences, and Ceilings: Contingent Conditions for Understanding the Knowledge Gap." *Communication Research*, 4: 179–202.

Eveland, W. P. (2003). "A 'Mix of Attributes' Approach to the Study of Media Effects and New Communication Technologies." *Journal of Communication*, 53: 395–410.

Ewen, S. (2000). "Memoirs of a Commodity Fetishist." *Mass Communication and Society*, 3: 439–452.

Ewen, S. (1996). *PR! A Social History of Spin*. New York: Basic Books.

FAIR. (2005). "Disappearing Antiwar Protests." September 27. (http://fair.org/take-action/media-advisories/disappearing-antiwar-protests/).

Farr, J. (1999). "John Dewey and American Political Science." *American Journal of Political Science*, 43: 520–541.

Farsetta, D. (2006). "Accuracy of Report on Video News Releases Affirmed: CMD Issues Full Rebuttal of RTNDA Claims." *Center for Media and Democracy*, October 9. (http://www.prwatch.org/node/5283/print).

Faules, D. F., and D. C. Alexander. (1978). *Communication and Social Behavior: A Symbolic Interaction Perspective*. Reading, MA: Addison-Wesley.

"Fear Factor." (2001). *Broadcasting and Cable*, July 9: 54.

Fengler, S. (2003). "Holding the News Media Accountable: A Study of Media Reporters and Media Critics in the United States." *Journalism and Mass Communication Quarterly*, 80: 818–833.

"Ferment in the Field." (1983). *Journal of Communication* (Special Issue): 33.

Feshbach, S. (1961). "The Stimulating versus Cathartic Effects of a Vicarious Aggressive Activity." *Journal of Abnormal and Social Psychology*, 63: 381–385.

Feshbach, S., and R. D. Singer. (1971). *Television and Aggression: An Experimental Field Study*. San Francisco: Jossey-Bass.

Festinger, L. (1962). "Cognitive Dissonance." *Scientific American*, 207: 93.

Festinger, L. (1957). *A Theory of Cognitive Dissonance*. Stanford, CA: Stanford University Press.

Fishman, M. (1980). *Manufacturing the News*. Austin: University of Texas Press.

Fiske, J. (1987). *Television Culture*. London: Routledge.

Fitzgerald, T. (2013). "Huh: Online Nearly Matches TV in Daily Usage." *Media Life Magazine*, April 9. (http://www.medialifemagazine.com/huh-online-nearly-equals-tv-in-daily-usage/).

Flavell, J. H. (1992). "Cognitive Development: Past, Present, and Future." *Developmental Psychology*, 28: 998–1005.

Fox, S., and M. Duggan. (2013). "Health Online 2013." *Pew Internet & American Life Project*, January 15. (http://pewinternet.org/Reports/2013/Health-online.aspx).

Framm, A., and T. Tompson. (2007). "U.S. Optimism Sinks to Record Lows." *TheLedger.com*, May 21. (http://www.theledger.com/apps/pbcs.dll/article?AID=/20070521/NEWS/705210376/1039).

Franklin, R. (2013). "Connectivity Conundrum." *New Republic*, January 26. (http://www.tnr.com/article/the-read/82164/children-technology-ipod-computer-dependent#).

Frederickson, B. L. (2013). "Your Phone vs. Your Heart." *New York Times*, March 24: SR14.

Fredrickson, B. L., and T. Roberts. (1997). "Toward Understanding Women's Lived Experiences and Mental Health Risks." *Psychology of Women Quarterly*, 21: 173–206.

Freedman, L. Z. (1961). "Daydream in a Vacuum Tube: A Psychiatrist's Comment on the Effects of Television." In W. Schramm, J. Lyle, and E. B. Parker, eds., *Television in the Lives of Our Children*. Stanford, CA: Stanford University Press.

Froomkin, D. (2012a). "How the Mainstream Press Bungled the Single Biggest Story of the 2012 Campaign." *Huffington Post*, December 7. (http://www.huffingtonpost.com/dan-froomkin/republican-lies-2012-election_b_2258586.html).

Froomkin, D. (2012b). "Yes, Iraq Definitely Had WMD, Vast Majority of Polled Republicans Insist." *Huffington Post*, June 21. (http://www.huffingtonpost.com/2012/06/21/iraq-wmd-poll-clueless-vast-majority-republicans_n_1616012.html).

Frost, R., and J. Stauffer. (1987). "The Effects of Social Class, Gender, and Personality on Psychological Responses to Filmed Violence." *Journal of Communication*, 37: 29–45.

Fukuyama, F. (1999). "The Great Disruption: Human Nature and the Reconstruction of Social Order." *Atlantic Monthly*, May: 55–80.

Funkhouser, G., and M. McCombs. (1971). "The Rise and Fall of News Diffusion." *Public Opinion Quarterly*, 50: 107–113.

Gadamer, H. (1995). *Truth and Method*. Translated by J. Weinsheimer and D. G. Marshall. New York: Continuum.

Galician, M.-L., ed. (2004a). "'Disillusioning' Ourselves and Our Media: Media Literacy in the 21st Century, Part I: Strategies for Schools." *American Behavioral Scientist*, 48: 1–136.

Galician, M.-L., ed. (2004b). "'Disillusioning' Ourselves and Our Media: Media Literacy in the 21st Century, Part II: Strategies for the General Public." *American Behavioral Scientist*, 48: 143–272.

Gamson, W. A. (2001). "How Storytelling Can Be Empowering." In K. A. Cerulo, ed., *Culture in Mind: Toward a Sociology of Culture and Cognition*. New York: Routledge.

Gamson, W. A. (1992). *Talking Politics*. New York: Cambridge University Press.

Gamson, W. A. (1989). "News as Framing." *American Behavioral Scientist*, 33: 157–161.

Gamson, W. A., D. Croteau, W. Hoynes, and T. Sasson. (1992). "Media Images and the Social Construction of Reality." *Annual Review of Sociology*, 18: 373–393.

Gamson, W. A., and A. Modigliani. (1989). "Media Discourse and Public Opinion on Nuclear Power: A Constructionist Approach." *American Journal of Sociology*, 95: 1–37.

Gamson, W. A., and A. Modigliani. (1987). "The Changing Culture of Affirmative Action." In R. C. Braungart and M. M. Braungart, eds., *Research in Political Psychology*. Greenwich, CT: JAI.

Gans, C. B. (1978). "The Empty Ballot Box: Reflections on Nonvoters in America." *Public Opinion*, 1: 54–57.

Gans, H. (2003). *Democracy and the News*. New York: Oxford University Press.

Gans, H. (1979). *Deciding What's News: A Study of CBS Evening News, NBC Nightly News, Newsweek and Time*. New York: Pantheon Books.

Gans, H. (1972). "The Politics of Culture in America: A Sociological Analysis." In D. McQuail, ed., *Sociology of Mass Communication*. Harmondsworth, UK: Penguin.

Garfield, B. (2013). "This Is No 'Golden Age' of Journalism. These Are the News Media End Times." *The Guardian*, March. (http://www.guardian.co.uk/commentisfree/2013/mar/27/no-golden-age-journalism-news-media-end-times).

Garfield, B. (2007). "The Post-Advertising Age." *Advertising Age*, March 26: 1, 12–14.

Garfield, B. (2005). "The Chaos Scenario." *Advertising Age*, April 4: 1, 57–59.

Garofoli, J. (2012, January 26). "Obama's Speech Echoes Occupy Movement Themes." *San Francisco Chronicle*: A1.

Garnham, N. (1995). "Political Economy and Cultural Studies: Reconciliation or Divorce?" *Critical Studies in Mass Communication*, 12: 95–100.

Garrett, R. K. (2009). "Echo Chambers Online? Politically Motivated Selective Exposure among Internet News Users." *Journal of Computer Mediated Communication*, 14: 265–285.

Gentile, D. A., H. Choo, A. Liau, T. Sim, D. Li, D. Fung, and A. Khoo. (2011). "Pathological Video Game Use among Youths: A Two-Year Longitudinal Study." *Pediatrics*, 127: e319–e329.

Gentile, D. A., P. J. Lynch, J. R. Linder, and D. A. Walsh. (2004). "The Effects of Violent Video Games Habits on Adolescent Hostility, Aggressive Behavior, and School Performance." *Journal of Adolescence*, 27: 5–22.

Gerbner, G. (2010). "The Mean World Syndrome—Media as Storytellers

(Extra Feature)." *Media Education Foundation*, February 18. (http://www.youtube.com/watch?v=ylhqasb1chI).

Gerbner, G. (2001). "The Cultural Arm of the Corporate Establishment: Reflections on the Work of Herb Schiller." *Journal of Broadcasting and Electronic Media*, 45: 186–190.

Gerbner, G. (1990). "Epilogue: Advancing on the Path of Righteousness (Maybe)." In N. Signorielli and M. Morgan, eds., *Cultivation Analysis: New Directions in Media Effects Research*. Newbury Park, CA: Sage.

Gerbner, G., and L. Gross. (1976). "Living with Television: The Violence Profile." *Journal of Communication*, 26: 173–199.

Gerbner, G., L. Gross, M. Jackson-Beeck, S. Jeffries-Fox, and N. Signorielli. (1978). "Cultural Indicators: Violence Profile No. 9." *Journal of Communication*, 28: 176–206.

Gerbner, G., L. Gross, M. Morgan, and N. Signorielli. (1982). "Charting the Mainstream: Television's Contributions to Political Orientations." *Journal of Communication*, 32: 100–127.

Gerbner, G., L. Gross, M. Morgan, and N. Signorielli. (1980). "The 'Mainstreaming' of America: Violence Profile No. 11." *Journal of Communication*, 30: 10–29.

Giddens, A. (1991). *Modernity and Self-Identity: Self and Society in the Late Modern Age*. Stanford, CA: Stanford University Press.

Gilmor, D. (2004). *We the Media—Grassroots Journalism by the People, for the People*. Sebastopol, CA: O'Reilly. (http://www.authorama.com/book/we-the-media.html).

Gillmor, D. M., and J. A. Barron. (1974). *Mass Communication Law. Cases and Comments*. St. Paul, MN: West.

Giner-Sorolla, R., and S. Chaiken. (1994). "The Causes of Hostile Media Judgment." *Journal of Experimental Social Psychology*, 30: 165–180.

Gingras, R. (2013). "A Reminder about Promotional and Commerce Journalism." *Google News Blog*, March 27. (http://googlenewsblog.blogspot.com/2013/03/a-reminder-about-promotional-and.html).

Giroux, H. A. (2011). "Youth in a Suspect Society: Coming of Age in an Era of Disposability." *Truthout*, May 5. (http://truth-out.org/news/item/923:youth-in-a-suspect-society-coming-of-age-in-an-era-of-disposability).

Giroux, H. A., and G. Pollock. (2011). "How Disney Magic and the Corporate Media Shape Youth Identity in the Digital Age." *Truthout*, August 21. (http://truth-out.org/opinion/item/2808:how-disney-magic-and-the-corporate-media-shape-youth-identity-in-the-digital-age).

Gitlin, T. (2004). "The Great Media Breakdown." *Mother Jones*, November/December: 56–59.

Gitlin, T. (1991). "Bites and Blips: Chunk News, Savvy Talk, and the Bifurcation of American Politics." In P. Dahlgren and C. Sparks, eds., *Communication and Citizenship: Journalism and the Public Sphere in the New Media Age*. London: Routledge.

Gitlin, T. (1980). *The Whole World Is Watching: Mass Media in the Making and Unmaking of the New Left*. Berkeley: University of California Press.

Glander, T. (2000). *Origins of Mass Communication Research During the American Cold War: Educational Effects and Contemporary Implications*. Mahwah, NJ: Erlbaum.

Glasgow University Media Group, eds. (1976). *Bad News*. London: Routledge and Kegan Paul.

Glasgow University Media Group, eds. (1980). *More Bad News*. London: Routledge and Kegan Paul.

Glasstetter, J. (2012). "Fox News Host Wants Federal Investigation into 'South Park' for Blasphemy." *Right Wing Watch*, September 9. (http://www.rightwingwatch.org/content/fox-news-host-wants-federal-investigation-south-park-blasphemy).

Gleick, J. (1987). *Chaos: Making a New Science*. New York: Viking.

Glynn, C. J., and J. M. McLeod. (1985). "Implications of the Spiral of Silence Theory for Communication and Public Opinion Research." In K. R. Sanders, L. L. Kaid, and D. D. Nimmo, eds., *Political Communication Yearbook, 1984*. Carbondale, IL: Southern Illinois University Press.

Goffman, E. (1981). *Forms of Talk*. Philadelphia: University of Pennsylvania Press.

Goffman, E. (1979). *Gender Advertisements*. New York: Harper Colophon.

Goffman, E. (1974). *Frame Analysis: An Essay on the Organization of Experience*. New York: Harper & Row.

Goist, P. D. (1971). "City and 'Community': The Urban Theory of Robert Park." *American Quarterly*, 23: 46–59.

Goldberg, B. (2009). *A Slobbering Love Affair: The True (And Pathetic) Story of the Torrid Romance Between Barack Obama and the Mainstream Media*. Washington, DC: Regnery.

Goldberg, B. (2003). *Arrogance: Rescuing America from the Media Elite*. New York: Warner Books.

Gonzales, A. L., and J. T. Hancock. (2011). "Mirror, Mirror on My Facebook Wall: Effects of Exposure to Facebook on Self-Esteem." *Cyberpsychology, Behavior, and Social Networking*, 14: 79–83.

Gonzales, R., D. Glik, M. Davoudi, and A. Ang. (2004). "Media Literacy and Public Health: Integrating Theory, Research, and Practice for Tobacco Control." *American Behavioral Scientist*, 48: 189–201.

Goodman, A. (2004). *The Exception to the Rulers: Exposing Oily Politicians, War Profiteers, and the Media That Love Them*. New York: Hyperion.

Goodman, M. (2001). "The Radio Act of 1927 as a Product of Progressivism." (http://www.scripps.ohiou.edu/mediahistory/mhmjour2–2.htm).

Gordon, R., and Z. Johnson. (2012). "Linking Audiences to News II." (http://cct.org/sites/cct.org/files/CCT_LinkingAudiences2012.pdf).

Gosling, S. D., A. A. Augustine, S. Vazire, N. Holtzman, and S. Gaddis. (2011). "Manifestations of Personality in Online Social Networks: Self-Reported Facebook-Related Behaviors and Observable Profile Information." *Cyberpsychology, Behavior, and Social Networking*, 14: 483–488.

Gottesdiener, L. (2012). "7 Highly Disturbing Trends in Junk Food Advertising to Children." *AlterNet*, November 29. (http://www.alternet

.org/food/7-highly-disturbing-trends-junk-food-advertising-children).

Gould, J. (1972). "TV Violence Held Unharmful to Youth." *New York Times*, January 11: 27.

Grabe, M. E., and D. Drew. (2007). "Crime Cultivation: Comparisons across Media Genres and Channels." *Journal of Broadcasting & Electronic Media*, 51: 47–171.

Graber, D. A. (1988). *Processing the News*, 2nd ed. New York: Longman.

Graber, D. A. (1984). *Processing the News*, 1st ed. New York: Longman.

Graeber, D. (2013). "Occupy's Legacy: The Media Finally Covers Social Protest Fairly." *Salon*, April 13. (http://www.salon.com/2013/04/13/occupys_legacy_the_media_finally_covers_social_protest_fairly/).

Grasmuck, S., J. Martin, and S. Zhao. (2009). "Ethno-Racial Identity Displays on Facebook." *Journal of Computer-Mediated Communication*, 15: 158–188.

Green, M. C., and T. C. Brock. (2000). "The Role of Transportation in the Persuasiveness of Public Narratives." *Journal of Personality and Social Psychology*, 79: 701–721.

Greenberg, B., and E. Parker. (1965). *The Kennedy Assassination and the American Public*. Stanford, CA: Stanford University Press.

Greenberg, J. (2011). "The Occupy Movement's Mobilization Dilemma." *The Ideas Lab*, October 26. (http://theideaslab.wordpress.com/2011/10/26/the-occupy-movements-mobilization-dilemma/).

Greenslade, R. (2012). "More PRs and Fewer Journalists Threaten Democracy." *The Guardian*, October 4. (http://www.guardian.co.uk/media/greenslade/2012/oct/04/marketingandpr-pressandpublishing).

Greenwald, G. (2009). "Jay Rosen on the Media's Control of Political Debates." *Salon*, January. (http://www.salon.com/2009/01/16/rosen/).

Grenard, J. L., C. W. Dent, and A. W. Stacy. (2013). "Exposure to Alcohol Advertisements and Teenage Alcohol-Related Problems." *Pediatrics*, 131: e369–e379.

Grier, S., and A. Brumbaugh. (2007). "Compared to Whom? The Impact of Status on Third Person Effects in Advertising in a South African Context." *Journal of Consumer Behaviour*, 6: 5–18.

Grier, S., and C. A. Bryant. (2004). "Social Marketing in Public Health." *Annual Review of Public Health*, 26: 319–339.

Griffin, E. A. (1994). *A First Look at Communication Theory*. New York: McGraw-Hill.

Gross, D. (2010). "You're Rich. Get Over It." *Newsweek*, February 3. (http://www.newsweek.com/id/232964).

Grossberg, L. (1989). "The Circulation of Cultural Studies." *Critical Studies in Mass Communication*, 6: 413–421.

Grossberg, L. (1983). "Cultural Studies Revisited and Revised." In M. S. Mander, ed., *Communications in Transition*. New York: Praeger.

Grossberg, L., and C. Nelson. (1988). "Introduction: The Territory of Marxism." In C. Nelson and L. Grossberg, eds., *Marxism and the Interpretation of Culture*. Urbana, IL: University of Illinois Press.

Grossberg, L., C. Nelson., and P. Treichler. (1992). *Cultural Studies*. London: Routledge.

Grosswiler, P. (1997). *Method in the Message: Rethinking McLuhan through Critical Theory*. Montreal: Black Rose Books.

Gulati, G. J., M. R. Just, and A. N. Crigler. (2004). "News Coverage of Political Campaigns." In L. L. Kaid, ed., *Handbook of Political Communication Research*. Mahwah, NJ: Lawrence Erlbaum.

Gunster, S. (2004). *Capitalizing on Culture: Critical Theory for Cultural Studies*. Toronto: University of Toronto Press.

Gunther, A. C., and K. Schmitt. (2004). "Mapping Boundaries of the Hostile Media Effect." *Journal of Communication*, 54: 55–70.

Gunther, A. C., and S. C. Chia. (2001). "Predicting Pluralistic Ignorance: The Hostile Media Perception and Its Consequences." *Journalism & Mass Communication Quarterly*, 78: 688–701.

Gunther, A. C., and J. L. Liebhart. (2006). "Broad Reach or Biased Source? Decomposing the Hostile Media Effect." *Journal of Communication*, 56: 449–466.

Gunter, B. (1987). *Poor Reception: Misunderstanding and Forgetting Broadcast News*. Hillsdale, NJ: Erlbaum.

Gurevitch, M., S. Coleman, and J. G. Blumler. (2010). "Political Communication—Old and New Media Relationships." *Annals of the American Academy of Social Sciences*, 625: 164–181.

Guttmacher Institute. (2010). "U.S. Teenage Pregnancies, Births and Abortions: National and State Trends and Trends by Race and Ethnicity." (http://www.guttmacher.org/pubs/USTPtrends.pdf).

Habermas, J. (1989). *The Structural Transformation of the Public Sphere*. Cambridge, MA: MIT Press.

Habermas, J. (1971). *Knowledge and Human Interest*. Boston: Beacon.

Hachten, W. A. (1992). *The World News Prism*. Ames, IA: Iowa State University Press.

Haelle, T. (2013). "Consumption Junction: Childhood Obesity Determined Largely by Environmental Factors, Not Genes or Sloth." *Scientific American*, April 9. (http://www.scientificamerican.com/article.cfm?id=childhood-obesity-determined-largely-by-environmental-factors&page=3).

Hafner, K., and M. Lyon. (1996). *Where Wizards Stay Up Late: The Origins of the Internet*. New York: Simon & Schuster.

Hall, S. (1982). "The Rediscovery of 'Ideology': Return of the Repressed in Media Studies." In M. Gurevitch, T. Bennett, J. Curran, and J. Woollacott, eds., *Culture, Society, and the Media*. New York: Methuen.

Hall, S. (1981a). "Notes on Deconstructing 'The Popular.'" In R. Samuel, ed., *People's History and Socialist Theory*. London: Routledge.

Hall, S. (1981b). "The Whites of Their Eyes: Racist Ideologies and the Media." In G. Bridges and R. Brundt, eds., *Silver Linings*. London: Lawrence and Wishart.

Hall, S. (1980a). "Encoding and Decoding in the Television Discourse." In S. Hall, ed., *Culture, Media, Language*. London: Hutchinson.

Hall, S. (1980b). "Cultural Studies: Two Paradigms." *Media, Culture and Society*, 2: 57–72.

Hall, S. (1973). *Encoding and Decoding in the Television Discourse*. CCCS Stenciled Paper 7. Birmingham, UK: University of Birmingham.

Hall, S., D. Hobson, A. Lowe, and P. Willis. (1982). *Culture, Media, Language*. London: Hutchinson.

Hallin, D. C. (1986). *The Uncensored War: The Media & Vietnam*. New York: Oxford University Press.

Hallin, D. C., and P. Mancini. (2012). "Comparing Media Systems: A Response to Critics." In F. Esser and T. Hanitzsch, eds., *Handbook of Comparative Communication Research*. London: Routledge.

Halloran, J. D. (1964/1965). "Television and Violence." *The Twentieth Century*, Winter: 61–72.

Hamelink, C. J. (2001). "Considering Communication Issues and Problems around the Globe." *ICA News*, November: 8–9.

Hampton, K. N., L. F. Sessions, and E. J. Her. (2010). "Core Networks, Social Isolation, and New Media: How Internet and Mobile Phone Use Is Related to Network Size and Diversity." *Information, Communication & Society*, 14: 130–155.

Hampton, K., L. Sessions, E. J. Her, and L. Rainie. (2009). "Social Isolation and New Technology." *Pew Internet & American Life Project*, November 4. (http://www.pewinternet.org/Reports/2009/18—Social- Isolation-and-New-Technology.aspx).

Hardt, H. (1999). "Shifting Paradigms: Decentering the Discourse of Mass Communication Research." *Mass Communication and Society*, 2: 175–183.

Hargreaves, I., and G. Ferguson. (2000). *Who's Misunderstanding Whom? Science, Society and the Media*. Swindon, UK: Economic and Social Research Council.

Harkinson, J. (2009). "Facebook's Privacy Faceoff." *Mother Jones*, February 17. (http://www.motherjones.com/print/21333).

Harmon, M. (2001). "Laboring to Be Fair: U.S. Network TV Strike Coverage." *Electronic News: A Journal of Applied Research & Ideas*, 1: 13–22, 39–40.

Harris, L. (2012). "Are Americans Too Dumb for Democracy?" *The American*, June 9. (http://www.american.com/archive/2012/june/are-americans-too-dumb-for-democracy).

Harris, R. J. (2009). *A Cognitive Psychology of Mass Communication*, 5th ed. New York: Routledge.

Hart, P. (2009). "Hard Times for the Overclass." *Extra!* November: 5–6.

Hart, P. (2005). "Why Is Labor Off TV?" *Extra! Update*, August: 3.

Hart, P., and S. Ackerman. (2002). "Patriotism and Censorship." *Extra!* November/December: 6–9.

Harwood, R. C. (2000). *Tapping Civic Life: How to Report First, and Best, What's Happening in Your Community*. Washington: Pew Center for Civic Journalism.

Hatemi, P. K., E. Byrne, and R. McDermott. (2012). "Introduction: What Is a 'Gene' and Why Does It Matter for Political Science?" *Journal of Theoretical Politics*, 24: 305–327.

Hatemi, P. K., C. L. Funk, S. E. Medland, H. M. Maes, J. L. Silberg, N. G. Martin, and L. J. Eaves. (2009). "Genetic and Environmental Transmission of Political Attitudes over a Life Time." *The Journal of Politics*, 71: 1141–1156.

Hatemi, P. K., R. McDermott, L. J. Eaves, K. S. Kendler, and M. C. Neale. (2013). "Fear as a Disposition and an Emotional State: A Genetic and Environmental Approach to Out-Group Political Preferences." *American Journal of Political Science*, 57: 279–293.

Hawkins, E. T. (2003). "Bridging Latin America's Digital Divide: Government Policies and Internet Access." *Journalism and Mass Communication Quarterly*, 80: 646.

Hawkins, R., J. M. Wiemann, and S. Pingree. (1988). *Advancing Communication Science: Merging Mass and Interpersonal Processes*. Newbury Park, CA: Sage Publications.

Hay, J. (1989). "Advertising as a Cultural Text (Rethinking Message Analysis in a Recombinant Culture)." In B. Dervin, L. Grossberg, B. J. O'Keefe, and E. Wartella, eds., *Rethinking Communication, Vol. 2: Paradigm Exemplars*. Newbury Park, CA: Sage.

Hayes, A. F., J. Matthes, and W. P. Eveland. (2011). "Stimulating the Quasi-statistical Organ: Fear of Social Isolation Motivates the Quest for Knowledge of the Opinion Climate." *Communication Research*, 38: 1–24.

Heath, T. (2010). "U.S. Cellphone Users Donate $22 Million to Haiti Earthquake Relief via Text." *Washington Post*, January 19. (http://www.washingtonpost.com/wp-dyn/content/article/2010/01/18/AR2010011803792.html?wpisrc=nl_tech).

Hellmich, N. (2004). "Obesity on Track as No. 1 Killer." *USA Today*, March 10: 1A.

Helm, J. (2002). "When History Looks Back." *Adbusters*, March/April: no page number.

Hendriks, A. (2002). "Examining the Effects of Hegemonic Depictions of Female Bodies on Television: A Call for Theory and Programmatic Research." *Critical Studies in Media Communication*, 19: 106–124.

Hendricks, M. (2012). "Growth Trend Continues for Newspaper Websites; More Visitors Stayed Longer in Q4 2011 vs. 2010." *Newspaper Association of America*, February 1. (http://www.naa.org/News-and-Media/Press-Center/Archives/2012/Growth-Trend-Continues-For-Newspaper-Websites.aspx).

Herman, E. S. (1996). "The Propaganda Model Revisited." *Monthly Review*, July–August: 115–128.

Herman, E. S., and N. Chomsky. (1988). *Manufacturing Consent*. New York: Pantheon.

Herzog, B. (2000). *States of Mind*. Winston-Salem, NC: John F. Blair.

Herzog, H. (1944). "Motivations and Gratifications of Daily Serial Listeners." In P. F. Lazarsfeld and F. N. Stanton, eds., *Radio Research, 1942–1943*. New York: Duell, Sloan and Pearce.

Herzog, H. (1940). "Professor Quiz: A Gratification Study." In P. F. Lazarsfeld, ed., *Radio and the Printed Page*. New York: Duell, Sloan and Pearce.

Hetherington, M. J., and J. D. Weiler. (2009). *Authoritarianism & Polarization in American Politics*. New York: Cambridge University Press.

Heussner, K. M. (2013). "Dr. Google Is as Popular as Ever—Can Real Doctors Adapt?" *GigaOM.com*, January 17. (http://gigaom.com

/2013/01/16/dr-google-is-as
-popular-as-ever-can-real-doctors
-adapt/).

Hill, W. G., M. E. Goddard, and P. M. Visscher. (2008). "Data and Theory Point to Mainly Additive Genetic Variance for Complex Traits." *PLoS Genetics*, 4: e1000008. DOI:10.1371/journal.pgen.1000008.

Hitler, A. (1933). *Mein Kampf: Zwe Bande in Enemband*. München: F. Eher.

Hobson, D. (1982). *Crossroads: The Drama of a Soap Opera*. London: Methuen.

Holbert, R. L., R. K. Garrett, and L. S. Gleason. (2010). "A New Era of Minimal Effects? A Response to Bennett and Iyengar." *Journal of Communication*, 60: 15–34.

Holbrook, T. M. (2002). "Presidential Campaigns and the Knowledge Gap." *Political Communication*, 19: 437–465.

Hovland, C. I., I. L. Janis, and H. H. Kelley. (1953). *Communication and Persuasion*. New Heaven, CT: Yale University Press.

Hovland, C. I., A. A. Lumsdaine, and F. D. Sheffield. (1949). *Experiments on Mass Communication*. Princeton, NJ: Princeton University Press.

Howard, P. N., A. Duffy, D. Freelon, M. Hussain, W. Mari, and M. Mazaid. (2011). "Opening Closed Regimes." *Project on Information Technology & Political Islam*. (http://dl.dropbox.com/u/12947477/publications/2011_Howard-Duffy-Freelon-Hussain-Mari-Mazaid_pITPI.pdf).

Huang, C. (2003). "Transitional Media vs. Normative Theories: Schramm, Altschull, and China." *Journal of Communication*, 53: 444–459.

Hudson, W. E. (2013). *American Democracy in Peril*. Los Angeles: Sage.

Hughes, C. (2002). *Key Concepts in Feminist Theory and Research*. Newbury Park, CA: Sage.

Human Rights Watch. (2009). "US: Drug Arrests Skewed by Race." March 2. (http://www.hrw.org/en/news/2009/03/02/us-drug-arrests-skewed-race).

Huppke, R. W. (2012). "Facts, 360 B.C.-A.D. 2012." *Chicago Tribune*, April 19. (http://articles.chicagotribune.com/2012-04-19/news/ct-talk-huppke-obit-facts

-20120419_1_facts-philosopher-opinion).

Huston, A. C., E. Donnerstein, H. Fairchild, N. D. Feshbach, P. A. Katz, J. P. Murray, E. A. Rubenstein, B. L. Wilcox, and D. Zuckerman. (1992). *Big World, Small Screen*. Lincoln, NE: University of Nebraska Press.

Hwang, Y., and S. H. Jeong. (2009). "Revisiting the Knowledge Gap Hypothesis: A Meta-Analysis of Thirty-Five Years of Research." *Journalism & Mass Communication Quarterly*, 86: 513–532.

Igartua, J. J., and I. Barrios. (2012). "Changing Real-World Beliefs with Controversial Movies: Processes and Mechanisms of Narrative Persuasion." *Journal of Communication*, 62: 514–531.

Inglis, F. (1990). *Media Theory: An Introduction*. Oxford: Basil Blackwell.

The Bias of Communication. Toronto: University of Toronto Press.

Innis, H. A. (1950). *Empire and Communication*. Toronto: University of Toronto Press.

Institute of Medicine. (2006). *Food Marketing to Children and Youth: Threat or Opportunity?* Washington, DC: National Academies Press.

"Internet Users in the World." (2013). *Internet World Statistics*, January 1. (http://www.internetworldstats.com/stats.htm).

Ito, M., H. A. Hors, M. Bittanti, D. Boyd, B. Herr-Stephenson, P. C. Lange, C. J. Pascoe, and L. Robinson. (2009). *Living and Learning with New Media*. Cambridge, MA: MIT Press.

Itzkoff, D. (2010). "You Saw What in 'Avatar'? Pass Those Glasses!" *New York Times*, January 20: A1.

Iyengar, S. (1991). *Is Anyone Responsible? How Television Frames Political Issues*. Chicago: University of Chicago Press.

Iyengar, S., and K. S. Hahn. (2009). "Red Media, Blue Media: Evidence of Ideological Selectivity in Media Use." *Journal of Communication*, 59: 19–39.

Iyengar, S., and D. R. Kinder. (1987). *News That Matters: Television and American Opinion*. Chicago: University of Chicago Press.

J-Lab. (2013). "Community Media Directory." *American University*

School of Journalism. (http://www.j-lab.org/tools/citizen-media-database/).

Jackson, J. (2013). "13th Annual Fear & Favor Review." *Extra!* February: 9–11.

Jacobs, T. (2012). "Facebook: Saving Lives, One Kidney at a Time." *Pacific Standard*, May 16. (http://www.psmag.com/health/facebook-saving-lives-one-kidney-at-a-time-42266/).

Jamieson, K. H. (1988). *Eloquence in an Electronic Age: The Transformation of Political Speechmaking*. New York: Oxford University Press.

Jamieson, K. H., and K. K. Campbell. (1997). *The Interplay of Influence: News, Advertising, Politics, and the Mass Media*. Belmont, CA: Wadsworth.

Jamieson, K. H., and M. E. P. Seligman. (2001). "Six Rules for Government and Press on Terrorism: Undercutting Fear Itself." Unpublished report, Philadelphia, November.

Jamieson, K. H., and P. Waldman. (2003). *The Press Effect*. New York: Oxford University Press.

Janus, N. V. (1977). "Research on Sex-Roles in the Mass Media: Toward a Critical Approach." *Critical Sociology*, 7: 19–31.

Jarvis, J. (2010). "Media's Evolving Spheres of Discovery." *Buzz Machine*, February 22. (http://buzzmachine.com/2010/02/22/medias-evolving-spheres-of-discovery/?utm_source=feedburner&utm_medium=feed&utm_campaign=Feed%3A+buzzmachine+%28BuzzMachine%29&utm_content=Google+Reader).

Jensen, J. D., J. K. Bernat, K. M. Wilson, and J. Goonewardene. (2011). "The Delay Hypothesis: The Manifestation of Media Effects over Time." *Human Communication Research*, 37: 509–528.

Jensen, K. B. (1995). *The Social Semiotics of Mass Communication*. Thousand Oaks, CA: Sage.

Jensen, K. B. (1991). *A Handbook of Qualitative Methodology for Mass Communication Research*. New York: Taylor & Francis.

Jensen, K. B. (1990). "Television Futures: A Social Action Methodology for Studying Interpretive Communities." *Critical Studies in Mass Communication*, 7: 129–146.

Jensen, R. (2010). "The Collapse of Journalism/The Journalism of Collapse: New Storytelling and a New Story." *Dissident Voice*, March 26. (http://dissidentvoice.org/2010/03/the-collapse-of-journalismthe-journalism-of-collapse-new-storytelling-and-a-new-story/).

Jensen, K. B., and W. R. Neuman. (2013). "Evolving Paradigms of Communication Research." *International Journal of Communication*, 7: 230–238.

Jensen, T. (2013). "Fox News' Credibility Declines." *Public Policy Polling*, February 6. (http://www.publicpolicypolling.com/main/2013/02/fox-news-credibility-declines.html).

Jeong, S. H., C. H. Cho, and Y. Hwang. (2012). "Media Literacy Interventions: A Meta-Analytic Review." *Journal of Communication*, 62: 454–472.

Jessell, H. A. (2012). "TV Helps a Nation Come Out of the Closet." *TVNewsCheck*, May 11. (http://www.tvnewscheck.com/article/59391/tv-helps-a-nation-come-out-of-the-closet).

Jhally, S. (1989). "The Political Economy of Culture." In I. Angus and S. Jhally, eds., *Cultural Politics in Contemporary America*. New York: Routledge.

Jhally, S., ed. (1987). *The Codes of Advertising: Fetishism and the Political Economy of Meaning in the Consumer Society*. New York: St. Martin's.

Johnson, B. (2006). "The Cost of Democracy." *Advertising Age*, November 20: 3.

Johnston, H., and J. A. Noakes. (2005). *Frames of Protest: Social Movements and the Framing Perspective*. Boston: Rowman and Littlefield.

Jones, A. S. (2009). *Losing the News: The Future of the News That Feeds Democracy*. New York: Oxford University Press.

Jowett, G. S., I. Jarvie, and K. Fuller. (1996). *Children and the Movies: Media Influence and the Payne Fund Controversy*. New York: Cambridge University Press.

Jowett, G. S., and V. O'Donnell. (1999). *Propaganda and Persuasion*. Thousand Oaks, CA: Sage.

Kahneman, D. (201). *Thinking, Fast and Slow*. New York: Farrar, Straus, and Giroux.

Kaiser Family Foundation. (2007). *Food for Thought: Television Advertising to Children in the United States*. Washington, DC: Kaiser Family Foundation.

Kalman, Y. M., and S. Rafaeli. (2011). "Online Pauses and Silence: Chronemic Expectancy Violations in Written Computer-Mediated Communication." *Communication Research*, 38: 54–69.

"Cellphone Study Shows One-Hour Exposure Changes Brain Activity." *Washington Post*, February 22. (http://voices.washingtonpost.com/posttech/2011/02/cell_phone_study_shows_1_hour.htm).

Kang, C. (2011). "Kid Apps Explode on Smartphones and Tablets. But Are They Good for Your Children?" *Washington Post*, November 17. (http://articles.washingtonpost.com/2011-11-17/business/35281254_1_app-stores-smartphone-samsung-galaxy).

Kang, C. (2009). "Cable Giants to Put Shows Online." *Washington Post*, December 3: A30.

KBOI Web Staff. (2013). No Premarital Sex on Television Please, Lawmakers Urge. *KBOI2.com*, March 14. (http://www.kboi2.com/news/local/Idaho-Premarital-Sex-News-198283721.html?tab=video&c=y).

Kaplan, M. (2008). "All the News That's Fit to Neuter." *Huffington Post*, December 2. (http://www.huffingtonpost.com/marty-kaplan/all-the-news-thats-fit-to_b_147703.html).

Katikalapudi, R., S. Chellappan, F. Montgomery, D. Wunsch, and K. Lutzen. (2012). "Associating Internet Usage with Depressive Behavior among College Students." *Technology and Society Magazine*, 31: 73–80.

Katz, E. (1983). "Publicity and Pluralistic Ignorance: Notes on 'The Spiral of Silence.'" In E. Wartella and D. C. Whitney, eds., *Mass Communication Review Yearbook 4*. Beverly Hills, CA: Sage.

Katz, E., J. G. Blumler, and M. Gurevitch. (1974). "Utilization of Mass Communication by the Individual." In J. G. Blumler and E. Katz, eds., *The Uses of Mass Communication: Current Perspectives on Gratifications Research*. Beverly Hills, CA: Sage.

Katz, E., and P. F. Lazarsfeld. (1955). *Personal Influence: The Part Played by People in the Flow of Communications*. New York: Free Press.

Kaufman, G. (2003). "Push the Courvoisier: Are Rappers Getting Paid for Product Placement?" *VH1.com*, June 6. (http://www.mtv.com/news/articles/1472393/20030606/puff_daddy.jhtml).

Keane, J. (1991). *The Media and Democracy*. Cambridge: Polity Press.

Kellner, D. (1997). "Overcoming the Divide: Cultural Studies and Political Economy." In M. Ferguson and P. Golding, eds., *Cultural Studies in Question*. Thousand Oaks, CA: Sage.

Kelly, A. M. (2010). "The Kids Are All Right: They Have Cell Phones." *MediaChannel News*, January 14. (http://www.medicalnewstoday.com/articles/113878.php).

Kenny, C. (2009). "Revolution in a Box." *Foreign Policy*, November/December: 68–74.

Kerlinger, F. N. (1986). *Foundations of Behavioral Research*. New York: Holt, Rinehart, & Winston.

Kim, H. S., C. A. Bigman, A. E. Leader, C. Lerman, and J. N. Cappella. (2012). "Narrative Health Communication and Behavior Change: The Influence of Exemplars in the News on Intention to Quit Smoking." *Journal of Communication*, 62: 473–492.

Kirkhorn, M. J. (2000). "Media Increasingly Ignore Poor." *San Jose Mercury News*, February 20: 3C.

Kirzinger, A. E., C. Weber, and M. Johnson. (2012). "Genetic and Environmental Influences on Media Use and Communication Behaviors." *Human Communication Research*, 38: 144–171.

Kistler, M. E., and M. J. Lee. (2010). "Does Exposure to Sexual Hip-Hop Music Videos Influence the Sexual Attitudes of College Students?" *Mass Communication and Society*, 13: 67–86.

Klapper, J. T. (1960). *The Effects of Mass Communication*. New York: Free Press.

Klapper, J. T. (1949). *The Effects of Mass Media*. New York: Columbia University Bureau of Applied Social Research.

Knight Commission on the Information Needs of Communities in a

Democracy. (2009). *Informing Communities: Sustaining Democracy in the Digital Age.* Washington, DC: Knight Foundation.

Knight, S. (2012). "Not the Video Game Blame Game, Again!" *Washington Monthly*, December 16. (http://www.washingtonmonthly.com/political-animal-a/2012_12/it_was_only_a_matter041822.php?tm_source=feedburner&utm_medium=feed&utm_campaign=Feed%3A+washingtonmonthly%2Frss+(Political+Animal+at+Washington+Monthly).

Knobloch-Westerwick, S., (2006). "Mood Management: Theory, Evidence, and Advancements." In D. Zillmann and P. Vorderer, eds., *Media Entertainment: The Psychology of Its Appeal.* Mahwah, NJ: Erlbaum.

Kok, B. E. et al. (2013). "How Positive Emotions Build Physical Health: Perceived Positive Social Connections Account for the Upward Spiral between Positive Emotions and Vagal Tone." *Psychological Science*, in press. (http://www.unc.edu/peplab/publications/Kok%20et%20al_psycscience_inPress.pdf).

Konijn, E. A., M. N. Bijvank, and B. J. Bushman. (2007). "I Wish I Were a Warrior: The Role of Wishful Identification in the Effects of Violent Video Games on Aggression in Adolescent Boys." *Developmental Psychology*, 43: 1038–1044.

Kost, K., and S. Henshaw. (2013). "U.S. Teenage Pregnancies, Births and Abortions, 2008: State Trends by Age, Race and Ethnicity." *Guttmacher Institute*, March. (http://www.guttmacher.org/pubs/USTPtrendsState08.pdf).

Kornhauser, A., and P. F. Lazarsfeld. (1935). "The Technique of Market Research from the Standpoint of a Psychologist." *Institute of Management*, 16: 3–15, 19–21.

Kornhauser, W. (1959). *The Politics of Mass Society.* New York: Free Press.

Kotler, P., and N. R. Lee. (2008). *Social Marketing: Influencing Behaviors for Good.* Los Angeles: Sage.

Krahé, B., I. Möller, L. R. Huesmann, L. Kirwill, J. Felber, and A. Berger. (2011). "Desensitization to Media Violence: Links with Habitual Media Violence Exposure, Aggressive Cognitions, and Aggressive Behavior." *Journal of Personality and Social Psychology*, 100: 630–646.

Kraut, R., M. Patterson, V. Lundmark, S. Kiesler, T. Mukopadhyay, and W. Scherlis. (1998). "Internet Paradox. A Social Technology That Reduces Social Involvement and Psychological Well-Being?" *American Psychologist*, 53: 1017–1031.

Krcmar, M., and K. Greene. (1999). "Predicting Exposure to and Uses of Television Violence." *Journal of Communication*, 49: 24–45.

Kreiling, A., (1984). "Television in American Ideological Hopes and Fears." In W. D. Rowland, Jr. and B. Watkins, eds., *Interpreting Television: Current Research Perspectives.* Beverly Hills, CA: Sage.

Krippendorf, K. (1986). *Information Theory: Structural Models for Qualitative Data.* Newbury Park, CA: Sage.

Kruger, J., N. Epley, J. Parker, and Z. W. Ng. (2005). "Egocentrism Over E-Mail: Can We Communicate as Well as We Think?" *Journal of Personality and Social Psychology*, 89: 925–936.

Krugman, P. (2011). "Sounds of Outrage Heard on Wall Street." *Truthout*, October 18. (http://truth-out.org/opinion/item/4074:sounds-of-outrage-heard-on-wall-street).

Kubey, R., and M. Csikszentmihalyi. (2002). "Television Addiction Is No Mere Metaphor." *Scientific American*, February: 74–80.

Kuhn, T. (1970). *The Structure of Scientific Revolutions*, 2nd ed. Chicago: University of Chicago Press.

Kuklinski, J. H., and P. J. Quirk. (2002). "Reconsidering the Rational Public: Cognition, Heuristics, and Mass Opinion." In A. Lupia, M. McCubbins, and S. Popkin, eds., *Elements of Political Reason.* New York: Cambridge University Press.

Kurtz, H. (2005). "The Judy Chronicles." *Washington Post*, October 17. (http://www.washingtonpost.com/wp-dyn/content/blog/2005/10/17/BL2005101700259.html).

Ladd, J. (2012). "Distrust in the Media and Confirmation Bias." *The Monkey Cage*, April 27. (http://themonkeycage.org/blog/2012/04/27/distrust-in-the-media-and-confirmation-bias/).

La Ferle, C., S. M. Edwards, and W. N. Lee. (2000). "Teens' Use of Traditional Media and the Internet." *Journal of Advertising Research*, 40: 55–65.

Laitinen, R. E., and R. F. Rakos, (1997). "Corporate Control of Media and Propaganda: A Behavior Analysis." In P. A. Lamal, ed., *Cultural Contingencies: Behavior Analytic Perspectives on Cultural Practices.* Westport, CT: Praeger.

Lakoff, G. (2011). "How to Frame Yourself: A Framing Memo for Occupy Wall Street." *Huffington Post*, October 19. (http://www.huffingtonpost.com/george-lakoff/occupy-wall-street_b_1019448.html).

Lang, A. (1990). "Involuntary Attention and Physiological Arousal Evoked by Structural Features and Mild Emotion in TV Commercials." *Communication Research*, 17: 275–299.

Lang, K., and G. E. Lang (1983). *The Battle for Public Opinion: The President, the Press, and the Polls during Watergate.* New York: Columbia University Press.

Lasswell, H. D. (1949). "The Structure and Function of Communication in Society." In W. S. Schramm, ed., *Mass Communication.* Urbana, IL: University of Illinois Press.

Lasswell, H. D. (1948). "The Structure and Function of Communication in Society." In L. Bryson, ed., *The Communication of Ideas.* New York: Harper.

Lasswell, H. D. (1934). *World Politics and Personal Insecurity.* Chicago: University of Chicago Press.

Lasswell, H. D. (1927a). *Propaganda Technique in the World War.* New York: Knopf.

Lasswell, H. D. (1927b). "The Theory of Political Propaganda." *American Political Science Review*, 21: 627–631.

Lavey, W. G. (1993). "Inconsistencies in Applications of Economics at the Federal Communications Commission." *Federal Communications Law Journal*, 45: 437–490.

Lazarsfeld, P. F. (1969). "An Episode in the History of Social Research: A Memoir." In D. Fleming and B. Bailyn, eds., *The Intellectual Migration: Europe and America, 1930–1960.* Cambridge, MA: Belknap Press of Harvard University.

Lazarsfeld, P. F. (1941). "Remarks on Administrative and Critical

Communication Research." *Studies in Philosophy and Social Science*, 9: 2–16.

Lazarsfeld, P. F., B. Berelson, and H. Gaudet. (1944). *The People's Choice: How the Voter Makes up His Mind in a Presidential Campaign*. New York: Duell, Sloan & Pearce.

Lazarsfeld, P. F., and R. H. Franzen. (1945). "Prediction of Political Behavior in America." *American Sociological Review*, 10: 261–273.

Lazarsfeld, P. F., and R. K. Merton. (1948). "Mass Communication, Popular Taste and Organized Social Action." In P. F. Lazarsfeld and R. K. Merton, eds., *The Communication of Ideas*. New York: Institute for Religious and Social Studies.

Lazarsfeld, P., and F. N. Stanton, eds. (1942). *Radio Research, 1941*. New York: Duell, Sloan & Pearce.

Lee, A. M., and E. B. Lee. (1939). *The Fine Art of Propaganda*. New York: Harcourt Brace.

Lee, E., J. Lee, and D. W. Schumann. (2002). "The Influence of Communication Source and Mode on Consumer Adoption of Technological Innovations." *Journal of Consumer Affairs*, 36: 1–28.

Leedy, P. D. (1997). *Practical Research: Planning and Design*. New York: Macmillan.

Lenhart, A. (2012). "Teens, Smartphones & Texting." *Pew Internet & American Life Project*, March 19. (http://pewinternet.org/Reports/2012/Teens-and-smartphones/Cell-phone-ownership/Smartphones.aspx).

Leonard, A. (2013). "Google's War against Fake News." *Salon*, April 10. (http://www.salon.com/2013/04/10/googles_war_against_fake_news/).

Leonard, A. (2010). "The Conservative Backlash against 'Avatar.'" *Salon*, January 5. (http://www.salon.com/entertainment/movies/avatar/index.html?tory=/tech/htww/2010/01/05/the_conservative_backlash_against_avatar).

Levy, M., and S. Windahl, (1985). "The Concept of Audience Activity." In K. E. Rosengren, L. A. Wenner, and P. Palmgreen, eds., *Media Gratifications Research: Current Perspectives*. Beverly Hills, CA: Sage.

Lewis, J. (2008). *Cultural Studies: The Basics*. Thousand Oaks, CA: Sage.

Licklider, J. C. R. (1960). "Man-Computer Symbiosis." *IRE Transactions on Human Factors in Electronics*, vol. HFE-1: 4–11.

Liebert, R. M., and J. N. Sprafkin. (1988). *The Early Window: Effects of Television on Children and Youth*. New York: Pergamon.

Lin, F., Y. Zhou, Y. Du, L. Qin, Z. Zhao, J. Xu, and H. Lei. (2012). "Abnormal White Matter Integrity in Adolescents with Internet Addiction Disorder: A Tract-Based Spatial Statistics Study." *PLoS ONE*, 7: e30253. DOI:10.1371/journal.pone.0030253.

Lind, R. A., and N. Rockier. (2001). "Competing Ethos: Reliance on Profit versus Social Responsibility by Laypeople Planning a Television Newscast." *Journal of Broadcasting and Electronic Media*, 45: 118–134.

Linn, S. (2004). *Consuming Kids*. New York: The New Press.

Lippmann, W. (1922). *Public Opinion*. New York: Macmillan.

Littlejohn, S. W., and K. A. Foss. (2011). *Theories of Human Communication*. Long Grove, IL: Waveland Press.

Littleton, C. (2008). "TV's Class Struggle." *Variety*, September 22–28: 1, 81.

Livingstone, S., and E. J. Helsper. (2006). "Does Advertising Literacy Mediate the Effects of Advertising on Children? A Critical Examination of Two Linked Research Literatures in Relation to Obesity and Food Choice." *Journal of Communication*, 56: 560–584.

Long, E. (1989). "Feminism and Cultural Studies." *Critical Studies in Mass Communication*, 6: 427–435.

Ludwig, M. (2013). "Labor Report: Four Major TV News Networks Ignore Unions." *Truthout*, April 10. (http://truth-out.org/news/item/15655-labor-report-four-major-tv-news-networks-ignore-unions#_methods=onPlusOne%2C_ready%2C_close%2C_open%2C_resizeMe%2C_renderstart%2Concircled&id=I0_1365631425422&parent=http%3A%2F%2Ftruth-out.org&rpctoken=71088189).

Lunden, I. (2012). "Analyst: Twitter Passed 500M Users in June 2012, 140M of Them in US; Jakarta 'Biggest Tweeting' City."

TechCrunch, July 30. (http://techcrunch.com/2012/07/30/analyst-twitter-passed-500m-users-in-june-2012-140m-of-them-in-us-jakarta-biggest-tweeting-city/).

Macdonald, D. (1953). "A Theory of Mass Culture." *Diogenes*, 1: 1–17.

Madland, D. (2008). "Journalists Give Workers the Business. Center for American Progress." (http://www.Americanprogress.org/issues/2008/06/pdf/world_without_workers.pdf).

Malamuth, N. (1996). "Sexually Explicit Media, Gender Differences, and Evolutionary Thought." *Journal of Communication*, 46: 8–31.

Mandese, J. (2013). "Study Finds More Parents Concerned About Media Than Guns." *MediaPost*, January 10. (http://www.mediapost.com/publications/article/190762/study-finds-more-parents-concerned-about-media-tha.html#axzz2I5R6LyhW).

Manly, L. (2007). "Brew Tube." *New York Times Magazine*, February 4: 51–55.

Marche, S. (2012). "Is Facebook Making Us Lonely?" *Atlantic*, May. (http://www.theatlantic.com/magazine/archive/2012/05/is-facebook-making-us-lonely/308930/).

Marcus, G. E., W. R. Newman, and M. MacKuen. (2000). *Affective Intelligence and Political Judgment*. Chicago: University of Chicago Press.

Marcuse, H. (1978). *An Essay on Liberation*. Boston: Beacon.

Marcuse, H. (1969). *The Aesthetic Dimension*. Boston: Beacon.

Marcuse, H. (1941). "Some Social Implications of Modern Technology." In A. Arato and E. Gebhardt, eds., (1978). *The Essential Frankfurt School Reader*. New York: Urizen.

Marsh, D. (2012). "Digital Age Rewrites the Role of Journalism." *The Guardian*, October 16. (http://www.guardian.co.uk/sustainability/sustainability-report-2012-people-nuj?ewsfeed=true).

Marshall, A. G. (2013). "The Propaganda System That Has Helped Create a Permanent Overclass Is Over a Century in the Making." *Alternet*, April 12. (http://www.alternet.org/media/propaganda-system-has-helped-create-permanent-overclass-over-century-making?page=0%2C0).

Martin, C., and H. Oshagen. (1997). "Disciplining the Workforce: The News Media Frame a General Motors Plant Closing." *Communication Research*, 24: 669–697.

Martin, C. (2004). *Framed! Labor and the Corporate Media*. Ithaca, NY: Cornell University Press.

Martin-Barbero, J. (1993). *Communication, Culture, and Hegemony: From the Media to Mediations*. Translated by E. Fox and R. A. White. Newbury Park, CA: Sage.

Martindale, D. (1960). *The Nature and Types of Sociological Theory*. Boston: Houghton-Mifflin.

Martins, N., and B. J. Wilson. (2011). "Social Aggression on Television and Its Relationship to Children's Aggression in the Classroom." *Human Communication Research*, 38: 48–71.

Massing, M. (2004). "Now They Tell Us." *New York Review of Books*, February 26. (http://www.nybooks.com/ articles/16922).

Mast, G., and B. F. Kawin. (1996). *A Short History of the Movies*. Boston: Allyn & Bacon.

Matson, F. M. (1964). *The Broken Image: Man, Science, and Society*. New York: Braziller.

Mattelart, A. (2003). *The Information Society,* Thousand Oaks, CA: Sage.

Mawhinney, H. B. (2001). "Theoretical Approaches to Understanding Interest Groups." *Educational Policy*, 15: 187–215.

Mazzarella, S. R. (2010). "Coming of Age Too Soon: Journalistic Practice in U.S. Newspaper Coverage of Early Puberty in Girls." *Communication Quarterly*, 58: 36–58.

McChesney, R. W. (2013). "Mainstream Media Meltdown!" *Salon*, March 3.

McChesney, R. W. (2004). *The Problem of the Media: U.S. Communication Politics in the 21st Century*. New York: Monthly Review Press.

McChesney, R. W. (1997). *Corporate Media and the Threat to Democracy*. New York: Seven Stories.

McCombs, M. E., (1981). "The Agenda-Setting Approach." In D. D. Nimmo and K. R. Sanders, eds., *Handbook of Political Comm-unication*. Beverly Hills, CA: Sage.

McCombs, M., and S. I. Ghanem, (2001). "The Convergence of Agenda Setting and Framing." In S. D. Reese, O. H. Gandy, and A. E. Grant, eds., *Framing Public Life: Perspectives on Media and Our Understanding of the Social World*. Mahwah, NJ: Erlbaum.

McCombs, M., J. Llamas, E. Lopez-Escobar, and F. Rey. (1997). "Candidate Images in Spanish Elections: Second-Level Agenda-Setting Effects." *Journalism and Mass Communication Quarterly*, 74: 703–717.

McCombs, M. E., and D. L. Shaw. (1972). "The Agenda-Setting Function of Mass Media." *Public Opinion Quarterly*, 36: 176–187.

McCoy, M., and O. Hargie. (2003). "Implications of Mass Communication Theory for Asymmetric Public Relations Evaluation." *Journal of Communication Management*, 7: 304–317.

McIntyre, J. S. (1987). "Repositioning a Landmark: The Hutchins Commission and Freedom of the Press." *Critical Studies in Mass Communication*, 4: 95–135.

McLeod, D. M., and B. H. Detenber. (1999). "Framing Effects of Television News Coverage of Social Protest." *Journal of Communication*, 49: 3–23.

McLeod, J. M., and E. M. Perse. (1994). "Direct and Indirect Effects of Socioeconomic Status on Public Affairs Knowledge." *Journalism Quarterly*, 71: 433–442.

McLuhan, M. (1964). *Understanding Media: The Extensions of Man*. New York: McGraw-Hill.

McLuhan, M. (1962). *The Gutenberg Galaxy: The Making of Typographic Man*. Toronto: University of Toronto Press.

McLuhan, M. (1951). *The Mechanical Bride*. New York: Vanguard.

McLuhan, M., and G. E. Stern, (1967). "A Dialogue: Q & A." In M. McLuhan and G. E. Stern, eds., *McLuhan: Hot and Cool: A Primer for the Understanding of McLuhan and a Critical Symposium with a Rebuttal by McLuhan*. New York: Dial Press.

McQuail, D. (2013). "Reflections on Paradigm Change in Communication Theory and Research." *International Journal of Communication*, 7: 216–229.

McQuail, D. (2005). *Mass Communication Theory: An Introduction*, 5th ed. Thousand Oaks, CA: Sage.

McQuail, D. (1994). *Mass Communication Theory: An Introduction*, 4th ed. Beverly Hills, CA: Sage.

McQuail, D. (1987). *Mass Communication Theory: An Introduction*, 2nd ed. Beverly Hills, CA: Sage.

McRobbie, A. (1984). "Settling Accounts with Subcultures: A Feminist Critique." *Screen Education*, 34: 37–49.

McRobbie, A. (1982). "The Politics of Feminist Research: Between Talk, Text and Action." *Feminist Review*, 12: 46–57.

Mead, G. H. (1934). *Mind, Self, and Society*. Chicago: University of Chicago Press.

Media Literacy Symposium. (1998). *Journal of Communication*, 48.

Meehan, E. R., V. Mosco, and J. Wasco. (1994). "Rethinking Political Economy: Change and Continuity." In M. Levy and M. Gurevitch, eds., *Defining Media Studies: Reflections on the Future of the Field*. New York: Oxford University Press.

Meehan, E. R., and E. Riordan. (2002). *Sex & Money: Feminism and Political Economy in the Media*. Minneapolis: University of Minnesota Press.

Meier, B., and A. Martin. (2012). "Real and Virtual Firearms Nurture a Marketing Link." *New York Times*, December 24: A1.

Meital, B., and T. Sheafer. (2010). "Candidate Image in Election Campaigns: Attribute Agenda Setting, Affective Priming, and Voting Intentions." *International Journal of Public Opinion Research*, 22: 204–229.

Mendelsohn, H. (1966). *Mass Entertainment*. New Haven, CT: College and University Press.

Mennem, K. (2013). "San Diego Ranked 2nd Safest Large City in U.S." *San Diego Reader*, February 12. (http://www.sandiegoreader.com/weblogs/news-ticker/2013/feb/12/San-diego-ranked-2nd-safest-large-city-in-us/).

Mehrotra, A., S. Paone, G. D. Martich, S. M. Albert, and G. J. Shevchik. (2013). "A Comparison of Care at E-visits and Physician Office Visits for Sinusitis and Urinary Tract Infection." *JAMA Internal Medicine*, 173: 72–74.

Merton, R. K. (1967). *On Theoretical Sociology*. New York: Free Press.

Merton, R. K. (1949). *Social Theory and Social Structure*. Glencoe, IL: Free Press.

Meyers, M. (2004). "African American Women and Violence: Gender, Race, and Class in the News." *Critical Studies in Media Communication*, 21: 95–118.

Meyrowitz, J. (2008). "Power, Pleasure, Patterns: Intersecting Narratives of Media Influence." *Journal of Communication*, 58: 641–663.

Meyrowitz, J. (1985). *No Sense of Place: The Impact of Electronic Media on Social Behavior*. New York: Oxford University Press.

Mickes, L., R. S. Darby, V. Hwe, D. Bajic, J. A. Warker, C. R. Harris, and N. J. S. Christenfeld. (2013). "Major Memory for Microblogs." *Memory & Cognition*, January 1. (http://link.springer.com/article /10.3758%2Fs13421-012-0281 -6#page-1).

Miller, K. (2005). *Communication Theories: Perspectives, Processes, and Contexts*. New York: McGraw- Hill.

Miller, N. E., and J. Dollard. (1941). *Social Learning and Imitation*. New Haven, CT: Yale University Press.

Miller, R. L., P. Brickman, and D. Bolen. (1975). "Attribution versus Persuasion as a Means for Modifying Behavior." *Journal of Personality and Social Psychology*, 3: 430–441.

Mindlin, A. (2009). "Web Passes Papers as a News Source." New York Times, January 5: B3.

Mitchell, A., T. Rosenstiel, and L. H. Santhanam. (2012). "The Explosion in Mobile Audiences and a Close Look at What It Means for News." *Journalism.org*, October 1. (http://www.journalism.org /analysis_report/future_mobile _news).

Mitchell, G. (2009). "Watchdogs Failed to Bark on Economy." *Editor & Publisher*, April: 16.

"Mobile Phone and Tablet Users." (2012). *Advertising Age*, August 20: 12.

Moerman, M., (1992). "Life after C. A.: An Ethnographer's Autobiography."

In G. Watson and R. M. Seller, eds., *Text in Context: Contributions to Ethnomethodology*. Newbury Park, CA: Sage.

Moody, C. (2011). "How Republicans Are Being Taught to Talk about Occupy Wall Street." *Yahoo! News*, December 1. (http://news.yahoo .com/blogs/ticket/republicans-being -taught-talk-occupy-wall-street -133707949.html).

Moon, S. J. (2011). "Attention, Attitude, and Behavior: Second-Level Agenda-Setting Effects as a Mediator of Media Use and Political Participation." *Communication Research*, 38: 1–22.

Mooney, C. (2012). "The Science of Fox News: Why Its Viewers Are the Most Misinformed." *Alternet*, April 8. (http://www.alternet.org/story /154875/the_science_of_fox_news %3A_why_its_viewers_are_the _most_misinformed?page=0%2C0).

Mooney, C. (2004). "Blinded by Science." *Columbia Journalism Review*, November/December: 25–35.

Moores, S. (1993). *Interpreting Audiences: The Ethnography of Media Consumption*. Thousand Oaks, CA: Sage.

Morales, L. (2012). "U. S. Distrust in Media Hits New High." *Gallup*, September 21. (http://www.gallup .com/poll/157589/distrust-media- hits-new-high.aspx).

Morales, L. (2011). "U. S. Adults Estimate That 25% of Americans Are Gay or Lesbian." *Gallup*, May 27. (http://www.gallup.com/poll /147824/adults-estimate-americans -gay-lesbian.aspx).

Morgan, S. E., L. Movius, and M. J. Cody. (2009). "The Power of Narratives: The Effect of Entertainment Television Organ Donation Storylines on the Attitudes, Knowledge, and Behaviors of Donors and Nondonors." *Journal of Communication*, 59: 135–151.

Morgan, M., and J. Shanahan. (2009). "The State of Cultivation." *Journal of Broadcasting & Electronic Media*, 54: 337–355.

Morgan, M., J. Shanahan, and N. Signorielli, (2009). "Growing up with Television: Cultivation Processes." In J. Bryant and M. B. Oliver, eds., *Media Effects: Advances in Theory and Research*. New York: Routledge.

Morgan, M., and N. Signorielli, (1990). "Cultivation Analysis: Conceptualization and Methodology." In N. Signorielli and M. Morgan, eds., *Cultivation Analysis: New Directions in Media Effects Research*. Newbury Park, CA: Sage.

Morley, D. (1980). *The "Nationwide" Audience: Structure and Decoding*. London: British Film Institute.

Morris, D., and E. McGann. (2008). *Fleeced*. New York: Harper.

Morris, J. S. (2007). "Slanted Objectivity? Perceived Media Bias, Cable News Exposure, and Political Attitudes." *Social Science Quarterly*, 88: 707–728.

Morrisey, J. (2011). "O.K., Downloaders, Let's Try This Song Again." *New York Times*, September 4: BU1.

Mosco, V., and A. Herman. (1981). "Critical Theory and Electronic Media." *Theory and Society*, 10: 869–896.

Moyer-Gusé, E. (2008). "Toward a Theory of Entertainment Persuasion: Explaining the Persuasive Effects of Entertainment-Education Messages." *Communication Theory*, 18: 407–425.

Moyers, B. (2001). "Journalism and Democracy: On the Importance of Being a 'Public Nuisance.'." *The Nation*, May 7: 11–17.

Moynihan, M. (2013). "Boston Marathon Bombing Media Errors Pile Up, as Does the Outrage." *Daily Beast*, April 18. (http://www .thedailybeast.com/articles/2013/04 /18/boston-marathon-bombing -media-errors-pile-up-as-does-the -outrage.html).

Moynihan, M. (2012). "Nicholas Lemann: Journalism is Doing Just Fine." *Daily Beast*, October 14. (http://www.thedailybeast.com /articles/2012/10/14/nicholas -lemann-journalism-is-doing-just -fine.html).

Mullainathan, S., and A. Schleifer. (2005). "The Market for News." *American Economic Review*, 95: 1031–1053.

Mulvey, L. (1975; 1999). "Visual Pleasure and Narrative Cinema." In L. Braudy and M. Cohen, eds., *Film Theory and Criticism: Introductory Readings*. New York: Oxford University Press.

Mumbry, D. K. (1997). "The Problem of Hegemony: Rereading Gramsci for Organizational Communication Studies." *Western Journal of Communication*, 61: 343–375.

Murdock, G., (1989a). "Critical Activity and Audience Activity." In B. Dervin, L. Grossberg, B. J. O'Keefe, and E. Wartella, eds., *Rethinking Communication, vol. 2: Paradigm Exemplars*. Newbury Park, CA: Sage.

Murdock, G. (1989b). "Critical Studies: Missing Links." *Critical Studies in Mass Communication*, 6: 436–440.

Murphy, S. T., L. B. Frank, J. S. Chatterjee, and L. Baezconde-Garbanati. (2013). "Narrative versus Nonnarrative: The Role of Identification, Transportation, and Emotion in Reducing Health Disparities." *Journal of Communication*, 63: 116–137.

Murphy, S. T., L. B. Frank, M. B. Moran, and P. Patnoe-Woodley. (2011). "Involved, Transported, or Emotional? Exploring the Determinants of Change in Knowledge, Attitudes, and Behavior in Entertainment-Education." *Journal of Communication*, 61: 407–431.

Muuss, R. E. (1988). *Theories of Adolescence*. New York: Random House.

Muwakkil, S. (2001). "Media's Warped Interpretation of Chaos." *Chicago Tribune News*, April 16. (http:// articles.chicagotribune.com /2001-04-16/news/0104160055 _1_youth-crime-violent-crime -homicides).

Nadkarni, S., and S. G. Hofmann. (2012). "Why Do People Use Facebook?" *Personality and Individual Differences*, 52: 243–249.

Napoli, P. M. (1999). "The Marketplace of Ideas Metaphor in Communications Regulation." *Journal of Communication*, 49: 151–169.

Naureckas, J. (2012). "Global Disaster? Not on the Agenda." *Extra!*, November: 6–7.

Naureckas, J. (2011). "They Are the 1 Percent." *Extra!* November, 7.

Naureckas, J. (2009). "Before We 'save' Journalism." *Extra!*, July, 5.

Naureckas, J. (2002). "Patriotism Vs. Jingoism." *Extra!*, January/ February, 2.

Negt, O. (1978). "Mass Media: Tools of Domination or Instruments of Liberation? Aspects of the Frankfurt School's Communications Analysis." *New German Critique*, 14: 61–80.

Nelson, C., and L. Grossberg, eds. (1988). *Marxism and the Interpretation of Culture*. Urbana, IL: University of Illinois Press.

Nelson, T. E., and R. A. Clawson. (1997). "Media Framing of a Civil Liberties Conflict and Its Effect on Tolerance." *American Political Science Review*, 91: 567–583.

Neuman, W. R., and L. Guggenheim. (2011). "The Evolution of Media Effects Theory: A Six-Stage Model of Cumulative Research." *Communication Theory*, 21: 169–196.

Neuman, W. R., Y. J. Park, and E. Panek. (2012). "Tracking the Flow of Information into the Home: An Empirical Assessment of the Digital Revolution in the United States, 1960-2005." *International Journal of Communication*, 6: 1022–1041.

Newcomb, H., ed. (2007). *Television: The Critical View*, 7th ed. New York: Oxford University Press.

Newcomb, H., ed. (1994). *Television: The Critical View*, 5th ed. New York: Oxford University Press.

Newcomb, H., ed. (1974). *TV: The Most Popular Art*. New York: Oxford University Press.

Newcomb, H., and P. M. Hirsch. (1983). "Television as a Cultural Forum: Implications for Research." *Quarterly Review of Film*, 8: 45–55.

Nichols, J. (2002). "Standing up for Dissent." *The Nation*, September 23: 24.

Noelle-Neumann, E., (1985). "The Spiral of Silence: A Response." In K. R. Sanders, L. L. Kaid, and D. D. Nimmo, eds., *Political Communication Yearbook, 1984*. Carbondale: Southern Illinois University Press.

Noelle-Neumann, E. (1984). *The Spiral of Silence: Our Social Skin*. Chicago: University of Chicago Press.

Noelle-Neumann, E. (1974). "The Spiral of Silence: A Theory of Public Opinion." *Journal of Communication*, 24: 43–51.

Noelle-Neumann, E. (1973). "Return to the Concept of the Powerful Mass Media." *Studies of Broadcasting*, 9: 68–105.

Nordenson, B. (2008). "Overload!" *Columbia Journalism Review*, November/December: 30–40.

Nyhan, B., and J. Reifler. (2010). "When Corrections Fail: The Persistence of Political Misperceptions." *Political Behavior*, 32: 303–330.

O2. (2012). "Making Calls Has Become Fifth Most Frequent Use for a Smartphone for Newly-Networked Generation of Users." *All About You*, June 29. (http://news.o2.co.uk /?press-release=making-calls-has -become-fifth-most-frequent-use -for-a-smartphone-for-newly -networked-generation-of-users).

O'Brien, S., and I. Szeman. (2004). *Popular Culture*. Scarborough, Ontario: Nelson.

O'Connor, A. (1989). "The Problem of American Cultural Studies." *Critical Studies in Mass Communication*, 6: 405–413.

O'Keeffe, G. S., and K. Clarke-Pearson. (2011). "Clinical Report—The Impact of Social Media on Children, Adolescents, and Families." *Pediatrics*, 127: 800–804.

Okrent, D. (2004). "The Public Editor: Weapons of Mass Destruction? Or Mass Distraction?" *New York Times*, May 30: sect. 4, p. 2.

Oliver, M. B. (2008). "Tender Affective States as Predictors of Entertainment Preference." *Journal of Communication*, 58: 40–61.

O'Malley, G. (2013). "Nearly 4 Billion Minutes of Video Ads Streamed in February." *MediaPost*, March 15. (http://www.mediapost.com /publications/article/195903/nearly -4-billion-minutes-of-video-ads- streamed-in.html#axzz2Nuo6zptn).

The On-Demand Generation. (2013). *Variety*, April 2: 62–63.

Oreskes, N. (2004). "The Scientific Consensus on Climate Change." *Science*, 306: 1686.

Oreskovic, A. (2009). "Facebook Makes Money, Tops 300 Million Users." *Reuters*, September 16. (http://www .reuters.com/article/ technologyNews /idUSTRE58E7ZK20090916).

Ott, B. (2009). "America's Safest Cities." *Real Clear Politics*, June 5. (www.realclearpolitics.com/articles /2009/06/05/americas_safest_cities _96815.html).

Otto, S. L. (2011). "Good Science Always Has Political Ramifications." *Scientific American*, November 24. (http://www.scientificamerican.com/article.cfm?id=good-science-always-has-political).

Packer, G. (2006a). "Knowing the Enemy." *New Yorker*, December 18: 61–69.

Packer, G. (2006b). "Keep Out." *New Yorker*, October 16: 59–60.

Page, A. S., A. R. Cooper, P. Griew, and R. Jago. (2010). "Children's Screen Viewing Is Related to Psychological Difficulties Irrespective of Physical Activity." *Pediatrics*, 126: e1011–1017.

Painter, J., and T. Ashe. (2012). "Cross-National Comparison of the Presence of Climate Scepticism in the Print Media in Six Countries, 2007–10." *Environmental Research Letters*, 7: 1–8.

Palmgreen, P., L. A. Wenner, and K. E. Rosengren, (1985). "Uses and Gratifications Research: The Past Ten Years." In K. E. Rosengren, L. A. Wenner, and P. Palmgreen, eds., *Media Gratifications Research: Current Perspectives*. Beverly Hills, CA: Sage.

Panousi, V., I. Vidangos, S. Ramnath, J. DeBacker, and B. Heim. (2013). "Inequality Rising and Permanent Over Past Two Decades." *Brookings Institution*, Spring. (http://www.brookings.edu/about/projects/bpea/latest-conference/2013-spring-permanent-inequality-panousi).

Parenti, M. (1992). *Make-Believe Media: The Politics of Entertainment*. New York: St. Martin's.

Park, D. W., and J. Pooley. (2008). *The History of Media and Communication Research: Contested Memories*. New York: Peter Lang.

Park, S. (2012). "Dimensions of Digital Media Literacy and the Relationship with Social Exclusion." *Media International*, 142: 87–100.

Pariser, E. (2011). *The Filter Bubble: What the Internet is Hiding From You*. New York: Penguin.

Patterson, K. (2004). "Violence in Media Linked to Aggression in Youths." *Providence Journal*, April 19: A1, A4.

Patterson, T. E. (1993). *Out of Order*. New York: Knopf.

Peirce, C., (1955). "Essentials of Pragmatism." In J. Buchler, ed., *Philosophical Writings of Pierce*. New York: Dover.

Penetration. (2010). Digital Market Facts 2010. *Advertising Age*, February 22.

Perloff, R. M. (2010). *The Dynamics of Persuasion: Communication and Attitudes in the 21st Century*, 4th ed. New York: Routledge.

Perloff, R. M. (1989). "Ego-Involvement and the Third Person Effect of Televised News Coverage." *Communication Research*, 16: 236–262.

Perse, E. M. (2001). *Media Effects and Society*. Mahwah, NJ: Erlbaum.

Petty, R. E., P. Brinol, and J. R. Priester, (2009). "Mass Media Attitude Change: Applications of the Elaboration Likelihood Model of Persuasion." In J. Bryant and M. B. Oliver, eds., *Media Effects: Advances in Theory and Research*. New York: Routledge.

Petty, R. E., and J. T. Cacioppo, (1986). "The Elaboration Likelihood Model of Persuasion." In L. Berkowitz, ed., *Advances in Experimental Social Psychology, Volume 19*. New York: Academic Press.

Pew Center for Civic Journalism. (2002). *Civic Journalism: A Living Legacy*. Washington, DC: Pew Center for Civic Journalism.

Pew Research Center for the People and the Press. (2013). "The State of the News Media 2013: Overview." *Pew Research Center*. (http://stateofthemedia.org/2013/overview-5/).

Pew Research Center for the People and the Press. (2011). "Labor Unions Seen as Good for Workers, Not U.S. Competitiveness." *Pew Research Center*, February 17. (http://www.people-press.org/2011/02/17/labor-unions-seen-as-good-for-workers-not-u-s-competitiveness/).

Pew Research Center for the People and Press. (2004). "Online News Audience Larger, More Diverse: News Audience Increasingly Polarized." *Pew Research Center*, June 8. (http://www.people-press.org/files/legacy-pdf/215.pdf).

Pfanner, E. (2013). "Music Industry Sales Rise, and Digital Revenue Gets the Credit." *New York Times*, February 27: B3.

Pickard, V. (2010). "Whether the Giants Should Be Slain or Persuaded to Be Good": Revisiting the Hutchins Commission and the Role of Media in a Democratic Society." *Critical Studies in Media Communication*, 27: 391–411.

Pickard, V., J. Sterns, and C. Aaron. (2009). *Saving the News: Toward a National Journalism Strategy*. Washington, DC: Free Press.

Piersanti, S. (2012). "The 10 Awful Truths about Book Publishing." *BKPExtranet*, March 6. (http://www.bkpextranet.com/AuthorMaterials/10AwfulTruths.htm).

Pingree, S., J. M. Wiemann, and R. P. Hawkins, (1988). "Editors' Introduction: Toward Conceptual Synthesis." In R. P. Hawkins, J. M. Wiemann, and S. Pingree, eds., *Advancing Communication Science: Merging Mass and Interpersonal Processes*. Newbury Park, CA: Sage.

Pippa, N. (1996). "Did Television Erode Social Capital? A Reply to Putnam." *PS: Political Science and Politics*, XXIX: 474–480.

Plummer, B. (2011). "America's Top Export in 2011 Was … Fuel?" *Washington Post*, December 31. (http://www.washingtonpost.com/blogs/wonkblog/post/americas-top-export-in-2011-was–fuel/2011/12/31/gIQAzlvgSP_blog.html).

Poindexter, P. (2012). *Millennials, News, and Social Media: Is News Engagement a Thing of the Past?*. New York: Peter Lang.

Pollitt, K. (2012). "What's the Matter with Creationism?" *The Nation*, June 14. (http://www.thenation.com/article/168385/whats-matter-creationism#).

Polo, S. (2012). "Jarrah Hodge Drops Some Feminist History on Us: Bra-Burning is a Myth." *The Mary Sue*, May 17. (http://www.themarysue.com/jarrah-hodge-drops-some-feminist-history-on-us-bra-burning-is-a-myth/).

Pooley, J. (2008). "The New History of Mass Communication Research." In D. W. Park and J. Pooley, eds., *The History of Media and Communication Research: Contested Memories*. New York: Peter Lang.

Pooley, J. (2007). "Daniel Czitrom, James W. Carey, and the Chicago School." *Critical Studies in Media Communication*, 24: 469–472.

Pooley, J. (2006). "Fifteen Pages that Shook the Field: Personal Influence, Edward Shils, and the Remembered History of Mass Communication Research." *The ANNALS of the American Academy of Political and*

Social Science, November, 608: 130–156.

Postman, N. (1996). *The End of Education*. New York: Vintage.

Postman, N. (1994). *The Disappearance of Childhood*. New York: Vintage.

Postman, N. (1985). *Amusing Ourselves to Death: Public Discourse in the Age of Show Business*. New York: Penguin.

Potter, D. (2001). "News for Sale." *American Journalism Review*, September: 68.

Potter, W. J. (2012). *Media Effects*. Los Angeles: Sage.

Potter, W. J. (2009). *Arguing for a General Framework for Mass Media Scholarship*. Thousand Oaks, CA: Sage.

Potter, W. J. (1998). *Media Literacy*. Thousand Oaks, CA: Sage.

Potter, W. J. (1997). "The Problem of Indexing Risk of Viewing Television Aggression." *Critical Studies in Mass Communication*, 14: 228–248.

Potter, W. J. (1991). "The Relationships between First and Second Order Measures of Cultivation." *Human Communication Research*, 18: 92–113.

Potter, W. J. (1990). "Adolescents' Perceptions of the Primary Values of Television Programming." *Journalism and Mass Communication Quarterly*, 67: 843–851.

Pratkanis, A. R., and E. Aronson. (1992). *Age of Propaganda: The Everyday Use and Abuse of Persuasion*. New York: W. H. Freeman.

Preiss, R. W. (2007). *Mass Media Effects Research: Advances through Meta-Analysis*. Mahwah, NJ: Erlbaum Associates.

Proctor, J. (2004). *Stuart Hall*. NewYork: Routledge.

Protess, D. L., F. L. Cook, J. C. Doppelt, J. S. Ettema, M. T. Gordon, D. R. Leff, and P. Miller. (1991). *The Journalism of Outrage*. New York: Guilford.

Putnam, R. (2000). *Bowling Alone: The Collapse and Revival of American Community*. New York: Simon & Schuster.

Quan-Haase, A., and A. L. Young. (2010). "Uses and Gratifications of Social Media: A Comparison of Facebook and Instant Messaging." *Bulletin of Science Technology Society*, 30: 350–361.

Radio-Television News Directors Association. (2000). "Code of Ethics and Professional Conduct." (http://www.rtdna.org/pages/media_items/code-of-ethics-and-professional-conduct48.php).

Radway, J. (1986). "Identifying Ideological Seams: Mass Culture, Analytical Method, and Political Practice." *Communication*, 9: 93–123.

Radway, J. (1984; 1991). *Reading the Romance: Women, Patriarchy, and Popular Literature*. Chapel Hill, NC: University of North Carolina Press.

Rakow, L. (1986). "Feminist Approaches to Popular Culture: Giving Patriarchy Its Due." *Communication*, 9: 19–41.

Ramasubramanian, S., and M. B. Oliver. (2007). "Activating and Suppressing Hostile and Benevolent Racism: Evidence for Comparative Stereotyping." *Media Psychology*, 9: 623–646.

Redlawsk, D. P., A. J. W. Civettini, and K. M. Emmerson. (2010). "The Affective Tipping Point: Do Motivated Reasoners Ever "Get It"?" *Political Psychology*, 31: 563–593.

Reese, S. D. (2010). "Journalism and Globalization." *Sociology Compass*, 4/6: 344–353.

Reeves, B., and E. Thorson. (1986). "Watching Television: Experiments on the Viewing Process." *Communication Research*, 13: 343–361.

Reimer, B., and K. E. Rosengren, (1990). "Cultivated Viewers and Readers: A Life-Style Perspective." In N. Signorielli and M. Morgan, eds., *Cultivation Analysis: New Directions in Media Effects Research*. Newbury Park, CA: Sage.

Rendall, S. (2004). "Meet the Stenographers." *Extra!*, November/December: 6–8.

Rettner, R. (2011). "Kids Under 2 Should Play, Not Watch TV, Doctors Say." *Live Science*, October 18. (http://www.livescience.com/16586-tv-viewing-young-children-media.html).

Richtel, M. (2010a). "Digital Devices Deprive Brain of Needed Downtime." *New York Times*, August 25: B1.

Richtel, M. (2010b). "Attached to Technology and Paying a Price." *New York Times*, June 7: A1.

Rideout, V. (2012a). "Children, Teens, and Entertainment Media: The View from the Classroom." *Common Sense Media*, Fall. (http://www.commonsensemedia.org/sites/default/files/research/view-from-the-classroom-final-report.pdf).

Rideout, V. (2012b). "Social Media, Social Life: How Teens View Their Digital Lives." *Common Sense Media*, Summer. (http://www.commonsensemedia.org/sites/default/files/research/socialmediasociallife-final-061812.pdf).

Rideout, V. J., U. G. Foehr, and D. F. Roberts. (2010). *Generation M2: Media in the Lives of 8– to 18-Year-Olds*. Menlo Park, CA: Kaiser Family Foundation.

Riesterer, T. (2012). "Stimulate Your Customer's Lizard Brain to Make a Sale." *Harvard Business Review*, July 31. (http://blogs.hbr.org/cs/2012/07/stimulate_your_customers_lizar.html).

Roberts, D. (2012). "A Chat with Chris Mooney about the Republican Brain." *Grist*, April 18. (http://grist.org/politics/a-chat-with-chris-mooney-about-the-republican-brain/).

Robinson, J. P., and D. K. Davis. (1990). "Television News and the Informed Public: Not the Main Source." *Journal of Communication*, 40: 106–119.

Robinson, J. P., and M. Levy, with D. K. Davis, eds. (1986). *The Main Source: Learning from Television News*. Newbury Park, CA: Sage.

Rogers, E. M. (2000). "The Extensions of Men: The Correspondence of Marshall McLuhan and Edward T. Hall." *Mass Communication and Society*, 3: 117–135.

Rogers, E. M. (1986). "History of Communication Science." In E. M. Rogers, ed., *Communication Technology: The New Media in Society*. New York: Free Press.

Rogers, E. M. (1962). *Diffusion of Innovations*. New York: Free Press.

Rogers, T. (2011). "Our Kids' Glorious New Age of Distraction." *Salon*, August 21. (http://www.salon.com/2011/08/21/now_you_see_it_interview/).

Rojek, C., (2009). "Stuart Hall on Representation and Ideology." In R. Hammer and D. Kellner, eds., *Media/Cultural Studies: Critical Approaches*. New York: Peter Lang.

Romano, A. (2011). "How Dumb Are We?" *The Daily Beast*, March 20. (http://www.thedailybeast.com /newsweek/2011/03/20/how-dumb -are-we.html).

Romer, D., K. H. Jamieson, and S. Aday. (2003). "Television News and the Cultivation of Fear of Crime." *Journal of Communication*, 53: 88–105.

Rorty, R. (1991). *Objectivity, Relativism, and Truth: Political Papers I*. Cambridge, UK: Cambridge University Press.

Rorty, R., J. B. Schneewind, and Q. Skinner. (1982). *Consequences of Pragmatism*. Minneapolis, MN: University of Minnesota Press.

Rosen, J. (2013). "Look, You're Right, Okay? But You're Also Wrong." *Press Think*, February 3. (http:// pressthink.org/2013/02/look-youre- right-okay-but-youre-also-wrong/).

Rosen, J. (2012). "So Whaddaya Think: Should We Put Truthtelling Back Up There at Number One?" *Press Think*, January 12. (http:// pressthink.org/2012/01/so -whaddaya-think-should-we-put -truthtelling-back-up-there-at -number-one/).

Rosen, J. (2009). "Audience Atomization Overcome: Why the Internet Weakens the Authority of the Press." *Pressthink*, January 12. (http://archive.pressthink.org/2009 /01/12/atomization.html).

Rosen, J. (1996). *Getting the Connections Right: Public Journalism and the Troubles in the Press*. New York: Twentieth Century Fund.

Rosen, R. (2013). "Is It Journalism, of Just a Repackaged Press Release? Here's a Tool to Help You Find Out." *Atlantic*, April 23. (http:// www.theatlantic.com/technology /archive/2013/04/is-it-journalism -or-just-a-repackaged-press-release -heres-a-tool-to-help-you-find-out /275206/).

Rosenberry, J., and J. Burton. (2010). *Public Journalism 2.0: The Promise and Reality of a Citizen-Engaged Press*. New York: Routledge.

Rosenblum, M. (2013). "Newspaper Advertising Makes No Sense in a Non-Linear World." *The Guardian*, April 4. (http://www.guardian.co .uk/media-network/media-network -blog/2013/apr/04/newspaper -advertising-online-non-linear).

Rosenwald, M. S. (2010). "Obsessed with Smartphones, Oblivious to the Here and Now." *Washington Post*, February 22: A01.

Rosnow, R. L., and E. J. Robinson. (1967). *Experiments in Persuasion*. New York: Academic.

Rowling, C. M., T. M. Jones, and P. Sheets. (2011). "Some Dared Call It Torture: Cultural Resonance, Abu Ghraib, and a Selectively Echoing Press." *Journal of Communication*, 61: 1043–1061.

Rozendaal, R., M. Buijzen, and P. Valkenburg. (2011). "Children's Understanding of Advertisers' Persuasive Tactics." *International Journal of Advertising*, 30: 329–350.

Rubin, A. M. (1998). "Editor's Note: Media Literacy." *Journal of Communication*, 48: 3–4.

Rubin, A. M. (1994). "Media Uses and Effects: A Uses-and-Gratifications Perspective." In J. Bryant and D. Zillman, eds., *Media Effects: Advances in Theory and Research*. Hillsdale, NJ: Erlbaum.

Rubin, A. M. (2009). "Uses-and Gratifications Perspective on Media Effects." In J. Bryant and M. B. Oliver, eds., *Media Effects: Advances in Theory and Research*. New York: Routledge.

Ruggiero, T. E. (2000). "Uses and Gratifications Theory in the 21st Century." *Mass Communication and Society*, 3: 3–37.

Russill, C. (2012). "William James: Among the Machines." In J. Hannan, ed., *Philosophical Profiles in the Theory of Communication*. New York: Peter Lang.

Russill, C. (2008). "Through a Public Darkly: Reconstructing Pragmatist Perspectives in Communication Theory." *Communication Theory*, 18: 478–504.

Russill, C. (2006). "For a Pragmatist Perspective on Publics: Advancing Carey's Cultural Studies through John Dewey … and Michel Foucault?!" In J. Packer and C. Robertson, eds., *Thinking with James Carey: Essays on Communications, Transportation, History*. New York: Peter Lang.

Ryan, C., K. M. Carragee, and W. Meinhofer. (2001). "Framing, the News Media, and Collective Action." *Journal of Broadcasting and Electronic Media*, Winter: 175–182.

Salmon, C. T., and F. G. Kline, (1985). "The Spiral of Silence Ten Years Later: An Examination and Evaluation." In K. R. Sanders, L. L. Kaid, and D. D. Nimmo, eds., *Political Communication Yearbook, 1984*. Carbondale, IL: Southern Illinois University Press.

Samson, L., and M. E. Grabe. (2012). "Media Use and the Sexual Propensities of Emerging Adults." *Journal of Broadcasting & Electronic Media*, 56: 280–298.

Sass, E. (2011). "56% of Americans Check Online News Daily." *MediaPost*, July 27. (http://www .mediapost.com/publications /article/154841/).

Scheufele, D. A. (2000). "Agenda Setting, Priming, and Framing Revisited: Another Look at Cognitive Effects of Political Communication." *Mass Communication and Society*, 3: 297–316.

Scheufele, D. A. (1999). "Framing as a Theory of Media Effects." *Journal of Communication*, 49: 103–122.

Scheufele, D. A., and D. Tewksbury. (2007). "Framing, Agenda Setting, and Priming: The Evolution of Three Media Effects Models." *Journal of Communication*, 57: 9–20.

Schiller, H. I. (2000). *Living in the Number One Country: Reflections from a Critic of American Empire*. New York: Seven Stories Press.

Schiller, H. I. (1989). *Culture, Inc.: The Corporate Takeover of Public Expression*. New York: Oxford University Press.

Schiller, H. I. (1973). *The Mind Managers*. Boston: Beacon.

Schonfeld, E. (2010). "Facebook Drives 44 Percent of Social Sharing on the Web." *TechCrunch*, February 16. (http://techcrunch. Com/2010/02/16 /facebook-44-percent-social -sharing/).

Schorr, D. (1992). "True Confessions of a Lifetime TV Journalist." *San Jose Mercury News*, May 17: 1C, 5C.

Schramm, W. (1954). *The Process and Effects of Mass Communication*. Urbana, IL: University of Illinois Press.

Schramm, W., J. Lyle., and E. Parker, eds. (1961). *Television in the Lives of Our Children*. Stanford, CA: Stanford University Press.

Schutt, R. K. (2009). *Investigating the Social World*, 6th ed. Thousand Oaks, CA: Sage.

Schutz, A. (1970). *On Phenomenology and Social Relations*. Chicago: University of Chicago Press.

Schutz, A. (1967). *The Phenomenology of the Social World*. Evanston, IL: Northwestern University Press.

Scruton, R. (2000). *An Intelligent Person's Guide to Modern Culture*. South Bend, IN: St. Augustine's Press.

Sedghi, A. (2011). "Addicted to Smartphones: The Latest Ofcom Communications Results." *The Guardian*, August 4. (http://www.guardian.co.uk/news/datablog/2011/aug/04/smartphones-usage-ofcom-report).

Segrin, C., and R. L. Nabi. (2002). "Does Television Viewing Cultivate Unrealistic Expectations about Marriage?" *Journal of Communication*, 52: 247–263.

Seitel, F. P. (2004). *The Practice of Public Relations*. Upper Saddle River, NJ: Pearson.

Severson, K. (2012). "Number of U.S. Hate Groups Is Rising, Report Says." *New York Times*, March 8: A17.

Shade, L. R., N. Porter, and W. Sanchez. (2005). "You Can See Everything on the Internet, You Can Do Anything on the Internet! Young Canadians Talk about the Internet." *Canadian Journal of Communication*, 30: 503–526.

Shafer, D. M. (2012). "Causes of State Hostility and Enjoyment in Player versus Player and Player versus Environment Video Games." *Journal of Communication*, 62: 719–737.

Shanahan, J., and V. Jones, (1999). "Cultivation and Social Control." In D. Demers and K. Viswanath, eds., *Mass Media, Social Control, and Social Change*. Ames, IA: Iowa State University Press.

Shanahan, J., M. Morgan, and M. Stenbjerre. (1997). "Green or Brown? Television and the Cultivation of Environmental Concern." *Journal of Broadcasting and Electronic Media*, 45: 118–134.

Sherman, A., R. Greenstein, and K. Ruffing. (2012). "Contrary to 'Entitlement Society' Rhetoric, Over Nine-Tenths of Entitlement Benefits Go to Elderly, Disabled, or Working Households." *Center on Budget and Policy Priorities*, February 10. (http://www.cbpp.org/cms/index.cfm?a=view&id=3677).

Schank, R., and R. Abelson. (1977). *Scripts, Plans, Goals, and Understanding: An Inquiry into Human Knowledge Structure*. Hillsdale, NJ: Lawrence Erlbaum Associates.

Shapiro, B. (2011). *Primetime Propaganda: The True Hollywood Story of How the Left Took over Your TV*. New York: Harper Collins.

Sheldon, L. P. (2012). "The Plan for a Gay (Domi) Nation." *Charisma Magazine*, July 31. (http://www.charismamag.com/life/culture/13906-the-plan-for-a-gay-domi-nation).

Sheldon, P. (2008). "Student Favorite: Facebook and Motives for Its Use." *Southwestern Mass Communication Journal*, Spring: 39–53.

Shen, F. (2004). "Effects of News Frames and Schemas on Individuals' Issue Interpretations and Attitudes." *Journalism & Mass Communication Quarterly*, 81: 400–416.

Sherman, S. (2004). "Floating with the Tide." *The Nation*, March 15: 4–5.

Sherry, J. L. (2004). "Media Effects Theory and the Nature/Nurture Debate: A Historical Overview and Directions for Future Research." *Media Psychology*, 6: 83–109.

Shils, E. (1962). "The Theory of Mass Society: Prefatory Remarks." *Diogenes*, 10: 45–66.

Shoemaker, P. (1996). "Hardwired for News: Using Biological and Cultural Evolution to Explain the Surveillance Function." *Journal of Communication*, 46: 32–47.

Shrum, L. J., (2009). "Media Consumption and Perceptions of Social Reality." In J. Bryant and M. B. Oliver, eds., *Media Effects: Advances in Theory and Research*. New York: Routledge.

Shrum, L. J. (2004). "The Cognitive Processes Underlying Cultivation Effects Are a Function of Whether the Judgments Are on-Line or Memory-Based." *Communications: The European Journal of Communication Research*, 29: 327–344.

Siebert, F. S., T. Peterson, and W. Schramm. (1956). *Four Theories of the Press*. Urbana, IL: University of Illinois Press.

Signorielli, N. (1990). "Television's Mean and Dangerous World: A

Continuation of the Cultural Indicators Perspective." In N. Signorielli and M. Morgan, eds., *Cultivation Analysis: New Directions in Media Effects Research*. Newbury Park, CA: Sage.

Signorielli, N., and S. Kahlenberg. (2001). "Television's World of Work in the Nineties." *Journal of Broadcasting and Electronic Media*, 41: 305–323.

Signorielli, N., and M. Morgan, eds. (1990). *Cultivation Analysis: New Directions in Media Effects Research*. Newbury Park, CA: Sage.

Silverblatt, A. (1995). *Media Literacy: Keys to Interpreting Media Messages*. Westport, CT: Praeger.

Simon, H. A. (1981). *The Sciences of the Artificial*. Cambridge, MA: MIT Press.

Simon, T., T. Atwater, and R. Alexander. (1988). "FCC Broadcast Content Regulation: Policymaking in a Vacuum." Paper presented at the annual meeting of the Association for Education in Journalism and Mass Communication, Portland, OR, August.

Singer, J. L., and D. G. Singer, (1983). "Implications of Childhood Television Viewing for Cognition, Imagination, and Emotion." In J. Bryant and D. R. Anderson, eds., *Children's Understanding of Television: Research on Attention and Comprehension*. New York: Academic.

Sotirovic, M. (2003). "How Individuals Explain Social Problems: The Influences of Media Use." *Journal of Communication*, 53: 122–137.

Skelton, A. (2012). "Social Demographics: Who's Using Today's Biggest Networks." *Mashable.com*, March 9. (http://mashable.com/2012/03/09/social-media-demographics/).

Slater, M. D., and D. Rouser. (2006). "Entertainment—Education and Elaboration Likelihood: Understanding the Processing of Narrative Persuasion." *Communication Theory*, 12: 173–191.

Small, G. E. et al. (2009). "Your Brain on Google: Patterns of Cerebral Activation during Internet Searching." *The American Journal of Geriatric Psychiatry*, 17: 116–127.

Smith, B. L. (1941). "Propaganda Analysis and the Science of Democracy." *Public Opinion Quarterly*, 5: 250–259.

Smith, A. (1991). *The Age of Behemoths: The Globalization of Mass Media Firms*. New York: Priority.

Smith, A., K. L. Schlozman, S. Verba, and H. Brady. (2009). "The Internet and Civic Engagement." *Pew Internet & American Life Project*, September. (http://www.pewinternet.org/Reports/2009/15--The-Internet-and-Civic-Engagement.aspx).

Smith, G. (2012). "'Digital Divide' Overlooked as Party Conventions Embrace the Web." *Huffington Post*, August 29. (http://www.huffingtonpost.com/2012/08/29/digital-divide-broadband-access-conventions_n_1833608.html).

Smith, S. (2013). "We're All TV Executives Now: Lurching toward Personal Programming." *MediaPost*, April 5. (http://www.mediapost.com/publications/article/197401/#ixzz2QFd7caQb).

Snowball, D. (1999). "Propaganda and Its Discontents." *Journal of Communication*, 49: 165–172.

Solomon, M. R. (1983). "The Role of Products as Social Stimuli: A Symbolic Interactionism Perspective." *Journal of Consumer Research*, 10: 319–329.

Solomon, N. (2009). "Media Absence of Class War." *Progressive Populist*, October 15: 16.

Solomon, N. (2006). "Media New Year's Resolutions for 2006." *Truthout*, January 3. (http://www.Truthout.org/docs_2006/printer_010306M.shtml).

Sotirovic, M. (2001). "Media Use and Perceptions of Welfare." *Journal of Communication*, 51: 750–774.

Soundbites. (2012). "Which Conflicts Attract NPR's Interest?" *Extra!* October: 3.

Soundbites. (2010). "The Quarter-Million-Dollar Middle." *Extra!* March: 3.

Soutar, G. N., and J. C. Sweeney. (2003). "Are There Cognitive Dissonance Segments?" *Australian Journal of Management*, 28: 227–250.

Sparks, G. G. (2006). *Media Effects Research: A Basic Overview*. Belmont, CA: Thomson/Wadsworth.

Sproule, J. M. (1997). *Propaganda and Democracy: The American Experience of Media and Mass Persuasion*. New York: Cambridge University Press.

Sproule, J. M. (1994). *Channels of Propaganda*. Bloomington, IN: EDINFO.

Sproule, J. M. (1987). "Propaganda Studies in American Social Science: The Rise and Fall of the Critical Paradigm." *Quarterly Journal of Speech*, 73: 60–78.

Stadd, A. (2012). "20 Twitter Stats from 2012." *MediaBistro*, December 3. (http://www.mediabistro.com/alltwitter/twitter-stats_b32050).

Stafford, T. F., M. R. Stafford, and L. L. Schkade. (2004). "Determining Uses and Gratifications for the Internet." *Decision Sciences*, 35: 259–289.

Stanglin, D. (2013). "Report: Conn. Shooter Kept Mass-Murder 'Score Sheet'." *USA Today*, March 18. (http://www.usatoday.com/story/news/nation/2013/03/18/newtown-sandy-hook-adam-lanza-massacre-school/1996455/).

Star, A. (2008). "Judgment Call." *New York Times Book Review*, August 17: 10–11.

Starkman, D. (2012). "Are Newspaper Audiences Really Shrinking?" *Columbia Journalism Review*, October 18. (http://www.cjr.org/the_audit/weakened_newspapers_expanding.php?age=all).

Starr, P. (2012). "An Unexpected Crisis: The News Media in Post-industrial Democracies." *The International Journal of Press/Politics*, 17: 234–242.

Steinberg, S. R. (2011). "Kinderculture: Mediating, Simulacralizing, and Pathologizing the New Childhood." In S. R. Steinberg, ed., *Kinderculture: The Corporate Construction of Childhood*. Boulder, CO: Westview Press.

Steiner, L. (1988). "Oppositional Decoding as an Act of Resistance." *Critical Studies in Mass Communication*, 5: 1–15.

Stepp, C. S. (2006). "The Blog Revolution." *American Journalism Review*, February/March: 62.

Stevens, J. (2012). "Political Scientists are Lousy Forecasters." *New York Times*, June 24: SR6.

Stevenson, R. L. (1994). *Global Communication in the Twenty-first Century*. New York: Longman.

Strasburger, V. C., A. B. Jordan, and E. Donnerstein. (2010). "Health Effects of Media on Children and Adolescents." *Pediatrics*, 125: 756–767.

Strupp, J. (2012). "Editorial Page Editors: WSJ Lack of Romney Advisers Disclosure 'Inexcusable" and 'Shameless.'" *Media Matters*, September 27. (http://mediamatters.org/blog/2012/09/27/editorial-page-editors-wsj-lack-of-romney-advis/190152).

Strupp, J. (2011). "Bill Keller Speaks Out on Judy Miller, Iraq War Coverage, and Fox News." *Media Matters*, June 3. (http://mediamatters.org/blog/2011/06/03/bill-keller-speaks-out-on-judy-miller-Iraq-war/180289).

Subervi, F. (2013). "Labor & Unions in National TV Network News: Preliminary Summary Report." Paper presented at the National Conference for Media Reform, Denver, April 7.

Sullivan, A. (2013). "Guess Which Buzzfeed Piece Is an Ad, Ctd." *The Dish*, February 24. (http://dish.andrewsullivan.com/?s=native+advertising+derek+thompson).

Summers, J. H. (2006). "The Deciders." *New York Times Book Review*, May 14: 39.

Suskind, R. (2004). *The Price of Loyalty: George W. Bush, the White House, and the Education of Paul O'Neill*. New York: Simon & Schuster.

Swanson, D. (2005). "Labor Media, or the Lack Thereof." *Truthout*, April 25. (http://www.truthout.org/issues_05/printer_042605LA.shtml).

Szalavitz, M. (2011). "Study: Whites More Likely to Abuse Drugs than Blacks." *Time*, November 7. (http://healthland.time.com/2011/11/07/study-whites-more-likely-to-abuse-drugs-than-blacks/).

Tatham, M. (2012). "15 Stats about Facebook." *Experian*, May 16. (http://www.experian.com/blogs/hitwise/2012/05/16/15-stats-about-facebook/).

Taylor, S. E. (1981). "The Interface of Cognitive and Social Psychology." In J. H. Harvey, ed., *Cognition, Social Behavior, and the Environment*. Hillsdale, NJ: Erlbaum.

Terkildsen, N., and F. Schnell. (1997). "How Media Frames Move Public Opinion: An Analysis of the

Women's Movement." *Political Research Quarterly*, 50: 879–900.

Tesser, A. (1993). "The Importance of Heritability in Psychological Research: The Case of Attitudes." *Psychological Review*, 100: 129–142.

Thomas, E. (2009). "Obama's Nobel Headache." *Newsweek*, April 6: 20–25.

Thomas, S. G. (2007). *Buy, Buy Baby*. Boston: Houghton Mifflin.

Thompson, D. (2012). "The Scariest Thing about the Newspaper Business Isn't Print's Decline, It's Digital's Growth." *Atlantic*, December 19. (http://www.theatlantic.com/business/archive/2012/12/the-scariest-thing-about-the-newspaper-business-isnt-prints-decline-its-digitals-growth/266482/).

Thomson, D. M. (2010). "Marshmallow Power and Frooty Treasures: Disciplining the Child Consumer through Online Cereal Advergaming." *Critical Studies in Media Communication*, 27: 438–454.

Thomson, O. (1977). *Mass Persuasion in History*. Edinburgh, UK: Paul Harris.

Tichenor, P. J., G. A. Donohue, and C. N. Olien. (1980). *Community Conflict and the Press*. Beverly Hills, CA: Sage.

Tichenor, P. J., G. A. Donohue, and C. N. Olien. (1970). "Mass Media Flow and Differential Growth of Knowledge." *Public Opinion Quarterly*, 34: 159–170.

Time/CNN. (2004). "Crossroads for Bush?" *Time*, May 24: 34.

Tonry, M. (2011). *Punishing Race: A Continuing American Dilemma*. New York: Oxford University Press.

"Top 15 Most Popular News Websites." (2012). *eBiz*, October. (http://www.ebizmba.com/articles/news-websites).

Trench, M. (1990). *Cyberpunk* [Mystic Fire Videos]. New York: Intercon.

Tsfati, Y., and J. Cohen. (2013). "The Third-Person Effect, Trust in Media, and Hostile Media Perceptions." *International Encyclopedia of Media Studies: Media Effects/Media Psychology*, 1: 1–19.

Tsukayama, H. (2013). "Why the Video Game Industry Has to Talk about Gun Violence." *Washington Post*, January 11. (http://articles.washingtonpost.com/2013-01-11/business/36313414_1_violent-video-games-games-and-real-world-violence-game-industry).

Tsukayama, H. (2012). "Amazon Introduces Kid-Focused Service." *Washington Post*, December 5. (http://www.washingtonpost.com/business/technology/amazon-introduces-kid-focused-service/2012/12/05/eae0c27e-3f11-11e2-ae43-cf491b837f7b_story.html).

Tuchman, G. (1978). *Making News: A Study in the Construction of Reality*. New York: Free Press.

Tuchman, G., and H. A. Farberman. (1980). "Facts of the Moment: The Study of News." *Symbolic Interaction*, 3: 9–20.

Tunstall, J. (1977). *The Media Are American: Anglo-American Media in the World*. New York: Columbia University Press.

Turner, J. H. (1998). *The Structure of Sociological Theory*, 6th ed. Belmont, CA: Wadsworth.

Turow, J. (2013). "How Should We Think About Audience Power in the Digital Age?" *The International Encyclopedia of Media Studies*. Oxford, UK: Blackwell.

Turrill, D. (2012). "The Cross-Platform Report." *A. C. Nielsen*, Quarter 2. (http://www.nielsen.com/content/dam/corporate/us/en/reports-downloads/2012-Reports/Nielsen-Cross-Platform-Report-Q1-2012-final.pdf).

U.S. Census Bureau. (2012). "Marriage and Divorces—Number and Rate by State: 1990–2009." (http://www.census.gov/compendia/statab/2012/tables/12s0133.pdf).

U.S. Congress Senate Subcommittee on Communications. (1972). *Surgeon General's Report by the Scientific Advisory Committee on Television and Social Behavior*. 92nd Congress, 2nd session, March 21–24.

"U. S. Divorce Rates for Various Faith Groups, Age Groups, & Geographic Areas." (2009). *ReligiousTolerance.org*, July 20. (http://www.religioustolerance.org/chr_dira.htm).

U.S. Election Project. (2009). "2008 General Election Turnout Rates." April 26. (http://elections.gmu.edu/Turnout_2008G.html).

Valkenburg, P. M., and H. A. Semetko. (1999). "The Effects of News Frames on Readers' Thoughts and Recall." *Communication Research*, 26: 550–569.

Vallone, R. P., L. Ross, and M. R. Lepper. (1985). "The Hostile Media Phenomenon: Biased Perception and Perceptions of Media Bias in Coverage of the Beirut Massacre." *Journal of Personality and Social Psychology*, 49: 577–585.

Van Aelst, P., T. Sheafer, and J. Stanyer. (2012). "The Personalization of Mediated Political Communication: A Review of Concepts, Operationalizations, and Key Findings." *Journalism*, 13: 203–220.

Van Vonderen, K. E., and W. Kinnally. (2012). "Media Effects on Body Image: Examining Media Exposure in the Broader Context of Internal and Other Social Factors." *American Communication Journal*, 14: 41–53.

Vanderbilt, T. (2012). "The Call of the Future." *Wilson Quarterly*, Spring: 52–56.

Vandenbosch, L., and S. Eggermont. (2012). "Understanding Sexual Objectification: A Comprehensive Approach toward Media Exposure and Girls' Internalization of Beauty Ideals, Self-Objectification, and Body Surveillance." *Journal of Communication*, 62: 869–887.

Vander Neut, T. (1999). "Do Violent Images Cause Violent Behavior?" *Risk and Insurance*, November: 38–40.

Verel, P. (2010). "Authors Advocate Government Subsidies for Journalism." *Fordham University*, February. (http://journalism.about.com/gi/o.htm? zi=1/XJ&zTi=1&sdn=journalism&cdn=newsissues&tm=7&gps=226_10_1231_580&f=00&su=p284.13.342.ip_p554.23.342.ip_&tt=2&bt=5&bts=5&zu=http%3A//www.fordham.edu/Campus_Resources/eNewsroom/topstories_1771.asp).

Verhulst, B., P. K. Hatemi, and L. J. Eaves. (2012). "Disentangling the Importance of Psychological Predispositions and Social Constructions in the Organization of American Political Ideology." *Political Psychology*, 33: 375–393.

von Zielbauer, P. (2007). "A Marine Tutorial on Media 'Spin.'" *New York Times*, June, K5.

Walker, R. (2006). "Gaming the System." *New York Times Magazine*, September 3: 18.

Walters, S. D. (1995). *Material Girls: Making Sense of Feminist Cultural Theory*. Berkeley, CA: University of California Press.

Ward, L., and K. Friedman. (2006). "Using TV as a Guide: Associations Between Television Viewing and Adolescents' Sexual Attitudes and Behavior." *Journal of Research on Adolescence*, 16: 133–156.

Warlaumont, H. G. (1997). "Appropriating Reality: Consumers' Perceptions of Schema-Inconsistent Advertising." *Journalism & Mass Communication Quarterly*, 74: 39–54.

Wartella, E. (1999). "Children and Media: On Growth and Gaps." *Mass Communication and Society*, 2: 81–88.

Wartella, E., (1979). "The Developmental Perspective." In E. Wartella, ed., *Children Communicating: Media and Development of Thought, Speech, and Understanding*. Beverly Hills, CA: Sage.

Wartella, E., and P. A. Treichler. (1986). "Interventions: Feminist Theory and Communication Studies." *Communication*, 9: 1–18.

Wegner, D. M. (2012). "Don't Fear the Cybermind." *New York Times*, August 5: SR6.

Weis, R., and B. C. Cerankosky. (2010). "Effects of Video-Game Ownership on Young Boys' Academic and Behavioral Functioning : A Randomized, Controlled Study." *Psychological Sciences*, 21: 1–8.

Westley, B. H., and M. MacLean. (1957). "A Conceptual Model for Mass Communication Research." *Journalism Quarterly*, 34: 31–38.

Wheeler, M. (2009). "This Miracle Brought to You by America's Unions." *Firedoglake.com*, January 16. (http://emptywheel.firedoglake .com/2009/01/16/this-miracle -brought-to-you-by-americas-unions/).

White, R. W. (1972). *The Enterprise of Living: Growth and Organization in Personality*. New York: Holt, Rinehart & Winston.

Whiten, J. (2004). "Bad News from Iraq? Blame the Source—U.S. Officials." *Extra! Update*, February: 13–3.

Whittelsey, F. C. (2003). "Dead Letter Office." *Extra!* January/February, 16.

Wicker, T. (2004). "Pressing Problems." *Editor and Publisher*, July, 62.

Wiener, N. (1961). *Cybernetics*, 2nd ed. Cambridge, MA: MIT Press.

Wiener, N. (1954). *The Human Use of Human Beings: Cybernetics and Society*. Garden City, NY: Doubleday Anchor.

Wilcox, B. L., D. Kunkel, J. Cantor, P. Dowrick, S. Linn, and E. Palmer. (2004). *Report of the APA Task Force on Advertising and Children*. Washington, DC: American Psychological Association.

Williams, F., R. E. Rice, and E. M. Rogers. (1988). *Research Methods and the New Media*. New York: Free Press.

Williams, R. (1974). *Television: Technology and Cultural Form*. London: Fontana.

Williams, R. (1967). *Communications*. New York: Barnes and Noble.

Windahl, S. (1981). "Uses and Gratifications at the Crossroads." In G. C. Wilhoit and H. De Bock, eds., *Mass Communication Review Yearbook*. Beverly Hills, CA: Sage.

Wolf, G. (1996). "The Wisdom of Saint Marshall, the Holy Fool." *Wired*, January: 122–125, 182–187.

Wood, G., and T. McBride, (1997). "Origins of Orienting and Defensive Responses: An Evolutionary Perspective." In P. J. Lang, R. F. Simons, and M. Balaban, eds., *Attention and Orienting: Sensory and Motivational Processes*. Hillsdale, NJ: Erlbaum.

World War II, The Propaganda Battle, Walk through the 20th Century. (1982). New York: PBS Video.

Wright, B. (2012). "Even Superman Can't Stomach What Mass Media Have Become." *Daily Advance*, November 2. (http://www .dailyadvance.com/opinion /other-views/bud-wright-even -superman-can8217t-stomach -what-mass-media-have-become -1323775).

Wright, C. R. (1986). *Mass Communication: A Sociological Perspective*, 3rd ed. New York: Random House.

Wright, C. R., (1974). "Functional Analysis and Mass Communication

Revisited." In J. G. Blumler and E. Katz, eds., *The Uses of Mass Communication: Current Perspectives on Gratifications Research*. Beverly Hills, CA: Sage.

Wright, C. R. (1959). *Mass Communication: A Sociological Perspective*. New York: Random House.

Yan, Z. (2009). "Limited Knowledge and Limited Resources: Children's and Adolescents' Understanding of the Internet." *Journal of Applied Developmental Psychology*, 30: 103–115.

Ybarra, M. L., M. Diener-West, D. Markow, P. J. Leaf, M. Hamburger, and P. Boxer. (2008). "Linkages between Internet and Other Media Violence with Seriously Violent Behavior by Youth." *Pediatrics*, 122: 929–937.

Yglesias, M. (2013). "The Glory Days of American Journalism." *Slate*, March 19. (http://www.slate.com /articles/business/moneybox/2013 /03/pew_s_state_of_the_media _ignore_the_doomsaying_american _journalism_has_never.html).

Young, K. S. (2004). "Internet Addiction: A New Clinical Phenomenon and Its Consequences." *American Behavioral Scientist*, 48: 402–415.

Young, B. (2009). "Human Capacity for Information Is Massive but Finite." *TechNewsWorld*, December 10. (http://www. technewsworld.com/perl/search.pl? query Human capacity for information is massive but finite).

Young, B. (1990). *Television Advertising to Children*. Oxford, UK: Clarendon Press.

"Youtube & News: A New Kind of Visual News." (2012). *Journalism.org*, July 16. (http:// www.journalism.org/analysis _report/youtube_news).

Ytreberg, E. (2002). "Erving Goffman as a Theorist of the Mass Media." *Critical Studies in Media Communication*, 19: 481–498.

Yu, B., and S. Renderos. (2013). "Seizing the Airwaves." *Extra!*, March: 12–13.

Zhao, S., S. Grasmuck, and J. Martin. (2008). "Identity Construction on Facebook: Digital Empowerment in Anchored Relationships." *Computers in Human Behavior*, 24: 1816–1836.

Zillmann, D., and P. Vorderer. (2000). *Media Entertainment: The Psychology of Its Appeal*. Mahwah, NJ: Erlbaum.

Zimbardo, P. G., and A. L. Weber. (1997). *Psychology*. New York: Longman.

Zywica, J., and J. Danowski. (2008). "The Faces of Facebookers: Investigating Social Enhancement and Social Compensation Hypotheses; Predicting Facebook and Offline Popularity from Sociability, Self-Esteem, and Extroversion/introversion; and Mapping the Meanings of Popularity with Semantic Networks." *Journal of Computer Mediated Communication*, 14: 1–34.

INDEX